T4-ABK-442

By the Same Author

A Piece of Paris – The Grand XIVth (1996)
Paris Now and Then: Memoirs, Opinions, and a
    Companion to the City of Light (2004)
Mediterranean Sketches (2005)
Situation Reports on the Emotional Equipoise:
    Collected Poems 1959-2006 (2007)
A Chronology of the Life and Times of Lawrence
    Durrell (2007)
The Time in Tavel: An Informal Illustrated Memoir
    of a Sojourn in Provence (2010)
Radovic's Dilemma: A Mediterranean Thriller (2012)
Travels in Greece and France (2013)
A Paris Chapbook (2013)
Shorts of All Sorts: Selected Prose and Poems (2013)
The Hemingway Log, A Chronology of His Life and
    Times (2015)
Almost to the End, The Shorter Poems: New and
    Old (2016)

"*A-a, kakaya raznitsa*," the corporal answers. "*Poshli napravo.*"

They come upon two gray uniformed Germans on the ground behind a streetcar lying on its side.

"*Oni mertvye?*"

"*Ne dvigayutsya.*"

"*Nu-ka prover'!* "

The corporal and one of his comrades each shoot one of the Germans in the face to ensure they are dead, the crack of their rifles lost in the barrage of a Stalin organ's swooshing blast.

"*Poshli otsyuda.*"

"*Smotri na doma.*"

As they slowly walk down the street in a zigzag pattern, five meters separating them as their orders specified, all three see movement in a doorway to their right. Spinning swiftly in that direction they fire their rifles three times in rapid succession. The corporal crouches and runs to the doorway, his finger tense on the rifle's trigger. He quickly turns around and comes back to his comrades.

"*Poshli otsyuda. Eto prosto patsan.*"

"*Aga, poshli poichshem devok. Kapitan skazal, chto my ikh mozhem togo... Oni eto delali s nashimi devkamio.*"

"*Davay sperva voynu zakonchim*," the corporal says with grim determination as they advance down the street.

The mother and sister of Gertrude Elizabeth Kleinschmidt, residents of Marienburger Strasse in the Prenzlauer Berg quarter of the city, will bury the ten year-old five days later after the fighting stops and before the soldiers of the victorious Red Army rape them in the same doorway.

The war has ended; the peace has not yet begun.

PART ONE

Waiting in Bad Nauheim, a less damaged suburb of Frankfurt-am-Main, Second Lieutenant John Ralph Schade, formerly Johannes Rainer Schadlerberg, briefly citizen of the Third Reich, faced the future in his former homeland with an uncomfortable sense of reluctance and anticipation. Many things troubled his mind, and this resulted in a chronic condition of indecisiveness that affected the most urgent question of his immediate future as a member of the conquering occupying forces. Indeed, he believed the ambivalence of his thoughts about his former countrymen might render him less than effective for the purposes of his newly adopted country. He served in its army with no particular reluctance, but also with no great enthusiasm now that they had defeated the barbarians. He wondered if his doubts about the correctness of certain aspects of his country's occupation policies would curtail his ability to make some contribution to the revitalization of a liberal German society. He also smiled at the idea of anyone in the military hierarchy taking seriously the hesitations of a second lieutenant, and one of foreign origin at that.

For the moment, his indecisiveness about his future restrained him from requesting demobilization despite his having accrued almost enough points to return to New York. An American citizen since the government drafted him into the military, he could not decide where to call home. Breslau, the place of his birth and early childhood? What did he remember about the place? What did he remember at all about the country of his birth that would form a bond between him and its terrible recent past?

Schade, in fact, remembered entirely too much: very European, very un-American. His mind carried his past and history along, dragging them from station to station like an unsuccessful salesman carrying his unsold samples, finally not wanting to sell them because they had become part of his existence, an existence which became impossible unless he did sell them. Very much aware of this he consciously tried to suppress certain memories.

The dubious analogy and equally suspect enterprise occurred to Schade again one afternoon late in June as he drove a battered jeep from Bad Nauheim to the small spa town of Wiesbaden several kilometers away to clear his mind in the relative isolation of the Stadtpark. The formerly luxurious casino town where well-off businessmen and their families went before the war to take the sulfurous waters and lose their money at the baccarat tables, had suffered less destruction than the larger cities. On that cloudy afternoon the few early summer flowers bloomed fitfully, small isolated splashes of color in the beige-green landscape, observed if not enjoyed by the few dowdy civilians wandering up and down the park's gravel pathways. The rain had stopped earlier in the day and the stunted flowers smelled fresh and new after the clogging dust of Frankfurt and its suburbs.

The flowers brought to Schade's mind his colleague and friend Makepeace's cautionary tale about his military training, one he tirelessly repeated to all new acquaintances, carefully measuring their reactions. "You know what the DI told us after we'd had our first target practice?" he asked Schade soon after they met. "Don't reach for the flower, that's what he said, don't reach for the flower. This was a warning to us. Luckily for me I never had to fire a gun after that, being in cultural affairs, y'know." The last phrases spoken in an exaggerated nasal accent, obliterating the residue of the Minnesota tones which constituted Makepeace's normal speech. "It was a butterfly," Schade had said. Makepeace ignored this. "In cultural affairs we do not fire guns, we turn them into messages of hope and the values of the democratic way." "A butterfly, William; the DI must have forgotten the scene." "I suspect he was not more than ten or fifteen when he saw it." "That's why he thought it was a flower." In the end Schade convinced Makepeace that the young German soldier in the final scene of the film *All Quiet on the Western Front* reached out from his trench for a butterfly, an action a French sharpshooter took advantage of to kill him at the very end of the war.

Schade left the jeep on the Kurparkallee in front of the shuttered casino and walked toward the large pond in the center of the park. The heat of the afternoon pressed on his neck as he stood at the pond's edge. He could see no one else in the park now and the sounds of military traffic on the streets dwindled in the distance as he moved slowly around the water deeper into the park. He sat on the one undamaged bench along the pathway. The glaucous liquid in the pond had emulsified into a dull surface that absorbed the pale light of the day as the porous night absorbs the remnants of the day. Nothing swam or floated in this pond and no animal drank from it. No wind moved the scattered flowers or the uncut grass, and no insect buzzed on that warm summer afternoon. The unexpected silence pressed on his brain as the sun weighed on his itching eyelids. He did not remember clearly when or why he had been in Wiesbaden before. Perhaps he had never walked in this park and this return was no return at all. This fit perfectly into his current frame of mind where definitions and memories blurred, but constantly pushed into his consciousness. Perhaps he could not recall the place because something pleasant had happened here.

He lit a cigarette and considered the matter chronologically. But how far back was he to go before tracing the progression of his memory forward again? No memory of his early childhood would focus on this pond, this bench. He remembered nothing out of the ordinary in that bourgeois household until the world depression of 1930. Prior to that everything melted together in the innocence of unencumbered routine that left no trail for his later mind to follow. Could it have been during a summer vacation when the family traveled for one month each year?

His mind shifted suddenly to another question he had for long been unable to answer: what should and could he make of his life given the circumstances in which he found himself? For many years he answered this question with a deceptively simple statement: I am going to be a writer of literature. The pomposity of the sentence both pleased and repelled his sense of reality, and in recent times, when anyone asked, he altered his response to: I am a writer, quickly followed by the inquiry: "Have you seen my latest story (or poem, or essay) in the *Phahnaughton Review*?", an obscure journal in which he had never published a word. No one, as far as he knew, had ever bothered to check his statement.

And while he did consider himself a man of literature, here he washed up against the shoals of a problem he would not easily resolve, with or without sophistry, the old conundrum of the exile and the émigré: what *was* his literature? German? European? Or that of his adopted country? Where did he fit into that scheme of things? He had written masses of words in both languages, passionately throwing them onto the paper, attempting to create structure and form for his life and the creative force he felt straining his mind. And on a more practical mundane level, how would he earn a living after being demobilized, a question his father often asked in his letters? Should he remain in this wasteland and join the reconstruction effort? Or should he allow himself to be drawn again into the dynamism of America and its exhilarating, well-fed energies?

He discovered the answer for the first time one snowy day walking in Washington Square Park during the winter of 1939 after the Germans invaded Poland. At the time he faced the dismaying prospects of graduating from college and decisions to make about future. Pondering this question in his usual withdrawn European manner, his head pulled down into his collar against the swirling snow the wind whipped down Fifth Avenue, he collided with a figure equally absorbed and they both fell to the ground. As he picked himself up and began to offer a hand to the other, he distinctly heard the young woman mutter "goddammit" in that easy manner which he admired in Americans of all ages. She accepted his hand, he apologized, they dusted each other's coats and picked up their books. He surprised himself by inviting her to coffee at Riker's on Sheridan Square. Surprised again when she shrugged and said, "Sure, why not, thanks." Later, he thought about her often, about how closely she resembled all the American girls with whom he had fallen in love since his first day at the public school in Washington Heights: relaxed with others their own age, they found only an occasional need to dissemble or hide behind the facade of social distance and caution, which Europeans had built into their lives and languages. This easy-going camaraderie never failed to intrigue him even if he did not fully understand it. Now, Schade thought her beautiful and immediately succumbed to her immense American enthusiasm and her unaffected American optimism; nothing could possibly be beyond her abilities to master. She knew no German but thought his residual accent cute and admired his ability to read Gerhard Hauptmann and Arthur Schnitzler in the original. Twenty-years old herself, she studied acting with intensity of her age and had just obtained a role in a play in one of the many small theaters in Greenwich Village. He adored her tumbled brown shoulder length hair which she tossed about with calculated abandon, her infectious flash of smile and light laughter; easily convinced of her acting talent, he decided to write a play for her. When it was time to go, he watched her hair float around her head as she skipped down the steps into the subway entrance. After she disappeared into the darkness he walked into the tiny park by the newsstand and jumped up and down in the snow.

Leslie Archer lived with her parents in Brooklyn Heights, and he still lived with his on the other heights at the northern end of the city, which complicated and curtailed the sexual side of their romance. The affair lasted five months; only toward the end did she "lose her cherry", as she somewhat embarrassed but smiling called their first complete sexual connection; "and it hardly hurt at all". She knew enough to have him pull away just before he experienced his first true orgasm and spread his semen on her brown delta hair and stomach. She rubbed it into her skin as if it were a lotion. The shyness that overcame them immediately after his coming for the first time did not recur the few occasions I which they were able to "be together", as she described their love-making, which did not mean she too reached the high pitch of satisfaction, though she came close twice. She did not know enough then to realize that his satisfaction and release should have been hers as well, a matter she only learned about with an older actor during the summer after she and Schade broke up. When she thought of him later in life she did not resent the absence of her own orgasms. Her sexual life as she grew older and demanded satisfaction blossomed into continual swerves from frenetic passion to a deep sighing release and back again. Schade did come to learn the necessity to satisfy his lovers and always looked back to his time with Leslie as a period of both bliss and anxiety that she might become pregnant despite the measures they took to prevent such an occurrence. The thought of Leslie always made him smile, a smile that from time to time turned to a grimace when he thought of his ignorance of how to completely satisfy her. But they were young, both inexperienced and naïve, new to the game, as he later admitted.

They saw each other whenever they could and listened to Ted Malone read love poems to organ music on the "Between the Bookends" radio show. He later of course denied ever hearing such sentimental drivel. She thought Bing Crosby's version of "I Surrender Dear" to be the best music for dancing; he tried to interest her in "Brother, Can You Spare a Dime," the Comedian Harmonists and Bessie Smith.

Early that spring he took her to one of the interminable meetings in the Yorkville quarter of the city attended by the separate groups of exiles and refugees from Germany and Austria. His mother, graying but energetic, asked him to bring his "Fräulein friend" to meet the family. Resisting this, he compromised by sitting with Leslie in the back of a small crowded room full of former citizens of the Greater German Reich gesticulating and making pronouncements. It seemed to Leslie that they all talked at the same time, and she understood not a word although she registered the serious concern that absorbed each of these men (rarely did the few women there speak to the group). She thought they all suffered from depression: they seldom ever joked or laughed freely. Perhaps, she thought, they did in private. Though they did not meet often, Mrs. Schadlerberg liked Leslie for many of the same reasons that motivated her son, most particularly her liveliness and politeness. The older woman appreciated the girl's directness, but was appalled by her cultural ignorance and inability to understand the plight of the anti-fascist refugees.

Schade's mother found it difficult to obtain any meaningful paid employment because she lacked any functional skills such as stenography, and she never learned how to operate the typewriter beyond the ability to hunt and peck at the keys with four slow fingers. This was an all too typical predicament for bourgeois women whose additional handicap was the lack of fluent English. So Mrs. Schadlerberg volunteered whenever she could with several groups of German-speaking refugees, serving coffee and the cakes she baked in her narrow kitchen. She passed out leaflets at meetings and on street corners, until a group of German-American thugs from the Bund pushed her around and tore up the flyers, whereafter the family refused to allow her to continue street work. She also helped raise funds for the most needy exile families, and occasionally volunteered at the American Joint Jewish Distribution Committee stuffing envelopes and operating a mimeograph machine. "Your father has a job; it doesn't pay very much, but it keeps us sheltered and fed. This is what I can do to help. It is what I want to do. There are so many less well off than we are. What's that? Well, the neighbors who helped us most when we first got here were Jews, weren't they? I am just doing my bit. Isn't that what one says in English?"

Her encounter with the American version of the nazi party hooligans increased her devotion to the Cause to the point where her husband began to worry and speak the word "obsession" aloud. Remembering how his own involvement with the Social Democratic Party had frequently kept him away from the family nights and weekends, he was reluctant to complain about his wife's occasional absence from the kitchen. Nonetheless, he worried because he feared the Cause would take over her life and push him and the children to the periphery of her concerns. Schade helped his mother whenever he could take time from his other pursuits and he learned more about the pain and humiliation of poverty in exile than he had experienced and came to appreciate how fortunate he and his family were, even though they had been forced to leave Germany and all their possessions, except what they could jam into two suitcases each.

The meeting to which he took Leslie quickly degenerated into a loud series of ranting solutions to problems the attendees never defined, but which clearly related to the curious lack of action by the Wehrmacht in France and the Low Countries and how much time remained to get as many refugees out of Europe at the least cost. They left the meeting before it ended. "I don't understand what's wrong with those people," she said, her voice shaking with astonishment. "It's their way of dealing with the fact that they can't do much to help and their guilt at being here and safe." "They could get run over by a truck tomorrow." "That's not the kind of danger that concerns them." They walked on, each thinking about what they had seen.

"Let's cross the street. Come on." "All right, but what's the hurry?" "See that bunch in uniform over there, American nazis." "Oh."

He finished the play, but it was not very good and mirrored too much his own life in its lack of any focus other than Leslie. In the late spring the play in which she appeared closed and her parents sent her to classes at a college in Massachusetts. During the summer he visited her once; the reunion was unsuccessful: they had outgrown each other, though each suffered for a while a low-grade melancholy. "You could send me a copy of the play." "It's not very well done." "But it *is* mine, isn't it." "Yes."

He had to make up the semester and did not graduate as scheduled. His parents did not censure him for this expression of youthful passion and he continued to live in a room full of books in the family apartment. It took months to overcome his desolation; the fact that both he and Leslie had told each other the last time they met in the drafty bus terminal that each understood that it had to end had not made things any easier. They had been very civilized about it all and for several days congratulated themselves on their maturity. But back in the city he took to drinking too much beer at the anti-fascist and refugee aid meetings, which he now attended with greater enthusiasm and a new argumentative voice.

> *Little mean things we were doing*
> *Must have been part of the game*
> *Lending a spice to the wooing*
> *But I don't care who's to blame.*

He did not give up the idea of writing plays and continued to jot down fragments of dramas, stories, and poems when he could steal the time from school and the endlessly demanding activities of the movement. His poetry remained for some time heavily influenced by the Imagists and in a sense he never could remove himself from that influence.

A nude lighthouse
shining on the wave
of my pillow

is representative of his work at the time.

He spent hours moving his eyes slowly along the rows of his small library of mainly second hand books without dust jackets standing on the dilapidated red brick and warped board shelving he had constructed from building materials found at sites in the city and laboriously carted back to his room in small unnoticeable increments. Lack of money dictated the size of the collection and he supplemented his reading with borrowings from the public library branch and his friends, which explained the presence of several overdue notices gathered in an envelope stuck between Ernst Toller's *Das Schwalbenbuch* (perversely inscribed in English "To young Johannes who will grow to be a swallow") and the unread *Feuerbach und der Ausgang der klassischen deutschen Philosophie* by Engels. The volumes comforted him and eased his heated mind allowing him however briefly an escape from the heart pain he knew he would bear for the rest of his life. He came gradually to understand that each of the books represented a gateway to a different and exciting world that he could enter any time he wished by the simple act of reading. At first this astounded him but he soon realized that while the act may be straightforward, the chewing over of the subjects he read was not simple at all and the connections he began to make among the strands of ideas, thoughts, and characters in wildly complicated plots deepened and broadened his ability to deal with the mundane in his life as well as the more complex issues of his soul and heartbreak. But the mere act of gazing at the books leaning against each other in no particular order helped him during dark and painful hours when he suffered from the withdrawal of love and the acts of loving.

He would occasionally run his fingers along the spines of dark cloth covers while slowly masturbating to some inner directed rhythm reading the titles to himself. *Absalom, Absalom! La condition humaine, Die Verwirrungen des Zöglings Törless, The Great Gatsby, Old Shatterhand und die rothäutige Apachen, Hiob, Of Time and the River, Preussische Wappen* (Gertrud Kolmar's poems given to him as a birthday present by his mother, which caused him to miss a stroke when he saw the volume), *Rote Signale* (a collection of poems written by leftists given to him by his father at which sight he did not miss a stroke), *A Portrait of the Artist as a Young Man, Der Untertan, Briefe einer Deutsch-Französin, To Have and Have Not, Manhattan Transfer, Grapes of Wrath, Die Leiden des jungen Werther, The Magic Mountain* (unread in English and way overdue to the library), two novels by Samuel Mithman in garish dust jackets, a collection of Heine's poetry in German with a terrible English face en face translation, *Les chants de Maldoror* in English, Countee Cullen's *The Medea and Other Poems*, the *Iliad* and the *Odyssey* in a one volume English translation ...

He went often to the Village, where he maintained his friendships with some of the young theater people he'd met through Leslie and continued to thrash out with them the ideas then animating their lives as they sat over cheap red wine and spaghetti in Aldo's. Several little magazines published some of his poems and stories and he acted in a minor role in one of the plays staged by his friends. But during this time he concluded that his future did not lie in the theater: he needed the expanded possibilities of the novel to express his messages, whatever they would turn out to be. He found this resolution to be a welcome relief and he immediately began to outline a long fiction about young Americans in the New York theater world, in which an almost exact duplicate of Leslie Archer played a prominent part. Later he was grateful that he left the torso unfinished and even later lost it somewhere.

And he continued to revel in the city, the great metropolis that contained both the Museum of Natural History and Julius' Bar! Many of his parents' generation stood at a different angle to the city. For those who crossed the Atlantic as adults, who had known Paris and Berlin, New York often seemed rather provincial, a backwater in which they feared they would stagnate. At best they feared they would be forced to generate their creative energies and motivations from within themselves since they seemed unable to find them in their neighborhoods. Their fellow exiles scratching out a living in the city might stimulate some form of energy to overcome the smiling philistinism of American culture and the paralysis of will faced by many who could not forget that their own culture had rejected them. They trembled at the edge of the abyss of mental if not emotional depression.

Even if they later learned to appreciate their parents' intellectual traditions, the younger exiles like Schade assimilated more easily because they saw no reason to resist the process. They discovered the city to be invigorating and full of wondrously interesting challenges: they had little in the past with which to compare it, so they took it as their own.

The German-Soviet non-aggression treaty and the occupation of Poland by both countries had brought about a bitter split in the left-wing political movement that spilled over into every aspect of the lives of those deeply concerned with the issues. The behavior of the two arch-ideological enemies shocked the left and isolated the communist parties. The internecine struggles ate the energy and time previously devoted to combating the enemy and aiding needy comrades. Confused and disoriented by these events, after the end of the affair with Leslie, Schade gradually withdrew from active involvement with the Cause and its politics to spend his own energies completing the requirements for graduation that winter, writing a long series of poems on the death of sex, reading Freud, and debating with himself the efficacy of going to the whores on 7th Avenue. The graduation ceremony at City College presented him with a liberal arts degree and the necessity of either finding a job to support his writing time or a scholarship to support his enrollment in graduate school. Without undue consideration he chose the former and thought about finding a cheap room in Brooklyn but finally decided to move his books and papers into a shabby but clean room in a Greenwich Village tenement. He worked during the day as a clerk in the bursar's office at New York University on Washington Square, in the evenings wrote page after page of the novel, and found kindred young people with whom he could gratify both his physical and mental desires. Eighteen months later, with little of his work published, but with a greater knowledge of the ways of the world, Johannes Schadlerberg received a form letter beginning with the word "Greetings." Shortly thereafter he officially became John Schade, an American citizen, and a private in the armed forces of the United States.

   The name change startled a number of his German friends and acquaintances who regarded him with a bent eye and the notion of betrayal. Since the change was more functional than ideological, if a somewhat perverse one given the name he chose, he rejected the idea of treason out of hand. Betrayal of whom, of what? His German heritage? What could be more German than Schade? And the nazis had already betrayed his German heritage, and forced him out of it. The German exiles in New York feared the idea of change: they already had lived through more than their share. He came to understand this and his anger at their reaction gradually dissipated. His name would have no effect upon his ability or willingness to carry the "better" and the "true" German culture into the future. This he saw as the great task of the emigration: to nurture and maintain the German cultural tradition suppressed and murdered by the nazis, the tradition which included Heine and Mahler as well as Goethe and Beethoven.

The change of name did bring with it certain difficulties: his German friends pronounced the new name correctly – soft "a" as in "ahh" and the "e" enunciated as in "uh" – many of his American friends spoke it as if it should be preceded by the word "window." The more literate among them made small jokes about Dante and hell.

Not that his German friends let him off that particular hook. Almost all of them played with the name at one point or another. Since the word in German means both "regret" or "unfortunate" and "damage" or "harm," he often heard the phrases *"Schade, du schadest nichts"* and *"Schade, dass du Schade bist."* The humor of which is lost when translated into English: "Schade, you don't harm anything" and "A shame that you are Schade". All of which he attempted to absorb with a disdainful tolerance and an ability to laugh at his own expense. The thin border between the self-deprecatory and condescension he sometimes crossed when introduced in the German fashion: one briefly barks one's last name while pumping the other's hand twice in a short jerking motion. He enjoyed the confused reactions when the others could not discern if he was insulting them or not because he could be saying "Too bad I am meeting you!" As he grew older the occasions on which he practiced this little experiment in sociology diminished in number, but he held the exercise in reserve in case he needed it.

> *When I reached the age of nineteen*
> *It didn't matter if I had a bean.*
> *Then at the age of twenty-five*
> *I found my life just full of jive.*
> *Now that I am so much older,*
> *Almost twenty-six or so,*
> *The old songs sound so much bolder*
> *Than I can sing them oh my oh.*

* * * *

Now, so much later in time and space, in Wiesbaden, Germany, 2nd Lieutenant John Schade could not remember when he had been there before the summer of 1945.

Returning his autobiography to a bottom drawer in his mind, he drifted into a blank doze, emptying his mind in the pale sunlight, an effective method for evading unbidden thoughts, which disturbed mental equilibrium and hindered action. He did not sleep, but closed his eyes to the spring warmth and the park's washed out brown-green landscape, escaping into the gentle numbness of silence and the sun's prickly rays on his face. He did not think at all, but fragments of inchoate notions lackadaisically nudged one another about the flat surface of his mind. The colors of the day sailed slowly across the edges of his consciousness, warm and comfortable.

"*Cave tibi cane muto, aqua silente.* Watch out for silent dogs and still water. Not quite apropos, but it is rather unwaveringly quiet here, isn't it?"

Sensitive to accents and origins, Schade's first mental reaction came immediately: English, American overlay, educated, somewhat insecure or perhaps only shy, unsure of the response to his greeting. Schade's first emotional reaction came simultaneously: a flash of visceral annoyance which he immediately repressed and opened his eyes. The tall, benignly overweight man before him in the uniform designed for civilian staff held a cigarette before his chest between two lavishly nicotined fingers. A layer of flesh full of shallow creases blurred what had clearly once been sharp facial outlines. A very unmilitary shock of light hair hung over his forehead when he removed his overseas cap. Somehow Schade knew he was not as young as he appeared. The intruder waved his arm vaguely at the pond, scattering ashes. "The soldier home from the hill." He smiled. "But we're not quite there yet, are we? Didn't mean to disturb you, but I did. You looked so peaceful, or at peace. I was quite envious."

"That's all right. I mean, you didn't disturb me." When the other grimaced skeptically, Schade added, "Time I was on my way in any case."

"You're German originally." He pronounced the statement in a light soft voice without accusation.

"Yes. I'll never lose the accent, I suppose."

"Why should you? I'm rather an emigrant myself. One never fully loses it. I've tried hard enough from time to time."

"The American school systems do not teach Latin as much as they should."

"Beware of the silent dog and still water. My generation still had to learn it."

"You're English," Schade said feeling thick and stupid, his brain still shrouded in the cotton nimbus of escape.

The other man lowered himself onto the bench beside Schade and smiled with a touch of condescension. "We are all Americans now, aren't we? It's the wave of the future to be American, like it or not." He sighed and stretched his legs.

Schade felt a surge of restlessness and resentment against the invasion of his dream-escape. "What are you doing here?" He had not meant the question as aggressively as it sounded, and the other emigrant politely ignored the hostility. "Oh, I'm with the bombing survey, yes."

Schade looked blankly at him and shook his head. "The United States Strategic Bombing Survey. Not sure myself exactly what we're doing. Supposed to survey the results of strategic bombing, psychological and physical damage done, that sort of thing. Interviewing top krauts. Eh? Sorry. Perhaps it will be useful someday to someone, in the next war."

"Should there be another war...."

"I suppose. Actually, in my case, it was a method of getting over here to see what's going on, wasn't it? I lived here for some time before the war."

"So did I." They both laughed and Schade relaxed a little.

"In Wiesbaden?" The surveyor offered his cigarettes and Schade took one.

"Thank you. No, Breslau, some time in Berlin."

"That's where I spent most of my time: Berlin. I remember spending a day or so here on a trip and walking through this park in the evening." He glanced around them sadly. "Much different then, of course."

"Yes. That's my experience, too. Traveling through."

"How does it feel being back here now, on the other side, as it were?"

"I've been trying to analyze that." Why did he feel so comfortable with this stranger, a man older than he by a decade? He felt a certain intimacy growing between them in the few minutes that had passed; perhaps because they shared the emigrant experience, though Schade's had nothing of the voluntary about it. "Are you a physician?"

"Lord, no! I thought of studying medicine once. No, I've been teaching for years, English literature. Poetry and essays do not make a livable wage, do they?"

"I've certainly never earned anything from my poems; perhaps they're just not very successful." They smoked in silence for a moment.

"Look at the bushes and trees over there," the older man said, waving a hand in the direction of the far side of the shiny pond. "They're so dark and forbidding, aren't they? What lies behind them, do you suppose?"

"Limbo? Inferno? Certainly not paradisio."

"We need a Charon to take us over in an old leaky rowboat creaking with age and groaning in protest."

"We'd be better off listening to Cerberus."

"Then we'd never reach the other side, we'd remain ignorant."

"Perhaps that's best, at least in this case."

"You've no sense of adventure in your soul, my friend, have you then? But you'll find out anyway. It's inevitable." Not knowing which of the various answers to choose from those his mind immediately provided, Schade did not respond for a long moment.

"Actually being back is confusing to me. I haven't been able to think about it in any organized way, but I find the whole matter ... ambiguous, I suppose."

"I've wondered myself how I'll react to England when I return, or how England will react to me. But of course it will be different from your case. I wasn't forced to leave, not in the usual manner."

"I'm not Jewish." Why had he blurted that out?

"No. But you had your reasons, or your parents did. And fascists didn't emigrate, did they?"

"Often I'm not sure what I am." Schade smiled awkwardly as he said this and wondered again what this man possessed which drew him out so openly, like an old friend not seen in years.

"Knowing what one is doesn't always solve the problem. Makes it worse sometimes." Then, as if feeling he had crossed some limit, he quickly added, "What are you doing here?"

Schade briefly explained his unit's mission in what he hoped was a neutral tone. (Poet or not, the civilian reported to someone higher in authority.) He added that his group would be moving on very soon, and, not knowing whether or not the army had classified the destination, he omitted to mention the city. The poet lit another cigarette and nodded. "Berlin, eh? I'm not sure I'd like to see Berlin at this point. The photographs give the appearance of unpleasantness. I doubt I'd find any old friends there now. And of course the shifty-eyed Ivans are there. That'll be a bucket of worms, *mein Lieber*, wait and see."

"The Soviet Union suffered more than most from the war."

"They bloody well ganged up on Poland with the nazis, didn't they?" The man flushed. His voice tightened and began to rise with emotion. His arms flapped in the air. "Look at what they did in Spain to the rest of the Left. Look at what they're doing now with their soldiers taken prisoner by the Germans. Of course we're not much bloody better, we're giving those poor bastards back. It's horrid and monstrous, a barbarous sin." He dragged deeply on his cigarette and scratched behind his left ear. In a softer tone, he said, "One is no longer sure of anything except death. A cliché, but not a trivial point. Surely the way one dies is important as well, don't y'think?"

Schade brushed his mustache with his thumb. "*Tod ist Tod,*" he murmured.

"I disagree entirely, Lieutenant, entirely."

"The race has come this far, it will go on one way or another."

"But that's not the point, is it? The point is the process, how we go on or don't. That's what will make it worthwhile or despicable. We're not worms, are we? Presumably we're human beings with brains and souls."

"I don't know about the souls, but I wonder what the next generation will think about it. What will it have to hold it upright? Art, perhaps, for some."

"God, my friend, the Christian god. He is available for everyone, even Jews, even Muslims, everyone."

Schade felt the old discomfort and annoyance begin to foment in his mind, as they always started when he faced a zealot so sure of his faith that no response except capitulation would satisfy. He leaned back on the bench and forced a measure of calmness on his reaction. "I don't think that's possible any longer, not after this kind of evil...."

"Unfortunately," the older man interrupted, "unfortunately that goes for both sides. No, I don't mean the camps and the atrocities, but the bombing. It's what I'm supposed to be doing, you know, studying this horrible messy affair. It is incomprehensible that we had to be so destructive of non-military targets. The cities, my God, there's never been anything like this. Just because the kraut swine are barbarians doesn't require us being down there in the slime with them, does it? There is something askew in this stuff. Of course we fought the good war, no one can deny that. It's the bloody *way* we fought it, it's the awful terrifying results. You've seen it, you know what I mean. It's your country as well."

"No!" Schade's response was immediate and uncompromising. "No, no longer. Not for a long time. It's not my country any longer. I disown it. I repudiate it. Perhaps it's still my heritage, but it isn't my country any longer."

"So you're a real American now." The man smiled and his voice descended as Schade's rose in shrillness.

"Well, I have an American passport in any case, or would have if I was a civilian. I wear this uniform. I serve the nation, But...." He waved his hand slightly. "I don't know. Does one ever escape one's heritage? And we have to get along with the Russians, especially here; we have no choice."

"I think you unreconstructed leftists will find it more difficult than you imagine."

"Perhaps, but what other choice is there, damn it!"

"That's just it, there doesn't seem to be any." The surveyor-poet shook his head firmly. "Britain barely survived the war, France is morally bankrupt and physically too weak to count for anything but talk, Germany is destroyed, deservedly. What does that leave? The alternatives are clear: the States and the Soviet Union. Obviously, my dear, we have only one choice, don't we? More than ever now America is the future. Believe me."

Schade inclined his head and looked at the ground, his thoughts chasing one another so fast he could not separate them. It came as a shock to him when he noticed that his interlocutor wore a pair of shabby brown carpet slippers with his uniform, the apprehension of which oddity completely derailed the younger man's train of thought.

"And there's no choice for the krauts either, as wicked as they may be," the other continued in his Anglo-American voice. "They must go with the Americans. If they're too thickheaded to see this for themselves, they must be shown the way. *That's* what you ought to be doing in Berlin, Lieutenant. Eventually the Russians will have to see it, too."

"I don't think they will; their ideology is too strong and they've invested too much in it, they're too committed. And all the Germans care about is food, for the moment."

"Which means now's the time to get at 'em," the surveyor interjected quickly. "They've no resistance left. The so-called Werewolf underground is a myth. Twist 'em, turn 'em, bring 'em around. They're so bloody sad they'll do anything for you, won't they. And if they won't, we can force them, for their own good as well as ours."

"You sound like a reorientation directive: We shall democratize the Germans in our own image blah blah."

The other snorted contemptuously and lit another cigarette. From behind the cloud of smoke he told Schade, "No, not that. But Germany has no independent role to play in the foreseeable future, does it? We have to guide it in our direction or the Ivans will take it all or the same groups that supported Hitler will return. Probably will anyway, one way or another."

"They will resist eventually. In the long run they cannot be forced; they have long traditions, too."

"That, my dear friend, is where your job takes on its importance. You must feed their little blonde heads as well as their disgusting bellies."

"Yes, that's the policy, all right. Feed them democratic ideas and democratic bread. All we need is the democratic circuses, and that's what my job is going to be, isn't it?"

"You can't possibly be sympathetic to this horrid country, even with your heritage."

"They weren't all nazis."

"Not all the time, perhaps, but often enough. No, no, you must purge your minds of such nonsense. It simply won't wash. Have a fag."

Schade took the cigarette and the light. In previous discussions on this topic he usually regretted allowing his doubts and hesitations to come so close to the surface. He well knew that most of his colleagues did not share his ambivalence, so he generally kept his confusion well covered with banalities and the superficialities of quick if vague agreement. This made his life easier, but he knew that at some point he would have to uncover his position on the issues, once he had been able to think about it all more deeply and once he had a more lucid point to make.

"Are you sure you're not some kind of a confessor?" He said this with a grin and the other laughed.

"You don't often have the chance to confess, do you?" After a moment he stood up and looked around the park. "I must get back to Bad Homburg. You know, lieutenant, I once walked in this park with the loveliest person, before the war when we were all so awfully young. Not much youth left in Europe now, is there? All used up. Take another generation or so to grow a new crop, and what will they resemble? Think about that. Well, nice chatting with you. By the way, my name's Auden."

Schade stood up to take the proffered hand. "Schade."

"I'll spare you the obvious puns."

"I've read some of your poems: 'September'...."

"I'm having that one removed from the canon, as it were. Don't like it anymore, my dear, not honest, y'know?"

"History doesn't lie."

"No, but we do, don't we? Well, good-bye; good luck in Berlin."

The surveyor-poet shambled off down the path toward the boulevard trailing cigarette smoke behind him. He rounded a curve and disappeared from view leaving Schade squinting slightly in the pale warm sunlight. He still could not remember when he'd been in Wiesbaden before the war.

* * * *

Once under way military operations leave little time for reflection by individual soldiers suffering Doubts about their own direction and National Policy Goals. About the latter, their commanding officers preferred they not think at all, and for the remainder of his brief time in Bad Nauheim the planned move to Berlin occupied all of Schade's waking hours. On some level of unconsciousness, however, the struggle toiled on, raveling and unraveling its tenacious coils like a roll of live barbed wire spasmodically mulching a half-ton of veg and potatoes into new forms and consistencies.

The unit's final staff meeting took place just prior to the move to Halle in the Soviet Zone, the last staging area for the swing north to Berlin. Lt. Colonel Graham McCrae, a colorless former mid-level radio executive in Chicago before being drafted (his "friend" on the draft board having missed the opportunity to move his file a sufficient distance from the active pile), recently appointed commanding officer of the Information Services Control Branch for the US Sector of Berlin, conducted the meeting in his usual fashion which Makepeace would later describe as "that balanced combination of efficiency and ineffectualness which arises when a civilian is put in uniform and attempts to behave like a military officer." McCrae himself preferred Paris but had been unable to arrange a posting there. On the whole, if he had to remain in Germany at all, Berlin appealed to him. It had been a big city and McCrae felt comfortable in big cities where he could do his job but remain anonymous. He had not thought much about the impossibility of this happening in Berlin under the circumstances of the defeat and occupation. Now he faced his staff without visible nervousness and spoke to them without notes, the sound of command in his voice, if not, as Makepeace noted, in the substance of his lecture.

"Gentlemen, what are we going to do with the goddam Germans?" he said with a swerve of his right arm. "In our case, the Berliners. Our job is to prevent anything related to the press, music, theater, movies and book printing from being done in our sector without our approval, that is without our licensing the project whatever it is. And on what do we base our license?" McCrae coughed and thought, there must be a better way of saying all this, but I can't think of it. "Part of the process will be denazifying our clients, by which I mean they'll have to fill out a long and thorough questionnaire called a Fragebogen giving their life histories. This will tell us when they joined the party which will tell us what kind of nazis they were. We check the party records wherever they exist to see if someone is lying, and they will, you can bet on it. In short, nothing gets done without our permission. They can take a crap or get laid without asking but everything else is our business."

Makepeace whispered, "What if they want to pick their noses?"

McCrae continued, "Of course the guidelines are all laid out in the occupation handbook written by the desk jockeys in Washington who've never even heard of Hansel and Gretel, and in the thousands of pages of directives we have to carry around with us. But I tell you, gentlemen, we won't know what we're going to do with the goddam Berliners until we get there!"

(Later Makepeace laughed and said, "Actually the handbook was written by a fouled up combination of ignorant policy makers and anti-nazi refugees who ended up in the Office of Strategic Services and the War Department. It still won't be of much use to us in the field, or in the city."

"How do you know that, Bill?"

"Word gets around, John, word gets around."

"Especially in certain circles, that's clear."

"As spring water, pal."

And Darkley said to both of them later as they accompanied him to Tempelhof airstrip for his flight back to headquarters in Frankfurt, "A friend of mine received a letter from Thomas Mann *castigating* the Germans, I mean *flaying* his countrymen. He said they have an abiding tendency toward meanness, they're egoistic, malicious, and *both* arrogant and self-pitying. I *quite* agree, of course.")

"But this is not the official view, and you need to know that so here it is: we've a fair idea of what it's like up there. OSS had a team in there last month, but we have no details of that report because it's classified. Typical. The situation, however, can be summed up in one word: bad. Some of our people have been up there already to work out the logistics and since we're going up in the second convoy, some quarters will have been cleared for us. At least that's what they tell me. You've been in the army long enough not to count on things like that. You'll probably get sleeping bags. It's summer after all. The quarters for the big meeting are located in Potsdam, somewhere outside the city, so we don't have to be worried about being bumped out of town by the big brass. Maybe. Our sector has been marked on the maps you've all been issued. They're not very good, but they are the best we've got for now. I think they're from 1916.

"Once we're there remember two things: we've got to take control as fast as possible in our sector. It won't be like anything we've experienced so far. The Russians have already re-established cultural life of sorts up there. They've been in business more than a month, so theaters are open, concerts are given, excetera, excetera. We're not sure what kind of denazification standards and procedures they're actually using. This means we may have to clean house in our area from the ground up. We'll meet with the Russians and the British to work out a common policy as soon as we get organized up there. The French are scheduled to come up later. The point is to let the Germans know we mean business. No nazis get licensed. If there are some working in our sector under Russian license, we revoke the license for our sector. The British have already concurred in this, more or less." McCrae's tall figure ceased pacing and his thick fingers scratched his brush cut graying hair. He appeared to be contemplating a possible bit of indiscretion in his last phrase. Having found none he could identify, he continued to walk back and forth in a slow, lanky pattern.

"So we have to move as fast as we can. The first few days will be reconnaissance, excetera, excetera. Find out what's going on, what's been done and what has to be done, get settled in, show the flag, excetera. When we've got our bearings, we go to it.

"The second thing to keep in mind is cooperation with the Soviets. As I understand it the Russians, the British, the French and we will run the city, that is, policy will be decided jointly for the entire city and implemented by whichever clean Germans we can find under our direction, excetera. Present policy emphasizes cooperation and getting along with the Russians, a solid Allied front against the Germans. So we do our jobs with that in mind, clear? It may not be easy at first. The situation is likely to be unstable until we shake it down.

"Okay. It's going to be primitive up there for a while. Keep your field gear in order. I don't have to remind you about the non-fraternization policy, excetera, but I also don't have to tell you that this applies selectively to our team. If we don't meet them, we're not doing what we should be doing. But the main thing is getting the job done." He stopped pacing and looked over the men of his command as if he wondered if he had expressed the image of a ranking military officer giving his men a realistic pep talk, some how intuiting that a pep talk is the antonym of realism. "We move out for Halle at 0630 hours. Any questions?"

* * * *

Schade and Makepeace walked back to their quarters after the briefing. The air cooled and began to swirl the dust in the street around their feet. In the darkening sky bulky clouds swollen with storm nudged each other uneasily. "It's going to rain." Then, "Obviously."

"John, we have one more meeting, just the two of us, in an hour, with the bigger brass. The rain will hold off." Makepeace sighed with either exasperation or annoyance, Schade could not determine which.

Schade was not surprised: meetings were unavoidable under circumstances in which most of those involved had no knowledge about plans and programs which would possibly change their futures and certainly alter their geography. "What's it all about?" "I'm not sure. Maybe they're going to enforce the directive that says no good old American GI with relatives in Germany can serve in the occupation forces. They want me there to restrain you. On the other hand, we did make an exception for you, John."

"Oh, yes. Me and seven hundred other military government personnel."

"But, John, you are the only one of them working with *us*."

"How do you define us, William?"

"Ah, yes, indeed, there is the nub of it, isn't it?"

"What if it isn't that ridiculous directive?"

"Well, it can't be anything good when the brass go over McCrae's head to the likes of you and me. It's bound to make our lives even more miserable. Not very military."

"Most people here aren't very military really. They're like us: civilians in uncomfortable uniforms."

"I still don't like it."

"They probably want us to pick up some souvenirs for them before the Russians get them all."

* * * *

Makepeace remained troubled, a not uncommon state of affairs, but one which, with practice, he learned to adroitly camouflage. William Thoreau Makepeace carried his literary name, the result of an argument between his New England-bred mother, who read *Walden* once each year, and his Minnesota father, with some inner discomfort, but with outward aplomb. Having reached the conclusion that he had little talent for writing literature despite his name and his mother's desires, he turned to studying novels and poetry in college with the vague idea of teaching at some indeterminate future. He planned to attend graduate school to obtain a degree that would allow him to join the faculty of an appropriately rated college somewhere in the East (according to his mother) or the Midwest (according to his father). That gentleman, a successful insurance executive whose family had been in St. Paul for generations, had not approved his son's choice of a profession, considering universities to be spawning grounds for liberals who supported "that son-of-a-bitch in the White House" (liberals being something akin to communists in his estimation). When he first showed signs of wanting to write, his father had driven him to Summit Avenue and stopped in front of a row of townhouses at number 593. "See that house? A writer lived there. Look at it; not even a real house. There's no garage. He's a failure, see? Nothing to show for his life except failure. A drunk, a real souse, couldn't take care of his family. A down and out failure. That's what happens to writers. We're ashamed that bum Fitzgerald was born here, I'm telling you. And you're not going to end up like that." And he stepped on the gas pedal and the car sped down the street and down the hill leading to downtown and the St. Paul Hotel where he had an appointment. The son took the bus home in a state of shock and disgust.

When they all discovered early in his school career that the young Makepeace naturally used his left hand to do everything all his schoolmates did with their right hand, the young boy harshly discovered, as he noted later to Schade, "There's something suspicious about lefthanders, even in the name: think of the Italian word for left." As a teenager he began to wear his watch on the right hand wrist, and when he finally earned a sufficient amount of money on his own, he bought a heavy-linked sterling silver wrist bracelet with his initials, no periods, engraved in Gothic script on its curved surface. He wore this ostentatiously on his left wrist and rattled the links against each other when his emotions rose above a certain level on his personal feelings gauge.

𝔚 𝔗 𝔐

"They tried their damnedest to get me to write with my right hand, but I refused, absolutely refused. Like Bartleby, I preferred not to. In the end I won that one. Not that I particularly liked being a southpaw, but at some point ya gotta draw the line, don't cha?"

In the summer they went to the lake for two months. In Minnesota "the lake" is a generic terms for any and all of the 10,000 lakes that the citizens went to if they could afford it. The specific lake where the Makepeace family owned a "cabin" was called Carlos near a very small town named Alexandria. Like "the lake" a "cabin" is the statewide generic term for any residence on the lake regardless of size. The Makepeace house had four bedrooms, two large screened porches and a dock for the small motorboat in which the males in the family went fishing for walleye from time to time. The drinking water tasted peculiar at the lake, like slightly decomposed mulch and the summer woods and water plants, unpolluted by city chemicals and purifiers. One of the younger Makepeace's jobs in the early morning was to pump fresh water up from the well into a blue enamel pitcher that he placed on the kitchen sink for the family to use when they brushed their teeth. He enjoyed the lake until he grew old enough to argue with his father. After that he no longer freely enjoyed the cabin and the lake and took summer jobs so he could not go there anymore.

The elder Makepeace had sent his son to Stanford on the theory that a degree from that university would allow him to teach anywhere. And if the younger Makepeace must go to college, the elder Makepeace also appreciated the reputation for conservative opinions attributed to that institution. He had stipulated, however, that his son take a year before entering college to work on the Wyoming ranch of a relative whose extreme antagonism to the New Deal surpassed even his own. The Makepeace relative firmly and loudly believed that the members of the Civilian Conservation Corps, the government's attempt to put unemployed young men to doing socially useful work in the middle of the most severe economic depression the nation and the world had thus far experienced, formed the nucleus of a secret communist army whose intent was to overthrow the capitalist system and the relative's very way of life. "That's what they're doing out there in the woods, right here in Wyoming, stirring up the jigaboos and the Indians." It went without saying that the leader of this revolution was "that son-of-a-bitch in White House."

The empty spaces of Wyoming proved not to be as onerous as the young man feared and the combination of open air work and the attentions of a waitress in a small café in town initiated him into several areas of experience during those twelve months. His studies thereafter were guided by a clever if very traditional aging professor of German literature whose left eye was in a constant state of twitch. He had left Germany in the mid-thirties because of a vocal disagreement with the extent to which the National Socialists carried their policies and their patent bias against traditional cultural norms. While his mentor did not turn him into a flaming liberal, the conflicting pressures of the times made him a centrist conservative cynic who damned both the right and the left with equal enthusiasm and disdain.

The arrival of his draft notice interrupted his studies and, after six weeks of basic training as a simple private, officer training school had made him, like Schade, a second lieutenant, which means an officer and, presumably, a gentleman, though the regular West Point officers doubted this. The vicissitudes of military processing and his knowledge of the German language and its culture had placed him in the psychological warfare unit instead of the infantry or quartermaster corps. While doing "sikewar" (psychological warfare) in Paris he met John Schade and they became unsurprisingly competitive and prickly friends, their friendship being conducted like porcupines meeting in the dark. While abhorring nazi theory and practice, Makepeace's offhand contempt for the left in general and the Soviet Union in particular concerned and frustrated Schade, who wondered out loud how well his colleague and friend would cooperate with their Soviet counterparts in Berlin.

"I suppose I'm as much a creature of my upbringing as anyone else. So it's understandable that I don't share your plebian left wing views." Makepeace did not smile as he said this.

"One can always break away from one's background, rebellion is always a possibility," Schade said with equal earnestness.

"Oh, I rebelled all right. Yes, indeed. Leaped from the family's extreme Republican individualism smack dab in the middle of the road FDR liberalism. Very dramatic it was, too. Father finally disowned me, but by then it didn't matter," Makepeace said with satisfaction.

They were drinking Calvados in a bar on the Rue Saint Jacques near the Panthéon, where the waiter eyed them with suspicion and distaste. American soldiers became obstreperous when drunk and broke things in fits of primitive enthusiasm. The waiter did not worry about the furniture, for which the proprietor was responsible, but he was concerned for his own well-being and that of the bottles for which he would be held accountable. The only difference between enlisted men and officers when in this condition was the fact that the enlisted men occasionally made an effort to pay for the damage they caused. These two officers concerned him, although they appeared to be so involved in their conversation that they probably would not come to hitting each other over the finer points of their disputes.

"But you've taken over his political views, your father's; you've got the same ideological blinders as he does."

"Because I don't agree with you hardly means that I'm blind to the real world."

"Not blind, warped –"

"Horseshit."

"—you need to be straightened out. Where's your good old sympathy for the underdog?"

"I was one myself, several times in fact."

"It's an American characteristic, you know."

"Rigid patriotism is the veil behind which the unthinking and the narrow minded hide their empty brains."

"Scoundrels."

"Them, too."

"So why can't you admit that socialism would be better for everyone, right through the whole society?"

"Ha! Like diarrhea through the bowels. Whoosh!"

"There's that warp again."

"You've too little humor, Johannes, like all you pinkos."

"Dead wrong, *mon chèr Guillaume*. I'm known in certain New York circles for my clown-like behavior and witty repartee."

"God save us! *Monsieur, encore la calva, s'il vous plait.*" Makepeace shook his head and bent to retrieve his hat. "Germans have a problem with humor. The more *Weltschmerz* the better they feel."

"But I am an American, got all the papers to prove it. Even the army agrees so there you are."

"No sense of humor, no wonder they've always caused trouble, read Tacitus –"

"*E pluribus aluminium excelsior.*"

"And now we're going to have trouble with our faithful allies from the east –"

"Certainly will if you think like that from the start without giving it a chance –"

"Oh, they'll get chances enough. We'll bend over backward to accommodate them, but soon enough the struggle will become painfully visible."

Schade bridled. "You can still be a socialist without following Stalin's line –"

"In the end it's the same and in your mind of minds you know it."

"You – we've had enough of this acid. I'm going to bed."

"You're not capable. I'll escort you."

"Since your bunk is about two meters from mine, sure."

Makepeace said in a soothing tone, "Rest easy, *mon capitaine*, we'll give it the old college try –"

"I preferred high school, actually."

"Incorrigible Teuton. Typical."

"Argh …"

"Precisely."

The waiter breathed more easily as the two officers cleared the doorway on their way out, but caught his breath in his throat when they staggered back into the room and walked past him mumbling something about "*fait le pipi.*" When they finally disappeared down the rue Clotaire toward the Panthéon he discovered to his surprise that they had left exactly ten percent of the bill as a tip.

* * * *

In Bad Nauheim the army had billeted them in the dining room of a requisitioned apartment previously inhabited by a party functionary whose activities in the past few years had been of such a nature as to cause his suicide immediately prior to the arrival of the American troops. Figures from other units came and went in the other rooms, shadows in transit like themselves.

As they entered the room after the briefing, a short, heavy-set captain with horn-rimmed spectacles on his nose looked up from the papers he was reading. "Hello. Kirshhof, Harald, called Hal. I've been assigned to Berlin Information Control. Newspapers is my racket, kay?" He spoke in the soft accents of the Midwest. "Hate to bust in on you guys like this, but the Colonel assigned me here for the night. Got anything to drink?"

While Makepeace searched the heavily waxed sideboard for a bottle, the other said, "Don't know how I got assigned here. My German's not all that hot. I was a reporter in Bloomington for a year before they drafted me. That doesn't make me a newspaper expert, does it?"

Makepeace located the bottle and waved it about. "Give up this peripatetic search for the holy grail of logic. You'll do naught but damage your mystified brain and obtain no answer in the end or final analysis." After intoning this he drank briefly from the bottle, gagged, and handed it to the newcomer to whom he said in the same pontifical tones, "You're Jewish, I presume."

Kirshhof did not gag on a swallow considerably larger than Makepeace's. "You presume right. Where'd you learn to talk like that? College? I went to college for a while, kay? Didn't work out. What'd I need college for to be a reporter? Yeah, I'm Jewish. Wanna see proof? Why just take a gander at these personalized identification tags I wear around my Jewish neck. Note the finely stamped 'J' right here where everyone can see it, even some nazi SS swine. Think about what happened to Jewish GIs who got captured. You think the J stands for Jesuit, kay? A goddamned gift to the kraut pigs! Oh, yeah, I'm Jewish all right."

Schade stood the bottle on the sideboard without tasting the contents. "You don't need to be defensive. We're on your side. It was just a question. Under the circumstances the question is understandable."

"Oy, another professor. This one from around here somewhere, kay? Listen, buddy, under the goddamn circumstances it's a goddamn offensive question." He looked at each of them in turn, a curious intensity glowing briefly in his eyes. Then his expression thickened and his facial features seemed to gain weight. "Listen. I try not to make my life anymore difficult than it is. You've got no idea what it's like to be a Jew in Indiana, even a non-religious assimilated Jew who's learned to say things like 'for christ's sake.' We all know what the fucking krauts did. Everybody'll know before long. Should have known long ago, kay. Yeah, I lost relatives in the camps. Sure I'm bitter, kay. I hate those fucking German pigs. You know what my ambition here is? To sleep with some female nazi and then tell her I'm Jewish. But what the hell, I've got enough points to get out and go home at the end of October. That's a true fact, kay? And I'm going. That's a true fact, too. So nobody's got to worry about me, kay? I won't shoot any krauts, I'll do my job just fine. Until October. Then I'll hate the goddamn krauts on my own time, kay?" He swallowed more alcohol without gagging. "What is this shit?"

"Evidently a local specialty," Makepeace answered carefully. "Goldwasser. We found it when we got here. Our predecessors apparently didn't care for it either, whoever they may have been."

Schade maintained his habitual skeptical expression. "What did you do before they assigned you here?"

"What is this, twenty questions?"

"No, just interest in a fellow worker in the vineyards of the good and the true, " Makepeace said and stepped quickly backward as a round dark object shot out from Kirshhof's right hand toward the sideboard, and just as suddenly shot back into his hand before it smashed into the furniture. "What the hell!"

"Arrgghh, sorry, sorry. When I get tense playing with a yoyo calms me down. You'd be amazed how effective it is." He shot the implement out and back several times, at the finale of the last trip the wood smacked against his palm and his hand closed over it. "I was an editor for the *Stars and Stripes*, not bad either."

"That makes you a newspaper expert."

"John, we have to be off. Welcome aboard, Hal. We'll be back shortly."

Kirshhof returned his attention to his papers. Head bent, he asked, "Where do we eat around here?"

"The officer's club is around the corner. You can't miss it. You'll find the garbage always surrounded by a large crowd of civilians." With this Makepeace loped out of the room adjusting his canteen. Outside, as they climbed into the jeep, Schade said, "He's going to be trouble."

"Hell, no," Makepeace replied with some asperity starting the motor with an unnecessary roar. "He wants to go home more than he hates the Germans. I'll bet he didn't even know those relatives in the camps. He'll be okay. But I wonder if he's better at the yoyo than he is at editing."

"I think he'll be trouble. He's too angry, too intense."

"Christ, we're all intense, future unknown. It's natural. And he just got here. You're always intense when you join a new unit. Stop worrying, we've got enough on our minds. Like continuing to whack the krauts, like this goddamn meeting, like not fraternizing *mit den Fräuleins.*"

"Perhaps, maybe...." Schade looked to the west above the houses into the early evening sky. "We ought to put the top up; it's going to rain."

Blue skies
Smiling at me,
Nothing but blue skies
Do I see.

* * * *

The meeting was confusingly brief. They spent more time maneuvering their way across town through the congestion of war material, blank-eyed Germans and ambiguous displaced persons crowding the streets than it took their superiors to give them their orders.

To Schade's surprise the very formal Brigadier General Thomas Sender, the chief of Information Control in the American occupied territories in Germany, presided over the meeting. "Good evening, gentlemen. Please sit down. Colonel Darkley is going to give you a special, top-secret assignment. My presence here is to ensure that you understand the seriousness of the mission. It has my complete support. And it must remain secret, totally secret." He smiled coldly and his steel-rimmed glasses glittered in the lamplight, sending coded signals confirming his statements. The smile seemed to say, "I need add nothing further. You understand me."

Darkley adjusted the blue eye patch covering his left eye socket, cleared his throat and began to speak in rasping tones surprising for a mild-mannered American aristocrat. "We have a *list* of Berlin cultural types who *will* survive denazification and be licensed to work in our sector. It is short. We do not know at present in *which* sector they live or work or *if* they are working. Most of them are theater people or musicians. Your job is to make sure they *work* and *live* in our sector. More specifically that they do not work *regularly* in the other sectors, especially in the Russian sector. You will interview them as *soon* as possible after setting up shop. Convincing most of them should not be *difficult*. If what we've heard about Russians' behavior in Berlin is *true*, you should have an easy time of it." No dying fall accompanied Darkley's finale, he simply stopped, as if there would be no further discussion, but of course there was.

"You look skeptical, lieutenant," the general said to Schade from the heights of classified knowledge. "You needn't be. We're not throwing out the policy of cooperation with our Allies. We are merely trying to ensure that our sector receives its share of the available talent. You will note the list is short. We have no intention of creating difficulties with the Russians or the others. In fact," the general smiled behind his glasses, "it wouldn't surprise me if our Allies had planned a similar kind of mission."

"The mission *is* highly classified," Darkley continued, "very low *key*, of course, but highly classified. In fact, it does not *exist*. As I said, you should have little trouble, but I urge you to be subtle. A hint is often more effective than a *flat* statement, and a hint is infinitely more *deniable*. Subtle, but *convincing*." Darkley allowed a smile to emerge and join the general's, but with a suspicious touch of warmth the general's lacked. "You won't be rated *by* the success or failure in *this* matter. It will remain among the *four* of us, more or less four of us, if you get my *drift*. Just do your best and don't *make* any waves. Understood?"

Both Schade and Makepeace automatically nodded. Darkley passed them a sheet of paper with eight names neatly typed on it. Only three of them had been misspelled, as Schade later pointed out. "Perhaps they are *already* in our sector. Then your job is to make certain that they *stay* there. I remind you again that this is *top* secret, for obvious reasons. Colonel McCrae has enough to *worry* about, so we won't *bother* him with this matter. As a *matter* of fact, *we* may never *mention* it again. Once you get to Berlin things *there* will undoubtedly be very hectic."

The general spoke again in flinty tones. "Nothing blatant. No promises that would embarrass us. No coercion. You'll work out the details of the situation after you've oriented yourselves in the target area." He turned to his deputy. "You will be on your own for a while, a month, maybe longer, until we fill out the roster with additional officers. You will have to recon all the entertainment fields, theater, music, film. Newspapers, books, libraries, and so on, others will take care of. Another part of the Information Control Division will take care of the American movies that can be shown in our zone. I think that covers it, Colonel."

Darkley rubbed his seeing eye and made the traditional closing comment. "Any questions, gentlemen?"

They had none they thought sufficiently innocuous to ask the general and the meeting ended, each of the younger men understanding different meanings.

Driving back to their quarters Schade shifted in his seat, even more than usually disturbed and annoyed. "This is not good, Bill, not good at all."

"It's not as bad as I thought. At least we're not hunting for autographed pictures of Adolf and Eva for the general's walls. What the hell, John, it could be exciting. Secret, hush-hush stuff. Swell." Makepeace laughed. "And diddling the Russkies a bit is no big deal. They've had time to set up there the way they want. No reason we can't stir up the bees' nest and see what happens."

"Bill," Schade said somewhat plaintively, "this is no way to *start* the occupation."

"Come on, friend, don't *start* to talk like Colonel *Dark*ley. Besides, they take a few from us, we take a few from them. What the hell? A little competition will do the krauts good. Show them how the system works." He yanked sharply at the wheel of the jeep as the vehicle barely missed an elderly couple trudging down the middle of the road pushing an old empty wheel barrow in the stygian gloom of the Central European night.

"Slow down, for Christ sake. That kind of competition we could do without. It'll give the Germans an opportunity to play us off against each other. We're supposed to be a solid front...."

"There you go, you unreconstructed kraut-sympathizer, with all that leftwing jargon –"

"Jesus, you are bloody exasperating. What is jargon about it? You know what I mean. What the hell are we here for anyway?"

Makepeace occasionally gave the appearance of deep seriousness, betraying his essentially pessimistic view of the future. "I think we are here to keep the communists out of the rest of Europe," he said with more deliberation than he had previously shown. The jeep's speed decreased noticeably. "I think they've got their Germans and we've got ours, especially in Berlin."

Schade suppressed a surge of anger and said with soft bitterness, "Asshole! We're here to make damn sure the Germans don't threaten Europe ever again. The Soviet Union has the same goals."

"*Bin kein Arschloch, habe aber eins*," Makepeace said in a conciliatory tone using the old German phrase "I'm not an asshole, but I've got one". "Maybe it won't work out that way. You can't deny the Russians are exporting class revolution for its own ends. The situation in Berlin is bound to be different in any case. Three or four victorious powers trying to rule a major city -- are you kidding? But frankly, given the nature of the two systems, I don't see how we can come to any long-term agreements with them. The point at hand is to deal with the Germans. On that we can agree with the Russians. One step at a time, didn't Lenin say that? We'll get the Germans first. You worry too much, even for a left winger."

Schade's smile bordered on the insulting, reflecting more the desire to end the argument than agreement. Makepeace seemed so sure of himself in many matters about which Schade did not feel secure at all. A true American trait, he thought with admiration mixed with a natural if mild presumption of European cultural superiority, a residue of his past he could not give up regardless of the color of his passport. "What about Kirshhof?"

Makepeace shook his head and cursed the dimness of the jeep's headlights. "Now that's another complication," he said, as willing as Schade at this point to change the subject. "But I doubt he'll cause any trouble. We'll keep an eye on him." Then in his professorial voice: "Let us assume that old EB is cognizant of the situation with reference to the man's antipathies and has arranged to maintain control over said situation." EB was Makepeace's derisive nickname for Lt. Col. McCrae meaning "equivocal brain."

"You slay me, Bill, you're so amusing. Watch that pothole! And I told you we should have put the top up."

"You worry too much; we're almost there." Makepeace rattled his ID bracelet.

Schade stopped for a moment in the hallway of the apartment to shake as much rain as he could off his uniform. "Why did they pick us for this stupid mission?" Makepeace looked blankly at him. "How come they set up this meeting through you?"

"They couldn't find you, I guess. What difference does it make?" Makepeace touched the crown of his head as if searching for some sign he would retain all his hair.

"Just wondered," Schade muttered, the beginning of suspicion entering the back reaches of his mind.

* * * *

He stood briefly in front of the mirror hanging on the grayish yellow wall. Brown eyes stared back at him, neither cold nor warm, underscored by dark splotches of exhaustion, his straight light brown hair, cut very short by a military barber, lay flat, without energy. Brushing his left thumb lightly across his closely cut brown mustache, he saw nothing unusual in his reflection.

Good night, Mrs. Calabash, wherever you are!

* * * *

The move to Berlin started the next day as scheduled. The trip to Halle went smoothly but at an excruciatingly slow pace. They arrived in the late afternoon and MPs directed each section to its overnight quarters. Schade's unit drove to a damaged school building where he and his colleagues ate their tinned C-rations and drank coffee laced with whiskey. Lt. Col. McCrae gazed meditatively at his tin of generic meat and muttered, "To think I used to eat at the Blackstone and the Drake five days a week back in Chicago." In another part of the building, Kirshhof said to Makepeace, "I really wish I could say I've eaten worse." "Weren't you ever in boy scout camp?" "Who, me?" They slept on the floor in their bedrolls and in the early morning after brief ablutions and a visit to the latrine herded into the school cafeteria where a crew of frightened, shabbily dressed German women of all ages with hesitant smiles served them a hot if tasteless breakfast. "Look at their eyes, John, they speak terrible words in silence. Vox populi. They know the Russians will be here in a couple of days; it's their zone. These poor wretches would do anything to go with us. They fear liberation as much as death."

Schade coughed. "That's bullshit. They are not being liberated, they are a conquered people. They fear the future in any form because they know nothing about it."

"Right now they fear the Red Army."

As they left the building, one of the women stopped Kirshhof, holding his sleeve, talking, her speech heavily distorted with the local dialect, pleading. He pulled his arm away and walked on. The woman remained motionless staring after them, her eyes blank with resignation. "Camp followers," Kirshhof remarked with contempt as he climbed into the jeep and took out his yoyo.

The long convoy of military vehicles proceeded north as fast as the bombed and buckled road allowed. The storm during the night had dispersed the clouds and the pale sun fixed the dust, sweat and curses raised by the column in its dim glare. As the soldiers wound their way through the smaller towns and villages squatting over the roads, they distinguished two different types of civilians, less by their clothing, which was quite similar, than by their behavior that was quite opposite. The Germans stood in silence, defeated crowds along the edges of the streets staring with astonished degrees of bafflement and tense curiosity as the variety of vehicles sped past them. When this particular column disappeared to the north, they continued their weary trek from somewhere to elsewhere.

The second type of crowd raised a muted storm of jubilation and, shouting in various tongues, cheered the Americans as they passed. Many of them spoke the crazy-quilt languages of Eastern Europe and beyond, but the noise constituted a babble of all known and some unknown patterns of sounds. However, the yelling possessed a curious weakness, the noise level rarely reached beyond a hoarse croaking, full of the desire to express joy and some form of gratitude. Some of these people spastically danced up and down in their excitement. They could not maintain this state very long; the camps and slave labor factories had robbed them of the spark of life beyond that of simple survival. It would take some time to recuperate their physical and spiritual energies. Emaciated into skeletal forms, weakened from inhuman exertion and malnutrition, they stumbled anxiously across the face of central Europe like a plague of exhausted locusts, millions of them, named by common consent "displaced persons," a horribly inadequate descriptive phrase culled from the drawer of some indifferent desk jockey safe behind the lines. These scrambled people constituted a major problem for the victorious Allies, for the vanquished and for themselves as they restlessly pillaged and foraged from one town or farm to another, clogging the breathing tubes of the already choking cities, drunk with freedom and life after years of prison and death. As the American military column disappeared to the north, the savage hunt for food and revenge continued.

    Schade and Makepeace sat with Kirshhof and a sergeant who drove the jeep, all of them in full battle gear, the officers with pistols; only the sergeant carried a carbine he could not use unless he removed his hands from the steering wheel. As they moved deeper into Soviet occupied territory, they passed convoys of soldiers and material moving in the opposite direction from theirs. The soldiers of the Red Army and the American Military Government greeted each other with curiosity and spontaneous friendly gestures. They yelled at each other above the swirling dust and the jangling roaring noises of the machines, exchanging mutually incomprehensible compliments congratulating each other on their common victory, enjoying the warmth of relief at having avoided death and dismemberment.

"*Privet, tovarischi!*" "How the hell are ya?!"

Some of them shot their weapons in the air laughing until the officers put a stop to that potentially disruptive expression of international camaraderie. After this Verbot they shouted their exuberance to one another until the officers moved on, where after they once again shot their guns into the sky and occasionally into the ground which made much more of an impression.

Ever the provocateur, Makepeace yelled above the uproar: "I wonder if they're the troops who took Berlin and raped the women?"

"What women?" Kirshhof shouted.

"Ninety percent of the women in Berlin were raped by the Red Army when they took the city," Makepeace yelled back.

"Holy shit! No kidding? No more than they deserved, but still...!"

"How do you know that?" Schade bellowed at Makepeace.

Forestalling any response, the sergeant yelled, "What the fug?" and Makepeace immediately pretended astonishment and said, "Why mention a stuffy and odorous place of confinement here in the great open air of this fine government-issue motor vehicle?"

"Sorry, sir, but I've got no idea what you're talking about."

Schade controlled his laughter and said, "In a saloon on the eastern end of Long Island I heard a monologue on a record called 'The New Soap'."

"O yeah?"

"It went something like this: Ladies here's a new soap guaranteed to wash your clothes better than anything else. So if Tide doesn't do it, if Oxodol doesn't do it, if Sears doesn't do it, Fug it!"

The sergeant looked puzzled and said, "I guess that's pretty funny alright. Wouldn't hear it on the Jack Benny show, though."

Kirshhof suddenly screamed something incoherent, pointing up the column of Red Army troops, his mouth open, the dark wood yoyo bouncing on the floor of the jeep. "Camels! I don't believe it! Can you believe this? *Camels!*"

"*That's* what I meant," the sergeant yelled.

The fully motorized Americans looked with astonishment at the slower paced Soviet convoy as men and various animals strained to move the heavy equipment down the road. Horses, mules, and an occasional exotic beast like the camel shared the burdens of haulage with the American lend-lease and Soviet motor-driven vehicles. Amidst the dusty turbulence and noise small groups of farm animals milled about, herded along by Soviet soldiers from the vast farmlands in that country of nations who knew all about the propensity of military supply lines to break down. The troops on foot or bicycles trudged on in tattered, eclectic pieces of uniforms, often unshaven and filthy from lack of opportunities to wash. The Americans had been ordered that morning to shine everything in the convoy including themselves and consequently they gleamed brightly as they cruised north on the road. The contrasts made little difference as the Allied soldiers continued to shout frantically at each other, excitedly waving in victory.

Kirshhof shook his head. "Can you beat that?! Can you beat that?! It's like pictures of the Civil War."

"These are the combat troops, they're the ones who beat the nazis on the Eastern Front. They bore the brunt of the war, no wonder they look like this," Schade said with open admiration.

"After we opened the second front and bombed the bejesus out of Germany." Makepeace held up his hands. "Yeah, I know, I know. They did a great job and took an ungodly amount of punishment. And they fought like wounded tigers, I admit. But you've got to think about the big picture." Schade repressed any retort.

A short while later Makepeace said, "You know, each country has a special smell about it which its armies carry with them, a distinguishing olfactory characteristic."

Kirshhof shook his head in disgust, almost convinced his colleagues conspired to make him feel linguistically inadequate. "Kay. And what, pray tell, are they?"

"Think about it, remember how the Russians we just passed smelled."

"The Russians were a minority among them, most were central Asians." Schade immediately realized he should not have said this, treading on ideological toes. Now both his colleagues looked at him in disgust.

"Filthy swine," Kirshhof answered.

Not allowing himself to be buffaloed, Schade added, "Shit and onions."

"Hal, you are no farmer, and John's read too much Irish literature."

"I'm surprised you noticed."

"There's a lot that'd surprise you, as you will no doubt discover as time marches on."

"What are you collegiate schmucks talking about?" Kirshhof asked in an aggrieved tone.

"What do you think, sergeant?"

"I don't get paid to think. Officers don't like it when sergeants think. What did I smell? Crankcase oil and nasty tobacco overlaid with the sweat of the steppes and unwashed beasts of burden." The sergeant intoned this in a voice drenched with indifference and lack of emphasis, a voice well-trained in conversations with superior officers. His eyes never left the road in front of them as it disappeared beneath the jeep.

They all looked at him in mock astonishment. "What did you say your name is, sergeant?"

"Norman, sir. In civvy life I was a mailman, but I read a lot of books from the county library." He shifted his helmet to scratch his dark tightly curled hair that pressed against his skull.

"Yes, well, that's fine." Makepeace cleared his throat and gestured royally with his left hand.

"So what are you talking about, for chrissake?" Kirshhof demanded impatiently.

After casting a look of suspicion at the driver, Makepeace raised his eyes to the sky and said, "Stop that incessant yoyoing, will you." Then he declaimed, "What indeed, my good fellow, what indeed? Odors, fragrances, aromas, scents, smells, stinks, the perception of taste without food on the tongue, those elements the olfactory senses of mankind have perceived over the centuries in distinct national components ... a result of the infatuation with the nation-state, no doubt, but not entirely unknown in more primitive societies. In short, my friends, and you too, sergeant, armies stink according to their nationalities.

"Regard: the Germans smell of doom, sweat, and sauerkraut. The Russians smell like a farm: black bread, newly threshed wheat and the farmyard. The French smell of bistros and red wine and black tobacco. The British smell of bland kitchens, milky tea, boiled ham and cabbage..."

"And the Americans smell of industry," Schade said. "Gunpowder, carbon monoxide, Spam, baked beans..."

"And chewing gum, and martinis."

"That's nuts," Kirshhof announced. "I've never eaten a baked bean in my life. And martinis don't smell, the gin does. And what about the Jews?"

"They have no state, thus they have no national smell."

"Palestine will be their country."

"Then they too will have a national smell. Perhaps orange juice."

The sergeant began to quietly hum several bars of *Sing, Sing, Sing* over and over. He kept his eyes on the potted road and uttered not another word until they reached the Berlin suburbs. Kirshhof continued to yoyo off the side of the jeep.

"What kind of leave do you think we'll get in Berlin?" he asked, snapping the wood disk into this palm.

Schade laughed. "Leave? What's that? Ha!"

"Only combat GIs get leave. Don't you read *Time*? That picture of the young lady in the striped jacket and plaid skirt, so coordinatedly French, walking down the sea shore in Nice with a GI on each arm?"

"They weren't officers?"

"Not according to the magazine. No brass hats, no saluting, and gentle MPs. What a life, eh?"

"But the war's over, for christsake."

"Doesn't matter. Ya gotta be in the infantry to get that kind of leave." Makepeace turned to the driver. "What do you think of that, Sergeant?"

"If I were paid to think, I'd probably say that as a member of the transportation corps it was probably a mistake to have sent me to the Riviera for a week last winter, not being in the infantry I mean. Not much different from Atlantic City in a different language. Not bad."

"Well," Schade said to Kirshhof, "you don't have to worry about it. We won't be getting any leave for quite long time. And the job takes up all your time seven days a week, just like before the war ended."

"It's a different kind of war," Makepeace said, "but it's still a war we'll be in."

"Thus spake the young pessimist," Schade intoned.

"Thus speaks the realist, Johnny me boyo. Wait and see."

"We don't have any choice about that, do we?" Schade drank from his canteen and wondered about choices.

When the convoy arrived at the outskirts of the still spavined city the extent of the damage became clear and they wondered how any of the Berliners could have survived the destruction. As they moved on, however, they could distinguish certain areas which had been randomly spared the bombing and the artillery that had obliterated the definitions and contours of the great urban landscape: an undamaged building standing irrationally in the center of blocks of erupted rubble; an entire block of houses physically untouched by the war facing a street which no longer existed except as a chaos of tangled craters; overturned streetcars and tanks like skeletons of prehistoric mammoths half absorbed by the earth; jagged plumbing pipes jutted up from the ground and out of buildings in grotesque contortion, hanging in the dusty air like the skeletons of extinct birds of prey. Although the Red Army had already cleared certain sections of the city to allow military traffic to circulate, the Americans and the British entered the center in a state of shock at the bleak and sullen desolation reflected in the broken city and in the eyes of its remaining citizens. On the side of the last remaining wall of a large old house they read the block handprinted statement, "*Das verdanken wir Hitler!*" They drove past a squad of Red Army soldiers operating a field radio set up on a Biedermeier end table in the middle of the sidewalk under a slogan painted haphazardly on the building facade: "*Berlin bleibt deutsch!*"

Later they discovered small sections of the city such as parts of Dahlem, which had suffered comparatively little damage, where the villas of the bourgeoisie squatted stolidly in their gardens, without windows but retaining much of the overstuffed Biedermeier character of the German nouveau riche. The victors confiscated the best of the lot and began the process of making their lives as comfortable as possible on the basis of the eternal military tradition: the higher the rank, the more luxurious the housing.

But the general effect on the Anglo-American troops was numbing; the filth and dust choked them; the smell of death gagged their throats; the ghostly lunar landscape overwhelmed their sense of proportion and bewildered even those familiar with the wreckage of Munich, Cologne, and Frankfurt. The incoherence of the blasted city in which they would live baffled them as they slowly wheeled along the narrow lanes cut through the dirt and stones of what had once been grand boulevards. The smells of cordite, rotten cabbage and horse piss assaulted their noses and throats with a force they had not previously experienced. The jagged remnants of buildings stuck into the sky at radical angles like a nightmare of bad abstract paintings, appalling in jerky gray and black strokes. And it had been worse when the Red Army first entered the city two months earlier, filled with frustration and hatred and great lusts for revenge and plunder.

Though he would later write with no small amount of perception and sympathy of the city during this time,

Schade always felt defeated by the destruction. The photographs which the newspapers and magazines printed, and even the film footage shown everywhere in the following years, failed to evoke the deadened response they all felt on first seeing the massive wreckage of the former capital. In the early days, before they became accustomed to the alienating strangeness of the place, Schade tried to balance his response to the city by comparing it to his reaction at the sight of the films and photographs of the concentration camps and their survivors. But he had not himself seen the reality of the camps in their pristine horror. He suffered a certain burden of guilt because his shock was greater in Berlin. He was never able to totally reconcile this fact with the idea that the camps destroyed people with an incomprehensible deliberateness, and Berlin was, after all, a collection of buildings, the destruction of which at first had moved him more immediately than the murder of countless human beings.

They saw few people moving about as they penetrated the core of the city. Grotesque shadows, seeming to prefigure the darkness of the grave, began to stalk the broken masonry as the evening crept out of the east and building remnants menaced the streets with threats of collapse, gray skeletons choking on the dust-clotted remains of their former structural integrity. They ate the bland C-ration food from their field packs and washed it down with water or whiskey from their canteens. Kitchen facilities would be established during the following day where after the quality of their meals climbed out of the wartime cellar of year-old tins to the first floor of mass-produced unctuous but nutritious food. The mess hall officers were already busy hiring unemployed German cooks to man the kitchens. These lucky individuals would eat far better than their fellow citizens.

A pale major told them their permanent quarters would be ready the next day and warned them not to leave the area that night. The military police had orders to shoot if no password came on request. The major did not know that night's password. As exhausted and benumbed as the others, Kirshhof let his hatred retreat to the bitter pool of his mind while they unrolled their sleeping bags and took them into a gutted building to spend the night under the distant stars. Makepeace contented himself with the comment: "Good thing it's not the middle of winter." Schade fell into a fitful doze and wondered if the plumbing would function in the house requisitioned for them. The banality of their thoughts reflected the dazed quality of their minds. The city disturbed everyone's sleep that night. The next morning, in the desolation of the pulverized landscape, they would begin their work.

Once I built a railroad
I made it run
Made it run against time.
Once I built a railroad
Now it's done
Brother, can you spare a dime?

PART TWO

> -- Ja, von Kultur zu reden, wir haben ja "Der Ritt der Walküre" und was haben Sie? "Ghost Riders in the Sky."
> -- Maybe, but you had Hitler and we had FDR.

Joachim Buchdow absolutely denied the hunger that gnawed at his belly and lightened his head. A full stomach indicated success and he desperately wished to appear successful. He knew the Americans respected success and looked with contempt upon failure. The one way to ensure the Americans would allow him to move his activities into their sector was to impress them with this success in the Soviet part of the city. This would be difficult enough since he had achieved none there. On the other hand, he had experienced no failure either. The problem lay in the fact that whatever successes he had achieved had been accomplished during the nazi time, and he doubted that the Americans would register these successes, as minor as they had been, on the positive side of his ledger. And there the rub abraded the city's skin: the victorious Allies looked for successful professionals, but success and professionalism had been earned and learned under the nazis, during a period when joining the party meant certain privileges which helped one's career. But the Allies also wanted no nazis in the new society. Apparently they had not as yet realized the conundrum they faced.

An anomaly. Another was the situation in which he found himself: he had been given clearance to work in the theater, a level one ration card for "irreproachable" cultural "workers," and membership in the Möwe Club on the Luisenstrasse, but had not been given a theater as he thought he deserved. Based on his previous experience he thought he deserved a theater of his own, but thus far he had only been able to join the rather improvised group that spent its time at the old theater on the Schiffbauerdamm. Since this house had suffered major damage in the fighting there was no question of performing in it for the time being. Everyone worked on restoring the building; the issues of scripts and roles would be decided after that work was well underway, or so everyone had been informed.

Buchdow did not believe this for a moment, but said nothing and continued to move debris from the building to the street with everyone else. At that point the war had hardly been over a week and he knew the Russians wanted the theaters and music halls open as soon as possible. This was part of their methodology for controlling the city's always volatile population. Bread and circuses, true, but nothing to sneer at when everything in the world had utterly collapsed. One had to eat, after all. *"Erst kommt das Fressen, dann kommt die Moral,"* as ratty fellow Brecht had written. What was that commandment in the paper the other day?

Hilf dem Bauer in der Not,
Dann hast auch Du Dein täglich Brot. [2]

The Russians making the decisions were not stupid, nor were the Germans who worked for them. There would

---

[2] The newspaper notice reads, "Help the farmer in his plight, then you'll have your daily bread." The phrase from *Die Dreigrosschenoper* (*The Threepenny Opera*) song has been variously translated; in the W. H. Auden version: "First grub, then morals."

eventually be the right kind of work and sufficient food. Gisela's drug habit would have to be broken. The supply was close to exhausted and he could get no more of the stuff. It had served its purpose in maintaining her calmness in the last weeks of the chaos during the battle for the city and her sanity after Red Army soldiers raped her during their mindless, vengeful rampage that plundered the city and its inhabitants in the weeks after the fighting stopped and continued to rage in spastic outbreaks of uncontrolled violence. She would have to break her dependence upon it. Fortunately she had not been on the drug long and was fundamentally a strong person. Food was the main concern at present and that meant work, but did it have to mean this kind of drudgery?

    No doubt the theater on the Schiffbauerdamm had to be renovated. But so much time was being wasted by a committee in the official Kammer der Kunstschaffenden (the Chamber of Creative Artists) that spent many hours considering which plays could be safely performed, which actors would be allowed to play in them, and most important for Buchdow, who would produce and direct them. Theoretically, he supposed, the Russians issued the guidelines and their German communist party lackeys made the decisions, but when in recent years had reality reflected theory? Perhaps the decisions had already been made. From conversations with colleagues he knew that the Russians were applying pressure to open the theaters and concert halls faster than their Germans thought appropriate. These latter garrulously complained they hadn't the capability to move so swiftly, the investigations and clearances could not be done with so little time. Concerts and cabarets had already started under primitive conditions in shabby quarters, often with no roofs or walls.

It came as no surprise to Buchdow when, after a week of clearing rubble, the officials of the Chamber requested his presence to discuss his future work. He was, however, somewhat astonished at the cursory discussion of his affiliation with the National Socialists.

"We note you were only a nominal party member, Herr Buchdow. No, you do not have to defend it now. Our Soviet friends have examined your case. We, too, have made our investigations." The smiles of these gray men in gray clothes were perfunctory and meaningless. No friendliness or warmth informed them.

While his stomach lay weeping from hunger they discussed plans for reconstructing the life of Berlin theaters. He sat before them nodding at the appropriate moments, saying little, regretting having given up his bread ration that morning so Gisela would have something to gnaw on at midday. He had arrived at the Chamber's offices in the old Reichskulturkammer building just off the Kurfürstendamm in the Schlüterstrasse with a lengthy defense of his activities over the past decade prepared in his mind. He did not regret that there had been no need to use it. He had been as non-political as possible under the circumstances and his membership, in fact, *was* nominal as far as he was concerned. Young enough to have escaped (as it turned out) becoming a well-known name as a director, he nonetheless had made a good start with three silly comedies the Propaganda Ministry thought necessary to stiffen the morale of the shell-shocked Berlin population. That he had joined the party was a given, after all. He would not have risen in his profession without such an act. It had not mattered to him, he thought only of the theater and himself. In the last year he had not paid his party dues because he had forgotten about the matter, and party officials had other things to occupy their time. This had been a piece of good fortune.

So they informed him he could join the Chamber, that he had received his *"Persilschein"* (as the vox populi termed that eagerly sought certificate of cleansing, named after the laundry detergent Persil), and that he would be given a play to direct and a theater in which to mount the production after certain "organizational measures" had been implemented. These bland officials had not clarified further and dismissed him. "We have many people to see, Herr Buchdow, thank you for coming. *Auf Wiedersehen*." Weeks after the interview the "measures" had not yet been taken, and he continued to direct a cart full of rubble instead of a theater full of actors. He also attended the Chamber's open meetings when theater questions appeared on the agenda. When it finally cleared two plays for production at the Schiffbauerdamm his disappointment pained him more than his hunger at being given a featured role in one of them but not appointed director.

With growing resentment and frustration against both his professional stagnation and the situation with Gisela, he continued to sit in on the Chamber's deliberations and rehearsed his role with the company. The meetings bored him. The questions debated inevitably involved political matters in which he had no interest except as they touched on the issue of a unified denazification policy for the entire city. He very soon noticed with some disquiet the emergence of two schools of thought on the question: the ideologues (not all of them hard line communists by any means) led by the young communist fanatic, Reinhard Woller, demanded rejection of all nazis whom they defined in various, often contradictory ways, and the pragmatists who accepted nominal nazi party membership in order to move forward with the revival of the city's cultural life. Buchdow strongly but silently supported the second group. And they all wondered what would result from the four-power meetings at the Allied Kommandatura on the subject of a unified policy for the city.

Now, as he walked the long trek down Unter den Eichen past the Botanical Gardens, ravaged like the rest of the city, toward the Milinowskistrasse where the American theater control officers had their office deep in the Zehlendorf quarter, he reflected on his situation, doing his best to ignore the razor-sharp reality through which he passed. The teeming wreckage around him absorbed the late afternoon's yellow sunlight. The city lay blasted on the Brandenburg plain, a place of jutting masonry and iron piping, all hard angles unmediated by the civilizing process of time. Great lines of these angular people clothed in eclectic collections of unmatched textiles, shuffled through the destruction in the sun hunting for relatives, a room to sleep in, food to eat or barter, or simply to reach another destination, to arrive somewhere else, preferably in the countryside where food could be more easily found. They moved slowly, expending as little energy as possible, hoping to find whatever they lacked, an escape, or affection. Multiple tones of brown and gray dominated the ragged streets. Lines of women moved blocks of brick and cement from one pile to another, straining under the weight and their malnutrition, bones pressed against the skin, eyes still numb and frightened. Young soldiers in jeeps and command cars ignored everything in their paths except potholes as they swept down the narrow corridors through the enormous mounds of rubble. Everyone prayed for rain.

Under posters plastered on the fragments of walls proclaiming Stalin's slogans ("*Die Hitlers kommen und gehen, aber das deutsche Volk bleibt bestehen*"[3]), which the Americans would soon silently tear down in their sector of the city, pedestrians all moved with apparent purpose on seemingly important missions toward some vital destination. No matter how slowly, they moved with determination, for to be seen at leisure or strolling meant immediate suspicion from both the occupied and the occupiers; it meant blackmail or favored position, especially if the stroller was young and female, but most especially if the stroller was young, pretty, and male. The threat of rape by Soviet soldiers hung like an ominous demon over the city; the wracked screams of young girls dressed in their summer clothes continued to haunt the nights. The residual Götterdämmerung atmosphere affected all in the city, even the soldiers of the victorious armies all of whom moved with a specific destination in mind, at least in appearance. The city had always contained a contradiction: speed at all costs but also the tradition of the flâneur, the latter of which now had no place in the broken anthill called Berlin. The sign hung at a slanting angle on the bullet-scarred wooden door of a building that no longer existed warning passersby not to touch the bombs, pay attention or die.

Achtung! Vorsicht!
Bomben nicht anfassen!
Aufpassen oder sterben.[4]

Stepping quickly out of the way of an old wood burning Opel sedan, Buchdow felt another twinge in his

---

[3] The Hitlers come and go, but the German people remain.
[4] Attention! Caution!/ Do not touch the bombs!/Pay attention or die.

belly and to alleviate it thought hard about the interview with the unknown Americans. He knew very little about them, but hoped they would be easier to deal with than the Russians and their Germans. At least seven theaters stood in fairly good repair in the American Sector. If he could get into one of them.... But he knew nothing of their clearance policies and whether or not his party membership would curtail his possibilities. If the Allies standardized their policies this would no longer matter, but this remained unknown as yet. Entirely too much remained unknown, but one had to take some form of action. Would they speak German? Buchdow's English was practically non-existent. He would learn it if he stayed in the American or British sectors, but this would not be much of a problem, he supposed. He had learned French and Italian without difficulty in a short period of time, at least learned it sufficiently to make his desires known. Would the Americans investigate his love life and discover his sexual preferences? Would that matter to them at all? Would they simply send him to the Magistrat, the city's civilian governing body, which housed the Chamber? If they did that he would have wasted a day's time and energy on a long weary walk through half the city.

Suddenly he felt urgently tired. Frustration sickened him with the bitterness of bile and a diffuse but intense rage spread through him like a rush a fresh adrenaline. Breathing heavily, he stopped and abruptly sat on a pile of broken bricks. Dust clogged his nostrils and lay on his suit and shoes; he felt the grit of the city in his pores; the vermin attacking his armpits and crotch itched maddeningly; the desire to weep and lash out simultaneously attacked him; the desire to scream choked him. Across the street from where he sat the charred and dusty accumulation of placards and posters hung away from the huge splintered wooden frame of the hoarding on the side of the building like a giant wing of a prehistoric bird. All the colors had faded to a uniform gray and the words of the last placard posted to the frame could barely be seen and only with memory's nudge could the advertisement for the painkiller Gelonida be deciphered.

Wer is da?
Gelonida!
Um die Schmerzen
Sofort auszumerzen![5]

He needed to concentrate his energies on the meeting and think of ways of mastering the Americans. If he could accomplish this, he could wash away the grit and only think about work and the resumption of his career. There was little else that mattered to him in any profound way. His affairs had always been brief and secretive; the nazis strongly supported the use of the provisions of paragraph 175 of the criminal code which made homosexuality in males a crime, but they also rarely bothered homosexuals in the world of culture who maintained their liaisons with discretion and followed the party's guidelines. He thought of Gründgens and others who would fall under the rubric of "*schwul*." One had to be so cautious that beginning a relationship was constantly fraught with tension and a certain amount of fear. His affair, if one could call it that, with Gisela had been a matter of survival for the group: he had made love to her because she expected it and because it made things more

---

[5] The placard text rhymes in German: "Who is there? Gelonida! To immediately get rid of the pain." It extols the benefits of a form of pain reducer.

normal for her, and containing her hysteria became a matter of keeping them alive. Now he felt only a vague sense of guilt and responsibility. If he had any success this afternoon he would ask the Americans to take Gisela as part of the arrangement; then his responsibility would be done. He would clean her up and present her to the theater officials. She would break the habit with encouragement and the chance to work again. There could be no question of her talent; he had immediately recognized her gift even in those asinine films she made during the early years of the war. Though her roles had been minor the depth of her abilities had been clear to the professionals, where the party hacks had seen just another lovely young face and possible conquest. Corruption of one sort or another would always be present, he knew, but the sheer incompetence of the party members placed in positions of responsibility by Goebbels and his assistants had been incredible. Corruption with skill and talent is very different from corruption with incompetence and arrogance. Not that such reflections would help him at this point, but one never knew.

Concentration required far more energy and will power these days; the external world thrust itself too readily into one's thoughts; in many ways the war had not ended. But the energy expended in cursing the situation did not brighten his mind or fill the hole in his acidic stomach; it did not return enough satisfaction to compensate for the expenditure. He stood up slowly, brushed desultorily at his clothes and continued his careful walk down the dusty ghost of the boulevard. Concentrating on his bargaining points, he dimly wondered why the Russians had not yet issued a work permit to Gisela and then, with some panic, if they hadn't would the Americans and the British? He shook his head, an act he found himself performing with increasing frequency. Drink that water when you come to that stream.

Breathing as shallowly as possible he trudged on, crossing the Dahlemer Weg and bearing right into the Schützallee, threading his way through the old men and women with bent shoulders and tattered packages. He avoided walking too close to groups of soldiers striding about the streets and remained constantly alert to the sound of vehicles. Too many civilians and soldiers had already been maimed because they had not been sufficiently agile to miss being smacked by a jeep traveling above the Allied speed limit posted in three languages around the city. The American soldiers particularly exuded animal good health and the promise of pleasure, someday perhaps. An occasional unarmed German policeman patrolled the neighborhood, bereft of his former glory in a plain uniform dyed blue that ran when it rained. Twice within four blocks some citizen collapsed to the ground and had to be carried to the nearest shelter while a physician, much too busy and hungry to come immediately, was summoned.

Joachim Buchdow averted his face and walked faster.

The building the Americans had requisitioned for the cultural control offices stood on a street lined with elegant residential villas strangely undamaged. Buchdow stopped at the beginning of the Milinowskistrasse astonished at the sight of these detached houses whose windows contained so many panes of glass. He would discover that these fully furnished villas of the Berlin bourgeoisie included double sinks in the bathrooms and crystal glasses in the kitchens. This kind of luxury he had not seen for years and had lived in for only the short period of time required for him to discover and reject the habits of a very rich, very nasty lover with more money than morals.

And the Americans used these houses as offices! The victors and the spoils, he thought with some bitterness. But it would not last forever: one of these days he would live in one of these villas.

"Hey! Watch it, you jerk!"

The shout snapped his attention to his surroundings. He looked up at the jeep bearing slowly down on him and stepped quickly onto the sidewalk. Concentrate!

Activity and rude health bustled up and down the street; soldiers moved rapidly in and out of the houses talking in loud voices he could not understand, doing jobs which would limit his own opportunities, driving motor cars he had no possibility of owning.... This kind of thinking would only lead to disaster. Concentrate.

All the healthy bodies in simple movement shocked his mind; they ate so well, they slept in the best beds, drove cars, drank so carefree, walked so loosely.... No! Concentrate. Move, you fool. Another deep breath, confrontation: a word he knew sounded similar in English asked of a passing soldier: "*Theaterkontrolle*?" The young man pointing vaguely over his shoulder and spoke words Buchdow took to mean" "That building over there." A jeep and a fairly undamaged blue Opel Kadet were parked in front of the villa: two Cerberuses before his personal hell. An empty-stomach belch forced its way through his clenched teeth. *Avanti*. Another soldier, arms full of papers, threw his head on the direction of the upper floor in response to Buchdow's one-word question. "Upstairs, mack."

He walked through the unguarded doorway and climbed the stairs toward the voices on the next floor. A soldier brushed by him running down stairs and Buchdow stopped to stare at the retreating figure. So they have women soldiers too, he thought, marveling at the radiant health of the young corporal. Near the top of the stairs he heard voices speaking English in one of the rooms; at least one of them spoke English, the accents and tones of the other two voices he could not place. The language sounded similar and he decided they must be Americans. To his knowledge he had never before spoken to an American. His stomach twisted into a knot with the desperate hope one of them spoke German. If he had to make his points in English, the whole effort would slip rapidly into disaster. At the top of the stairs he stopped and controlled his breathing. Here near the Grunewald the air seemed less redolent with decay and death. The Americans had chosen their sector well, however it had been done. Drawing air cautiously deep into his lungs and straightening his back, he walked to the door through which the voices flowed. A telephone shrilled. He knocked on the doorframe as he looked into the room.

    Three figures in clean pressed tan-colored uniforms sat scattered about the room filled with an eclectic collection of office and bedroom furniture piled with jumbled papers and books of various sizes and colors, typewriters, and a telephone into which one of the Americans spoke in a curious accent. The other two men had been speaking in lowered voices while they smoked American cigarettes, the price for one of which rose every day in worthless Reichsmarks. On the wall over one of the desks a small sign in soft script warned:

Fraternization with the enemy
FORBIDDEN
At all times.

At the sound of the knocking they turned to the doorway with vaguely questioning expressions. One of them wore a uniform with different markings. Buchdow did not know what they signified, but realized that their ages would make them junior officers. The man with the mustache at the telephone continued to speak into it with a muffled voice, his back to the doorway, gazing out the window.

"Yes?" One of the smokers said in a neutral voice, lazily touching the crown of his head.

Buchdow cleared his throat but did not step into the room. "*Entschuldigen Sie bitte. Spricht jemand hier Deutsch?*"

The two smokers looked at each other.

"My *Englisch ist* not good, *es tut mir leid, aber....*"

"We've got to hire a secretary to screen our callers."

"*Wir sprechen Deutsch. Was wollen Sie?*"

Relief swelling in him like a balloon, Buchdow pressed on in German. "My name is Joachim Buchdow. I am a director in the theater. I wish to work in the American and British sectors. I am not in the Russian sector. May we discuss this? I was not really a nazi. I want to work, but it is difficult with the Russians. I would...."

"This guy's got balls of brass," one of the Americans said in English.

It had begun badly. This perception started the panic and nausea seeping into his stomach. Dizziness from hunger and the cigarette smoke broke into his head; his hands began to flutter. He controlled this with a visible effort of will and spoke on, his sentences tumbling together, voice caught in a vibrato. "I am good at my work. May I sit down?" He had not meant for it to take this direction. He had to control the situation, but he realized he had already lost the initiative. Perhaps it would have been impossible in any case. His knees began to sag and he gripped the doorjamb as inconspicuously as possible.

The man at the telephone had not turned around. His compatriot in the same uniform motioned Buchdow to the only empty chair in the room. "Sure, sit down," he said in English.

Buchdow straightened and took the few steps to the chair slowly. "*Dankeschön*. It was a long walk to come here." His face formed a crooked smile. "One doesn't eat so well these days. It affects the energy." He hoped this did not sound like a plea for understanding, but he knew it did.

The American behind the desk said, "Would you like a cigarette?"

"Thank you, no," Buchdow answered carefully. "I no longer smoke very much. Also, it would make me sick, dizzy. Thank you."

The officer Buchdow took to be an Englishman looked at him with a bland, almost empty expression on his pale face, saying nothing, neither hostile nor friendly. The American held a scrap of paper in his hand, glanced at it briefly and returned it to his shirt pocket. "I am Lieutenant Makepeace. This is Leftenant Vasart of the British information control office. The gentleman on the telephone is Lieutenant Schade, my colleague." Schade continued to speak into the large black apparatus with his back toward the others.

Strange names these Americans have, Buchdow thought. While Vasart continued his neutral observation and Makepeace searched through a pile of papers on his desk, Buchdow fidgeted and hoped his stomach would not make vulgar noises. He felt much better sitting down, but his leg muscles still jerked in irregular spasms. They all looked so much alike, perhaps it was the uniforms. Each of them stood just under six feet tall, slim and young, though the Englishman showed the beginnings of a paunch and wore an elaborate RAF mustache while Schade kept his more severely cut; he also tended to slouch and dark bags of smudged flesh hung under his eyes.

"We need some information about you. Fill out this form, in the next room. I'll tell you straight away that there will be another longer questionnaire to compete later. This short form will allow us to begin the process. We'll call you when we're ready. Do you have something to write with?"

Buchdow nodded. "Only a pencil."

"Fine. To the right outside the door. We'll call you."

"Thank you." Buchdow turned and paused. "Is there a toilet for the defeated here?" An immediate plunge of his stomach resulted from this uncontrolled and, he feared, potentially dangerous, which is to say foolish if not stupid attempt at humor.

But Makepeace only grinned and touched the back of his head with his fingertips. "Well, there is and there isn't. Only one of them works. We have received a directive that specifies that Allies and Germans must use separate toilets. And if one is broken, you can imagine whose that is. What do you think of that?"

"I have never been in the Wehrmacht, but I understand one must follow the directives and the orders."

"Nice, very nice. Tactful." Makepeace grinned again and this time Vasart allowed the mere promise of a smile to touch his lips. "The toilet is to the right. You can use it for both purposes. Go ahead."

If the situation had been reversed, thought Buchdow as he walked slowly out of the room, I'd have had to hold it or find another pissoir. Were all Americans like this? If so, things should improve very soon. On the other hand, perhaps they could afford to ignore minor matters like this and would be very hard with more important aspects of the occupation. One just could not tell yet. When he entered the room to the right of the office he understood the meaning of Makepeace's last comment. The difference between the shabby hallway and this room was startling. The spacious interior contained not only a toilet, but also an ornate bathtub on lion's feet, a makeup table modeled after those in the best theaters, and a gilt-edged table that had served as some ambitious *Hausfrau*'s writing table. A large window with its glass panes intact gave onto the untended garden in the rear of the villa. His nervousness diminished as he sat in the plush chair with matching gilt and began to fill out the two-page questionnaire with a stubby pencil. The usual questions about personal background, profession, education, and then the questions about political affiliation, military service, membership in party-related organizations. He decided to fill out the form honestly and completely. They probably had access to the records of the former Reichskulturkammer, the nazi Chamber of Culture, and would cross-check the answers. Perhaps his records had been destroyed? It was not worth the risk. The Russians had cleared him, surely on the basis of his file there. Would these men do any differently?

    He sat for fifteen minutes after completing the questions, keeping his mind as blank as possible, scratching his groin and reciting some lines of Goethe and the banned Jew Tucholsky to himself to still the pains of hunger and uncertainty. He would have to stop at one of the clinics on his way back and finally go through the delousing process. Gisela, too, would have to be taken. It was terribly embarrassing, but everyone suffered from the same itch. All the civilians and many of the soldiers in the city scratched constantly at their private parts, under their arms, and at their skulls, although the situation had certainly improved with the dusty delousing program initiated by city officials.

"Buchdow!"

He walked stiffly into the other office where Schade now sat behind the desk and Makepeace talked on the ancient telephone. Vasart had gone and this surprised Buchdow because he had heard nothing. He prided himself on his ability to concentrate and shut out the external world, but had not been aware that he had done it so successfully this time. Confidence and assurance gradually began to creep back into his equilibrium.

"Sit down," Schade said in English, then continued in German. "Let me see your questionnaire." He glanced quickly through it. "You joined the party rather late."

"When it was no longer avoidable; to keep my job."

"And stay out of the army?"

"Tell him that's a lot of crap," Makepeace said loudly in English into the telephone. "Tell him we'll check with Yuri Tamirov this afternoon and get back."

"Joining the party did not keep one out of the Wehrmacht," Buchdow said. "But one had no choice if one wished to continue working in the theater. It was purely pro forma, of course. The same with the Reichskulturkammer. One had to join."

"So we've been told, over and over again."

"It is the truth."

"What kind of plays did you direct? These titles don't mean anything to me."

"They were comedies, not very good ones, but the Ministry thought them amusing. It was thought such things would lift the morale of the people in the city."

"Did they?"

"I doubt it, but those who sat through the performances were able to escape the present for a few moments, until the next wave of bombers arrived. I am not overwhelmingly proud of the plays, but we did them well."

"What did you do after the theaters closed?"

"I suppose I would have gone into the Volkssturm or have been sent to the front in some capacity if they had found me, but some friends and I hid out. We knew it would soon be over. It wasn't over soon enough."

"They never found you?"

"We were lucky, but it was not easy. Always on the run. Dodging police patrols and bombs, the Gestapo, the Volkssturm. Some got caught and shot or hanged in the streets and left there for the rest to see what happened to shirkers. Some of us held out. They were terrible months. When the Russians got into the city we had other worries."

Makepeace finally replaced the telephone on its cradle and sat at the other desk, requiring Buchdow to swivel his head between the two officers. "You worked for the nazis."

"How could one not? I worked for the theater, and myself, of course." This was not going to be like the interview in the Chamber; they had not accused him of anything.

"You were a member of party organizations," Makepeace continued, scanning the questionnaire.

"Of course. It was the only way to work steadily."

"Others didn't join."

"They didn't work very often either; they didn't get the good roles, unless they were well-known like Rühmann or Albers, then it didn't matter as long as they played their roles, and earned good money."

Schade asked: "Did you ask for a party card when you chose people for the plays?"

"Sometimes I had no choice in the question of who got which role. Sometimes it was necessary to ask, I'm sorry to say."

"You are an opportunist," Makepeace said evenly.

Buchdow surprised himself and repressed the smile. "I am sorry, but who is not?"

"We've just gone through a dozen years of people suffering and dying for their beliefs."

"I was really never interested in politics."

"I am not talking about politics. I'm talking about those who refused to compromise their values."

"Perhaps I was never put into a position where that became a question. Perhaps I was too young to learn such values before 1933, but once I started working no one interfered with me."

Schade said: "You've had rather safe properties given the circumstances, silly drawing room comedies...."

"I was lucky there, as it turned out."

"You didn't choose those plays."

"I was asked if I wanted to do them. The point wasn't the plays themselves, but the chance to direct them. My whole life is the theater. That opportunity was fairly heady stuff for someone like me without much experience." Buchdow wondered if he was being too honest, too flippant. Americans liked smart answers, so he had been informed. But these two remained passive, apparently indifferent; in spite of the sharpness of their words, a certain neutral quality shaped their tone. One of them clearly was a German, probably a Jew who got out before the war. They confused him.

"If the plays had been propaganda extolling the virtues of aryan superiority, would you have accepted the job?" Makepeace asked.

"I am grateful that they were not that, so I never had to face that question. But the answer would have been the same, I think."

"Disgusting, but honest. We get so little of that."

"You ask questions that are irrelevant now. What I *would* have done is less important than what I actually *did, nicht wahr*. I had nothing to do with nazi propaganda, or the party or anything like that. You don't have to like me personally, you can be disgusted with me, but I don't believe, I seriously do not believe I've done anything to bar me from being licensed."

"Your party membership alone is technically sufficient to reject you."

"The Chamber of Creative Artists cleared me...."

"We have our own vetting system and we issue the licenses for our sector."

"There are others who were party members like me who are working in your sector."

"So will you, inevitably, so will you; unless we come up with something during the investigation."

"There's nothing relevant you do not already know."

"Are you working in the Russian sector?"

"If one can call it that. I have been promised a play to direct, but nothing has happened. I have a role in rehearsal at the Schiffbauerdamm. But von Wangenheim is going to take over that house. I am not political, I don't think I'll have much of a chance there."

"There are other theaters in that part of the city."

"My experience has been negative thus far. It's been a month since they said I would have a play to direct."

"Von Wangenheim spent the war in Moscow, didn't he? So he's a communist and will get preferential treatment."

"I suppose so. I don't think it matters. He's very strong-minded. I have heard a great deal about him. I probably won't be happy working with him in any capacity. There's nothing political about that."

"What do you expect in our sector?"

"A freer chance to work, to do what I do well. I realize the necessity for manual labor to restore the theaters. I have done that. I will do it again here, but at the same time one wishes to begin again in one's profession."

"And what kind of works do you think should be performed now?" Schade asked.

Buchdow swallowed wondering how far he should pursue the opportunity. He had rehearsed his lengthy answer to this question all day and could recite it with some fluency if not eloquently. He decided to take the risk. "I presume there are certain plays which cannot be performed. It is that way in the Russian sector. That is understandable and I agree with it. Other plays must be given preferred treatment; I understand that also. I believe your Thornton Wilder plays will be done soon. Explaining the American way of life. I do not know these plays, but would like to read them."

"The Deutsche Theater is preparing *Our Town* to open soon," Makepeace said.

"I have only heard about these things."

Schade said, "I'd like to know your own opinion of the situation. What do you think should be performed? We are open to new ideas, as long as they are anti-fascist and uncritical of the occupation. They could even be interesting."

Makepeace added, "And you don't have to be teutonically tactful either. It becomes boring." He did not smile as he said this, but his voice expressed less hostility than a mild disdain. His German was fluent if somewhat ungrammatical and idiomatic.

Buchdow drew in two shallow breaths and began his monologue. "What we need is a new theater. We have to overcome the depredations of the past twelve years, but we cannot return to the Weimar time. We must go forward. Weimar is not relevant to us now. My colleagues and I have discussed this often, what we need to do now. The situation is entirely different. We have two things to do in the new German theater. We have to explain the past and show the path to the future. For this we need new plays, new ideas, new language. Some of my colleagues think the nazis destroyed the German language, corrupted and violated its tradition and usage. I am not sure that is entirely true. Any language evolves if it is to live and ours will develop to meet the new circumstances. Many of my friends are depressed, especially the writers and poets. But I think there are possibilities.

"People forget the past eventually, especially the negative aspects of it; they naturally want to forget, to get on with their little lives. In this case, too many have too much to forget; it is too terrible for them to remember because they feel too guilty. The burden of yesterday is unbearable for some of them. They will probably produce some new form of surrealism. but it will be an escape for them. But the world outside won't let us forget, will it? So we should begin to deal with it now.

"So I think we need more realism; we need to clearly tell what happened and why it happened. We need somehow to get into the German soul and lucidly examine it so people can understand. Romanticism won't work any longer. Schiller, Goethe...they would be struck silent by the massive destruction and so many killed and the camps. We cannot let that happen. We need clear eyes and reality, but things must be presented in the correct way. The philosophers will write books about the evil of the Hitler regime and indict or exonerate those who supported it even in passivity. Different levels of guilt will be argued about for a long time. But what does this mean to the common man? He doesn't read philosophical books; he does go to the theater.

"No, what we need to do is to present these new ideas in the theater where the immediacy of experience is intense and to the point. For this we need new materials, younger people with little baggage from the past; we need a new language, a revitalized language. A simple revival won't work. We can't go back to the Romantics, or the classical works, or even the great experiments of the Twenties. We're faced with the very different experiences of national socialism and occupation, we're totally defeated, we don't have a government and only a broken culture. We must rescue that part of our cultural heritage that can still be of use to us. What the nazis corrupted we must throw away. Perhaps there are some things the nazis distorted by lies and propaganda we can still save.

"The theater, yes, I believe the new German theater can help to overcome the past and allow us to come back to the values of European civilization. But we must start now. I realize it's quite chaotic and difficult; we have all lived through the same thing in the past months, here in Berlin I mean. Some of us in fact have not lived through it. We need to purge the culture of the evil with which it has been infected. We must renew our faith and confidence in ourselves to come to terms with what we've experienced, what we Germans have done to Europe. It would be too easy to lie down and moan mea culpa for the next five years, but we mustn't.

"We are obviously very much dependent upon the Allies at the moment. This is why we need your understanding and assistance. Right now we cannot accomplish anything just by ourselves, we have no recourse, but we have our minds and talents and ideas and we want to begin the reconstruction. At least some of us do. At the moment many do not know what to do so they ask for the old plays, the classics which will offend no one, those the nazis did not abuse. Perhaps for now that is all we can do until things settle down. That and perform those things that have been forbidden to us for twelve years.

"But that is not enough. We must create the new as well. We can start with Wedekind, Schnitzler, Tucholsky, and so on, and pieces from American and Russia, yes, but soon we must make our own stand and find our own answers."

He stopped. The effort exhausted and exhilarated him. He tried to control his enthusiasm, but it had taken over and run on with his tongue. He breathed in short gasps and closed his eyes as if fearing to know what effect his words had made. He thought his performance, however brief, had been fairly good. "I am sorry to talk so much, but these ... things are important to me."

"Doesn't want much, does he?" Makepeace muttered in English.

Schade continued in German, "Have you thought about acts of contrition, retribution, justice, punishment for unspeakable crimes, denazification, democratic reforms....?"

Through his exhaustion and hunger Buchdow showed some uncontrolled impatience. "Yes, of course, all these things will have to happen. We cannot just pray for rain and move on. I agree, of course, but without a new

85

vital culture of creativity these things will mean little in the end."

"We think these things must come first," Schade said.

"Then we have a difference of opinion philosophically," Buchdow replied shortly.

"That you can hardly afford at the moment," Makepeace snapped in a rough-edged voice and popped open his Zippo to light his Fatima with a jerking movement.

Buchdow sighed inwardly: he had made another mistake. Control, concentrate, diplomacy, no flashes of temperament.

"No," he said softly. "You are of course correct. I am hardly in a position to determine the sequence of things." He looked at each in turn: Schade showed no hostility, but concern of some sort could be seen in his tired eyes in their dark-rimmed sockets. Makepeace's expression betrayed his annoyance and Buchdow sensed the antagonism in him. "It has been a difficult time, yes. You defeated us, after all. We have been frightened and battered, deservedly perhaps. We are still frightened, we are confused and unsure of what will happen; nothing is predictable. Most of us welcomed the arrival of your armies in Berlin, but we have no knowledge of what you are planning to do. Will you continue the Russian policies, which are often arbitrary and contradictory? What is to be our fate? Whatever it is we must work, we must start to rebuild. We must also eat and rid ourselves of fear."

"I have no sympathy with your hard times," Makepeace said without rancor, but in a tightened voice. "Too many people died, too much...."

"But I had nothing to do with that!"

"Do you know how often we hear that statement? It's horseshit. You joined the party, you worked for the nazis, you didn't resist. Why should we have any sympathy for you?"

"The Russians cleared me of any complicity...."

"Nonsense! You're as guilty as anyone else. You didn't get sent to the concentration camps, you didn't go into exile, you didn't join the resistance."

"If I am guilty and everyone else who stayed in Germany and did not join the underground is guilty, surely there are differences of degree. And besides that, who is going to do anything now if you restrict and ban people from their professions? Who is going to do the theater? Who is going to direct the ... Ach, nein. Es tut mir leid, meine Herren, I apologize. It is not my position to question...."

"Let us move on," Schade said. "You will in any case have to be cleared, vetted by our intelligence people if you are to work in our sector. No promises, of course. Wait in the hallway for a few minutes. You will be called."

"Yes, thank you." Buchdow left the room with his emotions edging around the pit of despair. He had handled the whole thing badly, but what was one to make of these people? They were not so straightforward as the Russians. The Ivans might change their minds twice a day, but they gave a direct answer and their orders were usually clear. How could he reverse the trend of this damned interview without demeaning himself completely? If he only had something to offer them. Perhaps he could tell them that he had hidden Jews during the war? Or that he had sneaked some bit of anti-nazi statements into those pitiful plays? Or.... He studied the floor; a thin runner covered the center of the hallway except for the sections where military boots had worn holes in the fabric. The scuffing had battered the hardwood into random patterns of scratches in the wax and varnish that contrasted with the tiny deep blue and gray squares alternating in the carpet. He wondered if a formula existed for computing the number of squares.

"Buchdow!"

Only Schade sat in the office now. "Sit down. We understand you know the actress Gisela Albrecht rather well."

Buchdow was so surprised by this statement that he could not conceal it. He had forgotten her. Of what interest could she be to them? Was this come kind of trick? "Yes, I know her."

"How well do you know her?"

"We have been together since the theater closed. She was one of the group which went into hiding. We are close, I suppose."

"Yes."

"When I come to your sector I would like to bring her with me. She is a very talented actress and will be an asset to us." Why were they interested in Gisela? He had no answer and they probably would not offer one. Should he ask? The important thing was the interest itself. How could he use the information? Of what value could....

"I can tell you this much: assuming you pass the clearance, and you probably will since you were too small a fish to bother about frying, so if you come up clean you'll get the license to work in the American sector. All things considered it should not take too long and there is a certain leeway in allowing you to begin before the investigation is completed. If you don't come up clean, you are out. It would be best if you did not wait for us to give you a play or an ensemble or a building, which we might never do and you'd end up playing in other people's plays. Take the initiative. Free enterprise, within strict limits, of course.

Come up with a proposal. Forget about art and think of entertainment with a message. You get the picture, I'm sure. If we like the proposal we'll be of assistance. Now, do you have friends in the sector, a place to live?"

"Yes, I can find a place to live, but what about Fräulein Albrecht? I mean, I can't simply leave her...."

"Yes, what about her?" Schade thought for a moment.

"I can get her and bring her with me."

"We would prefer that you not return to the Soviet part of the city for the moment. We would prefer that you remain here and begin your work. We'll see about Fräulein Albrecht. Here is the longer version of the questionnaire, the *Fragebogen*. Complete it as soon as possible and return it. Is there anything in your apartment you need?"

Buchdow snorted. "Apartment? Hole in the ground. Just some books and papers, nothing else of value. A sweater ... the fighting destroyed everything else."

"We'll see to that when we deal with Fräulein Albrecht."

"She has not been well recently...."

"We'll do what we can for her. Now, I suggest you visit the clinic in Mainzerstrasse and get rid of the lice. Here's a certificate for that. Best return the *Fragebogen* tomorrow. Have you a ration card?"

"Yes, the Russians issued one when I went to work at the Schiffbauerdamm. But Fräulein Albrecht does not have one."

"We can do something about that. She has to go through the same process as you. After you've given your plans some thought, come back and we'll talk about them. You can see either myself or Lt. Makepeace." When he noticed the hesitation on the German's face, he added, "Lt. Makepeace is rather more rigid about the denazification process than some other officers. You'll find that most of them agree with him, however, so you might phrase your opinions a little more cautiously. Express them by all means, but a little more tact would not hurt your chances." Schade's smile held equal amounts of warmth and condescension, each canceling the other.

Confused, Buchdow said, "Your German is perfect."

Schade laughed. "That is being tactful, but it's rather heavy. I was forced to leave Germany ten years ago. We will not discuss this now. You have much to do. It would be beneficial if you begin immediately. I repeat that we have promised you nothing beyond the vetting. The rest is up to you. *Auf wiedersehen, Herr Buchdow*."

* * * *

"Can we do that?"

"Why not? Old EB will take our recommendation."

"But what if the CIC report is negative? And can we let him work before the vetting is done?"

"Why not? We can always ban him later. In this case it should be easy. We already know what's in his file at the Chamber and that's basically where CIC looks with little fish like this. He's not completely clean, but he's not so dirty as not to get a *Persilschein*."

"This whole business will never work. None of our Allies are going to push it so far. The *Germans* even complain the Soviets don't do enough denazification."

"Nonetheless, the policy stands. So far."

"Like non-fraternization, which is truly and perversely stupid."

"That's quite different and won't last much longer. Doesn't apply to us anyway. What did you promise that conceited prick?"

"The usual: that we'd welcome him but he's got to be vetted and then he's on his own, that he's got to come to us with his plans and proposal, that he'll probably be licensed. No more, no less."

"You do like those Americanisms, don't you?"

"They are extremely functional, and brief, like all such colloquialisms in all languages."

"What about Albrecht, the teutonic beauty?"

"I think he'd forgotten about her until I mentioned her name."

"Ironic, isn't it, that she's on the list and he isn't. We assume if he comes, she'll have no choice but to come with him. I hope the assumption is correct."

"I told him we'd pick up his stuff for him and talk to her about moving."

"Why? Hell, he could do it just as well, easier even. We don't know what condition she's in."

"I told him it would be better if he didn't go back to the sector for a while."

"Ah, your central European propensity for intrigue, mystery and deep dark danger around every corner. This isn't the Balkans in a Graham Greene thriller, for crying out loud."

"It may make him a little more malleable. In the future he'll think we did him a favor, saved him from some threat, deep dark or not."

"For someone who constantly bitches about this type of stuff, you certainly throw yourself into it with gusto."

"Europeans do not possess gusto. They are either too primitive or too sophisticated. Gusto is for the new world. But I do my job."

"Ah, yes, the efficient, conscientious German. You'd make a fine bureaucrat."

"Hell no, not me, my soul's too romantic."

"Your soul, Johnny me lad, is rather ambiguous. But let that pass. Do you think he believes all that he spouted? How long did he rehearse, do you think? Anyway, I hereby nominate you to make one of our nighttime visits to the blonde and delicious Albrecht. I've got to finish the weekly report before the electricity goes off and an early meeting tomorrow at the Chamber."

"Actually, I'd rather not go myself."

"I need my sleep. Furthermore, mein lieber Freund, I made the last one, you may recall. Still further, I think you should go early in case she has a problem or resists our irresistible offer. As long as things remain confused, we've got a better chance to move on our own. Gradually routine will set in and it will become more difficult."

"The lines are being drawn already. And routine won't mean any less time spent in meetings and writing reports. We spend half our time reporting on what we do the other half. Is this any way to run a railroad? And now we're secretly competing with the Soviets for actors!"

"It's not as if we're hijacking them, for Christ sake."

"Not as such maybe –"

"We're not grabbing them for ourselves like the scientists."

"Ur?"

"They'll still be in the city, not in Ohio or Krasnagorsk."

"Scientists …?"

"Not actresses, they stay here."

"Lucky them. What about scientists?"

"Both of us are clipping them and sending them to the fatherland. You ought to know that. It's only a secret to the American public."

"People disappear, yes ... but we are all shamelessly using these artists and actors for our own political purposes. This is not the way to reinforce the solidity of the alliance. Look at the blatant manipulation of old Gerhard Hauptmann – "

"By your own lefty reds, remember."

"We are all doing it."

"And the manipulated love it and praise the manipulators just as shamelessly thinking they are doing the manipulating, playing the Allies off against each other – a typical symbiosis, beautifully constructed, elegantly operated."

"That is so perverse it cannot even be discussed."

"Woof!" Makepeace sighed. "John, I've got to finish this report."

"All right, all right, I'll go as soon as it gets dark."

Makepeace sang,

As evening begins to fall about the town
And snowflakes start to dot your lovely hair
Then we'll begin to know about the moonlight
And once again know how to hunt the bear.

* * * *

Gray-blue smoke from his Dunhill cigarette curled into Yuri Vladimirovich Tamirov's weak eyes hidden behind glittering steel-rimmed glasses. Nothing else about him even hinted of weakness. Almost the stereotype Russian, he carried his two hundred pounds well supported by his six-foot height. He laughed a great deal and with pleasure, but the iron of his convictions remained close to the surface, just under his attempts at playing the role of the diplomat. Only his superiors in Moscow and someone in the Soviet Military Administration presumably knew his exact function; the western Allies certainly had no clear idea except everyone assumed some intelligence connection, but they had no details. He worked officially in the Soviet information control office and, after an initial period of little contact with his Allied colleagues, he now met fairly often with some of them, both formally in the Allied Kommandantura meetings and informally and irregularly on other occasions. This activity did not fit into the stereotype and worried his opposites in the western sectors of the city. For some reason he particularly liked talking with Makepeace, upon whom he practiced his professed diplomat role. "It's your inherent distrust of communists," Schade explained obscurely. "He's trying to convert you. He probably thinks you'd make a perfect fanatic Stakhanovite." Makepeace choked on his laughter and shook his head vigorously.

Now the future fanatic and his potential confessor sat drinking watered beer and smoking cigarettes in a small not very clean *Kneipe* off the Kurfürstendamm. Since the bar had very little to offer any customers, very few of them ever entered the unmarked door leading to the cramped odorous space filled with broken mismatched chairs and tables.

"Why do we meet in such smelly sinister places? Blah!" The look of disgust on Makepeace's face would have given pause to the most aggressively importunate whore. He inhaled Fatima smoke and touched the crown of his head.

"Tradition. Our types always meet in such places," Kransnikov said serenely.

"It is a good thing we are not secret agents, doing the expected."

"We meet in the opening, *kak nastoyashchiye bolsheviki*."

"You're such a card, Captain."

"Major, Lieutenant, I have been promotioned."

"*Tovarish*, we would like to have this Albrecht Gisela in our sector. What do you think?"

"Villum, take her."

"Buchdow is here and wants to stay."

"Villum, you can have that opportunistic pig. Besides, the sector borders are completely open. Anyone can live where they please. They are unimportant, too small for our concern, don't you agree?"

"They may be small fry, but they are the future and should be nurtured, as you know very well."

"The future will form itself as it desires, we must be attentive to the present, Villum, that is the reason we are here." Tamirov smiled with a broad façade of innocence. "Small fry, Villum? *Eto erunda*? Someday we should compile a dictionary of such amusing vernaculars."

"Like trading fours, Yuri?"

The Russian's body shook, but he controlled the laughter. "Precisely, partner."

"I suppose we are, in a way, still partners." Makepeace sounded skeptical, but resigned.

"Let us take advantage while it lasts, Villum."

"Yeah, you bring the caviar, I'll bring the bourbon."

"Better you bring the watermelon, I'll bring the vodka."

"The gray geese are flying across the evening sky."

"Perhaps in America. In Moscow we watch the cranes at twilight."

"Now Yuri, you won't try anything funny, will you?"

Tamirov rubbed a hand through his short gray hair and smiled back. "Funny? Funny? Unfortunately, we are rarely funny, Villum. Maudlin, sentimental, violent on occasion, yes, but hardly ever funny. Amusing on occasion, perhaps, even amazing...."

"Yuri, don't diddle me...."

"Diddle? Diddle?" Tamirov's body shook with laughter. He took the cigarette out of his mouth with thumb and forefinger, blowing smoke across the table. "What is that? Why don't you learn to speak Russian, Villum. Then we could really speak to each other, *kak druzhnye Soyuzniki.*"

"We could speak in German."

"Language of pigs. I only speak it to pigs, not our brotherly Allies."

"Your colleagues have been known to quote large amounts of Heine and Schiller in perfect German. Very well-read in the German culture, these fellows, better than many of their local clients."

"Yes," Tamirov responded thoughtfully. "We have many intellectual Jews from Leningrad in the ranks. But, Villum, they are *referenty po voprosam kul'tury*! Cultural affairs advisors, like you and me, but different, eh? We do not suffer *from katatskaya melancholia*, *kak,* saloon melancholia, I think." The Russian sighed, his spectacles glittering in the dim light, and raised his arms in an exaggerated gesture. "What can you expect?"

"We have several émigré colleagues who speak German only on the job when it is unavoidable. Even among themselves they speak English."

"Among ours they speak Russian, but they are all wooden heads without culture. Apparatchiks. Unfortunately we need them."

"Still, it's curious, rejecting your native language."

"The fascists degraded it so it is no longer civilized or useable."

"I fear these fellows will not rise to key positions in military government."

"Sometimes, Villum, you are, what is the word? *Napyschchennyy?*"

"Pompous? Me? Never!"

"Perhaps you should learn Russian. We may be talking much to each other."

"What you don't know, you suspect, is that it, Yuri?"

"You know, Villum, it is true we have our ways ... and our own sources of information. We will perhaps be here a long time; perhaps much longer than you; we must know a great amount of things. You have no idea how large our operations here are. You have only a skeleton of staff here. You are at a disadvantage. Why not admit it?"

"Yuri, we may seem small, but we're wiry."

"Wiry? You have tentacles everywhere? You have microphones in bedrooms? You listen to me snoring?" Tamirov's laughter boomed through the damp empty room.

"Like The Edge Bar we are everywhere."

"We just shut it down again, but for good in our sector." The Russian set a serious demeanor upon his face and grunted.

"It will reopen, like mushrooms after the rain."

"But not in our sector."

"Not yet."

"Not ever."

"Not under that name."

"Not ever."

"So be it. Just don't pull a fast one with this Albrecht...."

"There you go again, my dear, idioms, wise guy sayings. You, how is it, 'diddle' me, no?"

"Wouldn't think of it, Yuri. Never enter my mind."

"Your mind is as devious as the putative policies of your government, Villum – "

"No more than yours."

"- but have another drink, if you can stand this horse's piss. Next time we will bring our own."

"Thanks."

"Do not mention it."

"You bring that diesel oil you call vodka and I'll bring some fine Kentucky bourbon."

"I should be offended at this gross capitalist insult to our great national contribution to the world's progress toward the state of soporific bliss, but in the interests to international anti-fascist cooperation I will ignore it. Vodka comes in varying qualities, yes, but the result is usually the same: the first glass suffocates you, the second makes you bold like a falcon, after the third the glasses fly like birds. And remember what our famous genius-poet Mayakovsky wrote:

> *Better in fact*
> *to die of vodka*
> *Than of boredom!*

A fine Soviet hero, that Mayakovsky."

"Fine indeed, Yuri, but better dead and red than alive and bitter and possibly writing about it."

"But remember, Villum, the handwriting is on the wall." Tamirov sighed, whether with satisfaction or frustration Makepeace could not decipher.

"Perhaps, Yuri, but I think it's a forgery."

"It expresses the historical truth, the future, inevitably the future."

"It sure doesn't say *'mene mene tekel upharsin'*."

"No, most certainly not that. Of course."

"And there are no heroes anymore, Yuri, only protagonists and minor characters in the story, alas."

"Perhaps in the West this is so, but we still have our heroes, especially of the Great Fatherland War."

"You tend to change them, though; like Trotsky and Bukharin."

"The necessities of history require changes not easily understood by the masses."

"Or anyone else. Or everybody."

"Those of whom it is required understand sufficiently, if on various levels, it is true."

"And what about us, Yuri?"

"You and I, Villum? We have our roles and our masters, but in all probability the world will little note nor long remember what we have contributed."

"Literary theft is the second highest form of flattery in Russia?"

"Citation, coded or not, is sign of deep appreciation and perhaps even admiration."

"Honest Abe."

"A smart politician with a talent for fine rhetoric."

"Indeed. Now about Albrecht...."

Tamirov shrugged his massive shoulders. "She's yours, Villum, with my blessings, as it were."

"That's rather conditional."

"What more can I tell you? What more do you want?"

"You'll keep your mitts off her."

"Mitts? Something to catch ball with? What has this implement to do with theater nazis?"

"As in the bear's paws, to be kept off, Yuri." Makepeace smiled.

"If we wanted her, we would arrange to keep her. But why should we want a tramp, a drug addict? Easy come, easy go, as the Bulgarians say. Simple. How, Lieutenant Makepeace, how can you be so damned suspicious? Have we not an arrangement?"

"Of sorts."

"In these fragile times you can hardly ask for more, can you?"

"*Proshchay*, Yuri."

"Ah, you see, you are learning."

"Yes, I can do that, even as a bourgeois decadent end of the capitalist road boogie woogie zee, even I can learn a few delicate phrases in your native tongue."

"You have perhaps consumed too much of this sewer water. You talk in angles."

"Boogie woogie zee? A word play, Yuri, a minor improvisation on one of your favorite pejoratives—"

"Ah, ha! Bourgeoisie in English. How clever. I recall a statement made one night by that strange civilian fellow, Mister Morgan Tahni – someday you must wash yourself with me and inform me for whom he is spy – 'We'll hoist 'em by their own canard, those nasty middle class.' Too bad does not rhyme."

"Nor is there reason in it, Yuri, but I think he must have been angry when he said it."

"Villum, he had a truly beatific smile all over his face."

"Then he was very angry."

"Then I think he must work for the English. One can never tell what cooks in their heads. Their eyes are like kopeks, dull and opaque. I might get a rhyme out of that if I knew better the English, the language."

"Here's a melodic poem for you to learn, Captain Tamirov, just the thing for beginning your day, even in Moscow."

"I suspect I will not immediately grasp its meaning. And I come from Leningrad and have been promoted."

Makepeace sang,

> *A gentleman dapper*
> *Stepped out of the crapper*
> *Looked around the world*
> *And plaintively said:*
> *What's the story,*
> *Morning glory?*

"In Siberia, so they say, a toilet is a big stick for protection against wolves. And among friends we used the patronymic as well as the given name."

Makepeace moved the links of his silver bracelet against each other.

* * * *

What Schade really wanted was a stretch of peace and quiet in which to do his private work. Given the erratic and peripatetic existence he had lived since his twentieth year there had been no stretch of anything more than a few weeks during which he had been able to concentrate on what he thought of as his real work. He had written tens of thousands of words on hundreds of pages, but the few pieces he had been able to publish hardly constituted a test of his talent. And the vicissitudes of his life up to this point, particularly his last few years in the army, had fragmented his creativity, forcing him to write only short pieces, many of which turned out to be simply exercises and practice efforts. Before the draft notice arrived, his interest in writing plays diminished with the realization that he could not write a good one and the lack of inspiration so briefly provided by Leslie. What he really wanted to do was write a brilliant novel, but his constantly changing situation precluded any sustained thought about a suitable subject other than his own life and he did not wish to fall into that trap: could he write anything on the level of *Look Homeward, Angel* or *A Portrait of the Artist as a Young Man*? So he continued to drag behind him his duffle bag full of manuscripts in various stages of completion as he moved about the continent at the whim of military requirements. "Someday I think I'll live in a lighthouse," he told a skeptical Kirshhof. "Clean air, well-lit, simple functional furniture, simple food, regular unchanging duties that leave plenty of room for thinking and writing. A useful job. That's the ticket."

"Until the storm hits the shore."

"It is preventing ships from hitting the shore, that's the job."

Kirshhof flashed the bright green yoyo in a wide circle and snapped it back into his palm. "You're so romantic. Don't let the coffee get cold."

The vagaries of this unlighthoused, peripatetic life had brought him to his immediate preoccupation with attempting to safely navigate the massive piles of rubble and trash in the pitch darkness of the section of the city known as Mitte with the dubious aid of a small flashlight whose batteries were apparently of pre-war vintage. The stench eroding his sense of smell was even more odious, if less dangerous, than tripping over smashed masonry or an unexploded bomb still buried in the undulating ground. The reek of decay and lack of sanitation in the atmosphere resisted Allied and German attempts to purge the city.

During the daylight one could to some extent ignore it, but at night, with no lights in the streets and ominous shadows everywhere, every sensory unpleasantness intensified. Small noises, greatly amplified in the dark, rattled through the paths of rubble down the empty streets. Sound conceivably made by humans under these circumstances became even more alarming. Allied military police, notoriously short-tempered, automatically shot at unidentified moving objects at night and requested a password thereafter. These nocturnal excursions gave him no pleasure and left him shaken and exhausted.

Surprisingly, Makepeace seemed to enjoy them and usually went into the night to make the first contact if the person in question had not already appeared in the office. Some of the people they dealt with preferred for various reasons to conduct their business at night. These Germans still did not trust the political situation in which four disparate nations governed the city. Schade had to agree that the circumstances of his mission on these forays did not lend themselves to a comforting feeling of safety. In fact, he and Makepeace regularly attempted to manipulate this very distrust and instability in meetings with their nighttime "clients." The interviews had to be handled with discretion, the discussions carried out in oblique terms so there could be no question of an open rupture of the solid Allied front. As part of the occupation forces they had the advantage of authority over the Germans, but they wielded this power carefully: a client who believed he had made the decision himself served the mission more securely than one whom they forced into deciding in their favor. Thus far they had achieved an almost perfect success rate, the exception being a well-known musician who had been killed in the last days of the fighting. Schade felt no pride in the accomplishment because he continued to think the project misguided and politically suspect, but he had ceased arguing about it with Makepeace. In the end, they spent little time carrying out the order, and only a few names remained on the list.

    The Anglo-American bombing, carried out with devastating effect over the years, combined with the Soviet shelling of the city during its final weeks of agony, not only reduced much of the architecture to ragged empty skeletons, but also obliterated most of the street signs so that even in the daytime those who knew the city fairly well became disoriented and often lost their way. When the Americans first arrived in the city the Russians had replaced many of the name signs with their own in their own language. Too many old landmarks had disappeared while rats with a sure sense of direction scurried amidst the ruins. The night made matters even worse, and the fact that his mission could not possibly be considered in the spirit of inter-Allied cooperation added to his sense of foreboding and fright. Few people moved about at night, and those whom he passed probably had as little valid reason for their presence as he did. At one point a tall, familiar figure in ragged civilian clothes and a stained yachting cap covering his thinning brown hair loped by him. "Evening, Lieutenant." "Evening, Mister Morgan Tahni." "Watch out for the unexploded bombs, Lieutenant." "*Aufpassen oder sterben*, Mister Morgan Tahni." "That's right, Lieutenant. How's the novel coming?" The tall man did not pause, but smiled briefly as he continued on his way, his stride full of purpose and urgency. He appeared to be impervious to the nagging considerations that bedeviled Schade about being abroad at night. Makepeace could talk to his Russian contacts about the mysterious Mister Morgan Tahni, which seemed to be his full name. The city contained multitudes of such characters, each of them from elsewhere, most of them going somewhere, traversing the city's streets like living lines on a map, in constant motion, tracing their stories, but leaving no narrative behind them. Schade first saw the lanky fellow on the other side of Bismarckstrasse shortly after arriving in the city. Schade was admiring the large Lincoln convertible with the top down speeding through the newly cleared street, President Truman and three aides in their double-breasted gray suits and matching fedoras being taken on a tour of the rubble. On the other side of the street, Mister Morgan Tahni appeared and waved to the Lincoln's occupants, one of them waved back but Schade could not tell which one. When he looked again, the mysterious sailor had disappeared. Schade puzzled over the fact that only two jeeps with MPs, one fore and one aft of the limousine, accompanied the group of VIPs. The scene lasted less than twenty seconds and Schade remembered it for a long time.

Moving slowly around the corner of a large pile of bricks and dirt, Schade skirted a crater full of stagnant water to emerge onto the juncture of the street he had walked up and what once had been a wide thoroughfare. Now reduced to a narrow path between lengthy rows of rubble, it appeared to be little different from any other street except that paths had been cleared behind the rubble where sidewalks had originally been laid.

A recently acquired instinct vaguely informed him that he had almost reached his destination. He knew the small street he wanted lay somewhere off the former boulevard. Some of the houses on this avenue had not completely fallen into their cellars and as he proceeded he noticed a few dim lights flickering through the openings at street level where many Berliners lived in caves dug out of the dirt in the basements. At the next cross street the Russians planted a signpost giving the names of the streets in large Cyrillic letters, under which they tacked the names in much smaller German letters. Thus oriented, he walked sharply to the right for some meters and then following the beam of the torch turned into a break in the rubble to face the wreck of what had been an imposing four-story building. Little of it remained except the outlines of the sidewalls rent with gaping holes. The buildings on either side of this one had collapsed in upon themselves.

He found the tradesmen's door underneath the stairs leading up to what had been the main entrance, turned off the torch and, feeling somewhat embarrassed, knocked on the narrow piece of wood that served as a door. He expected no reply and none came. Setting aside the wood he entered and replaced the board behind him. Using the torch once more he fund himself in a small empty anteroom. Another door ahead of him emitted dull light through the cracks in the wood. On this door he also briefly rapped with the torch, then pushed the door forward.

Nothing stirred in the stale heat of the room, but life of sorts existed there. With no expression except the ghost of apprehension on her face, the young woman, dressed only in a torn and soiled undergarment, awkwardly rose from the tattered mattress on the floor and on bare feet began to edge toward him. Her painfully thin body moved spasmodically as if the joints had been disconnected. A glaze covered her eyes, which looked at him but could not define his presence. As she stepped forward with the exaggerated caution of a drunk, the matted, greasy blonde hair hanging to her shoulders hardly moved. A long rip in the stained line singlet exposed her undernourished thighs in the pale light of a short thick candle in a cracked smeared bell jar. Her breasts lay on her chest bereft of energy. A muscle in her right cheek jerked rapidly up and down, then stopped. Her shoulder blades pushed painfully against her blotched skin. This had been one of the loveliest young actresses of talent in the last years of the Third Reich. She moved now with the placidity of a sick giraffe stretching desultorily for a healing fruit on a branch just out of reach. His stomach twisted and nausea crept into this throat.

    Within arm's length of him, motivated by some torn fragment of memory, she reached out and placed her right hand on his crotch. Her pallid face twitched once, then settled into a placid blankness. She farted loudly but no recognition of it broke her expressionless gaze and she moved no further. "Doped up," he muttered in a strangled voice not hiding his disgust or his astonishment that he spoke in English. Her grimy paw automatically began to caress him. "And you stink." The hand stopped but did not go away. He could smell no ether or opium, but it could have been cocaine or some derivative. Even now in the city one could obtain anything in small quantities if one had the right friends and the ability to pay, somehow, anyhow, for what one needed. In her condition she had nothing left with which to pay; the last currency she possessed, her body, would not bring enough in the rawest back alley. "And you're filthy." His anger caused him to wonder why. In a hollow, grating tone she mumbled, "*Magst du ficken, Schätzchen?*" and giggled as if surprised by her own question.

    The muffled noise little resembled the voice he had heard on the soundtracks of the movies they had recently screened, except for the unusual grating edge, which had become a trademark of sorts. Harsh and empty now, it lacked the erotic undertone she once practiced so hard to achieve. Her eyes focused briefly and a pink flush suffused the sallow flesh of her neck and face as if she recognized the shocking vulgarity of the question. "You wanna fuck, sweetheart?" The blankness came again quickly and he could sense her mind retreating into itself, moving away from the pain and confusion of embarrassment. Almost as tall as he, she stood straight but swaying as the drug worked to take her further away from the fear and hurt. Through the mists of the narcotic she seemed to struggle against his anger and her condition, resisting and at the same time wanting to continue her travel in the milky landscape of her cushioned mind. He saw a residual strength in her that increased his anger and frustration.

Gently pushing her away from him, he resignedly muttered in English, "You've come a long way down." From somewhere in the neighborhood the sound of a clarinet climbed in the air playing an appropriate slow dirge combination of flatted notes. All we need now is the weeping clown, he thought with bitterness in his mouth. Impatiently his right hand brushed his mustache back and forth, then pushed his spectacles to the bridge of his nose.

For the first time he looked around the room. It resembled most of the caves and many of the above-ground rooms he had been in during the past weeks. The state of disrepair and improvisation, the dirt and trash, the desperate attempt to recreate an earlier existence were the same all over the city. In many of the caves signs of hope could be read in various ways: a bright splash of color, a small plant with blossoms, photographs of happier times. In this cave despair dominated the darkness; in this cave only a few accoutrements of a more civilized life lay scattered about the room: a coffee-maker with what appeared to be the residue of real coffee, a crushed packet of Russian cigarettes, a collection of phonograph records in damp cardboard jackets, several piles of waterstained books with torn covers, pieces of paper with handwriting and typing on them sticking out of stapled typescripts of plays, and bits of clothing on the floor, hardly more. The wan candlelight flickered valiantly struggling to brighten the night.

He wondered whether the coffee would help; they had not trained him for this contingency and his experience with drugs amounted to zero. Swell. A wave of anger broke on his mind and his bowels rumbled dangerously. Again he wondered why he was here witnessing the constant procession of degradation and the humiliation of the defeated trying to accommodate the victors. Doubts about the value of his work, questions about his own part in the charade being played with the Russians, beat against his mind like batwings. The sight of this shaking wreck of a woman whose youthful beauty had been breathtaking enraged his overheated brain and he growled sharply like a trapped animal.

He spoke in rapid German. "Now, how long ago did you take it? What is it? Come on, answer!"

She began to mumble and to sway back and forth. Taking hold of her arms, feeling the sinews where he should have felt flesh, he pushed her slowly toward a rattan chair by the small table piled with old typed play scripts. She slumped into the chair and lay her head on the edge of the table. Again she giggled absently. He quickly stuffed the books and play scripts into a duffel bag he'd had the presence of mind to bring with him and set it by the door. Then he began shaking her gently asking over and over how long ago she'd taken the drug, demanding she identify it, how often she took it, repeating the words with a great effort to overcome his growing sickness. The lack of response from the young woman increased his sense of helplessness. He shouted her name and she looked up at him, but her pale blue doe-eyes did not completely register his individuality. He began to will her to throw off the drug's effect, an effort he immediately believed to be hopeless. His anger rose higher, reaching to the upper register where mistakes could be made and misperceptions ruled. He now had little time and her condition would put everything behind the already tight schedule for the night.

Some restraint gave way in his mind releasing a flood of vicious and obscene invective of which he never before could have uttered even to himself in the innermost recesses of his brain. He lashed out at her in a stream of tight, harsh phrases describing her as the lowest of human dregs incapable of even licking the feet of her slave master, a willing victim with no self-worth, no pride, no future, a finished piece of human flotsam to be tossed into the gutter with the rest of the city's dreck. His shock at the cruelty of his words drove him on and the sharp, clipped tones began to penetrate her mind: she raised her head and something registered. Perhaps she had heard this before. He stopped the tirade and spoke her name in a normal tone of voice until she made a visible effort to concentrate and her eyes slowly started to focus. She shivered and small noises like sobs escaped her closed lips. Shaking her head, she rubbed her fist under her nose and coughed, spitting whatever it was she brought up on the floor. In a barely audible voice she said, "Who are you?"

"My name is Schade. I'm an American army officer, as you could plainly see of you weren't so goddamned hopped up!" Driven by anger, frustration and a feeling of helplessness, he perversely spoke in English.

"Wha d'you wan?" Her English came out with effort, ragged and slow; her torpid condition and the thick accent almost obliterated understanding. Swaying slightly, she sat straighter in the chair as if to regain some of the dignity she began to realize she had lost. Her eyes roamed slowly around the room as she raised her hand like an automaton to scratch her armpit. All her movements occurred as if under water. "*Kaffee, bitte.*"

He found a jug of fairly clean flat old water and began to make coffee with the residue of grounds on a small kerosene heater, hoping it would help. Perhaps it was like being drunk, and strong, black coffee would sober her up. This well-known technique had never worked is his own case, but the myth possessed such persistence that he thought there might be some truth in it. Where had they gotten real coffee?

"I want to talk to you about your work." How stupid that sounded. Embarrassment returned to nag him.

She raised her head and something approaching a wry grin tugged at her mouth. "*Sie haben vorher Deutsch gesprochen.*"

"All right, in German," he said in that language.

"I have no profession at the moment. I'm just a piece of shit on the streets." The uncontrolled giggle came and went like a hysterical bird briefly glimpsed in flight. She shivered again and slumped in the chair, one hand holding the table.

"You're an actress, aren't you? You want to work again," he continued in English.

"No more, not in a long time ... long time...," she mumbled in her own language.

"Do you want to act again?"

"Russians won't allow...." She struggled to sit up straight.

"That doesn't matter now."

"*Kaffee, bitte.*" Her head drooped and her eyes clouded over. He made the proper movements and wondered again if it was worth it. When it was over she would be totally exhausted and possibly wouldn't remember anything about it. Did she have anymore of the drug in the room? He could feel a tiny pattern of responsibility for her forming somewhere in the recesses of his emotions. Bloody directives written so far from the field. She looked so pathetic, like a half-drowned creature washed up under a pier. He tried to force his disgust to choke his sympathy and handed her the luke-warm liquid. "*Ja, danke.*" She sipped at the glass in short nervous gestures as if the coffee scalded her mouth.

He lit a cigarette; the smoke hurt his dry throat. He offered it to her but she only looked blankly at him and sipped the coffee. "Funny name."

"Not in English," he said, although it was just as unusual in both.

At a loss as to how to move the conversation forward he wondered if she would understand the situation in either language. Alternatives flew at him like silver flakes in a snowstorm, but they all melted in the heat of his indignation. He could leave and return the next day. Perhaps her addiction, if that's what it was, would make the whole thing impossible in any case. Perhaps he should write her off and go on to the others, but he knew he would stay. He had an obligation to at least attempt to make the situation clear to her. He would not, however, pity her; indulgence in that emotion he could ill afford. "How do you feel?"

"Far away ... but coming back...."

He briefly searched the rest of the room and discovered a small bottle of schnapps. It smelled oddly like crankcase oil. It tasted like crankcase oil. His stomach churned. Should have brought my own. "Can you understand?"

"Yes, I think so ... it comes and goes. When it goes too far I take more but there's no more now is there." With effort her voice gained depth and clarity. "But why ... What difference...?"

"What have you been doing for the last six months?"

"Hard times, yes ... horrible...."

"Did you stay in Berlin?"

"Couldn't get out."

"Did Joachim take care of you?"

A bitter, weak laugh gurgled in her throat. "Ach, poor Joachim ... didn't know what to do ... ran around crazy ... cried ... poor queer Joachim...." The laugh squeezed out again, now more like a sob. "Did find dope ... always running, moving, no sleep ... always thunder and lightning ... always hungry...."

"Didn't Joachim know any Russian officers?"

She stared at him, withdrawing again. "I don't know. We survived ... Mongols raped ... me ... behind the tank ... always hungry...."

"If you return to work you'll eat."

"Yes, Russians feed actors who work."

"So do the Americans. And the Russians haven't let you work." He leaned against the wall next to a torn reproduction of Dürer's etching *The Bath House*, where he wished he could be at that moment, waiting for her to finish the coffee or say something. He could not determine whether her responses were considered or automatic, but she appeared to grasp at least parts of the ragged dialogue. For some reason the Soviets and their Germans had not cleared her to work. Inertia? A personal vendetta? Something else official? Had she tried to work? Someone up the American chain of command wanted her in the American sector; and perhaps the Soviets did not care if she moved there. If he or Makepeace could find some oblique method of approaching the subject with one of their

Russian colleagues perhaps he would find out. But an answer probably mattered not at all. What difference did it make in the end? Robbing Peter to pay Paul. The whole scheme of manipulating each other's Germans was an absurd joke. They received the same rations; in fact, many "cultural workers" found it easier to work in the Soviet sector because the Russians paid only haphazard attention to denazification. The Americans pursued their own program with firmness and persistence if awkwardly like an elephant in a cornfield, and pressured the reluctant British to do the same, while the French followed their own idiosyncratic course. What could the Americans offer artists that the Russians could not? Both powers dictated what could be produced in the theaters and music halls and shown in movie houses. Schade felt uncomfortable playing on the common German fear of the Russians, or manipulating the bitter anger felt by most Berliners at the destruction and rape of their city, which they blamed entirely and unfairly on the Russians. He harbored little sympathy for the Berliners in general, but gradually he grew to actually like certain individuals like old historian Schadow and the erratic journalist Boltzmann, especially when they proved to be seriously facing their own responsibility for the catastrophe.

Sudden movement abruptly shattered his ruminations as the woman retched and stumbled from the room holding her stomach. He winced at the horrible sound, but made no move to help her. Disgust and anger continued to boil in him. Another swallow from the bottle offered no solace. He decided to end the conversation as soon as possible. The smell of the place nauseated him.

She returned to the room wiping her mouth with a fairly clean rag. "Why are you still here? There's nothing for you here."

"I won't be much longer. Do you feel better? Can you talk now?"

Struggling to maintain her focus she said, "What d'you want?" It came out both hostile and frustrated. "Leave me alone." When he did not respond she said with a tired sharpness, "Do you know Joachim?"

"We've recently met," he said with a sarcasm he immediately regretted, though it had no effect on her.

"He sent you here?"

"He provided the address."

"Where is he? Arrested?" The thought frightened her, but she took a deep breath and went on. "He was really no nazi."

"He is not on the automatic arrest list, no."

She sat down again and put her bony elbows on the table to hold her head, shivering from time to time in the heat. Schade wanted badly to sit down, but more than that he wanted to leave, and even more than that he wanted to do something. He remained standing, smoking a cigarette. Her position muffled her voice, already thick with the drug and exhaustion, but he understood her clearly. "He made a deal with you, didn't he?"

"He'll be cleared to work in the American sector, yes."

"What did he give you for that?"

"He thought he'd have a better chance with us."

"He was working here already."

"Perhaps he likes the Amis chewing gum better than the Ivan's tea." That at least was more in character: the wisecracking American victor. He relished this particular role not at all; playing the character seemed to him to be some form of betrayal.

She looked at him intensely, her vision continuing to clear in broken pieces of perception like an abstract jigsaw puzzle coming slowly together. "Victory," she said with bottomless bitterness, spacing her words with sour emphasis. "Allies. All together. You're all swine."

"Don't talk like that, you know too little."

"What makes you so different from the nazis, eh? Passing us around like pieces of furniture." He had no retort to this; it was too absurd, so unreal; he refused to respond and lit another cigarette. "You're stealing us from the Russians, aren't you? Fine Allies...."

"I'm offering you a chance to work." This was not true, strictly speaking; he had no authority to make such an agreement, but in the chaotic circumstances of the moment he could exert the necessary pressure: a bottle of whiskey, a carton of cigarettes, an introduction, the threat of arrest; and a favor to one of his own colleagues for a signature on a form ... many things could be arranged now that would not be so easy as everyone organized their programs in a more routinely bureaucratic manner.

She remained silent for a moment. "Do you have anything to eat?"

"Not here."

"Not stealing, buying us. The Russians feed us here ... we work, we eat here."

"You don't work, Fräulein Albrecht."

"Joachim, he works here, we eat."

"He won't be back here."

"How do you know? You did arrest him." Her eyes clouded with a despair, which began to suffocate the anger that had temporarily cleared them.

"No. He'll be in Kreuzberg." The pity started to well up in his chest. "You can do the same thing, you understand. We can arrange things."

"American sector...." The retreat began again as she looked deeper inside herself, rebelling as much against what she saw there as against the meaning of this healthy beast plaguing her with questions, demanding decisions.

He saw things going badly. Maliciously, but almost defensively, he murmured the words of the song of the hour: "*Ja, Berlin kommt wieder....*"

With a tremendous effort at deliberate irony she said, "But what will it look like? Russian? American? Or even German?" A cold, demanding hardness briefly pierced the residual film of the drug and exhaustion covering her eyes.

"You want to eat tomorrow, no? That is what you must think about." Anger battered his equilibrium, directed as much against himself as the situation.

"London ... I've always wanted to go to London ... I need time to think."

"And get off the drug."

"You needn't worry about that anymore," she snapped.

He could no longer talk to her. Nausea choked him, the smell overwhelmed him as he struggled against the other emotion rising in him. He could feel himself flushing with his own anger as he watched her scratching herself. Placing a piece of paper on the table he said, "Here's the address. Don't wait too long; don't bring any baggage, we'll pick up what you need later."

She dropped her head and waved a pale, thin hand. "... think about it. Leave me alone." In the distance the clarinet continued to bemoan the city, the past, a futureless existence, in tones of desperate exasperation. He could not decide whether or not to feel guilty about leaving her, so he repressed the thought. Outside, the stagnant air so full of death and decay did not clear his nausea, but walking calmed his anger. He retraced his steps through the night, cautiously avoiding the black market groups going about their business and the Soviet MP patrols, until he reached the American sector where he had to be careful not to be stopped by the American MPs. A soft rain fell making mud out of the dust. He decided not to do anything else that night. By the time he reached his billet the rain had soaked his clothes to the skin. The worst of it was that his sex had responded to her touch. He fell asleep immediately, but nightmares and the image of her gaunt face haunted him until daybreak.

> *Wenn zwei sich lieben,*
> *So steht's geschrieben,*
> *Sind sie ein Herz,*
> *Ach, da sind sie zwei Seel'n*[6]

* * * *

"The birds you are eating, Lieutenant Makepeace, sang this very morning in the Tiergarten, poor things. They simply moved too slowly to survive the voraciousness of the suppliers, you see."

"You don't mean to say we are eating black market birds?"

"They are not blackbirds, as far as I am informed."

"Yuri Vladimirovich, you serve a fine bird, well calculated to keep us in hunger pangs --"

"*Spasibo bolshoye.*"

"-- but also probably illegal under your own regulations."

---

[6]The lines can be translated as "When two love each other/thus it is written/they form one heart/but they remain two souls."

"We may not be well-known for our flexibility, Villum, but we do make do, on occasion."

"They are exquisite, Yuri Vladimirovich, exquisite."

"Would I serve you anything less?"

"Not with such a good cook; that is, for a German he's a good cook. What do you pay him?"

"He remains alive and he eats well. That is sufficient for the time being."

"You are a tough bunch, no doubt about it. You probably think we are too soft."

"We did worry about that briefly."

"But we nipped that in the bud, didn't we? Issued a very strict directive, you bet. No fraternizing. Period."

"Why bring up the Japanese, Villum? Are you having trouble with fraternization there as well?"

"Well, your troops certainly weren't soft, Yuri Vladimirovich."

"No, it's true of course. But we suffered massively at home when the German swine brutally occupied our homeland. You must not forget that."

"Tit for tat, I suppose, is justice of sorts."

"No need to be obscene, Villum. Have some more Rheinwein."

"Your English continues to improve. Congratulations."

"I am reliably informed that it is more American than English."

"Ah, that Ogilvy, he never gives up."

During the first harsh postwar winter they did not meet for several weeks. Then Tamirov called and they hunched next to a tile oven struggling to produce a modicum of heat in a cold small room located in the back of a half-gutted building in the Oranienburgerstrasse near the shell of the former synagogue. Makepeace offered the

Russian a Fatima and said, "You have been back to Moscow perhaps?"

"No, more's the pity. I've been substituting for my superior who had an emergency operation. Fortunately, he recovered quickly. He did have the best care, of course. Sauerbruck himself performed the procedure. Best surgeon in the city." He looked suspiciously at the cigarette. "Good smoke, odd name."

"But Yuri Vladimirovich, Sauerbruck was a big wig nazi."

Tamirov stated matter of factly, "We denazified him in time to operate. It went well, which is very good for the surgeon's health."

"I can imagine what would have happened had the general died under the knife."

"Yes, Herr Professor Dr. med. would no longer be at the Charité hospital."

"Or even in Germany."

"Perhaps under Germany," Tamirov said without moving a muscle in his face.

Makepeace smiled. "Yuri Vladimirovich, sometimes I think you actually own a sense of humor."

The Russian responded in a soft iron tone. "Villum, in my country no one owns anything."

* * * *

To the dismay of the American information control officers in the Milinowskistrasse building, the group squealed and bounded around the room with manic energy, tumbling and whirling at a speed that denied the officers the opportunity to determine exactly how many of them careened from one desk to another. Since some of them clearly could not read, but appeared to be quite excited at the prospect of answering the questions on the Fragebogen, they scratched their pencils and pens wildly across the surface of the paper, their high-pitched voices throwing questions and answers to each other about the meaning of the words they could not understand. The group of female, male, and child acrobat dwarfs from the former Marconi Circus wanted nothing more than to take up their profession in the Sebastian Circus being organized by the Sebastian family in the American sector. The noise level reached its peak of cacophony as Schade came into the building to meet his exasperated colleagues.

"What the hell is this? Is the place on fire?"

Felix Harrigan, the theater control officer who arrived several months after Makepeace and Schade, guffawed and sneezed. "They all smoke rancid cigars, even the women."

"It's a circus."

"Precisely," Makepeace snorted. "Can't we get them to fill out the damned thing at home?"

"Fill out what?" Schade demanded. "The *Fragebogen*? Are you mad? These people could not possibly have been in the party. They're midgets, for Christ sake! *Untermenschen*, or not even Menschen at all. Why should they bother with this?"

Oscar Monday, the music control officer new to the city, disentangled himself from a completely opaque conversation with two of the clan's elders and straightened his back. "The rules say they must be licensed. Everybody must be licensed. No exceptions."

"So give them licenses. This is ridiculous." Schade grimaced at the noise and chaos of moving small bodies, more like projectiles than flesh and blood. But a memory forced a rueful smile to his lips. The length and complexity of the questionnaire had of course evoked a multitude of sarcastic and comic responses from the Germans, in addition to annoyance and outright anger. One of the current jokes revolved around the addition of spurious questions to the document.

173: Haben Sie als Junge mit Bleisoldaten gespielt?
173a: Wenn ja, mit welche Regimentern?
174: Sind Sie nach zwölf Jahren noch am Leben?
174a: Wenn ja, warum?

(173: Did you play with tin soldiers as a kid? / 173a: If yes, with what regiments? / 174: After twelve years are you still alive? / 174a: If yes, why?)

    One of the gray-haired elders with a startling unlined face, questionnaire in one hand and a cigar stub in the other, somersaulted from a desktop onto the floor, bowed low to the ground, and with a flourish presented Makepeace with the paper. "I am Pfeffer and here it is!" he proclaimed in a thin high voiced German above the noise.
    A younger dwarf of ambiguous gender tumbled off another desk and flourished his or her paper. "And I am Salz, right here!"
    "And you," claimed what appeared to be a young person, pointing a stubby finger at Harrigan, "you are not Tabasco! Ha! Ha!"
    At which the entire group suddenly stopped whatever they were doing as silence took possession of the room for several seconds, following which the dwarves leapt into a pyramid of bodies and with a scurried shifting of their positions, began changing places in the cramped space of the office, singing at the top of their small voices a song in a dialect unknown to any of the Americans. The only words they could comprehend seemed to end each

verse in normal German: "*Und du bist nicht Tabasco*! Ha! Ha!"

With equal suddenness and speed, they collapsed the pyramid, leaping to the floor, where they retrieved their cigar stubs and stood staring at the speechless Americans, waiting for a response.

Schade took possession of himself and banished a sufficient amount of his astonishment to say, "Wonderful. *Grossartig*. Now, if you will take the papers away with you and complete only the name, address, and profession blanks, and one of you bring the papers back here tomorrow, we will stamp the appropriate annotations on them, and you will be cleared to work in the circus. Is that clear?"

They all looked at him with sly smiles and began moving out of the office in a line, all murmuring what seemed to be expressions of gratitude and the promise to follow the kind American's instructions and return the papers the next day. Once outside the building, the murmuring changed to small whoops of laughter and they careened in a mass around the corner.

Monday slumped in a chair and breathed deeply. "What could possibly follow that act? We might as well call it a day."

Makepeace shook himself loose from the state of incredulity in which they all found themselves. "Not likely. In fact, we've got several more cases to get through before we close up for the day. At least, Felix and I do. Let's open some windows here."

"I sort of resent being addressed with the informal 'du', after all I'm bigger than they are," Harrigan muttered.

"But not older," Makepeace noted.

"Christ, how can you tell with them?"

Without delays or much conversation Makepeace and Harrigan processed several unambiguous theater-related cases. As he read through the last questionnaire in the pile, Harrigan sighed and shook his head. "Does this guy Reger actually think he'll be licensed to manage a theater in our sector? He joined the party in February 1933 so he qualifies as an opportunist, if nothing else."

"Opportunism is not indictable, though there are times when it should be, and will not keep him from working."

"But his joining the party at that time puts him on the objectionable list and it's no license. The problem is that he has a long history of successes in his career. For twenty years he managed one of the most successful theaters in the city. There's no doubt we could use someone like that in one or two of our theaters right now."

"Let him manage the toilets. No license."

"You mean not yet, don't you?"

"I mean we're not giving him a license to manage a theater. Period. What's his name?"

"Reger. Hagen Reger. A thoroughly experienced professional. And we have some severe management problems."

"No dice. And no guff from you either, Felix."

"Oh, I agree, he's on the objectionable list, but he managed to stay out of the Volkssturm after the theaters closed. Wonder how he did that?"

"He says he was put to work in a factory making uniforms for the army. Now he's working as a clerk in the British housing office. No reason to even talk to him."

"No, I guess not. Let's have a drink somewhere before I go to check out a rehearsal of Offenbach's *La vie parisienne*, called here, unsurprisingly, *Pariser Leben*."

"A nice bit of innocent entertainment, but what's it got to do with the city in 1945?"

"As long as we don't provide anything new and different, we can't complain about the Germans picking up an obscure operetta they've never seen before." Harrigan could not completely repress the frustration in his voice.

"There's a lot we could have done differently, pal, but we're still stuck with what we've got. Enjoy the music."

* * * *

Schade remembered the great triumphal arch of the Brandenburg Gate much differently. The last time he saw the first of the city's classicist structures the burnished bronze Quadriga of galloping horses and wingèd Victory driving the chariot atop the roof of the monument glowed in the sunlight which bounced off the figures in bursts of golden waves. The streams of every type of vehicle known to western man clamored under the Gate's arches from Unter den Linden past the Reichstag through the Tiergarten down the Charlottenburg Chaussee toward the imposing Siegesengel monument gleaming in the unusual brightness and beyond. The din at street level stuffed his ears with great blocks of roaring sound and the well-dressed, stout, loud men and women wearing ruddy faces and hard eyes mechanically chugged about among the sallow, thin, less fortunate victims of the depression who marched less frenetically in search of employment and a bit of happiness or love, their eyes veiled in defense and chagrin.

Surely his young teenage jaw, which had thus far barely felt the razor's edge, had dropped at these dazzling sights and raucous sounds, but his memory held no such image. He did remember the large number of people on the streets wearing brown, black, gray, blue uniforms as police, military, and party officials charged through the city on apparently hectic missions of vital importance, the party members also sporting a red armband with the two intertwined twisted black crosses of the swastika on a field of white. The president of the Republic had recently appointed the leader of the National Socialist German Workers Party to be chancellor to form a stable government: the armbands identified members and functionaries of the party. The new government's repressive measures against the parties of the left forced his father and other Socialist Party members and officials to think the unthinkable: incarceration or exile. When the brownshirted thugs demolished the Party's headquarters in Breslau, his father knew that the future of the family was in imminent danger. His mother had added the final drop to the bucket of decision causing the overflow and their transient presence in Berlin: she refused to bring up her children in a nation the basis of whose government was terror. She would, she told his father, suffer the anxieties and frustrations of exile rather than wonder each day if her children or her husband would come home for dinner or end in one of the jails and concentration camps that had sprung up like poisonous mushrooms after a hard rain. The proximate cause of his being with his father and older brother at the Gate that afternoon was a layover between a change of trains to take them and his mother and sister waiting at the station to Bremerhaven and the passenger ship that would carry them into the safety of England and the United States. Then he had strained his neck to see the great arch in its sculpted glory, flanked by massive buildings through which the broad boulevard of Unter den Linden cut with the arrogance of its linden trees standing tall and straight all the way down the busy corridor to

Alexanderplatz. The Gate faced the Tiergarten to the west, then filled with thick trees and rose gardens of which the Berliners had been so proud. They considered this the center of their city, their Central Park or Bois de Boulogne.

He had felt no sense of dread at that moment, only the awe of youth when presented with the new and different, and he admitted later to being impressed by the newsreel footage of the giant party rallies and sporting events, but he had been very young then.

Now, as he and his British colleague, Captain Ogilvy Vasart, walked slowly eastward though the soft summer night from the Grosse Stern along the erupted pavement of the Charlottenburg Chausee, the landscape before them resembled a tormented geological catastrophe, devastated by some cosmic force in the process of making an error in design. An aura of crepuscular mystery and threat crept out of the darkness smelling of dust, decay, and scarred earth. The night whispered around them words they could not decipher, but which they perceived as vaguely threatening; nothing concrete they could define, rather abstractly ominous as the dark corners of cellars are to children and adults alike. The residual taunt of cordite tickled their nostrils like a recent memory already slipping away. It was after midnight and they had been liberally drinking from the Englishman's apparently inexhaustible nickel-plated flask with the raised Gothic-lettered initials "JWG," which he had filled at the British officers club earlier in the warm, pale evening. They had seen almost no one on the streets. Most citizens obeyed the curfew and those who did not moved cautiously, aware of the risk they took, or were too drunk to care. It had been a tiring day and the two men should have been in their billets, but had continued to walk, propelled by a vague restlessness neither could define.

The few marginally illuminating spotlights focused on the great stone Gate's classicist features dimly emphasized the darkness and camouflaged much of the shrapnel damage to the stone, massive chunks of which artillery shells had gouged out in the last hours of the battle for the city. Shell-fire had also severely damaged the Quadriga despite the efforts of the city officials to pile sandbags and wooden casings all around the sculpture in a vain effort to protect one of the city's landmarks. Artillery shelling had blown the heads of three of the horses to smithereens and warped the figure of wingèd victory. The war's ironfisted blows against the stone had reduced the edifice's elaborate grandeur to a pockmarked symbol of failure, palely illuminated by the victor's lights, draped in the victor's derisive red mantle, dwarfed by the city's explosive defeat. (The old historian, Emil Grüner Schadow, routinely denied any familial relationship to the sculptor of the Quadriga, Johann Gottfried Schadow, whose work in the classic style could be found throughout the city and helped to lend Berlin its aesthetic tone at the end of the 18th century. "If the Germans consider my books the way they considered his sculpture as part of the nation's patrimony, then my entrance into the Valhalla of academics is assured. Unfortunately, no Napoleon stole my work and took it to Paris so a marshal of the Prussian military could wrest it back again. Perhaps I am better off after all.")

Occasionally a military vehicle, roaring down the narrow lane cleared from the rubble through the middle of the Chausee, broke the crepuscular silence. As they neared the Gate they began to hear the softly sibilant rolling sea of hissing whispers spreading out like a blanket in the night: "*Zigaretten*! *Uhren*! *Neue Stiefeln*!" from the blackness where the trees had been, where now ragged craters and uprooted stumps defined the landscape. The area in front of the Gate and a block to the north by the gutted Reichstag building had become one of the main black-market centers of the city, only sporadically patrolled by British and Soviet military police where the Gate marked the border between the two sectors, though no signs as yet mentioned this fact. Schade noticed one sign chalked in swift white block letters just above a man's height on the Gate's south column.

KILROY WAS HERE!

Kilroy, like The Edge Bar, had been and was everywhere. Perhaps this name fit the peripatetic bartender at the ubiquitous saloon. But no, that could not be correct: bartenders killed nothing, certainly not kings, quite the opposite in fact.

As they walked, the shadowy bulk of the legislature loomed brokenly to their left. That formerly impressive citadel of Prussian arrogance which had witnessed so much drama in the struggle for democratic forms of government, the proclamation of the republic from its balcony (the first of two such announcements on the gray day in 1918), also had seen the prostration of the bourgeois parties in the last shabby act of the nazi march to power in the mid-1930s. Schade remembered the images from the newsreels and newspapers: the vast hungry crowd gathered in haste and desperation before this edifice in November 1918 longing for nothing more than an end to days of ersatz life and the renewal of some kind of substance in bread and fruit ("save at least my teeth for the future of a possible piece of beef..."). Salvation of sorts had arrived, but not providentially and only provisionally: the Germans forgot their history and 1945 crushed them far more extensively than the defeat of 1918.

Now the Red Army soldiers and their officers spent their Allied military marks freely for items sold by American and British soldiers. Some Germans, increasing in number as the summer grew older, attended this nightly agora, but what could they offer that the Red Army had not already taken? ("They don't even have the traditional offering to the victorious soldier, their sisters. The Soviets have already raped them all," the former newspaper owner, Helmuth Kronauer, said to Kirshhof trying to explain the palpable fear of the threat of sexual predators throughout the city. "And those they haven't raped absolutely believe they are next in line. This is unprecedented. In the first days of the occupation one short conversation dominated the city, very simple dialogue: '*Du gesund?*' '*Ja.*' '*Ich syphilis, komm*!' The fear of venereal disease is the great hidden wave surging underground through the city. That and pregnancies. Do you know what Salvarsan or Pyrimal costs on the black market? Two pounds of coffee or a hundred marks per injection. Who has that kind of wealth these days? Abortions are cheaper. Only the Allies have penicillin. God, what times we live in." Kirshhof kept his opinion on the matter to himself, but he knew that by the end of the first summer the victorious soldiers were consuming vast amounts of sulfa drugs.) Wave after wave of Soviet troops had confiscated a great deal more than sex and watches as they blasted their way through the German capital and the ground to the east of the city. They ignored the posters informing them of Stalin's difference between "Hitler's gang" and other Germans, preferring to recall the Russian writer Ehrenburg's demand that the Soviet armed forces burn, kill and rape anything German as vengeance for the German's treatment of the socialist motherland and its people. In the darkness of the Gate the Berliners and displaced persons from all the nations of Europe made the best of the situation, although, if they did not evidence the correct proportion of guile and subservience, the place could be dangerous. If they bargained too strongly they risked having to crawl home with a broken head or arm and nothing to show for the night's work but pain and an empty belly the next morning. The victors behaved as such and their level of tolerance remained erratic, unpredictable, and very low.

As Schade and Vasart neared the shell-battered Gate now crowned with red Soviet flags limp in the dim spotlights, they could make out small brief islands of light in the corners of the blackness. Matches flared suddenly to show off some item of trade; the low rolling murmur of voices crawled across the rubble-strewn ground. Occasionally the clouds opened and the pale moonlight partially dispersed the obscurity of the dealing. The broad expanse of the boulevard Unter den Linden lay in darkness all the way to Alexanderplatz: no electricity was available for the city's streetlights.

"Is this the real city?" Vasart asked the night. "A nightmare stinking of blood and sewage, reeking of human corruption? Out here to sell their mothers, or mine if they had her. The good sleep, eh? The nasties are out and about doing the night's business."

"There's that what should be done at night not in the day, too profound for light, *mein Freund*."

"It's a dark labyrinth we're in the midst of, lad, *keine Frage*."

"*Uri, Uri, gut Uri nik deuer Uri*." The slurred voice contained the savage winds of the steppes in its ancient history.

Vasart reacted automatically with the mild command, "Piss off there's a good chap."

"Took us for a client," Schade said astonished.

"We bloody well know what time it is and isn't."

"Ogilvy," Schade said with elaborate care, "Perhaps we should have gone another way."

"Quickest way, old man, isn't it?"

"But dangerous. Especially in our condition."

"Nonsense, old man. Don't arouse yourself. We're the conquering legions. No danger for us. Ur ... say, d'you ever lapse into German when inebriated? Sort of second nature, as it were?"

"*Nein. Niemals.*"

They reached the southern end of the Gate and stopped to sip from Vasart's silver-plated flask. "Should be careful," Schade mumbled.

Vasart smiled, his eyes slightly unfocused. "Just so. Let me sing you a scrap of verse from my college days. You'll like it. It explains many things. I've never quite figured out which, but there you are.

> *Cliomachus, O Clio,*
> *Hasrubal from Carthage*
> *Loved his bit of mopage*
> *More than his master Plato.*

Always cautious, John, always. That's why we won, donchknow. Keep a good lookout. Whoops!"

A short figure stumbled against Vasart and pulled away, stiffening. "*Ah, bouf! Bouf! Bouf! Quand même c'est pas le même chose parce-que c'est different, c'est précisement different parce-que ce ne pas la même, n'est-ce pas? Tout le monde comprend, voyons, tout le monde.*" The figure mumbled a series of additional sounds, stared at them and scuttled away into the darkness, searching for the perfectly formed excuse to justify his buying cameras in the Tiergarten Schwartzmarkt.

"What the hell was that?"

"French."

"Have they got here already? Might've known they'd find the black market first thing." Vasart was disgusted.

"Don't arouse yourself, Ogilvy."

"Don't like that, y'know."

"The French? They've had a hard time of it too. They're not bad. Venal, but not bad. I was in Paris not too long ago. Still the same. *Plus ça change, plus c'est la même chose, nicht wahr.*"

"No, no," Vasart shook his head vigorously. "The name, you sod, the name. My bloody sufferin' name. Don't like it at all."

"Why not change it, Ogilvy?" The level, neutral voice came out of the darkness near the last pillar of the Gate. They heard a low chuckle follow it and turned toward the sound as the clouds briefly parted for the moon to illuminate a tall man in a dark suit leaning against the pockmarked stone. The figure's pale white face cracked in a smile and moved a step toward them. In the dull moonlight he emerged from the shadows like a photograph image coming into focus during the emulsion process. "Why don't you change it, Ogilvy?"

"You should know about that, Harry. What are you doing here?" Vasart's voice suddenly assumed the tenor of sobriety and came out as level and neutral as he could make it: shock, dismay, no escape.

The pale skin seemed to absorb what little light remained. The man continued to smile; he was glad to see Ogilvy Vasart.

"I never expected to see you --"

"How have you been, Ogilvy?"

"-- here this early, Harry. How did --"

"One gets around these days --"
"-- you get here? Suborn a general?"
"-- and business is good here so far --"
"Still trading, Harry?"
"-- but it will change when they get organized."
"You're a proper criminal, Harry." Vasart belched, feeling suddenly alone in a reptile-filled swamp.
"It's not what you think or see, Ogilvy --"
"I know you, Harry."
"-- you only see part of it, you know."
"Have a drink."
"No, thanks. Watch it, you'll --"
"Doing just --"
"-- fall down."
"-- fine, jus fine."
"I'll help him," Schade said and took Vasart under the arm to pull him off the ground.
"Perhaps a little too much tonight, old man."
"You're okay, Ogilvy," Schade said.
The man named Harry chuckled again pleasantly. "Ogilvy, you haven't changed."
"Nor you, I suspect."
"You'll never learn --"
"Don't deal in black market medicine either, Harry."
"It's not like that --"
"Bloody hell --"
"-- you know, not all like that."
"Have a drink, Harry."
"Fine, I will. Thanks." He put the flask to his lips, then passed it to Schade who drank lightly. The distant silver moon edged out of the black velvet night, illuminating Harry's pale visage. Smiling, he said, "Taking care of him, are you?"
"No need, I think. He can --"

"He always needed --"
"-- take care of himself."
"-- someone on these peripheral nights."

Vasart laughed. "You don't know me *that* well, Harry, old man."

"Perhaps not. I may *need* you, though." Harry smiled at them from the shadows. It was all so unreal. Schade thought of Caligari and almost wept.

"What's that?"

"I'm leaving Berlin. There's a possibility I may need some official paper. Nothing much," Harry said with an insidiously pleasant tone.

"Not a chance --"
"You owe me a favor, Ogilvy."
"-- in hell I can do anything."
"But you can, Ogilvy --"
"Can't see it, old cock, can't see --"
"Something to get me on the train --"
"-- it at all."
"You'll see it, Ogilvy."
"Harry, old man, I may be drunk --"
"No doubt about it," Harry smiled at Schade.
"-- and I may owe you a favor --"
"You do, Ogilvy, you do."
"-- but I can't help you here. No power over such things." Vasart belched again and blushed at the vulgarity of it.

"I'm going to Vienna, Ogilvy, it's important." Harry spoke in a quiet convincing voice filled with inevitability.

They stopped talking and the rising and falling sounds of the unseen murmuring market took on a new amplitude. Clouds darkened the silver light. Somewhere in the Tiergarten two shots sounded. The murmuring continued, its rhythm unbroken, small flashes of dull matches burned shallow holes in the night. Vasart coughed and straightened.

"Here's a card. Phone number on it. Call tomorrow."

"I knew you'd not let me down, Ogilvy." Harry smiled that ostentatiously sheepish grin.

"Don't mention it." Vasart said this very politely, but without exaggeration.

"I won't, my friend, I won't." Harry laughed.

"You don't have any friends, Harry."

"There's you --"

"That's your trouble."

"There's you, Ogilvy," Harry said with the same soft intensity.

"We just help each other out at times, old man, what's that mean?"

"I'll telephone tomorrow. Watch that whiskey."

"You'd have a phone -- even here."

Surrounded by another chuckle, Harry began to dissolve into the Gate's shadows, his face pale and eyes bright. "See you in Vienna, perhaps."

"Doubt it, old man, really doubt it."

"So long, Ogilvy." To Schade he said softly. "Good night. See that he gets home, will you." He stepped back and was gone, the chuckle following him into the night.

As they walked away from the shadows into which the figure disappeared, Vasart said, "Old Harry, what a bastard. Steal his mother's bleedin milk if he could sell it." They drank from the silver flask.

"Ogilvy."

"Yes, old man."

"Ogilvy, what exactly is in this bottomless flask?"

"Well, now, I'm not completely sure I know but I'll tell you what it isn't."

"Tell, Ogilvy, tell."

"It is not absinthe."

"Why not?"

"I am a law-abidin' citizen of the Empire, John, law-abidin'."

"Of course you are."

"And besides it rots your brain, the cells decay from gray to yellow and y'can't think anymore. Not a decent condition for the victors, eh?"

They moved a few steps further down the dust-caked street in silence. "Why not lock him up?" Schade asked.

"I got the gen on him from one of the intelligence chaps."

"The true gen, Ogilvy?"

"Well, hell, old man, that will happen come Saint Geoffrey's Day, won't it?" Ogilvy giggled and slapped Schade on the shoulder, stumbling on a large chunk of mortar.

"Vorsicht!" Schade blurted automatically.

"One never knows about those chappies, does one? It's said he supplies information to our intel boys -- yours, too."

"Still should lock him up."

"Watch out for that rock! Some criminals are worth more outside; who knows?"

"Lock the bastard up. Schwein."

"Now let's not become aroused. You do speak fine German. No good becoming aroused. Let's see if we can arouse another little sip, say?"

"Not becoming aroused at all."

"Let's arouse another small tot, what?"

"Sure. Arousal. Nice sound. But not to get aroused."

"Surely not."

"Is he English?"

"Not sure."

"Sounds English."

"American, I think."

"How'd he get here?"

"Not all bastards are English, y'know."

"In a Lancaster probably."

"Never seen *him* aroused. A deep well, is Harry."

"Or in Monty's baggage."

"I say, John, old man, are you trying to *annoy* me?"

"Where's the flask? Don't want to become aroused. Monty's never aroused. Bastard Harry's never aroused."

"It's here somewhere."

"Nobody's aroused."

"*Ach, Scheiße*, as the krauts would say."

"Ogilvy, you too speak German."

"But I never admit it, old man, never, do I now?"

"British phlegm." They walked on. "Nobody's aroused."

"Dammit."

"Except us. We two are aroused, but undaunted, pal."

"Here tis, safe and sound and full."

They had walked from the Brandenburg Gate up Unter den Linden to what had been the Komische Oper and turned right into the Friedrichstraße, the former center of Berlin nightlife, now crowded with rubble and deep shadows.

"What's he got on you, Ogilvy?"

"What's that?"

"Why'd you give in?"

"I think I hear a jeep, old boy. We'd better duck in here for a bit. Shouldn't want any altercation with our Red Army allies. This is their sector, y'know. Don't think they care to have us roaming around like this. Not in our magnificent condition. Even if we are the victorious legions, what?"

"We'll be all right," Schade said following him behind a pile of rubble on the corner of Französicherstraße. The serene, objective moon, distant and silver, glowed palely in the dark brown night, and slowly crawled across the curve of the sky. After the jeep sped by they lit cigarettes and sat on the broken masonry.

"If we arouse ourselves anymore, we'll never get back. No taxis, no streetcars at this time of day. Trams, I mean."

"Could call the MPs perhaps." Vasart pondered this statement for a moment. "Not likely," he concluded. "Perhaps someone'll have a jeep at the club." The Englishman shook his head and belched softly. "You know, old chap, when I think of Harry, which I don't normally do, I automatically think of a poem in children's book I once read.

The world has held great Heroes,
As history books have showed;
But never a name to go down to fame
Compared with that of toad![7]

Doesn't he remind you of a toad? Eh?"

"More a lizard, or a chameleon, yes, chameleon is better."

"A toad, John, a toad. I prefer a toad."

[7] From Kenneth Graham's *The Wind in the Willows* (1908).

"Don't think about it now, Ogilvy. Concentrate on the directions."

They lurched on in the shifting deep and shallow stygian colors that appeared to reach out to clutch them into the fearsome but as yet invisible center of sinister intent. Schade shivered and attempted without success to walk faster. Vasart tended to wander off and they merged into the rubble-strewn side streets. The clouds unexpectedly parted to wash the irrupted cityscape in pale gray moonlight creating variegated black and gray shadows of shifting shapes and sizes.

The chances of falling over brick and mortar or a mislaid tank tread increased with each sip from Vasart's flask.

"John," the flask owner said plaintively, "I've lost my studs."

"Ogilvy, your uniform has no studs. Button your sleeves."

"Right-oh. By the by, what's studs in German?"

"*Manschettenknöpfe.*"

"By Victoria's great hymen, no wonder we won the war!"

Schade suddenly remembered their ostensible destination. Shaking his head, he told himself he'd have no more whiskey. Things were beginning to become too vague and he forgot too much. He had not allowed this to happen in a long time. After a certain level he lost control and sensed too much pleasure while his mind remained lucid and perceived everything with the clarity known especially to drunks. Straighten up and fly right. That was the key. "What club?"

"It's around here somewhere. Show us the way to the next whiskey bar. Music and women, maybe. Some musician told me about it. Been there before."

"Probably off limits." Schade thought of Gisela. A dirty business in the end. He wondered if she'd come to the office. She shouldn't have any trouble during the daytime. "What kind of music?"

"What difference does it make? Not interested in women, eh, old cock?" Vasart laughed but not unkindly.

"No. They're too weak and thin. Their eyes are empty."

"Ah, but with enough booze, my lad, they fill up fast. Must watch out for the VD however. No Veronika Dankeschön for us, thank you very much."

"What kind of music?"

They got up and carefully picked their way back to the street. The side streets were filled with stone piles and other debris, some of which partially filled the craters and potholes. At night there were times when the nasty odors remained underground. The moon reappeared and it became easier to navigate the unilluminated streets. The moon seemed friendly in this landscape and the air reeked of gasoline and burned motor oil.

"Boche jazz of some sort, I don't know for certain," Vasart said.

"Imitation Glenn Miller. Werner Müller Miller. It's all we need."

"Now listen, you've got --" Vasart stopped short, bugeyed. "My Gawd!" He rubbed his eyes rapidly. "Look! What the bloody hell was that?"

Schade had seen nothing being completely intent on not stumbling in the rubble.

"I must be absolutely blotto. How can I be standing?"

Schade glanced up at him and also stopped. "What?"

"From behind that pile of rubbish, ahh, rubble."

"What pile?"

"Over there. Someone ran across the street."

"Didn't see him. So what?"

"Had a bloody long red cape on."

"Capon? What's a chicken...?"

"No, dammit. A long red cape, like your Superman."

"Not my damn Superman, I deny ownership."

"'S the truth! Went across the street like a bloody rocket, din't he?"

"You are stony blind."

"Yes, yes, absolutely. Hallucinating. A long red cape. Flowing. Good Christ! A bloody red cape. Thought the bugger was going to take off, like a bloody red rocket. I've got to get me out of this bloody city. It's becoming too much for me. I'll go to Hamburg, yes, that's the ticket. Good city, Hamburg. Love the English there, they do."

Schade leaned against a wall fragment. It trembled slightly. "We just got here. Too early to leave ... Be here a long time yet."

"Not with freaks like that running around loose. I say, I mean, am I hallucinating or what?"

"Figment of your alcohol-ridden imagination. Goofy comic opera figure from the theater. Going to a costume party. Soviet superman, Stakhanov. Any number of possibilities."

Vasart squinted at Schade trying to focus. "But," he whispered hoarsely, "but what if he's, arrggghhhh, *what* if he's One of Ours?"

Schade took a deep breath preparing an answer with a suitably profound statement but felt an ominous tickle in his throat. After the coughing seizure passed he could only rasp out, "God help us," and lurched not ungracefully down the narrow stretch of open space through the rubble like a slow motion Chaplin tramp leaving the scene, rocking slightly from side to side. "Come on, come on. I'm exhausted. Where's this club? And why are we going there?"

"We could go to the Wunder Bar for a drink, eh? But the name is too, too cute."

"Yes. Right."

Holding the flask upside down Vasart stood in the middle of the street shaking his head mumbling, "What could have been in this rotty stuff, d'y'think? Sweet Jaysus."

"Hubba, hubba," Schade pronounced with raised left hand and finger pointed heavenward.

A mass of twisted steel and broken concrete curved erratically up before them and plunged into the water below.

"We'll have to find another way; this bridge is out."

"By the great Elizabeth's codpiece, John, you have a distinct flair for the obvious. You ought to bottle it. Is this a river or a canal? Whatever it is it stinks."

"Surely the Spree, long winding worm of a river through the metropolis, an watery artery bringing live's necessities to the people, like blood to the heart. Let us make our way to the right here, there seems to be an unblocked street going somewhere." Through the sub aqueous film around his mind, he thought he had become somewhat less drunk. A sure sign this was not the case, but Ogilvy definitely had to be taken care of. Someone should watch over him twenty-four hours a day. And night. With friends like Pale Harry of the Shadows and visions of rocketmen he needed help. Would he be any better off in Hamburg? Did that city contain any rocketmen? No, surely not, they couldn't afford to feed them, and only in Berlin could such things be seen. They formed part of the landscape in which few things made sense and everything happened suddenly. In the mind, the war still ground on, but the forms were different. Perhaps it was not too *early*, perhaps it was already too *late*. He shook his head to clear his vision and almost fell down. Righting himself he took a few more steps in some direction. "Come on, Ogilvy." Suddenly he felt completely sober and wanted one more drink. Then he would apply for a transfer. But where to? Where would it be any different? Where would he feel the pavement not moving like an escalator? "Ogilvy." A drink. Another cigarette. Even Glenn Miller second hand ... for a few more minutes before the problem of transportation had to be faced. The smell of the blasted city returned: ashes and excrement. Can an entire city stink of corpses? "Ogilvy!"

"Yes, a moment, eh?" Vasart picked himself up from the dusty street and pissed on a smashed building block. "All right, John, I'm better now. Need a drink, though."

"Hardly. Where's the club?"

"Not a club really. Just a cellar in a ruin. Like everything else. I say, you don't think I'm gaga, do you?"

"Just pissed."

"Yes, that's it, really. Just pissed. Just so. Come on now, let's get it on, this way. We'll find it in a jiffy. What's a jiffy, I wonder."

The next day Schade did not remember exactly where they found the cellar, but they did not walk very much further. The signposts carried the German as well as the Russian alphabets, but he spent his time watching the street for holes and masonry and did not notice where they went. He heard the music, however, and he again stopped short in groggy surprise, as if he'd burst out of a trap of wet cotton into an electrified fence.

In New York some years before, while awaiting governmental decisions which would shape his future, late on a balmy autumn night he had left his room to walk restlessly on the city, meandering aimlessly until he found himself slowly traversing the fascinating promenade of 52nd Street. Despite the lateness of the hour the street pulsed with a frenetic apparent chaos resembling a directionless circus that had lost control of its pace. Had he been drunk, the scene would have been a brain-fragmenting nightmare. Sober, the milieu increased the speed of his blood flow and sent his mind racing. He had been on the street before, of course, but for some reason that night it all seemed new to him, like the electric taste of whiskey for the first time. At the end of one block he turned and retraced his steps: he had been incapable of absorbing it all the first time. The people on the street moved in a fluid but irregular rhythm at a speed reminiscent of his Berlin memory but with very different colors. On the street the colors of their clothing splashed the gray, oil-slicked paved streets with a reflected brightness mirroring the gaudy electric signs offering the best of everything, come right on in. He stood still for a moment while his vision wandered among the crowds and the colors.

The names of the clubs in flashing red-yellow-blue neon brightness astounded his eyes and rang such pure trumpet bells in his mind that he never forgot: Onyx Club, Famous Door, Downbeat, Three Deuces, Samoa, Jimmy Ryan's, Carousel Club ... and those below-the-street bars that barely contained space for a stand-up piano, but made place for five young sweating musicians who played so fast and sweet as if they knew they had no futures and could only do this thing now.

Gradually he began to distinguish sounds beyond the street noises, but somehow accompanying them. The range of music swerved from traditional New Orleans through all manner of small group swing and singers crooning slow-drag ballads explaining that "love hurts." But from some of the clubs along this sliding sidewalk, he heard unknown and eccentric music, which perfectly fit the electric rhythms of New York. Strident yet melodic, the sound rushed with extraordinary swiftness out of the instruments, as if the musicians competed with one another to set a speed record for finger movement. The essence of the music seemed to be short, inventive melodic bursts held together by harmonic changes and a tight, light rhythm section propelling the melodies but holding the whole piece together. He did not recognize the names on the posters: Clarke, Tatum, Hawkins, Powell, Parker, Monk, Gillespie, but he knew then, immediately, that the sounds he heard would be his: acceptance was unconditional. At random he walked into one of the clubs and immersed himself in music whose linear structure reminded him of Bach but which sounded suspiciously like that strange Bartok stuff played many times faster than usual. He laughed freely out loud, exhilaration chasing the music through his head and accelerating his heartbeat. He heard bebop for the first time. "So beautiful and strange and new!"

Circumstances took him away from the city before he could witness the nasty side of nightlife on the street: the white servicemen's gleaming eyes full of violent hatred for black men, particularly musicians who played with whites and talked so freely with white women at the tables and on the sidewalks. He did come to know of the many incidents when with visceral, explosive contempt these whites ganged up and beat black men for any or no reason whatsoever. ("Man, they banged us up for walking down the street with light-skinned brothers and sisters! There's no end to that hate.")

Now, to his dulled surprise and bewildered astonishment the music he heard in this warm anxious Berlin night was bebop. The chopped notes blasted through the walls of the cellar and disappeared, running into the dark air.

"Is this it?" he asked, excitement beginning to flow through his mind, pushing the drink-induced mist aside.

"Righto, old bean. Behind that dirt pile in the back. Your bloody niggers making that bloody noise. Drinks are acceptable though. Black market. Big surprise, eh? Just let me adjust my costume."

A short thin man in a shabby tuxedo jacket and oiled hair smelling of pomegranate stopped them at the steps leading into the cellar. He began to sputter: "Bitte, bitte, meine Herren, Klub privat, kein Eintritt, private, off limits," until he recognized Vasart, and with the blink of an eye waved them inside with an ungraceful abrupt bow from the waist. They walked with tall, exaggerated dignity past the bouncer through a small curtained ante space and into the main room of the club.

"Amazing how these boche learn the right words so fast. Although he's probably a Romanian, or a Pole. Oh, I say, look at that lovely piece. Wish I wasn't so pissed. Bloody awful music, what?"

"It's beautiful, Ogilvy," Schade said, still astounded.

"No bloody taste," Vasart mumbled. "Sit here. Be back in a jiffy. Must have a chat with my tailor." He moved off into the darkness. Without electricity only candles and a few sputtering kerosene lamps that smelled and cast odd-figured shadows on the walls provided illumination. Figures in variously colored uniforms and civilian clothes, mainly men but with a number of women in old party dresses and bare feet in worn high-heeled shoes smoked and drank and laughed furiously, jamming as much fun as possible into the few hours they spent here excising their daily dulled existences by an immense joint act of will. Most of them ignored the music as well as they could and talked loudly above it.

    The place reminded Schade of other clubs on the left bank of the Seine which had opened since the liberation of Paris, created out of whatever space was available for a generation of young people anxious for the unique and original after years of static, nazi-approved culture. The long low-ceilinged space had been made by breaking down a wall that had divided the basement storage room. The soot blackened walls indicated one section had been used for storing coal. The entire space remained intact, or had swiftly been rebuilt; whoever operated the club had spent time ensuring that the room was sealed as far as possible to contain the music which the Soviet military police had never heard before and would automatically consider subversive, if not fascist. Tobacco smoke clouded the room and the odors of smoke, cheap alcohol, kerosene, and sweat congealed in the damp warmth. He ordered a beer from the undernourished ageless woman with a torn black apron and gratefully drank the tepid liquid.

    At one end of the room stood a backless upright piano being stabbed by the wizard thick fingers of a heavyset light-skinned Negro in a sweat drenched American Army uniform. Several paces away from him, a tall darker-skinned Negro also in uniform worked an old chipped alto saxophone with great bellows of gusto and pleasure, sweating magnificently. Behind him, two thin young Germans earnestly attempted to keep up with the furious music on a battered snare drum with a dun colored high hat cymbal and an old bass fiddle. The Negroes played as if they had been forcibly separated from the music for a long time and, facing an insecure future, had to play as many notes as possible while they had the opportunity. Even now this maddening city offered everything for those willing to risk its dangers. Schade shook his head in happy astonishment.

The music forced its way through the holes in the rubble and stabbed the air with a sharpness that transcended its physical parameters, shattering the European night and his emotional equipoise with lightning sequences of notes in the upper register, blasting the rubble surrounding the cellar and reforming it into new structures. For Schade, allowing the music to wash over and through his mind, the sounds did not destroy in their violence, but created a different tension, a renewed atmosphere that liberated the soul and sent it soaring. It thrilled him and took him out of himself. He tried many times afterward to describe this transcendental experience, but never succeeded in rendering the reality of its pure simplicity. He felt transformed in that brief but exquisitely enhancing moment of no known duration.

Vasart showed no signs of returning. Schade closed his eyes and thought of nothing, the music filling the vacuum, expelling everything else, the songs created out of melody fragments knitted together by the churning rhythm.

Abruptly the piano and saxophone stopped. Several seconds later the German rhythm section realized the song had ended and also stopped. Into the void rushed the crash of tightly raised voices and clattering glassware. Schade opened his eyes, disappointed the tune had not gone on. The Negroes exchanged brief tired but glowing angelic smiles. The piano player strapped his wristwatch to his forearm while the other packed his chipped and spotted saxophone in a battered case. They spoke a few words with the German musicians and began to wend their way through the maze of rickety tables and chairs to the bar in the back of the room, treading through uncomprehending stares and a few dazed congratulatory words. The volume of the clients' voices increased as closing time neared.

"Would you care for a drink?" He hoped they would, but would not have been surprised if they refused. He had by no means achieved a complete understanding of the black-white race relationships in the United States, but he knew that sensitivities were sharply honed and close to the surface on both sides. The system's obvious injustice and oppression was clear to him, but many of the subtleties and nuances remained as yet nebulous. He had always made an effort, perhaps too much of one, to be particularly polite to the Negroes he met, but he was never sure that he did not seem patronizing in his every attempt to treat them in the same way he treated white people he met.

They hesitated and eyed each other, the question unspoken but palpable. Schade quickly added: "We're off duty here...."

The tall dark-skinned Negro decided with a shrug and said, "Yeah, sure. Couple of beers. We've got to get back to the billets pretty soon."

"Yes, so do I. How did you find this place?"

Again the questioning look with narrow suspicious eyes snapped between the two enlisted men. The heavy-set lighter-skinned one leaned toward Schade and said, "Listen, man ... sir, as long as we're off duty here, are you with the MPs, or CIC?"

The thought had not occurred to Schade, but it was fairly obvious when one thought about it. "No, nothing like that. We just wandered in here. I work with Information Control. Please don't say 'sir'."

"Like propaganda?"

As usual the direct question posed no problem, but he always struggled to find a brief explanation of exactly what the Information Services Branch actually did, unthinkingly believing the matter to be too complex for a simple answer, an indication that he also believed many people would have difficulty in comprehending at all. "We try to keep nazis off the stage and out of the concert halls and newspapers. No anti-Allied programs or jokes."

"I can dig that, man. But it still sounds like the police of some sort."

"Not of the sort we need to worry about now, in any case," Schade smiled with warmth and said, "I like the music." The two musicians viewed this statement with some skepticism and gave no response, an awkward moment mediated by the arrival of the beer for which Schade insisted on paying a few worthless pieces of scrip paper. He held his glass up in a brief silent salute and murmured "Cheers," then smiled again and said, "It's true, really. I heard something like it a couple of years ago in New York on 52nd Street and in Harlem at Minton's. I like it. It makes sense to me."

"Are you a German or French of some kind?" the piano player said.

"I'm American now." With an exaggerated expression of innocence he asked, "How can you tell?"

"Just a wild-ass guess."

The tall saxophone player leaned back in the chair, but not far enough to break it. "Well, don't that beat everything. A Europe ofay who digs rebop. Whooee!" Schade could not decide whether this constituted sarcasm or a sincere opinion; not knowing the definition of "ofay," but suspecting it did not mean anything like connoisseur, he rather thought sarcasm described the statement. He did think it odd that they acted this way with a white officer, but the situation seemed to allow the opportunity. So he followed his usual pattern when faced with hostility still constrained by social obligations: he ignored it. And apparently thinking Schade as a European would play neither the race card nor pull rank, the two black men took the initiative away from him, an exhilarating if dangerous action. The piano player asked rather aggressively, "Who d'you dig in the biz? Billy Kyle?"

Before Schade could form a painful negative answer, the other Negro said, "Maaad mose Monk?"

The piano player followed this immediately with, "Joe the Guy?"

And the saxophonist laughed and said like a shot, "Charlie Jesus the Christian?" And the scat trading started picking up speed as the two men rapped out a beat pattern on their knees and the rickety tabletop to accompany their careening exchange of names.

"Artie Lahdiedahdie Tatum?"
"Kenneth Bomberman Clarke?"
"John Blowup Birks Gillespie?"
"Charles Birdmotha Mynah Parkah?"
"Nathaniel Augustine half-scobe Cole?"
"Augustine, man? Damn!"
"Coleman Flyon Majah Hawkins?"
"Gawd*dam!* Lester Phrapadapeen Young?"
"Cool! Benjamin Hipster full-scobe Webster?"
"Oscar Nineth Chord Flat Moore?"
"Clyde Bless-my Hart?"
"Oscar Bet-it-lord Pettiford?"
"Ole Bud Teenbopperager Powell?"
"Young Maxydaxy Teenbopperdopperager Roach?"
"Roy Little Jazzytoes Eldridge?"
"Noname Hotlips big-scobe Page?"
"Georgie Auldy baldy?"
"Nevahnevahdevahbevah!"
"Georgie Downinthemouth Wallington?"

152

"Little Georgie Porgie?"
"Porgie Audly Georgie?"
"Wallydolly Auldy Porgy?"
"Porgy Wally Folly Auldyness?
"Earl Daddy-of-us-all Hines?"
"Willy Count-his-blessing Basiement?"
"Alfonz Whiskeykeg no-scobe Haig?"
"Milton Roundnotes Hinton?"
"William Biggest Roll Collar Eckstein?"
"Theodore Skin-an-Bones Navarro?"
"Miles Bigarm mosest Davis?"
"Arthur Roll-elbow Blakey?"
"Denzil de Costarino Bestest?"
"Lucky Holy Collander Millinder?"
"Lucky Smooth-as-Silk Thompson?"
"Illinoise Screamass Jacket?"
"Jonathan Slick-as-a-Popsicle Jones?"
"Red-as-a-sunset-sailboat Rodney?"
"Salvation!"
"Mose heaven!"
"Redemption!"
"Halleluja!"
"Oh, my soul!"
"I be saved, lord!"
"Signify, brother!"

Strangled unembarrassed laughter in stretched back throats choked off their ability to pronounce the names or they could have gone on for an hour. Schade crammed his flushed embarrassment at the loud exhibition of exclusion deep into the pit of his mind, happy that he recognized some of the names, although the Negroes spoke so fast and in their own code, he could not make out many of them. As the two others mightily struggled to regain a certain decorum from the tangled remnants of their laughter,

Schade very seriously nodded and asked, "How did you come to find a place like this to play in?" While the Negroes broke into a renewed storm of laughter, he drank the last of the pale yellow beer and signaled to the woman to bring another round. The scene before him blurred from time to time but he believed he could still think clearly.

The saxophonist immediately shifted his facial muscles into the form of a blank mask. "Well, lieutenant, there's nothing doing for us in this town so we got to make our own party, see? So Barry Green," he indicated the lighter-hued piano player, "and me, Frederick Stoneland, and you note how I just introduced us without doing so formally, made some reconnaissance and found this dump. It's a long walk back to the billets, but the owner, or manager, whatever he is, lets us play for some Camels." Stoneland laughed. "Also we told him we'd beat the shit out of him if he dint cooperate."

"Schade, John, informally. And that's fraternization. Streng verboten."

Barry Green downed his beer and grinned in the dim smoky light. "Shit, man, that's old news. That stuff was never going to go down. Besides we're only here a couple of times. They keep a tight watch on us."

"What do you mean?"

"The Man don't want us moving around too much; afraid we'll make trouble or something. Don't want us dipping into no white poontang, German or not." Barry Green said this quietly, just under the sound level of the rest of the room but Schade heard it clearly. "Hell, man, we're trouble for them just being here. Democracy in action. Segregated military. We a goddam embarrassment for them just being here. They don't even like us being truck drivers. Not that they'd ever give us any other kind of job."

"It's true," Stoneland added, "so they keep us on the job and in the billets. But me and Barry Green here, we want to play, so we get out whenever the Man is looking the other way. Can't keep us out forever, and we can move about whenever we want if we're careful. The only fraternization the Man is worried about with us is with the white women, man."

"Listen," Barry Green said, his tone verging on the edge of anger. "Last week the CIC found a secret group of krauts somewhere in the south called the Black Panthers and arrested them. Know what they were going to do? Any German girl who went with a black soldier they'd cut off all her hair and parade her around the town like a whore. There's nowhere we can go, man!"

"Tell me something," Schade said. "Why do you refer to everyone as 'man'?"

"You want a lot for a couple of beers at this time of night," Stoneland said seriously, shifting his slender frame in the chair.

"Yeah, lieutenant, we're not going to let you in on all our secrets, sir." Barry Green grinned and drank from his glass.

Schade lit a cigarette to cover his confused embarrassment, not sure how to navigate through the conversation. "I just wondered...."

Stoneland shook his head slowly. "You haven't been called 'boy' all your life. It's an equalizer. Call everybody the same name means everybody's the same, equal, you dig? Maybe that's it."

"Language as a process of self-definition." As soon as he said it he realized how absurd the sentence might sound and his neck turned warm and a pink coloring suffused his face. "I mean, part of your jargon helps define who you are...." It wouldn't do at all, but he felt trapped in his own mouth.

The Negroes seemed to reflect on the thought, at least they did not react with derision. In situations such as this Schade found it difficult to predict any response at all. Sometimes he did not know whether his statements were perceived as insults or praise.

Stoneland leaned forward with some intensity and said, "Listen, man, it's like the music we make. We got to keep a step ahead of the ofay cats, you dig? You understand what ofay means? Well, okay, we got to keep one step ahead of the white man or else we lose everything. Everything we invent he takes and changes it, see, whitens it up and says it's his own."

"And makes more money selling it," Barry Green said with open bitterness.

Schade did not dig completely, the long night of whiskey and cigarettes had at last begun to wear away his ability to pay attention and think about complex matters.

"Look, man, lieutenant," Stoneland said trying to be helpful. "Everybody knows that Goodman cat got all his real stuff from Chick Webb and Jimmy Lunceford, you know? You know them cats?"

Schade was pleased he could nod his assent. "Yes, but Goodman also publicly integrated his bands."

Barry Green looked hard at Schade. "I don't see no Count Basie leading no big money band at no Carnegie Hall, man."

"Well," Stoneland continued, leaning his body against the wobbly table and drinking the beer. "If we gonna have anything of our own to keep we got to always make something new, see. So now we play rebop fast and complicated. The ofay cats can't do that."

"Yeah, but they will," Barry Green said, "they damn sure will. They're gonna take it over like everything else. Someday Sinatra's going to be scatting, man. Wait, you'll see."

"Then we got to make up something else, something new, like always. That's the way it is, man."

Schade murmured, "Sad...."

Barry Green narrowed his eyes. "What say?" It came out as a demand wrapped in hostility.

Schade, too deep in his own thoughts to notice, simply responded, "I said it was sad."

"Shit, man, it's always been that way. Like Freddy says, things don't change like that." He shook his head savagely. "How long are we going to be able to keep it up, s'what I wanna know, how long?"

Stoneland drank the last of his beer and laughed. "Hell, man, we're a creative people." He pronounced the last two words in an oddly affected manner. "Keep the faith. We'll always stay a step ahead of the Man, no other choice. We talk riddles and he don't know what the hell's going on, present company excepted of course, lieutenant. Lord, we can talk riddles forever! And we can play the godammed music forever too!"

"If we survive," Barry Green said. "If we keep shining their shoes and picking up their motherfucking garbage from their motherfucking back porch and shuffle around the motherfucking crackers babbling 'Yassuh, yassuh' and let 'em fuck our women and grin like pickaninnies just having a grand time over in the motherfucking slave quarters. Oh, yeah! Sure!"

Stunned by the intensity of the outburst, Schade finally made an intelligent comment. "You're going to be dangerous someday."

Barry Green laughed rawly. "Hell, man, we're dangerous just by being here."

"Let's split," Stoneland said rising from his chair. "We gotta go back to work for the Man tomorrow. Today, that is. It's cool you like the music, lieutenant, I mean like it is now. You can like it, that's fine."

"Can't find it here very easily," Schade murmured.

"Try *Jubilee* program, lieutenant," Stoneland said.

"What's that?"

"Amazing what you can hear on the Army radio these days. Sometimes they try to give us something. Too little, too late, but it's still ours."

"For now," Barry Green interjected. "For now but how long?"

"Man, you are one badminded cat tonight. You need a little taste, fix you up for the road."

"Naw, I don't need more of that kerosene. What I need is sleep."

Schade stood up and held out his hand to them. Stoneland hesitated for a brief moment, then laughed and slapped his open palm down on Schade's. "Later, man."

Schade stood rigid in instantaneous confusion and rage for the second it took him to remember and relax. "Dig you later," he said feeling foolish, like a child in an adult world who has just aped an adult custom and cannot anticipate the reaction. Stoneland smiled and walked toward the door shaking his head. Barry Green shook Schade's still outstretched hand briefly, then stuffed his hands into his pockets. (Schade later thought this natural act precluded saluting the officer, but that had hardly been necessary.) "See you around, maybe."

Sitting down again Schade wanted to hear more of the music. Everything had happened so fast. Fragments of the evening drifted through his mind as in a crazy cold-cuts dream. Suddenly he realized that everything had left him, that he had become empty inside. Tobacco and alcohol would not taste good anymore that night. Copper settled into his mouth. He walked to the bar, behind which a stained cardboard sign in a bent brown metal frame read in old German script

Guaranteed Aryan Whorehouse.

"Found it on the Kantstraße in the rubble," the bartender told Schade later, "thought it would remind some people what it had been all about." He dragged Ogilvy away from the half-dressed blonde woman at the bar and another officer drove them to Schade's quarters. At some point Schade incuriously asked the name of the club. "The Edge Bar," the officer said, "it's everywhere." Vasart spent the rest of the night in a spare bed in Schade and Makepeace's part of the Dahlem villa. As he lay down controlling his dizziness, Schade knew the next day he would be singularly ill from more than the effects of the whiskey. Before he fell into an erratic sleep he remembered the name of the slim figure that bumped into him as they left the Edge Bar: Mister Morgan Tahni. For a man who appeared to belong nowhere he seemed to end up everywhere. Outside the night carried on its whispered monologue, now exhausted, weary blues.

Salt peanuts! Salt peanuts!

* * * *

Schade's woozy analysis of his morning-after condition proved to be correct, much to his peevish disgust and dyspeptic discomfort. His head felt as though a team of large blackjack-wielding furniture movers had sapped it during the night. Two aspirins, breakfast of real eggs instead of the powdered military variety and a cold if rather watery American beer helped to dissipate some of the noxious fumes clogging his brain, but did not improve his disoriented stomach. The fact that he had known worse states of dissipation did not alleviate his current malaise or give dispensation for his nighttime transgressions. Nonetheless, he dragged his tired body and aching head into the office in the Milinowskistraße shortly after eight o'clock in time to reluctantly join a vigorously pursued argument bouncing among Makepeace, Kirshhof, and a Counter Intelligence Corps captain.

The Counterintelligence Corps (CIC) Captain, a tall muscular Texan named Irving Feldman, whose pale blue eyes startled those who looked into them because of their rock-like hardness, had written the final report for an investigation into the background of Walter Boltzmann, a journalist who had applied for permission to work for one of the civilian newspapers scheduled to begin publication in the American Sector. The argument concerned the last sentence of the report that noted the CIC could not recommend the man be employed. Makepeace attempted to convince Feldman to change the recommendation; the Captain stuck to the letter of the directives; Kirshhof held a new bright red yoyo in his left hand, the string looped over this index finger, and expressed the view that it didn't matter, even if the kraut was a good reporter, there were others just as good hungry for work. Schade entered the discussion with little enthusiasm noting that if the Americans failed to clear him, he would probably be cleared by the British or the French. If the man were any good it would be a shame to lose him. Schade did not mention the possibility of Boltzmann working for the

Soviet Sector papers: Boltzmann made no secret of his vehement contempt for what he called "perverse Stalinism." A man of the left, to be sure, but like Schade's socialist father severely critical of the Soviet Union where, he said, socialism had been betrayed by Marx and Lenin, and completely perverted by Stalin.

The fact that many CIC officers tended to view the left with the same mistrust as membership in the nazi Party formed an additional reason for Schade's silence about Boltzmann's political opinions. In this case, Captain Feldman had located Boltzmann's name in the membership lists of the nazi journalists' organization, not an unusual fact since membership had been mandatory to work in the profession. As a successful free-lance reporter, Boltzmann had written on every conceivable subject from bathing beauty contests to political affairs objectively but in a style laced with sarcasm and mock disbelief that such a thing, whatever it was, could possibly have happened in a modern, rational society. A certain bombastic anarchy occasionally forced its way into his work and this, coupled with the power of his language, made him capable of great invention and creative effort, but also showed a potential for great destructiveness, which he did not always recognize as such, especially when drunk, which condition often appeared to be his natural state, similar to that of his colleague and friend, Joseph Roth. His journalism was widely read in the liberal centrist newspapers of the city, but his behavior often bordered on the intolerable for his friends when he would shove his great red and pitted nose into their faces and bellow his contradictions to whatever they had said. Mathilde Kronauer labeled him "dangerous and fascinating," a description that said as much about her perception as it did about his Falstaffian character.

Boltzmann had left the city in 1940 to return to his family's farm in the Eiffel region of western Germany because he found no further outlet for his work. He began to labor at farm tasks, but shortly after his arrival the Wehrmacht drafted him despite his 47 years. An erratically aimed artillery barrage killed his wife and several villagers early one morning as they waited for thin gray bread at the local bakery late in 1944. Strained at the end, their marriage had produced no children, which had embittered both of them. Wounded on the eastern front with the resulting loss of his left arm, he had been in a military hospital in Potsdam when the Red Army captured the city. Somehow he survived the liberation of the city and avoided the deportation to the Urals of Germans who had fought in Russia. Now he wished to return to his former profession and remain in the city: he firmly believed that if a new Germany was to be created it would be done in Berlin, insofar as Moscow and Washington would allow the Germans any leeway in being present at the creation.

Makepeace used all of his inventiveness including a number of sophistries and in the end managed to convince Feldman to reconsider his recommendation. Kirshhof shrugged his shoulders but said he would rather have the man than not. With that the Texan and Kirshhof went off to their own offices elsewhere in the building, the yoyo gently walking the dog. "Lord, do I ever get tired of these same arguments every day in and day out. They inevitably end in the same stalemate: the need for qualified personnel has priority over everything else, but the denazification process has priority over everything else, so the guy's political background tilts the scales." Makepeace smoked a Fatima in disgust. "We put people into positions one week and remove them the next when we discover they'd joined some party organization at an unacceptable level. It's no wonder civil affairs on the local level are in chaos. It's a wonder they don't throw up their hands and tell us to run the damn place ourselves."

Schade did not find the fact of the argument itself odd, but the position Makepeace took on the issue surprised him. Previously, his colleague had consistently supported a tough and rigid application of the denazification directives, as in his hard-nosed stand on the question of licensing Hagen Reger. After Kirshhof and Feldman left their office, Schade mentioned this in passing, not intending to make an issue out of it, but curious to know the reason for the change of position.

Makepeace, the inveterate newspaper reader, snapped open a copy of the *Stars and Stripes*, sheepishly harrumphed for a moment, but finally muttered, "I know the guy, all right? He needs a job, he's good at his work, and he wants to work in our sector. He's got a fine background as a reporter. He's hungry and needs work. And he's no nazi, as anybody but a thickheaded CIC operative can plainly see." Schade found it curious to see Makepeace so disconcerted.

"He was in the party."

"No, just the journalists' organization. And I know what you're going to say, so don't bother." He turned to a pile of papers on his desk and lit another Fatima.

"I met him last week, but I didn't know you had," Schade offered invitingly.

"I ran into him during one of our first field surveys here. He speaks English and hates the Russians."

"He's a socialist, despite the one arm missing, William, a Red...."

"Don't bait me, John. I know where his political heart lies. We had a long conversation about the future. Someday we'll need Germans like that in our corner.

Now's the time to get them there. If he can stay relatively sober."

"I'm not convinced we'll fall out with the Russians, anymore than the French. They're both prickly, with reason."

"We don't have to worry about the French, they're not here."

"Your sources haven't been keeping you au courant. The gen is that they'll get a piece of ours and a piece of the Brits and make it a four-power Kommandantura."

"We still don't have to worry about them, not in the long run. And I knew that bit of information."

"The short run could ruin the whole matter if we're not careful. And the French aren't going to be easy either."

"Enough, enough, for christsake! Has the new Marlene Dietrich come in yet? That theater guy Buchdow turned in his *Fragebogen* and I started the process moving along its merry counterintelligence way. He acted very reserved, but much more gracious not to say ingratiating. Didn't grovel on the floor, though, for which I was personally grateful."

"He's a bit afraid of you. He thinks you don't like him."

"I don't have to like our clients, do I? By the way, the stuff in his cave has been taken care of: he's got his incomprehensible notes and his ratty sweater. The blonde bombshell was nowhere to be found but her stuff was there. That's not her real name, you know? It's Albrechtsburg, Rheinland aristocracy in the background somewhere. Shortened it for the marquees she hoped to inhabit. What do you want to do about her?" The question had begun to consume ever-greater amounts of Schade's mental and emotional energies; he wished he could provide an answer.

For the moment, however, his hangover made him nauseous and he vowed to give up alcohol forever.

> *Ich werde nur noch ein kleines trinken*
> *Denn meine Augen fangen an zu sinken*
> *Eins, zwei souffa!*[8]

("Fresh eggs!" Boltzmann had roared in the Neukölln café as he gnawed on a piece of stale brown bread, unable to escape the subjects of food and drink. "They went out of existence in 1941 along with fresh chickens and everything except guns and ammo! Only the victors have fresh eggs. As it should be, no doubt!")

> *Come, Bacchus, why regret*
> *All that booze we didn't get?*

---

[8]The meaning of the lines from the German drinking song is "I'm going to have one more little drink / because my eyes are beginning to close / one, two, down the hatch!"

PART THREE

Es gibt Untaten über welche kein Gras wächst.[9]
                 -- Johann Peter Hebel, ca. 1850

Gisela Albrecht fell down on a small stretch of cleared sidewalk along Unter den Eichen while making a trek similar to the one Joachim Buchdow had previously undertaken. Fear, hunger, and withdrawal shortened her breath and she remained on the ground until her vision cleared enough to look around her in panic to see if any Russian soldiers had seen her. Relieved at seeing only a small crowd of old men and women with very young children gathered around her, she began to breathe without gasping. Between the legs of her unintended audience she glimpsed the furniture long moving van, motor now disemboweled and draw by two unhealthy horses, slowly making its way down the street with its load and washed out sign along the side:

         Zieh aus, zieh ein
         mit Silberstein[10]

---

[9] There are nasty things over which no grass grows.
[10] Move out, move in / with Silberstein.

I remember that, yes, I did see it years ago, I remember it, I do.

Embarrassment colored her face and paradoxically briefly loaned her an almost healthy appearance. The crowd murmured offerings of advice, most of which involved the consumption of nutritious food, which everyone dreamed of but few had eaten in months. When she thought a sufficient amount of oxygen had entered her lungs and she could see the creases on the faces of the old men she allowed them to help her up and dust off her dress. She checked the water bottle in her stained brown shoulder bag and wiped the sweat from her forehead. As she walked slowly on, the old men and the women shook their heads and slowly went about their own affairs. Such things happened too often to shock them any longer. The noise of the city continued unabated.

Actually, she felt better than she had in some weeks. Although Buchdow had not returned after the American's visit to their cave with his obscure but foreboding announcements, the dark spectre haunting her mind gradually faded as she forced herself to confront her new circumstances. As usual, she received help; someone always appeared to offer support when she needed it most, whether she deserved it or not. In this case, having little choice, she gladly accepted it. When the American left she fell into a state of paralysis that ended only in a liberating unconsciousness. Throughout what remained of the night, deeply escaping into sleep, she shivered in the enveloping cotton warmth of the summer. Early the following morning, Claudia Kaufmann entered the basement room to see Buchdow about a playscript she needed and found Gisela lying on the mattress, her breath coming in short, shallow bursts. Claudia knew of the other woman's addiction and despised Buchdow for his role in starting that dependency. She also knew, however, why he committed the cruel act: Gisela's tendency toward hysteria in tense circumstances. Buchdow would have done anything short of leaving Gisela alone to prevent her from endangering the small group's erratic movements as its members scrambled to survive during the final weeks of war in the city. Claudia had also been with the group in hiding and, though she experienced an occasional twitch of discontent about this, felt a sense of superiority over the other woman because she had gotten through those weeks and the rapes without any artificial assistance.

Bending over the frail body now, she bit a fingernail and could not help uttering, "God, you stink." She felt the other's chest and wrist, then covered her with a blanket. A quick search of the room discovered no food or water, nor any sign of the drug. Fetching water in a dented coffee pot from the spigot across the street after twenty minutes standing in line, she returned and washed the unconscious woman's grimy face and began to force small amounts of water into her mouth hoping the liquid had not been contaminated. Under these ministrations, Gisela suddenly began to choke and opened her eyes. She coughed and lay back, but her eyes remained open. She made a visible effort to focus on the dark figure kneeling at her side, to identify and remember.

Finally she groaned and muttered, "Water" in an almost inaudible voice that sounded like a small cat scratching on a door. Claudia fed her another sip of water and said, "Gisela, can you get up? Do you need a doctor? Can you move?"

"Claudia ... what ...? Where's Joachim?"

"I don't know. Listen, my dear, you've got to get something to eat and you've got to bathe. Can you walk? Where are your clothes?"

After a while, Claudia managed to pull a wrinkled but clean dress on the other woman and lead her out of the cave into the daylight. Gisela moaned and shut her eyes against the sun's pale yellow wash. Claudia decreased the length of her normal long stride to accommodate the faltering pace of her patient. So by slow increments of steps and pauses, supporting the blonde woman's meager weight, Claudia directed them toward the house in which she lived with several others who worked with her at the theater on the Schiffbauerdamm. It was not far away but the walk exhausted both of them; at least Gisela did not collapse again. As they stumbled through the dusty cluttered side streets, Claudia kept the other talking, answering questions no matter how silly, anything to keep her mind working and aware. They passed a house without a façade and smelled gas in the air; both of them shuddered: one more Berlin woman who could no longer cope with rape and hunger. Once Claudia lost her fragile patience when Gisela whimpered a singsong complaint about her discomfort. "You're not alone, you know," Claudia hissed at the tottering blonde girl. "Others suffered the horrors of the last months as well as you. You never had to get up at three in the morning to be in the factory at five and screw pieces of ridiculous machinery together none of which made any sense with no food and the bombs all the...." She stopped and straightened her shoulders, tightening her grip on the other's fleshless arm. Everyone had suffered losses. "*'s hot keen Zweck*. Keep moving."

Twice Claudia's breath stopped and pain twisted her intestines when she spotted Russian soldiers and turned into the nearest doorway until they passed on, shielding Gisela so she would not see them. The sight of uniforms often panicked rape victims, calling horrifying attention to themselves, and Claudia, although having also suffered that violation, had no idea of the uniform's effect on Gisela in her present condition. None of the civilians on the streets paid any attention to them: the sight of people stumbling about the battered city disturbed no one's equilibrium. When they finally arrived at the house with no roof or window panes, Claudia helped wash her charge in the large ornate bathtub with a minimum of cold water and rough detergent soap. With the same soap and an old razor she shaved Gisela's armpits, groin and legs to facilitate delousing. "After you've eaten and slept some more, you go to the clinic on Bernauerstrasse and get puffed. You'll feel a thousand times better after that."

The pale figure attempted a smile, but her face refused to participate. "I feel better now, except for the pain ... thank you, Claudia."

"You can be thankful I'm not rehearsing today. Put the dress on; it's too big but it covers you. Here's some of your underwear; after you eat, wash it, then sleep, then to the clinic. Then we'll talk. Now eat. Not much, but something."

She ate a little of the dark sour bread and the cold cooked turnips, and drank a large pitcher of water. Her hands shook and her legs protested carrying even her underweight body. The withdrawal pains in her head and abdomen relentlessly made their presence an unavoidable part of her existence. She forced herself to squat over the turkish toilet, her thigh muscles trembling, then to wash her under garments in the baroque tub and hang them over a chair to dry in the day's heat. Finally, gratefully, she fell asleep on Claudia's bed, the tranquilizer of exhaustion obliterating the despair in her mind.

A few hours later she awakened with a start in the early afternoon's rising heat. Darkhaired Claudia Kaufmann sat across the room smoking a foul-smelling cigarette, worrying a fingernail with her front teeth, and reading a soiled playscript, making small movements she later would expand into elaborate gestures when done on the stage. Convincing herself that the pains had begun to diminish, Gisela washed her face, dressed, and taking Claudia's arm they set off for the clinic. "Don't worry, there's nothing to it. Come on." A tired voice of optimism, Claudia wondered why she bothered with this lovely wreck every time she stumbled and gasped aloud in annoyed frustration at her own inadequacy. They walked as quickly and with as much purpose as Gisela's condition allowed.

The nurse gave her a packet of vitamins from the hospital's sparse supply and informed the two women that Gisela's constitution was essentially strong as far as he could determine and with care and the right food she would be back on her feet in no time. He laughed at his use of the old cliché. "How easy it is to slip into the old phrases that don't mean anything anymore. 'Eat the right food.' Such nonsense. We're lucky if we find more than one meal a day and that's never enough. We count our intake in calories, not satisfaction." No one made any reference to the drugs, and the nurse appeared oblivious, hastening to the next patient. *Keine Zeit, keine Zeit, keine Zeit*! No one had any time.

"I don't feel too bad," Gisela said as they walked back to the house. In fact, her chest felt less hollow and her face less solid, but her shaven parts itched constantly and the DDT smelled offensive. "But I can't tell whether it's because of my general condition or because I'm throwing it off. But I'm awfully hungry."

"You're hardly alone there. When was the last time you took it?"

They turned automatically into a narrow side street to avoid a group of drunken soldiers loudly arguing among themselves on the road ahead. Two of them held pistols pointed at each other. "I don't remember, a couple of days ago, no, early yesterday, or the day before. I could use some now. No, no, of course not. Don't have any now anyway. Joachim was going to get some more and give it to me in smaller doses until I don't need it anymore."

"You have little choice at the moment. It's almost impossible to find in the city. All the old sources have dried up."

"I must in any case. I've got to find work. We can't go on living on just Joachim's ration card; it's not enough for one as it is. Maybe the Amis or the British will let me work in their districts. I'd like to know why the Ivans won't give me a clearance. Lots of actors closer to the Bonzen than I was are working. It's not fair. Maybe some bastard denounced me. They haven't even tried to get me to lie down for clearance. Every time I go to the Chamber they just say the investigation hasn't been completed." Her voice picked up speed and began to rush, a stronger timbre and determination growing in volume. "I don't know what's going on. I must have work. I've got to eat, don't I? I've got to stop these pains. Goddammit anyway! I could scream." She stopped and leaned against a bent headless lamppost, a small smile hovering about her lips. "Sorry. Almost went off again, but it did feel good! I am going back to work, Claudia, thank you, you'll see." She hugged her protector, kissed her dark hair and giggled. "Yours could stand a wash as well."

"Come on, we're almost there. Eat some more, sleep some more. I'll take Fred's bicycle and go to the Chamber and ask if there's been any change. If I can find Fred's bicycle: he hides it to keep it from the Ivans. Watches, bikes, and women, in that order."

Gisela pressed the other's hand and promised to make it up to her soon.

When Gisela asked about Joachim, Claudia hesitated and did not answer for a long moment as they skirted a large group of chattering women passing chunks of gray rubble hand to hand to fill in a crater in the street. "I've heard he's found a better situation in the American sector, didn't he tell you? Fred has taken over his lines at the Schiffbauerdamm. Fred has become quite good for someone so young."

"I've been so out of everything, I don't remember. Maybe the Ami told me the other night."

"I'll stop by the cave after the Chamber and see if he left a message. Get something to eat. And stop scratching."

With Fred's agreement, Claudia untied the skeleton of a bicycle from its anchor in a closet and wheeled it outside. Gisela slowly chewed the bread and turnips and drank water in the spare kitchen, exchanging in passing a few words with two of the other actor inhabitants of the house as they left on errands. His eyes bright with a form of desire, Fred watched her carefully, smiling sympathetically, nodding his finely chiseled blonde head as if he knew what she had gone through and empathized. She smiled wanly back at him, her mind elsewhere. The itching gradually ceased being a major concern but the disinfectant powder continued to smell bad; she was too exhausted to wash her hair again and returned to Claudia's room where she fell asleep immediately. As she drifted away from consciousness, she prayed briefly to an amorphous deity for the strength to balance her life. Then the prayer, too, fell away and she slept.

* * * *

Now as she moved slowly down Unter den Eichen clutching the scrap of paper in her dress pocket, Gisela's body expressed its demand for the drug in sharp tines of pain. She had gone back to the cave to pick up her clothes after the night at the group house and saw that Buchdow had taken his few possessions away. Changing her clothes she found the piece of crumpled paper on which the Ami had written the address and telephone number. On the table stood a bottle of water and a brown paper packet tied with new string containing some bread and cheese, which she assumed had come from the American; where would Buchdow have gotten new string and cheese? She ate the food and drank the water in small portions very slowly chewing carefully so she could digest without regurgitation. Then she folded her clothes into an old suitcase; the water bottle she could fit into the old brown shoulder bag of ersatz leather. She would take the suitcase to the group house and then begin the trek to the American office in Zehlendorf. Someone would move into the empty cave before too long: regardless of condition no housing remained unoccupied for more than a few hours: too many homeless people shuffled through the city desperately searching for shelter of any sort. The itching continued to gnaw at her body, but she learned to repress the automatic impulse to scratch. Perhaps the streetcars would be running again.

    A few had in fact started their short schedules, battered, without windows, driven by women, in some cases hauled by thin horses which had somehow escaped being slaughtered and eaten, the torn flaps of old advertisements clinging along the sides under the empty window frames, like the one for safety glass: no miracle.

THORAX-SICHERHEITS-GLAS.

KEIN WUNDER....

But none ran along the larger, more active streets describing the shortest route to her destination. At least she did not have to take the smaller less populated roads, always the most dangerous during the daytime since by now all but the drunkest Red Army soldiers had stopped molesting women in the presence of the general public.

After a while she sat down to rest her leg muscles and allow the sweat on her face and back to dry. She had not undertaken such physical exertion in weeks. The pain of withdrawal continued but did not increase and the food she had consumed during the last thirty-six hours gave her more energy than she had felt in a long while. She would later tell her sometime mentor, the old historian Schadow, that she had actually felt rather good as she sat there in the sun, her dress dusty but drying, trying to make sense out of the events of the past several days. Except for the pains and the inability to finish the digestive process, her body was returning to near normal in terms of its functions. Even the constipation she viewed positively, thinking the longer the food remained with her the more energy she would receive from it. How long the pain would last, she had no way of knowing then, but for the moment she believed it would be bearable until it disappeared. She vowed that she would never again fall down in the street.

Dust and smoke from the wood and coal burning vehicles on the streets clogged her throat and she drank some of the water. City noises assailed her. If she closed her eyes the sounds reminded her of those before the war, but she could no longer move about with her eyes closed. A brief rush of adrenalin suddenly made her dizzy, a feeling not unlike the rushing cloud elevation of the drug. She smiled and for a moment anyone who knew her a year ago, looking at her now, would have recognized at least the bright blonde face. The rush soon subsided but the optimism remained in her mind. She told herself over and over: now is not the time for illusions. Nothing is solved, nothing resolved. With that thought she stood and began walking again. No, nothing had been solved. She knew no more than before, but for reasons she could not then explain, she felt better about the future. She would work, throw off the need for the drug, work and eat regularly. She would eventually ween herself away from any dependence on Joachim as well. After all, he had his own life, his own circle. If the Russians refused to give her a work permit, the Americans would, or the English; that Ami with the funny name had said so, or had he?

She could not remember that night clearly. They had argued about something, perhaps Joachim's working in the American Sector. The Ami (what was his strange name?) would not have left the address for her unless Buchdow had asked them to. Doubts pressed in upon the fragile construct of her optimism like rain eating away at dust piles in the street. Her past had ill-prepared her to deal with this kind of unstable situation, and the lack of such knowledge had resulted in her falling apart when they had gone into hiding as the Red Army surrounded and then fought its way into the city. Buchdow had done her a disservice in the longer term by using drugs to quieten her hysteria, but she was grateful that she and the others had gotten through without permanent physical damage, though she and countless other women suffered heightened anxiety about possible pregnancy and venereal disease after the rapes. She was at least alive and could go forward; she would not only survive, she would succeed in reconstituting her career in the theater and the cinema.

After all, she continually told herself now, she had gotten this far.

But she could not have done this by herself; she had rarely done anything by herself, but she knew when to smile an invitation and when to fake a gorgeous orgasm. The steps from school to brief acting classes to the stage and then the film studios she had taken without particular difficulty. She possessed a great talent, showed herself willing to learn and was extraordinarily attractive. And her father's acquaintanceships in the theater and film world smoothed a few sharp corners. While her mother's image had become distantly comfortable in her mind, her father had always surprised and amazed her as she grew up. A successful banker, he combined business acumen with an interest in culture and an appreciation of the arts to an extent unusual in his circle. When she mentioned this to him after her first success on the stage, he laughed and said he was carrying on a tradition from before the 20th century when bankers were not all philistines; then his face clouded and he softly murmured that many of them had been Jewish. The family name, Albrechtsburg, of the old Rheinland aristocracy she had shortened to Albrecht for professional reasons, much easier to remember.

When she was small Rilke had been an overnight guest in their house on his way to being a guest in someone else's house or villa, Harry Kessler's wit had graced their dinner table, Ernst Barlach had spooned soup in her mother's kitchen and made a drawing of her sitting at the piano. She retained a vague recollection of one of Rilke's young friends making a drawing of her as a child sitting on the poet's lap, but the young man refused to show the results of his labor, and she could no longer remember his name, though she thought it might have been Polish. She had, of course, rebelled against her father's culture in the process of intellectual and sexual maturing, but the severe control the party watchdogs exerted over public cultural life limited in equally severe measure the parameters of youthful rebellion, channeling with narrow vindictiveness the younger generation's uproarious energies into politically useful and acceptable vehicles. Rebellion remained a private activity and thus dulled and blunted in its extent and satisfactions. Her experiences with the party bureaucrats, theater managers, and official culture just before and during the war taught her the varied methods of obtaining the important contracts and acting assignments. As the war's progress shrank German life to a minimum she could measure her minor but constant successes against the general lack of success in the wider spectrum of national life. The winter of 1944-45 shattered all this and she had not known how to behave in the new and radically threatening situation. A rare strain of tuberculosis killed her mother early in the war; she had not seen her father for many months and did not know whether he was alive or dead. He left Berlin early in the year to conduct some unspecified business in Bavaria before the Russians surrounded the city. However, someone was always there to be of assistance for an appropriate reward.

  Her step faltered and she wobbled on the brushed satin high-heeled shoes saved months ago from a bombed apartment building whose inhabitants had disappeared. Slowing down, she looked about her in panic. It served as no consolation to her that almost everyone she knew suffered the same spasms of panic and moved about in similar states of ignorance and fear. Joachim, who rarely spoke of his family, had occasionally mentioned the feeling of helplessness and desolation that washed over him when he thought of his parents and brother. When last heard from they still lived in the family home outside Hamburg, but he had not seen them for years and had no news of them since Christmas 1944. Everyone had a similar tale to tell, but few mentioned the situation voluntarily. The women did not discuss the rapes, even among themselves, even as they feared a recurrence every day and night. She pushed that thought away and concentrated on her mental script for the interview and her concern about its success. She touched her hair and wished she had saved some makeup, at least a tube of lipstick. Claudia had explained, "When you go to the Amis use it sparingly, they like things minimal with us. The Ivans don't care because they've had us in every way already. The Brits don't like any at all and the French like to see it on us applied poorly, it makes them feel more like victors." All well and good if one had the stuff, which she didn't, but the opinion could be correct; she would find out soon enough.

Questions swooped into her mind like bats frightened by a bright light: what if the Americans followed the Russians in denying her a work permit? Would the English be any different? Would they coordinate their practices? Where was Joachim? Would she have to return dejected to Claudia's house and ask to stay longer? Would anyone let her work? When would the withdrawal pains stop? What could she do except act? She could join the *Trümmerfrauen* who shouldered the city's rubble from one place to another in return for a ration card. She could join the queues of frightened women who sold themselves to the soldiers for a few cigarettes with which to barter for food. She could find an officer to live with, and be passed on to his successor when he left the city, a ragtag piece of material, made in Germany. She had no skills other than those of an actress; she had to use those skills, no matter at what. Did such things atrophy with lack of practice? Certainly her life in the past few months did not involve acting, unless it was to convince Joachim of her need for the drug, and recently she had little success there, for which she could now be grateful. The painful, unanswerable questions seemed unending. Drawing in a spasm of breath, she wanted nothing more than to scream or weep in frustration, and she stopped so suddenly the old woman leading a small thin child behind her bumped into her shoulder.

"*Entschuldigen Sie, bitte,*" she said automatically.

"*Ja, ja, es macht nichts.*" The woman smiled absently, her thoughts elsewhere, and moved on down the street past the blackened shell of a tank in which some children played with whoops of enjoyment. Torn posters advertising dancing classes and a few new theater programs covered the sides of the tank.

No, she thought, if there was to be a resolution to these questions, she would have to answer them herself. The pain in her body seemed to spur forward some barely conscious process of decision. She *would* change the situation. She would see the Americans and find Joachim; she would work and obtain a ration card; the interrupted chain of achievement would be stitched together again. And she would start now. She had no other acceptable choice.

When Makepeace many years later wrote the novel, *The Violent City*, about a character very much like Gisela Albrecht, he had her move from this point directly to the office he shared with Schade for the confrontation. It did not happen that way, of course, nor was she motivated by any political consideration, as Makepeace described. Her motivation was the ambition to go beyond survival and succeed regardless of the altered life around her, to once again feel the warm rush flow through her body as the curtain fell on a fine performance. And she did not go directly to their office because as she reached the neighborhood of the Milinowskistrasse, panic and confusion again wrapped themselves tightly around her intestines; their intensity almost pushed her over the edge of consciousness. In her fright she remembered that the piece of paper Schade had given her contained a number. After breathing deeply against the fear and pain she set off with desperate deliberation to find a telephone that worked.

After they had become lovers, Schade asked her why she had telephoned instead of walking the relatively short distance still separating her from the office. "I don't remember. I'm not sure I even knew then. It was a way of putting off the meeting. I wasn't sure what we had talked about when you came to that cave. I only knew that I had to see you or someone there, but it came out indirectly. For some reason it was easier for me that way."

"What would you have done if you hadn't had the number?"

"I don't know. Eventually I would have come to you, I suppose. My choices were so limited. I spent a long time finding a telephone that worked."

* * * *

Makepeace wrapped his hand around the mouthpiece of the antediluvian black bakelite and grinned not unpleasantly, but with some sarcasm. "I do believe it is your teutonic goddess, John, *mein Lieber*. She doesn't quite remember your name. You must have made a terrific impression on her."

"This is Lieutenant Schade," he said in English.

She spoke German and identified herself, "...you remember?"

"Yes, I remember," he replied in German. The flash of annoyance that sped through his mind was not caused by the fact that she called, but because his hand suddenly trembled slightly and his throat dried. "Are you coming here? Where are you?"

"I'm a few blocks away, but I don't feel well ... weak, you know. I am sorry. Where is Joachim?"

"I have his address, he's living in Kreuzberg. We want to talk to you."

"Yes, I know, fine, but I want to see Joachim, his things are gone. Thank you for the bread and cheese, it was good and the water." Her sentences came swiftly and ran together. He heard her make an effort to calm down and speak with more deliberation. "I would very much like to see Joachim. Then we can talk. Can that not be arranged?"

"All right. Where are you? Can you come here?"

The static in the telephone system cut across her reply and the line went dead. He sat for a moment stupidly staring at the instrument in his hand. "Wake up, John, there's work to be done, cows to be milked, fields to be ploughed, no pun intended, und so weiter."

"Ur?"

"Is she coming or not? You don't have to be so gentlemanly, lieutenant, order her to show up. Never mind now. We've got a meeting at the Titania Palast scheduled with the Special Service imbeciles. EB wants this problem worked out immediately, not ASAP, remember?" Makepeace said this not harshly, but with a certain impatience. He admitted later to Schade that he had at first believed the non-fraternization directive was essentially correct and necessary, an opinion he changed abruptly somewhat later. That original opinion and the constant friction with the Special Service officers, who wanted the theaters and music halls for troop entertainment, which they believed had a greater priority than allowing the Germans to use the facilities, made Makepeace impatient.

Schade shook himself mentally. "Right, yes. *Jawohl, Herr Leutnant Mekpiz, zu Befehl!* The line went cockeyed and cut out. SOP. I assume she'll be here, said she was nearby. Or call back. Where'd she find a telephone? When is the meeting? We can get someone to tell her to wait here until we get back. Hmm?"

"Why don't you just leave Buchdow's address for her and have her come back tomorrow? That would be the reasonable thing to do, don't you think?" Makepeace intoned this in an eminently neutral voice that was another way of indicating his dissatisfaction with the course of events.

"She reminds me of Schiele's nudes, an intriguing combination of sex and starvation."

"Who is Schiele?" Makepeace asked, actually wanting to know.

"An obscure Austrian artist, dead and generally unknown, who painted his sexual fantasies on canvas in lurid images."

"So how do you know him?"

"I've got a friend in Vienna. Or I had one, don't know if he survived. Probably not -- he's Jewish, or was."

* * * *

Claudia Kaufmann rode the bicycle west to the Chamber of Creative Artists offices in the Schlüterstrasse to ask about the Albrecht case. As a fairly well-known theater personality with pronounced anti-fascist sympathies (she had not appeared on the stage during the last years of the nazi regime because of a verbal blacklisting by officials in the Propaganda Ministry, earning a minimal income teaching a children's acting class and posing for several banned painters who sold their work privately), she was able to see an assistant to the president without much delay. He had no information on the case beyond the fact that the Chamber's own investigation had finally cleared Albrecht to work in the city but Soviet officials had not yet given their approval. Without this, the Chamber would not issue the certificate and the ration card. There was nothing to be done for the moment. The assistant, who knew very little about any part of the denazification process and nothing about specific cases, allowed as how, perhaps, the situation would change now that the British and the Americans had begun organizing their own clearance systems. Fräulein Albrecht might discuss the matter with them. As far as the Chamber was concerned, she could work any time, but the Chamber could only do so much without the approval of the occupation authorities. Terribly sorry, Fräulein Kaufmann, but you do understand our position. *Und so weiter*.

On the other hand, the assistant grinned openly, if we had some decent coffee around here matters would surely move much faster. One spends so much time running around for such basic stuff there's so little left over for business. Claudia smiled and allowed that she could certainly understand, the same situation could be found all over the city. Such a shame. She leaned forward toward the assistant's file-strewn desk. Yes, all over the city. The coal vendors require cigarettes as well as ration cards, the hairdressers need more than the price of a shampoo, don't they, a cup of sugar, a half pound of coffee, six American cigarettes. *Und so weiter*.

Riding the bicycle through the streets crowded with increasing numbers of returning soldiers, liberated camp inmates, and displaced persons, she felt her energy begin to fragment and her mind began to form a crystal of resentment against her own offer to help. She should have been studying the playscript or using her time to search for food. She decided not to visit the cave where Gisela had lived with Buchdow. Wherever he was he would either contact her or not, and she could find him tomorrow or the next day or next week. Everyone in the theater eventually knew where everyone else lived and worked. The group in the house would find space for Gisela, but the rest she would have to do on her own. There was a limit to what one could do these days, even for a colleague.

* * * *

Buchdow no longer itched, but still suffered the knife of hunger in his belly. Going over stage directions with two colleagues in the small theater near the Hallesches Tor in Kreuzberg, he believed he had again gained some control over his future and this belief gave him both satisfaction and the desire to move with determination and speed in mounting his first production, a safe, pre-Hitler comedy which had been a success in the early Weimar period. He would have preferred something new, a piece that built on the past rather than reprising it, but no one had as yet written such a play, and the Americans might not approve it even if he had one in hand. He felt this compromise deeply but had no answer to the problem. Civilian communications remained uncertain so he lacked knowledge of what his colleagues were up to in other cities; indeed, for a complex of reasons he felt terribly alone. He needed a partner, not only for the physical comforts and excitement, but to think with about all these matters so crucial to his future: unfortunately partners generally came in two qualities: physical and intellectual, rarely did he find these qualities in the same person. He should attend more of the soirées at Count Nishtikontov's apartment on the Kurfürstendamm at the corner of Uhlandstraße. Everybody, including western allied control officers, CIC agents, and occasional slim French-speaking Russian officers whose desire for the bright colors of youth and a different culture outweighed their fear of their morality police, showed up at one time or another. But the bulk of those who attended the Count's parties consisted of homosexual theater and music people grateful for an elegant locale in which to freely gather after the brown years of oppression, and certain criminals from the demi-monde of the city. On the other hand, perhaps Fortuna would smile upon him one night at the bar Bei Barth.

One person, with whom circumstances now required him to meet more often than he liked, he had not yet been able to make sense of: the massively cynical and coldly distant Felix Harrigan, the American theater control officer, whose authority over theater business in the American Sector, while not absolute, lay like a heavy hand suspended over the scene, ready to drop at a moment's notice. The man, whose brown horn-rimmed spectacles fought for dominance of his face against the blue cold glitter of his restless eyes, was simply unknowable: at one moment Buchdow believed the American looked at him, his eyes choking with desire, and seconds later the look metamorphosed to one of indifferent, bland contempt. He seemed to believe in nothing, neither the goals of the victors' mission in the city nor his own future; his main concern, as he bluntly expressed it himself, was "to cultivate the talent for keeping boredom at a sufficient distance not to require my suicide." Kronauer remarked at one point after having met the American several times that he was reminded of one of the maxims of Marcus Aurelius:

"'One philosopher goes shirtless; another bootless; a third, only half-dressed, says 'I have not a breadcrumb, yet I cleave to reason.' Which only proves the hollowness of rational man when his entire life is led in his brain. And in Marcus Aurelius' time, grown men did not chew gum." Buchdow did not believe for a moment that Harrigan lived only in his brain: he had seen however briefly the cynic's eyes engorged with longing. Exactly what Harrigan longed for, he did not know, but perhaps he should find out. Something organic and wild lay beneath the icy condescending demeanor, perhaps it would be worthwhile to penetrate the facade, it certainly would be a challenge. If only one could get enough to eat. His dreams recently had been stuffed with sauerbraten cooking in its own juices surrounded by peppercorns, bay leaves, onions, carrots and celery, served next to a mountain of white mashed potatoes sprinkled with chopped chives awash in pure yellow butter, closely nestled by a pile of brussels sprouts drizzled with fresh ground pepper, accompanied by an endless supply of fresh Bauernbrot and liters of sparkling Lübeck pilsner in tall sweating glasses....

  But that challenge would have to await the appropriate circumstance, after the success of this stupid piece of fluff, when his self-confidence had attained a higher level and he could move with more assurance through the city's web of sexual and political relationships. After a number of conversations with Makepeace and Harrigan, Buchdow no longer worried unduly about his final clearance. Even if the information control committee of the Kommandantura issued a set of guidelines for the entire city, he would be able to continue. Let the Allies worry about the bigger fish like Gründgens and Heinrich George; let Buchdow get on with his career and this goddamned play which at present caused him so much trouble with its requirements for a large cast and lavish sets. Neither of these could be duplicated under the present circumstances and had to be improvised out of the meager personnel and material available to him. The casting problems might be solved on schedule if the Americans continued to clear actors and musicians at a reasonable rate, for example that fellow Fred who took over his role when Buchdow moved to the American Sector. Getting him to move there should not be too difficult: the young man was a natural climber ready to take advantage of anything and anyone who could possibly be of help to him. And he had talent, and those blonde good looks.

However the scenic material simply was not to be had. Perhaps he could convince the Americans to borrow some materials for the sets from the Admiralspalast in the Soviet Sector. Makepeace was a devious fellow, even more so than Harrigan or the émigré, as Buchdow thought of Schade. And Makepeace had at least appeared to promise that the necessary material would be made available for set construction at some point. This ostensible promise helped Buchdow not at all now as he sat in the small room below the stage with his production assistants discussing how they could re-use pieces from one set for another without disturbing the flow of the performance.

"Joachim?"

He looked up to see her standing in the doorway holding her shoulder bag in front of her as if to protect her against what he knew would be painful for both of them. Her face reflected the confusion and hesitancy, which had dominated her since they had gone into hiding. Later, he told himself that he had detected a new resolution in her eyes, but that could easily have been in retrospect, after they had accustomed themselves to their new relationship, after they both realized each of them possessed the depths of ambition that would lead them to pursue their lives with a ruthlessness neither suspected in themselves or the other.

He pronounced her name with as much joy and spontaneity as he could squeeze past his guilt and annoyance at being interrupted. They embraced quickly and stood back hesitating for a moment until he dismissed his co-workers for a few minutes. They left the room wrapped in their annoyance like capes they had flung over their shoulders. "You're looking much better, *Schätzchen*, much better."

"Why didn't you come back? You left me helpless." She embraced him again, holding him tightly, a feeling of loss and anger burning her emotions. He tried unsuccessfully to restrain his body from registering the conflicting emotions which raced about his mind; the sudden rigidity, however, he could not control and he knew she felt it.

"Sit down for a moment. I haven't much time right now, but we must talk. I have a lot to tell you. Things are going to be fine. Sit down, please."

Things were not fine that afternoon during the half-hour she spent in the theater with Buchdow. As he talked she make an effort to maintain a reserve, a distance between what she felt and what her told her. Her physical weakness had worn down her ability to resist the splashing tears and hurt rage that demanded some form of release. But even her weakness did not disable her enough to stop her from tearing into an angry denunciation of Buchdow and men in general when he mentioned as kindly as he knew how that she would have to transfer her dependence on him to another figure or to herself, that he would no longer be able to play that role in her life because he had a new life to create for himself, as they all did, as she did.... The end of the war changed everything; the defeat made everything twice as difficult. They must all reinvent themselves as best they could. The theater basement smelled of decay, cheap tobacco, and thirty years of actor sweat. On other occasions this smell exhilarated her, but now each breath brought a choking sense of nausea. Her rage centered on Buchdow, driven by her knowledge that she had been too dependent upon him, as she had been on her father and his contacts in the world of artists when she began her career, and the manipulation of sex she had endured and committed during the reign of party officials in the film industry. Realizing that Buchdow would truly no longer share the burden of her life fed her panic, intensifying the brutality of her frustration. The fact that he had truthfully described her situation did not meliorate the unendurable drumming of insecurity that pounded through her chest, and she lashed out at him with accusations of manipulation and advantage-taking until she exhausted the reservoir of lamentation. Finally, she ceased weeping and combed her long blonde hair. She had already decided never again to allow herself to become so vulnerable, so dependent upon anyone, no more dependence, no more love which meant leaving herself open to pain. That this would prove impossible, she of course did not consider then and the determination, once made and reinforced in that hot odorous dressing room, allowed a partial return of the faint optimism she had felt earlier in the day.

"I won't bother you about our relationship anymore, Joachim. But I am going to need some further help from you. I want to start work again. The size of the role doesn't matter at the moment. I have to bring myself back under control, and that includes getting out of the drug habit. I think I can do this if I don't have to worry about where my next meal is coming from, you understand. I am not about to sell myself for a few cigarettes. I have not talents to be a secretary. I will not become a *Trümmerfrau*. I want to take up my career and get on with my life. Not so unusual, is it, rather a cliché in fact, no? Let me finish. Under the circumstances this is not going to be easy. I need help. What you can do is let me join your theater group and let me act. I don't know for how long, but it won't be forever. You won't have me around your neck either. I need the ration card, I need to eat regularly. You owe me that much."

He agreed, of course. Her talent, which he never doubted, would take her far and it would benefit his own career. That part would not be difficult, but the American vetting process might be problematical. When he mentioned this to her, she said she would find out about it later that afternoon. She would talk to the Americans. "And you won't have to be my lover anymore," she added with a small twisted smile. Comprehending the new element of determination in her mind, Buchdow felt an immense burden disperse in the smelly room. He drew in a deep breath of the wonderful stink and quickly gave her his new address. As he walked her up the stairs to the empty theater orchestra his mind had already returned to the interrupted considerations of sets and cast. His two co-workers swished past them huffing with sarcasm as they descended beneath the stage. "They're amusing," Buchdow told her. "But more importantly, they are very good at what they do and when you come to work they will fawn all over you. Beauty and talent they appreciate."

As she walked out of the building into the fading sunlight and the mounds of rubble piled like monuments to a ruined civilization, she swore in the basest terms she knew both at herself and the world that permitted her to be so degraded and hurt. She turned south from the Hallesches Tor into the Mehring Damm and almost wept at the thought of the long trek back to the office in the Milinowskistrasse. Then, from his open jeep, she heard Schade say, "Fräulein Albrecht?"

She climbed awkwardly into the passenger seat. The sun and exertion forced sweat pearls out of her skin on her back and armpits. She tried to force a smile of gratitude on to her lips without success. Her facial expression expressed bafflement and fleeting touches of resentment. This would not end well, she thought, holding her purse in one hand and the windshield frame with the other. Her hands were slippery with the sweat of exhaustion. Her mind raced and for some minutes she could not speak. She did not remember his name, but with a soldier this did not matter: he had a rank. *"Danke, Herr Hauptmann,"* she said with, finally, a hint of a smile.

"*Leutnant John Schade zu Befehl, gnädiges Fräulein,*" Schade said with a grin. "Where does the lady wish to go?"

Her head weighed heavily on her neck. With an effort she turned and looked into his eyes. She could not believe he could find her attractive in her condition. Her eyes watered diffusing the bright red broken capillaries. Rebelling against the lack of substance in it her belly gurgled and she blushed, but he did not seem to have heard this common complaint. "I think you know my destination, Lieutenant."

Of course he knew. What he was unsure of was his behavior vis à vis this human wreck. Something in her character promised a change, something he could not yet define hinted at reserves of will power beneath the defeated façade, the weakened body and clouded mind. In fact, her mind seemed perfectly clear: he thought with a fleeting touch of pride that she had not taken the drug since their encounter in the cave. He believed he could see or intuit an energetic beauty beneath the exhaustion and flaccid appearance. She had been a beautiful young woman he knew from the publicity photographs: the shimmering long blonde hair brushing her shoulders, the sparkle in the eyes and bright smile – posed to be sure but she would look like this away from the studio lights and photographer's brush. And he was now convinced she would again. His reluctant pity flowed into an attraction he did not want to resist, and began to form that pool of fluid emotions from which would slowly bubble a desire to possess and be possessed, to experience a return to her former physical beauty and mental activity she had attained before the war destroyed her equipoise and before that swine Buchdow fed her the drugs to control her disintegration and fervid panic. In short, though he could not yet admit this to himself, he wanted to simultaneously heal and make love to her. He did not allow the thought that these desires might be contradictory. She invaded his mind and tightened his scrotum. As he cautiously explained to Schadow much later, "I became obsessed with the notion of being both her lover and physician. Not a very prescient start for a relationship, I know."

"Not a very stable foundation, no. Albert Schweizer and Hans Albers in one person is rather unbelievable. But what do I know about such things, *nicht wahr?*" Schadow murmured.

Wenn mein Schatz sich so fröhlich benimmt,
dann regnet's den ganzen Tag lang, oh ja, oh ja[11]

* * * *

---

[11]When my sweetheart behaves so happily / then it rains all day long, O yes, O yes.

The man in the uniform raincoat and garrison hat expected no more than a wet walk around the island before his interview with the refugees from Poland, and he did not expect much from that either. What he discovered here, however, would in time alter the course of his future and his relationship with the city and its denizens.

Rain pummeled the tall grass and the dusty leaves of the island's linden trees, pressing the sparse but overgrown vegetation to the earth with the special intensity nature reserves for unexpected summer cloudbursts, beating down the underbrush and snapping off weak branches.

This small platter of earth in the waters of the Kladower Seestrecke stretch of the Havel River in far southwestern Berlin called the Pfaueninsel, the island now bereft of peacocks, bore its name with proud indifference, having witnessed an astonishing variety of human foibles committed to and on the "island." During the medieval period the island was known as Große Werder and somewhat later as Pfau Werder, the name stemming not from the name of the bird (peacocks were first introduced to the island in 1797) but from the middle German designation "page/pau" for horse. Since then the lords of the land had used and abused the space in various ways: toward the end of the 17th century a chemical laboratory was established to create new substances and develop industry in the region, an embarrassing failure for the chemist and his patron; at the end of the 18th century during the age of revolutions, Friedrich Wilhelm II had a series of buildings constructed including a hunting lodge and a small castle in the form of a ruined Roman country estate for his mistress, the Countess Lichtenau, but he died before the structure could be completed and the Countess never got her pleasure garden; a dairy farm, an exotic animal park later turned into a research zoo, and several royal buildings eventually open to the public were constructed during the 19th century. Early in that century, the architect Johann Gottfried Schadow designed a brick-glass building to house palm and other exotic trees; several decades later the building burned down. ("No, no! We're not related at all!" as the old historian found it necessary to explain throughout his long life.)

Now on this late summer afternoon the temperature required the flimsiest of clothing to be worn by flâneurs on the crisscrossing paths that allowed visitors to traverse the hints of hillocks and dales, which dotted the island's dusty verdant surface. The city's citizens had not yet cut down all the trees in preparation for the winter's bone marrow-freezing cold. Somewhere in the green-yellow landscape a small bird, which had somehow escaped the ravenous hunger of the city's hunters, sang its thin sweet tune in the damp field.

The darkhaired woman strode slowly in the unexpected but refreshing rainfall making no attempt to keep any part of herself dry; her thin blue summer dress absorbed the rainwater as rapaciously as the sandy earth beneath her feet. Indeed, so deeply was she involved in her own thoughts that she seemed not to have even noticed that the sun shower had suddenly begun with its dense blue-gray curtain of sparkling water falling from the bright cloudless sky. Her hair color plunged so deeply into its darkness as to turn black against her pale face and slender neck, its pile of wild, pinned length now flattened to her head by the driving force of the rain. She moved like a panther in the rain, her dress so wetly pressed to her body's curves and crevices as to provide no cover of modesty, which she neither required nor desired. She had seen no other person on this part of the island so the fact that the soaked dress sticking to her body made her appear more naked than nude did not concern her. The amount of suffering which she may have born did not appear on her face or in her stance as she moved at a slow stride through the tall grasses ignoring their wrapping themselves around her legs. She did not hear the strange calling of birds to one another in the rain.

Reaching the top of a small rise, she stopped and tilted her head far back on her neck, allowing the clear sweet rain to dissolve the salt of tears on her face. The gentle curtain of the rain fell slowly now to the parched earth so dry that no puddles formed as the land swiftly absorbed the water into its arid depths. The grass and the leaves on the remaining trees, cleansed of the city's dust, reluctantly dribbled the raindrops to the voracious earth. The woman's body shook with a series of spasms that almost felled her as a muffled cry fled her lips pressed together to suppress it. Head bent back to the rain her hands clasped her breasts in a violent gesture and her fingers squeezed her nipples until the pain stopped the spasms and her body slowly relaxed, her head falling forward to stare at the ground. One burst of distant thunder rumbled through the air. Her hands slowly, unconsciously, traced the contours of her body through the cloth of her wet dress and briefly pressed the meager flesh of her belly, as her arms dropped to her sides and she stood in the rain legs apart, arms akimbo as if rooted in the earth. The next roll of thunder gurgled from a greater distance as she lowered her head and wiped the rain and tears from her face to look out over the expanse of the Havel River. One lonely sob broke through her pressed lips followed by the hiss of a sudden intake of breath and a last shudder before she determinedly turned on her heel and began to move in her long strides back the way she had come through the chilled rain, back into the city.

    She gave no indication that she had seen the uniformed young man standing under a tree some meters away, who had watched her with a look of glorious fascination on his face. Witnessing but not understanding motives or causes, Makepeace felt a violent dislodgement of his being. Terribly moved by the scene, he would carry this image of the woman clutching her breasts in a posture of paralyzed sexual abandon as an erotic talisman with him for the rest of his life: in moments of stress when he needed a distraction from the discomfort of mental pressure he would reach into the cavity of his memory and draw forth the picture of the woman in the rain on the island like an exotic fetish stashed away in a drawer to be taken out only on ritual occasions. Even after he learned the true nature of the act he witnessed with such strong emotion, he continued to achieve satisfaction by using the frozen image on the surface of his mind as a device to distract himself from unpleasantness.

I saw you there one wonderful day...

* * * *

Felix Harrigan came to Berlin from a position in the army's entertainment branch called Special Services. Before being drafted he had been a producer in the Boston theater world, an experience which left him with a resentment, mildly felt but clearly defined, of being just a mite provincial when in New York or London: there no one's eyes lit up with recognition when he mentioned the theaters in which he had mounted productions. This syndrome only reinforced his already pronounced tendency toward cynicism as a response to that world's indifference. He had come to believe that very little in his life and environment possessed any lasting value, and while he carried out his duties efficiently enough he could not bring himself to find any real meaning in the results of his work. This made him difficult to work with if his colleagues and German clientele sought forms of sympathetic understanding and friendship. He responded best to a straightforward clear proposal based on a distant but professional presentation. The cynicism and a demeanor bordering on the haughty protected him from most of the unwanted intrusions which others thrust upon him, but did not slow the roller-coaster motions of his ambiguous sexuality. As his last male lover in Boston put it, the night before he left for basic training camp: "You don't have to jump off the fence on one side or the other permanently, you know. You may have to come to terms with both sides, even if you favor one over the other." In this well-meant advice he found no comfort or surcease, and the brief flashes of hunger for another person, which Buchdow had seen but did not understand, expressed as much his desire for love as his confusion as to where to look for it.

    Despite the pressure of some of his friends' readings of Freud's theories about human development, he could not find the cause of his distress in his mother, or his father for that matter, though he left sufficient mental space should he have to fill it with either of these ideas. His Boston Irish father operated a successful music store in the city and had disciplined the young Harrigan when necessary but on the whole had attempted to give him emotional and intellectual support whenever he thought he should. Harrigan's mother was a secular Jew whose family had been in New England as long as his father's and whose arrangement with the elder Harrigan resulted in Felix growing up with no religious affiliation at all. At the age of bar mitzvah and confirmation, his mother took him to a synagogue on a Monday so he would know what one looked like. His father took him to a Roman Catholic church the next day for the same reason. Neither parent ever wavered from their agreement, made when his mother became pregnant, but his father felt the tickle of doubt in the back of his mind from time to time. "You can decide when you're grown up," his mother told him. That was perhaps acceptable in America, but he also came to know that his choice of a religion, or the lack of one, would have made no difference in Germany: one of his parents was a Jew, ergo he was a Jew. And, ironically, only in Berlin did he begin to feel a nascent curiosity about what it meant to be a Jew. But this he kept to himself; his name protected him from any suspicion that he was not completely as Makepeace jokingly called him: "That wild young mick."

He made an exception with Schade one evening when they stood at the counter in The Edge Bar drinking whisky and listening to Barry Green noodle his way through a twenty-minute improvisation on the theme of *Stella by Starlight*. They had been talking about problems in making the Anglo-American documentary film about the atrocities in the concentration camps without mentioning the Jews as the main victim of the mad genocidal behavior of the nazis and their collaborators. "It's all of a piece, my friend. Think about the reason we've sent so few Jews to Berlin with the military government. Our so intelligent leaders and planners are afraid the Germans will resent having their biological inferiors telling them what to do. Hell, if they knew I'm half Jewish I'd have been stationed in Italy until my tour is up. Fortunately - or not - I always put down 'none' in the space for religion. Which is true enough. Of course, here I'm a Mischling and for the orthodox I'm a complete Jew since for them being a Jew is a matter of maternity. Until the last few months I've never even felt like a Jew. But I never felt particularly Irish either. Perhaps I'll take up the cabala and study *Ulysses*."

He chewed spearmint gum with a consistency worthy of a passion, let his wavy black hair grow longer than regulations allowed whenever he could and dropped sarcasms from thin lips whenever the chance arose, appropriate or not. While this did not endear him to his colleagues, Makepeace, who shared this proclivity, and Schade, who admired it, appreciated the cutting edge of Harrigan's sour wit. He surprised everyone, perhaps even himself, when he later signed up for an additional tour in the army on the condition that he remain in the city.

* * * *

Ulrich Kramer, the former theater critic, like everyone else in the city attempting to return to his profession or find a new one compatible with their interests and talents, stood outside the Deutsche Theater on Schumannstrasse in the late afternoon with Schade and Makepeace. Hand lettered posters on the theater facade announced the performance of Schiller's *Der Parasit*. A slight breeze ruffled Kramer's thinning hair and Makepeace touched the crown of his own head to check the progress of a similar biological process. "The theater scene in this burg is amazing. They've got little or nothing, it rains on the stages through the holes in the roofs, but anywhere there's room they're doing theater. Amazing." Makepeace sounded truly astounded.

"They haven't got much else, have they?" Schade said.

Kramer's stomach gurgled softly in agreement, expressing its desire to be filled. "A poet can write a poem, a painter can paint a picture if he can find oils and a canvas or a piece of paper, but there's no way these things can be communicated, the delivery system has not been repaired. Most Berliners cannot get out of their own districts. There are no printing facilities for civilians, very few galleries, no mail system for invitations to be sent. But there is the theater, all over the city there's theater. You've taken our radios and there's nothing on Radio Berlin except Allied news anyway. But there's theater ... even if it's just a reading or a shabby review with the old songs. It may rain on us, the chairs are as hard as stone, this winter we'll freeze in the halls, but every new performance is an act of liberation. Don't you see, everything that was forbidden for twelve years is now available, assuming the Allies approve, of course. There's a great need to catch up, an unquenchable thirst for the old which was banned for so long, and perhaps for the new."

Schade interrupted quietly: "There's nothing new yet, there's been no time."

"It will come. The new for us is perhaps the old for you because we've not seen anything freely since 1933. All of that which you take for granted, we've not had in twelve years. Think of all the plays, films, books, ideas the nazis banned! My god! It will take us years to catch up. The one aspect of that we can deal with now is the theater. We have no newspapers of our own, books take too long to publish, making films is too expensive, but the theater: we'll go to any lengths to do it, to perform it, to see and hear it ... I tell you, as long as ration cards exist, as long as these terrible limitations on our daily lives continue, as long as what we don't have dominates us, as long as others rule us, no matter how benignly, the theater will flourish in this city as a kind of substitute freedom, a surrogate for the past. You can bet on that. We'll take coal bricks with us to heat the theater in the winter...." Kramer stopped talking, his breath panting slightly from emotion and the effort.

"The great escape," Schade said pensively. "Wrap up all the cares and woes, *panum et circensus*, eat cake, and give them something to patch up the gaping holes in their spiritual lives. Is that what the theater should do here and now?"

"We must take the longer view that this is a beginning, the start of a process whose course we cannot exactly predict, but whose end we should know and plan for. The Germans must be given back a spiritual life, secular or religious, or both, because they no longer have one. They gave it up years ago."

"That's a hell of a burden to expect the theater to carry. And the Germans are going to have to create their own spiritual life; who's going to give it to them?"

"The theater is only the beginning, as I've tried to explain--"

"Tell Lieutenant Schade about the risks of going to the theater, Herr Kramer," Makepeace interjected with a grin.

Kramer's laugh sounded like a small dog barking. "Ach, ja ... that hasn't happened since then, I am happy to say, but to others ... it goes on all the time, I'm afraid, so many displaced persons, people hungry ... I think of the experience as exemplary of what we've been talking about. I was on my way home to Nollendorfplatz from the premier of *Der Parasit* in this theater - not an easy trip to make if you have to cross two canals with bombed out bridges. The smoke from the fires still lay over the city. I passed by Red Army troops camped in the Tiergarten: an unquieting experience, I assure you. They looked at me very skeptically. What shortly before had been a routine ride on the number one bus had become a great adventure. It was the sixth of June....

"In any case, I was on my way home in the twilight to be there before curfew, just on the Grosse Stern, when a band of thieves blocked my path and stole the last few Reichsmarks I owned. They tried to take my relatively new wedding band, unsuccessfully I am happy to say, but they beat me into unconsciousness. When I came to my senses it was already dark, after curfew. I remained in the Tiergarten, full of fright, hiding in the bushes, not daring to sleep. When I arrived home the next morning my family had given me up for dead. People disappear so easily." The critic barked again. "It's ironic, Lieutenant, no? I mean coming from a Schiller play and walking into a situation described in his ballad."

Schade could not decide on the appropriateness of a smile or a simple nod of the head. Makepeace had no such qualms and laughed. "*Die Räuber*," he said. "Interesting isn't it that on just that day the Russians arrested the theater's director who was in the middle of rehearsals for *Die Räuber*, coincidently enough."

"Yes, we've not been able to find out why they did that. Gründgens was no better or worse that many others in the theater; he sold his soul to the nazis, but he broke no laws. Not so coincidently, that play was the last one put on at the Staatliche Schauspielhaus on the Gendarmenmarkt before the theaters closed. Gründgens has a sense of continuity."

"Then we won't give him a license," Schade said with a firmness he did not quite feel. "He can't work in the Schauspielhaus, in the Soviet sector, because it was destroyed in the bombing last winter."

"Perhaps he will recognize the necessity for disjuncture. When he is released, if he is released. But going to the theater in those days just after the end of the fighting was quite an adventure. It remains so, of course, but somewhat different now. You see, one is already nostalgic about the first days of the occupation. A human foible which makes the present easier to live with, I think."

"Like the theater," Schade murmured. He looked at his watch and offered the critic a cigarette. Makepeace was painfully withdrawing from his dependency on tobacco, a process which occurred at regular intervals. "You know, of course, what this is worth on the black market," Kramer said meditatively, holding up the cigarette. "Ten Reichsmarks. The thieves got three from me on that night, marks that is. Not that there's much to buy, unless you know the right people."

"Hell," Makepeace broke in, "you know what a $1.00 carton of Luckies is worth in this town? Between 1200 and 1500 Reichsmarks. That, my friends, is $120 to $150 when cashed in at the Army post office. But they're occupation marks."

"You know what a semi-skilled German worker takes home in a week?" Kramer asked with some bitterness. "Eighty Reichsmarks."

"*Touché.*"

Schade looked at his Chesterfield with mild disgust. "They'll have to do something about it before too long."

"They will, they will," Makepeace retorted.

"Thus speaks the Voice of Knowledge."

"It can't go on; they'll stop it." The others smoked in silence; Makepeace listened to the sounds around them: fragments of conversations ("Look, captain, I was just helping the old lady with her bags across the street." "You're up for fraternizing, sergeant, that'll be half a month's pay in fines."), the occasional motor vehicle, the humming noises of bicycle tires on damp pavements, the tubercular coughing of the citizenry, the shuffling movement of refugees constantly heading east or west in their millions. The sun dried all but the largest puddles and the water-filled craters that had not been filled in. The cigarette smoke hung lazily in the warm air around their heads replacing the rubble dust the rain had temporarily soaked into the ground. "Why do you think the Russians pushed so hard to open the theaters and get the nightlife started, Herr Kramer?"

The critic immediately became cautious, his eyes narrowing, his face taking on the pinched look of the suspect under interrogation. "It is hardly up to me to question the politics of the victors, lieutenant."

"I understand. But surely you have an opinion. Expressing your opinion is hardly questioning Allied policy. At least not here, with us."

"I am not entirely sure of that. It could be construed as such."

"Part of democracy is expressing your opinion," Schade said with a firm smile this time, and added, "Don't worry, we won't turn you in."

"*Danke, Herr Leutnant.*" Kramer bent his body slightly at the waist in an ironic bow. "Well, I think there are probably many reasons. First, it could have been a politically calculated maneuver to distract the public from the horrendous conditions in the city, to direct their energies toward a politically harmless form of participation in some public activity and take their minds off their hunger and despair. Something like that. On the other hand, the Russians are a very culture-oriented people on the whole. They're driven by an almost idealistic, missionary concept of art. Thus perhaps they view the theater and art as a method of reconstructing the German mind, even the

German soul. The Russians are very soulful, you know, they tend toward mysticism, especially when drunk."

"They're very shifty, too," Makepeace interjected, slowly rolling his left wrist back and forth.

"In any case, they may think this is a way to purge the decadent soul of Germany, to enlighten us, to recreate the German mentality. Who knows? Perhaps this is all to prepare us for the political domination of the German communists when the parties are licensed again. Having met a number of the Russian cultural officers, I tend toward the former answer. They are well educated and know German culture remarkably well, at least those in Berlin. I think they really believe they can - how shall I put it? - make over these Germans, to re-educate them in the values they lost during the nazi nightmare. And as I've explained, I agree with this policy and fully support it. This should not be difficult for you to understand. After all, you Americans surely have some sort of re-education policy, don't you? I suppose you will also try to reform the German soul and you will support the theater for basically the same reasons."

"What about creating art as an end in itself?" Schade asked.

Kramer barked a sour laugh. "I write journalism, Lieutenant, not art. My erstwhile colleague, Boltzmann, you know him I think, says that writing journalism is easy, especially what he calls 'cultural stuff.' All you have to do, he says with some asperity but not much sincerity, I hope, is read the flyleaf or the theater program and sound authoritative about whatever you write. Book reviews are best written after reading only the dust jacket and the introduction, he says. To say that I disagree with this cynicism is to state the obvious."

When Schade later mentioned this to the old historian, Schadow said, "Very similar to academics discussing books in their fields. You get the man's point in the introduction and go to work showing that it has no basis or support, is misguided at best and perverse at worst."

Now Schade said, "Who writes for the critics and the professors? One writes for the intelligent few who buy your books and hope that a sufficient number of them do so to pay your rent. Look at Tommy Mann."

"For every Thomas Mann or Lion Feuchtwanger, there is an Alfred Döblin who needs his medical practice to pay the rent. What does that tell you?"

"I understand he's working for the French in Baden-Baden, Döblin, editing a literary journal," Makepeace said abruptly. "So he's paying his rent again without practicing medicine, at least not in the usual sense. Let's drift, we've got work to do."

Later he said to Schade, "John, if you're going to persist in using Latin tags, at least get them right: *panem et circenses*. And we've got to keep an eye on that Kramer: he agrees too much with the Russians."

"*Quisquis plus justo non sapit, ille sapit.*"[12]

"Bingo!"

* * * *

Dissecting each other with their eyes, their tongues too swollen with emotion to intertwine, they lay amid the gray unstarched sheets like corked champagne bottles shaken too hard.

---

[12] The Latin tag can be translated as "Whoever is not too wise, is wise."

*

During the peak of passion she sometimes cried out his name in the tones of a hungry sparrow: "Johan! Johannes!" He discovered he did not mind the name in her mouth as much as he resented it in anyone else's. Until one day early in the winter, "My name is John, remember."

"I don't like it, it's too foreign. I'll call you Jonathan."

"All right, but I am foreign, you know."

*

The tumultuous momentum of their passion (they could not in truth call it love), broken by exhaustion and the pressures of work, traced the jagged curve of reckless encounters across the graph of their lives.

"I want to love you": murmured in hopelessness, his face in her neck. "But you can't": spoken with mild indignation while she continued to stroke his sex.

Their love-making afforded them bright release and occasional joy. The determination with which she attempted to snap the chains of lassitude he saw develop into a more playful acceptance of the act as something beyond contrition or abandon. They both played roles they thought the other required to disguise their individual inadequacies in loving.

As her body hair slowly softened from stubble to flax she became more energetic and ambitious in their sexual conjoinings. "It was embarrassing. You might have thought I had lice and been put off. I did have, but that was before we met."

*

Fiercely he longed for tenderness and soft caresses ... with growing physical indifference he accepted sensuality and hoarse yelps of orgasmic delight. "Go ahead, please," she murmured as she rolled onto her stomach and arched her back. "It's the place the Mongols never got. Now it's yours."

*

Drinking real coffee in his room, she sighed at the physical pleasure of the black liquid and gazed at him through the cigarette smoke. "Why do we have to call it 'making love' when we don't love each other?" "Because anything else is vulgar ... and there's always hope." "Wouldn't it be nice to be able to take a hot bath." "I'm moving soon so you will be able, when there is water."

*

"I am damaging you, aren't I? I don't mean to; you give me so much ... in every way." How like her, he thought, to use the word "damage" instead of the more intimate and personal "hurt." A rueful smile: "You even feed me. It isn't easy for me either, you know. You've no exclusive possession of anxiety in this city. It's the current disease, an epidemic, along with lice, hunger, edema, rape and all the baggage of defeat." Then with a certain sad kindness: "Do you want me to love you? I wish I could. I would like to be able to love you. But it is not possible ... I've none to give, not now. Anything else, anything, but not that. Wet and dry passion you can find in the city now, but love and tenderness no longer live here. Anything but that, my darling...." And she wept for both of them and he fumblingly comforted her. They fell on the bed and emptied themselves into each other trying to extort love with sensual fervor. They blackmailed each other's bodies with drenched sex clotted with the dust of the city's rubble and insecurities.

*

They diligently maintained their individual private worlds, but both believed they could continue their relationship and provide each other's need for what they found together. Their problem was to define these needs with sufficient clarity as to afford them a foundation upon which they could be together. Without articulating the matter, they thought they could maintain a relationship without growth or intrusion on the other's emotions and interests; indeed, they thought this the basis upon which they could continue into the future without crashing against the barriers of their interior lives. They convinced themselves without discussion that they could do without the flowering development of openness and confidences that make and sustain love. If they could not have love, they still wanted each other; the pleasures and sensualities they exchanged in lieu of love would be enough to carry them to the point at which one or the other would leave. This is what they thought they understood, and reluctantly accepted, like one accepts the existence of a virus once it has infiltrated one's body, knowing it will go away if treated correctly.

*

Early in their affair, when neither was quite sure where the limits of knowledge skirted the unacceptable, he asked her about the drugs. "It was a horribly stupid thing to do, even under the circumstances. Perhaps Joachim's kind really do hate women underneath it all. You know how it started, now you see how it is ending. I no longer need it. That is all." A hesitant smile barely lightened her face. "It is not easy, but it is not as difficult as I thought. Besides, it is almost impossible to find now. The price is too high. So there's no choice, you see? That part is over. Look, feel here: I'm gaining weight. I thank you for that." He was tempted to allow her smile to destroy his thoughts, but he suspended his disbelief and hoped she was right.

*

So they exchanged their physical gratification of sexual release with as much pleasure as each could give and accept. Schade thought of these acts as making love, if not loving, but he realized she did not or could not share that emotional alibi. He thought she was being too ruthless in what she considered to be honesty. This, however, she tried to explain as the only basis upon which they could continue their comforting of each other's needs and weaknesses. "I can't call what we have love because I don't know what the word means." She uttered this with profound sadness and kissed him with renewed passion.

* * * *

Watching them dancing at the newly renovated Bar und Tanzpalast am Rande just off the Kurfürstendamm late that winter, Makepeace said to Harrigan sotto voce: "It's not going to work. An ambiguous American and a hungry German. He only knows where he's been and she only cares about where she's going."
"She's eaten well enough since she met him."
"Whisky has eaten your brain."

*

Being Makepeace, he did not conceal that he found Schade's relationship with Gisela difficult to believe, and he occasionally ragged his friend about it. "Since you are so deficient in social skills vis à vis the opposite and most important sex, I'm always surprised when you end up with a girlfriend."

"I am not entirely without wiles."

"Yes, there was after all that French floozy in Paris."

"She was hardly a floozy."

"But it runs together so well. Like flat foot floogy with a floy floy."

"She didn't have flat feet and she never wore a floy floy, never."

"But she was a floogy."

"Only by stretching the meaning beyond the edge."

"Ah, but she certainly was a rugcutter. You know, Johnny, all I ever wanted to be is a rugcutter."

"Well, Willy, I'll just bring the scissors!"

At which point Makepeace sang a few lines from the well-known 1920s dance number:

My, my,
Crabapple pie.
Seabirds fly,
Why don't I?
If I put on my knuckleduster
Do you think I'd pass the muster?

"You know I sometimes am reminded of a line from Whitman's 'Broad-Axe Poem,' do you know it? 'Weapon shapely, naked, wan...' does sort of describe her. Only the line, of course, not the title." Makepeace gently rattled his bracelet.

So it was with a certain amount of quid pro quo that Schade responded to the eventual news of Makepeace's fall from non-fraternization grace.

* * * *

Surrounded by piles of Fragenbögen, routing slips, various scraps of paper and the incessant ringing of telephones, Makepeace sat at a desk on the second floor of the villa orchestrating a report with all ten fingers on an ancient German typewriter, swearing at the reversal of the z and y on the keyboard. The window overlooking the Milinowskistrasse gaped open flooding the room with light; although it was early evening according to their timepieces, daylight remained: in order to conserve electricity the western Allies had set the clocks to a radical daylight saving time so that darkness did not begin until 9:30 or later. The Russians still officially operated on Moscow time, an addition to the list of anti-German humiliations, so well deserved, but annoying to the others who sometimes were confused about the times of meetings. Gray clouds blotched the pearl blue sky with the promise of rain.

Schade stopped pushing his fountain pen aimlessly across the inkspotted sheet of foolscap on the desk in front of him. "Someday it had better be worth it." He said this to no one in particular; Makepeace typed and swore; Vasart, there for a conference once more postponed, spoke in low tones rapidly into the old telephone receiver. Finally, Makepeace looked up. "A generation later it's always worth it."

"That's too long, much too long. It must be worth something now, the problems that exist now, we need the answers now. All this paper, tears and hysteria!"

"Do I detect a tinge of hysteria *here*, humm...?"

Disgusted, Schade lit a cigarette and sipped coffee from a mug with a large UFA symbol on it. "You wish to analyze me, mein lieber Freud?"

"Why not? Beats writing this report no one will read except some dusty historian thirty years from now in some dusty archive. Where shall we start? Pre-natal? Infancy? Adolescence, perhaps?"

"Write the report. You're better at that. Add another batch of paper to the pile. And what happens when we send the questionnaires and reports? CIC investigates, oh yes. Investigate? If they did their job thoroughly we'd never clear anyone; it would take years. All they do is run over to the document center and look up the name in the party membership files and the SS records, and maybe, maybe talk to someone who knew the person. What the hell does that mean? Everybody lies. What does it matter? These people are starving and want to work, that's all. We know most of them weren't anything but nominal nazis. Most of the real swine don't come out of the woodwork to ask for clearances they know they won't get; probably be arrested and tried for war crimes. Anyway we know those who were more than *Mitläufer*. We don't seem to draw the line close enough, we throw them all in the same bad bag. We've got to make some distinctions here."

"What side of the goddamned bed did you get up on this morning? Yes, yes, the world ain't perfect. But you're too sympathetic to these people, John, you're too involved and while that's understandable, you can't stand on both sides of the fence. You want a swine like Reger to simply go back to his old job, as if nothing happened between 1933 and now? Without bastards like that supporting them the nazis wouldn't have gotten to first base, or Warsaw."

"I'm trying to do my job and the regulations make it very difficult. There are too many contradictions, contradictions everywhere. It's not a matter of being sympathetic to the Germans...."

Vasart replaced the receiver in its cradle and said thoughtfully, "After what they did in the Soviet Union, Bergen-Belsen, Auschwitz, I hardly think they deserve any sympathy at all."

"Listen, I am more aware than most of what the nazis did. I agree that there must be retribution for the crimes; I agree there must be expiation for the sins. The gas chambers are incomprehensible, but they existed, yes, but how are we to punish an entire nation in a way that makes any sense? I just don't think we're going about it in the right way. Are we going to force the entire nation to fill out the bloody *Fragebogen*? The idea is absurd, yet we seem to be trying it. The Soviets don't have a system like this, so where does it leave us and Allied cooperation?"

"They have other ways of proving value and guilt, I suppose, don't they, at least for their own purposes," Vasart said without much conviction.

"But that's the point. If we don't have a common system the whole thing falls down. We're not going to achieve anything this way. We've got to come up with something else? What about the British?"

"I must admit that we follow you Americans reluctantly in this matter. We certainly agree on punishment, but we generally think your method is unworkable. We are not very enthusiastic in implementing our own denazification policy, are we? It gets in the way of other things, like running the cities and the countryside. But the boche must be punished, no doubt about that. But how...?" Vasart shrugged.

"And this whole idea of competition among the Allies in Berlin for artists. Everyone knows about it, or suspects it, no one says anything, but everyone knows. It's ridiculous."

"I agree, old chap, I agree. Doesn't seem to make much difference where the buggers live or work, does it?"

Makepeace looked up from the typewriter. "It will."

"Ah, the Voice of Doom, the Tones of Cassandra creeping out of the mind of Our Own Oracle. I say, Bill, you are rather a bit of a pessimist about all that."

"It doesn't make any sense, the Soviets have already said they want the Philharmonic in our sector," Schade's voice climbed another notch on the scale.

"That surprised me, I admit. Very nice. Now we have to find room for them."

Vasart laughed with velvet in his voice. "And you chaps weren't supposed to talk to them, eh? Non-fraternization, indeed. How did you propose to do that? Cut off the GIs' balls?"

Schade grinned at Makepeace's discomfort. "It was rescinded soon enough, Ogilvy. We were exempt anyway for business purposes."

"Rather odd policy, though."

"Have you seen the propaganda the army put out to support the policy?" Makepeace rummaged in the desk and pulled out a batch of clippings. "I'm saving this stuff for posterity." The cartoons portrayed the activities of a full-breasted germanic harlot engaged in luring bright-eyed enlisted men (officers evidently did not consort with teutonic bawds) to her bed for a variety of fleshly, if speedy, pleasures, the results of which ineluctably led to medically disastrous consequences for the poor innocent sap of a soldier. The lusty Teuton's name was Veronika Dankeschön. "Get it, Ogilvy, V.D."

"My, my. Rather obnoxious stuff, what? Do our boys have to read trash like that, I wonder?" They laughed together, secure in their superior knowledge. Later that year when Vasart displayed symptoms similar to those so graphically depicted in the cartoons he roundly cursed the Countess with whom he had dallied and demanded massive amounts of penicillin. The others laughed then with even more superiority, but with sympathy. "Should have watched those bloody awful training films more carefully, what? Not that it would have made any difference, I suppose." Vasart shifted his feet. "Speaking of films, do you have any idea where the decision was made about the movies you're showing here?"

"Certainly not in Berlin. We would have known better," Schade said.

"You had a chance to not only entertain these people but teach them something as well. All these bits of fluff and escapist frivolity. *I Married a Witch* instead of *Mr. Smith Goes to Washington*, *Gold Rush* instead of *The Great Dictator*. Missed opportunity there."

"Ideally," Makepeace said, "we should have arrived here with dozens of films with German soundtracks with the same propaganda message we sent them over the airwaves about the values of democracy and the American way of life, sure. Would have had a deep and lasting effect. But we didn't. Don't know why, except the decisions made in Washington got tangled up with the Hollywood studios and the military bureaucracy. The studios needed to give permission to show the films and wanted a return in cash. Couldn't be done, so they got unexportable bank accounts here and distribution rights. But the process took so long to work out, we ended up with crap at our end."

"How do we expect the Germans to take us seriously when we give them this stuff, badly captioned if at all?" Schade's voice bled with disgust.

"We'll improve as time goes on, no doubt, but currently I must admit the situation is ridiculous. Washington sends the most goddamned unrealistic directives all the time. They don't know what's going on here!" Deliberately changing the subject, Makepeace asked Vasart, "And how are things in your office, Leftenant?"

Vasart waved his hand and replied with an edge in his voice. "Oh jolly, jolly. After the elections no one seems to really know how far and in which direction they should move. Not that Labor has all that much choice, do they? The Army chappies don't care, of course. They just follow the bloody directives. The flush of victorious Britannia still on their cheeks and all that. They can't really do much else, y'know." He brooded on this for a moment, puffing on a Woodbine. "There seems to be a lack of energy in England. It's rather distressing. Everyone's worn out, exhausted, the whole nation's tired from the burdens of empire and the war, I suppose, dispirited. They want to know why they've got rationing when we won the bloody war. Hell's bells, we eat better here than I would in London at the moment, even the military food here is better. When I think of the Berliners and the spirit and enthusiasm that they show, at least the people we deal with...." He began to sing *Berlin kommt wieder*, but a spasm of harsh coughing interrupted the recital.

"Have you seen a doctor about that, Ogilvy?"

"John, I've seen them all at one time or another, haven't I? They all proffer the same advice: give up everything that makes life bearable here and now. It's not advice one can take without serious contemplation, is it?" He swerved the conversation back to the previous subject. "Perhaps, y'know, it's the guilt that makes the difference. Between the English and the Berliners, I mean. We've got nothing to feel guilty about, nothing to pay for...."

"Except your colonies," Makepeace interjected.

"Yes, well, don't know about that, Bill. Who thinks about that problem except for the bohemians in Soho and the marxists, eh?"

"All the colonials, perhaps," Schade said, smiling.

"They don't live in England, old man, at least most of them don't." Vasart's father had served in the British imperial cause in India and Egypt his entire adult life, which had come to an abrupt and violent end on a dusty Cairo street corner when an Arab without a driver's license ran over him in a large British army truck carrying stolen rifles to a sect-like group of Egyptian revolutionaries determined to take advantage of the war to throw the hated imperialists out of their country. The idea that this project, if successful, would only change the nationality of their rulers from British to German did not enter their minds. Vasart believed he understood both sides in the colonial struggle, as his father believed in the sacred mission of the Empire to bring the soothing benefits of Christianity and British efficiency to those in the realm who did not completely recognize these phenomena as being desirable or required for their future health and wisdom. The son thus harbored conscience-biting reservations about the efficacy of the Allied mission in which he served.

"But the Germans have a great deal to feel guilty about, don't they? Perhaps this outbreak of spirit in the city is their way of doing penance of sorts, as well as evading the subject, and making up for lost time, lost opportunities after the last twelve years...."

Sternly, Makepeace said, "You know, for a former tabloid theater critic, you can be horribly deep at times."

"My dear boy, what do you mean 'former'? And 'tabloid'? A large metropolitan newspaper, I should say. Bloody well paid, too. Furthermore ..."

"Yes, well, we all have our crosses to bear. Look, how well do you get along with Yuri Tamirov, our erstwhile shifty-eyed counterpart?"

"Like most Russians I've met in the last months, I find him rather opaque, don't y'think? Can't quite get the hang of him. Seems all right, but distant. I suppose it's their training: all us capitalists are the enemy and all that. He makes an effort to appear rather friendly, and he's shown us cooperation whenever we asked for it. Why d'you ask?"

"I understand he's going to be the Soviet representative on the cultural committee in the Kommandantura."

"Oh that. Surely our all-powerful lords and masters could have thought up a better system for running this blighted city, couldn't they? Four-power control seems rather fragile, cumbersome what with the different ideologies, and so on. Does it work any better in Vienna, I wonder." Vasart coughed gently.

Schade came out of a mild trance. "It seems to have worked out thus far."

"Sure," Makepeace said, "because we agreed to let things stand as the Russians set them up before we got here."

"Don't really know what we could have done in any case, old man. The city is running. Badly, perhaps, but under the circumstances running fairly smoothly," Vasart remarked in a neutral tone.

Makepeace turned to Schade, who was staring at the unusually silent telephone as if willing it to ring. "Did Udo come in today?"

"I haven't seen him, but I've been out a lot."

Vasart said, "Udo? Who's he when he's at home? Haven't heard his name before, have I?"

His chair moaned as Makepeace leaned back and lit a cigarette, breaking yet another vow to give up the demon tobacco. "Udo Siegmeister is a very interesting fellow. Going to work for us after we get him vetted, and that, at least, should be easy. Had you ever heard of him before the war, John?"

Schade snorted. "No, Bill, I didn't know everyone before the war. I was a kid when we left, and a young man at the time and living in New York, remember?"

"Anyway," Makepeace looked with resignation at Schade, as if he should have known at least Udo Siegmeister before the war. "This guy came into the office a few days after we arrived, all skin and bones like most of them. Speaks English, or a form of it, and asked if he can work for us if we're going to do anything with movies. Well, hell, we get this all the time. But this guy's different, see? First of all, he's a Jew, and, secondly, he wasn't in a camp. It's amazing, but he spent the whole time in Berlin. Calls himself a U-boot. He went underground and made it through the whole thing. Not that it was easy. Must have been hell for him, but he made it. Before the nazis tossed him out he was an agent for one of the Hollywood studios here. Distribution, dubbing the films, stuff like that. That's his story anyway. We're checking with the studio to see if he's telling us a cock and bull story."

"How on earth did he survive all those years? Never ran across anyone like that before."

Schade said, "There are a number of Jews and Mischlinge who hung on, one way or another. I've heard stories about them, but Udo is the only one I've met thus far. They're surely more of them who survived, hiding in the city."

Vasart nodded. "Yes, one hears all kinds of stories these days. Apparently our Russian allies did not differentiate between Jews who survived and other Germans when it came to plunder and rape. Insisting 'y a yavreye!' offered no protection from the stiff Soviet prick."

Makepeace looked pensively at the paperwork on his desk. "All kinds suffered the same fate. Yuri Vladimirovich fell out of character the other day and told me about two women, lesbians evidently, who were good communists, party members, belonged to the resistance, the whole thing. They scrounged around the entire twelve years doing what they could for the cause, writing slogans on the walls, waiting for liberation by their comrades. Lived in shacks and scrounged food during the last year. Damn near died of malnutrition, always on the lookout for the SS and the Gestapo, afraid of being denounced. Christ, what a life it must have been. Anyway, they held on, kept their faith in Uncle Joe and the party brightly burning. And when the Ivans finally did get to Berlin and liberated the joint, guess what happened? The first soldiers they saw, they ran out their hiding place filled with joy, waving their party cards with happiness, and bam! Raped. Party members, sure. The goddamn soldiers probably couldn't read. Wouldn't have made any difference anyway. Bam! Just another couple of kraut women. Bam! Bam! Geezopete."

"Tamirov told you this?"

"Yeah. He thought it was a funny story. The Russians have a perverted sense of humor. Probably comes from living with Stalin all these years."

"Maybe even German communists are Germans first. Think about what the Germans did to the Russians," Schade said in a carefully neutral tone.

"A perceptible lack of sympathy, clearly."

Schade looked at the telephone again. It had not made a sound in fifteen minutes, which could mean the line had been disrupted by the usual unknown forces. He brushed his mustache with his right thumb and repressed the urge to call the theater where Gisela rehearsed. Tonight he had no official nocturnal duties trekking around the city with his flashlight, burrowing into the pasts and present of certain Berliners. Tonight he would be able to go to bed early, if not to sleep then to make more notes in his crimped script to add to the pile of diffuse jottings that refused to congeal into a coherent fictional structure. Or perhaps he would talk to Kronauer about the future of the city, a discussion that seemed to go on interminably in that house, like a floating crap game with endlessly rolling dice but no money to cover the betting. Schade found these mental exercises invigorating and enjoyable if at times acerbic and emotionally loaded, especially when Mathilde Kronauer loosed her considerable intelligence and waspish manner against anything she considered to be stupid or immoral, the list of which seemed to lengthen each time they met. If Mathilde could not cover her bets with cash, everyone around the table accepted her IOUs with anticipation and speculation about the method of payment.

Suddenly he thought of onions, fresh, salacious, odorous onions, and could not remember when he'd eaten the last one. How long ago had it been? Surely in Paris. He closed his eyes and thick slices of yellow onions on a wooden platter stained with their juices appeared. His salivary glands splashed his mouth with the sharp tang of memory, and he remembered the smell of onions mixed with the deeper scent of nicotine on his fingers. He sighed. The telephone rang with preternatural loudness.

Makepeace said into it, "Information Control. Lieutenant Mapepeace" and grinned at the others. He was not particularly fond of his surname and often mumbled it in odd ways into the telephone. He straightened slightly in his chair, fingering the crown of his head. "Yes, sir. Where do they want to go? Tonight?" He covered the mouthpiece and muttered, "Shit." Then into the large old mechanism, "Yes, sir. What time? Yes, sir. One of us will be here." He replaced the receiver and looked at Schade. "What do you think about that? For christsake."

"I could think much more efficiently about whatever it is if I knew what it was." Vasart giggled and added, "Yes, Bill, do we have to bribe you or will you volunteer the info?"

"The brass have arrived and wish to be entertained for the evening. Can you beat that? As if we don't have enough to do. Our psykwar general boss and some civilians here for the big meeting want to see the sights. A little Berlin festivities for their highasses. Something perhaps a leetle risqué, humm?"

"Ur."

"Exactly. They even know where they want to go. A brief drive around town and a few stops at some cabarets, especially the Kaberett der Komiker, the old Kadeko as the Berliners call it in the interest of saving their precious time. I'd like to have seen that in the old days before the brown plague. Old Willy Schaeffers has got some publicity outside the city, it seems. Ogilvy's lot tossed the Kadeko out of its theater so the NAAFI could have it."[13]

"Not my doing, old man," Vasart interjected, holding up a hand. "Quite the opposite, in fact. I went to the bat for Schaeffers, the cricket bat, of course."

---

[13] NAAFI: Navy, Army, Air Force Institutes: the organization supplying the British military with goods and entertainment, not used by commissioned officers who had their own mess facilities.

"Of course."

"Did have a problem with the NAAFI and the Renaissance Theater, though. Just after we took over our sector they put on a '*Wedekind-Schnitzler-Abend*,' readings and short scenes. Very amateurish and the newspaper critics blasted them the next day. The NAAFI shut the production down to use the theater for troop entertainment. I tried, but couldn't stop them. Most regrettable since we'd just appointed the former head of the Jewish theater in the city to run the Renaissance. Don't know what we're going to do with him now." Vasart shook his head at the generic unfairness of world at large and his part of it in particular. "Did you know that at one time the theaters in this city were half empty on Jewish holidays? It's a fact."

"A true fact, Penrod?"

"A true fact, Sam."

"Knock it off for a second, will you?" Makepeace pleaded in exasperation. Turning to Schade, he continued his peroration. "A stop at the Femina, perhaps, where the blackmarketeers are so thick on the ground that the MPs have taken to raiding the place. That would be a treat for the brass. And they want a guided tour. Hear that, John? A guided tour! Ain't that swell."

"The city has become one big tourist attraction for the diplomats and the brass. The ruins are tourist sites, for chrissakes." Schade's indignation brought a faint redness to his neck. "And the journalists!"

"They want to confirm how terribly they defeated the Germans," Vasart said.

"They want to confirm that they've had their revenge on the enemy and what utter destruction humans can inflict upon one another." Schade's voice rose a decibel.

The Englishman looked out the window toward the tall pine tree that blocked their view of the dull late afternoon beige sky. "We go out of our way to visit Roman and Greek ruins from antiquity in Italy and Greece. A thousand years from now they'll be coming to Berlin to visit the ruins of nazi civilization."

Schade shook his head. "The city as museum? No, that would not be a good idea because it would also be a memorial to the nazis. We need memorials all right, to the victims not the criminals."

Makepeace grimaced at the turn of the conversation. "The city will be rebuilt, no doubt, but we've got more pressing things to deal with here."

"That's one of the problems, isn't it?" Vasart said. "And there's another thing: the danger of taking them around to show off the destructive power of the bombing is that the sights may be so terrible with all those ghosts wandering through the ruins that they begin to sympathize with the citizens as victims instead of seeing them as criminals to be punished."

"Perhaps they have been punished enough, the civilians as a whole," Schade said softly.

Makepeace laughed sharply. "Ah, John, you're such a goddamned romantic."

"*Scheisse.*"

"The tour, gentlemen, the tour presses upon us."

"No doubt they requested you by name to lead it." Schade said with a minimum of hope in the back of his voice.

"Not by a long shot, pal. Ogilvy here obviously can't do it—"

"Could, but won't," Vasart muttered smugly.

"— although that would be an experience for him -"

"Had quite enough of those, thank you very much."

"— and for them. We'll just have to flip the old coin, John. The loser gets the brass. Very democratic. Objective."

"Ur."

"Right again. Heads or tails?"

"Ur."

"Come on, man, get on with it! Praise the Lord and pass the ammo!"

Schade lost. Makepeace told him where to meet the party, after which the loser mumbled an obscenity and said, "See you tomorrow." To which Makepeace responded, "If some trigger-happy MP doesn't knock you off with the brass. Wouldn't that look great in the *Stars and Stripes*. And I'd have to go to all the meetings and write all the reports myself. It would reach the point where I'd be reporting on writing reports because there'd be no time for anything else." But by then Schade was descending the stairs into the city streets, dulled gray and brown under clouds covering the early twilight sun. The rubblewomen and companies of refugees had widened and swept some of the major thoroughfares for the meeting in Potsdam: clean streets bordered by piles of dirt and masonry against a background of skeletons and stubs of buildings, reminding the victors of their victory and the defeated of their losses.

* * * *

In two army-green Chevrolet limousines the group drove off from American Military Government headquarters in the Kronprinzenallee to begin the tour. General Sender, Colonel Darkley, his eye patch now blending in with the falling darkness, a number of unintroduced colorless colonels and generals, including the Assistant Deputy Military Governor for the American occupation zone, a gray-haired, exquisitely suited diplomat from the State Department, and Second Lieutenant John Schade: ten in all. Schade and one of the colonels drove the cars. Adhering to the curfew meant they could not remain in anyone place too long. Schade and Darkley had quickly planned a schedule of stops ending at Sender's villa near Wannsee, taking into account the frustratingly slow pace of travel in the city even for the victorious Allies in their national vehicles and confiscated German limousines.

They began with music. Behind a wrecked concert hall without proscenium stage or rows of upholstered seats or vaulting roof they sat on rickety chairs placed in the grass while the denazified members of the Berlin Philharmonic cautiously played the previously forbidden Mendelsohn-Bartholdy's "Fingal's Cave Overture" and Smetana's "Moldau," the musicians perched on a cracked cement terrace. Almost 800 of the city's denizens and a scattering of uniformed Allied personnel sat on the chairs and listened intently to the swirling melodies, some in the audience remembering with pleasure the sonorities their government had banned many years ago. During a brief stop at what had been Max Reinhardt's Deutsches Theater in the Soviet Sector to watch a few scenes of the new production of *Our Town*, called *Unsere kleine Stadt* in the German translation, the director of the piece took Schade aside to inform him that this would be the last performance: the Russians had banned the play until further notice. The official reason appeared to be a lack of agreement among the Allies regarding "responsibility" in cultural affairs, but the director thought the Russians viewed the play as too passive and poetic, "too much pure art" to be politically appropriate in the present circumstances. Schade said he would look into the matter, but he knew nothing would come of it; the play would have to await its opening in the

American sector. Later, Tamirov unofficially explained to Schade, "Too pessimistic, Lieutenant, much too pessimistic for these people. We want them to be happy they've been 'liberated,' not feeling oppressed by the fact that they've been unconditionally defeated."

Darkley and Schade discussed the possibility of taking the group to the Hebbel Theater to see the new production of *Die Dreigroschenoper*, but decided against it. Harrigan had seen the piece when it opened and reported heavy emphasis on sarcasm and indirect comment on the current situation in the city. Harrigan had, in fact, suggested to the director that he tone down the closing song in the second act sung by Macheath and Spelunken Jenny containing the refrain "*erst kommt das Fressen, dann kommt die Moral*," which had been mightily applauded by a hungry, resentful audience. At this point such an Allied "suggestion" required an appropriate German response and during the next performance the actors sang the line almost inaudibly and caused no untoward applause.

Schade remembered the night earlier that summer shortly after he arrived in the city when he stumbled upon a crudely hand-lettered poster, attached to an overturned tireless truck lying on a street corner like a dead turtle on its back, announcing a performance of the Weill-Brecht collaboration in what had been a theater in the Soviet Sector. Intrigued, he decided to include a visit to the theater as part of the survey work his unit had undertaken. The building had no roof and part of one wall had fallen into the street, but the red plush seats remained intact, a jarring colorful reminder of better times among the dull colors of the present. Most of the audience consisted of Soviet military personnel; if they did not understand the German lyrics they nonetheless appreciated the music and had been informed that the play, written by a radical leftist bourgeois intellectual and a communist, was to be considered a weapon in the class struggle. For this they willingly endured the stench of decay and death that lingered still in the open auditorium. When the music began Schade forgot the smell of ashes and unwashed bodies. The performers had no props, the orchestra lacked half its members and played badly. The singers had no need for greasepaint to realistically play the roles of beggars: their haggard appearance was real, their rags were their own. Some of them had recently been released from the camps. They sang poorly, but with the enthusiasm of those who have been given a precious gift and wish to express their happiness at receiving it. After the performance, Schade spoke to some of the actors. One of them told him: "When some of us got together after we were liberated we found it easy to agree on the first play we wanted to do. Nothing else but *The Threepenny Opera* would do, you see. Then we began to organize it in a haphazard way -- you saw, and heard, how amateurish we are, no materials, few instruments -- everyone agreed this must be the first piece. It is fitting, nicht wahr? Perhaps we all thought that if we did Brecht again, we would prove that the nightmare was really over; if we could do Brecht it would be like pinching yourself to be sure you're not dreaming. You see?" Like many such pickup groups they didn't last more than five or six performances; no one paid them, many of the ensemble moved on to roles in the newly established theaters, the musicians found more lucrative employment playing in the canteens of the victors or in the licensed night spots. The Hebbel Theater staging was the first professional mounting of the play, but for Schade it did not have the same spontaneously exhilarated feeling of the earlier performance.

Darkley mentioned the cabaret and they drove to the Kaberett der Komiker, newly ensconced on the Kurfürstendamm after the British equivalent of Special Services ejected the group from its theater in that sector. The Ku'damm had become a center for the city's bedraggled youth. The thin, knife-faced young men with long civilian haircuts meandered up and down the boulevard trying to snarl at the world they had not made. Pretty young women with long hair held up with brightly colored combs, much less sullen than their male coevals, strolled about swaying their skinny bottoms on the arms of uniformed Allied soldiers, blatantly ignoring the non-fraternization rules. They swayed past bars spitting the sounds of hot swing over the sidewalk promising all that had been missing for many years, but serving only hot tea in glasses with a small amount of watered rum and no food. Small groups of soldiers and civilians sporadically gathered around a seller of a cup of sugar, a packet of condoms, five real coffee beans, American cigarettes (Pall Malls being more valuable because longer), or anything not otherwise available, then as quickly dispersed, their eyes darting about them to ensure no surprises before they could enjoy the results of their purchases and sales. Behind the facade of the street rose mounds of rubble and debris in front of gutted buildings with empty windows inhabited only at night by lonely souls and their comforters for five or seven minutes.

Achtung! Vorsicht!
Bomben nicht anfassen!
Aufpassen oder sterben.

The performance had sold out, which meant ten Germans lost their seats so the Americans could enjoy the show, but the management regretfully refunded their entrance fees. Schade wondered how much of the show these VIPs would understand, but tactfully did not offer to translate for them, a task which would in any case have been hopeless. The large room barely contained the smoke and noise of raised voices and clattering glasses containing watered whisky and just plain water. He thought the timing and talents erratic and undisciplined, moving between the awkwardly provincial and remarkably high levels of smooth professionalism. The latter was undoubtedly due to the talent of the star and director of the show who also served as master of ceremonies, Willy Schaeffers. He bounded onto the stage following a long announcement in Russian and informed the audience: "In German that means the same." Several Russian officers and enlisted men in audience enjoyed the attention of an attractive young blonde actress in a short red skirt and frilly, cuffed white blouse provided by the house to translate the sketches and jokes into fluent Russian. The Russians and the politically smart Germans awarded her loud applause, but her work disrupted the pace of the show. Schaeffers asked to be pardoned for the fact that he had not yet mastered English well enough to gloss the performance in that language. Birgitte Mira performed "*Berlin kommt wieder*" as a solo and gave an energetic rendition of the song as the show's finale.

> *Berlin kommt wieder*
> *Das ist das Lied das jeder singt*
> *Und das jetzt wieder*
> *So schön in ganz Berlin erklingt!*
> *Jawohl mein Schatz*
> *Am Alexanderplatz*
> *Am Stern, am Zoo, am Knie*
> *Ertönt auf's neue diese Melodie,*

*Und wer sie einmal hört
Der vergisst sie dann nie
Berlin kommt wieder.*

  ...

*Doch ganz genau
So wie nach dunkler Nacht
Die Sonne wieder lacht
So werden Unter'n Linden Linden blühen.
Berlin bleibt doch Berlin!*[14]

On the way out Darkley remarked quickly to Schade: "I'm not *sure* about that song. I don't know if the *sentiment* is the right one for this time: Do we *want* Berlin to return? It smacks too much of the past, the desire for return -- we want them to *look* to the future."

"They mean the city before the nazis. It makes the Berliners a bit more cheerful to believe that. I think the song is harmless enough." Schade wondered if Darkley had understood the lyrics or intuited the meaning.

"I'm not *so* sure we want them to go back to Weimar either. We may have to do something *about* it."

"Did you know, sir, that Schaeffers appeared in a revue called *Bitte einsteigen!* with Josephine Baker back in the 20s?"

---

[14] The lines from "Berlin kommt wieder" can be translated as Berlin will return/That's the song everyone is singing/That now once again/Sounds so lovely all over Berlin!/Yes, my sweetheart/At Alexanderplatz/At the Stern, the Zoo, the Knie/Once again this melody is heard,/And whoever hears it but once/Will never forget it/ Berlin will return./That's exactly it/Just as following the dark night/The sun laughs again/So on Unter den Linden/Lime trees will /blossom again./Berlin will remain Berlin!

"Words *and* music by my friend Friedrich Hollaender in the Theater des Westens during the 1928 season, music *played* by the Weintraub Syncopators, lieutenant?"

"Unlikely he emphasized that during the last twelve years?" Schade could find no other comeback; Darkley could always best him in the game of one-upmanship.

They attempted another cabaret in the American Sector, but it appeared so shoddy and unprofessional that they quickly moved on. Walking to the automobiles, the diplomat, silent thus far, asked, "Are they mostly that bad?"

"We try to limit the worst as best we can, but they spring up overnight," Schade said, and could not resist adding, "like mushrooms after the rain" with a straight face. "As soon as we close one down, another opens."

"One might admire the persistence of the business mind," the diplomat said quietly and rebuttoned his dark double-breasted suit jacket.

"Usually they don't last long. They close after a few days when no one shows up to pay the entrance fee."

One of the generals looked at the warped skyline, pulled his Eisenhower jacket down over his belly, and said with wonder in his voice, "Brother, it's going to take more than a dime to get this burg back on its feet. It's gone to hell in a basket!"

Standing by the limousines, General Sender announced to the group that they would make one further stop. "Although officially it's still daylight, we're going to take you to a nightclub. The club is off-limits to Allied personnel, but I doubt if any MPs will bother us and we'll have no trouble getting in, I assure you. It is also a black market club, in fact *the* black market club in our sector. It's called the Femina. Did I pronounce that correctly, Lieutenant? Heh. We tolerate this club for a number of reasons: Germans who can afford it have to have some place like it to let off steam, something more than potato soup to let them get away from reality for a while. We may consider some of these people to be engaged in somewhat illegal ventures, but this is what keeps the civilian economy going at the moment, and this will be the basis for the future economic health of the city, like it or not. We certainly can't maintain the economy, nor can the other Allies. Congress is already moaning about the cost of the occupation. Also, if we closed this one, another would take its place. We cannot stop this kind of thing completely so we let this one go on and keep an eye on it. Furthermore, Intelligence tells me they find the place useful. We won't talk about any confidential matters there. Heh, heh. It will give you a taste of Berlin that doesn't appear in the reports you read." He nodded to Schade and they climbed into the limousines.

Schade had been to the Femina earlier that summer during a survey trip; he did not like it because of the aura of penury, false gaiety, and heavy nostalgia that penetrated its corners. The smell of cigarette smoke and stale grease hung so thickly in the air that no one breathed very deeply of its damp and sticky joys.

In the 1920s the Femina had been one of the city's biggest lavish nightclubs, its billboards in front of the building festooned with photographs of naked girls laughing invitations to passers-by. After 1933 the club began to feature awkward Italian jugglers more to the taste of the nazis' warped petite bourgeois puritanism. Now what passed as entertainment consisted of the inevitable pretty young blonde singer in a low-cut dress who could not stay in tune, supported by two tone deaf musicians with brilliantined hair and greasy shirt collars who abused a piano and accordion. Schade thought with pleasure and frustration about the bar in which he had heard the two Negroes playing bebop. The Femina served bad drinks and meager food, but it was always crowded. The maitre d' swiftly found two tables for the high-ranking Americans in uniform. Schade and the four others at his table ordered cocktails (cheap watered whisky or gin without ice: "English style" the waiter proudly informed them), then wine and the *Gedeck* or fixed menu. They talked desultorily in the loud voices of the conquerors.

The shabby failed attempt at elegance pained Schade; he had seen so much of it in recent weeks. Indeed there were occasional glimpses of former individual style to be seen through the damp smoke: a tall slender man with a Prussian haircut and a pressed tuxedo somehow saved during the battle for the city but cut for its owner at a time when his body carried far more flesh than at present; a middle aged woman in a gown stylish fourteen years ago hanging from her angular shoulders, the few pins unable to contain the pile of ill-washed hair; the well-tailored English tweed suit out of season in the Berlin summer, its owner sweating mightily, a forced grin on lips between which hung an unlit tobaccoless cigarette; a waiter ("You may call me Fritz, sir") who had worked in the opulent Café Kranzler in another life, spare and formal, whose trousers did not match his badly repaired jacket; the bartender going through the motions of mixing elaborate cocktails with professional élan but no ingredients.... The gaunt faces trying to remember real pleasures, the unpressed brown and gray clothing -- it all depressed Schade as much as it left the others In the group indifferent and impatient to move on. In the Femina, "das Ballhaus Berlins," the customers worked hard at enjoyment; only those who had been able to intoxicate themselves with ersatz whisky, who could forget the smells of their unwashed bodies and broken drains, their worthless currency, and the barely endurable pressures on them during their waking hours displayed any spontaneity; even these lacked sparkle, even when recent memories could be repressed, and most assuredly when one had no desire to repress those memories. All the refugees and every German in the city shared the necessity for some form of escape, if only for a moment; those who could afford it and had a residual taste for artificially induced mild decadence came to the Femina and its imitators.

Schade repressed the urge to vomit. On the other side of the room he recognized Claudia Kaufmann, in a pale blue dress which would have magnificently set off her figure if it fit correctly, gnawing at a fingernail, sitting with two men in dusty suits and yellowing shirts and a wraith-like figure of a woman who talked intensely; he wondered what kind of black-market deal she was arranging; or were the men theater producers hoping for the chance to mount a production if the money and the licenses could be obtained? The young actress appeared wan and tired, but she spoke with animation to the older of the men. Schade tried to concentrate on her dark hair unstylishly piled up on her head, and the dress that should have emphasized the curves of her breasts and bare back, but the noise and smoke limited his vision.

Sitting next to Schade and Darkley, the gray diplomat watched a thin despairing couple of 50 years at a nearby table progress into sad inebriation. "You know, a colleague of mine in the FO, an Ambassador to one of the Balkan countries one can't seem to keep track of, described to me one shabby night in Sofia the three stages of getting tight: 'slightly dappled,' 'progressively pooped,' and 'downright marinated.' I can't recall his name, Lawrence Antro-something, I think, but I've found his to be a fairly accurate measuring device. Alas." He sat back and averted his eyes as the woman struggled helplessly with a box of matches. Her partner had fallen asleep.

Their food arrived with a tired flourish as the singer climbed on to the stage and stood next to the piano, a blonde smile pleading for acceptance saying this time it will be better because it gets better each time - it really does. On their plates lay a sliver of meat alleged to be beef (*"Nur das erstklassigste Rindfleisch bei uns!"*), a minute amount of potatoes, embellished with a teaspoon of thin colorless sauce, and a small round object resembling a baked roll. "Generic meat," someone at the table said. "For the Germans this is probably luxurious," a general added. "Maybe we should have left it for them." But most ate something from their plates and hesitantly sipped from their glasses. Darkley leaned toward Schade. "Get the *bill* as soon as you can. I *think* we've had enough of this." The hard blonde barely made the last four high notes of the torch song about the waiter whose girlfriend fell in love with a bear in the zoo as the group scraped their chairs on the floor and marched out of the club, several of them politely clapping their hands together as they went. The bill totaled 152 Reichsmarks and Schade paid the meaningless sum without thinking. He knew the club had charged them the legal rates but that a German would have paid double or triple. What difference did it make, after all? The money had no value, barter drove the city's economy, not cash, unless the cash was dollars or pounds sterling. Possession of these currencies automatically made Germans into criminals and few of them had access to anything but their own worthless paper scrip. Schade felt relief when they emerged into the light evening air and he breathed deeply to clear his lungs and brain.

General Sender announced that they would motor to his quarters "for a real drink." As they walked into the commodious living room they could not help noticing the large black-white-red flag with the twisted cross in the center covering the couch. Schade thought it a strange war trophy and no one mentioned it. Since none of them felt they had actually eaten supper, the general had his cook prepare what appeared in comparison to be an elaborate meal, which they consumed with relish and gusto, desultorily discussing their tour, the condition of the country, and the methods for best administering the chaotic mess. The general had a table big enough for all of them to sit without battering their neighbor's elbows and the middle-aged German houseman served with a professionally detached but attentive manner so smooth they hardly registered his presence.

As they settled around the table ("No, lieutenant, stay and have some wine and food. We'll not stand on ceremony this evening."), the houseman opened several bottles of prewar vintage white Bordeaux and Rhein-Hessen, but left it to the men to pour their own, trusting they would find none of the bottles so inferior as to be undrinkable. The general regretted not having the appropriate glasses, to which the old diplomat responded, "General, we thank you for a wine of this quality, which will taste the same in either a water glass or Rosenthal crystal." Schade found the German wine far too sweet so drank sparingly of the Bordeaux. The houseman laid out china anointed with the von Kalckdorff family crest and silverware from the army quartermaster supplies. The makeshift meal consisted of sliced tomatoes ("By god, Sender, where did you find these? Haven't seen a tomato in months!") drizzled with olive oil and dried herbs; fresh white bread baked that afternoon for the officer's mess; yellow margarine, which the cook melted over the boiled potatoes sprinkled with dried parsley; followed by apples and an unidentified but pungent soft cheese.

General Sender told one of his "occupation stories" as he called them ("We all have one or two, don't we? Heh, heh."). "What happened to the Rühmann fellow, Lieutenant?" Without waiting for an answer he turned to the company at large. "This fellow was a famous actor on the stage and in the movies, sang too, I think. A star, close to the nazi bigwigs. Anyway, this is his house, villa. We requisitioned it. One day not too long ago he came into the office here and asked if he and his wife could have some linens and photographic equipment from the house. Haven't got the faintest idea where they're living now. They had to leave rather quickly when we took over here. So they want this stuff. How about that? Well, we're not unfeeling monsters and these people have to live as best they can, don't they? I mean, this guy's no war criminal. So we gave him the linens. The equipment is still here somewhere, unless it moved to Frankfurt." The general coughed his chuckle and the others laughed briefly, politely, with more indifference than interest. Everyone had one or two occupation stories. Schade never had the opportunity to answer the question, although he could have told them precisely what had happened to Heinz Rühmann.

As Schade wondered what he was doing there and wrestled with the question as to why he felt slightly drunk on so little alcohol, someone asked him whether the Russians cooperated with his office. He allowed several answers to flit through his mind before he settled on one that would provoke as little response as possible. "We don't see much of them, but so far we've had no more trouble with them than with the British. The French haven't opened for business yet." He hoped this constituted a cautious statement; it was true enough.

The gray diplomat coughed and drank deeply from his French wine, looking much older in the bright lights of the general's dining room than he had in the half-twilight in the city's streets. "I don't hold out much hope on that score. Frankly, my experience in Moscow these last years gives me little encouragement that we will achieve harmony in foreign policy vis à vis Germany. I wish it were otherwise; after all, we've just fought a horrible war as allies, but we have to face the situation as it exists, not as we might desire it to be. I may be an old man, gentlemen, and I'm set in my ways, and I'm certainly a firm believer in the free enterprise system, but I know the Soviets and I tell you it's not going to be easy, and it may turn out to be impossible. If we aren't very hardnosed in the negotiations from the start it simply is not going to work. I've sat across from Stalin at the bargaining table often enough these past years: he respects only power and the willingness to use it. If we don't show him immediately that we mean business and hold them to the agreements, they'll take whatever they can get. The antagonism, the hostility between us already exists - how can it be otherwise? - and will continue to grow, and Germany is where the conflict will be played out. Anyone with half an eye and a peabrain can see that. I've told the president and the secretary that. Unfortunately, I don't think they're convinced. They don't realize yet that the inherent tendency of the communist system is to expand, as is capitalism to be sure, but our system is a natural process, not one forced at the end of a gun. We're the big competitors, it's clear, we always have been. The president's still too new in the job. He'll learn though." His gravelly voice made the last statement so flatly that no one said anything for a moment, during which the diplomat drank more wine. Gradually the conversation resumed with the diplomat at the center, answering and expounding on his theme, adding examples and elaborations in a quiet, assured tone in a vice-grip of conviction. No one disagreed with him out loud.

    Schade contributed nothing further to the discussion as befitted a very junior officer in the presence of so much brass. He drank and smoked too much, exhibiting the only visible signs of disturbance, but no one noticed as helpless dismay filled his eyes. When the group broke up, General Sender and Colonel Darkley thanked him for his labor, and the general had his guests sign the blank front page in a leather bound copy of *Mein Kampf*. "My guest book, heh, heh. Not bad, eh?" None of the officers offered Schade a ride, so he walked to his quarters, numb and shaken, and he could not sleep that night.

> *Erstens kommt es anders, zweitens als man denkt.*
> *Was du unternimmst: es wird dir nichts geschenkt.*
> *Darum leg dich ruhig schlafen*
> *Oder macht mit allem Schluß:*
> *Es kommt alles wie es kommt,*
> *Es kommt alles wie es muß.*[15]

* * * *

Notionally aware of each other's needs, they tried not to make excessive demands on the other. After the first weeks they met whenever they could arrange to be in the same place at the same time; the demands of their work, the difficulties of transportation, and their guilt left such

---

[15]First it'll be different, second as one expects/Whatever you start, nothing is free/So lay quietly down to sleep/Or end it all now/Everything will happen as it happens/ Everything will happen as it must.

meetings to the consistencies of sexual and other desires. Their lovemaking ratcheted up and down the scale of intensity like an erratic fever measured by a thermometer overfilled with the mercury of passion, leaving them both simultaneously depleted and fulfilled. The ambiguities of their relationship exhausted and exhilarated them, creating an unintended push-pull emotional swing that somehow drew them together.

After a judicious amount of rationed whisky and unregistered cash, a clerk in the billeting office requisitioned a room with a separate entrance in a small villa not too far from Milinowskistrasse where they could be alone, and he moved into it under a hailstorm of Makepeace's sarcastic witticisms. Her room in the house near the Schiffbauerdamm, which she shared with Claudia Kaufmann and the others, embarrassed both of them when he stayed overnight there because the circumstances afforded no real privacy and the presence of an American soldier, officer or not, made everyone uncomfortable. "In the morning one of us goes out to the spigot for water. The pipes in the houses on that street have not been repaired. When the electricity is on we drink ersatz coffee and heat water for washing. If not, we wash cold. Our hair tends to be greasy. It's fine now, but when winter comes...."

"Your smell is erotic."

"When I start to stink you won't think so. You Americans can't stand sweaty bodies."

"But I'm not fully American, am I?"

She continued to gain weight; not the puffy flesh of an ersatz and starch diet with little nutrition, but a few solid pounds that rounded her malnourished angles. She remained slender but the food he inevitably provided began to hide her ribs and shoulder bones; the dark pouches under her eyes lightened and gradually blended into her cheeks.

He delighted in the new firmness and weight of skin and flesh, the new curve of her bottom. Laughing one evening, he said, "Your breasts stand up to say hello." In indeterminate anguish she swayed between guilt and satisfaction, and with terrible seriousness answered: "Will you smile when they say good-bye? Tell me, I want to know." He could not answer and spoke of other things.

* * * *

Harrigan wondered aloud at the premiere of her first play since the surrender: "Why did McCrae put John in charge of movies? He'd have been perfect for the theater - and could have done it as well as I can, with his connections."

"That's why you're in charge of theater and he isn't," Makepeace replied affably. "Old EB knows what he's doing."

"I suppose you actually think that makes some sort of sense. Wouldn't surprise me if you put him up to it."

"It's time to go in, the curtain's going up. And stop chewing that gum for a while. I've heard this is a good one." It wasn't, of course; it was the harmless bit of fluff Buchdow put up as his first production while he worked to create something new that would satisfy his striving after art and pass the Allied censors. Gisela, however, transcended the inept script and chockablock improvised sets to invest her character with a brittle, light pattern of behavior perfect for the role.

* * * *

Schade sometimes asked about her past, but always lightly, as if it were of little consequence, as if he were showing polite interest, a ploy which fooled her not at all, but which she appreciated nonetheless. He did not wish to interrogate her or seem unduly inquisitive, but he could not deny the impulse of natural curiosity and he urgently wanted to know about her life, what experiences had formed her, even though he realized that many of these had been painful and humiliating. In some small way he thought she owed him her past, or at least a version of it, so he gently but firmly persisted. And she always answered his questions, though in different ways. When preoccupied or secretive, she responded as briefly and circumspectly as possible, making the most limited interpretation of his inquiry. At other times, she allowed the story a fullness of detail that astonished him. Even if the tale she told was not a happy one (the inevitable demand for sex in return for roles, once with a well-known woman director; the loss of her first puppy to a yellow Mercedes in the Tiergarten; the separation from her father at the end of the war, from whom she still had no word...), she often remembered it to him in refined images with a concreteness and objectivity he sometimes found painful. In a strange way his pain pleased her and she often related details she normally repressed because they caused him pain.

"My father had some connections which helped me get into acting school. I have a certain amount of talent it seems so I got the usual small roles in those awful pictures and some in better plays. But after that I had to fuck my way into the bigger parts too often. If the war had gone on I probably would have had to fuck Goebbels or Heinkel to get the starring roles. Does that shock you?" It did not shock him; he knew enough about the film and theater business in any country; still he cringed inside. He may not have loved her in a clear and profound way, but he felt a great need and affection for her. "No, but it's vulgar," he said, meaning it was sad.

"Well, I have no intention of doing that again. It's too humiliating. Only twice was it different: he took time to undress and at least pretend there was some genuine emotion, and with the woman it was somehow cleaner. But I will not submit to that anymore." Then she stopped, her eyes widening dangerously, as if her freshly drawn eyebrows would lose themselves in her tumbling blonde hair. Laughter burbled up from the back of her throat beginning in the low register of arid amusement, and quickly rising to the edge of hysteria and helplessness. "Oh, god! What am I doing now?" It took him a long time that day to soothe her lacerated nerves, but he failed to convince her that a difference existed between then and now.

And inevitably she had to speak of the violation of women, herself, so common in the early days of the occupation. "They did it to me right there in the street three of them an old man tried to stop them they shot him and kept on when the third one was finished the first wanted to go at me again but they saw another girl and chased off after her when they couldn't do it again so soon they became angry and beat her to death but I got away hiding in the rubble until it was dark when I got back to Joachim and the others I was hysterical and he gave me the drug again that let me forget for a while." She told him this in a dull, metallic voice as if reciting something memorized. And like all of the men to whom the women told the story, he had no adequate response and felt ashamed. He would learn later that this was only one of the versions of the story she told.

*

"Do you know Helmuth Kronauer?" she asked as they walked through the Grunewald in the brightness of the early evening. He had heard of him, of course, but they had not met. "He used to own a newspaper in the city, before 1933. The nazis put him out of business soon after they took over the government. They 'requisitioned' his newspaper for the duration. I don't know how he and his wife survived, but they did. Their daughter was not so lucky. She was killed in Poland. Worked for some party organ confiscating art works and books. I don't know the details.

"My father knows him well, Kronauer; they belonged to the same club. Very English they were, almost as if they'd come from Hamburg. Helmuth loves the city. But he's terribly frustrated because he doesn't know quite what to do about it, the city I mean. The British are looking at his application to start the paper again, but the process is very slow, even for an anti-nazi."

"There are so many frustrated anti-nazis in Berlin, thousands of them. In fact, everyone here was an anti-nazi if you ask them. In any case, the Brits are more flexible about these things than we are; he's lucky he applied there."

"Don't be so defensive. I know the situation. Would it be helpful if you talked to your friend Ogilvy? After all, what's the use in having influence if one doesn't use it, don't you think? Playing up to the victors has always been the role of the defeated." After a moment she said, "I'm sorry, now I'm sounding defensive ... and mean. We're all horribly frustrated. It's part of our lives now. Like hunger, disease, infant death, rape. We can't escape it. Some friends of mine found a way to get to Munich; it's not as bad there, only one victor to deal with, but it's similar. Many people are trying to get out of the city; they think food will be easier to find, jobs.... Helmuth is going to stay, of course. He still has faith in the ability of the people here to snap back. *Berlin kommt doch wieder*. You know, it's fun rehearsing again. At least I've got a good part, even if the show is stupid. Joachim is really a fine director. But that's not what I wanted to say."

"Ogilvy probably can't do anymore that I could, but I'll mention it to him. Perhaps he can speed up the process. Why doesn't he apply in the French sector?"

"I think he has an arrangement with other publishers in the French and American sectors not to compete for licenses if possible. The British is the only one without a licensed newspaper."

"So much for our idea of democratic free market capitalism. I'll talk to Ogilvy."

"Thank you, Jonathan. But please don't mention this to Helmuth."

"I don't know the man."

"Ah, that's the point. He's inviting some people to his house to discuss the situation. I've told him about you, something about you. He wants you to come, if you wish."

"How open are they going to be with an American officer at the table?"

"You could wear civilian clothes."

"Don't have any here. We're in the Army now."

"It will only be a small group, darling, and you know some of them already: Walter Boltzmann, and I think he invited Reinhard Woller, though I can't see why. He makes me uncomfortable, and his breath is foul."

"Perhaps...."

"Surely it would be of benefit to know what the Berliners are thinking about...?"

"We know what they're thinking." Schade laughed sourly. "We have our sources."

"I don't like you very much when you speak like that."

"Circumstances aren't what we'd like, but we do have to act, don't we? We have to move forward. The means are not the best, but we have to use what we have."

"Filthy informers ... just like the nazis."

"Not so filthy. Not informers in the usual sense either. They want to build a new Germany as much as the Kronauers do. At least they realize it cannot be done without us."

"It would be good, I think, if you talked to Helmuth. Not in your office, not officially."

"I'll think about it."

"You might learn something."

"No doubt, no doubt...."

*

"You know, you don't really love me either," she said.

"I know that, but knowing it doesn't make things any better. We both want to love each other, but we can't. The reasons may be different but the results are the same."

Her smile did not quite fill her eyes ... her lips expressed what she was capable of feeling. "Think of the opportunities that gives us for knowing each other. We don't have love as an obstacle to our development. That's a marvelous thing, no? So full of possibilities."

"Do you believe that?" He looked out the window at the empty street.

"No, but it's nice to think about it that way. We enjoy each other in spite of this crippled situation, don't we? We indulge each other's desires with less and less restraint. Yesterday I had a wild urge to perform an obscenity on you in the park. That is new for me, it is exciting! We're as healthy as we can be under the circumstances, no? If sex is the only way we can reach

each other, let it be so. Stop picking at the scabby edges of our wounds."

"Have you been studying psychology?"

She refused to talk to him any further and, wrapping herself in indignant silence walked out of the room leaving the door open. He did not see her for a week. To his surprise her absence did not cause him as much discomfort as he anticipated. He worked later than usual and filled the time he might have spent with her doing other things. Images of her remained with him, of course, often erotic, sometimes tender: her face relaxed into vagueness when sleeping ... her body rigid in orgasm as she brought both of them to climax with her fingers ... the moment of glorious fulfillment after a good performance rewarded by the audience with a standing ovation ... the sweat-drenched face and blonde tendrils of hair as she pushed her body off the floor over and over again to strengthen her arm muscles....

* * * *

In the dim yellow chandelier light spreading into the brown darkness of the dining room, Kronauer's heavy Biedermeier furniture appeared to stand watch in the deeper darkness over the five people sitting around the large oak table covered with a fine lace cloth, upon which stood three open bottles of old wine, five bulb-shaped wine glasses with dark green stems, several short thick unlit blue candles on saucers, bright red and orange ceramic ashtrays and packets of American cigarettes. Later Schade remembered them in a dark sepia Victorian vintage photograph, as if the photographer had caught them all unaware and they all wished they had been sitting in different positions. Despite the open windows and the faint stirring of cool autumn evening air, smoke suffused the room and caused the low-watt bulbs, flickering dangerously close to extinction from time to time when the city's electricity weakened, to shed less illumination than stipulated on their labels.

    The great old house in Dahlem near the Botanical Garden, barely damaged by the war, had been requisitioned by a Red Army colonel in May shortly after the German surrender, a situation which saved the building and the Kronauers from further depredations by the rank and file. ("At least I could stop making myself look absolutely ugly in my own house," Mathilde expostulated. Gisela envied the other woman's supply of makeup: actors found very little of it available in the city so they appeared on the stage, even under the weak lights, much paler than they actually were.) When the Russian moved out with his orderly, the Americans moved in and proved to be distanced and mostly absent but polite guests who left the Kronauers almost completely to themselves, paying a small weekly sum for "services," which mainly consisted of washing their bed linens and making breakfast for them on the occasional weekend when they left for work later than usual. The Kronauers, and most other Berliners, observed with some bafflement the fact that all the officers and enlisted men worked seven days a week and only took time off as they could. The "guests" provided their own food and coffee, which after the first weeks they shared with their hosts whenever they ate there. And although these rooms remained requisitioned until the end of the military government, there were periods when no Americans lived there, and when they did, their presence did not influence the fact that the house became a focal point for various social events as well as tense, heated meetings about what the Germans could do to influence the course of their own economic and political development under the occupation and thereafter.

It was in this grand house that in the early days of each year the Kronauers' friends met for drinks and olives before they all went off to the annual ball at Walterchens Ballhaus, "where homos and heteros greet, meet and mix," as the maitre d' never tired of saying when tipsy. The Kronauers felt fortunate that they had been able to maintain ownership of their house throughout the lean years of the Third Reich; others thought this fact somehow incriminating because they could not solve the mystery of how the Kronauers actually earned an income during those same years, a mystery the suspects themselves declined to unravel.

Now at the head of the table presided the silver-haired, still rather portly Helmuth Kronauer, former and future newspaper owner, relentless devotee of the city's good life and unofficial popular culture, the things he had sorely missed since the mid-1930s. To watch him enjoy the first swallows of a freshly opened bottle of wine was an experience no one forgot and indeed discovered that it helped them to better appreciate the liquid of the gods themselves: half the pleasure came from Kronauer's luxuriant appreciation of the wine, the other half from tasting the wine itself. As the Third Reich continued its attempt to destroy recognizable European culture, these experiences became rare as the wine became less available and the occasions to drink it with enjoyment collapsed into fear and war. Those years, particularly after the Gestapo finally closed down his newspaper after a process of slowly throttling it by increased reductions of the amount of newsprint he could buy, resembled a massive hole in his life, an empty space in which nothing lived or died, a void he could not entirely comprehend, but which his memory constantly attempted to penetrate in a driven search for something of positive meaning to remember. The abruptness of the rupture had startled him, knocking him off balance: his life style had not changed until he no longer had the newspaper and an income, but then it radically altered when he could no longer move about the city's nightlife as he had in the past, not only because of his own material circumstances but because the city's life itself had radically altered. When his daughter, Ulrike Cleopatra, joined the party and then, during the war, went to work for that fatuous ass Rosenberg's cultural plunder commando in the east, Kronauer teetered on the edge of the abyss of hopeless despair. When she disappeared in the violence of the Red Army's juggernaut campaign to crush German military resistance, he maneuvered the memory of her into a deep pocket of his mind and did not think of her; Mathilde refused to mention her name as long as a chance existed that Ulrike might have survived.

After the loss of his newspaper, although he learned to adjust to the new environment, Kronauer never ceased missing the old culture in which he felt so comfortable. "I suppose I simply could not, or refused, to accept the permanence of this utterly barbaric society in which I did not feel at home. But somehow one had to accommodate oneself, no? After all, one had to feed one's family and pay the bills. Resistance is all well and good to contemplate, but what if it is clearly futile? What could we do at the time but plot and talk. Perhaps we didn't have the right connections. Not all of us are capable of martyrdom and many of us are cowards."

At the other end of the table, Mathilde Kronauer radiated the confidence and security she had learned at a young age as the necessary characteristics to be successful as a woman at a certain level of society. Noted in the city as a flirt when young, she maintained her reputation as a very feminine woman while at the same time silently announcing a seriousness that enforced a certain distance between her and the men or women with whom she conversed, a distance her children did not escape, though she favored her daughter and did not suffer the young woman's defection to the barbarians as much as her husband. The simple but elegant and costly clothing she wore, the sparse use of makeup and jewelry, and her severely pinned up deeply auburn hair ("Thank god one can find coloring again, not that I need more than a tint now and then.") contributed to her image as a controlled and controlling personage to whom a certain respect had to be paid even if one loathed her. Her brilliant smile did not always conceal the diamond hard brilliance of her deep seablue eyes.

Most people with whom she dealt thought of her as a formidable woman to be treated with caution and respect, an attitude which suited her own needs and did no harm to her husband's interests in the city's cultural and financial worlds. Colonel Darkley, who came from a similar level of society in New York and Connecticut, once described her as "a tyrant who clothes her imperiousness in polite charm." Reinhard Woller expressed the matter somewhat more bluntly when he said to Harrigan at a gallery opening, "Her suggestions have the effect of orders; one must obey them, although later one often wonders why one has done so." Harrigan never completely understood why she chose him to seduce: he could, after all, do nothing for her husband directly since newspapers did not fall into his bailiwick. This was, of course, the reason she made the effort: her mind worked through twisted passages and she believed everyone else's worked the same way. "I presented her with a challenge, I suppose: she knew I didn't particularly want sex with women, but I always thought that was the least of it, actually. Lovely, but devious."

Harrigan quite naturally talked about her husband's case with Kirshhof and his successor, Kenneth Farisse, as well as with their British counterpart. But only later did he come to believe in a real connection, and by then they had become friends of sorts and Helmuth Kronauer had his newspaper license. "Mathilde could never have gotten to first base with Kirshhof, but Kenneth would have jumped at the chance. I'm not at all sure why I went along with her. Nonetheless, I actually almost had fun. A less than noble experiment, but one should be flexible in these matters." (It was Harrigan who brought them the welcome news that their son, Jürgen, had not been killed in action, only wounded, and that he now served a different master as a prisoner of war in a French labor camp working in the mines near Strasbourg.)

Mathilde Kronauer in no way believed that she or her family should become martyrs of any sort, although she believed that she had never compromised with the nazi regime on any important issue. She did find it disturbing how often her mind turned these days to food, something most people in Europe understood to be a natural reaction to the lack of sustenance. She found herself dreaming while wide awake about white fish filets poached in court bouillon served with a large mound of mayonnaise tartar sauce and cold sliced potatoes sprinkled with chopped green onions and drizzled with vegetable oil accompanied by a large glass of cold beer and a freezing glass of Steinhäger. To her dismay her mouth watered and she quickly swallowed the dream before anyone noticed.

Now, dressed in a gown made for her figure at a time when she ate well and regularly, she watched her husband and their guests with wary, glittering eyes, ready to pounce on any idea she considered ill-conceived or potentially a threat to her family's well-being. In her eyes one could also read the sad sense of loss: recent history had reduced her once scintillating weekly salon evenings to this shabby caricature: only the house was the same, but now it sheltered a meager skeleton of the past.

She had not deliberately patterned her salon on those of Henriette Herz and Rahel Varnhagen, whose weekly gatherings included most of the intellectuals present in Berlin at the end of the 18th century. The two Jewish women were aware that the city possessed no university and each in her own manner offered a useful and interesting substitute as a center of intellectual exchange where ideas could be analyzed and discussed in a milieu free from pomp and inhibitions. The subjects thus discussed ranged more widely over the cultural and political spectrum than those in ostensibly Christian houses. Alexander von Humboldt often referred to his family seat as Schloss Langeweile (Boredom Castle). Differences among the salons existed on many levels. Rahel Varnhagen held hers in a spare attic room at Jägerstrasse 54, not in a drawing room of a polite bourgeois house like Herz, whose husband lectured on philosophy in theirs. The topics at Bettina von Arnim's salon tended to be more political and the opinions expressed there were more liberal. When a senior bureaucrat in the Ministry of Foreign Affairs once compared Mathilde Kronauer's gatherings to von Arnim's, she snapped, *"Ich bin keine Bettina von Arnim. Die war doch eine Kommunistin!"* No one would deny she was not Bettina von Arnim, but one might have gagged at the notion she was a communist.

Upon hearing this, Schadow chuckled and murmured, "Says more about the speaker than about the subject. Bettina was far from being a communist."

On the other end of the spectrum of women in the city who successfully swam in the streams of various social levels, Kronauer was fond of mentioning the *ur-Berlinerin*, known as Madame du Titre, who in her old age allegedly made the statement, "*Wenn ick so denke, wer von meine Verwandten all det scheene Geld erbt, mocht' ick am liebsten jarnich sterben.*" Like any other dialect in any language, the Berlin version is difficult to translate, but the meaning of the passage is stated easily enough. "When I think about my relatives who'll inherit all this gorgeous money, I'd rather not die at all."

As soon as it became clear that the Allies would defeat Germany, Mathilde began to think about reviving her salon. Once she accomplished this she would know their lives had again achieved the social plateau they had once inhabited so comfortably. She had not been prepared for the nature of the defeat and the severe strictures and depredations of the occupation. On the subject of the rape she preferred repression to analysis, but she would not give in to the impulse to join the hundreds of women who resolved the matter by suicide. If revenge were possible, she would eat it cold. If not, she would recreate her life as closely as possible to what it had been and conduct herself as if the violation had never happened. She was grateful for the penicillin Helmuth somehow procured from the British military hospital that cured the gonorrhea given to her, but she resented the necessity for the gratitude. She promised herself that none of this would retard her progress in lifting her family back onto the stage of city life it had once occupied.

Boltzmann loomed above the side of the table, his gaunt length propped up by a bony elbow, his hand engulfing a wine glass and an unlit cigar as if he considered dueling with it. His face resembled a loose watchspring: it contracted and expanded at unexpected junctures in time and place. And one rarely knew his true feelings until the clockwork achieved a form of equipoise and settled into a recognizably human pattern of responses. Unusually subdued because drunk from the generously poured Kronauer wine sloshing about in his empty stomach, he concentrated on making his points lucidly and concisely, not trusting himself to handle long, syntactically complex sentences. The only visible indication of his condition appeared on the unnaturally red skin of his flushed, tired face, a coloring that began a startling transformation into a bright shade of mauve when his mind slipped into overdrive at some contested notion in the discussion. It required a great effort of will on his part to restrain his proclivity to bellow at such points. Mathilde Kronauer ignored his occasionally raw behavior, remembering earlier times when this good friend and colleague of her husband conducted himself with perfectly proper manners and graced her dinner table with charm and wit. Since the death of his wife and daughter in an artillery barrage late in the war, and his experiences on the eastern front including losing an arm to a *"Frikadellechirurg"* (meat grinder surgeon), Boltzmann depended upon a certain level of alcoholic bluster to maintain his emotional and mental balance. He suffered from a recurring dream in which round-edged brown young girls just beyond puberty bathed him in milk with their long, deep black hair. To her friend and former lover, Ursula Opladen, Mathilde Kronauer described Boltzmann as "dangerous and fascinating."

Gisela barely touched her wine as she followed and contributed to the conversation with a chilly passion whenever a subject that interested her came up. Her honey-blonde hair had now grown quite long, and she wore it unpinned to her shoulders, which allowed her to toss it out of her face with some regularity, a gesture she thought accentuated her femininity, but which annoyed Schade who thought it affected. The Kronauers understood the motivation and appreciated the pleasure one could obtain from freshly washed hair after so long without the possibility.

Schade smoked and drank in moderation, torn between the desire to represent his adopted country's interests and the equally persuasive urge to simply participate in the thrust and parry of the conversation without the necessity of defending actions and policies with which he did not always agree. From time to time his attention wandered to the high bookshelves that lined the wall he faced on the other side of the table. Although he could not read the titles on the spines, the missing volumes, victims of the victorious army's depredations and primitive notions of plunder, left gaps in the rows that stood out like missing teeth in the wide mouth of an amateur boxer. ("I am sure none of them, including the officer who stayed here, could read a word of the books they took. They could barely read Russian much less German, French and English, but they somehow knew the books had value.") The complete collection of Schadow's works once graced these shelves; Schade promised himself he would replace them if he could. Kronauer would appreciate that gesture and it would allow him a certain amount of satisfied pleasure. Schade knew of no other dining room that boasted a wall of books.

Through the open windows the muted sounds of the city's suburb effortlessly penetrated the house. Though no clock remained in the house to show the time, it was after ten-thirty and only the most foolish or courageous Germans remained on the streets.

"The city has been badly damaged, but not beyond repair." Dressed in a pre-war black suit, silk tie and highly polished if battered English brogans, Kronauer lifted his wine glass to his lips with the deep satisfaction of one who has abstained for a long period from an indulgence in a pleasure that chased shivers of exquisite excitement through his sensory switches. "We are fortunate the members of the victorious Allied Armies did not find this -- but we hid it well. The Gestapo, not to speak of our local Dahlem police, never found it either, but they didn't search too strenuously. We are not Jewish and what did those cretins know about fine French wine? In fact, this was once a very fashionable wine, everyone drank it. Unobtainable in the city now. Fashion, indeed," he mused staring into the wine. "In Berlin at present we have no time to be fashionable. Let Paris and London be fashionable. I lived in Alexandria once, before we married, did you know that, Gisela? Do you remember what Morgan Forster said about it? All those beautifully well-dressed people eternally driving back and forth, along the Corniche, wasn't it...?" Mathilde smiled at her husband, softening the angles of her face. How like him to allow them to believe he thought they would, of course, know the writer Morgan Forster and his book about Alexandria. She was sure that only Schade at the table, other than her husband, actually did know of the Englishman; she herself certainly had never heard the name before. "We may have had some of that here, once, but now we can only walk or stumble along, and we're in rags. Well, more or less, metaphorically for certain. Not that we don't deserve it. Eventually we may have better, or at least newer clothes and drive new but not better automobiles -- nothing is eternal about this city anymore." He sighed and grimaced. "Was anything ever eternal here?" Then he looked at Schade with a glint of amusement in his eyes. "We have two of your colleagues staying with us, you know. At first they did not speak to us because of the non-fraternization policy. Economists, I believe. It was all rather amusing. Well, no actually amusing is not the appropriate word. Silly, perhaps."

"I'm surprised they allowed you to stay."

Boltzmann snorted and lit his cigar, but said nothing. Kronauer shifted his stiffened leg under the table and sipped his wine. "Ah, at first they planned to kick us out, but we were able to adjust the matter with the officials who make such decisions. It helps to have a reputation of sorts on such occasions." He said this with a smile somewhere between self-deprecation and pride.

"You're too modest, Helmuth," Gisela murmured and turned to Schade. "One is never quite sure with him. His connection with the resistance, for example. He keeps the details to himself ... a useful habit, no doubt. Only one hears things...."

The older man laughed briefly. "The fact that the nazis shut down my newspaper early is well-known and that is helpful now, I must admit. In any case, our two Americans are rarely here and surprisingly quiet when they are." He tapped his walking stick gently on the plum-colored rug. "I knew your father slightly, lieutenant, did you know that?"

"No, not at all."

"He came to Berlin quite often on business or to visit the SPD central before the nazis shut them down. Our meeting is not as strange as it may appear. Regardless of where my own sympathies lay, and they did not lie on the left, my newspaper based its reputation on its objectivity. Very unusual in the city. We attacked both left and right, or praised them, with equal vehemence. In the end, of course, this did not help us survive the *Gleichschaltung* after 1933. You needn't be surprised. Gisela has told me of your name change. That's amusing. There's also a touch of irony in your presence here, no?"

"No, not irony, a grotesque twist of fate, perhaps. There are a number of us who have come back with a different nationality if not new names."

"But not with a new character, or a completely new culture, I suspect. It must be difficult for you from time to time."

"Not particularly." Schade was annoyed that she had given the information, but Kronauer's charm and wine offered him the welcome opportunity to contain this feeling. In the silence that followed someone's stomach audibly growled an organic protest against the lack of substance in its pouch; no one at the table reacted: it happened to everyone all too often.

"Perhaps not," Kronauer continued smoothly. "We can discuss that at another time. More pressing at the moment is the situation of the city. We are all deeply concerned about the future, Herr Schade. We are not convinced the Allies have concrete practicable plans for reconstruction that they can agree on and that are reasonable. The news we've heard about the Potsdam meeting is not very reassuring, frankly. Too much has been left unsettled. Perhaps the plans are still secret...?"

"I'm afraid I'm not privy to the government's secrets. I know little more than you do about the larger picture."

Boltzmann put down his glass and blew cigar smoke at the ceiling. "I find that difficult to believe, *Herr Leutnant*," he said, clearly attempting a smile to remove a modicum of the sharpness from the remark, but placing a slight emphasis on Schade's rank.

"Alas, it is true." Schade returned the smile and did not feel insulted. "As a lowly junior officer I am hardly privy to such things, as I'm sure you understand, *Herr Feldwebel* (corporal). I suspect there may be a grand plan, but in the nature of things, with such different points of view, agreement on details is difficult to negotiate."

"Yes," Boltzmann said, puffing hard on his cigar. "That is understandable given the two antagonistic systems of society and government, but something must be done about rebuilding the city, and the rest of the nation. A prostrate Germany is in no one's interest in the long run. We are in a strange set of circumstances in Berlin, aren't we? This is, or was, the capital, the epicenter of our national existence and culture--"

"I know some in Munich and Hamburg who would vehemently disagree with that statement," Kronauer remarked, "but it is still the truth." He paused for a moment, but all of them waited, such was his natural authoritarian presence, knowing more would follow. "I love the city. I've lived all my 58 years in it, with brief interludes elsewhere. I know it as well as my own body -- or did until recently. Berlin cannot be allowed to die. One way or another there must be a center for society, a generally agreed upon point of reference around which people can organize themselves. Especially now when everything is fragmented and the recent past is quite correctly denigrated. But to forbid the music of Wagner and Strauss is foolish. Are we to have no past upon which to build the future? Are we to lose Nietzsche? Or Goethe? This is worse than foolish, it is stupidity. One cannot create a culture out of a vacuum."

"No," Schade interrupted, something he would not have done in his former life. "The point is to create a new society out of the less destructive parts of the past. Of course we can't throw everything in the trash bin."

Boltzmann could not control himself and blurted out in English: "Accentuate the positive, blah blah the negative, don't *fummel* around with the center!"

"And who is to decide which parts are the good ones?" Mathilde Kronauer demanded, an edge in her voice, which most of their friends had learned served as a warning of sharper, more biting things to come, unless one retreated from whatever position one espoused, or at least refrained from further expression of it in her presence.

"German or American?" Boltzmann demanded in turn, gulping more of the exquisite chardonnay, causing Kronauer to groan softly at the waste. "Russian? Soviet? British? Latvian?"

The patrician lover of his city sighed and deliberately digressed. "Ah, yes, the Russians. We've had the Russians, en masse, here before, you remember, Walter? During the twenties thousands of them lived here. They were different then, of course, the opposites in fact: émigrés from bolshevik Russia. They lived all over the city in a kind of genteel poverty making ends meet somehow. They had their own restaurants (remember, Mathilde, we used to eat that piquant borscht at the Prince Igor? They were always princes of course.), their own press, their own publishing houses ... remember that young writer who thought he knew all about butterflies? Everything in Russian, of course, few of them ever learned German, they all expected to go back someday soon. I don't think we influenced them very much ... they hardly left any traces here either, though we enjoyed Chaliapin's voice, la Pavlova's legs, Piatigorsky's songs, and some of the novels of that butterfly fanatic, Sirin, I think, were published in German ... but most of them were poor and hungry like most of us until 1924 or 25 when many of them began to live better, like most of us. How they all earned a living remains a mystery to me. Many of them were Jews. Lord knows where they are now. But, you see, the city learned to deal with them, not absorbing them, since they remained isolated in their own communities, but making room for them. That gives me reason for optimism today."

"Helmuth, *des is jo quatsch, manne. Die sind ja keen Mongollen jewesen, wie heut mir die hob'n.*" Boltzmann relaxed into his idiosyncratic Eiffel-Berliner dialect, meaning the Russians then were not the same as the Mongols who marched through the city now.

At the same time, Schade said, "That may be, but the situation is totally different now; the ability to absorb or tolerate is at an end. The destruction is too great and the number of DPs too high." At this Kronauer smiled and tolerantly shook his head, condescending to what he clearly viewed as analytical weakness, if not ignorance of historical fact. "The point is," Schade continued, ignoring the older man's brief gesture, "that the Germans, and the Berliners, can benefit from some elements of American society -- and they'll get them, one way or another."

"Quite right," Mathilde Kronauer interjected. "Perhaps, however, not your racial strictures, lieutenant. We remember all too well our own equivalent of benches 'for colored only'. Still, we have to be left to decide ourselves which of those elements, or else the graft won't take, will it? In any case, we have our own tradition of democracy, as incomplete and blunted as it may be...."

"Nevertheless," her husband interrupted with a brief smile offering his apology, a gesture only those who have lived together for many years can make without failure. "Nevertheless, we need a center, a focal point, if not for a highly centralized government, at least a cultural point of reference. All countries have one. New York, London, Paris, Rome...." He halted for a moment. "Berlin has played this role since unification, despite the claims of Munich. If the nation is to be rebuilt, Berlin must be rebuilt."

Schade had no adequate response to this passionate *Lokalpatriotismus*. He could only nebulously and theoretically envision a Germany other than the one in which he now struggled to play out the current act of his life. No vivid personal memory of the country encompassed this totality. "Yes, it's very complicated, doubly so by the fact that this country must be punished as well. You cannot disagree with that, can you?"

"*Einverstanden*! Many of us agree with denazification and the trials, and agree evil has been committed, a barbarism unknown to the history of mankind, which we haven't quite completed understood." He spoke in sad but emphatic tones, as if working out a problem that resisted a rational solution. "These crimes must be expiated. Retribution will be done, sins will be punished, as they should be. Let us not get into a fruitless argument about that. But a line must be drawn somewhere; destruction must cease and reconstruction begin. Taking the industrial capacity out of Germany for reparations is hardly reconstruction. Are we really all to be made into farmers, harmless peasants tilling the fields to supply the rest of industrial Europe with bread and cheese? Ach, there goes the damned electricity again. Speak of the devil, eh? Though that is hardly the proper phrase in these times, is it? Mathilde, be so kind and light the candles on the sideboard."

He passed around packets of wooden matches and each of them leaned forward to light the candle stumps on the table. Mathilde Kronauer had painfully and carefully hidden the candlesticks beneath the garden surface many months before the final battle in the city. Now, the polished silver reflected the pale flickerings of light projecting a festive if not jolly atmosphere into the room.

She resumed her seat. "*Berlin kommt wieder*," she said. "That must be more than a whimsical hope and the last line of that sloppy sentimental song."

Boltzmann looked up from his contemplation of the wine he swirled around the sides of his bell glass and shifted his left shoulder and its arm stub. "There is no way around Berlin as the center of German culture, god help us. I'd personally prefer Hamburg, where at least they speak decent German."

"The Allies are thinking about banning that song," Gisela murmured with some bitterness.

"No order has been given for that," Schade interjected, "but they are thinking about it. Perhaps it's foolish, but understandable. There must be no return to this city's brown past."

"But Berlin was always red," Mathilde Kronauer snapped, "wasn't it? Look at the voting records. Or have we been misinformed?"

"Berliners have nothing to be happy about, isn't that the theory behind it? It's all part of the punishment, no?" Gisela's voice sounded like cracked ice splashed with cold water.

"Gisela, my dear...," Kronauer mediated.

"Yes, that seems to be the idea. Penance before happiness," Schade admitted in what he hoped was a neutral tone.

"There's little joy in the city now in any case, understandably, but there is a tremendous amount of energy here, underneath the surface of apathy and resignation. It may be energy born of insecurity, defeat and hysteria, but it is a far better sign for the future than depression. Yes, yes, I know, there's enough of that around, it lies on the city like a dreadful choking fog, but the fog isn't suffocating everyone. This city has been the urban spirit non plus ultra since the beginning of the century. We have to foster what's left of that spirit and enthusiasm, the drive and ambition, even the old Berlin kiss-my-ass attitude -- it's the only way to get through this nadir in our history, isn't it? Only through the native vitality can we overcome the past and the occupation (for we'll have to get over that, too, you realize). So much ambition and creativity has been repressed for twelve years, we must nurture this now. If the Allies have any sense of history and any intelligence about the future, they will play their part as well." Kronauer sat back in his chair, exhausted by the expression of these thoughts, the candlelight working shadows in the crevices of his face.

"If the Allies cannot come to a common policy for Germany, will they allow the Germans to develop their future by themselves?" Boltzmann demanded, waving his hand over the wine glass.

"No," Schade said in a monotone, "not now, not yet, perhaps not until it is too late. The Germans must show they've earned anything they're allowed to do."

"Except fuck the victors for cigarettes and a decent meal," Gisela defiantly but softly interjected, blushing, but solidly committed to her statement, tossing her hair back. Kronauer looked pained, and Mathilde quickly added, "Yes, that, too, if put rather strongly," but she smiled and looked with sympathy at the younger woman.

Ever the considerate host, Kronauer said, "You know the reason why one clicks wine glasses before drinking? Wine affords delight to many senses, taste, smell, sight, even touch, but not sound. Ergo, the click to add to the richness of the wine drinking experience. A reasonable theory, don't you think?"

At this, Boltzmann drank off the last wine in his glass, no longer completely sober yet not obfuscated by the alcohol. "The city is like an animal that has been beaten almost to death but still breathes; blood still circulates; it can still eat and digest, but barely. It needs medication and a good diet to survive, to regain its health." His hand began to thump the table in a rhythm approximately matching his verbal pace. "But this particular animal also needs mental and spiritual sustenance. It doesn't need a ridiculous 1200 calories a day, it doesn't need censored newspapers, it doesn't need incomprehensible Russian or American plays, it doesn't need the dismantling of all its industry, it doesn't need the public degradation of its women, it doesn't need the inability of its occupiers to reach an agreement, it doesn't need all this, but this is what it has! God, how long it's been since I pissed asparagus!"

"Our problem has always been an excess of one thing or another," Mathilde Kronauer said sharply. "If we could change that...."

"Excess?" cried Boltzmann. "What is excess here? How do you define it? Berlin is an excess of everything you can possibly imagine, always has been: the excess of Friedrich the flautist, the excess of Otto the international intriguer, the excess of Wilhelm the fatally flashy, the excess of the bloody trenches and mustard gas, the excess of the twenties, economic chaos, bread a billion marks a loaf, hurrah! All the norms shattered, homosexuals everywhere, the motor vehicle takes over our lives, and Hitler! Holy mother of Christ's pecker and the balls of the goddamned prophet! And now? An excess of defeat, occupation, an excess of renewal, an excess of what? Punishment? All the ex-party members are running around scouring the city for documents to show how many Jews they risked their lives to help to save.

Gottverdammtnochamoll! How can there be any normal excess in a city that is itself an excess? It will only get worse. Mark it!" Thus saying, he carefully poured golden wine into his glass and drank deeply.

No one responded immediately to these impassioned statements, but Schade, somewhat embarrassed by the passion exhibited by the older man, wondered how "normal excess" could be defined. They all retreated into their own thoughts, attempting to connect their personal circumstances with the larger condition that sparked Boltzmann's anger. Had Schade not been present, or so he believed, that anger and frustration, fed by hunger and guilt, would have shot forth from each of them into the gloom. Now he said, "No one really knows what will happen. I'm not sure that we even know what we want to happen. Part of the problem is a definition of our responsibilities in Germany. That's been only vaguely negotiated by the governments. Most Americans want to forget the war and get on with life. I can't imagine it's not like that in the other countries as well."

Kronauer smiled sourly. "To the victors belong the spoils of reconstruction. That's irony for you, isn't it? The spoils of war end in the responsibility for the defeated. The final absurd destination of national welfare care for the citizens."

"In the long run you'll have to be responsible for yourselves; you won't be able to depend on us forever...."

"But we don't want to depend on you now!" Gisela's voice contained a plaintive note, but the ice in it did not melt.

"You've no choice now. You committed horrible atrocities, and you lost the war. Now the starvation alone-"

"This isn't the first time Berliners have gone hungry," Kronauer gently but firmly cut Schade off.

"We've been through it before, those of us who are old enough remember. We remember very clearly our empty bellies in the winter of 1916-17, the turnip winter, and the winter of 1918-19 in the defeat and revolution. So much meaning in so much confusion that year. A triple defeat then: the war ended but not the Allied blockade; the Kaiser crossed into Holland never to see the city again; the shaky twice-proclaimed republic ... the city gave itself up to chaos, peace, and revolution. Very exciting, but fatal for many, of course, including our friend Helga Opladen. All of us, regardless of our politics, suffered one thing in common: hunger. Do you remember it, Mathilde? Do you remember, Walter, the fighting in the streets and the dead horses and what happened to them? Weak from malnutrition men and women fell on the horses with whatever sharp object they could grab from the bars and stores along the streets. Some of the animals weren't dead as the knives cut into them. It didn't matter. The people cut them up and went home covered with steaming blood and cooked the flesh and ate it with relish and haste. It didn't help for long, of course; soon enough they were hungry again, and there were no more horses."

Boltzmann growled: "There's an old Berlin saying, of course.

> *Wenn ich einst gestorben bin,*
> *Geh zu meinem Grabe hin,*
> *Leg auf meine kalte Brust*
> *Eine warme Leberwurst.*"[16]

---

[16]The saying can be translated as "When I am finally dead/go visit my grave/and lay a warm liver sausage/on my cold chest." See also endnote.

Kronauer turned slowly toward Schade and Gisela. "So, you see, hunger, too, is nothing new to the city. The difference is that then no foreign army occupied us and Berlin hadn't been bombed into a landscape that looks like a bad expressionist painting."

"More Cubist, I think," Schade offered.

"But that's French," Boltzmann expostulated in all seriousness.

"In any case," Kronauer went on inexorably, not to be deflected from his point. "In any case, that is the major difference, obviously --"

"For women there's another major difference that no one speaks of, isn't there?" Mathilde said quickly, running her words together in a rush to make the point, while her husband plunged on.

"But we went hungry during the mass inflation of the twenties also. For two eggs one could buy a shave, but few of us had two eggs. Money meant nothing, certainly the Reichsmark meant nothing. There was too much of it. Fifty million marks for a turnip! God, how we hated turnips after that. It was best to barter if you had anything. Even better was to have dollars. Many of us went hungry anyway. Hungry and cold ... sometimes we were rather drunk, too; even without money one could always find schnapps. It helped against the cold and hunger." While Kronauer spoke the truth as it affected millions in Germany then, he and his family did not suffer unduly as the owners of a financially healthy newspaper with access to a certain amount of foreign currency, the much sought after Valuta. Nonetheless, the spirit of his peroration held against the standard of historical truth.

"Does history repeat itself? Only partially perhaps. Today's situation can hardly be described as a farce except by some Zeus-like historian on some future Olympus. In those days some made paper fortunes, Stinnes built an industrial empire by manipulating paper money. That cannot happen today, of course, not yet, but who knows what the economy will look like in three years. Of course there is a difference, many differences. One thing remains the same, however. The dollar was king then as it is today. Dollars represented value, marks meant nothing ... that remains the same."

"Except in this case it's cigarettes and Allied occupation marks," Schade said.

"The dollar is still the basis of it all, isn't it? But we've had enough nostalgia, Helmuth, *n'est-ce pas*?" Mathilde Kronauer's thin lips smiled briefly, dismissing the subject.

"Yes, that is correct," her husband continued, unwilling to cease gnawing at the bone of the problem. "Nostalgia is something we cannot afford now. It would be difficult in any case, would it not? I mean nostalgia for the brown past would be foolish at best, at worst evil. The older people are in danger of harking back to the Kaiserzeit or Weimar, but that is self-defeating: we cannot recreate these times. And we shouldn't want to. Still, under the circumstances many Germans have nowhere to look but back to the past, even if they didn't live it, because their imaginations are in a state of suspended animation so they cannot envision any future. *That* is what we must struggle against. Objectively, for us there is nothing *but* the future. It is a very interesting position, don't you agree?"

Boltzmann nodded his bristling head, more from the wine than agreement. What he meant as a laugh emerged as a sarcastic bark. "But Helmuth, that feeling of *Kriegskameradschaft* lends itself to nostalgia, especially after a defeat. Look at the experience after 1918 ... all those front-line troop organizations, all that literature yearning for the days in the trenches when everything was simple and clear and right. The storm of steel as an uplifting, almost religious experience for the nation! Hell, even Remarque's book was an exercise in nostalgia of sorts."

"No, no, there won't be much of that this time. The whole experience was different. The cause was wicked and everyone knows it. There won't be a repetition of that 'youthful comradeship in the trenches' feeling; there won't be any Freikorps. The Allies will see to that since they are in our streets now, and there weren't any trenches this time. No, the defeat has been too final, too public, the cause was too sinful, too negative to motivate that kind of nostalgia."

"So we're left with nothing but the future -- and we've no idea at all what it will be or what part we'll play in it," Gisela cried.

Mathilde Kronauer moved her eyes coldly over the company at her table. When she spoke her voice was colored with bitterness and frustration, the sound of raw iron rasped in her throat. "We *do* have a past we can be proud of and look to for models! There are some of us who do not have to hang our heads like convicted criminals for our own behavior, only for that of others. We *have* been a people of a rich and deep culture; we can and will be so again. We did *not* escape the effects of the Enlightenment. Nor do we need this facile masculine nostalgia for the intimacy of battle and blood lust. We have a heritage we can look back on and learn from."

"Unfortunately, you and those who believe this are a small minority at the moment," Schade said with sadness and arrogance.

"It is this minority which will shape the future," she snapped. "It can be no other way." The finality of her tone expressed an arrogance equal to Schade's. "Our suffering was quite different from the émigré experience, *Herr Leutnant.* We remained here in our homeland, we experienced the criminal regime on our own backs, beating down our own spirit...."

"A comparison of the quality of suffering is not the issue," Schade began in a sharp, angry voice, "resistance or the lack of it is."

"This will get us nowhere," Kronauer interrupted.

Gisela shook her blonde head in short, quick arcs. "We must make our own plans, take our own responsibilities, not just for the past but for the future as well. We can't just wait for the Allies to tell us what to do. I see it all the time in the theater and the Chamber. They wait for orders, they've no initiative. What we *need* is initiative!"

Boltzmann grinned crookedly. "Thus speaks youth. No, no, I mean that positively. That's a fine, healthy attitude, but at the moment unrealistic. We do not have to succumb to the magnetism of national masochism that appeals to so many these days, but we do have to look reality in the face. Illusions such as yours cut off too many possibilities for us. The Allies and our circumstances are limiting us enough as it is."

"And how do you propose to increase our freedom of action if our minds are double trapped in the past from which we cannot escape and which the Allies demand we repudiate?" The question exploded in a reedy voice from a thin dark-suited figure in the doorway. No one had heard him enter, but Reinhard Woller knew how to make an entrance with his intense, burning presence. Woller's habit of speaking swiftly in long sentences arose from the dual experiences of the resistance and the concentration camp: in both, information had to be communicated quickly and clearly. Not everything he communicated, however, was clear to those receiving the information. A communist by conviction, if not party membership (firebrands being viewed with suspicion by the current leadership under the watchful eye of the Soviet "friends"), a student of philosophy and mathematics, he had immersed himself in the creation of what he referred to as the "new, possible Germany." Most people who knew something of his life attributed his frantic activity to the fact that a Ukrainian *Ostarbeiter* killed his father while the latter served as a guard at a factory in Rostock at the same time the Gestapo beat the son with truncheons for suspected treason. Ostensibly he served at the moment as the secretary to the president of the Chamber of Creative Artists, but the CIC officers Schade dealt with believed that Woller gave the political direction to that institution while the aging actor in the presidency, whose moral authority stemmed from having spent most of the nazi years in Moscow, served as a figurehead without any real powers. Woller was an imposing personality, but he abraded people with his unrelenting intensity and intellectual acuity. ("Smart as hell, but wouldn't know a joke if one fell on his head," as Harrigan put it). He also discomfited those who came into close physical proximity to the stink of his breath emanating from a mouth filled with rotting teeth and a stomach permanently sour from various privations and lack of decent food. This was hardly an unusual phenomenon among Europeans, but his colleagues believed that Woller's intense demeanor increased the pungency of his breath.

(To Gisela, the old historian Schadow once quoted Marcus Aurelius on the subject of patient admonition as a method of dealing with others' knotty problems. "Do unsavory armpits and bad breath make you angry? What good will it do you? Given the mouth and the armpits the man has got, that condition is bound to produce those odors

... Apply your reasonableness to move him to a like reasonableness; expound, admonish. If he pays attention, you will have worked a cure, and there will be no need for passion; leave that to actors and streetwalkers." Immediately after having thus so pontificated, the old man burned crimson with embarrassment and hotly apologized for his lack of consideration. The actress shook her hair and laughed, assuring him that actors and whores both needed passion for essentially the same reason: to convince the clientele they were experiencing something real. Schadow's sense of humiliation at his thoughtlessness never quite left him and made him more cautious in his conversations with the young woman who evoked in him such contradictory desires.)

Few, including Gisela, doubted Woller's courage -- he had just broken the curfew and risked arrest or being shot -- but equally few wished to sit next to him.

"Ah, my dear Woller." Kronauer indicated a chair next to his own, showing his willingness to make sacrifices for a discussion of the issues, allowing a radical range of opinion. "Mathilde, remind me to repair the lock on the door. Woller, you push the limits of probability with these nightly perambulations. But we are glad you are here. You know everyone, I think."

"There's never sufficient time and the stupid curfew makes things even more difficult than they need be. Yes, I think I do." He shook hands all around, pausing momentarily in front of Schade as if silently questioning his presence in the gathering. "*Guten Abend, Herr Leutnant.*"

Boltzmann leaned onto the table and grinned. "Do y'know, Herr Woller, why do you click glasses before drinking wine?"

"For the same reason one does it when drinking beer. In jail one learns many obscure and useless things. One of my cellmates thought himself to be a connoisseur of such things. A plumber and active in the trade union and our party, he had been inside for years before I met him. A very brave but not very clever man. He collected such facts, possessed a refined talent for extracting these nuggets of nugatory information from everyone they put in his cell. He said it kept him from going mad. It did nothing to save him in the end. They shot him two days before the end of the fighting."

"Herr Woller, you have a talent for depressing the company," Gisela said with some impatience.

"Now what was that about a mental prison in which we Germans find ourselves?" Kronauer asked lightly, but anticipating fireworks which got his own adrenalin running beyond its usual exhausted pace. For this reason he regularly invited Woller to these discussions despite the good chance of having them degenerate into a sterile but loud exchange of banal political slogans and vituperative personal attacks.

Woller smiled in a slight, artificially self-deprecating manner; once his entrance was made he contented himself with a less dramatic presentation that did not, however, lose any of its intensity. "Perhaps my fatigue has made me somewhat pessimistic about the future, but I believe we Germans have trouble learning from the past. We repeat our history like a small child who doesn't draw the lessons from being thrashed by his elders. Hitler's imperialism repeated the Kaiser's from before 1914; the same bourgeois-capitalist syndrome occurred: war. We learned nothing. The stupid racism of the nineteenth century remains part of our existence; the only difference now is that we've taken it to its final extreme and tried to exterminate a whole people. I wonder what German racism would have been like if we'd had a colonial empire in which to play out the same foul drives. The Germans are even now trying to reestablish the old class structure and yet again repeat the past. But clearly this will not happen because the Soviet Union and the progressive forces of the west will not allow it to happen again. On the other hand, having a new system imposed upon us is the wrong way to go about it, we have to create the system ourselves or it won't take. It is we Germans who must flush the past down the drains, we must not only be the actors in the drama, we must also write the script, we cannot remain merely the observers of the determination of our fate. And we must actively pay for our sins to earn the right of an active existence in the new world. This is why I and my colleagues welcome the denazification policies of the Allies, especially the western Allies. But we must be allowed to do it ourselves through the anti-fascist organizations we've created for just the purpose of preparing for the new society. We must be allowed to purge ourselves of everything associated with the nazis because only then will we be ready for the new society, you see, only then will we have *earned* it." By this point Woller's audience included all of Germany and the great capitals of Europe, yet his high-pitched voice did not scream, the stridency remained modulated to the size of the space in which he spoke. After once listening to him, Schadow noted that the young agitator had welded his own talents to techniques he learned from the theater rather than from recent political oratory.

"You believe the new society will be communist, allied to the Soviet Union?" Schade asked, knowing the answer but wanting to hear its form.

"Eventually a communist Germany will be allied with the Soviet Union, without question; but the rest of the world will also be communist, or socialist, as well, inevitably. But this is in the far future. Germany today does not deserve to have the socialist system simply given to it; its sins against humanity have to be expiated, reparations have to be paid for the atrocities Germany committed against mankind, especially in the Soviet Union. When the Germans have purged their own kind and have taken positive action to change society for the better, toward socialism, then we will be ready for communism."

Schade smiled. "Not every society is ready at the same time, each develops according to its own schedule. And the notion of imposing socialism from the outside is hardly part of the canon."

"You verge on the Trotskyite blasphemy," Woller rejoined lightly, "but you are correct that socialism is not a gift but a stage of development which must be achieved, earned, and struggled for."

Kronauer shifted his stiff leg with some impatience. "You admit yourself that your theory necessitates a long duration, Woller. In the meantime you may write the script and play the parts, but Moscow revises the script and directs the play. What concerns us now is the immediate present and how to deal with it. It seems to me that denazification and reconstruction must be undertaken at the same time."

"I don't believe that is possible; we must denazify and purge ourselves first. No one who was associated with the nazis and their crimes must be allowed to hold any position of responsibility. That is the first law we must follow. Otherwise rebuilding is worthless; in any case, we must not be so concerned with reconstructing the old, but rather with establishing the new. That's the important thing to remember. And now is the time to do it. What better circumstance than this, in the wreckage and flux and chaos? We must take advantage of the opportunity circumstances have given us. May I have a glass of wine?"

Mathilde Kronauer colored slightly at her social faux pas and quickly took a glass from the sideboard and poured it full. No one else at the table recognized the error, except her husband who automatically forgot it as he readily forgot other aspects of her behavior in order that they could continue to live together in a relationship relatively free of tension and conflict. He had long since learned the prices he would pay for loving his wife.

Schade said, "You know that the Soviets pay less attention to denazification than we do."

"There are admittedly certain problems in this area. But they will be cleared up. We have the example of the Americans before us, don't we? Sometimes we must provisionally keep on a few of those infected with the nazi bacillus while we train others to take their place, but that does not negate the validity of the principle."

"That kind of mass denazification isn't really feasible," Kronauer said. "But certainly something like it must be done. The war crimes trials are a start--"

"But only a start, don't you see, only a start. They deal with the very top of the criminal list. We must also punish those who did not sit behind desks and sign papers. The little nazis have too much blood on their hands to be allowed to go free. If we return to the old ways, we will surely repeat the whole shitpile. This cannot happen."

"But what about right now?" Gisela interjected. "What do we do about the city now? It's dying as we sit here babbling about principles."

"No, Fräulein, I don't think the city is dying. That's a mistaken notion. You yourself are an example of exactly the opposite. Those who cry *'anno null'* are misguided and simply laying the groundwork for another myth. The city is not very healthy, but it isn't dying. The Allies will not let it die, for one thing. No, I don't think we should be entirely dependent upon them, but you will agree that we must be realistic."

Boltzmann nodded his head vigorously but erratically, indicating the amount of wine he'd enjoyed. "S'actly what I've been saying all along. Realism above all! Face the facts."

"We are acting now," Woller continued. "We are cleaning our house of the filth that's inhabited it for too many years. It will take time, to be sure, but we've made a start. Now we must ensure that it continues: licensing newspapers, theaters.... Patience is not a characteristic for which the Germans have been well-known, but we will have to learn it, or some form of it. We no longer control our fate completely, of course. The expansion of our control will come with the progressive purging of Germany by *us*, not the Allies. Are we mere integers in the landscape? Are we not characters in our own stories rather than only personalities expressing some idea we're perhaps not even aware of or understand?"

Schade noticed Mathilde Kronauer controlling a fidget with difficulty and knew she would close the discussion soon. One further question chased itself around his mind and he asked it. "And what role do the members of the resistance play in the new Germany, as the only people who actively struggled against the nazis?" He expected an immediate reaction from Mathilde to reinforce her opinion that only those who remained behind had the moral high ground and could thus take the stage in national life after the defeat of the nation. He had at that point no idea whether or not she and her husband had been active in the resistance, and she disappointed him in offering nothing but a slight smile. Woller's answer Schade already knew having read his colleague Henry Alter's report of an interview with Woller some weeks ago.

"We in the resistance failed in our task of overthrowing the fascists. Consequently, we have no right to ask for a privileged position or to make demands. Not at the moment. On the other hand, who is better placed from experience and moral stature to take on those tasks?" Woller seemed to sink into himself for a moment. His empty stomach joined the symphony of the city and gurgled aloud and a burp escaped his lips. "No, we did not achieve our ends. But this is not all bad because if we had achieved an early end to the war by overthrowing Hitler, Germany would not have gotten the necessary amount of punishment and suffering required for its rebirth, the development of historic necessity would have been broken and the process stopped too soon."

"One can see your Hegelian training, my dear Woller," Kronauer said, "but that is a most horrifying thought. If Hitler had been assassinated or imprisoned, hundreds of thousands of lives would have been saved."

"What makes you so sure that removing Hitler would have meant the end of the war? The system would have continued the war in one form or another. The system had to be defeated. Because there is reason in history. Hegel saw that, so did Marx and Engels. The historic process of the 20th century demanded imperialist Germany should be destroyed in order to build a new society. That is the dialectic. I believe it is true, yes, despite the deaths." He said this with such force that silence dropped over the table.

Restlessly unhappy with this level of ratiocination, Gisela broke into the silence. "That doesn't help us with what we are to do tomorrow morning."

The discussion continued, revolving around the same points like a manic merry-go-round without a brass ring, until fatigue, the wine, and hunger slowed the machine to an exhausted crawl. The silences lengthened and finally Mathilde Kronauer spoke, rubbing her eyes, the metal in her voice only slightly mediated by the lateness of the hour. "We will not decide anything tonight, I fear."

"All of us are doing what we can at the moment," Kronauer said, drawing a long breath and brushing his silver hair back from his forehead. "We must continue that. It is hardly a satisfactory situation but it is the one we have to deal with until things stabilize."

Gisela began to expostulate against the passivity of that attitude, but Mathilde Kronauer murmured something to her husband about the curfew and the next day's appointments. "It is late, my friends. We can continue this discussion another time. Walter, you can sleep here tonight. Herr Woller, there is a bed for you as well. Presumably the Lieutenant can navigate Gisela safely home without being arrested." Woller demurred saying he would find his way without incident to his next meeting. Boltzmann unbudgingly murmured, "*Où sont les bifteks d'antan?*" Then he nodded briefly and fell asleep, his head bent to his chest and right hand surrounding the empty wine glass. Gisela and Schade made their farewells. Kronauer took Schade aside for a moment and asked if he could send an envelope of letters through the military mail system to the United States, assuring him that they contained nothing that could damage the interests of the Americans. Germans could not normally mail letters abroad and such requests were not uncommon. Schade accepted the envelope with a nod and he and Gisela walked to the blue Opel in front of the house. Woller had already slipped away into the dark on his mysterious rounds.

As they drove through the dimly lighted empty streets, both wrapped in silence she wondered where it would all end and fought against the frustration that comes from feeling so helpless. Schade experienced the same emotions, but, remembering the gray diplomat's conversation, wondered if it would ever begin.

* * * *

Through the autumn and early winter certain matters conjoined to disrupt Schade's inner life, and shift the nature of his relationships with others and his role in the occupation of the city. The walls of the compartments into which he had divided his life began to crack open and break down, threatening to unbalance the equipoise they previously allowed him to achieve in order to focus his existence with purpose and sanity. He became increasing preoccupied with his ill-defined affair with Gisela Albrecht and his inability to completely understand what he considered her anarchic emotions and his role in her life beyond the obvious one of provider. He thought often of Gisela's increasingly coherent desire to atone in some manner, a desire that manifested itself in an ambition to lift the city's theater into the stratosphere of brilliance and profundity equal to any high point in its history. If she could play a major role in this creation, she believed she would have at least shown that the Germans were still capable of achieving a level of culture that could be recognized by the rest of the world.

At one point in their interminable discussions he told Makepeace, "We all have our Pyrrhic victories but the struggle never ends because the causes of the problem are systemic – only a radical change in the system itself will allow us to be free enough to pursue our destinies and develop our talents to their fullest – and this is ever more unlikely as we chase after a restoration of the pre-1933 past rather than a new post-fascist future."

"Did you read that in old mad Marx's logorrheic ramblings or have you been perusing the pseudo-background papers the left-wingers write for the generals, who don't read them of course. And what the hell is a 'post-fascist future'? If you can describe it maybe we can work on it. At the moment all we can do is stuff the Germans with USA-approved American culture and non-nazi German works, that I may remind you can only have been written before 1933 or in exile. 'Post-fascist' is horseshit at the moment. Much too early for it. The sheets of paper are only now coming out of the desk drawers, very slowly. There's not much of it, is there? So we give 'em Thornton Wilder, Aaron Copeland, and Walt Whitman, along with fluff like *Hokus-Pokus*."

"Your friends in the east are not so finicky about such things and they're not afraid to give them real dramas and serious books," Schade said with a distinct irony.

"Pro-communist propaganda. What the hell. You're too naïve. Grow up and look around you."

"I've seen enough."

"You haven't, yet, but you will," Makepeace said in a neutral tone. "You will because you're too honest not to."

His disagreement with the direction of the hard-line American occupation policy regarding denazification made his work a frustrating experience, continually repeating the case of the journalist Boltzmann: the fact that a person's name appeared on the membership rolls of a party organization did not suffice in Schade's mind to automatically disqualify that person from receiving a license to work. He increasingly resented the lack of spare time to devote to writing, and his unsuccessful search for an appropriate theme for a grand novel ate away at his mental composure like acid on an abstract etching. Equally disturbing, the ambiguous response bordering on contempt of many Germans in the city to those forced into exile, who now wished to return to the country of their birth, both chilled and angered him. As a result, his perception of life around him and his place in it gradually broke into quanta pieces of discordant mental energy and emotions, refusing to meld into a coherent whole on the basis of which he could act. As a response to this fragmentation, he redoubled his attention to his job in an attempt to override its frustration. Lt. Col. McCrae, in fact, commended him on his energetic pursuit of the unit's mission. Indeed, command headquarters began to suspect too much energy on his part, as he learned some years later: Makepeace eventually saw a copy of a report, which included a passage noting that Schade "may be trying to arrange an agreement on film distribution with the British excluding the Russians. This must cease immediately." Nothing had resulted from the report because the information was inaccurate. When Makepeace told him about it afterwards, they could laugh. "Given your political views at the time, it's absurd to think you'd have done anything to *exclude* the Soviets!" But at the time he occasionally drank rather too much, and the moments of oceanic angst came ever more frequently. All of this led to restless nights of too little sleep and only his tremendous supply of energy, generated by his youth and enthusiasm for life per se, allowed him to maintain the accelerated pace.

Tamirov eyed him one night at a reception as he sat in a corner with too much vodka, smoking too many cigarettes, thinking too many thought fragments. "You should not be so involved with the Germans, Lieutenant. I say this kindly." Schade laughed, unsuccessfully attempting lighthearted repartee. Finally he said, "Must be this 500 proof potato juice you serve. I'm fine."

* * * *

Under different circumstances the captains Oscar Monday and Claude-Jean Leseur would have shared an apartment until one or the other married and moved on. In the circumstances of their lives in the city, they never had the opportunity to discover whether or not they would have been compatible as roommates because their respective military authorities provided them quarters confiscated from Germans unlucky enough to be absent from the city or who joined the party too early. They became fast friends and spent a great deal of time together on and off the job. As "music control officer" ("Imagine anyone thinking music can be controlled?!") Monday served on a sub-committee in the four-power Kommandatura the Allies created to govern the quadripartite former German capital and also served on the committee as the general cultural factotum for the small French sector. "We've just not got enough qualified people to do the job properly; they're all in Paris celebrating the great French victory over the fascists. Much more pleasant to do there than here, n'est-ce pas? And you know the French hate to travel outside the country. Why bother? Everything is there, and in the other countries no one speaks French.

"My superiors?" Lesueur continued. "Bouf! I report to a colonel who is more interested in 12th century

Arabic manuscripts than telling the boche what music they can listen to. You would not believe the stuff he's found hidden away in the city. He reads them at his desk and makes notes for a magnum opus, which he will never complete of course: he has too much fun reading and making notes. He reports to the commanding general, so what can one do? My few colleagues and I do the work and he gets the medals. Business as usual, *mon ami*."

And so they met and, during several weeks of talking about the tasks of making over the city's cultural foundations, they graduated to their own interests outside the parameters of their work. They would meet for drinks and dinner several times during the seven-day work week, usually at the French officer's mess since they both preferred even a vin ordinaire to watery beer and taste-numbing hard liquor, the usual fare at the American officers club. The food was equally poor in both kitchens, but the French knew better how to camouflage low quality raw materials with a zesty or piquant sauce of some complexity. "It is most difficult for me to understand how your country can be so powerful militarily, with such a vital culture, by which I mean your black jazz music and your detective literature - I am less impressed by skyscrapers and I understand nothing of baseball - and yet you have no national cuisine worth a franc. Otte dugs?! Why dugs? We Franche do not eat dugs, otte or culd. Amburgers? There is no am anywhere in them. Corn we feed to pigs. Ow is this possible?"

"Look at the map, my friend," Monday explained. "How many hexagons would fit into the States? In all those parts of the country we've got different styles of cooking. Perhaps we have no single national haute cuisine, except an importation of yours, the grandiose dimensions of which we've reduced to blander tastes. That's what makes life there so interesting. Have you ever been to the States? No, I thought not. You're right, however, the *echt* national cuisine of America, if it has one, is not haute but plebeian, as it should be in the world's first true democracy where the so-called common people are seen as exemplars, at least in theory, of the good and true life. Pot roast, chicken in every pot, beef steak red in tooth and claw, canned veg, watery coffee with dinner, thin beer in smelly dark bars, white gravy drowning indigestible lumps of dumplings for Sunday ... one could go on but why bother?" He pressed his left hand to his side, just under the rib cage, a habitual gesture of preparation readying him to contain either laughter or panic, one or another of which constantly lurked in his brain threatening to overwhelm him at any time with ventilating palpitations. He lived in the midst of an ever-present emotional struggle to balance his reactions to the threat as they erratically rebounded among the extremes of reductive hysteria, pandemonic joy, and sudden terror. "Don't knock the hot dogs until you've eaten a kosher dog at a baseball game on a Saturday afternoon, with a cold bottle of beer."

To which Captain Leseur, not entirely unaware of his colleague's fragile equipoise but committed to treating him as he would any other friend, lifted his pointed nose in the air, looked down the thin proboscis, and pronounced himself satisfied with his ignorance of the hoi polloi American kitchen, and, in any case, he had no time for useless discussion about a subject that did not even exist: the sparkling Marybeth Mullen of the flaming red hair awaited his sophisticated presence for a magnificent dining experience in a new black market restaurant in Reinickendorf managed by the Countess and her mother with the silent backing of several ranking French officers. Somewhere they had discovered an Algerian cook with swift, light hands who fabricated miracles of culinary wonders by adapting Escoffier to local circumstances, thus transcending the bleak quotidian conditions in which they all found themselves, some more fortunate than others. His essence de faux truffle sauce d'oise was reputed to have wondrous aphrodisiacal effects on male and female alike. Alors.

Monday once commented on his name: "Well, it may have been Montag at some point in the family history, but I've never been sufficiently interested to look into the matter. I rather like being Monday: a fresh new week in front of me at all times."

He did not attribute to music any extra-musical characteristics, quoting a passage from Euripides' *Medea*:

> *If music could cure sorrow it would be precious;*
> *But after a good dinner why sing songs?*
> *When people have fed full they're happy already.*

When he heard this, Darkley added, "Full bellies make less trouble than empty ones. Keep the vox populi well fed and the people will be happy on their own." And Woller naturally contested the notion one night in The Edge Bar. "We have seen that belief can replace a full belly. The people must believe and work. After all, Euripides also said, 'Pious words and idle hands bring in no breakfast'." The burly journalist, Wilson Tompkin, running his fingers through his blonde-silver full beard, eyes shining, stared at the intense undernourished intellectual with the unfortunate rotten breath. "I can't believe you just made a joke, Woller. How unlike you!"

"About ideology and food there can be no joking."

"Did Marx or Lenin say that?"

"That I have said."

"Well I'll be dipped!" Monday said in English. "Ur?"

* * * *

Monday spent most evenings sitting at the mildly off-key piano in a dusty, echoing rehearsal room splattering sequences of notes across sheets of lined foolscap with a blunt dark lead pencil, scratching and scraping, erasing and humming the score of his "new old world symphony" score. "This will turn the music world on its head," he promised one and all. "This goes beyond Ives but remains deeply American. Instruments haven't been scored like this ever. Perhaps I can get the Berlin Philharmonic to premier it. I'll conduct myself of course. As long as we have so much influence here, what the hell, eh? What do you think?" Since no one had seen or heard a note of the piece, and Monday refused to show or play it in its incomplete form, his colleagues answered his questions with smiles and shrugs. They all agreed, however, that it would be a fine thing if he set the music world on its head.

Schade had heard one of Monday's pieces in New York before he entered the army. Indeed, various pickup bands had played Monday's work in a variety of small avant-garde venues, but New York audiences mainly knew his incidental music for the theater which he wrote for several notionally progressive productions of modern European and ancient Greek dramas. Schade had found the music for a production of one of Aeschylus's lesser-known tragedies, written for flute (long fluid lines of C-scale notes) and trombone (short barks up and down flatted scales), to be too deliberately alienating, too energetically radical, but fortunately very incidental.

In Berlin, Monday played other partially improvised pieces on the piano which Schade liked, and over a weekend in the second summer after the war, a chamber group made up of members of the Philharmonic and several theater bands played two evenings of Monday's music for the public in the Schlosspark Theater, which split the critics into two reluctantly opposing camps, each attempting to review the concerts honestly, but not offend the occupation forces on either side of the political spectrum. On the whole the newspapers on the radical political left throughout the city, stumbling between the desire to be on the progressive edge and the requirement that the music serve the interests of the international proletariat, bashed the pieces as decadent claptrap of no social or musical value, but praised the performers and Monday as a conductor doing the best one could imagine with such poor material. The liberals thought the music exciting, interesting, and that it had an anticipatory quality to it: the sounds pointed to an undefined future. The conservatives thought the composer had gone off the edge and out of the canon. One of the works was entitled "The City at War" and had caused headaches for the musicians and the conductor alike because the piece made use of war noises simulated on the instruments (whooping air raid sirens, cascades of whistling bomb trajectories, thurumpfs of artillery shell explosions, chain rattle of machine guns, thump-thump of anti-aircraft batteries, the whahgah-whahgah of ambulance sirens, and the like). The work, filled with great sheets of dissonant glissandi and contorted scraps of atonal melodies like the plaintive cries of seagulls swooping over the turbulent roar of an angry ocean, lasted a bare seven minutes, and baffled most of the audience. Gisela and Schadow attended the concert together and walked away afterward in two different states of shock.

"Clearly they'd never heard of Satie or Antheil," Monday sniffed after the performance to Leseur as they severely damaged several bottles of Moët-Chandon in the latter's BOQ.

Reinhard Woller proved to be an exception, opening his review with the statement, "The war concerto rejects the entire Romantic movement from Beethoven (excepting the late quartets) through Wagner and Tchaikovsky to Ravel and Erich Korngold." He devoted the rest of his text to a thoughtful essay on the question of where serious music could go after the work of early Stravinsky, late Richard Strauss, and the music of Schönberg and Bartok, with all of which he seemed to be familiar. This surprised Monday because the works of these composers, with the exception of some harmless Strauss, had not been heard in Germany since 1933 and Woller was too young to have heard it before that. When asked about this his eyes brightened. "Radio, records, writings, imagination ... everything possible." Which of course did not satisfy Monday, but Woller refused to divulge any additional information on the subject.

None of those who wrote about the concerts, except Wilson Tompkin whose New York newspaper printed his short review as a news item, mentioned the fact of the composer-conductor's Jewish heritage: most knew nothing about it and, even if they did, for Germans to talk about such a thing in public could easily ruin reputations and result in unemployment. And, after all, his music did not *sound* Jewish; at least it no longer did: under the nazis it would have been described as "decadent Jewish-Bolshevik trash," less for the ethnic or political characteristics of its composer than its discordant 20th century tonality.

"If we didn't 'control' music in this city, I'd never get the piece played here: too much nostalgia for the military, too much memory of death in the bombing. Probably won't be able to play it in London either, or Leningrad, they remember too much and it's too early. Paris is a possibility, or Rome, or Stockholm, certainly New York or Chicago. Who do we know in Stockholm?"

Monday persevered in his work and on the job, repeating to himself and to some of his friends that the German music world could and would be healed and that his new symphony would knock them on their duffs. "He never tells you who 'they' are, of course," Makepeace complained only half in jest.

Late one afternoon in early autumn of the first occupation year a tall, gaunt, hawknosed German musician sat nervously on the other side of Monday's table that served him as a barrier between him and those who, willfully or not, disturbed his concentration. The thin German shifted nervously about on the hardwood chair. They spoke in German and the musician, a bassist who occasionally played late at night in The Edge Bar with American Negro soldiers, lit a horrid smelling cigarette with a battered box of Welthölzer matches, at which point Monday shoved a large square blue glass ashtray at him. "Put that out please, it stinks, and I don't smoke." (When Leseur asked him if the smoke from the acrid black tobacco filled Broyards the Frenchman constantly puffed on bothered him, he pressed his left hand to his side just under his ribs and claimed he liked the smell even though he did not himself smoke. Leseur did not believe this, but he also did not stop smoking the fat yellowpaper cigarettes in Monday's presence.)

"Yes, of course, sorry. My name is Wolfgang Käsebier," he began hesitantly. "I would like to give you my Fragebogen, if you don't mind."

Monday read briefly through the document and found nothing unusual in its entries in slanting German script.

"How long will it take to process my papers, do you think?"

"I don't usually deal with the more popular musical forms so I can't really tell you how long you must wait for a response. Symphony orchestra musicians usually wait for several weeks, but occasionally some have taken much less time."

"I tried to stay out of the party, you know, but when it came down to the unspoken but clear choice between that and the army, what would you have done? Yes, I know that is irrelevant, sorry. I joined and continued to be a civilian musician playing Wienerwalzer for the Bonzen. Never even shot a gun. Never saw an Allied soldier."

"You played with Teddy Stauffer?"

"Briefly, very briefly, before they sent him back to Switzerland. Fortunately my name seems not to have been added to the band's paperwork so I experienced no negative effects from that job."

"Do you have any recordings by his band?"

"No. All my records were destroyed in the bombing."

"Too bad."

"Yes. The collection was not very extensive, but quite good.

"Your Fragebogen does not mention whether or not you were in the Volkssturm."

"Supposed to be, never went. Actually tried to disappear in the last winter. Went underground, so to speak. Not very pleasant, but one survived and didn't have to shoot anyone, not even one Ivan." Käsebier bent his long frame over the table as he leaned forward to add in a softer voice, "Not that some may not have deserved it, what they did to the women and the girls in the city." Straightening in his chair with an abrupt movement which seemed to indicate he might have gone too far, he said, "Not that we didn't do nasty things during the war in the East, to the civilians I mean."

"What are you doing now?"

"Playing for the Russian generals in Karlshorst in the evenings. They like popular kitsch and go to bed early, contrary to their reputation as vodka-soaked knee dancers. Very serious people."

"Pay well?"

"Not particularly, but every Friday, consistent. And there are other benefits, mainly food. Hate Russian cigarettes, but they are good currency on the streets."

"What do you play?"

"Russian folk songs and American songs from Benny Goodman and Glenn Miller."

"How did you learn those? That swing music was banned in the Third Reich."

"It's a myth that you couldn't find jazz here under the nazis. Even with all the crap from the *Reichslügenmaul* - that's one of the names we gave to Goebbels: State Lying Yap - and his asskissers, we could listen to jazz in Berlin. Oh they yelled and raised hell against '*Negermusik*' and you couldn't find it anymore on the radio, it's true. But one could always buy records. Early in the war I found a jam session with the Jew Benny Goodman openly sold in a store in the Tauentzienstrasse. There were other stores that sold good stuff, but never advertised it, of course. And we could always find small group jazz in certain bars. They changed the titles, you understand. 'Saint Louis Blues' was French, made it sound okay, yes, 'La Tristesse du Saint

Louis' or something like that. 'Tanz mit dem Tigerchen.' I don't know the original name, but we played the real stuff."

"Tiger Rag."

"Even more well-known types like Teddy Stauffer in the Femina Bar in the Nürnbergerstrasse after 1933 before he was deported because he jazzed up the 'Horst Wessel Lied,' imagine that? If he'd been a German they'd've thrown him in a KZ and beaten him to death. I wonder what he's doing now? Kurt Wittmann and his band played the real stuff at the Imperator in the Taubenstrasse. Man, did he swing that band from his drums, and when they really got into it he'd grab the cymbal and bang out the beat on his head. Very effective as a show but they played good jazz almost until the end. Never saw many girls in those places, not many girls seemed to be interested in that music. Not even the thrill of the forbidden drew them in to those bars. Too bad, no? Things aren't much different now, but some girls do show up to listen or to dance. The new music from New York isn't very danceable, is it? Very difficult to play and we've got no records yet to study. Challenging stuff, *nicht wahr*. Very interesting. Very difficult, but very interesting. No girls, though."

"I grow tired of hearing your voice, Herr Käsebier."

"Then I will relieve you of the discomfort, *Herr Hauptmann*."

"You will undoubtedly hear from us about your application."

"I am happy to know this."

"In the meantime, practice the bebop. It has a great future."

"I will most definitely keep the captain's words in mind," he said in accented English. "*Auf Wiedersehen, Herr Hauptmann*."

"Possibly," Monday replied and turned to the papers on his desk as the thin bassist loped out of the room. "Ichabod Crane."

When he next saw Leseur he asked, "Do you know the character?"

"I think not," polishing his one minor medal. "Is it one of Poe's?"

"No, Washington Irving."

"Do I ask you if you know the characters of Frédéric Mistral?"

"No, but you would if you knew them yourself."

"Insult! Swords at dawn!" They spoke English, which limited Leseur's effectiveness in repartee, and he spoke the word "sword" as it appears in print, a faux pas Monday ignored as a kindness to his friend.

"I prefer flintlock pistols myself."

"*Quoi*?! *Qu'est-ce que c'est flintlock?*"

During the winter a small group of colleagues met from time to time in the early evening at The Edge Bar in its new location near the Savignyplatz, resplendent in its new decor that Manning-Lehman, a British political intelligence officer friend of Makepeace's, called "shabby Hawaiian." Schade, Udo Siegmeister and Leseur sat with Monday at a table in the back of the room listening to him tell the story of the recent premier of one of his serially dissonant "Fables of an Anti-Semite" performed with several other short pieces by other avant-garde composers before a small audience in the Brandeis University auditorium. "Preaching to the choir, of course." A friend had written him a letter describing the reception of the "Fables."

Holding the letter between his fingers, Monday related the story with a sardonic grin. "Silence at first, of course. Then bafflement slowly changed into hesitant clapping, can't really call it applause - more like mice scratching around looking for a hole to crawl into. Then silence again. Fortunately the conductor, a friend of mine from Julliard, quickly gave the downbeat for the next piece, although an intermission was scheduled, and the band played what clearly was more understandable, if not totally enjoyable, to the poor auditors who, apparently, did not know what the bloody hell was going on. At least they seemed to accept the Copland, though that piece is rather astringent. The one review in the Boston paper several days later made no mention of my piece. The reviewer is obviously an anti-semite."

And later: "When I came to Berlin I thought I had prepared myself sufficiently to handle the situation and my tour here. It all seemed so *einfach* when I got the orders cut in London. I tried not to create my own personal Berlin, which would be battered and smashed by the real thing. That was before I got off the train and walked into the city. The real thing generates such intensity that one is forced to create a counter image to balance that reality or go mad. I've not yet been able to do this, but I'm working on it." He pressed his left hand to his side with particular emphasis and lifted his glass of black market aquavit to his mouth. "May the good fates vanquish the nasties and watch over us poor fool mortals." They all nodded and drank the icy liquid fire.

"I decided that as a double alien: an American and a Jew, I would penetrate this disastrous culture, so prone to violence and gross sentimentality. Perhaps I could discover some answer to the question we all continue to ask in rising exasperation: how could the nation of the big Bs create a mass industry of racial murder?

"Well, it didn't work, of course. I could no more become one of them that I could become a Zulu. Even outfitted in the shabbiest of DP clothes and a filthy fedora and two days stubble on my chin. Even with old Schadow's mentoring I couldn't do it right. Oh, he tried to help. Nice old fellow. But my German isn't up to it, not to speak of the *mentalité*. So that ended that. You, John, you could do it, perhaps, but we, Claude-Jean, we cannot. And you, Udo, have already done it and moved on."

"Perhaps you should have another aquavit, *mon ami*, you are beginning to make sense."

Siegmeister thought for a moment then said, "Yes, even if you called yourself Montag you would not have been able to assimilate. Not only too American, but too Jewish. In the end the assimilation was a lie, a murderous lie."

"No doubt this is so," Leseur murmured slowly nodding. "And names are no camouflage in the end."

Monday shivered and broke the chain. "Names, ha! Yours, my friend, just won't do either. The name is simply wrong for the tongue. Whatever possessed your parents to reverse the names like this? Everyone knows Claude must come as the adjunct to Jean. The reverse just does not sound right."

"What can I say? My grandmother named me. She was very eccentric: wealthy, she lived in a hut in the *garrigue* outside Uzès in the south."

"Ah, well, that explains it then."

"But my sobriquet, *comment dit-on...? Oui*, nickname, in school was 'Grisbi'. I've forgotten why. *Drôle*, no doubt, but also something of an embarrassment. Since I was smaller than most of my classmates they would regularly beat me up until the director told them very strictly '*Touchez pas au Grisbi!*' *Très drôle, n'est-ce pas*?"

Several aspects of Claude-Jean Leseur's character may have been amusing or eccentric to his colleagues and, on occasion, to himself as well, but his physical appearance was not one of them. At the university one of his professors, when asked to describe him, gave his summary opinion in one word: medium. "Everything about this young man is medium, his height, his ears, his common brown hair color, his temperament. What can one do with such material?" This professor became known in certain circles for his statement that during his entire career in the academic profession he had taught only one really bright student, a young man named Brasillach, who would make something of himself. The professor's tightly constricted patriotic sensibility could not recognize the icy, fast, and occasionally brilliant mind of his erstwhile student with the curious name, and in this he was not alone. (But as the student later phrased his reaction to this and other misapprehensions, "*Chacun son pain, chacun son hareng!*") The war offered Leseur the same opportunity it presented to others in his position: a permanent detour away from a road leading to a frustrating career of mediocrity and boredom. What he lacked in talent for action he made up for with competent organizing of actions and brilliant reporting on their results. With the liberation of France, neither he nor his superiors knew exactly what to do with him and before the latter decided to muster him out into civilian life he arranged to be posted to the French sector of Berlin where he anticipated nothing more than time in which to think about his future and plan a program to ensure a modicum of success in whatever he discovered to be that future. What he did not reckon with was meeting Marybeth Mullen, whose mind contained the same amount of ice as his and whose controlled sensuous appetites, if less refined than Leseur's, met his on a flat playing field where neither one lost and both lay victorious in the end.

Sergeant First Class Mullen, underworked chief secretarial administrator in the American military occupation government Economics Division, lent a certain aura of meaning to Leseur's life once they decided that being together was more satisfactory than not being together. "But now I must remain in this horrid place, eh? France is just now not such a good location for an American accustomed to sufficient food and warm apartments in the winter. In Avignon we have no heat and poor food. An impressive palace for the pope, it is true, but the rooms there are very cold in winter. So, if I am to be with Marybeth I must stay here, n'est-ce pas. *Mais attend*! What if she is transferred out of Berlin? What if she is demobed? Can I go to America? I must ask the general. Do they have baguettes in America? This could be terrible. What do you think?"

They first met in a place neither particularly wanted to be. The Russian count's grand apartment on the corner of Uhlandstrasse and the Kurfürstendamm reeked of multigendered sex and unwashed clothes; everyone with any pretensions wanted to be there. "Full of gunsels and wild ducks flirting with each other and stealing the count blind," Makepeace said to Schade after spending an hour there one night. What he neglected to tell his colleague was that he met Tamirov there from time to time: no one there thought it odd for them to talk as long as they required. However, given the Count's erratic but constant anxiety of being kidnapped back to Russia by Soviet secret police, Tamirov always came in mufti, a sartorial camouflage which fooled no one but one which neatly conformed with the Count's illusions. "You can't *imagine* how relieved we were to find that we lived in the *American* sector, but the reds still kidnap people so we always have to be on the lookout." The fact that their apartment actually lay in the British sector in no manner diminished the relief the Count and his mother felt at being somewhat protected by the accident of geography.

During one visit in the first winter of peace Makepeace looked around at the motley collection of hangers-on dashing in and out of the blue smoke in the rooms and said, "Zille would have loved this."

"So would Grosz, but I think Wilhelm Busch would have rendered it more accurately," Tamirov replied.

"Perhaps, but not with the same affection."

"A bourgeois affectation with no place in socially useful art."

"Ah, Yuri Vladimirovich, you know better than that."

"Never in public, Villum."

On another occasion that found them both in the apartment, Makepeace suddenly stopped in front of a painting on top of a pile of battered art history reference books leaning against the stained yellow wall in the living room. Puffing furiously on a cigarette, he glared silently at the canvas as if willing it to perform some act of recognition.

"You *would* like such picture like this, Villum."

"Ur."

"Decadent bourgeois trash, perfect symbol of western capitalist social degeneration. But lovely, of course, curiously liberating for the viewer, one might say. Not that I would."

The lavishly colorful painting portrayed a nude woman lying on mauve-red-blue Moorish cushions with green bracelets around her ankles and a red band encircling her slender throat. The artist had hastily sketched in the background so no specific location could be discerned: the fleshy pink and beige young woman seemed to float in bright sunfilled space that had no relation to any contemporary reality; she existed only within the mind of the artist. Astounded to the point of confusion, Makepeace immediately recognized Claudia Kaufmann as the model.

"I wonder if the Count will sell it to me?"

"The Count will sell anything but his mother to anyone. Ask her."

Makepeace did not buy the painting from the Count then, but it eventually ended up in his possession.

("It was cold," she told him later. "Opladen had some money, a private commission, I think. And I very much needed money then to pay the rent. So we made an arrangement. I posed in the nude and he paid me a model's fee. I think that was the last time he could afford such a thing. Very straightforward. It was autumn and cold in his atelier. I don't know how it ended up at Graf Valdy's."

"One of his punks probably stole it."

"It meant a few month's rent then."

"It means much more now."

"You're such a romantic fellow."

"Yeah, but it's still a good painting."

"And I know he did this one himself."

"Claude-Jean says it's a blatant imitation of Matisse's style."

"Opladen studied with Matisse."

"That's no excuse."

"No, it isn't, but it explains a lot.")

* * * *

The public never received invitations to the parties at Count Vladimir Nishtikontov's eight-room apartment in the former social center of the city, but those elements of the public which constituted the usual mix of types coming and going throughout the rooms on Friday evenings always knew when a party was on. Graf Vlady, as he was known to his friends and clientele, appeared physically incomplete because the depredations of the war and its aftermath ensured such an intense life that he never regained the weight of flesh necessary to fill out his natural shape. He always seemed to be on the verge of finishing his growth, but not quite achieving it; somehow his features remained only partially formed giving him the appearance of an overgrown child with the residual anxieties of adolescence. He also suffered from his addiction to young energetic street thugs he incessantly picked up in bars, much to his mother's dismay since the rough trade inevitably left the apartment in the early hours with some piece of stuff the Count had secured in order to sell it at a considerable profit. Sometimes they beat up the Count when he protested too much, and on at least one occasion his poor old mother, Melodya, suffered a mild concussion when one of the street punks hit her on the head with a precious antique lamp. From time to time, one or another of these juvenile gangsters showed up on a Friday night, but given the motley collection of types who paraded through the rooms only the youth of the *Strichjungen* set them apart from the others puffing on black market cigarettes and washing the lack of anything to eat down with stolen American rye whisky.

  The main business of Graf Vlady's parties was business, usually conducted in whispers in the corners, but from time to time done openly when the items being bought or sold or bartered were not too extremely hot, such as Heinrich Opladen's paintings which the Count's mother liked because they reminded her of the great Matisse paintings she had seen in the Moscow house of the tragic collector Shchukin. No one was quite sure how the Count and his mother had swerved from czarist Moscow, where the family maintained social relations with the wealthy bourgeoisie as well as the well-placed aristocrats like themselves, to Berlin at the end of the 1920s where they seemed to be able to pay the rent on their expensive flat throughout the nazi years. Fama reported that they had escaped the vulgar bolsheviks with the family jewel collection intact and well hidden. With Melodya's parsimonious selling techniques, they could have maintained a level of wellbeing acceptable to most of the émigré Russians who had fled the October Revolution and ended in Berlin where they formed a large minority culture complete with their own newspapers, publishing houses, and restaurants.

    The Count's apartment evolved into a provisional safehaven for homosexuals during the brown years when contravention of a reinforced paragraph 175 could mean imprisonment, sterilization, internment in a concentration camp or death. After the war Graf Vlady's parties became notorious for a relaxed freedom from gender limits, a liberation from the threats of persecution and camp death threatened by the previous regime. The events allowed both queens and the closeted the chance to come out at least for a night without fear of being beaten up or thrown in jail or losing a job. They served as a source of great relief for that section of the city's denizens, now that the Count could hold his open house openly without resorting to the conspiratorial measures necessary during the repressive previous era. These citizens remained at some risk, however. As Buchdow exclaimed to Harrigan at one point, "When the Allies threw out all the nazi laws they considered 'anti-democratic,' whatever *that* meant to them, we thought they would get rid of 175, but they never got around to it. Isn't that surprising? Not much has changed." To which the Count censoriously replied, "My dear Jokey, they don't *enforce* it at all like those misguided thugs. That's the difference." As one of the Allies himself, Harrigan unwrapped another stick of spearmint gum and judiciously remained silent.

The Nishtikontovs survived with certain shabby *élan* and sufficient food in the postwar chaos of the city, and the economic basis for their existence after May of 1945 was clear to anyone who cared to see it. One defined criminality in many flexible ways when one's existence teetered so precariously between disaster and a modicum of comfort. Boltzmann, who detested American rye whisky but drank it because it was free, and often the only refreshment available at the Count's parties, proclaimed that the Russian would have been even more successful in his wild capitalist endeavors if he had not been such a fan of alcohol in its various forms and tastes. That Boltzmann himself had become an expert in this field made his judgment unhesitatingly acceptable to his listeners.

The Count and his doting mother dealt in old furniture and jewelry, which they insisted was "antique," even if they could not locate the item in one of the dozens of reference books scattered throughout the apartment. As Melodya explained to a skeptical fellow émigré friend, caressing a jade ring in the form of a coiled snake all the while, "If it is older than the filthy revolution, well then it is antique. And should be paid for as such, don't you agree?" The Count's slender form glided from smoke-filled room to room, making a deal to trade two Biedermeier chairs for a first edition of Ludwig Börne's *Briefe aus Paris*, exchanging a whispered confidence about a flight of sexual fantasy, arranging a rendezvous at the Eldorado, or organizing an assignation in the Grunewald.

It was in this apartment late one night, amidst the noise and smoke and suffering from an intense headache that Monday composed the title song for a musical theater piece he never completed. "Couldn't do it after all; never found the right creative milieu again. Probably because I was in such pain and the Count's piano was so wildly out of tune." Nonetheless, in his own circle the verses of the song that survived the depredations of time, accident and alcohol gnawed their way into the minds of his friends to pop out at odd moments. "In the Sanjak of Novi-Bazar" became, if briefly, one of the city's most well-known unwritten musicals.

Mitzi
If you're looking for someone with clout
Or a fine round popo to mount
They're easy to find, if you're of a mind
To visit this one of a kind

Chorus
In the Sanjak!
In the Sanjak!
In the Sanjak of Novi-Bazar.[17]

The fact that a uniformed American female soldier attended one evening of the Count's unending open house party was not in itself unusual, but the appearance of Marybeth Mullen in her slightly too tight uniform ("I am engaged in an eternal struggle with pounds, sometimes I lose, sometimes I win, but it never ends."), nylon stocking seams just slightly off center, tieless and blouse opened two buttons below the neck, and startling red hair electrically

---

[17]For the complete lyrics to this song, see the endnote.

loose about her head and shoulders, at some point drew the eyes and the attention of everyone else in her vicinity, from the oldest (an ancient drag queen in stale prewar makeup trying to forget his camp experience) to the youngest (a pale runaway fifteen year old girl from Neckargemünd just arrived in the city to become the next Margo Lion, longing to sing a duet with Marlene Dietrich).

But for most of the guests only the eyes and attention were drawn: the American's demeanor made it clear that she desired no companionship to make the evening complete and that she would rather be elsewhere. Leseur never found out exactly why she came to the place; she left the explanation with the statement, "It was a mistake. I thought I was going somewhere else. But it did let us meet, didn't it?" Consequently, she had not exchanged more than distanced pleasantries with some of the guests as she wandered from room to room looking at the eclectic collection of paintings and objects on the Count's yellow watermarked walls until she stood in front of a recent small Opladen oil canvas splashed about with garish primary colors among which slashes of blue and yellow predominated.

Standing next to her in a crumpled uniform of the French forces, puffing heavily on a Broyard, Leseur was so enraged at the painting that he did not at first apprehend the physical characteristics of his neighbor. "One has rarely seen such shit!" Although she did not understand French, the meaning of this sour ejaculation could not have been clearer. "It is not so complicated," she responded in a neutral tone. "The painter is telling us that she's tired of the war and wants desperately to return to a life of peace and other kinds of excitement."

"The man is clearly an incompetent derivative of Matisse and Dufy who has lost or never had an ability to draw people or things!" Leseur sputtered this in English.

"She's not painting people or things, she's painting a desire, an emotion."

"What do you mean she? How do you know it's she?"

"I can see it in the painting."

"But that is nonsense...."

"I feel it in the painting, can't you?"

"No, no. One doesn't feel such things, one thinks about them."

"You can feel a painting with your eyes."

"Where did you get these outlandish notions?"

"I can't explain it; sometimes I know things. I understand things without knowing why. It doesn't happen very often."

"For which we can be grateful, n'est-ce pas?"

Continuing the conversation they drifted to the bar and drank a glass of prewar Scotch whisky from the Count's diminishing supply and smoked at each other's ideas until a distracted American colonel appeared out of the din to take her back to her quarters. She gave Leseur her office telephone number and said she looked forward to carrying on the discussion. For the first time that evening she flashed a rosy smile at him and he noticed the small gap between her large but not protuberant incisors of sparkling white against the deep red of her painted lips. He moaned to himself at her departure and in anticipation of their next meeting.

"I tell you, Oscar, she is bursting with health and the future. Her smile is that of gamin and her body one of a 19th century courtesan. What a combination! How can I resist?" "What if the resistance is from her side?"

"Impossible, but nonetheless ... I must call her immediately." "That will have to wait until the morning. There are no phones in The Edge Bar." "Well, let us provide some. This is of vital importance. Lives may depend upon it. Perhaps even mine."

When they met in the dim light of the pre-Hawaiian Edge Bar off a large square in Prenzlauer Berg in the Soviet sector, she wore her hair smooth as red velvet in a stark contrast to its crinkly electric splay in the Count's apartment. Her uniform snuggled around her plumpness with a sigh of satisfaction and her tie fit closely to the buttoned neck of her sand-colored blouse. Leseur was entranced and desired nothing more at that moment than to drown in her black eyes, very rare in red-haired people. "They are terribly non-committal, her dark bottomless eyes, but that is all right. We have time." Leseur liked to think of himself as an optimistic pessimist: there might just be a chance of success, so why not act on this belief. In his ignorance of the physical characteristics and behavior of redheaded American women, Marybeth Mullen kept him in a state of amazement that edged up to obsession. His eyes widened in astonishment upon first seeing her naked body sprinkled with a light dusting of freckles ranging from hard pink to pale red, as if in infancy her parents had dipped her ever so briefly into the warm spotted bath where freckles grow, and gently shook her dry leaving her soft skin curiously dotted with sweeping patterns of color. "Me, I have never seen anything so extraordinary in my life! Magnificent, n'est-ce pas?"

Later he buried himself in her hair, which he thought smelled like electrically charged raspberry jam. He could not repress the astonishment he experienced each time he saw the varied styles of her hair, the most immediately visible physical characteristic she presented to the world through which she sailed with the aplomb of one who rarely encountered a storm that could not be successfully navigated. "It's the shampoo and the time. I can wash my hair whenever I want to, something the German girls can't do: they have no shampoo so their hair is greasy and stringy. What I don't always have is time so mine looks different every time you see me." Whether or not the relative conditions of their hair formed the motivating force of their social relations, the German women employed by Marybeth's office eyed her with a certain amount of caution and suspicion. The men in the office attempted unsuccessfully not to eye her at all fearing the effect on their collective equilibrium. She treated them all with the same vaguely indifferent distance that neither drew them to her nor rejected their daily pleasantries. Having found a space in which to manipulate a healthy balance between the tepid shoals of commitment and the sharp-edged ice bergs of independence, she sailed as close to the shores of love and passionate attachment to other human beings as she found comfortable without the panic of emotional shipwreck.

  Late one freezing midnight deep in the city's howling winter of peace, Eden the Bartender whispered across the bar, "Mademoiselle Mullen strides forward, always forward, with that American informality and unrestrained looseness of limbs so impossible for Europeans tightly accustomed to rigid patterns of social and sexual behaviors. That typical American naturalness where gawky youthful lack of coordination strangely evolves into a freedom of movement that some unthinking person might think was indicative of a certain looseness of morals; especially a European bourgeois might think this, not knowing how else to react to the phenomenon, mon." Astounded at the presumption and insulted to his toenails,

Leseur expostulated with soft plosive sounds: "But that is, you will forgive me, complete merde! I myself stand here as an example of exactly the opposite of that wholly inaccurate assessment. Alors." To which Schade responded, "Eden is a comment machine, like all perfect bartenders. What else can one expect?"

Although she felt a jittery thrill as the focal point of Leseur's concentrated attentions, she had no particular desires as to how she should fit into that future with which he thought she effervesced. So she was satisfied to remain for the while in Berlin where life was chancy and restrictive for female military personnel but those limitations formed a chain of security links for those who were not entirely sure what they wished to do with their lives. She did not love Leseur, but was happy in his company and appreciated his artful sexual hijinks. "And I think his accent is amusing," she told a disdainfully skeptical Mathilde Kronauer one night, "especially in bed." Marybeth intended the latter bit of information to further discompose the condescension the young American felt emanating from the older woman, who thereafter began to consider both Marybeth and Leseur in an expanded light. The American's unsettling black eyes simultaneously reflected hidden promises and bold amusement, which Mathilde Kronauer perceived as an unspoken challenge, one which she silently accepted as they smiled their frosty antagonism at each other. "She does so well in the role of the wide-eyed innocent. It is a lie, of course, so American," the older woman remarked to her husband. Marybeth may or may not have heard about the remark, but one evening she commented to Oscar Monday, "She can dish it out, but she sure doesn't like to take it."

A short time later, with some archness she could not conceal, Mathilde Kronauer said to her, "I understand you like Opladen's work, Fräulein Mullen. We have several of his paintings here if you would like to see them. Unfortunately, we are no longer able to entertain as we once did, but we still hold the remnants of a salon together from time to time. You know what I mean?" Marybeth did not take umbrage at the question, but smiled her answer. "Ah, then come to the house next Friday." Marybeth could not refuse the offer, and she asked Leseur to explain the history of the salon in the city. He rolled his eyes and insisted on the French origin of the phenomenon, then gave her an elaborate analysis of the subject. Marybeth thought she would have enjoyed being there and meeting Varnhagen and Herz. "I don't think I would have liked all those clothes, though; I have enough trouble with these awful girdles."

    That evening she stood for some time looking at the canvases, feeling them with her eyes, for a brief moment no longer aware of her surroundings. "We are acquainted with the artist, if you would like to meet him. Yes? Bring some easily digestible food with you." It was there at the Opladen studio-apartment that Marybeth met the old historian, a friend of the painter and his first wife, Helga, from the old time before 1914, when for a brief several months Schadow and Helga conducted an intense but circumspect affair that ended badly in a painful and expensive abortion. It was also here that the young American's examination of the recent Opladen canvases confirmed her perception that his current wife, Ursula, had painted not a small number of them.

    As if he dimly caught the thread of her thought, the prematurely aged painter squinted and rewarded her thoughtful house gift (a container of boiled rice with peas and carrots) with an invalid's tirade about his suffering. "I damn near died of starvation during the early years of the brown stained nightmare. Perhaps I should have left with the others. Only through the charity of friends like the Kronauers who bought pictures they didn't want, great splatterings of color they really thought signs of madness and stuffed them in the attic not on the walls where they dissolved in the fires of the bombing. You never needed that kind of charity no the Amis didn't get bombed no blood in the streets and everything worthwhile smashed to dirt poor Ursula and I were sometimes invited out to eat so often our stove remained cold for weeks on end poor Werner never went to school he died of scarlet fever but malnutrition caused that the Amis never had to fry potatoes without fat did they tossing very thin slices about the frying pan very quickly back and forth they usually got black before they got done stunk up the whole house when the war started I worked in a factory making blueprint drawings until they found out I was one of the degenerate artists then I made ersatz leather pouches in which the soldiers carried bullets and we ate no better but more often my contribution to the war effort we don't eat much differently now but thanks anyway for the food Ursula still suffers from malnutrition. What? Oh, yes, I always attempted to paint allegories, like Vermeer. You know him? No. No matter. My allegories always turned out to be too real, too colorful, eh? No smudges, no possibilities for interpretation beyond what the bloody paintings simply *were* – no Vermeer or Hals was I! Now, of course, I paint no longer. Impossible. Who can paint now who can represent reality who can contemplate anything without blood on it I mean real blood no more sunflowers from Arles they're all withered now either we go back to the beginning or commit suicide no in-between we've committed too much sin."

"Some found it in themselves to resist."

"No one of importance." At which point he sank within himself exhausted and bitter.

Mathilde looked at Ursula with deep sympathy and smiled in an attempt to console. Marybeth watched the gray haired painter for several moments in silence then turned to the other women. "Thank you for letting me see the paintings. I have to go now."

Thereafter she regularly returned to the Opladen studio apartment and she and Ursula grew into a friendship that their friends could not quite understand, but which both accepted as part of their lives without preface or epilogue. They discovered a liking for each other and formed an increasingly intimate bond of affection and shared interests. They did not speak of Marybeth's perception that Ursula had painted many of Opladen's final works until after the painter died, but the knowledge forged the links of the relationship into a strong mutual attraction. They held the secret together which both of them treated with gentle caution: Ursula controlled a repressed fear of exposure and Marybeth was careful not to use the secret to dominate her new friend. She was amazed how far what she had considered her limited German could carry her. Fortunately, many of those she met through Mathilde Kronauer's social relations spoke English with some fluency, albeit a form of English she occasionally had difficulty in understanding because it originated in Oxbridge, not Dayton, Ohio.

Gradually she learned to know the parameters of the Opladen saga, the rise to a respectable level of success in his work, the shooting death of Helga during the days of revolutionary chaos in the city immediately following the end of the war, the marriage to Ursula and the death of their son, the removal of his works from the museums, and the bare survival of the increasingly disaffected couple. What pained Opladen most intensely was the disappearance of his paintings from the museums and the art market; the fact that the authorities sold some of his work in Switzerland at laughable prices hurt him almost as much as the destruction of other works by the same authorities, who burned them with philistine pleasure. Opladen's situation also bothered his friend, Mathilde Kronauer, who one evening turned on Schade to snap in a sharp, clearly antagonistic tone, "And what are you doing about this?"

He realized that "you" meant the Allied Military Governments, but also he himself personally. "What should we be doing about it?"

"Something must be done."

"We are registering what we've found. The lists are endless. Perhaps we'll be able to find the owners, perhaps not."

"What will happen to the works with no owners?"

"I don't know. Put them in a museum until someone comes to prove ownership."

"Not a very satisfactory solution, Lieutenant."

"Perhaps not, but what would you substitute for it?"

Mathilde regarded him stonily and changed the subject by allowing the other talk in the room to fill her angry silence.

During one visit to the Opladen studio while the painter himself trudged about the streets calling on old patrons in an attempt to obtain additional commissions Marybeth remarked on the very different look of an early Opladen landscape done in the late German impressionist style. "That is the only one we have left," Ursula replied. "He was influenced then by Max Liebermann, before he went to Paris with Helga and studied with Matisse. Do you know Liebermann's work? We've not seen any of it for the last twelve years. A Jew and a modernist. His is another of the sad stories we all know so many of and tire our friends with constant telling of them. He had a large studio on the west side of Pariser Platz by the Brandenburgtor. From his window with some friends he watched the SA and party types in those horrid muddy brown uniforms with blazing torches march through the Gate in January '33. They remember him saying 'Ick kann gar nich so viel fresson, wie ick kotzen möchte.' He cultivated his Berlin accent all his life. I'm not sure how to translate that. Something like 'I couldn't eat enough to vomit as much as I'd like.' They threw him out of the Academy because he was a Jew and two years later he died at 88. Only three gentiles walked in the funeral cortege to the Schönhauser Allee cemetery; they should be remembered for that: Hans Purrmann, Käthe Kollwitz, and Konrad von Kardorf. We did not go. Liebermann had made a nasty comment about Heinrich's painting under Matisse's influence twenty years ago so we stayed home. I regretted that and still do. In '43 the Gestapo came to deport his 82 year-old widow to the death mills in the east and she threw herself out the window. Perhaps in America there have been some exhibitions and catalogs?"

  Opladen had radically altered his style yet again during the war years before he stopped painting altogether. Especially the blotted oils edged up to the border of abstraction, swirls of bright colors which short curls and lines of black formed into vague but recognizable shapes of things and the human body. His inner passport had no visa to cross the frontier to enter the alien country, which he had always been able to avoid, bypassing this scrambled landscape, flying over it or skirting its edges on his way in and out of his own stylistic changes. In fact, he had passed through the vortex of European art and arrived at his fundamental style which allowed him endless variants without losing his early absorption in the Fauvist joy in primary colors and forms reduced to their essences: no shadows marred his images until the middle of the war when its overwhelming presence throttled his optimistic indifference to the reality in which he lived. He had not considered emigrating and refused to listen to Ursula's pleas to at least move to Italy. After this submission to his country's tortured history his work contained nothing but shadows as the colors darkened into dull browns, and deep blacks, and garish reds. The war amputated his ability to feel and express joy: he felt personally offended by the bared necessities of the city under bombardment and by the end he made only small drawings of flowers and birds in slashing strokes of such violence that the pencil often ripped holes in the paper.

"We cannot cancel the last twelve or thirty years, nor should we, but what I am trying to do with paint and canvas is to offer an alternative and a vision for the future that incorporates the past and transcends it. Not utopia or paradise, but a reality that – dare I say it? – ennobles man rather than oppressing him into infantilism, into the ignoble savage." Ursula Opladen paused. "This is what Heinrich would be doing if he were healthy and had his old energies."

* * * *

Some of the thousands of aliens resident for shorter or longer periods in the wreckage of the city developed "Berlinitis," that emotional and mental syndrome of opposite attractions: the city drew them in and repelled them at the same time. Had she thought about it, Marybeth Mullen would have considered herself one of the curious but defensive foreigners who landed for so many different reasons in the shell of the former capital. She thought about many things: why she had enlisted in the WACs, why god had plagued and pleasured her with that mass of uncontrollable fiery red hair and black eyes, whether or not her affair with the French officer would last until she transferred back to the States, whether a hysterectomy would stop her menstrual cycle which gave her so much pain, whether she should seek a promotion and remain in the service, why her office mate, a vibrant young woman from San Francisco, stared at her so often, why her nature had given her such prominent incisors with that gap between them so praised by Claude-Jean that she wondered if all foreigners liked failures of beauty ... she thought many things, but not about her relation to the city which she came to know in the superficial fashion of the sympathetic tourist -- she did not think about this because her relation to her environment was so natural that it required no thought.

Less enamored of her charms, Makepeace expressed his opinion to Schade and Manning-Lehman in unadorned language: "Empty heads do not think, they provide a staging area for hair, eyes, nose, and other necessary human accouterments, but thought is not one of them." But Monday's friendship with Leseur brought him into proximity with the dazzling red hair more than any of his colleagues and over the weeks and months he learned to appreciate her sense of the absurd ("Does my embracing Claude-Jean mean I am taking France into me? Am I devouring a whole culture?"), her fast wit, and, he admitted with some reluctance, the way her ever so slightly overweight body pressed against the confines of her uniform.

The notion of foreigners and their place in the city crept into conversations from any number of angles and perspectives, the nature of which depended upon the individual mixture of experience, expectations and prejudices. "There is a certain pleasing irony in the fact that normally foreigners are outcasts of one sort or another in a society," Monday explained to Schade in an attempt to clarify his own thoughts, "but here it is the natives who are the outcasts trying to reenter their own society which we, the putative foreigners, dominate and control. At least we think we do."

"I'm not so sure, Oscar. These are perhaps unhatched eggs so it is too early to count the chickens."

"Ouf!"

"Quite right. In any case, underneath - or alongside of - our superstructure the Germans go on with their lives, their own society exists along with the one we superimpose."

"You must know, John. Of all of us, you should know."

"Few of us are here because we want to be. I don't mean the Germans now. As individuals most of us would rather be elsewhere. We're not exiled here: we can return home or go somewhere else after our tours are over. If we're exiles, it's a very different form of exile. And some of us would prefer to live away from our homelands, it's true, but too often we are not fitted for the place of exile either. In fact, those unfortunates fit nowhere at all."

"You speak of yourself now?"

"No, not yet, but that time may come some luckless day. Look at Mister Morgan Tahni."

"But perhaps we are in fact exiles of sorts here after all. We live our lives here far from home, except you, John, although you no longer think of yourself as German. We work here. We're not all here by force majeur. I mean we could have requested duty elsewhere, but that would have meant not doing what we are most fit to do, at least for this short while. I think we might qualify, although not like those who fled Europe before, no, not like those unlucky devils."

"Luck may have played a greater role than you think," Schade said with sad weight in his voice. ("There they are," Makepeace once proclaimed when he saw Monday and Schade together, "the time and the pity." He felt mildly insulted when someone failed to recognize the puns.)

Some of Monday's colleagues did not immediately share his fondness for the Frenchman. Schade did not at first care for Leseur and his excessive patriotism. At their first meeting the Frenchman said, "Well, in 1914 we yelled '*à Berlin*!' It took us until 1945 to get here, but the important thing is we made it."

"That's stupid sophistry," Schade replied sharply. "If you'd gotten here in 1914, we wouldn't be here now."

"*Alors*, who is the sophist here now, eh?"

"Gentlemen," Monday interjected with a growling laugh, his left hand pressing his side just below the ribs, "let us drink to the great antifascist allied cooperation effort which defeated the common enemy in a historic struggle of good against evil."

"*Merde!*" "Bullshit!" Expostulated simultaneously with great gusts of laughter.

* * * *

Oscar Monday steered the blue Opel into a side street off the Grosseallee and quickly turned off the motor as he braked to a stop. Uncleared rubble blocked the passageways between the gutted buildings so they could not see into the inner courtyards. They could, however, hear the sounds of activity beyond the rubble. As Monday and Schade, followed by a middle-aged German policeman and a young American MP, got out of the car, the composer rapidly whispered, "This is not exactly where I should be, you know. I'm in the music business, not a chaser of illicit film productions. I should be out there making sure the composer of 'Lili Marlene' and other German propaganda music is banned from following his career in music while the song is a big hit in England. Vera Lynn, Anne Shelton. Nothing like Lale Anderson, of course, but her version never sold much in 1939. All women singers of a song so blatantly from a male perspective, interessant nicht wahr, good old Norbert Schultze, let's keep him outta de biz cause he so *brown*!"

"Enough already!" Schade snapped, then shrugged. "Always shorthanded, need to be flexible, one car, half a jeep, and too many clients. Old story. Let's go."

As quickly and as quietly as possible they climbed over the rubble and strode into the courtyard. Two older men balanced a battered 16-millimeter film camera on a makeshift tripod pointed at a younger man and woman holding each other and speaking in soft, earnest voices. The production had neither lights nor sound equipment. The group froze when they heard the others enter the area and with panic in their eyes looked unsuccessfully for a second exit. Their shoulders sagged in unison and they turned to the Americans, resigned but without despair. Across the courtyard a line of women and old men with pails and pitchers slowly made its way to the faucet from which a narrow stream of brownish water sluggishly fell into the containers. The water carriers paid no overt attention to the scene played out between the Americans and the filmmakers, but they listened intently, eyes on the faucet and dust in their throats.

Glancing at their old equipment and threadbare clothing, Monday murmured sadly, "Pitiful, really. Probably can't even develop the film."

"Where they got it is the question," Schade replied. "All right, Herr Sagedorff, ask them for their license." The policeman spoke in German.

They had no license to make a film in the American sector, or anywhere else in the city. The dark haired older man in a clean white shirt explained in a Bavarian accent that he had served for many years as a second unit director at the UfA studios in Babelsberg and Geiselgasteig, and now, with one of his former cameramen and the two young actors, was frankly taking advantage of the chaotic conditions in the city to finally make his own movie about the resistance ("What else would he tell you," Udo Siegmeister scoffed.) and a doomed love affair ("That must have appealed to you, Johnny," Makepeace chided.). Yes, they realized they needed a license, but everything was so complicated and time consuming, and they had all been cleared by the Chamber of Creative Artists, their denzification papers were in perfect order.

"Ask where they got the film," Schade said in English without waiting for Sagedorff to translate the Bavarian's explanation.

The cameraman looked at Schade with the wary red-veined eyes of the convinced alcoholic and ignored the policeman who did not say a word. "Im April als die Russen kamen, hab ick's versteckt," he assured them in the narrow tones of the Berliner.

"Where's the rest of it?"

"*Der Rohfilm?*"

Schade did not respond and the man finally said, "*Es gibt's nichts mehr.*"

"So this is the last scene in the film?"

"*Nein, nein, eigentlich nicht, aber –* "

"So you must have more film. Where is it?"

"*Es gibt's tatsächlich kein Meter mehr, Herr Leutnant.*"

Waving his arm, the director said in English, "We shoot whenever we find more rawfilm." He shrugged. "*Wir können nichts anders.*" It was hot in the midday sun and they had all begun to sweat. "It is not the most efficient method, ja, but it is only one we have now."

"Where's the sound equipment?" Monday asked in German.

The director, relieved to speak his own language, quickly said, "We have none that works at the moment. We will synchronize the voices later. We have no choice but to improvise, you see." His voice sounded hollow and tired.

"What about the script?"

"Ach, we haven't one of those either, only an outline; we improvise the rest. It's the only way we can work under the circumstances." The director rubbed a hand over his jaw and shrugged. "What can one do?"

The actors did not appear old enough to have had much experience. Perhaps this made them better improvisers. The situation clearly frightened them and they thought the Americans might arrest them. The two older men knew this would not happen, but already regretted what would.

"Corporal," Schade said to the MP, "confiscate the camera and the film. Don't expose the film. Herr Sagedorff, please take down names and addresses and tell them to be at the office in two days for further processing of their case. We'll wait by the car."

"*Herr Leutnant,*" the director said in a tightly controlled voice. "Might we finish please at least the shot?"

Schade did not look at Monday. After a moment, he said, "*Aber schnell.*" He nudged Monday's arm. "Come on, Oscar, let's get out of here."

As they climbed back over the rubble, Monday said quietly, "You could have saved time and spoken German, John."

"They understood well enough and who knows what they did during the war."

"The Kammer cleared them to work. You saw the papers."

"But we didn't. Unlicensed use of rawfilm is forbidden. By order of the commanding general. Period."

"Semicolon, maybe. You confuse them, John. You swerve unexpectedly from antagonistic tough guy to sympathetic tough guy."

"An expression of my ambivalent character, no doubt."

"Perhaps. More likely a confusion of identities."

"You're as bad as Makepeace. Are you all psychoanalysts?"

"You don't need an analyst, my friend, you need to make some decisions in your mind."

"Yessir, captain, as soon as I find a free moment."

Monday laughed softly. "You let them finish the scene. That's not in the regulations."

"No, they don't say that, but what can one do?"

"I think you may be just a bit *meschugge*. I have an uncle in Connecticut like that. He's a rabbi. His parishioners don't know whether to love him or fire him. For the time being they love him."

"Our parishioners don't have to love us and can't fire us. The comparison is inept."

"I don't think so, only on the surface, perhaps. But it doesn't matter right now. Here is our team with the confiscated goods. Don't you think the girl looks Jewish?"

"No, she's much too dark."

"You couldn't make a dime on the borscht circuit."

"You're right. Heights scare me. All right, Corporal, put the stuff in the trunk. We'll drop you and Herr Sagedorff on the way. Our colleagues need the car and we're late."

Monday laughed again as he climbed behind the wheel. "*Meschugge*," he said, shaking his head and smiling.

In the courtyard behind the rubble, the water carriers moved a few inches forward as one of them finished filling her pail and began to carefully walk to her windowless apartment and her thirsty children down the street. A vial in her pocket contained four iodine pills the British soldier had given her on his last visit. The children would not suffer from drinking this water and he didn't hurt her the way the Russians had.

PART FOUR

> If I ever write my memoirs, I'll begin with
> a footnote. How will that look on the page, eh?
> Wonderfully *academic*, no?
> -- Professor Dr. Schadow

The agèd Schadow edged into the orbit of Schade's existence obliquely and unobtrusively, much as the old man had endured his life during the past twelve years: remaining out of the way and quiescent, he had survived the mutilations and humiliations of the brown years after his removal from the university where he had spent his entire career. ("I was beyond retirement age, you see," he once mentioned to Schade, "so it was easy for them. But it caused me some pain to be so summarily dismissed. I should have expected it, of course. You see, I belonged to a race of creatures locked up in the academy as if in a cage and we were all some kind of rarefied birds pecking away at this or that; scribblers, you see, *charakitai* in Greek: scribblers on papyrus rolls. Curiously, there's a bit of word play here because *charax* means enclosure in Greek -- birds in a cage scribbling away at some impenetrable tome weighty with obscure useless knowledge for the delectation of the cognoscenti -- at least that's how the people in the street saw us, and who knows, perhaps they are right.")

In no way radical in his scholarship, he had enthusiastically pursued his research into what was known as *Geistesgeschichte*, that typically Germanic study of the history of ideas, in the traditional manner. His colleagues respected his work for its skillful delineation of the effects ideas caused on the development of human society (a Hegelian idealist, he had no patience with the materialists in the field, although he enjoyed arguing with them from time to time) and the stylistic grace with which he composed his writings, more French in their lucidity than the ponderous complexities of academic German. There was in Schadow something of the intellectual bully and he openly condescended with great hauteur to those he considered his mental inferiors. A number of his critics did not fail to note that his work could be considered more style than substance, but he had always been able to defend his positions with both élan and what he was fond of calling in English "the meat of the matter." (With some embarrassment he would recall to Schade his meetings with the dying Nietzsche. "It was hardly a missed opportunity, you see, because it was already too late for both of us. He was beyond answering questions of real substance. I always wanted to ask him, "My dear Nietzsche, how do you eat?" Here Schadow motioned to Schade's mustache. "That massive soupstrainer, you know. But I never did, more's the pity. I simply hadn't the nerve. In the end, he never talked at all. So much for the *Übermensch*, though that wasn't what he meant either. That soupstrainer is good, eh? Especially for him, who rarely ate and never with any real pleasure. Even at the end when he knew the end was coming, the rage still emanated from him in his comatose state. Such people get little pleasure out of physical sensation, like eating well. I used to be like that myself.")

His students sensed his essential indifference to them, but this too was part of the tradition in German universities and did not cause him to stand out. However, his articles in the feuilleton sections of the liberal press (many of them published in Kronauer's newspaper until the Gestapo unceremoniously announced that no further newsprint would be available and the paper closed down) made it clear that he had no sympathy for the brash right-wing movements that aggressively clamored onto the public stage with such violence after the defeat in 1918. In fact, he detested any ideology that lauded blind instinct over reason and he had nothing but contempt for the unrefined incoherent ravings of the movements' spokesmen. That the descendants of Attila's Huns should one day rule the German nation was a concept that could not penetrate his mind; such a thing was very simply unthinkable. Not that he was a political naïf (he had foreseen the results of the Kaiser's policies in 1912 and publicly warned against them, and he had reluctantly seen the necessity for the republic in 1918, becoming a *Vernünftrepublikaner* like many of his friends and colleagues), but it had proven impossible for him to believe that this street rabble could come to power in his Germany: they were totally irresponsible and their emphasis on blood and race made no sense. He did not extract the lessons to be learned from the rollercoaster 1920s, and he continued to disbelieve the possibility of the radical right being awarded the highest political prize until it happened, and the events following January 1933 shocked and disoriented him. The impossible had come to pass and his mind slid precipitously close to the edge of madness. Realization of the danger came too late and he never resolved the trauma and guilt in his mind at having not seen and resisted it sooner in a more effective manner. Privately, he felt a secret shame that the new masters of the nation did not consider his carefully crafted articles of sufficient import to arrest him. They had simply posted a notice on the door of his seminar room advising that Professor Dr. Emil Schadow would give no further lectures or seminars at the university. He viewed this as an insult, but was then powerless to respond. (Later, he would quote with great sadness a line from Verdi's *Nabucco*: "*Io sono dio!*" noting, "at that point lightning struck Nabucco down. Unfortunately, nature's electric axe did not cleave Hitler's crown and head before he did his dirty work.")

A man of precisely calculated reasoning, he found his ejection from the academy, the only society he had ever known, and the years that followed, mentally confusing and exasperating. So much no longer made any sense in any rational way, and the pervasiveness of what he could only consider to be stupidity and horror forced him to a re-evaluation of his own intellectual development and the entire course of German history, which he painfully conducted in the depths of his mind, daring to jot down for future reference only cryptic phrases in his notebook. He felt betrayed both in his citizenship and his professional knowledge, so he continued to think and read and make notes in an attempt to understand the past that had so violently expelled the unacceptable but agonizing palpable present. He never forgave himself for not perceiving the outlines of the future until after the barbarians had irrevocably crushed the citadel in their envious lupine embrace. "That paladin of virtue, Marcus Aurelius says something about not allowing the future to disturb you. This foolish innocent tells us we will meet the future with the same weapons of reason with which today we are armed against the present. But, of course, he knew nothing of the twentieth century, did he?"

The loneliness of those solitary years he bore with gritty patience and hard-won equilibrium. After his only child died on the Eastern Front in 1943, he steeped himself further in his studies and weathered the forlorn days with an emptiness he could not fill or share with his wife, Elfriede, because she had left his life by dying of cancer several years after his dismissal from the university. They had never been particularly close; passionate love had not brought them together nor kept them together, but they had grown into each other's lives and accustomed themselves to one another's presence and idiosyncrasies, much as one becomes accustomed to a favorite piece of furniture or pet animal as one grows older and more detached from individualized personal commitment. When she died because her weakened, malnutritioned body could no longer fight off the disease eating away at her insides and he could not find any medical man with a cure, his isolation from human warmth and companionship deepened and he had little more than his private work to occupy his intellect and his time. For a while he thought she had deliberately starved herself and had given in to the disease, but since this would have meant she no longer wished to be with him, he pushed the thought far into the recesses of his subconscious. The last time he touched her was to remove her gold wedding ring, which he henceforth wore with his own on the ring finger of his right hand, in the old tradition. The phrase "ashes on her breath" came unbidden into his mind as she lay dying. They buried her in the Französische Gemeinde cemetery under a gravestone upon which the cleanly chiseled Roman letters read:

Elfriede Maria Schadow
geb. von Adamsen
Erfurt 1891 – Berlin 1936
Sina doctrina, vita est quasi mortis imago.
– Dionysius Cato

"She would have understood that," he told his friends, but they did not believe he was correct: she had suffered, they agreed amongst themselves, from his overabundance of learning, which for her meant, if not the image of death, an existence inadequately filled with the passions of life. One of his closer friends hazarded the ironic speculation that the phrase *"nihil est melius quam vita diligentissima"* might have been more appropriate for her gravestone, but no one spoke to him of such thoughts.[18]

Weather permitting, he continued to take long walks with several of his former students and their friends who still wished to learn something about the Greek, Levantine and oriental gods ("Isn't it interesting that the further east one goes, the more humility and passivity one finds in the gods?"), the thought of Nicolas of Cusa and Ockham's Razor, the mythology in the Dante's *Divina commedia*, or trace the idea of progress from its optimistic beginnings to its current degradation in a Europe dominated by German fascist ideology. The introduction of wartime safety measures and the drafting of the young men into the military and the young women into the munitions factories put an end to the perambulating seminar.

Friends and a few of his former colleagues continued to visit him, and still fewer of them accompanied him to the theater and to restaurants, until the lack of anything real in either dried up any desire to be there. "Unfortunately, I was too old to go abroad, or at least I thought so at the time. Now, of course, I'm not sure. After

---

[18] Dionysius Cato's statement: "Without learning, life is but the image of death." The next Latin tag means, "Nothing is better than a most diligent life."

all, I do know Latin, French, and English and some Serbo-Croatian."

Too old to be of any use to the war effort and apparently forgotten by the new rulers and their minions in the police and educational departments of the party and government, he spent the war years in a small room on the eastern edge of the city eking out a living on his diminished pension and, for a year or so, on payments for his historical essays that Kronauer published until he lost his newspaper; the university brownshirts reduced his entitlement when he applied for it following his dismissal, but he was grateful to have even a part of it. Being neither Jewish, a member of any political party, a member of any resistance group (too old, too old), nor an outstanding public figure despite his feuilleton pieces (as he discovered to his chagrin), the regime did not threaten him with internment in the camps, which he would not have survived. Still, he lived in constant fear that one of the savages might stumble on one of the articles, or one of his former colleagues or students might remember and denounce him, allowing an obscure bureaucrat to decide he constituted a threat of some sort and order his arrest. For reasons he never discovered this did not happen, and he worked with the few volumes he saved from the book-lined study in his former apartment when city officials forced him to move after his wife died. (Ironically, those same officials offered the apartment to Wilson Tompkin's news agency for dollar payments [ah, sweet Valuta!] and Tompkin himself occupied the premises for a brief period before the regime's anti-American campaign deprived him of those large but cramped rooms stuffed with heavy *Gründerzeit* furniture.)

Schadow never knew who lived there after the Americans left, a matter of indifference to him except for a residual concern for the fate of his extensive library.

During the war the building suffered the fate of many Berlin structures collapsing one night under a direct bomb explosion. Thus, although long since gone from the building, Schadow lost everything except what he had been able to take with him in two suitcases a decade earlier.

His work done in what he described as his scriptorium saved him: in addition to his search for signs of the present in the past, which he thought would help explain the terrifying condition of the incoherent world in which he now lived, he sought out in the sources remaining open to him the obscure and unfamous personages who illuminated their times more precisely than the more well-known historical figures. He looked into and analyzed such themes as he could research: the arcana of 16th century intrigues and the squalor of peasant life during the so-called Reformation, and the social violence behind the mythical façade of Arcadia. The resulting few essays he had no hope of publishing, but writing them kept the hounds of hell from the door of his mind. He read and wrote to maintain his sanity and protect his heart from shriveling out of loneliness and despair. Although the Party had seen to it that the public libraries no longer contained any books whose ideas might pollute the nation's intelligence with alien notions, he found the classic literature of Rome and the Enlightenment to be a balm to his restless mind. One of the librarians at the university on a few occasions surreptitiously pushed a "decadent" book across the table into his briefcase, thus saving it from official destruction.

Indeed, it was the old man's Apollonian Hellenism that had placed him outside the world of National Socialist irrationality and savagery. He could no more have entered that world as a believer than he could chop off his right hand. In any case, the barbarians had shut the portals to deny him entrance.

And thus he survived, as Fortuna protected him from being killed in the bombings and the battle for the city at the end. After the war began, his age and the lack of public transportation made it difficult for him to get about the city, especially to the libraries which eventually closed for the duration, even during the day or during the pauses in the bombing raids. The diminishing number of friends not afraid to be seen with him took him to a nearby restaurant or café until they realized that they could not talk freely in public places, and that they could not obtain anything eatable that they could afford in those places. Thereafter they brought food and his favorite beer and ate in his room or went for walks after the all-clear signals. In this way, the old man maintained his friendships with the Kronauers, Gisela and her father when they were in the city, and some of his former colleagues, many of whom had also been removed from their positions in one way or another. He also maintained a desultory acquaintanceship with the odd Piekheim family in the house behind the garden where he sat in the sun from time to time and attempted with Gisela's help to grow vegetables. Georg Piekheim the philologist at the university and Mechtild his wife, a published poet, and their three sons survived the war. The half Jew Mechtild survived because her husband was a gentile, but in Auschwitz her German fellow-citizens murdered her daughter by a Jewish painter from before she knew Georg. Broken by this wrenching event and by the bone disease that bent her body, she devoted her time to her family and writing acerbic poems about the impossibility of love in the time of the barbarians. Schadow, guilty at not having spent more time talking to them, now discussed the events of the day and questions of language with them over the wire fence that separated their garden from the one at the back of the house in which he had his room.

The atomization of society during the battle for the city and its aftermath temporarily snapped the links in the chains of these friendships, but gradually, as the city and its conquerors painfully began to repair its broken parts and cautiously fit them together again, he and his friends also began to weave together the skein of their relationships and met with increasing frequency. Regardless of their individual circumstances, all of them suffered the common condition of hunger. The old man's thoughts turned increasingly, disturbingly to the image of sour cream on large boiled potatoes spiked with marinated onion strips, and a full blossom glass of light red wine situated at a neighborly distance from his hand. Each of them, in fact, entertained an image of a meal on blinding crisp white linen (Claudia Kaufmann's table cloth sparkled with the bright blues and yellows of the south of France), which popped into their inner visions at unexpected moments, from which they attempted to achieve some form of satisfaction and repletion. When the dilapidated streetcars began to reduce the distance between the eastern and western sections of the city, he made the frustratingly slow trip to Kronauer's house in Dahlem and extended the parameters of his social activities, which increasingly became limited only by the physical disabilities of his age. ("The *Strassenbahn* groans pitifully in protest against its age and battered condition as it lurches down the tracks only partially under the driver's control as he pounds his foot down on the warning bell's button," he wrote in his daybook as a draft for a letter to a colleague who had emigrated to London at the right time.)

When they met at Kronauer's "at homes," Schade's immediate reaction to the former professor was ambivalent. As the younger man came into the room the conversation revolved as so often around the topic of hunger, and

Schadow was saying, "I would rather bite the cloud than the dust; best would be a bloody beefsteak, but under the circumstances even fresh tuna would do." After Kronauer introduced them, Schadow cast a sardonic eye on the younger man and murmured, "Schade, the end of summer in Germany, a time to regret the dying of the season and the oncoming long winter. But you are surely too young to regret much of anything."

"I don't regret the changing of the seasons, only the necessity of having to become an American," Schade answered a little too sharply, meaning the battered and bloody history of the twentieth century and the acute pain of exile.

Schadow ran his pale thin hand lightly across his bald corrugated head, feeling the bones of his skull jutting against the yellowish skin, and pushed his wire-rimmed spectacles against the bridge of his nose. "Yes, there's that, to be sure." Then, as if to ease the discomfort of his comment: "My name is also rather odd, *nicht wahr*, especially in English. If I went to England it would give me an aura of chiaroscuro, no? A bit of crepuscular mystery and intrigue, perhaps, like in those wonderfully inaccurate but exciting cinema thrillers they do so well there. Do you think it would help me to charm the ladies?" Saying this he adjusted his face into what he called his "cocktail lounge smile," which appeared as a vulpine leer quite inappropriate to the shallow settled folds of his cheeks on a face still affected with the residues of malnutrition and professorial hauteur. "I never figured out what the tail of a rooster has to do with drinking in dark smelly places, but no doubt it has something to do with seduction and lust, don't you think?" They shook their heads and laughed. "Well, yes, perhaps I am too old for that kind of thing. Certainly long out of practice. Never saw myself as Professor Unrat anyway. I'm much too thin, don't you think?"

Schade quickly discovered that Gisela visited the old man in his room as often as possible, bringing him books and food and an occasional bottle of wine over which they discussed the great questions of her life and the possible whereabouts of her father. (Once when she brought him two apples, Schadow reminded her of Aristotle's description of animal cravings being basically founded on the sense of touch, which explained the gourmand who wished for nothing more than the throat of a crane so that he could enjoy his food for a longer stretch of time as it slowly worked its way down from mouth to the alimentary canal.) The young woman always gave him a mild jolt of physical pleasure, manifested in that slight, all too brief tickle in his genitalia, whenever she appeared at his door. From the vast distance of age he could still appreciate her sensuousness and beauty, which traces of hunger and the ravages of her recent life had not completely obscured, albeit in the same way he took pleasure from his beloved Greek statuary. (A volume of photographs of these cold symmetrical images had been among those things he'd been able to rescue from his apartment, in addition to the reproduction of Dürer's woodcut of the bath house, which he pinned to the window curtain and chuckled over each time he examined the hidden and not so hidden meanings the artist had crammed into the image). They had lost contact with each other in the last months of the war and their mutual expressions of delight at finding the other had survived the war and its ravaged horrors moved them both to tears. The sight of her thin form and haunted visage saddened him, but somehow he knew she would regain the energy and beauty she naturally possessed. Over the years, Schadow had observed her passing through the stages of growth from infancy through adolescence and early adulthood with the detached concerned attitude of avuncular affection. He never offered advice unless asked, something she rarely did directly. Like her father, who had once been the old man's student, she felt comfortable discussing matters with him because he never demanded that she act in any specific pattern; his opinions, most of which she respected, he made clear through an informal Socratic dialogue of gently phrased questions eliciting answers which contained the seeds of the decisions she had to make.

When they walked through the eastern part of the city in that first weird winter of peace when the cityscape resembled more the ruined lunar landscape of some demented extraterrestrial archaeological dig than anything recognizably human in creation and construction, she tried to explain what appeared to be a typical Berlin, mutually beneficial, arrangement of GI and Fräulein, victor and defeated: the damp primitive pleasures of sexual congress for the gross satisfactions of stilled hunger and cozy dry warmth. "One cannot condemn us for this; it is a way of surviving in order to accomplish our work."

"Do I condemn you? I, too, eat the Allies food and accept their books. We all fraternize to one extent or another. What a curious word to describe the biological imperative to satisfy a hunger."

"Not only biology is motivating this behavior. We are faced with the necessity of developing a new theater, a whole new language with which we can differentiate ourselves from the perversions of the past. Does anyone disagree with this? How can they? How can we use the words 'special treatment' any longer?"

"It is not a matter of disagreement in principle, but differences of opinion on the methods and timing, isn't it?"

"Yes. And in the meantime I trade sex for food and the opportunity to work with some freedom. Where does that leave us?"

"The defeated have to accommodate the victors," he murmured with great sadness in his voice, "at least for a time. Have you no real feelings for the Lieutenant?"

"The relationship is not all a business contract, no. There is some affection. We are trying to love each other so we do not feel guilty about the affair. It is not easy, but I suspect we will both survive the experience."

"I am saddened by such cynicism in one so young, although I think I understand it." He thought about what he knew of her brief but flashy career in the past several years and hastened to add: "There is a greater reason, nicht wahr, for all this, what shall I say, eh? Without being vulgar, but if we can't avoid it, for all this fucking. Without such a transcendent reason we'd all be rutting in the pig stall of conscienceless sex. And we wouldn't want that now, would we? Or would we?"

"Dear Professor Schadow, would that it would be all that simple!"

"Oh, I think I understand complications, my dear, but the sex I'm not sure I get at all!"

"Perhaps you will, perhaps you will."

"I should live so long!"

"In any case, it is difficult to find a difference between what one did to succeed with the nazis and what one does now to get a license, eat decently and stay warm in the winter." Her voice carried within it the resignation of the age-old lessons of not only the victor-defeated syndrome, but also the dichotomy of the female in a society directed by and for the male.

"It would be of little use to you if I attempted to convince you of what seems to me to be the difference, but my point would be more ideological than emotional."

"You mean trading sex for things is justifiable as long as we lay down for the Americans, but it was shameful and disgusting when one did it with the nazi Bonzen!"

"Do *you* see no difference?"

"Not at the moment," she snapped.

"Perhaps in time you will, because there is one. But it is for you to determine for yourself. You will believe it only if you discover it, don't you think?"

She did not answer and they walked on in silence.

"You may be saving too much of yourself for yourself. The receiver does not have to be Lieutenant Schade, it is probably too late for him and he is not my concern – but at some point you must give more deeply of yourself to someone, not to some *thing*, like an idea or 'the theater'. If you do not, the result will be a form of sterility, you see."

"I cannot spend what isn't there."

"But it is, lying nascent, waiting for you to rediscover it."

"You mean love."

"I mean a sufficient amount of yourself to be called that."

"I don't know if I can …"

"And I know it is not easy, but I also know it is vitally necessary."

"This does not seem to be the time for love."

"Now is when we need it most, I think. It is too easy to fall into resignation and displacement of emotion."

"One can try, I suppose, but I don't see much chance of success. And besides, I don't have the energy for both the theater and love."

"But you will, I hope."

"Perhaps."

Like Nietzsche, Schadow admired Socrates, that "mocking enamored monster and pied piper of Athens," believing that knowledge could be best achieved by forcing people to think through the consequences of ideas and actions. He regretted not having been more successful with this practice in the case of some of his more intelligent former students, and he tended to generalize the failure onto that of his profession per se. ("My method has failed; you have only to look around you to see the results of unthinking ignorance, arrogance, which leads to stupidity and madness. When Nietzsche said that god was dead, he meant we are no longer able to believe in god, that we would have to find something else to satisfy our need for faith. For him this was man himself, but a rational man of wisdom, not a racist barbarian. We have not yet understood his teaching either. And now we are forced to face the idea of evil without redemption.")

One of those intelligent former students, Abraham Buschelsohn, a Jew who had survived the camps and now worked at some unspoken but clearly evident mission, met Schadow during that first summer of peace by coincidence at a slapdash concert of chamber music put on by a pickup group of amateur musicians who played in the open air of Treptow Park. The younger man walked with Schadow to the old man's room not far distant, where the discussion turned quickly to the catastrophe of the attempt to exterminate the Jews of Europe, for which Buschelsohn used the Yiddish word "Hurban."

"Now we need to create new models, we need to see a new type of Jew, the one inherent in Zionism. Neither the assimilated secular Jews nor the ghettoized yiddische Jude. We need the Jew with his own country, fierce and proud, secure and convinced of his equality with any Goyische, a nationalistic, strong Jew with his own army to support him. Neither assimilation nor isolation. Never again. We came too close this time."

"Your only problem, then, is to remove the Arabs to make room for the Jews. Not a very good start, not a very stable basis for a new state."

"The Arabs can live with us, if they choose. They can be citizens, but not too many of them so they become a problem. Maybe they should convert, who knows. We are very sensitive to the condition of second-class citizen. We know better than to foster that."

"Herzl's dream cannot be realized because it is a dream. It makes no allowances for reality. Certainly not the realities of Palestine. Good Christ, man, it's too complex. The Arabs already fear the Jews and removal, or at least being dominated by the Jews there. The riots before the war showed that."

"Christ has nothing to do with it. A minor Jewish fringe radical taken up by dissatisfied elements of the Roman have-nots. The Arabs will have to educate themselves out of their stagnant ignorance."

"And the Jews will no doubt teach them."

"Why not? We're good at that."

"So there will be an Arab university across the street from Hebrew University?"

"That would only reinforce the differences. No good, too divisive. They can attend Hebrew University."

"The better to assimilate them?"

"Of course. The difference is - so you don't catch me here! - the difference is they have a safe haven to go to very close at hand. We didn't."

"If they love the land as all peasants do no matter how inhospitable and barren, they won't move easily.

You'll have to deport them or live with a permanently disaffected minority within the nation. I've no need to tell you what that means - ethnic and religious hatreds combined are the devil's playing field. We've had that here for the last twelve years. You cannot tell me you wish this to happen again."

"It will not happen again, definitely. We've learned the lessons, but above all else the Jews must have a homeland, a nation state to protect them against the destruction of the race. That is the non plus ultra. The Arabs of Palestine can only benefit from a Jewish state. It will raise them out of ignorance and sloth, it will allow them to emancipate themselves from misery and hunger. What could they have against finally entering the twentieth century?"

"They may not want any of that."

"You mean they may not yet know they need all that." Buschelsohn said this with a certain sadness.

"They may wish to travel at their own pace."

"Let them do it elsewhere then," Buschelsohn snapped. "Besides which, none of us has that choice anymore. You Germans have seen to that. And the British helped with the Balfour Declaration, can't forget that. The Jewish state is now inevitable. As soon as the powers see this, they will not be able to stand in our way, nor should they want to. The Arabs aren't going to bring the Middle East into the modern age, nor are the imperialists, they're too dependent on Arab oil, and their time is past anyway. We will do it. And now we have moral right on our side."

"From that angle, the price was too high."

"We did not pay it willingly. And we will never pay it again. Your argument is specious sophistry."

"And yours, I fear, is irrational."

"That no longer matters, does it? The force of history, as you well know, is undeniable, and it is now with us."

"I heard that kind of argument in Munich in 1923."

"And in Paris the year before the Grand Army marched off behind Napoléon, and in Vienna and Berlin in 1914, and in Macedonia when Philip let his son loose upon the world, and and and -- it has always been so in human history. Now it is our turn. We've paid our dues. *Carpe diem*, my dear professor."

"This conversation has saddened me to the point of depression."

"We will not ask your help, Herr Professor."

"No, I am too old and feeble for that."

"No, you think too much. What we need now are fighters, committed secular warriors willing to die to save the race. Our first priority is to move as many of the young and strong of the She'erit ha-Peletah, the surviving remnant, to Eretz Israel to work for the Yishuv."

"Without that youth and energy, the communities here will never be recreated," Schadow murmured with a question in his voice.

"Europe has seen the last of its Jews; we need them in the homeland."

"But surely there are Jews who still feel an identity with European culture and traditions, who want to rebuild the communities here, they are after all German."

"You ensured that there are no longer any German Jews, only Jews forced to live here for the time being."

Schadow's eyes flashed for a brief moment with the old fire of angry rebuttal. "Not all Germans killed Jews! We are not all guilty of that."

"You are much too intelligent to deny the responsibility of all Germans for the hurban. This is no place for Jews any longer, this is the killing earth too soaked in our blood."

"I think you are wrong, Herr Buschelsohn. I am told the Berlin *Gemeinde* is coming together again, what's left of it, and finding new members from among the DPs who do not wish to return to their homes. Immanuel Weinraub and others are very active in rebuilding the communal organizations. Their point, I believe, is to deny the nazis a posthumous victory: a Germany free of Jews."

"They are suffering from a deep lack of understanding and are missing the Zionist vision. And the British support them because they don't want too many Jews to move to Eretz Israel. The British need oil and are pro-Arab so of course they support the local communities. The Americans follow the British, half-heartedly perhaps, but they too support the so-called rebuilding. Weinraub argues with me every day. Doesn't matter, Herr Professor. We will win."

"Then the future will be as bloody as the past. I am grateful I won't see it in its full catastrophe."

"You so-called Aryans have no right to tell us what to do, or to criticize. Your guilt is as unequalled in human history as your industrial murder of our people. And if you think we are or will be satisfied with the Allies holding trials for every war crime imaginable except the mass murder of Jews, you are wrong, very wrong. We will deal with the murderers ourselves!"

Schadow sat in the dark silence, as shrunk in upon himself as a rail-thin old man can shrink, his face an image of desolation in the knowledge of the future. Exhausted and unable to speak, he moved his left hand weakly, indicating his withdrawal from the present.

"I will leave you now, Herr Professor. We probably will not meet again. I move about a great deal, as much as my health and the military governments allow. We've much to do. I cannot say meeting you again has been a great pleasure. I no longer find it agreeable to speak to Germans, but who knows?"

"In the end I taught you nothing," Schadow murmured softly, despairing. "I regret that also."

"Oh no, Herr Professor, you taught us all too well. Goodbye." The last word he spoke in English: he did not want to indicate any possible "*Wiedersehen*." The fact that they did see each other again did not lessen the despair that gnawed at Schadow's mind when he contemplated his failure. The old man remembered all too clearly the brief exchange they had somewhat later when they met by chance on the street and Schadow incautiously mentioned Faust. "Apparently we cannot get away from the Faustian bargain."

"And some don't try very hard," Buschelsohn snapped.

"The nation made that bargain with the brown shirts and paid the price."

"The price for six million Jews will never be paid."

"I suppose not. Others suffered as well."

"No doubt, but it's not the same, is it?"

"I don't know, Herr Buschelsohn. What is the sense in comparing the quality of suffering?"

"You made the bargain with that devil and you've no choice but to pay."

"I take it that the 'you' is the nation in general?"

"I fear you personally are also part of the nation."

"I could say that I have already paid enough."

"You could, Herr Professor, you could."

"But that would be meaningless …"

"Precisely."

"Nonetheless, I contributed nothing to the killing of the Jews or the war. I am too old and they threw me out of my profession."

"You cannot escape being German and the collective guilt of all Germans for the hurban and the war."

"Under other circumstances, I might risk the statement, 'You too drive a hard bargain,' metaphorically of course."

"Of course. But at the moment that would be walking very close to the edge of anti-Semitism."

"Yes, I suppose so. There is so little room left for humor."

"For some of us there is no room at all."

* * * *

Gisela, again like her father, did not always follow the oblique advice Schadow placed before her; despite her natural rebellion against the practices of older generations she appreciated the opportunity to talk over the various alternatives with a critical, but sympathetic mind. When he did criticize her actions he surrounded his phrases with affection: a sharp condiment mitigated by a bland sauce. ("You see, even our analogies and metaphors are those of the alimentary canal these days!" Boltzmann roared one well-watered evening.) During the war when she traveled to Munich to act in movies at the Geiselgasteig studios, they wrote each other frequently if cryptically because he correctly feared the Gestapo might read his mail (so many men did not relish duty on the Eastern Front but could be helpful to the police on the home front). The letters she received from him, written in his angular idiosyncratic old German script in red ink, brought a measure of relief and wisdom into her life when she felt awash in that peculiarly totalitarian atmosphere of corruption, cynicism, and mercantile sex.

In preparation for writing those graceful letters and his essays, he had to wipe the barrel of his fountain pen with a rag he kept on his writing table for that specific purpose. Surprised by the first tentative Royal Air Force bombing of the city early in the war, he dropped the pen, opening a small fissure in its barrel, which thereafter seeped bright red ink into the cap and discolored his fingers. When Schade once asked him about the pen and the seemingly permanent stain on his hands, he said, "I've written some fine essays with this pen in the last twelve years, all for the desk drawer, to be sure. The instrument has emotional value for me; it is a talisman. And besides, one cannot replace it today." During the winter Schade gave him a new Parker fountain pen for which the old man politely thanked him. Then he put it away in its case, preferring to use the broken one. Schade understood this when he discovered that the historian's wife had given him the pen as a present upon the publication of his last book in 1932. The black and gold Montblanc comforted him with its association, while simultaneously drawing a dim sense of retrospective guilt from his conscience for not having loved the giver of the gift with more passion and solicitude. So he continued to write with it and bore the red stain on his fingers as a private heraldic sign, the understanding of which only he possessed despite its more obvious symbolic significance. The stain became part of his identity; his aging brain, crammed full of the bric-a-brac of the 20th century jostling against chunks of the deep past, remembered his personal losses whenever his eyes fell upon the color of his fingers. "Not that there is any *political* meaning in it, you know," he seriously and unnecessarily told Gisela.

Schadow liked the young American-German because of his openness, friendliness, and mind that chewed over his thoughts before expressing them. He asked Gisela to bring Schade occasionally and enjoyed the interchange of literary and historical allusions, which they exchanged in mock competitions, which Schadow usually won. Schade proved to be willing to continue his learning process and Schadow stood, or at this point in his life sat, ready to continue his mentoring function, an activity that made him feel alive. For his part, Schade enjoyed the challenge presented by the older man's still agile mind, but maintained an emotional distance from him, as if fearing a too powerful influence. Caught up in the tension between his American and German selves, Schade paradoxically needed and rejected the traditional intellectual methodologies of thought and analyses offered by the sympathetic but not uncritical former professor. Sometimes it seemed they also shared the smaller and larger packets of guilt that the history of their unprecedented and horrifying times planted in everyone capable of thought and even a minimal amount of compassion. It was with Schadow in his increasingly manuscript and book filled room that Schade talked through the idea for his novel.

* * * *

In the autumn gaudy leaves of fiery colors would have come tumbling down, but none remained to fall. The final blasts of the battle for the city had stripped the trees of all their foliage and most of their branches, and the most perspicacious among the citizens were already busy cutting down the trees themselves in anticipation of the winter winds off the Brandenburg plain which would freeze the water in the pipes and the blood in their veins. (Early in the next spring a survivor of the winter, a drawn and gray middle-aged man in stained bib overalls and a worn brown cloth cap, his breath crystallizing in the still cold air, would guide two thick farm horses, steam snorting from their noses, harnessed to an ancient plough making furrows in the sandy earth of the treeless Tiergarten beneath the battered isolated Victory Column surmounted by the ironically triumphant angel statue. Passing the scene with Makepeace, Boltzmann would note with resignation dampening his voice into the depths of his throat, "What better comment on our condition.")

> *Am Brandeburger Tor blühen die Tomaten,*
> *Am Grossen Stern wächst Sellerie und Suppengrün*
> *...*[19]

Kirshhof, a dead cigar between his fingers and uniform necktie unmilitarily loosened, worked hard filing another negative report on a journalist's application for a work permit, saying to Schade one afternoon: "It's because you seem weak, y'know? That's what makes you so attractive to people. You appear to be so goddamned vulnerable, even some intelligent people think they have to protect you somehow, kay? No, not me; I'm essentially indifferent to your charms. You never really crossed me, but I'm not your friend either. I'm waiting to see where you land when you make up your mind to jump. Maybe we can be friends then. It depends on where you land. Kay?"

---

[19] Lines from KaDeKo review *"Melodie der Strasse"* (1947). "Tomatoes blossom at the Brandenburg Gate/Celery and soup greens grow at the Grosse Stern."

Schade demurred, unable to agree or disagree with the apparent but not substantive obscurity of the other's discussion. Kirshhof shook his head at this unwillingness to face the facts and relit the thick cigar, blowing a huge cloud of smoke over his desk. "John, I even *like* you, but that doesn't change anything. You've got to make up your mind, you've got to make a choice. You can't stay on the fence for long, not around here, for Christ's sake! Don't you see that? Do you need a weather vane to tell where the wind is blowing? It's the hard line, kay; we can't be soft on these swine; they don't deserve it; they've got to be punished, kay. They're not really human, y'know. There's no in between: either they grovel in the dirt at your feet or they beat the shit out of you with arrogance and a whip. We'll denazify them all right. Damn good. Listen, I know you come from here, but that doesn't make any difference, does it?"

There could be no rational argument with him on this subject, although otherwise he could be a reasonable colleague, and after several days of working with him, few made the attempt. Harrigan voiced the common concern with an old cliché: "The Jew's a time bomb and nobody knows when he's going to explode; not even he knows." Makepeace told Kirshhof after one outburst: "It's not that you're wrong - or right - it's that you're getting in the way of us doing our jobs. The Germans have got to be allowed to run their own show some time. The sooner the better, or don't you read the papers about Congress cutting the military government budget? You're no help here." Following this conversation Kirshhof rarely voiced his obsession in their presence, but he could not, or would not, let up. The dull chains of his concerns had metal spikes in them and the pain they caused drove him incessantly. Feldman, the fast-talking CIC captain, told Schade: "The bee in his bonnet stings him every day into a permanent state of rage." At one point, his yoyo madly doing one loop-the-loop after another, Kirshhof yelled at no one in particular: "Show me a fucking kraut and I'll show you a Jew-killer!" The blatant irrationality of this idea did not deter him from his increasingly demented course. Schade, Harrigan, and Makepeace, in veiled conversation with some of their colleagues, decided to recommend to Lt. Col. McCrae that Kirshhof be transferred as soon as possible to a post outside the occupation zone for the last months of his duty tour. They concluded that the prospect of his imminent discharge actually spurred him to even higher levels of intense concentration and activity. In fact, it became clear that Kirshhof's intercourse with Germans, inevitable in the job, only increased his hatred since he had become incapable of making distinctions, and therefore each German he met reinforced his conceptions of them. Of course, they arrived at their decision too late: early that winter, shortly before his transfer to the States for discharge, on a still, cold evening, Kirshhof murdered a German by shooting him in the heart with a US Army-issue sidearm. Harrigan's first reaction was to say: "I knew they should have taken those things away from us before this." Schade, stunned, could only mumble, "We should have gotten him out before this. What will they do about it?"

  The news came through the telephone from the office of the American Sector commanding officer where Kirshhof had gone to surrender. (Schade later wondered why he hadn't simply walked away from the body: how thoroughly would anyone have investigated yet another death, even a murder, among so many? The German police had thus far only been organized to deal with traffic control, not homicide.) Makepeace answered the telephone and talked to several people, then briefly to Kirshhof himself, although he could barely understand his colleague's disjointed phrases. "Shock, deep shock, as if he couldn't believe what he'd done. I think he was faking it, but that won't matter now." Makepeace finally talked to the CO himself and then made a series of short calls. The telephones functioned more efficiently than they had during the early days of the occupation, but delays and broken connections still bedeviled the system. His responses became increasingly cryptic and his final conversation on the old black apparatus mystified Schade, who paced about the office smoking furiously, raging at Kirshhof's stupidity and the delay in doing something about it.

"Hello. This is Lieutenant Makepeace, sir. Yes, Kirshhof. I've spoken to them ... Yes sir. I think so ... Yes sir, if we move fast enough ... Right ... Yes sir." He replaced the receiver on its squat pedestal and turned to Schade. "John, can you go over to Colonel Howard's office and keep Hal company for a while? It won't take long. Take the Opel."

"What the hell is going on?"

"We're going to get him out today, the lid is going on the whole thing."

"That's crazy."

Makepeace smiled briefly, his face already haggard with fatigue. "Nonetheless, my friend, that is the decision. Don't say anything to Hal about it, in case something goes wrong. The best laid plans, y'know. Just keep an eye on him, talk to him. They're afraid he might go off the rails completely and kill himself - or someone else."

"If this gets out there'll be hell to pay."

"You do use those Americanisms correctly, John."

"Dammit, we're supposed to be setting an example here," Schade replied angrily.

"We're also the victors here, remember? Listen, we can argue about it later. The decision has been made. We've got to move."

"Who were you talking to? Who made the decision?"

"Later. Take the Opel. Go. I'll use the jeep."

*

Harrigan remembered his amazement at the sight of Kirshhof bedazzling a group of Germans at Alexanderplatz standing around him with open mouths and awe-struck eyes as he flashed yoyos in each hand with a speed that blurred the coordinated actions of his arms, wrists, and the flying round pieces of color sizzling out from his slightly crouched torso to snap back into his hands with the sound of a sharp slap of wood against flesh. The look of utter contempt and sneering condescension on the yoyoist's face as he fascinated his audience disturbed Harrigan enough to mention it to Makepeace, who responded with a voice bordered with impatience: "What do you expect?"

The Soviet city commandant's office formally complained in the next meeting of the inter-allied cultural affairs committee about the undermining of Soviet authority in its own sector. "An unidentified American officer deliberately performed a provocative act with a round object and a length of string, knowing this would provoke a negative effect among the population relating to the policies and procedures of the Allied military occupation governments. The Soviet Military Administration demands that appropriate action be taken by the American command to assure that such a provocation is not repeated and that the offending officer is appropriately punished." Harrigan and Schade had not found this as amusing as their colleagues.

*

Schade drove as fast as he could through the dark streets without crashing into a crater or knocking over any of the shadowy figures plying their trades in certain areas. The women's rubble brigades had cleared many road surfaces, but it remained dangerous to drive too fast on the side streets and the MPs had become notorious for their hair-triggers. One nervous young MP corporal had shot and killed an Army captain in the Re-education Division who for some unknown reason did not stop his jeep on command. Another shot one of the more politically acceptable German orchestra leaders whose driver simply had not understood the young soldier's thick Alabama accent, thus adding to the official tribulations plaguing Oscar Monday's life and adding another legend to the city's already bulging storehouse.

At the CO's office, they expected Schade: Makepeace must have made another telephone call. Kirshhof sat subdued and alone in a small side office smoking a cigar. One unobtrusive MP guarded the room from a desk outside the room. Otherwise Schade saw only the usual contingent of young men with the distinctive white on black armbands patrolling the perimeters of the building, whose skeleton crew at this hour went about their business in the unperturbed, almost distracted manner of all who work the graveyard shift. Evidently they knew nothing about the shooting.

Schade closed the door. "Hal?"

"Hello, John. I didn't expect they'd send you."

"There was no one else in the office when the call came."

"Where's Bill?"

"Trying to make arrangements. We're not sure how these things are done ... MPs ... CIC...."

"I heard some of the CO's talk on the phone, kay ... I haven't been arrested ... What's going on?"

"I don't know exactly. What happened, Hal?"

Kirshhof shifted in his chair sheepishly and puffed on the cigar. "I lost my head for a moment." He smiled grimly. "I guess I might lose it permanently now. They took my ID card and my yoyo. What's left?"

"How did it happen?"

"It's getting cold, you know?" His eyes retreated into his mind and silence ensued. Finally he began to speak as if from within a depth within himself of which he had previously been unaware. "Actually, it was easy. I mean, I remember everything, kay ... I think ... you just pull the trigger and he falls down and doesn't move anymore ... I even remembered to pull the slide back before the trigger. It made a loud noise ... haven't heard that in a long time. He must have jumped back three feet before he fell down ... I mean it seemed like he jumped ... actually, John, he probably didn't jump because he was dead ... the bullet must have thrown him back, kay ... the look of surprise, as if it couldn't possibly be happening to him, the fucking pig. Christ, did it ever feel good! Damn, damn, did it feel good to shoot that bastard ... but it hurt my hand all right, still tingles, kay. Then I must have blacked out for a while, not very long, seconds. Then suddenly everything came rushing back and there I was, kay ... standing there like a moron with the gun in my hand ... you know it's funny he pissed his pants ... after I shot him, after he died, I guess. That was very disconcerting. It made him so ... vulnerable, almost, maybe human ... for a while I didn't know what to do, kay ... there was nothing I could do. So I came here and turned myself in. It's not like I expected, John ... they haven't arrested or booked me or anything ... haven't even seen the MPs yet but I know there's one there outside the door. It'd be different in Bloomington, kay, I'll tell you that."

"Why, Hal?"

"What?" The puff-puff on the cigar seemed to give him some solace, but his concentration wandered from one subject to another somewhere in the depths of his whirligig mind.

"Why did you shoot him? Who was he?" Kirshhof's apparent indifference vexed Schade, but he repressed this as unworthy under the circumstances; a sympathetic attitude of understanding would be far more useful. Speaking of a middle-aged novelist no longer able to write after returning from a British POW camp, Ulrich Kramer had said, "Another *mutilé de guerre*. The psyche, you know, is all too often affected even when the body remains healthy. A condition shared by victors and defeated alike." Schade tried to think of Hal Kirshhof in that way.

"A kraut, just a kraut, a half-blind kraut, no more, no less." Kirshhof made the statement in a neutral voice that trembled around the edges. "Like all of them, John. I've told you before, remember? A soulless lout, but an intellectual, a journalist, for crying out loud!" He fell silent as if mulling the matter over, line of concentration etching soft indentations on his pudgy face. Cigar smoke drifted into his eyes but he did not squint. "It's what he said, John. What he said is what he is ... they'll never learn. We'll be here forever, kay, have to ... can't let them alone or they'll go right back to it ... until there's not a Jew left on earth." His voice cracked in a muted growl of hopelessness.

Schade groaned.

"Yeah, I know you don't believe me, but you'll see, you'll see it happen, kay." He looked up suddenly, clear-eyed. "Sit down, you're not my judge. I could plead temporary insanity, y'know. With a good lawyer I bet you I'd get off. He wouldn't have to be a Jew either. Maybe that's what I'll do. What do you think?"

"Perhaps. I don't know. Who was he, Hal?"

"Late this afternoon, I was in this bar, kay, the Florian where the guys from the old papers hang out. I wasn't drinking much at all. Hell, there's not much there to drink unless we bring it, a few beers, just talking to some of the guys we've cleared and some of our guys about putting out the new paper in our Sector. The locals are worried about the supply of newsprint like everyone else and we were talking about that, kay. And I was getting tired of the bellyaching when this tall skinny guy comes over to the table and won't sit down. He's missing one eye, y'know, just an empty socket, ugly as hell, with a red scar running up through his hairline, proud of it, no patch like our friend the colonel. Wanted everyone to know he fought in the war and suffered for his country. I could tell he was one of those arrogant bastards who forgot they lost the war but remembered all the Jews they'd saved from the gas chambers. I could tell it just by looking at him, thin lips and hard eye. You get a talent for that after a while, kay. He introduces himself, Hinrichts or something like that, says he needs to talk to me about getting a license for a magazine he wants to publish. Well, hell, normally I'd tell the schmuck to come around to the office, but the beer in the Florian was especially bad today and I was tired of listening to them complain about the lack of this and that and everything else. So I said okay, we could talk about it. I thought we'd walk back to the office and I'd give the bastard the forms and find out what he had in mind, y'know.

"Got a match, John? This cigar's gone out. Thanks." Puff puff puff. "This aint a bad cigar, y' know. Want one? Jesus I'm tired, could sleep forever. Wait, no not forever, too much like dying ... I've been thinking about that, kay. It's so easy over here. Every day you see people in the streets wheeling bodies back and forth ... dying is all around us. What's another life, especially a Jew-hating fucking kraut! He *was* one, y'know. That came out pretty fast after we left the Florian. As we walked out of the joint he asked if I was a German, originally, like you, kay, given my name, which around here isn't necessarily Jewish. Well, I didn't lie, I told him yeah my grandparents came from the Rhineland, but I didn't tell him I'm a Jew ... I never do. You find out a lot about these creeps if you don't tell them you're Jewish; they feel more comfortable and say things they usually wouldn't if they knew.

"Well, we don't get too far when he asks if we can stop at his apartment for a minute so he can pick up some papers for the clearance, references, stuff like that. I told him he could do that later. I thought for a moment he might be queer, wouldn't that have been something, but he didn't really act like one. He said his place was just around the corner and it wouldn't take a minute and he had examples of a magazine he'd published before the war there so I could see he was legit. His English wasn't too good but he made himself understood well enough, kay. He told me he'd published a magazine on popular archaeology before the war ... this was what he wanted to start up again. Said he was in the army until last winter when he was wounded and they shipped him to a hospital in Potsdam ...

Probably in the SS, the prick. Anyway I finally said what the hell, okay, and his place was only a block away. Pretty well bombed out, but one room had walls and a ceiling. I don't know why I agreed to go, never did before, curiosity maybe.

"When we get inside he says, 'I couldn't talk to you there in the Florian, too many Jews around,' and gets this look of disgust on his face, kay. I could feel myself starting to go off, but I just looked at him as if to ask what he meant, y'know? Maybe I should've stopped it there, but I was sort of fascinated by him, like being hypnotized by a goddamn snake. I'd never personally heard even a kraut talk like that before, not personally. He blamed the Jews for losing his goddamned magazine, in 1938 for Christsake! He kept going on about the Jews being the cause of all Germany's problems, the whole usual nazi shebang, working himself into a fit. He kept saying the words 'hep, hep' as if they were a litany, smiling like we had a conspiracy, the two of us, a big secret, 'hep! hep!', kay, and the strange thing is I knew what he meant because I'd just read about it in a book on the middle ages by that Schadow historian. 'Hieroslyma est perdita,' kay, 'Jerusalem is lost,' which they shouted in the pogroms while they beat up the Jews. If I hadn't known that maybe it would have been different, but I doubt it, kay, because of that smile. At one point I wanted to yell at him "Jesus was a rabbi!" but I didn't, wouldn't have made any difference, he wasn't Christian. All this shit coming out of him and he got madder and madder, losing control, talking a crazy mishmash of German and English. He must have been demented, his wound must have gone right through to his brains. Or maybe they ran out of the hole. Talking like that to an American officer. Meschugge. I think he forgot I was there. In the end I damned sure reminded him that I was still there. The madder he got, the colder I got, kay. I became like an ice block, y'know, removed from the place, just listening to this bastard run off at the mouth with this filthy kraut stuff. I knew this was a bad sign but I couldn't stop it, couldn't move, like being hypnotized. My mind was super clear, but off near the ceiling, kay. Maybe I even nodded my head. I don't remember that.

"As I listened I started analyzing what he was saying, breaking it down and automatically thinking up arguments against each piece. It was like arguing with myself. It was crazy. Standing there listening to him, but my mind working like mad, like a machine, an engine running too fast in neutral, kay. I never experienced anything like that." He stopped talking and stared at the cigar between his fingers. It had gone out again but he made no move to relight it. Clearing his throat with a growl, he shifted his weight in the chair and looked blankly around the room without moving his head.

"Finally, in the middle of the argument in my mind, I registered that he was saying something about not enough Jews being gassed and how we'd be better off if a better job had been done of it. Everything screeched to a stop then. My mind went completely blank, totally. Something snapped, kay. I *heard* it snap. Maybe it was the sound of the gun when I pulled the slide back. I remembered to do that. He didn't realize what I was doing, I guess, too full of his own craziness. He kept talking right up until I pulled the trigger. When he finally caught on he was surprised, not panicked, he didn't have time for that, just surprised, as if no one could possibly disagree with him. When I killed the bastard he was still surprised. I didn't even tell him I'm a Jew." Kirshhof shook his head sadly. "I should have told him. There wasn't time, I guess. He jumped back and fell down on the floor. Must have died right away. Who knows what camp he worked in probably was a guard ... who knows how many Jews he killed. I blanked out for a few seconds, then came to and wondered what the hell I should do. Maybe I should have just left him there and walked away, but people had seen me with him just before. So I came here and told the story to Colonel Howard. Had to raise hell to get to see him at all. What's he care about Jewish captains, kay. He didn't do anything at first except look pissed off at having to bother with the whole thing. Then he told me to call McCrae and tell him the story, but I misdialed and got onto Bill. When Howard heard who it was, he talked to Bill himself for a bit then left and told me to sit here, kay. He seemed to know Bill. What's going on? What are they going to do, John?"

"I don't know, Hal, but we'll find out soon."

"You know, I could've made a million with the yoyos. The kids at least love them."

"No one here has a million to buy anything, Hal."

"Lord, am I tired. I got the shakes. No wonder, eh? They won't give me the chair or anything like that, will they?"

"Probably not."

"After all, I'm an American Army officer, dammit, and we won, didn't we?"

"That's what they say, Hal, we won. But we didn't win for this, did we?"

"Then what the hell, John, what the hell?"

At that point Makepeace rushed in carrying Kirshhof's ditty bag, accompanied by a sergeant and corporal Schade had not seen before. "Hal, you stupid son-of-a-bitch. You're more trouble than you're worth. But the decision's been made to get you out of here. Understand? The fix is in, you jerk. There's a plane to Frankfurt in an hour. You'll be on it. These men will make sure you get to

Tempelhof and go with you to Frankfurt. From there you'll fly to CONUS where you'll sit out the very short rest of your not very brilliant military career in some boon dock base. Probably less than a month. Am I getting through to you?"[20]

"Ur."

"Good. You'll forget about the whole matter, verstehe? Sign this paper, it's a mild form of blackmail just to ensure you keep your mouth shut. You've got every reason to do that, Hal. I suggest you don't even think about it anymore. What a stupid thing to do."

"What about my yoyos?"

"Most of them are in the bag. All right, sergeant, take him off. Your other stuff will be shipped to you, Hal. So long." Makepeace shook his left hand slightly and no one heard the heavy bracelet links rub against each other.

And so Kirshhof went, still baffled by the speed at which everything happened. His life in those hours seemed like a film strip accelerated far beyond the normal speed of projection: a blur he did not quite comprehend, leaving him breathless, and not sure that he wanted to understand or that it would be of any benefit to him if he did. As he and his escort left the office, the words of the American song played on someone's old radio accompanied them.

> *You'll be my dreamboat forever*
> *because I'll never leave you, never.*

Later, Makepeace and Schade sat smoking and drinking coffee with Colonel Darkley in the office he used on his trips to Berlin. "At this point, gentlemen, it was

---

[20]CONUS: Continental United States; also known as the land of the big PX.

decided we had no choice but to send him home. You can *imagine* the problems involved if we had held a trial here, what with the *other* trial in Nüremberg. This is no case of some drunken private first class assaulting some German in mitigating circumstances. This was a military government officer in an important position *dealing* with Germans every day, potentially influential Germans, newspaper editors and journalists. The results could be horrendous. And, as a member of the tribe, so to speak, having a Jew kill a German at this point would not *help* our situation in Germany, would it, no matter how much you or I may *sympathize* with Kirshhof. This doesn't help the American cause, or the Jewish cause. As I wholeheartedly support both, I had no hesitation in authorizing this action, with the appropriate clearances from *above*, of course. We simply cannot afford a public scandal now, especially with such newshounds as Tompkin in the city. I tried to get him for the radio network, did you *know* that? Despite the example of Bill Shirer, I was unsuccessful. Don't know why. Well. The German pig will simply disappear, another *victim* of the postwar chaos. Unfortunate, but necessary. No leaks, you understand. No one should have anything about *this* to remember. Now, there are some matters of business to discuss before I return to Frankfurt myself. Colonel McCrae is waiting for us." Darkley rubbed his uncovered eye and stood up. "*Allons-y!*"

Schade doubted Kirshhof would ever be able to forget the incident, but he soon pushed it into the further recesses of his own mind. Occasionally a phrase or a piece of landscape reminded him of the man with the yoyos whose visceral hatred broke his equilibrium. Once he drove past the ruins of the old Adlon Hotel, much frequented by foreign correspondents, movie stars, and diplomats before the war, and remembered going past it with Makepeace and Kirshhof one day. Makepeace had stopped the jeep to gaze abstractedly at the rubble. "I always wanted to stay at the Adlon. It has such sharp associations of dark modern romance: whiskey, trench coats, beautiful women in slinky low cut gowns, foreign intrigue, a whiff of danger ... Now look at it: a busted symbol of someone else's past and my youthful fantasies." Kirshhof had said thoughtfully, "They'll rebuild it. The krauts are like that." "Not likely."

With the exception of the yoyos, Harold Kirshhof as an identifiable individual disappeared from the city's memory and, in the rush of daily events and concerns which involved all of them who stayed on in the city, as they became increasingly caught up in the fragile web of public and private relationships the citizens and their conquerors wove with such weakened social and sexual threads, his colleagues too gradually lost their images of the man and forgot his deranged act unless reminded.

Not even Schade brooded on the subject of Kirshhof and his act of misguided revenge, but, almost alone among the denizens of the city, he did not forget the man himself entirely. Shortly after Kenneth Farisse, Kirshhof's replacement, arrived in the city he said to no one in particular, "I should have brought a couple of yoyos with me. They would have made for a continuity, a smash hit among the natives, yessir, they would." No one in particular contradicted him and the Kirshhof yoyos entered the city's mythology even as the person disappeared from living memory.

* * * *

Pale and squarejawed Kenneth Farisse was not what his parents would have called a "well-rounded" individual:

After a tempestuous youth in San Diego, he settled down to four years of college in the state system during which he spent an inordinate amount of time drinking Rheingold beer, eating cheap meals and chasing girls. He took his academic work just seriously enough to pass his courses, but what really interested him was writing stories so he joined the staff of the campus newspaper and wrote two or three pieces a week for two years before becoming the assistant editor-in-chief. He loved words even more than he loved females of all ages and shapes. He excelled in literature courses and the teachers always gave him top grades on his papers, many of which he turned into articles for the newspaper. During his last year at the school he slept very little because the local police arrested the editor-in-chief for creating an incident in a sailors' bar near the harbor and the college forced the unfortunate coed to drop out of school. Farisse took over full responsibility for the thrice weekly appearance of the paper, a job he carried out conscientiously with verve, while simultaneously pursuing several undergraduate girls and two faculty wives, studying for his classes, and writing fiction, some of which appeared in the year's final issue of the campus literary magazine devoted entirely to the work of graduating seniors. He had more pieces in the issue than anyone else.

Noticing the increasing sallowness of his skin and the dark pouches under his constantly bloodshot eyes, the newspaper's faculty advisor, a kindly middle-aged man who wrote and published modernist poetry under a pseudonym and who would recommend Farisse for a job on the *Des Moines Dispatch* where he had a friend on the staff, mentioned one day the advantages of monogamous relationships between the sexes, especially the dubious morality of squandering one's seed, so to speak, so widely and so often.

"Professor Clancy, I know exactly what you mean, but you know, would you eat peanut butter sandwiches every day for years and years?"

"Some people do."

"Not this one."

At that point the professor sadly left off any further advice to the young man that dealt in any way with his sexual activities, but continued to advise him about the operation of the newspaper until graduation day, whereafter he never saw the aspiring journalist again. Farisse did write from time to time to let the older man follow his progress from one ill-paid position to another on one newspaper after another. At least he worked steadily at his profession, when many newspapermen were being laid off as the depression deepened and spread. The last letter the professor received from him was postmarked Sarasota, Florida, noting that the draft had finally caught up with him, and enclosing a postcard with a photograph of a circus elephant with one of its front legs seeming to rest on the rearend of a scantily dressed young woman lying on a beach.

Kenneth Farisse hated the army, but knew enough not to broadcast this to all and sundry. As soon as he left boot camp he found a way to be transferred to a military government training center at a university in New York City where the senior officers ignored the fact that he had studied Japanese for two years in college and marked him down for service in Germany, giving him a crash course in the language of that country. "They were going to put me in the public safety division, but I had got to know the secretary to the boss by then and she nicely fixed my paperwork so I went to Frankfurt in the press control section. I never saw the army move so fast as when they transferred me to this burg after old Hal left so quickly on emergency leave. Sure must have been a big emergency. Say, what about a beer and some peanuts? I know some loose women down at the Wunder Bar. Clean, and not bad looking either."

* * * *

Darkley and Schade skirted a gutted Soviet tank skewed over the sidewalk and street like a prehistoric beast fatally sunk on its haunches. They walked slowly and somewhat stiffly as if they had just met and had not yet decided whether they liked each other well enough to continue the conversation. The mild sun warmed their backs as they picked their way through the rubble and potholes, dodging the shaky bicycles that served as the Berliners main form of wheeled transportation if they could keep them from the endlessly greedy hands of Red Army soldiers. The colonel walked with his head held tightly upward, the seeing eye straight ahead, his barrel chest and round reddish face thrust forward like the prow of a sailing ship ploughing the waves. Schade wondered how he missed the holes and jagged edges of concrete. He also wondered why they had left the office; Darkley had merely said he wanted to walk, giving no destination, and Schade now realized they had none. As they stepped aside to allow passage for a middle-aged couple pushing an old wheelbarrow containing the shrouded corpse of a small child, Darkley shook his head. "How much more of that?" His eye was bleary with fatigue.

"Not enough medicines, not enough food, living exposed to the rain ... there's a lot of death here. Winter is almost here so it will get worse."

"There's not *much* of that in Bad Nauheim, or Frankfurt, anymore. This city *is* another world. Depressing."

"I'm not sorry we don't have to deal with public health. We're lucky in that, I suppose."

"Yes. We're *more* interested in mental health." They walked in silence for several meters before Darkley, visibly if mildly ill at ease, cleared his throat and turned his head slightly to Schade. "That special *mission* we gave to you and Lieutenant Makepeace has been cancelled. That's what I wanted to tell you away from the others." Schade inhaled dust and carbon monoxide fumes, his face squinted into a questioning appearance. "You understand, lieutenant, that it is still classified top secret. It is finished but it *remains* classified. Is that clear? Good." The colonel stopped walking to adjust his blue eye patch and began walking again. When Schade indicated that they had almost completed the mission in any case, Darkley responded, "Yes, well, *that's* that then. You might be interested to know that the desist order came directly from the top. Somehow General Clay got wind of it and ordered it to cease immediately. The General wants nothing to *impede* cooperation with the Russians. Personally, I don't think this would have made any difference, but we have no choice in the matter now. I'd like to know how he *found* out about it. Any ideas?"

Surprise tussled briefly with gratification in the younger man's mind: that the deputy military governor for the American zone strongly emphasized cooperation with the Russians pleased Schade's sense of balance and concern for the future. The whole mission had been stupid and self-defeating, the same results could have been achieved in the course of events without the nightly forays. Quite suddenly he realized what lay behind Darkley's question and he felt a warm flood of annoyance-driven embarrassment flow up from his belly. Did Darkley think he had informed Clay? Absurd. He'd only seen the general from a distance on several occasions, never said a word to him. Lieutenant generals do not often converse with unknown junior officers and Clay had the reputation for being efficient but demanding, cold and distant with his subordinates. The idea was too incredible. Schade had never been able to hide his skepticism and doubts about certain aspects of American policy in Germany, and had discussed them with Makepeace and others, but ... Perhaps this had caused the colonel's odd question. After a few steps he said: "No sir. But it was hardly a well-kept secret, frankly. The Brits had a similar policy for a while, and the Soviets make life easier for artists and the intelligentsia in their sector. Everyone knows that."

"That does not *change* our policy, Lieutenant."

"No sir, but people *are* disappearing, to the east, I'm told. Weren't we trying to counter that?"

"What we were *doing*, with some success, is to ensure proper control over events in our sector. We continue to do so. If our methods *change* from time to time, our mission does not."

"No sir."

"We do not *kidnap* people off the streets and make them disappear the way some of our Allies are *prone* to do. We like to think our methods are more subtle and our motives less paranoid. In any case, Lieutenant, your *change* of method is clear, is it not?"

"Does Lieutenant Makepeace know about the change?"

Darkley nodded and quickly grabbed Schade's arm, yanking him off the sidewalk into the middle of the street. "That *wall* is going to fall down. Watch it." They retreated to the other sidewalk and after the noise and dust settled continued up the street. "Those crummy buildings are *rickety*, lieutenant, *rickety*. Good Lord, will this town ever be repaired? Too long. Well, I won't *be* here to see it. My demob orders have been cut. Back to private life and industry. Radio of course, the old network, but television, lieutenant, television *is* the future. No future here." Darkley's voice filled with a weight of bitterness Schade had not heard there before. "I couldn't rise any higher in the service. Too many Jewish generals already."

Schade allowed himself a sudden informality. "Did you lose family in the camps?

"In the camps, in the ghettos, on the roads, in the forests ... yes."

Schade heard him speak without emphasis or inflection only this once, and never mentioned the subject again, not then or later in New York City when Darkley helped him find a publisher for his novel.

"Yes, Makepeace has been informed. Officially no one *else* here knew about it; no one does *know* anything about it, you understand, lieutenant."

"Yes sir, completely."

"Fine. I always doubted the *efficacy* of it. Didn't think it necessary. *All* we had to do was let the Russians *behave* like Bolsheviks for a while and they'd force the issue. They may give *their* Germans payok packages and the Möwe, but we'd *give* them intellectual freedom."

"Within reason," Schade ventured.

"And *within* policy directives, yes, of course. Couldn't be any *other* way, could there?" Darkley changed the subject to the conflict between Special Services' demands for troop entertainment theaters and McCrae's cultural control unit's requirements for the same theaters to be used by the Germans for the Germans. From this they went on briefly to other matters concerning Schade's office until the colonel said, "Ah, there's my jeep." By some process of extra-sensory perception the driver must have known when Darkley desired to leave the conversation, or had he given a hidden signal? Schade never discovered the answer, but accepted that such things happened only to field grade officers. "I'm returning to Frankfurt tonight. I'll inform General Sender that the question has been *settled* satisfactorily here. *He* can report to General Clay. You know, one of my ancestors lived in the Frankfurt ghetto more than two hundred years ago."

They made their farewells short and the colonel drove off down the street the way they had come, sitting straight and round in the passenger seat, the one-eyed prow ploughing the waves, completely conscious of the image he presented to the public. Schade stood on the sidewalk underneath a sign warning of the presence of unexploded bombs and removed his soft overseas cap to run his hand through his hair and brush his mustache with his thumb. Junior officers could always walk back to their offices. He plunged into the gloom of the first building he saw with a sign indicating beer. Two glasses of the dimly yellow concoction did nothing to cool his anger. ("Schultheiss?!" raged Kramer one night when an unfortunate Manning-Lehman ventured the opinion that Berlin beer tasted somehow "beerier" than the typical English lager. "Schultheiss?! That rhino piss hasn't tasted like anything but American shit for decades. Now a good pilsner, that's different!") Walking back to the office, he decided to take the Opel and visit the theater in which Gisela was rehearsing, if the Opel was available. What would he do if someone else had it out? Pound his desk with his fists, drink some whisky, smoke a few Chesterfields, and do some paperwork? Or go to The Edge Bar for a glass or two of whisky purloined from either the American or British rationed stores? At least there he could talk to Eden, the Perfect Bartender, who always nodded sagely in all the right places and at all the right moments. He decided on The Edge Bar and skirted the sign hanging by a thin string from a headless lamppost.

>*Achtung! Vorsicht!*
>*Bomben nicht anfassen!*
>*Aufpassen oder sterben.*

"The owners are thinking of building a hotel to shelter the Bar, mon. Perhaps even finding a satisfactory building somewhere near the Potsdamer Platz, the crossroads of the world where east and west meet, although these days it may not be so healthy to meet the east, nicht wahr? Someday before too long this city will be back to its old glory, don't you think? That's what the owners think. The town could do with a fine old hotel, they think, now that the Adlon is kaputt, like the Cecil in Alexandria or Shepheards in Cairo - one of the owners is Egyptian, y'know - top class, or the Hotel Europe in Avignon, something along the lines of the Danieli in Venice, do you know it? No, I don't either, but I've heard good things about it. I have been told the Monteleone in New Orleans might be another example, but I've not been there either. Now that the Adlon is gone what is there left in Berlin, they ask. Soon it will be time to make another hotel like that. The time will be right, and the people, the highest tip-top class of course, will need such a resting spot. This the owners think, and who knows but that they may be accurate. They don't ask my opinion, of course. Quite right, too, because, after all, I am only Eden The Bartender at The Edge Bar, mon. Would you care for another

Oulahtanga Cocktail? Mister Morgan Tahni's favorite. He taught me to make it even without the papaya juice."

Eden The Bartender possessed no apparent nationality and Fama reported that he owned a Nansen passport, but other rumors made it South African, Chilean, and Texan. He mastered most languages sufficiently well to carry out his functions including listening to tales of heartbreak, remorse, betrayal, and occasionally good fortune, at which point he quietly opens a bottle of champagne, the quality of which depends upon the depth of the customer's joy at his, or sometimes her, good luck. Only Mister Morgan Tahni flummoxed him one night by ordering the Oulahtanga Cocktail in a Polynesian dialect. No two people ever described Eden The Bartender's physical characteristics in the same terms, they all remembered him differently, but they all had one thing in common: they all held the memory of him as a Perfect Bartender. A memory-cypher chameleon.

The mysteriously invisible owners not only considered building a hotel to house the Bar, but constantly renovated it in their endless search for the perfect design ambiance to match their Perfect Bartender. Each renovation brought with it a move to a new locale: they began in the cellar of a damaged building in what became the Soviet Sector, then moved to the British, the American, and the French sectors, then back to the British sector and no one doubted this pattern would continue until they either built their hotel or found the decor to match their employee behind the bar. As that worthy person explained it to Vasart and Schade one slow night, "It got too dangerous in the Soviet quarter, mon. They closed us down all the time on no pretext at all, but we knew it was because we are The Edge Bar and our exemplars are Manhattan and London and the Raffles of Singapore. They know that. So we are not here in the west for good - or until the reds develop a different sense of saloons."

"Eden, I don't remember you behind the bar the first time I came here. That was early on when you were in the east and I heard the group playing bebop."

"If I may say so, Lieutenant, you may not have seen me, but I was there, and your condition on that evening slightly worse for the wearing, sir, if I may say so."

"You may, Eden, you may. And now a small glass of Johnnie Walker, if you please. Black. I have had a disturbing day."

"*Aber natürlich, Herr Leutnant. Ein Eisberg gefälligst?*"

* * * *

When Harrigan met Hagen Reger for the first time, his immediate reaction was one of offended disgust: he preferred not to deal directly with questionable petitioners seeking licenses to work in the American sector of the city. Now, watching the short, thin-haired former theater manager sitting in front of his desk, Harrigan lit a cigarette and wondered when the man would begin to squirm. But Reger showed no signs of squirming, indeed he presented the image of studied neutrality, neither arrogant nor humble, his eyes staring blandly behind dark-rimmed spectacles.

"I understand there is some question of my receiving a clearance to be licensed, Captain. Could you tell me if there is anything I can do to be of assistance in moving the matter along?"

"Your case is hardly any different than many others, Herr Reger. One might say that your past is your present, if you know what I mean."

"I am not sure that I do. I understand that certain things one might or might not have done in the past may influence decisions in the present, but, as you say, my case is not different from others, who have been cleared already."

"Membership in the party before a certain date is sufficient reason for denying a license. You know that already."

"Captain, I wish to work at what I know best how to do, work at which I have achieved a modicum of success, if I may be somewhat immodest. I am good at what I do, which has never had anything to do with war crimes or service in the Wehrmacht or the SS. I was never sent to the fronts and have always been a civilian."

"You were fairly good friends with Goebbels."

"That surely is not a crime. One can be misguided in the choice of one's friends, but we were never friends; friendly on the few occasions we met, but never friends."

"Your party membership is unquestionable."

"Why should I not admit joining the party? I wished to continue to manage one of the most successful theaters in the city. I worked hard, I achieved success and the commensurate rewards."

"Yes, Herr Reger, we have talked to several young actresses who provided you with some of those rewards, which you forced from them in one way or another."

"Captain Harrigan, we are both men of the world and sufficiently sophisticated to appreciate that very few men in any profession are saints. I must say that if my wife understands this, surely the American army can."

Harrigan smiled thinly and mentioned the names of several actresses including Gisela Albrecht.

Reger sighed and just stopped himself from a shrug of the shoulders. "Over the years, there were many. I can't possibly remember each of them individually. The Albrecht is the blonde with the cigarette voice, I think. Very talented. The others…. This situation was not very unusual, Captain, although deemed morally doubtful in some circles. I doubt that the situation is much different in New York or Hollywood."

"There is one big difference, Herr Reger."

"Oh? What is that?"

"There was no nazi party in power there. And you lost the war."

"That is hardly a reason for not allowing me to work."

"It will do for now. *Auf Wiedersehen*, Herr Reger."

* * * *

Wilson Tompkin found a deep satisfaction and sensual pleasure in rejecting social invitations and remaining closeted in his room with a large vase of sweetly odorous flowers near his bed while lying naked, his cat asleep rising and gently descending on his belly. The soft pressure of warm fur and the light grind of the animal's purring, he insisted, allowed him to formulate brilliant openings for his articles. "Imagine: if I spent most of my time like that, I would write the Great American Novel. Better than Proust. Unfortunately for world literature and fortunately for my editor, there's nary a cat to be found in Berlin these days." Most of those who knew Tompkin found the image incongruous: the tall burly reporter with a full curly silver and blonde shaggy beard and a hairy chest balancing the thinning hair atop his head, hand curved around a whisky glass like an iron glove, fit the boxing ring more appropriately than the Beardsley decadence of heavily fragrant blossoms and small furry animals. That image also did not accommodate itself to the apparently ineluctable expression of the digestive process his body suffered from time to time after he had imprudently overindulged his appetite for too much greasy food - he who dreamed of rendered goose fat mixed with blackened bits of onions, salted on brown bread for breakfast with cold beer after a prophylactic shot of Jägermeister "to prepare the stomach for the cold beer." He belched in short fragmented melodies, which despite their fragmentary and blurted nature, Monday insisted could be fingered on the piano or actually sung if put together properly on music manuscript sheets. "Well, that's better than farting like a pig smelling like a hog, which me sainted mother told me was not de rigueur in polite society. That's why I don't chew gum: gives me gas." He paused to adjust his goldrimmed spectacles. "Y'know, I don't think pigs do fart, not in America anyway."

Tompkin arrived in Berlin for the third time in the late summer of that first year of the occupation to report on the city for the Overseas News Service, for which he had worked since the mid-1930s. A large collection of Americans and British appreciated Tompkin's stories of his tour of duty in Berlin, with a brief interruption in Bucharest, during that grotesque period between 1939 and 1941 when the United States remained neutral in the war. His talk and stories about the city during that intense time had become justifiably famous, and he narrated them with a detachment and enthusiasm, which covered whatever emotions he felt about that period of this life. And told them to whomever expressed an interest, and to many who did not as the night wore on, with gusto and wry humor. Makepeace found this intriguing and mentioned him to Schade who shook his head, not understanding detachment from matters concerning Germany and plagued by continuing ambiguity on the subject. Consequently, he did not attend the court occasionally held by the reporter in one of the officer's clubs or in his rooms (quite near his old space in Schadow's apartment and the new Overseas News Service office in Neuköln). Thus he missed witnessing the night when the American reporter met Walter Boltzmann for the first time. They prowled around each other like two suspicious tigers trying to clarify the other's intentions. Indeed their behavior patterns were similar in so many ways that they did not become friends until the episode with the one-legged whore and the candy bar, whereafter they formed a mutually supportive fan club whenever they met, which fortunately for both of them rarely happened. "You know Willy, it's a good thing we did not know each other the last time you were here, but I had already left the city for health reasons." "Just think, Wally, if we had met, would history have been any different?" "Ours would have, no doubt."

Tompkin had reported what the censor would allow about the real situation in Germany at war with the civilized world. The Berlin police, acting on higher authority, revoked his residence permit at the end of November 1941, whereafter he wrote a long series of articles based on his diaries from the time, colorfully portraying the paranoid style of German officialdom and the oppressed restlessness of the German citizens, explaining why the nazi state had to be defeated as thoroughly as possible. "Of course that asshole Hitler made it easier by declaring war on us after Pearl Harbor."

"In the end, during those last months in the city, we wrote harmless crap which we knew could get through the censors. We said we destroyed our notes, loudly and in public, any pieces of paper with writing on them; one radio reporter even erased the marks and marginal jottings in his books, and that's a true fact. Perhaps it was being overly cautious, but you never knew.... We knew our phones were being tapped, so we learned to speak like Hemingway, only even more cryptic. Gestapo interrogations were not pleasant and they would pick us up for any or no reason at all just to harass us. In those days you could cut the anti-Americanism with a knife.

"The crazy bastards were everywhere. Once they showed up at the Embassy wanting to investigate the ladies' john, which they did and rather sheepishly left. Turned out the architect was an American with a little German and had noted the word "Pulverkammer" on the blueprints. He thought it meant powder room. The Gestapo knew better and thought it meant powder magazine. Swell, eh?

"As the Germans piled up victories like baseball scores many of us became lethargic; whatever had brought us to Berlin lost its magnetism; we despaired. Friends and colleagues began to leave either under pressure from the government or because they became sick in their souls. Those of us who remained began to snap at one another; friendships broke off, then picked up again. We called it the "Berlin Blues." It was like a woman having a period: with regularity we fell victim to a sort of spiritual illness, a depression. As time went by the sickness became sharper and more difficult to recover from. It was so bad we never even made up any words to a song about it.

"At one point I had to get out, anywhere would do, but I wanted to be able to get back so I took a couple of weeks and had myself transferred temporarily to Bucharest, a nation very friendly with Berlin. Sort of a leave from the cauldron here, except it weren't since the Iron Guard marched all over and blood flowed in the streets when they attacked the Jews and the communists and anyone considered liberal, however they defined it. Sometimes it seemed they considered anyone not themselves to be a Jew and thus to be chopped up like minced meat. Like the Germans at Kristallnacht. I got to know a playwright there, a Jew called Sebastian; he was symptomatic in that he never knew from one day to the next, hell, from one hour to the next what might happen to him. An absurdly paranoid life, played hell with his ability to write. Quite the little ladies' man in spite of it all. Wonder what happened to him. Anyway, I got out of there as soon as I could. Not even those well-padded hookers at the Athénée Palace could keep me there. Why trade the real thing for a bloody imitation. I went back to Berlin as soon as I could. Everything unhinged there - and everywhere else in Europe. We said then that Europe had turned into a lunatic asylum with the patients in charge, but it was worse than that. The doctors committed the entire society to the looney bin and turned it into an abattoir. So much blood in so many gutters....

"Before they threw me out, the only thing that kept us going, except for the schnapps which is always around even when it's not for sale, the only thing that gave us any hope were the RAF raids. That ass with ears, Göring, had promised the city no bombers could reach that far or get through the Luftwaffe's defenses; people could call him Hermann Meier if one bomb fell on Berlin. No one ever did to his face that I know of, but plenty talked about it in private after the RAF started bombing during the second winter of the war. At first the Propaganda Ministry made sure we saw the damage, how petty it was. 'Pinpricks' they called it. They sent cars around so we could get to the bombed areas right after the allclear sounded, usually at three or four in the morning. It was damned exhilarating speeding around the city in the blackness, stopping in bars to telephone the office with the descriptions of the fires.

The office would then get on the wire to Zürich for transmission to New York with the story. All that stopped, of course, when the British kept it up. Suddenly it became a matter of espionage even to mention the current raid. The High Command finally put its Prussian boot down on the Propaganda boys and put the kibosh on the whole thing. In the end you could only send the communiqué issued by the Germans, badly written tripe that admitted nothing. No commentary or you went to jail in the Prinz-Albrecht-Straße, the happy Gestapo hotel.

"You know, the Brits should have continued those raids. Don't know why they didn't. Even if the damage done wasn't near what the krauts were doing to London, the effect on the morale of the Berliners was terrible. People stopped wishing each other good night when they went home and they started saying 'bolona' which meant 'bombenlose Nacht,' bombless night. Hell, even if the RAF had sent only one plane without any bombs, it would have kept the city in the cellars, in the cold and dark for a few hours in the middle of the night.

"It may not have made any difference in the end. The mass bombing later in the war didn't have much effect on the morale of the people. They didn't rise up and overthrow Hitler and stop the war, true enough, but who knows ... my experience was that it made them grumpy and morose. Created chaos with the traffic the next day, too. And I saved it all, not like the other guys. I kept my notes, my diary, and I got it out in pieces, partly through the Embassy pouch, but mainly in a phony suitcase bottom just like in the movies. Scared the bejesus out of me going through the control points. Couldn't piss for days.

"How about another shot of that schnapps? Doesn't anybody in this town know what ice cubes are? Another thing I miss here these days is the old Berlin jokes. The

Berliner Schnauze seems to have gone down the drains with the rest of the place. Berliners were famous for their cynicism and sarcasm; you don't hear that anymore. Understandable, of course, but still ... maybe it will return when the food situation gets better and the rapes are forgotten. I remember when the Propaganda Ministry held a giant press conference to announce the victorious end to the war in Russia, only some mopping up operations left and all that. Well, of course, that was pure hogwash, which everybody knew. Never found out why they did that. Stupid. Resulted in fewer people buying newspapers; couldn't believe a word in them. The Berliners had enough lies, but could still work up a joke about it. One of the big papers was the *Berliner Zeitung*, called *BZ* for short. The joke started with the question: why were the Berliners only reading the *BZ*? Because it only lied from B to Z while the others lied from A to Z. Hell, the Berliners would make jokes about almost anything, wasn't much held sacred at all. They formed a kind of passive resistance to the anti-Jewish campaign. Red Berlin never went for the nazis in a big way. A lot of Jews even lived out the war in the city and they couldn't have done that without help from other Berliners. Why they even joked about the yellow star the Jews had to wear as a measure of resistance; some of the Jews I knew told these jokes too. Probably trying to take the sting out of the humiliation. They called the star 'pour le sémite,' a takeoff on the 'pour le mérite' decoration. The answer to the question 'Who's going to win the war?' was 'It's written in the stars.' Pathetic, eh? One gag had it that the word 'Jude' really meant 'Italiens Untergang, Deutschlands Ende.' Stuff like that. Of course, this was before we knew what was going on in the East, before the extermination centers. When I was here last, Berliners groused all the time, but still made a joke about everything.

I reckon the city doesn't have much to joke about these days. One of the things I'm going to look for is that sense of humor, probably all gallows humor now. That's the only kind we'd print anyhow. People in the States don't want to read about krauts laughing, even at themselves."

Makepeace and Harrigan laughed every time Tompkin told the stories of his stay in Paris just after the city had been liberated. Even Schade, after he finally met the reporter, enjoyed hearing about the city that held such a fascination for him because of its place in the history of the anti-fascist exiles and their organizations' activities. Makepeace felt the city's magnetism because of its literary history, and Harrigan liked Paris because, while passing through on his way to Berlin, he had enjoyed a successful sexual experience with a charming older man.

"I tell you," Tompkin began, slumping comfortably further down in his chair, "there's no place like Paris for whorehouses. Know what they call them? 'Maisons de tolérance.' How about them apples? Tolerance. Jesus. After the liberation a roll in the sack cost 2500 francs, something like fifty dollars, but hell, the GIs at least had a lot of dough. They thought it was play money, those liberation francs we printed, and they couldn't spend them at Normandy. Oh, the MPs put the joints off-limits and the trade declined, but any soldier worth his pecker can get around rules like that. Say, you got anything to needle this coffee? Eh? Rum's the best, of course. No? Ah, well ... let's have at the slivovitz then.

"I remember one place, the most fantastic cathouse I ever did see. Called the House of All Nations behind the Bibliothèque Nationale, where I also did some work, believe it or not. What a building! Well, a large black woman from one of the French colonies opens the door and you go into a parlor and sit at a table with one of the working girls who's wearing a pair of satin slippers and a smile and you drink some champagne. After a while the lady of the house rounds up a group of GIs and the tour of the world begins. I tell you, I've never seen anything like it, that's the god's honest truth.

"I did a story about it but the censorship wouldn't pass it. Anyway, I was with a group of about ten young guys when we toured the twenty-four rooms, all of them decorated in the style of some exotic spot. Fabulous. And that madame was one smart cookie, too. This was last winter, see, and she inadvertently took us at one point to the Japanese room. She was fast on her feet all right, and before anyone could react, she immediately started talking about the wonderful Chinese and their great war effort. Ha! We saw the Italian room, too, but no one said anything. It had a gondola paddle small enough to whack bottoms, and posters of Florence on the walls. They had a room called 'Wagon-Lit Cook' with upper and lower berths and a small diorama that rotated the countryside past the bed when you pushed the right button. For those with a taste for America the joint had a room named 'Le Miami.' You'll never guess what was in there so I'll tell you: piles of sand and beach umbrellas. Can you beat that with a stick? All the guys in the tour went downstairs and came back up with one of the girls. I went off to write the story, needless to say. What? Well, actually I chose the Scandinavian room. Ah, those ice cubes and meatloaf.

"Of course, there's nothing like that in this city anymore, I suppose."

"Not yet," Schade answered with a grin, "but no doubt soon."

Schade first heard the stories of Paris after he met Tompkin when the reporter appeared in the doorway of the Milinowskistrasse office, a sardonic but friendly inquisitive expression on his bearded face. "Is this where it's all happening? It's zooy enough. How do you stand the noise?"

Tompkin carried his large body well except for a slight stoop and roundness in the shoulders which resulted from a lifetime of bending to listen to those who did not reach his six and a half feet in height, but who may have had something interesting to say. Now that the Allies had defeated the Germans and opened the atomic age in the Pacific ending the conflict there, Tompkin laughed a great deal, an attribute of his character which annoyed many who considered this a sign of shallow philistinism rather than a facade from behind which the reporter could operate more effectively. He had learned the techniques of subtle interrogation as well as the hail-fellow-well-met facade bordering on the boisterousness of fraternity initiates or businessmen trying to make a deal. "Hi ya, fella! How's it going, guy? Say, have you heard anything about the great 1941 Inglenook cabernet sauvignon? I tell ya this is going to be the exemplar, even for the French. Astounding, isn't it? What? Well, no, I never actually got to taste it, but between us we could probably find a bottle, what d'ya say?" This worked well with high-ranking officers after two drinks at the club and Tompkin had made a solid, if flamboyant reputation as a war correspondent ("Is there any such thing as a 'peace' correspondent?"). Using both techniques when appropriate he'd been able to come up with telling information from both ends of the military ranking system in addition to his German sources ("My German is not so lousy as they think."), which gave his stories the touch of both the particular and the universal: his stock-in-trade had become the individual trying to make sense out of wartime events on foreign shores. Now he applied the same techniques to the broken societies of postwar Europe, convinced things were happening that no one outside a small elite group of officials knew anything about, a paranoid view of an otherwise inexplicable world gone off the edge of rational considerations into an abyss of entropy where no beginnings or ends existed. "People can't find answers anymore, so I provide them with what they need all neatly wrapped up in an easy to read newspaper column of 2000 words or less. Of course, I have to simplify a bit, but it's all there."

The news service had offered him Rome as a base, but he insisted on Berlin. "The future is here, isn't it? And so is the past, so this is the place to be. Hell, I've lived in discomfort in this city before. It was pretty bad just before Pearl Harbor. The nazis started the anti-American program long before that and they harassed us up one side and down the other, gave us all kinds of guff. And it wasn't only the censorship either. Hell's bells, you could get arrested or beaten up for speaking English in restaurants, things like that. Food was, in fact, a big problem. By then almost everything we could get was ersatz of one sort or another and there was never enough of it, had no taste and little nutrition. Housing was bad: the krauts kept requisitioning our apartments and we couldn't find rooms; some of us slept in our offices. Oh, we had enough money, but you couldn't buy anything, the shops were empty as a hobo's pockets. By the time I got out I looked like a hobo myself and that's a fact. The longer we stayed the more ragged we became. Whenever anyone left to go stateside they sold or left us bits and pieces of their clothing. Didn't help me much, not too many of my size around. Once I got a pair of shoes from an Embassy official's wife who bought them for me on a trip to Switzerland; all the guys envied me until the first time it rained and the shoes shriveled up and died. Don't know where the shaft came from that time: the Swiss or the Embassy wife. And, Christ, did we smell! The soap was ersatz, too, and we didn't get much of it. Thank god for the booze. Oh, yes, I've lived in Berlin during hard times."

Now he eyed Schade with some skepticism and sat on one of the office's wooden chairs. "What is it that you do, Lieutenant, exactly?"

"I doubt if there's a story for you here," Schade answered in a voice empty of any identifiable tone.

The big reporter smiled broadly. "Hell, Lieutenant, there's a story everywhere if you know what to look for or if you recognize what you hear when you hear it."

"What are you looking for?"

"Listen, part of the American public is interested in what's going on here, a small part true enough, but it wants to know why the government insists on the GIs staying here. There's a voluminous lack of information about the occupation in the States, denazification, Germany's role in Europe's future, punishing war criminals, and so on. That will change, of course, if it goes on too long. Too much money is going to be spent. Congress is already gnawing away at the War Department's budget. Another part of the public, the larger part isn't at all interested in Germany and the occupation, but it should be, don't you think? So tell me what you do. I can keep a secret." He made the sign of a wavy cross vaguely near the left side of his chest. "So help me."

Schade laughed under the waves of warm volubility emanating from the innocent smiling bear on the side of his desk. "I'll bet." He drew a long breath and looked out the window at the darkness creeping through the city leaving shadows in its wake. He lit a cigarette and brushed his mustache with a thumb. "There's nothing secret about what we do. It's rather simple compared to some other offices here. My job is to look after the film situation in the American sector of the city, to make sure the theaters show the approved films and the newsreel we make every week with the British. We run the distribution agency for American films in the city. The money goes into blocked accounts for the studios. We vet the Germans who want to make movies again, though there's little enough raw stock and equipment around for that. We get proposals for scripts all the time, documentaries, shorts, features. These have to be reviewed and approved, the producers and actors licensed, and so on. But no films are being made here now. It's all dreams and illusions."

"Do you conduct the background investigations?"

"Sometimes, if the case is simple. We depend on the CIC for the most part. Everyone has to be cleared, in theory anyway. We check the files in the so-called Kammer der Kunstschaffenden, Chamber of Creative Artists, the old Reichskulturkammer where the nazis kept personal files on everyone in the 'culture business.' You'd be surprised what we find in there. Even if the Russians cleared people before we got here, we do it again if they want to work in the US-sector. The files are in the Schlüterstrasse in the British sector, so we have no access problem. The nazis registered everyone."

"The Germans who work at the Chamber are all communists."

"Not all of them, but the most important of them, yes. What do you expect? The Russians gave them their jobs. They do their work well enough."

"I understand the Russians aren't as rigorous as we are in denazification."

"They are a bit more haphazard about it."

"What do you think of the denazification program, personally, I mean."

"A soldier doesn't have a personal opinion in public."

"I'll call you 'a reliable source'."

"I'd appreciate your doing that in any case, but I still don't have an opinion on the matter for publication."

Tompkin sighed and grinned. "I've talked to countless men and women in the city and in the Zone about this. Opinions range all across the spectrum from the ideological hardliners who want to ban every party member from any job except day laborer to the pragmatists who just want to get the job done and will use anyone to do it. Everyone knows there's no unanimity of opinion on the subject."

"It is a highly complicated issue," Schade said carefully. "As long as the policy stands, we'll carry it out."

"Maybe you could tell me, within your press guidelines of course, tell me what the policy is expected to accomplish?"

"It's a form of exorcism, I suppose, a method of rooting out an evil from the past so the future can take care of itself."

"The French call it 'l'épuration,' and they are just as haphazard about it. My old drinking pal Brasillach gets shot and others who did much worse get off scot-free."

"What I'm thinking about cannot really be purged. That's too superficial for what's needed here. This warped ideology is too deeply rooted: it must be exorcized."

"Put behind us, shoved into a dark corner of the mind and forgotten so we can get on with living. Is that it?"

"No, shoved out into the open, in public where everyone sees it and admits to its existence. And certainly not forgotten, that will not be possible here, nor should it ever be. This particular past will gnaw on the German mind like the eagle eating Prometheus' liver for eternity."

"It was a vulture, and it only lasted thirty years. So you mean penance followed by redemption?"

"Can the creature who machined-gunned a village full of Jews – or Gentiles, think of Oradour – can this monster ever find redemption? I think not."

"To forgive is a Christian attribute."

"I never claimed to be a Christian."

"So the guilty should be *seen* to be guilty and suffer the consequences?"

"The crime is so inconceivable that we've not yet figured out what the consequences should be! Execution may be too easy. But no matter what, the evil must be exorcized and to do that we must admit that evil exists. We seem to have a hard time with that concept."

"Okay, Lieutenant, I think maybe we'll get back to that later. How do you work with our Allies? Do you find the Russians difficult to deal with?"

"Not particularly."

"You're being very diplomatic."

"I am giving you the facts."

"What else do you do?"

"I attend endless meetings."

"Does anything get decided?"

"Sometimes."

They both laughed. "You were originally German, I understand. Does that make things difficult for you in dealing with these people?"

"No."

Tompkin's grin came quickly and intimated that they both knew that could not possibly be the whole answer or even the true one, but that they would keep the matter to themselves for the time being. "I've got a lot of people here somewhere ... who work around here I should talk to...." His hands scrambled about his clothing like two small animals, making a show of searching for the piece of paper. "What do you know about Harold Kirshhof?" he asked offhandedly while patting the pockets of his civilian uniform.

"He transferred out some weeks ago, back to the States, I think."

"So I gather. Rather sudden, wasn't it?"

"Not especially. There's a great deal of demobilization going on these days."

"Yeah, the mothers of the country want their sons back home pronto. They don't understand the occupation."

"Evidently not, but we all want to go home."

"You too?"

"Of course, why not? I consider New York my home. That's not so strange."

"I didn't mean it that way. No need to be defensive. Just wondered if you might have thought about the need for people with your background...."

"You've been talking to Makepeace."

"Sure. I talk to everybody. It's a shame about Kirshhof. I wanted to talk to him, too. There's a story there, being Jewish and dealing with the Germans."

"There are plenty of other Jews in military government."

"True, but I understand Kirshhof was quite vocal about his dislike of the Germans. It would have made an interesting piece."

"Probably not," Schade said. He did not want to talk about Kirshhof to anyone, much less an intelligent newspaper reporter. "He did his job like everyone else. That's all."

"Okay," Tompkin grinned again behind his shaggy beard. "Well. Lieutenant, I'll be on my merry way. You're not the easiest officer I've interviewed, but that's okay. Why don't we have a drink some time when we're both off duty?"

"When is a reporter ever off duty?"

"Never, actually, but a good reporter doesn't always write everything he hears either. Some reporters you can even trust, believe it or not."

"I'll believe it when I see it."

"Try me."

"Perhaps. A drink at some point can't hurt."

"Hell no. I'll regale you with stories about the city. I know a million of them."

"So I've heard."

"Say, have you got Helmuth Kronauer's address, by any chance? I knew him slightly before the war and I'd like to see him again."

"He's living in the same house."

"I never knew his address. We always met in a dark bar or on a street corner or in the gents' clothing section of the KDW department store. It wouldn't have been healthy for him to be seen with an American reporter in those days. We met at odd hours and never at his home."

Schade gave him the address.

Tompkin left wondering how long it would take to become friends with Schade; he thought the gauntlet had been nicely thrown down, the challenge subtly issued. Now when would the young officer pick it up. Schade sat for a moment wondering if he would ever like Tompkin or if he could ever trust him. The answers to these questions came in circumstances unanticipated by either man.

* * * *

"In all honesty," Tamirov began.

"A concept alien to your way of thinking," Makepeace interrupted with a grin that contributed nothing to softening the sting of his interjection.

"In all honesty, as I stated, a concept we new Soviet men well understand."

"But rarely practice."

"Can one practice a concept, Villum? No, do not bother to respond. Just listen for a change."

Makepeace made his face solemn as that of an Anglican priest listening to a particularly juicy confession and nodded.

"In all honesty, I am not at all convinced that these Germans will ever change. They are all too trapped by tradition, their past is their prison."

"Our policies here are based on the assumption that such change is possible," Makepeace replied.

"Are we engineers of the souls of men?"

"We believe society and its citizens can be reformed, through education and example."

"Lenin said the same thing," Tamirov said with a grin.

"Americans have a saying about that."

"So do we, so do we all."

"But ours is so pungent and to the point."

"I can barely restrain my erupting curiosity and please do not speak of cats."

"Not a word about felines. It is this: no matter how you shake and dance, the last few drops fall on your pants." Makepeace spoke the saying in English.

"What is drops?" Tamirov asked in English.

Makepeace told him in Russian and they returned to that language. "Ah," Kransnikov smiled in triumph, "but it doesn't rhyme in Russian."

"The effect, however, is the same, and nothing rhymes in Russian, at least in the Soviet version."

"I don't know why I put up with you, Villum, truly."

"Oh yes you do - for the same reason I put up with you: our bosses have so ordered it. And I occasionally add to your hoard of vulgar Americanisms."

"True, true, but nonetheless it is not easy dealing with the class enemy at such close quarters."

"*Da*, some of our doomed ideology might become too attractive, eh?"

"Not for me, Villum," Tamirov uttered with a small mild sigh, not quite of resignation but as close as he would allow himself to approach that unsoviet state of being.

"Go piss up a rope," Makepeace said in English.

"*Shto?*"

Makepeace explained.

"That is a fine saying. It requires no further explanation. *Khorosho, khorosho!*"

"Just don't use it on your bosses."

"Of course not. It is too fine for them. They would not understand its metaphysical properties. I shall save it for an appropriate occasion."

"Like your hanging?" suggested Makepeace.

"Oh, we no longer hang anyone, Villum. That procedure is not modern, very primitive and takes too long."

"Ah yes, you require mass production methods to meet the demand."

"That is close to the danger point, my friend, let us change the subject before we go over the edge here."

"Agreed, but our time is about up. Shall we discuss the baseball series?"

"The everlasting triumph of Moscow Arsenal would be preferable."

"But did you not invent baseball, Yuri Vladimirovich?"

"So some have claimed, but I certainly have never figured out how the rules make sense."

"They don't have to make sense, they just have to be followed."

"Now you sound like an agitprop apparatchnik."

"Who's on first?"

"Ur?"

"Time's up. See you next time, Yuri Vladimirovich."

"Piss up rope," Tamirov said in English.

* * * *

PART FIVE

> *Wie um das dümmste Mädchen*
> *Sich sonderbare Fädchen*
> *Nachts durch die Strassen zieh'n*
> *Die Dichter und die Maler*
> *Und auch die Kriminaler*
> *Die kennen ihr Berlin.*[21]
>
> --Joachim Ringelnatz

He awakened gradually, by ascending stages of consciousness, his face comfortably resting on the curled blonde hairs of her armpit, breathing the musky smell of body sleep, his erection tight against her thigh. Neither resisting nor encouraging the rebirth of his consciousness, he lay for as long as needed to gather and arrange the sensations of the morning, his eyes closed against the pale light edging reluctantly through the glassless and shadeless window opening on the courtyard below: the tickle of soft hair on his lips, muted tang of her skin when he gently

---

[21]Ringelnatz, approximately: As around the dumbest girl/wonderous threads/wend their way through the streets at night/poets and painters/and also criminals/they know their Berlin.

pushed his tongue against its taut surface, muffled groan as she turned slightly against him, pressure of his feet against the bedboard many miles from his head, sparrow's chirping song somewhere in the courtyard, the pulse in his erection straining against her flesh, the dim knowledge that the day belonged to them and neither had to work until the evening, the small pang of disappointment with the realization that they lay in her bed, not his, in a house full of other people, the pasty taste of decayed cardboard in his mouth ... the day took shape like a photograph coming into focus in a tray of developing solution, slowly clarifying the outlines of form and content.

    Carefully he pushed his dog tags over his shoulder and began to extricate himself from the tangle of their bodies and the gray sheets. She murmured a garbled question, dreams still holding her consciousness, struggling against the process that would result in awakening. He whispered consoling sounds and stood up, putting on his spectacles. How absurd to say, "just have to pee," how inadequate in any language when the bladder is full to bursting and painful. He rinsed his mouth with water from the glass on the floor beside the bed and spat into the chamber pot. Pushing aside her pile of typed playscripts and his copy of Klaus Mann's precocious autobiography *The Turning Point*, he picked up the unadorned white vessel of chipped porcelain and moved a few feet from the bed to end the pressure and pain in his bladder. No one emptying this pot would think him a god like Demetrius's son. Sighing with the inevitable relief and regret, he placed the rag over the pot and returned to the bed. She shifted again so he lay with his head on the thin pillow, hand behind his neck to watch her breasts move slowly to the rhythm of her breathing. He slipped his hand under the sheet to gently scratch her pubic hairs, then placed it between her legs with a minute amount of pressure and closed his eyes. Flushed pleasure ran over his skin as he watched her when she slept or when she was unaware of his gaze; he grasped a certain naturalness about her movements, a certain nonchalance which excited his nerve ends. When she reached into her clothing to hold her breasts, as if measuring the weight gained now that she ate well and regularly, a strange sense of satisfaction sped through him like a rush of adrenalin, a second's thrust of pride and possession which he knew to be unreal, more a matter of his inchoate desires than based on Gisela's feelings or perceptions.

A muscle spasm shook her leg and she moved closer to him. The spasm made him think of the drug: that she seemed to have no further need or desire for it pleased him and lessened the pressure of guilt simmering in one of the dark pools of his brain. His awareness of the fact that their affair would end, his inability or unwillingness to do anything about it, his dread of the end, and his feeling of responsibility toward her combined to form that littoral of guilt which all too often threatened to choke him. The previous night she had spoken openly and with finality about the drugs, with the objectivity of one who stood above personal involvement, the pride of one who had defeated an enemy, and repressed the memory of the battles lost. As if to confirm her independence she talked to him about the city and its drug-haunted past. ("We can't get away from the city, can we?" he had remarked. She looked at him for a moment with a confused expression of helplessness that turned resentful as if she had bitten into a peppercorn. "You can," she said and turned her head away.)

Cocaine flooded Berlin in the years between the wars, the elite and would-be elite drug, readily available and not very expensive: young women sold it in nightclubs always saving a packet of the "snow" for themselves; struggling artists sold it to make enough to eat; doctors prescribed it to patients as a painkiller ("I heard even your friend Freud published a paper praising cocaine." "He's not my Freud."); maimed veterans, themselves hooked on morphine as a result of their treatment for war wounds, sold it on street corners in small envelopes. Morphine was the second most available drug. So many veterans suffered so much pain and morphine smoothed out the ragged edges of their agony; Göring's addiction to morphine was a badly kept secret in the city. For those who could afford them, or steal them, drugs allowed for some brief respites from the crushing oppression of the instabilities and hungers of the Twenties and the great economic depression that followed; they gave temporary depth to the shallow souls of the confused population who rushed about like lemmings eagerly seeking the nearest abyss. For others, drugs provided an artificially induced transcendence that fueled the creative thrust at the edge of tolerance. The young dancer-actress, Anita Berber, bursting with kinetic energy driven by drugs and alcohol, loving women and men indiscriminately, selling her slender vibrating body to the highest bidder when she needed cash or a quick fix, a legend in her short lifetime, uttered the line that became famous in certain circles of the city's night life: "Where do you think I get the energy to throw these pearls before those swine every night?"

"She would show up late at the Pyramide, a well-known lesbian club, often without changing her costume from her last performance that night, with another famous *Nachttänzerin*, Celly de Rheidt. She always made the place more electric, more exciting. Her body was her art. What else did she have? What else did she need? She must have been a wonderful thing to experience."

"How do you know this?"

"People tell me about everything. But certain hypocrites who loved her in the clubs wouldn't have her at their parties. She'd go and the servants would throw her out. They were swine and still are. I regret that I never saw her dance, but I was too young and she died in 1928 of tuberculosis. I never even saw the films she made in the early Twenties. No one remembers her anymore, even though Otto Dix painted her portrait. We forget so easily some things and always remember others, usually the worst. She was only twenty-nine. Porcelain figures of her were very popular after the war."

("Women loving women," Claudia once explained to a skeptical Makepeace, "means many different things. In my case, most of the clubs had been closed down by the time I needed them, but one could always find some place. If you were known as a lesbian, you see, most of the *Bonzen* left you alone; it was a matter of protection as well. This didn't help when the Ivans got here of course. That experience created lesbians, at least temporarily, as a way of healing I suppose. For me, I think I've gotten over that. I mean the rapes." And she began to hum the cabaret song "*Wenn die beste Freundin*," the lesbian anthem of the interwar era.

> *Früher gab's den Hausfreund,*
> *doch der schwand dahin*
> *Heute statt des Hausfreunds,*
> *gibt's die Hausfreundin!*[22]

[22] First there was the boyfriend/but he disappeared somehow/ Today instead of a boyfriend/there's a girlfriend at the house.

Schade murmured, "Before it was male house friend, but he disappeared; today instead of a male friend, there's a female house friend. How the hell do you translate that into English? Impossible."

Gisela said, "Both my father and Helmuth Kronauer told me the story of an actor, quite well-known, world famous in fact. In the middle of a heavy film schedule he became ill with a skin infection that was quite painful. The studio doctor treated him with a drug, Luminal, I think so he could sleep. One night he took too much. To counteract that, the doctor treated him with cocaine and continued to supply the stuff until the film was finished. After that, the man was on his own, but coke was readily available and he had enough money. Of course, he began to depend on it, you know. Finally, two French nuns on a train shamed him into giving it up. They prayed for him. I don't know how much that helped, but he got off it. He left Germany in 1933 and went to America. So you see...." She laughed and hugged herself, nodding her head. "But I would like a cigarette please."

They had both sipped a fair amount of Scotch whisky from the endless depths of the flask borrowed from Ogilvy Vasart as they walked to her room from the theater where the audience had at great length applauded her performance. Neither of them had gone over the edge from tipsy into inebriation, and so remained on that plateau of gaiety and mild recklessness at which they could laugh at silly jokes one moment and swerve into deadly serious dialog the next and return to laughter without insult or injury.

"Given the size of them, do you think dinosaurs' toothaches were more massive than ours?"

"No, their brains were too small to register large doses of pain; rather more like a cow, I should think."

"How big is a cow's brain?"

"They have extraordinarily small teeth."

"I've never seen a cow's tooth."

But no matter how hard they tried, they could not long escape the encroachments of the city and their own consciences on their affects and behavior. The weather had turned sharply chilly, a happenstance they recognized only later. As they turned the corner into her street, a child's laughter danced into the street with unusual abandon. Momentarily sobered, she began to speak of the soldier returning from the prisoner of war camp, painfully finding his way back to Berlin, his former apartment, and his family. Hungry but filled with happiness at finding the building still intact, he rang the bell on the door. A child of twelve opened the door, a child he had not seen in years, a child who turned her head toward the interior of the apartment and called out, "Mama, there's a beggar at the door!"

"That's not very funny."

"No, unfortunately, it isn't. Kiss me now, quickly."

Moments later they discovered something which may not have been very funny either, but about which they could laugh. Their laughter often held the slight taste of bitter almonds, the barest hint of a sob, but it carried them down the pitted streets, past the bent and gutted buildings, through the decaying air until they finally reached the windowless building in the second rubble-filled courtyard which at one time had been the center of four linked five-storey blocks of apartments. One of the blocks had been bombed and partially fallen in on the courtyard; a scruffy line of Trümmerfrauen had carried most of the useable stone out to the street where the pieces stood in neat squared off piles awaiting future reconstruction. They passed through the first courtyard by the pitted enamalled sign reading

> Das spielen der Kinder
> auf Hof, Flur und Treppen
> sowie
> das Umherstehen vor der Haustür
> ist streng untersagt![23]

Now no children played in the courtyard, hallway and stairs and no one hung around the doorway. As they climbed the stairs to her room, hugging and bumping into the wall, their arms around each other, she said, "You've heard the expression 'vitamin B'? That's how to get things done in this chaos: *Beziehung.* Influence. Some kind of influential relations with the bureaucrats and the politicians who can make decisions. You must use vitamin B whenever possible. For the Allies, it's easy: an order, a bottle of whisky, cigarettes, a job, medicines ... but for the Germans it's more difficult: they have so little or nothing left to give: heirlooms, sex, jewelry, food if they have any at all. Hah! At first the Ivans simply took whatever they wanted, in the open, they didn't care, raped women in the streets ... women still have to be careful but now it's best to have a relative in the countryside with a garden. That's worth a fortune: an egg is a priceless commodity, fresh vegetables are miracles, real milk from a cow is

---

[23]Children are strictly forbidden to play in the courtyard, the hallway and stairs and to hang around the door to the building.

unthinkable. But with the right *Beziehung* most things are possible."

He stopped on the stairs and, in a desperate and feeble attempt to wash away her past, clothed his voice in the uniform of officious greed and oily charm: "Why now, just what does the little lady desire, little lady?"

"How about electricity for my electric toothbrush."

"Electric? What an imagination! Fritz Lang, listen up!"

They laughed too loudly and someone in the building yelled at them to be quiet. As they continued to climb the stairs, Schade sang softly, "*Veronika, der Lenz ist da …*"

"Where did you hear that one?"

"My parents had the record. And they came to America on a tour."

"Some of them moved to America, I heard somewhere."

"The Jews, yes."

"I never saw them; too young. But we heard the records, evening during the war with people we trusted. They would've had to change their name if they stayed together. English names frowned on, you know. Comedian Harmonists."

"Never any chance in this country with three Jews in the group."

"Do you remember the line about asparagus growing? How we giggled at that, even as young girls we got the meaning."

Veronika, der Lenz ist da,
die Mädchen singen tralala.
Die ganze Welt ist wie verhext,

Veronika, der Spargel wächst![24]

They leaned against the wall and choked on their laughter.

In her room they took a long time to undress as one of them thought suddenly of something vitally important to say and stopped removing pieces of clothing to relate the information, which they both immediately forgot. The duration of the laughter and the sober statements decreased as exhaustion edged its careless way into their minds and muscles. Broken sentences remained unfinished, spoken in voices soft with weariness and desire.

"You know," he said, drinking a sip from the flask, "in my memory I grew up in America, in New York City, but I didn't grow up in America somehow. I went to school with Americans, some of my friends were Americans, I worked in American factories during the vacations from school, but we remained a German family, speaking and thinking in German, reading German books and newspapers ... We all believed everything would be temporary and Hitler wouldn't last long. My mother worked with a refugee relief agency and we organized anti-fascist demonstrations, collected money for the cause, did whatever we could to help. We held on to our Germanness. The fate of exiles, I suppose. Yet we became Americans too, somehow, we had to, especially those of us still young."

---

[24] This might be translated as "Veronika spring is here/the girls sing tralala/The whole world is as if bewitched/Veronika the asparagus is growing." But this translation misses the sexual connotations as the use of asparagus as a symbol for penis; Lenz is also a reference to turning 20 years old, a time of hyper sexual excitement.

"So you're a story of two cities," she laughed as she pronounced the sentence in English.

"I think it's 'a tale of'...."

"No, Makepeace says women are 'tails'...."

"Makepeace is a vulgar plebeian." He laughed with her at the strange mishmash of languages, but added, "Yes, two cultures...."

"But you're an American here."

"True, but still...."

They offered kisses and caresses to one another to make the air less abrasive and wipe away ideas which did not contribute to the night as they wished it ... even as he put his mouth to her breast the back of his mind toiled with the juxtaposition he could not resolve.

"When does a Berliner feel most naked?"

"When he's forgotten his briefcase."

"*Jawohl*!"

Then later: "What do you call those metal things around your neck?"

"Dog tags," he said in English.

"*Hunde* ...?

"The Americans tag dogs with their names and addresses in case they get lost, so the soldiers call these dog tags."

"Why do you have two?"

"One for your mouth, the other for the company clerk when you're dead."

"That's not funny."

"Wasn't meant to be. It's only the truth."

"Tell me a funny lie then."

That night their lovemaking contained a suffusion of tenderness and distance, opposites in the confusion of their lives caught between the needs of their affections and the consequences of events which became the atmosphere of their irresolution, they struggled to maintain their equipoise and dignity. They dosed each other liberally with sexuality and cautionary thoughts unspoken but felt as they used their bodies to protect themselves from their minds; they attempted to shut out the otherness of the world with the parentheses of kisses and caresses, finally falling into sleep holding each other's sex as if it would save them from drowning.

 Rising only partially from the depths of oceanic sleep when he softly rolled out of bed, she swam even further toward the surface upon his return. Feeling his hand between her thighs she luxuriated in his gentleness and the sharp pressure of her bladder. She put off the necessity for relief in favor of the continued sensuality of his body and its morning warmth, ignoring the dull ache in her temples reminding her of the whisky the night before. Fragments of thought and sensations crept gradually into her consciousness: the almost empty toothpaste tube on the sink by the door, the sound of a bird in the courtyard, the weak sunlight on her eyelids meaning it would perhaps not rain, the scene in the play she had not quite worked out on the stage, the nascent rumble of her internal plumbing announcing the imminent arrival of her period, the abrasion on her left nipple where his teeth had been during the night, the strained hearty pleasure of stretching the length of her body in the chill of the morning air....

 As she stretched she felt him turn toward her and she reached for his body, lightly clasping his risen-again sex. Still under the waters of sleep, unwilling as yet to break the surface, she mumbled sounds repeating his earlier message and with half-closed eyes and early morning clumsiness stepped across the room to the chamber pot. Hunched over, listening to the urgent stream splash against the side of the basin, she wondered briefly how long her conscience would allow her to continue to appropriate his affection. She tried to balance her unease with the thought that she gave him of herself, that this situation was of a different category and magnitude from the manipulation in the past ... Closing her eyes completely she put the question away; today would be sufficient, perhaps tomorrow ... enough for now. Returning to lie next to him she turned to kiss his neck enjoying for a moment the prickling of his unshaven cheek. "*Nun, komm Schätzchen....*" And in the cold late autumn morning their bodies told each other of desire and need and pleasure, rocking gently back and forth, now of the surface of the waters like two canoes riding on the swell of the underground currents.

    Afterward, he would have watched her move about the room in the long mirror on the back of the door, but there were few mirrors left in the city. The war and its immediate aftermath had conveniently destroyed the old ones and the new had not yet been made. Thus from his position on the mattress he saw only a series of fragments of her body as she moved in long strides in and out of his vision. Later he put the fragments together in his memory.

    When they got up they had a "soldier's wash": cold water from the street tap poured into the sink in the room and sparingly applied with much shivering to the appropriate surfaces and crevices of their bodies. "The officials of the district say we'll have water in the house within a week, but one can't count on that these days." "Not enough vitamin B?" "I am becoming quite obsessed with washing. You saw me at my worst, ugly and smelling rotten. Now you must see me at my best, or as close as possible under these circumstances. The picture in your mind must be a beautiful one." "You're a pretty beautiful picture already." She laughed, saying, "Lying swine."

They breakfasted quickly in the damp crepuscular communal kitchen two floors below, grateful that none of the other residents appeared until they had almost finished. These had long since given up being surprised at the sight of a uniformed soldier from the occupation forces at the breakfast table. The second floor kitchen faced the courtyard into which the sun penetrated only in bits and pieces. Through the paneless window they could see the narrow path that wound through the junk and rubble toward what had been the rear entrance to the third block of buildings with its own courtyard, the last of the complex's quadrangle of buildings and courtyards for which the city was famous: cramming as many people as possible with relative comfort into the smallest space resulted in building complexes with one, two, and sometimes three courtyards surrounded by five story apartment blocks, which the *vox populi* called in "*Mietskaserne*."

Dry bread and ersatz coffee, the typical Berlin breakfast of the day. The bread crumbled in their mouths and the brownish liquid tasted of iron and iodine. For once they did not complain and Schade repressed the equivocal combination of guilt and annoyance at knowing he could have provided fresh bread and real coffee. Gisela did not think about the matter.

Silently smoking cigarettes with the last of the would-be coffee, the bluish smoke curling and recurling in a vague spiral, they nodded to the still sleepy figures who awkwardly passed in and out of the room, Gisela's colleagues at the theater and their own companions finding shelter from the increasingly chilly nights. Claudia Kaufmann, the one member of the house community with whom they felt at all comfortable, did not appear that morning. They both felt the flush of embarrassment if for different reasons.

Gisela suddenly lifted her blonde head. "Listen, Jonathan. Have you ever heard that? It's amazing. I haven't heard that sound in years. It's beautiful, isn't it?" Softly she sang,

> *Lieber Leierkastenmann,*
> *Fang noch mal von vorne an,*
> *Von dem schönen Spree-Athen,*
> *Wo sojar die Blinden sehn.*[25]

Schade did not think the music beautiful, but it did astound him to hear it. The rumbling metallic sound rise up from the courtyard, its steely dissonance sharp in their ears: an old Berlin *Leierkasten,* a venerable hurdy-gurdy, a memory of the city as it had been in better times, playing those subtle mixtures of folksong sentimentality and show business. They rushed to the window and saw in the middle of the narrow pathway a shambling, shabbily dressed skeleton slowly grinding the handle of a dilapidated out-of-tune music machine. The sounds emanating from the box were made all the more tortuous to the ear by the fact that the man seemed not to have the strength to turn the handle fast enough to recreate the melody built into the guts of the mechanism. What should have been a sprightly song from the period before the war emerged as a dirge-like perversion of the original intent under the slow methodical grinding of the thin atrophied arm. The old man appeared not to notice anything amiss and blissfully grinned with closed eyes as he churned. "He's hearing it the way it should sound," she muttered sotto voce as if the skeleton

---

[25] Dear Mr Hurdy-gurdy man/play it again from the start/about the beautiful Spree-Athens/where even the blind can see.

should not hear her voice. The machine, once known as the poor peoples' symphony orchestra, continued to rattle its shrill dissonance slowly across the courtyard and through the window frames now filled with figures watching the performance with varying degrees of pleasure and pain. Several of the more sensitive musicians who lived in the block ran out of the buildings and arrived at their appointments early that morning. The skeleton turned the handle with decreasing speed, the rhythm devolving inexorably toward silence as exhaustion and malnutrition wearied the strength in his arm. The expression of beatitude on his face denied knowledge of his physical frailty and the dolorous anguish of his mechanical sonata's diminishing noise. When the sound stopped he stood there, head held upward, his turning arm at his side, like a conductor at the podium waiting for the audience's applause. Moved by an irresistible impulse, which the skeleton seemed to extract from them, the people at the windows began to clap their hands and mutter, "How nice," "What a surprise," but the skeleton gave no indication that he heard them. Unmoving he waited. "He's waiting for his reward," she said and Schade groped in his pocket for change. "No, wait. He doesn't want money. There, look." On the floor of the courtyard, two young children edged hesitantly across the dirt and rubble toward the man and the machine, one holding a piece of brown bread, the other a cup of liquid. They could see the children hand him the food and drink, but could not hear what they said to him. The children stood starting at the music box with open curiosity, the skeleton in rags held no further interest for them: skeletons in rags were a commonplace in the city, but a machine, even splintered and rusted like this one, they had never seen before. When he finished, the skeleton handed back the cup and began dragging the *Leierkasten* out of the courtyard on to his next performance, felicity still shining from his face. Later on the stairs they heard the children telling others that the man was deaf, with one eye covered with white stuff, and that he talked strangely. But by then they had made their plans for the day and refused to allow anything to crack the fragile shell of brightness they wrapped around themselves.

> *Du wahst mein schönstet Jlück auf Erden,*
> *nur du - von hinten und von vorn.*
> *Mit uns zwee hätt et können werden,*
> *et is leider nischt jeworn.*[26]

She suggested they walk through the center of the city to see "some of our past" meaning the sites of cultural and social activity related to the creation of varied popular art forms she and her parents' generations remembered. Although she could not then have rationally explained the motivations behind her decision, she instinctively felt the necessity to show him a positive side of the city to counterbalance the obvious unspeakable depths to which it had been dragged. To some undefined degree she also needed this experience to reassure herself of the existence of a tradition that linked her own activities to an acceptable past even through the dust and blood of the present truncated cityscape. She needed to reinforce the structure

---

[26]The lyric, in Berliner dialect, might be translated into Brooklynese as:
> Youse was my prettiest joy on oith
> only youse - backward and forward.
> Sompin couldda come of us togedder
> but sadly nuttin evah happeened.

of her own life, to shore up her choice of acting as a worthwhile profession, to make a connection between herself and a believable future.

(Schadow, in attempting to explain the inexplicable, once wondered aloud to Schade: "Perhaps it was the impenetrable nature of the Prussian character. Nothing penetrated the garrison cast of mind except sex, alcohol, and winning wars. Some obstacle occluded access to other forms of human expression, art, music ... Which of our leaders since the second Friedrich really understood music? And he was as bloodthirsty as the others. We have been ruled by the soul of the bureaucrat and the heart of the machine gun. What's worse, we embraced them with enthusiasm.")

The issue of the past became disruptively and intrusively real: the more she learned about the events of the recent past, the less she was able to justify if not her lack of resistance to the evil in which she had lived, at least her willful refusal to acknowledge it, which might have forced a confrontation within herself she feared she would lose. The more she experienced the desolation of the city, the more difficult it became to rationalize her own privileged situation. The common phrase of the day, "I knew nothing about it," applied to her as much as anyone, but lacked resonance in her mind. It did not convince. Like so many she had doggedly ignored those scraps of information, which would have disturbed the delicate equilibrium of her life and the pursuit of her career, but now she could no longer simply refuse to listen and to comprehend. Unlike many of her fellow countrymen, she discovered she could not continue to dissociate herself from some form of responsibility. When, in a spasm of puritanical zeal of which he was later ashamed, Schade took her to see the American-British documentary film about the concentration camps (called *Die Todesmühlen*, The Death Mills), she had not wept, the subject had gone far beyond weeping, and she to some extent believed the film's directed message about the necessity for collective responsibility. The British and American psychological warfare experts who made the film succeeded with her as they failed with most other Germans who viewed the film. (After viewing the film, Makepeace said to Monday, "Odd, isn't it, that the Jews are never mentioned." "The point is to reinforce German guilt, not enumerate the victims, I suppose," Monday said, irritation deepening his voice.)

Untrained in the procedures of connective ratiocination, Gisela intuited this sense of responsibility rather than reasoning it through the nervous processes of her mind. "And isn't there a difference between guilt and responsibility? How can I be guilty? But am I not in some way responsible, as a German? Even if I did nothing? Or because I did nothing?" In lengthy exhausting discussions Schade tried to convince her that knowledge so obtained would not last, that she would lose the feeling because it was not rationally founded, like losing a character's lines in a play when a new role had to be absorbed. She did not argue the point as much as believe it was irrelevant for her. This was the way she achieved knowledge; her epistemology was that of the theater, not the university seminar. Schade could not accept the validity of this method when related to anything profound: an idea not thought through would not last because it had no structural foundation. That intuition could be a meaningful mechanism to achieve knowledge he would not at this point admit. He also found it difficult to discuss the essentially private nature of her struggle, which he associated with the nation as a whole. "This is not a public demonstration. I refuse to take the burden of the German people, whatever that means. I have enough trouble with my own problems." Neither convinced the other, but they used the opportunity to stretch their mental capacities against each other's agruments, momentarily lifting their concerns away from the crushing claustrophobic atmosphere of the city's struggle to revive, to remember, to forget, and their own erratically defined relationship.

The general unpopularity of her opinion caused her to discuss it with few people beyond Schade, whose attitude toward the durability of her hard-won resolution annoyed her no less than Buchdow's off-hand claim that such things could only block her development as an actress and keep her from learning her lines. "How can you allow yourself to forget your lines on opening night or your movements on stage, worrying about something you had nothing to do with?" "But we all had something to do with it. We let it happen." Kronauer and Schadow accepted her position as valid, but both in their separate ways insisted she had to take some form of action to resolve the apparent conundrum in which she was caught. Kronauer told her: "Thinking about the problem and forming a notion of yourself in relation to the issue is not enough. How many of us did exactly that vis à vis the nazis? How few of us actually did anything other than think?" Schadow told her: "Yes, we're all guilty or responsible to some degree, but such feelings can be terribly destructive if not handled correctly, positively. We've had enough destruction. We cannot let a sense of guilt, no matter how appropriate, to bring us to an impasse. You're young enough to be able to manipulate your emotions into an act, as horrid as that formulation may be. Work harder, justify your life. I know this sounds outrageous, but if you are serious, the only other alternative is suicide, and you don't feel *that* guilty. I don't mean to diminish the stress you went through to reach these conclusions." All this advice seemed too obvious, even if correct, to be of any help to her at the time.

"What I feel most guilty about ... Oh all right, *responsible* then. What I feel most responsible about, what makes me sometimes loathe myself, is not what I did to survive, and not primarily what happened in the camps - who can comprehend that? - but that I did nothing to resist, that is what is inexcusable." As Schade much later learned to appreciate, this constituted only a part of the complex mechanism of her memory.

And so she picked her way through the dagger-like thorns of the city searching for blossoms wherever she could find them and often wondered how her father would react to her thinking, her life. As the months slowly blended into one another she no longer anxiously read through every handwritten scrap of paper posted on every available public wall space offering and requesting information about lost family members in all the languages of Europe, sad leaves clinging forlornly to barren trees. Her mind refused to give anchorage to the possibility of her father's death, it floated like flotsam on the surface of her consciousness, immanent but unrealized, occasionally bruising the underpinnings of her mental stability with melancholy frustration.

As she walked with Schade out of her building that chilly noon, she turned to him with narrowed eyes and said with a sudden brutality, "Will you ask about my father in Munich?"

He nodded. "Yes. Of course."

"Good. Then I won't think about it anymore today. Thank you, Jonathan."

In fact, without telling her he had informally requested information on Axel Albrechtsburg some weeks earlier. What disturbed him was the apparent lack of any news at all regarding the banker. Then, too, his quiet attempts to discover the whereabouts and condition of some of his own relatives had been almost completely without success. Most of them had lived in the eastern parts of Germany and those who survived could be anywhere amidst the mass migrations taking place, or still in their homes, or with neighbors....

As if she perceived the direction his thoughts might take, she smiled brightly and said, "Come, we'll start with the Romanische Café. Have you heard of it?" This too was part of her self-administered therapy to straighten the labyrinth of her emotional state: the continual reference to the sites of her cultural heritage, which she decided would balance the scales of morality and her own fragmented feelings of guilt. She refreshed herself to deal with the present by dipping into the unbloodied pools of art and cultural nostaligia, the pre-nazi past: theaters, restaurants, apartments, cafés, studios ... wherever she could find flowers in the thorny thickets: the landscape of culture as priest for remission of sins. And Schade, who had himself once prowled the streets of New York City like a young panther ready to attack or love, hesitantly joined these raids into the past of another, for him still unknown, city. He doubted the efficacy of this emotional nostalgia as therapy, but in his own turmoil, evoking his own forms of guilt, he supported whatever she found helpful and hoped to add to her happiness, if she was actually capable of being happy. At the same time he took every opportunity to learn about the city and its citizens. We take our individual inspirations wherever we find them. These excursions required a great effort at imaginative recreation: too many buildings lay mutilated in the rictus of a very modern kind of death, a fatal paradigm of technological invention (who could name it "progress"?) and the infinite capacity of the human spirit for paroxysms of self-destruction in the name of salvation.

At one point during their walks she gestured toward a half-destroyed brownish black apartment building leaning close to the sidewalk like a drunk against an invisible lamppost. Indifferently she said, "That's where your colleague shot his German. Oh yes, it's hardly a secret anymore. Rumors and gossip always fill the vacuum left by lack of information. Somebody blurted out something about it after too many drinks. Foreigners always assume the local servants speak only their own language, and that badly."

He did not care that the secret was no longer a secret; nor did her indifferent dismissal of another's life strike a particular chord of surprise: a stranger's existence, or loss of it, held no personal obligation to mourn after the savagery of the last years. But her phrase "shot his German" elicited an underground response in his mind which began with the question, "If Kirshhof had 'his' German, did he have to shoot him?" and ended with the further questions, "Does each of us have 'our' German to deal with in some way that does not require death but other forms of suffering, like love or loneliness or sexual obsession? And by extension, in some perverse way, do we all have our Doppelgänger here? Am I 'my' German?" No immediate answers dissolved the questions, but the idea interested him sufficiently to make a few notes about it later that night.

Now he nodded and said, "Yes, we must all sooner or later leave this place for a while. It will become too intolerably close." The streets, gapped like the decayed mouth of a dispossessed beggar, took hold of them again, sliding past their vision like a slowly rotating panopticum.

They entered the wreckage of the Tauentzienstraße, by now cleared of much of its rubble, a block or so before devolving into the triangle it formed with the Budapesterstraße at the apex of which stood the stunted remnants of the Kaiser Wilhelm Gedächtniskirche on the Kurfürstendamm, what had been the city's great shopping thoroughfare. By the streetcar rails which once coursed down the middle of the street stood a large white sign board with black letters identifying the area as "British Sector" in three languages and a small facsimile of the Union Jack painted smartly at the top. Next to it another wooden sign warned

> *Achtung! Vorsicht!*
> *Bomben nicht anfassen!*
> *Aufpassen oder sterben.*

Behind them, on Wittenbergplatz, lay the remains of the famous department store of the west, Kaufhaus des Westens, which the Tauentzienstraße connected at its other end with the memorial church (Taufhaus des Westens, baptismal store of the west, as Berlin wit had it). The store had once had the reputation as being the Harrods of Berlin: one could purchase everything from toothpaste to crocodiles - and did. No shoppers entered the lumped pile of stone and steel now, although many people still came to look at it and remember.

"There," she said, pointing to an empty street level storefront. "That was the Café Zuntz. When the nazis with intellectual pretentions took over the Romanische, the other intellectuals came here around the corner to talk and drink, but the milieu had changed, the excitement of the times was too negative, too much wondering whether the man at the next table was Gestapo....."

"*Kommt Zuntz auch wieder?*" He forced a laugh, paraphrasing the song of the hour, "*Berlin kommt wieder,*" trying to keep the day as light and carefree as possible. The absurd element of her therapeutic notion was clear to him in the midst of this maimed city. He questioned the value of her gnawing at the past like a child nibbling at a sugar stick to absorb its energy, an attempt to resurrect memories she could not possess first-hand, but only through stories she had heard or read. He feared the delicate membrane that separates madness from mental balance would be strained to bursting by her self-administered therapy and she would disappear in the promontories of insanity or indifference where he could not follow. The diseases of the times.

But she returned his laugh with ease and said, "Someday .... something like it. The Romanische will surely be rebuilt. It's our equivalent of Le Dôme."

They turned the corner and stopped in the middle of the short stretch of space at the apex of the triangle formed by the two streets. This had been the famous gathering place of the city's artistic and literary stars and starlets. The outdoor area once filled with tables and chattering tourists jutted out like a carapace from the building proper onto the sidewalk. None of the regulars ever sat there; they frequented the two rooms inside with the less noisy smaller room occupied by those who needed relative quiet to think, write acerbic letters to the editor, meet a married lover (the waiters always more discreet than the regular clientele, who spread the news as soon as they heard it), sip wine or coffee and talk, plan a new poetry journal (avant-garde, of course, if one could get a poem by Ernst Toller or Joachim Ringelnatz...). Mixed among the poets and journalists sat those odd characters attracted to the intellectual life in all urban centers who exist on very little and never create anything but verbal wind, who occupy a chair all afternoon and half the night arguing obscure anarchist theses or bits of gossip behind a single cup of coffee, occasionally dipping a chunk of the free bread into the plate of goulash belonging to a more prosperous neighbor (who usually took no offense), while continuing the argument without pause, a nod of the shaggy head considered a sufficient indication of gratitude. (One had to commit some truly outrageous offense in order to achieve Lokalverbot, being banned from the premises: starting a fist-fight with a regular over some cutting witticism, spilling beer on a regular halfway through a swerve in an attempted waltz, or not being able to pay one's tab once too often....)

Kramer, the theater critic, inevitably told the story of the fly in the coffee: A clerk from a nearby bank sat one afternoon on one side of the room under an advertisement for Kantorowicz liqueurs and orangeade ("auch im 'Romanischen'") and ordered a coffee. He looked into the cup before taking the first sip, scowled and called the waiter back, saying, "Please take the coffee back. I cannot drink it. There is a fly in it." "Terribly sorry," the waiter said, "I'll have to call the manager." This personage thusly summoned made his way through the tables nodding to those clients he recognized or thought he should know. At the bank clerk's table he stopped and looked down his nose at the fellow. "So, what's wrong? You want the coffee taken back? You don't like the taste?" The bank clerk began to explain. "Look, I can't drink a coffee with a fly. Who said anything about taste?" The manager took a step back from the table. "A fly? A fly? *One* fly?!"

Kramer chuckled and added, "Perhaps apocryphal, who knows. As a young man I kept a small dog for a while. It too refused to drink its water if an insect invaded the bowl."

425

As Berliners never failed to note, the Romanische Café lost its artistic élan after January 1933 and its windows in the bombing of 1943-44, a statement that applied with equal appropriateness to all public meeting places in the city. When Gisela and Schade stood before the building, it had also lost its contours and the once bright neon sign spread across the front just above the ground floor ceiling level now read "...MANISCHE ... FE", the tubes of light long since smashed. The ruins of the plant box fence around the outdoor terrace and the steel-girded marquee lay crushed against the windowless facade. Inside one could see only dust hanging in the pale light radiating through the holes in the ceiling and broken furniture amidst puddles of water on the floor. A clumsy, handwritten sign tacked to the doorway, written by a would-be Polish or Russian entrepreneur with an incomplete knowledge of German, read

Achtung! Gefahr!
Eintritt auf eigene Gewähr![27]

Of what use could this be to her?
"Perhaps we could get inside somehow and see the small back room." With some difficulty they found they could enter the building through the glassless window. "If we go quickly, without looking around, people will think we belong to the place. Come." Schade had a brief vision of their embarrassment when the MPs or the German police asked for their papers and purpose, but nothing of the sort happened. None of the pedestrians gave them more than a

---

[27] Attention! Danger!
    Entry at own risk!

brief questioning glance without stopping to wonder ... his uniform lent them a certain authority with civilians. Inside it smelled of wet ashes and pulverized cement. The long bar still flanked the wall of the main room, but the elaborate mirrors and variously shaped bottles, the gleaming coffee machines and faux marble-topped tables, and anything else of potential value had long since disappeared. The back room resembled the front except for one undamaged chair that somehow had escaped the carnage. One wide beam of sunlight shone through the hole in the ceiling, falling through similar holes in the floors above.

Gisela placed the chair in the shaft of light, pulled her skirt up to her waist and sat down with the chair reversed, her arms crossed on the wooden back. Grinning, she began to sing softly in a growling voice.

> *Ich bin die fesche Lola,*
> *der Liebling der Saison,*
> *ich hab' ein Pianola*
> *zu Haus' in mein Salon*
>
> *...*
>
> *doch an mein Pianola*
> *da lass' ich keiner dran.*[28]

True to the spirit of the occasion she sang the words slower than the original tempo dictated, more as a moody ballad than the metallically rhythmic, slightly risqué chanson from the tumultuous 1920s when everything seemed possible including the gorilla who had a villa in the

---

[28] I am the clever Lola/the darling of the season/I have a pianola/at home in my salon/.../but I let no one get at my pianola.

zoo. He wondered where she had learned the words; surely such songs had been banned by the empty-minded minions serving their masters in the former Reichskulturkammer. Her father perhaps? As Schade's interest in this mysterious figure increased so did his anxiety regarding the man's situation. At the moment there was no way of knowing what that might be, but the prognosis tended toward the negative: the possibility that any individual presumed lost would turn up in good health with all his material resources in hand existed to be sure, but the odds stood overwhelmingly against such an event. For most of those lost turned up, if at all, sick in body and spirit, often maimed, without resources of any kind. Perhaps he'd been in a concentration camp, but from what she'd told Schade there was no reason to suspect this to be the case. Had he been on one of the Allied arrest lists, which contained so many suspect names? A definite possibility; he could be in some military stockade accused of any number of things from crimes against humanity to belonging to one of the nazi party organizations, several of which he had indeed joined. He could have simply disappeared in the cauldron of the war which boiled over in the final days before the ceasefire. What had the banker done during the war, especially during the final years of the total war effort? Schade hoped G-2 would provide some answer before too long. Now he put the elder Albrechtsburg out of his mind as his daughter began another song fragment, remaining in the same position, erotic but equivocal.

Es gibt nur ein Berlin
und das ist mein Berlin
...
so lang' die Welt sich dreht

> *so lang' die Zeit vergeht*
> *so lang' die Bäume in Frühling blüh'n*
> *gibt es nur ein Berlin.*[29]

The great chansoneuse Claire Waldoff had always performed this song in a medium fast tempo, the quickened snappy style of the between wars' cabaret. Gisela slowed the tempo to an almost dirge-like Moritat generating a funereal atmosphere, which negated the image of vague sensual hungers expressed in her position on the chair under the shaft of sunlight. Her blonde hair combed straight across her forehead glittered as she tilted her head back on her neck, eyes closed in concentration, tightening the muscles of the slender stalk of her throat. The emptiness of the shattered room absorbed the light and the hoarse voice so that it left no echo; a few meters away the low crooning threads of sound could not be heard. Street noises did not penetrate the room. The pylon of sunlight illuminated the dustmotes lazily turning on their own axes as if too freighted with questions to rise or fall.

Was this Berlin? Was this the real end of the city? A thin, beautiful woman in the ruins lamenting the passage of time and history with nostalgic popular songs; the final defense of the defeated: memories achieved second-hand. They could not carry the weight of the present, as beautiful and as achingly appealing as the image was, it would be unable to shore up the strengths needed for the future. What of the other end of the cultural spectrum? Liszt? Beethoven? Bruckner? Wagner, robotically beloved by

---

[29]There's only one Berlin/And that's my Berlin/As long as the world turns/As long as the trees bloom in the spring/There'll be only one Berlin.

the nazis because the Führer found in him a fellow mythomane and anti-semite? The manipulated, senile Richard Strauss? Would they transcend their abuse and debasement to return to an honorable place in German culture? Would the banned "degenerate" music of Mendelsohn-Bartholdy, Erich Korngold, Schönberg, Kurt Weill, Ernst Krenek, Hindemith be enlisted solely to reconstitute German musical life? (A stray thought flitted briefly across the screen of his mind: "What could the Germans possibly think if they heard the music of Thelonious Monk? "Unerhörte Niggermusik! Chaos!" It would no doubt blow their minds into a state of traumatic amazement.)

With a quick gesture she shifted her body in the chair and grinned with a lasciviousness unusual for her. Laughing she hiked her skirt higher. "Listen," she said.

> *Jonny,*
> *wenn du Geburtstag hast*
> *bin ich bei dir zu Gast*
> *für die ganze Nacht...*[30]

She broke off abruptly and stared blankly at him, squinting in the sun at his figure in the jagged shadows. "No. That's certainly not very appropriate, is it? Well...." She stood up and began walking around the room peering into the corners. "There's really not much left, is there? I wonder

---

[30] "Jonny, when it's your birthday/I'll be with you as your guest/the whole night long." The plain words without the music do not give any indication of the sultry, deeply sexual connotation of the song, especially when sung by a woman with a low, seductive voice.

what it was really like, before the war. Perhaps someday someone will make a movie about it and reconstruct the whole thing."

"It won't be the same...."

"Of course not, but it might help us to know."

"Where do your colleagues go after the performance?"

"A few tables, ersatz coffee, powdered milk if we're lucky, hardly ever anything to eat, two walls missing and no heat. The merest hint at a beginning."

"It will grow."

"Yes. Let's go. We've had enough of this. It smells too much like decaying teeth."

When they reached the sidewalk they faced the Gedächtniskirche, its spire missing as if a giant fist had snapped it off in a fit of rage. In the pale sunlight the fireblackened pillar appeared darker still, a reminder of the evil quivering beneath the surface of human life, as if the broken root had burst upward from the earth bellowing like a wounded bull. Now silent and dark, there remained only the nub of the matter, acted upon by a destructive force torn from the control of human hands and mind, a beastly unthinking act committed by an enraged animal that perceived itself in danger of losing the kiss of eternity. Here Schade's mind rebelled: it was after all just another building, by happenstance a Christian church erected in memory of a would-be Caesar in an attempt to mix the strengths of church and state into cement to support the nation's destiny, just one more structure slammed into broken masonry and glass shards by a modern extension of politics ... could one ruin alone bear the burden of such an elaborate metaphor when the entire city symbolized the end of an epoch?

She interrupted these confused intellections. "They tell me that I was at a service there as a child. I have no memory of it. Many Berliners say it's more decorative like this than it was before the bombing. The style is terribly pompous. Let's see what it looks like inside."

Crossing the square he said, "I can't imagine New York being like this. It's too full of life and energy."

"Then you can't imagine what Berlin was like before the war."

Ropes and warning signs prohibited their entrance into the stunted building.

Achtung! Gefahr!
Bomben nicht anfassen!
Aufpassen oder sterben.

Under the direction of an old man, a line of women passed pieces of stone through the only viable entrance, piling the brick rubbish on the street to be cleaned off and reused in the reconstruction of another building. Berlin wasted nothing except the lives of those who could not accommodate themselves to its character and pace. This is an apt symbol of the developments in the city: the past cleaned off and used to build the future, the cement newly mixed according to the most up-to-date recipe, but the past had already tainted the bricks. ("You will persist in looking for symbols and metaphors," Schadow told him. "I am beginning to think you're one of those artist souls who have to elevate everything to metaphysics and poetry before they can understand it. Isn't it enough just to see things as they are? Can you not comprehend the city directly, without the screens of art on which to project the images? Look at it! How real do you want it to be? Can reality be any simpler and starker than this?")

When they turned away from the church and its cleaners, a bell began to toll its stately bonging sound into the square. Their heads swiveled around to stare at the church in amazement: the bell tower of course had been blown away. Then they smiled as if comforting each other. They heard no mid-afternoon aural ghost: the weak, metallic volume of the ringing indicated a recording played through an old loudspeaker system. At certain hours during the day when the electricity worked church officials had permission to play the recording even though services could not be held there: another link in the chain of tradition being closed. "We've got ghosts enough to bedevil us as it is," Schade said.

"Yes."

The tall, pale figure in faded blue dungaree shirt and pants loped by in white plimsolls with the purposeful stride of those who possess false identity papers. "Hello, John. Pretty lady." "Hello, Mister Morgan Tahni. Her name is Gisela." "I know. So long. And how many words did you get done today?" After he loped off, she said, "Nothing should surprise me any longer, but something always does."

They walked in the direction of the Hallische Tor and Buchdow's theater where she would perform that evening. "Yes, that symbol has the beauty of simplicity and clarity. That must come from the American part of your mind. The danger lies in just that simplicity, doesn't it? We Germans too often prefer the density and complexity of a symbol. Our reappraisals fall into categories of labyrinths, turning in on one another, expressed in sentences with no endings, but highly charged beginnings...."

"Like the one you're building now."

She laughed happily, as if surprised at her ability to do so. "*Natürlich, Schätzchen.*"

"Undoubtedly I will chew over the notion until it is as complex and as deep as Schopenhauer would wish. After all, I am also German."

"Who is he? Should I know him? Did he survive the war? Was he a nazi?" At first he could not tell if this was seriously meant or a joke. She turned a totally blank face to him like a child waiting for an answer to an off-hand question asked of an adult. He began to laugh, drawing the sound from deep in his belly. Tears squeezed from his eyes and his body shook with the shudders of the first unconstrained and natural laughter in months. Staggering under the lightness of the attack, he drew in a few shallow gulps of air and, shaking his head, tried to still the peristaltic waves reaching up from his stomach. Wiping the tears from his cheek with a quick movement of his arm, he said, "I'll introduce you at the first opportunity."

In the voice of an old maiden aunt she answered, "Yes, that would be nice, I'm sure. We'll have him for tea and biscuits once we get the buttery back to normal. That will be very nice indeed."

His laughter redoubled and he held his abdomen with both hands, helpless to curtail the waves that washed up and over him. "Was it that funny?" she asked and he shook his head, gasping for air, leaning on her arm. "No," he said between gulps, "but the idea of laughing like this ... it's been a long time. This may be hysteria, but it feels so good." Finally, under her smiling eyes, her arm in the crook of his elbow, they began to walk again. He screwed down the spasms to a short giggle with long gulps of air until his stomach settled into its usual state of tension and he breathed regularly.

"Laughter is our great weapon against the indifference of the universe. Unfortunately, some of us have to think of time and place these days before we indulge in it; it might be taken as unseemly, certainly unwarranted. At the moment, when Germans laugh, it's taken as callousness."

"Provisionally, yes. Laughter in times like these becomes something extremely personal, to be let out only in private. The public face is one of heavy seriousness, as it no doubt should be. But none of us can afford to lose the private laughter. As hopeless as the situation may be, on any level, laughter stands between us and suicide. It is more important than art, isn't it, it is salvation in our secular age."

"You do run on. Must be the German part of you. And since when do you consider anything more valuable than art, even as salvation or redemption?"

"I've been thinking. Don't make that face. I occasionally allow myself the luxury of entertaining an idea or two. Yes, it is true."

"If what you say is true, then we had better stop giggling on the streets."

And in fact, shadowy pedestrians had begun to stare at them with various expressions, but with a common denominator: only the uniformed victors and their German whores had the possibility of laughter at their disposal. This popular opinion expressed considerably less than the complete verity: Germans, too, laughed in many ways: bitterly, raucously, drunkenly, sweetly, ingratiatingly, hysterically, happily, totally, in all the ways any human laughed. But they did not laugh in public in any way.

The troubled young couple walked in silence down the Schöneberger Ufer along the canal still partially filled with the jagged, rusting flotsam of war. Choosing a subject he knew would sober both of them, he asked her about Buchdow.

"I thought I knew him, but my concern with myself allowed me only to see his surface. Which many say is all there is to the man, but I don't agree. I know him better now and it's true his self-concern is even greater than my own. And he has such an important element of his being to hide, you know. The infamous paragraph 175. How they criminalize love. But I think he is brilliant, one of the best directors we have. He's not got the balance of maturity that someone like Boleslaw Barlog or Karlheinz Martin has, but that will come with time. His ideas on what the country needs in the theater are exciting but fantastical: a new language for the new times is a stimulating idea, especially after the way nazi propaganda abused our language, but how does one go about creating a new language? Can it be done deliberately, which means artificially, can it be forced like the breeding of a new species in the laboratory? I don't know. I think it must come naturally from within. This can only happen when the young writers have digested the experiences of the last years and begin to work them out at their desks, or in the theater in groups of concerned artists. How long will it take? I don't know.

"Certainly we need new subjects, new themes. We must rework the old myths into something meaningful for the present, that's Joachim's idea, and he's not alone. We must take back the last twelve years, or at least come to realistic terms with them. We can't make up for all that with art. How can we recompence for the camps with literature or the theater, with anything at all? But we must face it and understand it in all its ugly barbarism. Perhaps that's what he means by the idea of a new language, something to give us the tools to do what we must. I don't know the answer. It's confusing to me. I've a great deal of emotional energy whirling around inside my brain and my belly, but I haven't been able to straighten it out the way he has. I've got to learn to think more clearly, more rationally, you see. I've got to reconcile my own part in it all. Joachim is a great help to me in this."

"I meant, how are you getting along with him?" Schade asked softly.

"Yes. That at least is not so confusing anymore." She smiled. "You have no need to be jealous, Jonathan. We haven't worked everything out completely, but our relationship is a professional one now. There are still resentments from the past, but they diminish as time passes. We both try to forget much of what happened, but I'll never forgive him for the drugs, but he saved me from being raped more than I was, he protected me even if his method was despicable. The sex with him was too brief and meaningless to think about it now. And he's back with his own now. We've come to a mutual if relatively unspoken agreement to concentrate on the present and the future. It is working out one way or another. In fact, that relationship is much less problematical than ours. But let's not talk about *that* today. Please. Anyway, I won't be working in his theater after this play, at least for a while - I've got a part in Barlog's new production, a nice comedy called *Hokuspokus*, in the Schloßpark Theater. You'll like it."

"It's not bad, safe and funny, but hardly breaking new ground or contributing to the new language."

"But it's something we haven't seen in many years; it's something to entertain the public who have little to enjoy these days. We can't do everything at once."

"I'll come to see you opening night."

"Whether we're still together or not?"

"Of course."

"Perhaps we'll still be together...."

"When do you open?"

"Early March."

"I'll be there in any case, but -"

"Can we please get something to eat? I'm hungry and I've got to be at rehearsal soon."

The nervous ambiguities of their situation continued to gnaw away at the edges of their thoughts as they ate a sparse, overpriced meal in a small dank Kneipe near the theater. As the time approached for the rehearsal she withdrew more and more into herself: before he left her at the stage door she had taken on the characteristics of the role she played; her goodbye was perfunctory and absent-minded. Once in the theater she plunged into her part with a concentration that sometimes frightened Buchdow as he guided his ensemble on the stage. A few days later he spoke to Schade about it, saying, "She's burning herself up. I don't pretend to understand the complexity of things driving her, but I know about this so-called therapy process she's using to resolve whatever confusion and guilt she suffers from. I am obviously not entirely without feelings for her, regardless of what you might think. I do worry about her. This notion of working out her neurosis through the theater is essentially healthy, I suppose, even constructive. After all we all play roles of one sort or another all the time, don't we? But if she continues to attack it with this obsessed intensity she'll break down before anything is accomplished except some marvelous performances. Hardly worth the price, is it? Admittedly her performances are a great selling point for the play and the theater, she's become very popular and there is no question of her talents. But the cost, Lieutenant, the cost! There must be something that can be done to remove or resolve at least part of this incessant pressure. Please don't let your opinion of me interfere with our discussion. I am thinking of her health and future."

Schade supposed Buchdow meant that his relationship with Gisela constituted that aspect of the problem that could most easily be resolved. He had of course spent much time mulling over the very point the jittery stage director was making, chasing it up and down the byways of his mind into hidden corners and shadowy doorways when the process became too painful: if their relationship ceased, that element of her psychic turmoil would be removed and presumably she could concentrate on resolving the remaining pieces of her psychological imbalance, or at the least work out some form of equipoise for living with the emotional and spiritual penury which she perceived as her condition. All very fine if one could make the requisite decision and act on it, but Schade too much enjoyed being with her, the shared flashes of nerve-end excitement of their love-making ("Perhaps it isn't love, but it isn't just sex either." "Oh yes it is; why can't you admit it? The thrill won't be lost"), the very involvement with their entanglement as a problem filled some void in his life and provided a level of satisfaction for him that compounded his guilt in the notion of his conspiring with himself to prolong the affair, playing with her own weakness in being unable to end it but constantly expressing the awareness of their suspicious motives for continuing.

And how could he think of his place in her life as completely negative? Indeed, the age-old notion of lovers in quandary nudged his whole being: he thought he gave more than he received. He could not think of himself as a cause of her placing him below her ambitions for her career and her country without facing his own bankruptcy of the heart, and this he was not prepared to do. That would mean his acceptance of the relationship as manipulative and superficial (as she often described it to him and he had just as often rejected): their relationship existed only because it made their lives easier under the circumstances, nothing more. His romantic consciousness rebelled at the thought while at the same time his rational brain informed him of its validity.

They had both admitted that the word love could not describe the sticky adhesive that held them tenuously together. So deeply involved with their own ghosts and internal conflicts, yet they found that they needed each other, that each satisfied some desire for physical connection, for emotional comfort and support in the other. What they could not accept was that while their affair possessed all the outward characteristics of passionate love, it remained passion without the obligatory forms of commitment. While Gisela appeared to, Schade had difficulty in accepting that they did not love each other in a traditional manner, but behaved as if they did so. So in fact they used each other to assuage what bruises on their emotions they could and held each other for whatever uncommitted happiness they could give. (One day during a break in rehearsal one of her fellow actresses said, "It wouldn't trouble me at all to be eating that good Ami food. What's a little sex if that's the only way you can eat well?" The statement was only in part directed at her and of course she did not respond to it, but she no longer talked to the women except about professional matters.)

Schade's conversation with Buchdow had been unsatisfactory for both of them. Schade did not consider making a preemptory gesture to inform the director that the matter was none of his business. Nor did it enter Schade's mind simply to dismiss Buchdow and walk away as the victor turns his back on a prostrated enemy because

Buchdow's concern was obviously honest, if prejudiced by his professional concerns, and Schade's opinion of the director had changed over the months since their first meeting: he had come to respect the man's devotion to his art and his talent even if this was ruthlessly and coldly rationalized and lacked spontaneity. Nevertheless, at the moment Buchdow spoke to him he had no time for a lengthy discussion (which he would not have entered in any case, his sense of privacy being one of the strongest elements in his nature) and put him off with a few words allowing that he was aware of the situation and that he was not acting in a capricious manner. If he had to talk to someone about it, that person would not be Buchdow, who bore more responsibility for Gisela's increasingly stretched balance than he was ready to admit.

  For his part, instead of confronting his own responsibility, Schade decided to pursue what he considered to be another ingredient in the goulash of inter-related psychological problems that cooked in the recesses of her mind: her father. Though he could not define the extent to which the problems had their origins in the relationship between father and daughter, he knew that the lack of knowledge about his well-being sorely troubled her, that she possibly blamed herself for her father's condition (assuming it was bad) because she had taken on responsibility for other events and included her father in that whirlpool of self-renewing doubts, guilt and recriminations. Anything could be tossed into the pot: like a giant stew cauldron, her psyche could absorb almost anything that added to the guilt simmering in it. If he could remove one of those ingredients, perhaps the others might be rendered more easily digestible, and then dispatched before they did irreparable damage to the entire system.

* * * *

Gisela and Schade were not the only seekers who prowled the streets of the city in search of respite, or knowledge, or revelation. Makepeace spent much of his sparse free time stepping slowly through the lanes and thoroughfares around the piles of debris amidst the derelict buildings and the exhaustion-gray citizens, absorbing the city's past, the stories and conundrums, history and songs that reflected their own present rather than a long tradition-ridden past. Only the architecture mirrored the past now, the signature of the builders' generations erecting a skyline indicative of and evoking grand dreams of space and time, power and majestic desires for a place in history ... also the small-minded meanness of the peasant digging a living out of the barren sandy plains of Brandenburg. Berlin's history began late and ended early, spanned but a brief duration when measured against Athens or Paris, but its density and heartlessness made up for its brevity: the now devastated grandiosity of its architecture, its claims and will to greatness which had led to hubris and destruction, contrasted absurdly with the artistic creation madly spewed out during the few years of its hectic existence - all of which crashed blindly against the cynical humor of the average Berliner for whom the giant buildings, projections of an injurious compulsion to prove national strength and vigor, meant little except employment during their construction and a source of sardonic humor when completed in their pomposity and inhuman scale.

    Such thoughts wound through Makepeace's mind as he walked once again up the street and stopped just east of the Brandenburg Gate in the Pariserplatz in front of the wreck of the massive building that had been the luxurious Adlon Hotel. In the cortex of his brain the notion of not having been there during the city's history pressed him to take these solitary perambulations. The stunted shell of the Adlon had become the symbol of times he had not experienced himself but was determined to learn about and absorb into his mental make-up. What this all meant, this drive to know the city, he could not say at the moment, but the compulsion was sufficiently strong to push him on to the broken pavement time and again: he had become addicted to the city as if it were a drug offering a thoroughfare to some as yet undefined nirvana. Nostalgia, resentment, and excitement brewed in the stewpot of his mind. He would possess the city in his own secret struggle: victory would come with knowledge. A phrase of Brecht's, the poet who never liked Berlin, came to his mind. "Everything is overflowing with dreadful tastelessness. But on what a level!" But taste could be a matter of choice and Makepeace, who would read a great deal about the city without understanding it all, made his choice: the contradiction between the present condition of the city and its still visible past fascinated him. Perhaps he had an advantage over those such as Schade, who he thought would become one of the city's victims, who carried an intimate association with Germany ineradicably stained on their consciousness. Makepeace came fresh and oddly innocent to the contemplation of this contradictory urban ruin, armed only with a fundamental political cynicism that allowed nonetheless a belief in certain political structures and the skeptic's view that everything must be personally verified.

    Now he stood before the shell that had been one of the great modern hotels of Europe with the formidable address Unter den Linden 1, honored by the presence of the Kaiser himself at its opening in 1907 and since then the temporary residence of crowned heads, senior diplomats, stars of the stage and screen (as the hotel's own brochures once proclaimed), the headquarters of the international press corps: a symbol of the urban metropolis for those who could afford its luxuries. He tried to visualize its form and texture before the bombs and fire transformed it into a massive skeleton of steel beams and marble columns black against the pale eggshell sky. For some reason a huge Red Cross flag hung from the windows of what remained of the façade, one of the few touches of white and bright red amidst the dreck of defeat. The image of the former glory of the building, that cost 20 million gold marks to erect, refused to clarify, and he realized he was trying too hard.

"They came into the hotel with guns ready to fire, but when they saw only wounded lying in blood in the halls and the cellars, they left again." The voice at his elbow melded pain and residual shock, so typical of Berlin voices that year. He turned to see a white-haired elderly woman bent at the hip, her eyes filled with the image he had been unable to see. She spoke as if to herself in an unusually slow Berliner drawl, pronouncing the words with caution as if they were precious gems to be protected. "Wasn't the first time we got shot at here. Just after the other war, revolution in the streets, shooters right there across the Pariserplatz shooting down the Linden from the Tiergarten through the Brandenburgtor. People died trying to cross the street to the hotel. I saw a woman killed trying to cross the square in the snow. Shot the windows out, too. Defending the Fatherland or international proletarian solidarity. All the same to the dead. But nothing like today. They came again and took all those who could stand to clean up the rubble at the corner of Wilhelmstrasse. Other soldiers came to examine the building more carefully and leather suitcases, watches, silverware, jewelry disappeared."

Without looking at him she asked for a cigarette and coughed the smoke into her dust-filled lungs. "The final stage happened when a group of Ivans looking for watches and whatever else they thought valuable, found the wine cellars. Once we had over 25,000 bottles stored there; now there's not one left. On the same evening the trucks began pulling up to the door and soon the entire collection disappeared. They probably drank it like beer. The end of the wine cellar meant the end of the hotel. They left the cellar full of broken wine cases and packing straw. One of them must have set it on fire. There was no way to stop it; the flames moved very fast, drawn by the empty windows and shell holes in the walls ... floor by floor it ate its way to the roof. It was over quickly. The building had withstood the war, the bombing, the fighting in the streets ... to end in flames after the fighting stopped. It was not a glorious sight: those who could walk tried to move the wounded out onto the center strip of the boulevard where they'd be safe from the burning fragments falling around us. Many remained in the street, too old, too infirm ... In the midst of all this we heard the sirens blaring in the distance coming toward us. Trucks pulled up in front of the building, people started shouting orders in Russian and unloaded equipment in the street: a few newsreel cameras filmed the end of the Adlon Hotel, the flames, the dead and wounded in the street, the rubble. The last pictures of the grand hotel dying by fire in the middle of the inferno, the capital of the Reich. If you see the Russian film *Kampf um Berlin* it's all there, the final minutes. And that's all that's left, over there. Rubble and dead stone. Oh, the Ivans and their bootlickers are using some of the undamaged rooms as offices and bedrooms, but still ... rubble and stone.

"I spent most of my life in that hotel, cleaning the rooms. I liked my work. I was happy there, my husband

and I met there, I saw them all, the foreigners with money, the Kaiser, Stresemann, that lowlife Hitler and his vulgar pals, the Americans and journalists, Chaplin ... Most of them tipped well. I'm too old now, you see, and it doesn't exist anymore. The Adlon is gone, who knows what they'll build there now. I won't be around to see it anyway. A blessing maybe. It doesn't matter, it doesn't matter. Thank you for the cigarette. Can I have another? Ah, the whole packet, eh. You must feel bad about something, no? Doesn't matter. *Auf Wiedersehen*, perhaps." She spoke the last phrases softly as she walked away down the Linden toward Friedrichstrasse, her back bent, eyes straight ahead. She did not turn around, she had no need to look another time.

    Makepeace wanted to tell her that it did matter and the hotel would live on in her mind, but he made no sound, his tongue would not form the words he knew contained at best a truth for himself and not the old woman. She had lived the experience in the city, he vicariously tried to reform it in his brain and so indulge his curiosity and desire to know the city. His was an abstract exercise, a deliberate mental construct to recreate a milieu in which he had not lived, but in which he thought it would have been exciting to live. The old woman did not have to attempt to intuit or read to taste the city's history in her mind and mouth. She would not have understood his desire and he envied her life as much as he resisted her defeatism. She held in her memory vast quantities of knowledge he would never attain, psychological and physical knowledge that was forever beyond him: flavors, smells, colors, signatures ... for those like her, Berlin would not return. The thought saddened him equally for the old woman and himself. Struggling with a demon whose shape he could not completely perceive, he refused to believe the city and its history would not continue some way, in art if not in the collective memory of its citizens. Kronauer and Schadow were right: the city could not die, but in what form would it live? Turning, he walked toward the Gate and made a decision: he would contribute whatever he could to the life of the city and its reconstruction. Exactly how this would happen he did not know, but explanations would come with time and circumstances. The city might not need him, but he suspected, in a burst of self-understanding, that he would need the city. He would stay.

Gently shaking his left wrist, he walked through the huge pockmarked stone colossus with the red flag barely stirring on its crown. An old man and a young boy passed by him, the old man holding the boy's hand. He heard the boy ask, "Grampa, did people always build ruins?"

Das ist dein Milljöh
Das ist dein Milljöh
Jede Kneipe und Destille
Kennt den guten Vater Zille.[31]

* * * *

Glowing with inner sunburn, Makepeace met Schade on the stairs of the villa in the Milinowskistrasse. "John," he confided with an iota of irony, "I've broken the non-fraternization rule." Schade laughed: the policy had been unofficially retracted weeks ago as being unenforceable. "John, I made love to a woman from the other side. I've

---

[31] This is your millyo [milieu] /This is your millyo/Every bar and saloon / Knows good old papa Zille.

consorted with the enemy, John." Satisfaction beamed from his face, his eyes sparkled in the morning sunlight.

"You've had fleshly knowledge of a communist!?" with mock horror.

"Don't be flippant, you Weltschmerz creampuff. Ah, the world takes on a different hue in the morning. We glide outward into the daylight, slide into the new day a dawning with light hearts and empty balls...." This he accompanied with broad, dreamy slow-motion gestures.

"You've fallen in love again."

"Don't be asinine, I don't even know her -- yet."

"So you got laid."

"John, really, this has gotta stop. You're becoming impossible."

"Just trying to be precise in description."

"Save it for your reports, fella. Ta ta." Makepeace, slapping a rolled newspaper against his leg, bounded up the stairs singing *Hoppla, jetzt komm' ich!* loudly in the expressive Hans Albers style, but wildly out of tune.[32] Shaking his head, Schade followed his colleague wondering where this would lead.

When Harrigan heard about the affair, he ceased chewing gum and sang a verse of the enlisted man's Berlin anthem.

So it's squeeze, squeeze, squeeze
as many frauleins as you please
how can you pass up such a tease
but watch out my friend for those vigilant MPs.

* * * *

---

[32]See endnote for the lyrics to this song.

No one Ogilvy Vasart knew amongst his Allied colleagues ever discovered whether the Countess could validly claim her title or not, though a number of sniffy fellow-Englishmen certainly made noises suggesting a less than noble birth and upbringing. It is possible that many Germans in Berlin knew the truth of the matter, but if so they kept it to themselves. Vasart said it made no difference to him, but it did: his bourgeois soul swooned at the thought of squiring the nobility, even if that particular representative had fallen upon rather less than the best of times. He met her one warm dusty summer afternoon at the beach along the shore of the Wannsee where Germans were not allowed, and he did not particularly wish to be. The skills he had acquired during his youth in London did not include swimming, and, while he vaguely appreciated sunbrowned human flesh in theory, he had no great liking for baking and sweating in the merciless sun like a greasy bratwurst on gritty sand, the grains of which inevitably snuggled their way into his bathing suit like a salmon swimming upstream. He had diplomatically agreed to spend an hour or so by the lake that afternoon only to please one of his colleagues who processed travel orders, an acquaintanceship he thought potentially useful.

    Sitting white and beached on the rocks and sand in his army regulation shorts and polo shirt, he watched with mild disgust as his colleague amiably thrashed about in the tepid water. The Americans, in whose sector the lake lay, had given up by this time the foolish policy of non-fraternization, but along with the other Allies maintained certain areas off-limits for Germans so their soldiers could enjoy themselves off-duty without the contaminating proximity of the former enemy. The young soldiers of course entertained their own ideas of the effects of such contamination and continued to ignore the prohibitive clauses of their superiors' policy. This meant, among other things, swimming in the lake and sunning themselves in the company of young German girls to whose hollow laughter they seemed completely indifferent. The stomachs of these young women did not gurgle and rumble on such occasions because the chronologically equally young GIs thoughtfully supplied food for the day, which the young women consumed in haste but with a certain forced casualness of movement as if they had no real hunger, an unspoken quid pro quo from which both sides benefited and the venereal disease rate increased. The ubiquitous military police regularly patrolled the area but usually made no attempt to enforce the regulation unless they were new to the city, or suffered from either aggravation brought on by not having sufficient points to go home or a massive hangover.

 Vasart never knew which of these conditions motivated the two burly young hillbillies to demand the papers of the woman he came to know as the Countess when she walked out of the shallow gray water some meters from where he uncomfortably sat, removing her white rubber bathing cap and shaking out her short black hair. In the end, of course, it did not matter, the die had been cast, the bread buttered, so to speak. Two things immediately struck him: the woman's noble bearing in the heat of a humiliating situation, wearing a thin bathing costume of a decade-old style, and the fact that she did not belong to the same generation as the more prevalent numbers of German (or American and British) females on the lake shore. She stood calm and straight in front of the gawky MPs whose apparently permanent grins infuriated Vasart, answering their questions with a scarcity of words he admired straight away. She behaved in a neutral and distanced, but completely correct and self-possessed manner, and later confided to him that she knew the rules but it had been such a lovely day and the water seemed to promise refreshment and simple pleasure....

He rarely saw such polite aplomb in the defeated Germans and this, combined with the way that her wet swimsuit outlined her tall slender figure lending prominence to her mons venus and protruding nipples, captured his admiration and stirred his sex. Finally, unable to bear anymore of the scene, he grabbed his identification card and strode up to the confrontation in his best officer's demeanor to put a stop to it. Ever a gentleman, he thought of it as a rescue mission, although the damsel did not appear seriously distressed, and his shining armor consisted of his slightly sunburned but essentially milk-white flesh and his aggressive English superiority whilst facing down those of inferior social rank.

Showing his identification card with studied casualness he informed the gawkers he would see to it that the lady did not further trespass upon forbidden ground and indicated they were relieved of further responsibility in the matter. The fundamental lethargy of combat troops in peacetime and an inbred fear of authority common to the low-born, despite their brief police training, allowed him to take putative charge of the lady without resistance from the MPs. The latter tossed him an ironic salute and, as they sauntered away along the shore, he turned to his charge who vigorously rubbed her shoulders and arms with a thin towel. "Thank you ever so much," she said in a bright but reserved British English voice, as if he had just given her directions to the local opera house.

Undeterred, having practiced his own aristocratic tones and timbres for many years before attempting entrance to Oxford, Vasart asked, "Would you like something to eat before you go?"

Later that afternoon she did leave the lakeside, but by then she had lost some of her carefully constructed reserve and at least partially filled her stomach. Afterward she told Vasart, "I belong to *les gens qui vraiment aiment manger.* That's what I would like on my tombstone. Life is extremely frustrating these days, you know." Within a short period of time he came to wholeheartedly believe this. Like most Germans, she talked incessantly about food; unlike most Germans her background had been one of excellently prepared meals served on blinding white tablecloths by dark-coated servants. Thus she knew whereof she spoke when she fantasized about *quenelles de brochette, paté de canard truffé avec les petits oignons à la grecque*, and those fine wines whose names meant nothing to him. These things had been out of the bounds of possibility for many years, but the memory of them remained as permanent as the art of Brillat-Savarin. Or so she let him believe. An additional similarity with other Germans was her thinness resulting from gastronomical deprivation. Vasart thought she had probably seen close to forty years and the lack of weight he did not mind: he thought it was becoming in a countess. Of course he accompanied her when she left the lake, much to the barely hidden dismay of his colleague from the travel section who had made other plans for the evening with his new friend Ogilvy.

Over the brief period that they knew each other Vasart discovered bits and pieces of her past which he stored away in the rummage closet of his mind; all of it fascinated him and led him to make social judgments which could only be described as misguided at best and perverse at worst: even Germans of the faded and discredited aristocracy were not acceptable partners for officers of the British Army of the Rhine especially when forced on the society of the mess and drawing rooms of field-grade officers. Vasart did not seem to care. In tones plummier than usual he moaned, "I can't help it. It's the grand passion. I'm enraptured, my soul is captured, a victim of sex and fate!" He and the Countess had an easier time of it in the presence of junior officers in the American Army with whom he worked. Schade and his colleagues, none of whom considered themselves hypocrites, enjoyed the company of the odd pair. They too took some pleasure in her ever shifting stories of the noble milieu in which she grew up, though none of them approached the matter on bended knee as their English colleague did. (Kenneth Farisse, the newspaper editor who replaced Kirshhof, snidely noted that in that position Vasart's tongue did not have to work so hard.)

"You'd think the revolution of 1789 never happened," Makepeace said shaking his head in wonderment. Schade smiled and replied, "In Germany it didn't." "Ogilvy is British." "It didn't happen there either."

Piecemeal and vaguely she alluded to her family history: during the 18th century her family had owned a large armaments factory and invented a new weapon for one of Friedrich the Second's wars, whereupon the grateful monarch ennobled the family, whereupon the patriarch and his younger brothers sold the firm for an immense amount of gold bullion, which they divided according to some arcane standard of family distribution, whereupon the Countess's direct relation (the self-same patriarch) purchased a landed estate near Königsberg in East Prussia and property in the garrison town of Potsdam outside Berlin. Until 1939 the family lived in the grand style on the income from these properties, though it did not escape the depredations of the defeat in 1918 and the economic depression following 1929. Early in the war, when the

British began bombing the city, the unwed but not quite virginal Countess and her still attractive if erratic mother, Roswitha , moved to the East Prussian property to avoid the inconveniences of the air raids and to suffer the boredom of country existence. The advance of the Red Army banished the ennui of the bucolic life and shortly after celebrating a sparse 1944 Christmas, mother and daughter fled the onslaught scurrying back to Potsdam where the soldiers of the victorious Soviet empire finally caught up with them. Gang-raped in the garden of their house by rampaging and rutting soldiers from the Urals and beyond, the two women retreated to a room in a large apartment owned by friends near Tegel airport in what would become the French sector of the city. Soviet generals requisitioned without compensation their houses and property in Potsdam; the East Prussian property now served as a military base which they had no hope of regaining.

Life in the city that summer was not easy for the last two members of the von Mouton family. (The Countess never said a word about the fate of the male family members, but Vasart harbored the suspicion that they were either dead in the war or in one of the prisoner of war camps, since he silently assumed they all avidly served in the Wehrmacht or the SS until Stalingrad, after which they just served. "I mean, weren't they all, the aristos, weren't they nazis, after all?" he plaintively asked Makepeace at the start of the affair with the Countess, before he learned otherwise.) Regardless of the wide spectrum of problems they faced, the Countess only ever complained about the lack of food, the one subject that obsessed her and made her tiresome to everyone but Vasart, who found even this aspect of her character enrapturing. No one knew exactly how they survived, and Vasart never dared to cross the line of decorum to ask, but Makepeace hinted that she and her increasingly detached mother, who never mentally recovered from the rapes, gave German lessons to high-ranking French officers who appreciated with sympathy the situation of the nobility down on its luck. There existed in some quarters a distinct suspicion that the Countess gave not only language lessons to the French officers, but this Vasart discounted as jealous viciousness with no basis in empirical fact. "Just another sign of our mean and evil times, old man, that's the nub of it."

The distracted and infatuated former theater critic spent a great deal of his time thinking up ways to cook the fare available at the Allied commissaries which would satisfy the Countess's salivating memories of earlier and more gastronomically pleasurable times. Not that he actually cooked the ingredients he carted to the apartment on the (European) second- floor of the corner building; the Countess and her mother depended upon their friends, the owners of the apartment, for that service. With the advent of the French in their sector and the opening of the language lesson business, not to mention the start of the younger von Mouton's affair with Vasart, food of various nations began to flow through the kitchen at regular intervals and the owners of the apartment thought it in no way demeaning to cook for their aristo friends as long as they themselves partook equally of the results of their culinary labors.

Whenever he could find time away from his work, and she from hers, they spent a few hours together attending the few good theater performances, the newly reopened concert series, listening to many bad cabaret performances, walking in the Grunewald before a meal, lying in Schade's bed where their spontaneous acrobatics surprised both of them. The Countess frankly informed

Vasart one afternoon that, while her experience of love and its physicality did not reach the breadth of some of her friends, she had nonetheless sufficient experience to be able to judge that his performance must be classified at the level of the incredible. "D'you really think so?" he asked, rather taken aback by the notion. Fortunately for them, Schade had recently moved into his own room on the second floor of a large villa near Schlachtensee, which afforded him, and thus them, a private space with a bed as one of the few places available to them for the constantly stunning performances. Vasart shared quarters with two other officers, both confirmed boche-haters, and the apartment the Countess and her mother shared with their friends clearly was of no use to them for this purpose, especially since her mother never left it anymore. They also occasionally attended an official function where he could take her with some equanimity, but the risks of creating a Nasty Scene, as his commanding officer put it, hovered around such gatherings like yellow London fog invading a garden party. He did not care for himself, but strongly felt his responsibility to her in the social sense and only rarely suggested that they appear at these functions. Real trouble only occurred once, and that occasion became legendary throughout the British command.

Early one evening at a reception for a visiting fireman Vasart stood at the bar of the officers' club with one arm around the sloping shoulders of the Countess, elegantly dressed in a barebacked gown fashionable in the mid-thirties, and the elbow of the other arm hooked on the old polished wood, drink in hand. He was not entirely sober, but not quite drunk enough to excuse his behavior. They had come directly from a particularly inventive and energetic half hour in Schade's ever-welcoming bed, which may have added a layer of meaning to the motivation for his actions, or more directly, his words, since he undertook few untoward actions, but did wave his free arm about his head and spill a shower of scotch whisky. The complex of causes lay deeper in his consciousness than the effects of the whisky, which, however, loosened the restraints usually sufficient to keep the cauldron of his inner rage from boiling over. Now the embarrassment at the pressure of his companion in the milieu of that unthinking anti-German atmosphere of the British mess compounded the confusion out of which The Incident would explode. "All bloody snobs and working class climbers," as he later attempted to explain, "no bloody class at all!"

Too many of those present, while not above a dalliance with a local Fräulein themselves, nonetheless remembered all too well too many relatives or comrades whose lives the German war machine had abruptly ended. This, in various ways both subtle and offensive they made known to their wayward colleague. The fact that the Countess's command of the English language exceeded that of many of those who denigrated her presence made both she herself and her stalwart companion acutely uncomfortable and woodenly stubborn. Makepeace told him later that he should have brought her to the American club, if he had to take her anywhere at all, where feelings on the subject ran less high among the male officers. On the other hand, there they would have faced the catty remonstrances of the American women who resented the ready availability of young and willing German girls, even though the Countess did not properly fall precisely into that vaguely defined category, but she was undeniably, devastatingly attractive, especially now that she had added several pounds of well-placed flesh to her figure. As Marybeth Mullen informed Harrigan after the Nasty Scene had been played out, "Her English is too good to be true, and her tits are too tight. I think she's a spy." Harrigan laughed at the time, but later wondered about the acuity of the redhead's insight.

But all of that was post facto since Vasart and the Countess did attend the reception in the British officers' club, and he did give forth his infamous monologue. In fact, he always thought of his "Lecture in the Humanitas," as he occasionally referred to it, as a moment of glory. His friends made no secret of the fact that they thought him insane, at the least twisted, for having committed such an intimate action in public, but they had not been present to hear the glorious outburst among the hostiles and the dumb.

It began quietly enough with Vasart attempting to answer the question, "How do you think we should really treat these Huns?" asked in a snidely sarcastic tone by one of his fellow officers who stared at the Countess with an open attitude of contempt as he spoke. After several minutes of rationally balancing the pros and cons of the "hard or soft" occupation policy alternatives, Vasart became aware that his interlocutor had ceased listening, but looked intently at the Countess's breasts with a supercilious twist to his lips. This annoyed Vasart and he allowed his annoyance to instantly undergo a seachange to rage. He stuffed his nose into his glass and swallowed a sizable dollop of whisky, during which pause the fellow officer filled the silence with the steeljacketed statement, "But they're all so ... despicable." At this Vasart's gorge rose to his brain with the swiftness of a gazelle in heat, at which point anger, embarrassment and alcohol reached the critical mass of detonation.

"What you really want to know is whether we should be kind to them or not, isn't it? Whether they're all guilty or not, eh? If they're all guilty, cut off their balls and rape them. Would that make you feel better? Would we really have won then? Beaten them to nothing? Demented. There can't be any question of sentiment in our relations with the Germans; there's no place for it. How do you want to punish an entire nation? Oh yes, punishment there has to be, but how do you want to do it, eh? Make 'em all farmers and hang half of 'em? Which half? Look around you, dammit, there's punishment all over. They've made their own prison and they're in it. You want to starve them? They're starving now, many of them, selling themselves for a piece of stale bread. How much can a starving worker produce, you fool! Are we supposed to support them for the next fifty years? If they're going to work they've got to eat. Even you should understand that. The rain may fall on the guilty and the innocent. We're not gods but we are responsible. Ironic, isn't it? Or don't you understand irony either? If there's a German problem, it's our problem too, isn't it? They brought it on themselves, oh yes, but who's got to deal with it now? We're not liberators, no, we're the conquering army, by Christ, and now we've bloody well got to do something with what we've defeated. You want to treat the nation the way you'd treat an individual? Bash morality and punishment into their heads with a gun butt? Expand the colonial empire? Keep 'em down like the bloody wogs in Africa? You can't have justice by bashing indiscriminately about, you bloody beefeaters! You've got to have some standards of measurement for responsibility not a bloody unthinking blanket condemnation. Where's your balance, man? You've got your brains stuck halfway up your bleeding arse!"

As Vasart's voice rose in pitch and volume, the unfortunate captain began to back away and look about him for support as if he feared this madman would hurl himself physically upon his body. With the inevitability of an unbraked locomotive, Vasart began to follow the retreating captain. The crowd surrounding them parted slowly as they moved erratically across the floor of the barroom. The Countess had long since retreated into herself, seeking the protection behind that carapace of reserve, which cares for those of high birth in embarrassing situations. Vasart stalked after his prey with the ponderousness of a juggernaut, unmerciful and unstoppable, following his own flaming arc like a fleshy V-2 rocket without a stabilizing gyroscope.

"You're one of those who feel shame when you do something reasonable for them, eh? Someone might consider this *humane* behavior. That won't do, will it? All those years of free aggression and hatred still rule you, don't they? No, wait, we've just gotten started, old chap. You don't want to run away from it now, do you? You've got all the fucking answers, you're so bloody sure of yourself, what? Everything's been laid out for you in the directives, hasn't it? By Christ, you don't have to think at all!"

At this point Vasart, very much self-involved in his ranting harassment and, in truth, enjoying it in a perverse way, ignored or did not hear the growing exclamations of outrage and the muttered "ahems" which spread throughout the room like rolling molten lava increasing in impatience and heat. Throwing his arms wildly about his head, his glass, now emptied of its contents on the clothing of those closest, describing crazy patterns in the air, the unstoppable Vasart plunged on.

"Where's your humanitas, eh? Do you think repeating their behavior is the way to do it? Jump Fritz I'll give you liver? Lie down and I'll toss you a biscuit? Is that the way it is? Use your noggin for a change, man! You with your brains in your ballocks! Who does anything out of kindness or indifference? We act out of necessity, don't we? We do things because we have to, in our own best interests, yes, but we don't have to shit on 'em, do we? Look around you, you bloody panjandrum: they're covered with shit already! Must we add another pound or two? How much more do you want to weigh them down? They've weighed themselves down forever, we all know what they've done, the bloody Huns, it's clear, we're trying them in Nüremberg, but what the hell, man, what the hell? Eh? Where's it supposed to stop? What about *our* humanity? Have you forgotten about that? Where does it end? Six years of war and you want it to go on ... where's the return in it? Why don't you think a bit, exercise your bleeding intelligence if you've got any, you fucking moron!

"Let me tell you, captain, you are a captain aren't you, this is an officer's club isn't it, but where are the gentlemen? Where certain standards of human decency are observed, isn't that correct, old bean? That means not reducing ourselves to the beastly level of the nazi monsters, doesn't it? Hang the hangmen by all means, punish the guilty, all of them. But if we lose our own civilization in the process where does that leave us? Where does it leave you, you pompous ass? You and your kind *nauseate* me, the whole thing *nauseates* me! I disown it all. I refuse to give in. And you" (Here he threw out his arm in the direction of the hapless wildeyed captain.) "and your kind can have the whole bloody fucking wicket!" Saying this Vasart threw his empty glass against the nearest wall where it smashed with a gratifying crash, grabbed the stoney Countess and made a hurried exit from the pandemonium roaring behind them.

Some time after The Event, a quieter, calmer Ogilvy Vasart sat with Schade and Makepeace in Schade's room drinking whisky and discussing the incident, not quite a wake, as Schade noted, but not quite a celebration either.

"Actually, they'll probably disown *me*. Don't know what got into me. Should've known better, needless to say, but they annoyed me so, y'know. The CO had me in the next day for a chat. Very nice about it, actually, a good man that. Sympathetic to a fault." He sighed and looked into his glass. "Got a fag? These Woodbines are boring. Thanks. I wonder if they'll cashier me. That might not be too bad, Lord knows I've been in this ruddy uniform long enough, haven't I? What's worse, the Countess now refuses to see me. A bit too much for her, I expect. Understandable, I suppose. Nasty business, but that's a bit much, don't you think? I mean, after all, I did it on her bloody account. She'll be all right, of course. Lots of French officers learning German these days. Well, what about dinner? I've got an early meeting tomorrow morning."

There were those, of course, because there always are, who rumored that she did love him, after all, in about the same way that a wallet loves a hundred dollar bill. But they who rumored such things suffered the racks and ruins of jealousy and wished they had a countess to do all those wonderfully nasty little aristocratic things to them in strange sheets surrounded by colorful wall paper.

Never printed anywhere, for no one, particularly not Vasart, could remember exactly how it developed, his haranguing defense of the world's common humanity passed on in the ancient oral tradition of Homer, developing ever more outrageous phraseology until it reached a point of such distortion that the further telling of the tale gradually came around closer to the truth as it continued cyclically from mouth to ear. Vasart became so notorious through this oral tradition that his superiors saw no other expedient than to have him transferred to Vienna and, when the Word arrived in that quadripartite city of shadowy danger and intrigue, seriously considered shipping him back to London for discharge. This action, as it turned out, Vasart preempted by suddenly resigning his commission and entering into a partnership of sorts with his old friend Harry. ("You have no friends, Harry." "There's you, Ogilvy, there's you.") Makepeace expressed some skepticism when he heard this news: "The great god Momus was with him that night; who's to say it still isn't?"[33]

    Shortly before he left the city, Vasart discovered that even a countess could be a Veronika Dankeschön, but by then his transfer orders had been typed and he had little time for anything other than penicillin shots and preparations for travel. The French officers would have to look out for themselves.

> *Amor syphlliticus dances among the lovers*
> *Scattering bacilli like rosepetals at the break of dawn.*

* * * *

"Yuri Vladimirovich, be reasonable, or I'll be forced to really believe that old proverb: *Grattez un Russe et vous trouverez un Tatare.*"[34]

---

[33] The Great God Momus - ancient Roman god of satire whose barbed wit at the expense of other gods finally caused his expulsion from the heavens. For example, when he could find nothing but perfection in the naked body of Venus, he chastised her for making too much noise as she walked, improper in a goddess of beauty.

[34] "Scratch a Russian and you'll find a Tatar." Tatars: A Turkic-Mongol people historically prone to violence (15th century).

"Villum, I prefer my fish unadorned, as you should. An old Russian proverb has it, on the other hand, I admit, that a man without a mustache is like an egg without salt."

"Sometimes, Yuri Vladimirovich, no one wins."

"A thought like that wins only a visit to the reeducation centers. There are more pleasant ways of learning."

"But the lessons really remain."

"There is really no choice is there, if you want to remain alive."

"Perhaps there are some things worse than death."

"So I've heard. But I've thus far been fortunate enough not to have personally experienced them."

"Oh, there's still time, Yuri Vladimirovich, there's still time."

"That phenomenon, dear Villum, may not be on your side."

"Maybe."

PART SIX

Junge Dame, Büroangestellte, gibt Abendstunden in Demokratie nach sechs.
--Newspaper advertisement Autumn 1945[35]

Certain women are resented by other women and men not because of their arrogance or condescension, but because of their ability to project self-assurance and self-contained enjoyment in being alone; they render others unnecessary. This quality is particularly visible in public restaurants where assurance and decisive knowledge of what one wants are characteristics appreciated by very busy waiters and waitresses. The ability to make a cynical, tired waiter actually enjoy serving one is a trait to be carefully nurtured in the learning process. One can also see this at bus stops and railroad stations where the correct change and a confident smile can evoke a brightening of the eye in all but the most hidebound civil servant. Few men and even fewer women possess it and all others are baffled by it and envious of those who have it. Men, of course, especially those without it, resent it in women because it offends their sense of maleness.

Claudia Kaufmann possessed this quality, deliberately acquired after she decided she would not suffer fools with tolerance. She had taught herself to enjoy being alone when dining (though this was not often necessary), to

---

[35]"Young lady. Office clerk. Offers evening classes in democracy after six."

carry herself with authority but not arrogance, to speak firmly but politely in communicating her decisions, to accept reasonable suggestions but not be dictated to by waiters and other sales people, and thus to behave in a manner thought to be more masculine than expected in a woman. Although during the brown years official society had frowned on attributes such as these, she had incorporated this behavior into her life to the extent that it now came automatically whenever required. She enjoyed the consumption of food and drink with a pristine satisfaction and visible pleasure, while also able to uphold her end of the conversation with intelligence and wit. In earlier days when good, if not elaborate meals could be prepared, gourmets such as Kronauer and the elder Albrechtsburg gladly added her to their dinner lists. At one of the prewar Albrechtsburg dinners she met Gisela, at home on a rare occasion, and while they did not become fast friends, they did see each other from time to time, though increasing less often as the war lurched toward its end, then again for several weeks on the run together in Buchdow's group of renegade theater people. Now, at a time when people scrounged in the garbage of the victors for their next meal, former gourmets gave few dinners and former hostesses only rarely could organize an "at home." Food and one's attitude toward it had become of consuming importance to most Berliners.

* * * *

At one of the rare evenings that sufficient vegetables and potatoes to make up a semblance of a full meal had been located, Kronauer spoke of Lucullus, who at one point had grown tired of his elaborate menus and the fantastic costs of his dinners and decided to have his cook prepare a meal for one person. When he remarked on a certain lack of succulence and tang in the taste, his major domo informed him that the kitchen had thought there would be no reason to prepare a fine feast when the master dined alone. In tones that can be imagined, Lucullus replied, "It is when I dine alone that particular attention must be paid to the food. After all, Lucullus is dining with Lucullus!"

"The luxury of this kind of thought," Kronauer nodded sadly, "we can no longer afford. Most of us are happy these days when the potato soup contains a real potato." Kronauer was fond of quoting Juvenal's description of the great Roman bon vivant:

> *Stretched out on the unsocial couch, he rolls his eyes*
> *Over many an orb of matchless form and size,*
> *Selects the fairest to receive his plate,*
> *And at one meal devours a whole estate.*

After a pause, Kronauer would say with a wry smile: "Who in this century could afford that kind of largesse? Only industrialists and the bankers - and they lack the stomach and imagination for such gastronomic splendor. They prefer nightclubs and empty-headed mistresses or the comforts of grandmother's bourgeois kitchen."

One of the guests, Schadow or Boltzmann, shook his head. "The German worker returns home weary and hungry from the daily toil of trying to reconstruct the city and his life. Slumping in his cave he inquires of his wife about the evening meal. 'Ah,' she says, attempting to make the best of a desperate situation, 'tonight we are having sauerbraten, mashed potatoes with gravy, kohlrabi, fresh bread and your favorite beer.' The worker stares bleakly and unbelievingly at her. That night he eats turnips and a small boiled potato washed down with acorn coffee. He goes to bed hungry and dissatisfied with himself and the world. He's too depressed to make love to his wife. But what if he'd gone along with the spirit of her sudden attempt at humor, her unexpected flight of fanciful imagination? What if he'd stretched his own imagination and *thought* the turnips into the braten and potatoes with gravy? Eh? Would that have made any difference? Perhaps it is true that *n'est pas gourmand qui veut*, as Brillat-Savarin said, but surely imagination can help an empty stomach faced with an insufficient meal. You must taste the food in your mind."

* * * *

Not all Claudia's hungers could be assuaged by food and drink in any form or quality. A certain turmoil of fear and frustration roiled her emotions and mental balance making the achievement of her self-confidence the result of a powerfully fought struggle against the void of depression and the possibility of suicide. The release of the tension with which she struggled every day she found in only a few activities including the theater, long striding walks away from other people and the unfortunate habit of gnawing at her fingernails in moments of stress, a rare instance of her inability to control her behavior.

Thin summer rain warmly soaked the flimsy blue summer dress to her slender lithe body and pressed her long blue-black hair to her neck and cheeks as she moved as if blind down the path on the edge of the Pfaueninsel, that small island in the Kladower Seestrecke of the Havel River named after the peacocks that the citizens had long since eaten. Intended by one of the Prussian kings as an edenic escape from the overly sophisticated complex formalities of the rococo court system and the pressures of governing that unforgiving patch of central Europe called Brandenburg, royal servants attempted to create a natural rural setting for the ruler and his personal entourage including a dairy farm and a rustic inn which lacked none of what the late 18th century court considered modern conveniences. The royal retreat had not escaped the depredations of the bombing raids and the destructive impulses of the victorious Red Army: the meadow more resembled a blasted heath than a peaceful somnolent dale and the small wood lacked cohesion. Several remaining buildings all suffered torn walls and lacked glass but housed loose confederations of displaced persons and outlaws resting on their way to somewhere from nowhere. (Schade and Makepeace suspected that Mister Morgan Tahni lived here when not roaming about the city like one of Franz Hessel's flâneurs.)

She had come over to the island with two officials from an American Jewish relief agency to help with translating as they sought out fellow Jews among the suspicious DPs and hostile criminals congregated there. The cloudburst had surprised them and they all sought whatever shelter they could find, except Claudia, whose language skills a DP with fluent English, Yiddish and Polish made redundant. She wandered toward the river in the rain, her mind filled with the pain of loss made doubly unendurable because she possessed no contemporary image of the lost object: she had known her daughter for only four months and could not call up a likeness of what she must now look like. She profoundly and guiltily mourned Rebecca as if she had died - something Claudia did not know but accepted since to hope for its opposite allowed for the possibility of final disillusion and irreparable despair.

Standing in the meadow beyond the trees, she stretched her body upward and straightened her arms over her head. The rain fell like notes of music tantalizing her body with singing sweeps of melodies one after the other until she felt as if she could no longer remain stretched toward the sky, but must move to the magnetic mystery of each phrase of the falling melodies, pushing and pulling her leg muscles, as the songdrops drove her through the rain and the tall grass in wide springs and soft leaps of a dance that knew no beginning and no end, but only the continuum of motion pressing beyond the level of exhaustion and despair into the realm of nirvana and the singular consciousness of oblivion. Coming to a sudden halt, she again stretched her muscles upward, striving for the sky as if she could touch the crown of the heavens before the spell ended and her mind forced her body to return wearily to the exasperations of mundane life in the city.

    With a cry wrenched from her belly, she swung around and ran blindly out of the low meadow. As she neared the river's edge, weeping soundlessly in the rain, she felt an overpowering urge to die and end the bright orange pain that so often permeated her being until for moments at a time it became her existence. Throwing her head back on her neck she grasped her breasts and squeezed her nipples with such preternatural strength that for the necessary instant the physical pain displaced the crushing emotional upsurge. Her arched body staggered and shuddered beneath the frail cotton dress, and she dropped her hands to her sides, one massive sob tearing at her lungs. Gasping for breath in the rain, she turned and walked purposefully in long strides across the meadow to return to the city, shivering in the wet heat.

    These occurrences of what she accepted as the intrusion of moments of insanity attacked without warning and she usually controlled herself when they threatened to take over her mind in public: she retreated into silence which people took as meditation about whatever the subject of discussion. Alone, she succumbed visibly until the wave passed and the bright fog dissipated. When she asked the Mossad agents, they assured her they knew nothing about a six-year old Palestinian Jew named Rebecca Rosensaft, but they attempted to comfort her by saying they couldn't know about all the Jews in the Yishuv. They would, of course, ask their colleagues, but communications remained difficult....

Claudia refused to relinquish the hope, but gradually worked the pain and the fog into the pattern of her private life, never forgetting but pushing the despair deeply enough into the endless wellsprings of her mind to allow her to continue to live and occasionally to surprise herself by finding pleasure in her life. She gradually realized that in repressing the razor-sharp memories and claustrophobic pain of loss, she also suppressed the vitality of her natural life-force, which had been so powerful in her that she often quivered with its strength and intensity. The deep conflicts these antagonisms created brought her to the edge of her mental stability and threatened to shatter that fragile membrane of hope with which she maintained a modicum of emotional and mental equipoise. So she forced herself to learn the appropriate proportions of pain, despair, hope, and natural vitality, which enabled her to continue her life instead of taking it or entering the empty universe of catatonic trance.

*

She had not yet achieved that plateau of self-control described by Kronauer, and unplacated hunger belabored her stomach when she later in the year she walked on her way to the appointment with the other Jews. She passed in front of the Schöneberg sub-district office with the ancient public address system mounted above the window and stopped briefly to join the large crowd silently listening to local news spurting erratically from the loudspeaker connected by a telephone wire to Radio Berlin by way of the Greater Berlin city hall. Starved for information of any kind, the citizens of the district filled the square long before the broadcasts began. After listening for a moment she walked on in the direction of the Femina nightclub, her emotions in conflict and some fear sharing with hunger the vacuum of her belly.

The damp smoke and the noise of the club served many Berliners in various ways. For the two men and a woman, all dressed in shoddy clothes, sitting with Claudia against the far wall in gray darkness it meant they could seriously talk without the danger of being overheard: behind their laughter they discussed the sensitive subject of the fate of Europe's remaining Jews. The Femina, Claudia thought, was the perfect cover. The more experienced Jews with her knew that this both was and was not true: they could talk without being overheard, but half the customers there did business under the table and another fourth were intelligence agents of various nations and organizations. Consequently, if conducting clandestine activities was the object of business, one went to the Femina only once for that purpose: too many people began to take notice of those who appeared in the place more than once. Claudia flushed when her tablemates pointed this out to her and she did not make that mistake again. From that point forward the Jews chose the venues and they met in less dramatic and more open surroundings, never in the same place twice, basic practice in the clandestine trades. They did, however, take advantage of the din to discuss their business, if in desultory and cryptic manner, so the evening was not a waste of their time. For Claudia it had a positive aspect as well: she recognized Schade on the other side of the room sitting with a group of officers and a well-dressed civilian who appeared to be slumming and not enjoying themselves. She turned her Grecian profile to the others at the table and nodded. "I think I may have someone else for you, but I will have to talk to him first." Shortly thereafter one of the men and the woman left and several minutes later Claudia and the third man walked out of the smelly club into the darkening evening where they parted, each hurrying on his or her way to avoid being caught after curfew.

Now she faced the problem of communication, a matter frustrating even the victorious occupation forces, though less intensely: delivering a message of any confidential nature presented the Berliners with serious obstacles. The telephones could not be trusted even if she found one that worked; the chances of meeting Schade in a social situation wherein she could talk to him privately could not be counted on since time was a vital factor in the general calculations and she did not trust Gisela sufficiently to serve as an intermediary. As long as she worked in the Soviet Sector she had no need to be cleared by the Americans, so that avenue remained closed. She could not take the time for the lengthy trip to his office in the Schlachtensee villa without an appointment because Gisela might be there or he might not be. Travel took an inordinate amount of time and the more she thought about the problem the more her frustration reformed into annoyance and anger. In no position to dispute the importance of the matter, she found it eating into her time and energies, devouring those she should have been devoting to negotiating her next roles, learning her lines, and discovering new sources of food.

The deus ex machina turned out to be Buchdow, a role he delighted in playing and in which he admired himself tremendously. In this instance he discovered his role only years later, but this in no way diminished his self-appreciation. When she finally told him the story he laughed happily and murmured: "You see, those of us with genius sometimes perform such acts without being conscious of it. *That* ability is genius."

Buchdow sent word to ask if she would be interested in a major role in a new production at his theater for which she would need the approval of the American authorities, who had already given permission to perform the play. Fortunately, one of the recently reopened sections of the tramline enabled her to travel faster if not more comfortably to within a few blocks of Buchdow's theater in Kreuzberg where he lent her a bicycle to finish the journey to Milinowskistrasse. The battered and windowless old tram reminded her of better days before the war, although then she and the others jammed onto the wooden carriage certainly smelled better in those days. The old man driving the car, brought out of retirement for the purpose because younger men with experience were either dead or in POW camps, wore his official cap at a jaunty angle on his bald head and with great pleasure tromped his foot on the floor bell warning pedestrians and vehicles to give way to his priority. So she appeared in Harrigan's office to complete the preliminary requirements and receive the long Fragebogen which she looked at with distaste. She knocked on the doorjam to Schade's office and with some awkwardness introduced herself, overemphasizing her friendship with Gisela. They arranged to meet the following evening for a drink at the Möwe Club in the Luisenstrasse, which was not far from her room in the Soviet Sector: as did most military officials, Schade understood the fact that civilians could not match the ease with which Allied officials could move about the city. She simply said she had something of importance to discuss with him that had nothing to do with his job.

Schade knew the Möwe: a club the Russians established in the old Bülow Palais early in the occupation to pamper Berlin artists and "cultural workers" whom they allowed to perform or publish. Ulrich Kramer informed Schade that the Möwe represented another indication of the Russians' love for and awe of culture, especially the theater, a thought Schade was disposed to accept. He admitted with regret that the Americans expressed no such attachment to German culture: they had opened no club for Berlin intellectuals. The Möwe required a membership card, which entitled the holder to ration cards for food and drink; the food was plain and not plentiful, and the drinks consisted mainly of ersatz fruit juices and coffee, although beer and wine could occasionally be had if the Russian suppliers received the relevant orders. Nonetheless, people crowded the rooms during opening hours. The club served mainly as a meeting place, a club in the proper sense, for the exchange of information, the laying of plans, for hurried whispered conversation between lovers, a center for intelligence agents of various sorts and loyalties concerned with fulfilling the desires of their bosses, those officers concerned with denazification and the revival of the city's artistic worlds, and an occasional musical performance or poetry reading. The low ceiling, stained brown and yellow by smoke and humidity, pressed the necks of those sitting at the scattered tables, some in animated conversation smoking cigarettes with jerking movements, eyes blazing and bellies aching. Others absently stirred cups of cold acorn coffee for minutes on end staring into the middle distance, their eyes reflecting none of the chaos twisting their minds. Crowds always packed the Möwe, but the decibel level varied, lower in the evening when performers worked. And there they sat in their soiled clothes, drinking weak tea with no milk feverishly making plans to outfox the occupation authorities and create a new world in their own images, which at the moment meant a swath of drab gray textiles broken by an occasional burst of bright color in a dress or scarf.

"The matter is very simple," Tamirov explained to Makepeace at one of their frequent meetings around the city. "Our experience with artists and intellectuals has shown that they are much more malleable, much less resistant, when you give them some things the normal citizen does not possess. Clubs, extra rations, dachas outside the city, good apartments, paid holiday trips. On the other hand, some of my colleagues show an exaggerated respect for German intellectuals, especially if they call themselves '*Herr Doktor*'. In any case, we feed them and they dance to our music. You should learn how to pamper them, Villum, you pay too little attention to such things." "We'll get around to it, Yuri Vladimirovich, one way or another."

Entering the wide, low room Schade experienced a momentary dizzy sense of deja vu: how often had he entered similar bars and cafés in the Village and Yorkville before he'd been drafted and later in the Saint-Germain cellars of liberated Paris. The excitement of art and experimentation, politics and sex shimmered palpably throughout the room. He could almost smell it, like a pungent spiced stew simmering in a small kitchen; but this kitchen smelled too much of human sweat and sharp disinfectant. He shook his head and walked across the room to Claudia's table. His head ached and his mouth felt like soiled cotton. The concierge had not asked for his membership card: the uniform of the victors served that purpose, but it also isolated him in the space where military dress was rare. (He had of course complained often about the regulation of military dress. "Bill, we've got to get permission to wear civilian clothes, we stand out like lepers in a nudist camp." "John, civilian suits wouldn't make a damn bit of difference. We're too well-fed, well-housed, and well-washed.")

They smiled at each other with some embarrassment, each with different reasons. The beginnings of social relationships always made him awkward and she had come to no solution to the problem of approach. He immediately regretted lighting a cigarette, but did not put it out. She accepted a Chesterfield and drew smoke deep into her lungs. She looked viciously at the cigarette and parted her lips to speak. "Please," he said quickly, holding up his palm and smiling. "I know all about its value on the black market."

Her eyes hardened for a moment then relaxed, a short burst of laughter echoed deep in her throat. "Yes, I guess you do. Who doesn't these days? I was searching for a subject so we could make small talk. It is easier that way in the beginning, but not absolutely necessary."

"There's no reason we can't speak of the inconsequential. I didn't mean to be rude."

The Möwe stocked beer in unlabeled bottles that day and when the waitress placed two of them and glasses on the table he opened a small tin, shook out two white tablets and swallowed them with the beer. It was flat and tasted like nothing at all. "How long will it take for the real stuff to become available, I wonder?"

"You have German beer in America, no? The names are German: Schaefer, Rheingold, Budweiser, Hamms ... I've seen the advertisements in American magazines."

"Originally they may have been German, now they have hardly any taste and are always served too cold. Americans do not like beer so they hide the taste as well as they can. Better than this though."

"Are you ill?"

He shook his head. "No. A headache, no more. I often find it necessary to take aspirin with beer. What can I do for you, Fräulein Kaufmann?"

She hesitated. "Well...."

"You know," he said, attempting to ease the situation, "I am no longer directly concerned with theater matters now."

"Yes, I know that," she replied and quickly moved on to gain time to gather her thoughts. "We certainly have enough problems here to keep everyone busy. One of the biggest is lack of printed playscripts, the approved plays. The libraries and publishers' stocks were destroyed. The Culture Chamber advertised in the newspapers for plays from private citizens' libraries, but the response has not been good, as you might expect. No one wants to give up anything when there is so little of everything." She stopped again and shook her head, annoyed at her procrastination. And she had also learned a lesson several days earlier. She bit briefly at a fingernail. "That's not what I wanted to discuss with you. Can we go for a walk? It's very close in here." "Gladly."

They walked aimlessly in the prolonged watery twilight, breathing shallowly to avoid inhaling too much rubble dust, stepping carefully around the potholes and craters, averting their eyes from the public expressions of desperation and frustration which accompanied the passage of daily life in the city: the sudden outburst of pitiful aggression against a neighbor; the plaintive wailing of people driven beyond their powers of resistance or understanding; the furtive scramble to arrive safely at home with a small sack of potatoes; the frantic pursuit of coal briquettes to provide some warmth now that autumn ground inexorably into winter ...

("Listen, no matter how badly off they are, this is nothing like Belsen or Auschwitz." Oscar Monday rarely lectured his colleagues, and almost never on this subject, but at times it seemed to him that they tended to over-emphasize the plight of the Germans and forget the reasons for it. "If some of them are freezing right now, too goddam bad. Next winter they'll be warmer; in the camps a warmer next winter never came. Let's keep our priorities straight here." None of them, of course, could confound his argument, although some of his colleagues shared the dislike or distrust of Jews in the aggregate, even as they considered some individual Jews to be their friends. "The assumptions here," Monday insisted to Leseur, one of the few people he talked to about the issue, "the assumptions are so out of whack, so insanely irrational and warped." "Let us face it, my friend," Leseur assured him, raising his glass of rubyred cabernet sauvignon, "in the end we may make the Germans feel the guilt they deserve, but our own anti-semites are beyond our ministrations.")

And the city's ability to minister to itself slowly became visible on the streets. Someone always helped a person up who had fallen from exhaustion, hunger, or resignation; a minute amount of food could often be found for a refugee relative; a place to sleep, shelter from marauding bands of criminals; some hopeful phrases ... Death and evacuation had halved the city's population by the end of the fighting, but now waves of new groups began to fill the streets and stretch the city's facilities to the breaking point: ragtag remnants from the camps; the refugees from the eastern reaches of Central Europe escaping their experiences under Soviet communism; Jews who, in fear of further persecution and death, refused to return to their homelands where they no longer had any homes; soldiers returning from prisoner of war internment in the west; all bringing psychic and physical problems that the city could not adequately solve even though many of these ragged figures only passed through Berlin on their way elsewhere, millions of people on the move toward something better than the present that would help them forget the past.

At the corner of Luisenstrasse and Reinhardtstrasse at Karlsplatz they stopped to let a Russian soldier giving two small grinning children a ride on a rickety bicycle swoop erratically down the street.

They turned into the Luisenstrasse and walked in silence for several minutes. Claudia stopped and said, "I think Marx lived here when he was a student at the university." She pointed to a pockmarked façade with little behind it.

"Since this is the Soviet sector a plaque will no doubt appear on the front door announcing the fact," Schade said with a grin.

"Schleiermacher lived somewhere on the street with Friedrich Schlegel before the poet met his wife," she said in a distant voice.

"There will be no plaque announcing that fact."

"Probably not."

"I am amazed at how much Europeans know about their history. Americans know much less. They only teach it in the schools superficially."

"I am told that our schools did not do such a fine job recently. Who is your equivalent to Christian Morgenstern? He lived here, too, somewhere."

"I'm not sure we have one yet."

"Your Samuel Mithman lived here in the neighborhood."

"I read a couple of his novels before I was drafted. How do you know about him? He's hardly world famous."

"He was well-known in Germany and France. I met him once just before the war, at a party celebrating something, I think. He pinched my bottom. His books in German are out of print. Not that there's a connection. Probably considered degenerate by the party."

"What was he doing here?"

"I don't remember. Let's go to the left here into the Marienstrasse; somehow the war missed it."

"I suppose literary ghosts haunt this street as well?"

"René Schickele. Otto Flake. Hellmuth von Gerlach. Hermann Bahr. Adolph Menzel, yes. Ghosts."

"Menzel was a painter and we're avoiding the subject."

With an effort Claudia forced her mind to return to the present. "I would like to tell you a story. I know you are busy and will keep it short. It will help you understand, I think." Suddenly she stopped walking and looked into his face with a hard but almost pleading glare in her eyes. She stood like a caryatid fixing him at the end of a potentially dangerous thought. When she spoke again the forced neutrality of her voice contrasted with the intensity of her facial expression. "Please, this must remain between us, no matter what you decide. It would be very damaging for me...."

Surprised and baffled by the force of her charged personality, he nodded, but feared an intimate revelation, which would demand some form of commitment.

"Before the war I met a young man and we fell in love, of course, and I had a child. The man is dead and the child lives in Palestine. My lover was a Jew. I had the child in great secrecy because I wanted it. Lev smuggled himself and the girl out of Germany to Palestine while it was still possible, at the end of the summer in 1939. She was four months old when I last saw her. I didn't know she had survived until a few weeks ago. I never saw Lev again either. We were very young, at least I was; it seems like yesterday, you know. No, wait, please let me finish. I haven't thought about this rationally in a very long time, not in any concentrated way, you understand. It is difficult." She smiled briefly, her expression combining bitterness, pride and confusion. "Perhaps I should have rehearsed this scene, it would have come out with greater logic. Lev was in Germany in the underground helping Jews out of the country into Palestine. He belonged to an organization called Mossad that was in charge of illegal immigration to Palestine. I think that's all they did. I never knew too much about it. They were efficient, but their time was limited and the danger staggering. I never knew all the details of the work; I only knew I loved Lev and it was exciting. Our affair was brief and blinding, hardly more than ten months. Perhaps I could have arranged an abortion, those things were still possible if you knew how. But I wanted to have his child. I was very naive. I didn't tell him until it was obvious. Under the circumstances I thought having the child would prove my love for him. He never really believed it, you see, that a goyische German could love a Jew, but I did.

"He took our daughter with him when the organization ordered him to leave. I barely had time to see how much Jewishness peeped through in her features. At that point a non-Jewish German could not easily get into Palestine. It was for the best, or so I convinced myself. It turned out I was right, unfortunately. The child is alive and healthy living on a kibbutz in the desert. She's almost seven years old. I've never seen her, of course, not even a photograph. Lev was killed during the war fighting for the British." She continued to walk automatically, unseeing, after the words stopped.

Schade could think of no phrase that sounded appropriate, but he felt the need to make a sound of sympathy or understanding, knowing how artificial and inadequate it would be. "It must ... have been very difficult."

Stopping, she sharply drew in her breath and again stared at him with that ancient aura of profound sadness controlled by an immense effort of will. "I almost went insane. The war and the instinct for survival saved me, I suppose. I tried hard to forget them, but never could. They are always somewhere in my mind, especially since we've discovered the meaning of Auschwitz and Treblinka, or some of us have. Perhaps it is my own form of atonement for what we did, my own small Wiedergutmachung. Perhaps not since she was born before that necessity arose. I don't know." She smiled distantly. "Let us continue our walk. Now that you have heard the story you understand why it must remain secret, for her, for Rebecca, if that is still her name. They told me she would be better off not knowing her mother is a German goy. And here? As you well know, there are still many anti-semites in Germany; it is better no one knows about my daughter. You know the British are allowing only a tiny number of refugees into Palestine. And I hope you understand better now what I am going to ask you."

"I will try my best."

"You are German, Lieutenant." Meaning he could not truly understand the Jews.

"American. But you too are German." Meaning they had more in common than she would allow. He wondered whether he should tell her the story about the brief period in high school when he wore a young girl's Star of David on a chain about his neck, but decided it would be out of place.

"The Mossad evidently began making plans early to help what Jews remained in Europe after the war and the mass murder. They call the project 'brichah,' Hebrew for flight. Lev gave them names of people he knew in Germany who might be of assistance to them after the defeat of the nazis. Brichah's mission is to move as many Jews as possible to Palestine. Lev gave them my name when he returned to Palestine ... before he died ... and Mossad agents contacted me some weeks ago. They gave me few details. I don't even know what she looks like. Perhaps it's just as well, she no longer belongs to me. In any case, I cannot do much for them given the conditions here, but I can pass on names of others who are in a position to do something to help them."

"You gave them mine?" he asked in soft astonishment, knowing the answer.

"I said I would speak to you. If your response is sympathetic, they will discuss any cooperation you can offer them. I don't know the details, I am only an intermediary."

"Have you told your story to others who might cooperate?"

"There haven't been any others, yet. You're the first, but if necessary, I'll tell it again. It isn't very pleasant for me, sharing that secret, but if necessary...."

"Why did you choose me? I'm not a Jew, for one thing, as you so charmingly put it. You don't know me at all."

"I felt you would be sympathetic to their mission. Intuition, perhaps. I know little about you, it's true, but what little I do know makes me think you'd at least listen to what they have to say. Gisela talks about you occasionally. That's only natural. You're a thoughtful man. I've been told you take the side of the underdog."

"Being one myself, you mean?"

"That you must decide. Will you talk to them?"

"Frankly," he said slowly, "I don't see what I can do for them. I assume the illegal part of their work is still going on. There are official agencies in charge of legal emigration to Palestine."

"If you talk to them, they will explain everything and answer your questions. After all," she smiled, "I am just the intermediary."

"So you said." But Schade wondered and never came to a solid conclusion in his mind concerning Claudia's role in the matter. After he left Germany it ceased for a while to be the subject of immediate concern, but he thought about it occasionally as he followed the developments in the Middle East. It did not surprise him that he agreed to talk to the brichah agents. He deliberately repressed any inquiry into his own motivations for the decision, preferring to allow the obviousness of the issue from his political point of view and his knowledge of the "final solution," as it came to be known from German documents, to stand unanalyzed in his mind as reason enough for his actions. Eventually, of course, he would have to dive into the roiling sea of his mind to explain to himself why he followed this particular course.

* * * *

The timing and place of the meeting did surprise him: it occurred in the middle of the day. He had rather expected the message to state the time and place of the meeting for midnight in some grimy corner of the city, not early afternoon in a building three blocks from the American Military Government headquarters. The apparent incongruity of the situation added to his vague bemusement and he experienced a mild surprise when he saw the small typed sign tacked to the pocked gray wall announcing the organizations within as the American Joint Jewish Distribution Committee and the Jewish Agency for Palestine. He grinned briefly at his propensity for projecting mysterious meetings in dark corners; perhaps Makepeace was right about his conspiracy-oriented Central European mind: he expected intrigue and shadows, but here the building contained perfectly legal and military government approved relief and rehabilitation agencies. Even his mother occasionally helped to raise money for the Joint in New York. He shrugged; perhaps he was being naive.

Sitting behind an orderly desk an intensely thin middle-aged woman spoke into a large black telephone in a rasping language Schade could not identify while simultaneously reading through papers before signing them. Concentrating her entire energy on both tasks she remained unconscious of his presence until she looked up to dip her pen in the ink well on the desk. Her expression did not change as she waved him into a chair and continued to work. Gray and dark brown colors intermingled in her closely cropped hair through which her long fingers habitually crept as if searching for something lost. He judged her age to be around fifty years, although her voice sounded younger. When she lifted her head again he noticed a number of thin scar lines around her clear brown eyes, pulling back the tissue and giving her an oriental appearance. She wore a plain brown dress with short sleeves and an unmarked British military winter blouse draped over her shoulders against the chill in the unheated room. His eyes automatically looked for and found the blue-black number tattooed below her elbow. The frenetic energy bursting around her made him uncomfortable: he felt that somehow he too should be doing something other than simply sitting in a chair waiting. She would be hell to work for, he thought.

Behind her he could see through an open doorway into a second room in which two dark-haired young men in British Army uniforms stood over a table covered with papers and maps talking in quiet tones surrounded by thick layers of smoke from their cigarettes. The taller of the two had been in civilian clothes with the group talking to Claudia in the Femina; Schade envied their ability to exchange their uniforms for mufti. From time to time one of them made a pencil mark on the maps. He noticed something odd about them, something out of place: perhaps their curly black hair grew too long even for the British military, or their shoulder tabs somehow did not match their khaki blouses. He brushed his mustache with a thumb and desultorily wondered about the oddities he had seen in the city since his arrival almost six months ago. Retreating briefly into his mind, he allowed chapter headings for a book on the events and types of people in the city's ruins to haphazardly form themselves as if written faintly in chalk on a blackboard then erased at once by an invisible hand.

On the wall beside the woman's desk hung a great map of Europe festooned with markings denoting camps of various types and sizes. Each new group of refugees coming into the city brought with them word of new camps to be added until the face of the continent resembled a visage ravaged and pitted by some monstrous plague. These refugees passed on information about those who remained in the camps because they had no other place to go. These camps were in many cases the old nazi camps with different guards, many of whom struggled through indifference to a modicum of sympathy, but perceived themselves helpless to do much about the situation; the bystander mentality dominated their thinking which focused more immediately on the number of days left in service before they could return to their homes. The irony, if few saw it, was painfully exquisite. The Joint and the Jewish Agency did what they could to provide medical and other forms of relief in the camps, but could do little to bring about their disappearance.

Finally the woman rang off and ran her fingers through her hair. She replaced the pen in its stand and picked up a box of matches which she moved back and forth between her fingers during the entire time he spent in the efficiently organized room. "You are Lieutenant Schade." The statement washed over him like an accusation. She spoke in heavily accented English.

"Yes." He nodded once automatically.

"Can we speak German?" she asked in that language. "Though it is not my mother tongue I speak it better than English and I wish to be clear and precise in what I tell you." Then as an afterthought "Do you mind?"

He felt another accusation: if he did mind of what sin would he be guilty? In any case, she had made the decision and the question was nothing more than pro forma. He shook his head.

"What do you know about our situation here? When you tell me that I will be able to complete your information insofar as it concerns our possible future cooperation."

He shifted in the chair, somewhat put off by her studied formality, a device which maintained the distance between them with which she felt comfortable. "I know very little, I'm afraid. There are two movements of Jews out of Europe, one legal the other not. This is not altogether a secret. Most of the survivors want to immigrate to Palestine, but the British have severely limited the numbers in the quota. The Jewish Agency is charged with organizing the legal immigration, at least that is what I thought up till now. I don't know the Joint's exact role, but it does relief work in the DP camps and helps people emigrate."

Without smiling she said, "You may continue to think that, Lieutenant."

"Obviously then there must be another agency to handle the illegal movement. I've been told it is called Mossad. That is about all I know."

"Would it surprise you, Lieutenant, to know that we have already checked on your background?"

He grinned. "Yes, it would. There's a certain amount of irony there, no? Checking on the checker, so to speak."

"Perhaps. The point is we have talked to people in New York and have been informed of your work there with the anti-fascist exiles, many of them Jews, of course."

"My work, as you put it, consisted of helping my mother in some of her tasks with the refugee relief groups. Most of what I did was minor and mundane. Hardly a recommendation for me in your eyes I should think."

"Our information is perhaps more complete that you are aware, but that is not the point. We are satisfied that you are to be trusted, within certain limits, of course. That means I am going to tell you certain things to explain the situation, which must remain confidential. This will become clear to you as we proceed."

"No doubt."

"Fine." She paused for a moment, the matchbox stilled as she ran her fingers through her hair, and stared at him with hard, bright eyes. "People tend to confide in you, don't they?"

His grin appeared and went as briefly as the smell of witch hazel on a freshly shaven neck. "Some do, yes. I should have been a psychoanalyst. Papa Freud, Onkel Jung ... but the commitment is too great." He waved his hand in dismissal.

"It must be tedious for you."

"Only if it drags on too long."

"Quite right." The telephone on her desk rang loudly. Raising her voice she called to the young men in the other room in what Schade took to be Hebrew and the ringing stopped as one of them picked up the extension under the maps. "Let us get to the nub of the situation. My official job here is with the Jewish Agency to organize the legal immigration of Jews to Eretz Israel, the Yishuv, within the quotas established by the British White Paper of 1939. These, as you suggested, are very limited. To evade these limitations we created another organization called the Mossad Le'Aliyah Bet, or institute for B, that is: illegal immigration. Our mission is to move as many Jews as possible to Eretz Israel in any way we can. We have just begun the task but have achieved a measure of success. The point is to increase that measure, to constantly ship increasing numbers of us from this catastrophe. Do you know any Yiddish? No? I thought you'd know some, coming from New York. The Yiddish word for the fate of the Jews in Europe is "hurban," destruction of unthinkable proportions. We are moving those who escaped the hurban to the homeland where we belong."

Fanatics, Schade thought, are always dangerous, if occasionally useful. "I do not intend to debate the merits of Zionism with you."

"You've done that too often before, yes? Nor do I, Lieutenant, we have no time for it now, and besides things have gone beyond the point of debates. There are tens of thousands of Jews fleeing Eastern Europe, especially from Poland. The majority of them wish to make aliyah, you know what that means: you will understand it as 'to go home'. Under the British Mandate quotas they cannot make aliyah. We intend to see to it that they do. To be honest, Herr Schade, the Yishuv needs these Jews as much as they need the Yishuv. We are struggling against two forces to achieve our goal and become the national homeland of the race: the British and the Arabs. We need people there to end the struggle successfully. If they must come by illegal means, so be it. But they will come. If we had a Jewish state before 1933 the hurban would not have happened. All the lessons of escape we learned before and even during the war, we are using now. Am I making sense to you, Lieutenant?"

"The times are different now, I think."

"Let me phrase it this way: there is a difference of quality between the movement of Jews before and during the war and the present: the gas chambers and the crematoria are no longer working. Do you see what I mean?"

"Today they are moving from unpleasant conditions to what they hope will be a better life, they're no longer escaping death."

"Precisely. On the whole, although they are still dying from the conditions under which they live here. Nonetheless, even without the threat of death at their throats, these people are absolutely determined to get out of this charnel house and live in the sunshine of the *Yishuv*, the Jewish community in Palestine. We are determined to create the homeland on historic soil. But my main point regards conditions in central Europe today. Since the end of the war too many Jews remain behind barbed wire, some of these are notorious concentration camps, the center of an inconceivable evil! They are crowded, unsanitary, grim, you understand. The inmates remain isolated from the outside world, they have nothing to do and sit idle all day, planning, always planning. How has their situation changed from before liberation? Liberation is something of a joke to those still in the camps."

"They may be idle and dirty, but they're not being systematically murdered."

"Correct, but they are still forced to live like pigs." She spat the last word at him with particular passion. "Some of them suffer from malnutrition, though the Allies have been very helpful in feeding them. Still, they are hungry, there's not sufficient food; the clothing supplies are almost non-existent, most wear the striped camp uniforms, that's all that's available. How do you think this makes them feel?

"There's little for them to do except brood and fabricate grandiously unrealistic schemes for the future. They have no work to do and a bare minimum of cultural or social programs to occupy their time. What is left for them in these places except to pick at the scab of their frustrations and ulcerate their empty stomachs with dread about an uncertain future? They are very confused, these Jews.

"When we were still in the camps I worked in the *Schreibstube* where they forced us to register the mass murder of our families - we dreamed of rescue, it would be a miracle. We dreamed that should the miracle happen we would with certainty be welcomed, succored, given sympathy, kindness; in short, the world would welcome us with open arms and warm smiles and food, after what we had suffered. Well, it did not happen that way, did it? The miracle did occur, true, but only half of it, the certainty and welcome never materialized. Most of us are still in the camps guarded behind barbed wire by armed men." She paused, her thin chest breathing heavily from the exertion of saying so much so fast in order to stuff it all into his head without wasting a minute, as if the faster she accomplished this, the greater the number of Jews would land on the shores of the homeland.

"All of Europe is confused," Schade replied in a less than convincing tone. "There is chaos all around us. These things take time. At least they are not being murdered."

"You keep repeating that! Yes, yes, we are no longer being murdered en masse," she said quickly, nervously shifting the matchbox between her fingers. "But this is no longer enough of a justification for keeping us in the camps on the verge of starvation. There is no longer enough of a justification for treating us like animals instead of human beings."

"The problems are overwhelming given the sheer numbers," Schade began, "but progress is being made. You're painting conditions blacker than they deserve. There is a move to give a maximum of self-government in the camps, group activities have been organized, in some places they have their own internal police and court systems--"

"The authorities have abolished the camp courts run by the DPs," she interjected.

"Listen, you are correct, the situation is not good. We are doing what we can as fast as we can. There are massive problems."

"These problems are only going to get worse, Lieutenant. If the present rate of migration continues, we estimate there will be over 30,000 Jews moving west from Poland alone by the end of the year and even more after that. Let me tell you, in 1939 many Jews fled the nazi occupied areas of Poland into the eastern parts taken over by the Soviet Union. Now, the Soviet Union permits repatriation of these people to the new Poland and many of them return there but few want to stay. The Poles are violently anti-semitic, pogroms have begun again, in Krakow, elsewhere ... the Polish government gives them exit visas to get rid of them and they migrate to the US zones of Germany and Austria. But they don't have entry or transit visas for anywhere else. Most of them want to emigrate to *Eretz Israel*, the Land of Israel, they expect to stay here for only a short time, you see. And what happens to them? The camps again. This is happening all over Eastern Europe, there are more Jews on the move every day, and most of them want to go to the *Yishuv*. You see where this is leading us, Lieutenant?"

Schade could not help but smile. The woman's attempt at a rhetorical trap was so transparent, especially for anyone experienced in the argumentation techniques of those Jewish Marxists, both native American and central European exiles, in New York City during the purge trials in Moscow, the crises in Spain, and the Molotov-Ribbentrop treaty. "They want to emigrate to Palestine but there are too many of them for the legal quotas. They might be able to get papers for other countries."

The woman bristled with impatience. "Perhaps, but again, not enough. One hundred here, seventy-five there.

The United States is good about that, but that's not the point, is it?"

"In any case, you do not want them anywhere but Palestine, legally or not."

"That, Lieutenant, is totally correct. Bravo."

"Your condescending attitude begins to annoy me, *gnädige Frau*. You obviously want something from me and this is not the way to go about getting it."

She looked at him blankly, then smiled for the first time, briefly and with little warmth, but a smile. "My apologies, Lieutenant. I sometimes forget myself. The opportunity to speak like that to a person in uniform occasionally makes me lose my head for a moment. It is a weakness of character I must learn to curb." She smiled again, her expression demanding an unspoken understanding of her methods with the arrogance of those who have experienced unspeakable suffering vis à vis those who had not.

"What is it you want of me, Frau ... how shall I call you?"

"Since we shall probably never meet again, it is hardly necessary for you to call me anything. Ach, there I go again. Let me rephrase that. For the purposes of this mission I have been given a code name: Lazarus. You may call me Frau Lazarus. An appropriate name, no?"

"It has literary flair, Frau Lazarus."

"We had little time to read in the camps, Lieutenant, but many of us are highly educated." She waved her arm in dismissal. "But let us indeed get to the point at hand. We wish you to help us smuggle Jews into the American zone." She waited for a reaction, but Schade merely nodded and offered her a cigarette, which she refused. The matchbox continued its repetitive journey between her fingers. Finally, she grinned and ran the fingers of one hand

495

through her hair. "That apparently does not surprise you, Lieutenant."

Schade may not have been surprised, but he did experience in a rush the dizzying lift of vertigo, and he was somewhat bewildered. Slowly he drew in air and sighed. "No, Frau Lazarus, not surprised, but I don't understand how I can be of help to you."

"But you do not reject the idea out of hand."

"My sympathies for the underdog are apparently well known," he replied with sarcasm.

"True, but this concerns illegal activities."

"There is on occasion a higher morality above certain laws and regulations that is understood by rational people. But that's your line, isn't it?"

"Relativism, Lieutenant, can work both ways, for instance the Nuremberg laws ... but we take whatever trustworthy help we can get under the circumstances. Let us not debate morality. We are not interested in your motives, however fascinating they may be to yourself and a psychologist. What we need is action."

"On the other hand, I don't want to end up in the stockade either."

"There is little chance of that if everyone is careful and does his job. We have not achieved our successes so far by being careless; we control the situation as far as possible. At some point, however, one just has to trust the fates, as in everything else in life, but we try to arrange the most propitious circumstances. There are a number of Americans helping us one way or another, so you do not have to feel alone. I assume some form of baksheesh is not required in your case, but something can be arranged should it be ... ah, well, good. But time is short, much too short. Some of us are too busy with the *She'erit ha-Peletah*, the saved remnant, to sit shiva for more than an instant, for about as long as it takes to say Kaddish, you know, '*y'hey shlama raba min shmaya* ... amen'. So let me quickly explain how it works, in general terms of course. What you do not need to know, you should not."

"I have never thought that a particularly useful adage myself. I like to understand as much as possible."

"Yes, no doubt. We find dealing with intellectuals who are not totally committed to our cause to be problematic and often a headache: they want to know everything before they can act."

"But you make do with intellectuals...."

"When necessary." She smiled briefly. "Some of my good friends are intellectuals. I used to be one myself. I've no time for it now. I've become more of a fanatic, you see. It makes things so much easier when one emphatically and completely believes in what one is doing. One reacts much faster. That is of obvious importance I should think."

"Then let us hope I do not find myself in a situation where an immediate response is necessary. I might ruin everything by thinking excessively."

"Hardly likely, as I said, but possible. What we need here in Berlin are guides of a sort, camouflage guides. The refugees come across the Soviet Zone with valid exit papers from Poland. The Russians know they are in transit and rarely make any problems at the checkpoints: a bottle of vodka, a wristwatch ... they look the other way. The real problem begins here. We do not want these people stuck in the American Army transient camps for refugees here in Berlin. The Americans will register them and ship them to DP camps in the Zone and there they will sit, of use to no one including themselves. So we run them from Berlin along the access routes set up for the western Allies from and to the American Zone preferably in American military trucks with forged papers. Sometimes we cannot get papers and send them through hoping the checkpoints can be bribed with whisky, money, or ideology. From the American zone they go through Austria to Italy or to a port near Marseilles, then by ship to Palestine, where they either land safely or the British capture them and intern them in camps on Cyprus. That is in essence the way the system works. I think I do not have to explain the political reasons for this, in addition to the moral and ethical imperatives? Good. What we want you to do is be at the city checkpoint on the American-Soviet sector border where the truck will pick up the refugees, then accompany the truck across the American Sector through the crossing into the Soviet Zone. This means clearing the truck through the American and Soviet guard posts, a fairly simple and almost always an automatic procedure. Once you are out of the American Sector and in the Soviet Zone, someone else will take over from there and transfer them to a different truck. Your truck returns to the city empty and drops you off. You needn't know the rest. If you should be stopped, you simply say that you are taking them to one of the transient centers for processing. You will have some papers to support that claim. It is always good to have an American officer on these trips, you understand."

"It sounds too easy."

"There are risks for you, of course. An overachieving military policeman ... and in your case there is no reward. Your motives are your own, as are your satisfactions. I will not give you the spiel about helping the Jews to build their homeland, though that will certainly be the result of your participation."

"You would never be a success as a personnel recruiter for an American corporation," he said smiling.

She returned his smile, briefly as always. "No, but even if I had such a job, I would not be recruiting people like you to sell candy bars, would I? Intellectuals do not make good salesmen. That is why the world is so devastated. We do not have time to motivate anyone other than those who are in the pipeline to the Yishuv. We have to take what help we can find as it is."

A young woman with short dark hair dressed in a British army uniform with large blue and white shoulder flashes of the Jewish Brigade bustled into the room carrying a large pile of US Army blankets followed by a thin young man in an American uniform with sergeant's stripes on his sleeves straining with a cardboard box labeled "C-Rations." They hurried into the room behind Frau Lazarus where they placed their burdens on a table and with a brief smile and a wave of their hands in what might have been considered a minimalist salute to Schade they retraced their quick-steps out of the office.

"Is this a test?"

"Test, Lieutenant? Test of what?"

"My ability to not see certain things."

"Herr Schade, we all have our blind spots. There is an old Jewish saying—"

"There always is."

"Precisely. 'What you do not see or know will not return to bite your *toches* when you least expect it'."

"Is that really an ancient proverb?"

"As old as mankind, Lieutenant, or perhaps older."

"There's something else," Schade began.

"There always is," the woman retorted with clear impatience. "What is it this time?"

"Isn't the Joint supposed to be helping rebuild the Jewish communities here? You Zionists are taking the Jewish brains and brawn out of Europe, legally or not. There's a contradiction here, or am I thinking too much?

Aren't you working at cross purposes with the people who employ you?"

"I personally do not believe there is room for Jews in Germany any longer. I grew up here and believed in the symbiosis, the possibility of complete assimilation. I no longer believe this. I was wrong to ever have believed it. We all were wrong to depend on it. That stupid illusion cost us six million lives in a very short time. The only place for Jews is a Jewish state with a Jewish army to protect it. That is what we are building."

"There are others who find it possible to accept the necessity for both a Jewish homeland and Jewish communities in Germany. I've spoken to Immanuel Weinraub recently about this; he believes it, and he's doing his best to make a place for Jewish life here. He seems as intensely convinced of this as you do of your mission."

"I have experienced many interesting and passionate discussions with Herr Weinraub. They are often unpleasant and painful. He has his supporters, but there is no future for Jewry in Germany or east of here. The Yishuv needs Jews. We are providing them." She spoke the sentence with a finality that cut off further discussion.

"All right," he said and she turned to the two young men in the other office, who had continued their rumbling discussion as her conversation with Schade proceeded. "Chaim. Yossl. We need you now." They came into the room and she did not introduce them but said, "These men are *shilim*, emissaries from the Yishuv; they organize things. They will tell you what you need to know."

Chaim, who had been with the group in the Femina, squinted through his glasses at Schade as if wondering whether or not they were making a mistake. Yossl, whose uniform fit him imperfectly giving him something of a clownish appearance, remained impassive except for his shrewd eyes, which judged Schade's character but came to no immediate conclusion. The two men cultivated their physical similarity, which the uniforms reinforced: seeing them only briefly few could tell which they had seen, a distinct advantage in their present business.

Chaim smoked his cigarette in short jerking movements and explained in English some of the practical matters facing the brichah. "Border crossings without proper papers means bribes and danger, false visas and transit papers, forged identification papers, night movement, and lots of chutzpah. You know the word? Good. Sometimes we have our own train or trucks. Mostly we walk, hike over the mountains, which isn't good for people coming from the KZs, they're too weak. Trucks are good if we can get them, like we do here. In the south the Jewish Brigade in the British Army helps. Funny, isn't it? The British are the enemy as much as the Arabs yet their soldiers help the *brichah*. Very funny, yes? We're moving thousands, tens of thousands, from the east down to the Mediterranean ports. The ships are derelicts, they leak, they stink, they're too small, but they mostly get to the Yishuv. The British capture many and put the Jews in camps on Cyprus or return them to Europe. Also funny, yes. They should be used to it by now, these pesky Jews, always making trouble, yes? But thousands make it through the blockade, and thousands more will follow. They are needed to secure the national homeland. You don't have to be a Jew to be a Zionist, Lieutenant."

"I suppose not."

"Actually, we don't care if you're doing this just for the thrill of it as long as you do it."

"You are all so welcoming to the new recruits. You'd make fine drill sergeants in boot camp. You know what that is? Good. Now just what is it you want me to do?"

"How American: right to the point and the hell with motives."

"Things are more efficient that way, and you surely need efficiency. And I've already had this conversation with your colleague here."

"*So meine Herren, toches ahfen tish*, if you will pardon the vulgarism. Chaim, please explain the Berlin route to the lieutenant." Shifting the matchbox between her fingers, Frau Lazarus's tone afforded no denial; and lighting another cigarette Chaim obeyed her order. At the end of the recitation, Frau Lazarus turned her attention to the old Torpedo typewriter and began to belabor the keyboard, clearly dismissing the matter for the present. Yossl walked with Schade to the street and murmured in German, "The lady may exaggerate somewhat, but not by much. And Chaim exaggerates not at all. Let me tell you a story to show how serious we are about this. Two sixty-year old Jews from Tel Aviv volunteered for the Jewish Brigade and gave their ages as twenty years younger. The authorities found out and told them they were much too old to fight so they immediately went on a hunger strike. Shortly thereafter the Brigade accepted them and also their sons and they fought together in Italy. They are still armed and defending a kibbutz north of Haifa, but their life expectancies are not very optimistic. There will be a war with the Arabs. We have no choice but to move as many of the *She'erit ha-Peletah* to the Yishuv as fast as possible while the situation remains so chaotic on the ground. Even revenge, even executing criminals must not deter or detour us.

"*Auf wiedersehen, Herr Leutnant.*"

Eventually Schade learned that the refugees crossed the Western Zones into France and Austria to French and Italian ports where they shipped out to the eastern end of the Mediterranean and their fate: either safely landed or again interned in camps on Cyprus. And he soon wondered what Frau Lazarus's reaction would have been had he mentioned the notion that Hitler Germany's main war crime was not the destruction of the European Jews but the war itself that first allowed Auschwitz to exist and that killed many more soldiers and civilians than six million. Later still, he imagined she would look at him with some exasperation, squint, and say it depends upon one's point of view, doesn't it?

* * * *

Not unexpectedly, the first time was the most difficult for him. When he started walking to the rendezvous point, it reminded him of his nightly forays earlier in the year on behalf of Sender and Darkley, but worse because this activity was clearly illegal and clearly more dangerous. The illegality per se did not overly trouble his conscience because he believed in the higher justice of the Jews' cause and understood the necessity of the mission in pursuit of that cause. But the tightness in his belly indicated that he did not relish the notion of being arrested by a trigger-happy MP, American or Russian, and he truly did not want to spend any time in the stockade. A vaguely formulated but acutely present combination of sympathy, pity, and guilt proved to be stronger than his fear while not diminishing the trepidation. He soon discovered that he welcomed the excitement and anxiety of the adventure; it shoved aside his more complex problems, and the immediacy of the danger fully occupied his mind. After the first time the tension became almost automatic, and he savored the thrill of it. But the first time caused him the most difficulty.

He appeared early at the cross-over point where the truck would pick up the group for transport through the US Sector. Reading Eric Ambler and Graham Greene had given him a modicum of knowledge about clandestine activity: the agent invariably appeared early for the meeting in order to make a reconnaissance of the area so he could get out fast if betrayed and caught in a trap. The dimly illuminated juncture shared the same characteristics of every other street corner in the city, its sole defining feature being the border between the Soviet and American sectors marked by a primitive sign noting that fact. The streets contained the usual admixture of building skeletons and rubble hidden in deep shadows: only every fifth or sixth streetlamp functioned during the hours of electricity. Few people moved about in the night, although as the winter began to chill the city, the Allies enforced the curfew with increasing laxity. As he walked up the street, Schade could see the thin clouds of his breath in the brittle night air. Tension tightened his stomach muscles and scrotum, and a slight but penetrating pain radiated from the back of his head to his temples: he'd forgotten to eat aspirin. His heart pumped blood through his arteries faster than normal and his breath came in short puffs of condensed moisture. The urge to urinate came and went unexpectedly.

He briefly walked a few meters up and down the street to ward off the chill and the tension, repressing the question of his motivations again. He hummed the melody to the tune *Berlin kommt wieder* and he did not hear the truck until it turned the corner and stopped in the shadows. Fine secret agent on his toes, alert to every sound, ready for action. The sudden silence as the driver turned off the motor emptied his mind for a few seconds. It had begun. The sound of a harmonica listlessly playing a tuneless air entered the street as he moved slowly toward the vehicle, then stopped, taken aback at the sight of the white circled star and lettering on the door identifying the truck as belonging to the US Army. A voice as deep and black as the night, but richer in timbre said: "That's the signal; right on time."

Schade stepped closer to the cab of the truck, but he still could not see the face of the driver. Feeling foolish, he uttered the password: "Lazarus." A beam of light cut through the darkness startling him and he jerked his head back as the driver shined the torch in his face for less than a second. Dark laughter rolled out of the cab to blend with the night. "My, my, we do get around, Lieutenant. You don't mind if I don't throw you no salute, man, but it's kinda cramped in here." Barry Green's basso vibrated in a restrained chuckle. "Didn't expect our fan club to be here, did we, Freddy?"

"Hello, Lieutenant."

"What are you doing here?" Schade blurted and immediately regretted the question: the obviousness of the answer rendered it superfluous. A flush of embarrassment wriggled across his face and the pain of his headache increased. "No, forget it."

"Just out for a drive in the cooool night air, Lieutenant, just a little break in the monotony of occupation duties." The sarcasm boiled just below the surface of Barry Green's statement and, although he could not see him in the dark, Schade knew that the man's expression contained nothing but blank innocence. "And you, sir? Out for a stroll before bedtime?"

"Yes, just a break in the monotony of duty."

Stoneland cut off Barry Green's reply. "There they are."

In the quiet they could hear the shuffling of feet in the dust of the street moving quickly toward them. After a moment the figures emerged out of the night. Stoneland climbed out of the passenger side of the cab with the caution of those experienced in being able to disappear quickly and stepped to the back of the truck where he lowered the tailgate. "Lazarus," one of them whispered. Stoneland replied in a normal voice: "Shalom." Schade could feel the relief roll outward from the group of five refugees, each carrying a small valise and each very nervous. The sixth member of the group, a young man dressed in the same motley of shabby clothes as the others but clearly not one of them, Schade recognized as Chaim of no last name from Frau Lazarus' office. "Special group. Very important, yes? Engineers."

"Usually a hell of a lot more of them than this," Stoneland said, holding up the flaps of the canvas cover.

"Special group," Chaim repeated. "They are yours now."

"Okay, man, we know the way."

"I will go back now."

"Sure. Adios, Chuck." Stoneland turned to Schade. "That aint his real name, but I can't pronounce that, it's long and full of esses and zees, so we call him Chuck."

Chaim grinned and said, "Yeah. Later, man."

Schade could not place the accent, but thought it sounded like Czech or Hungarian. The curly headed Chaim turned and headed back down the side street into the night.

"We taught him some of our lingo. Seems like a good Joe. Too young for this business. But what the hell, age don't seem to matter much here."

From the cab Barry Green's voice stabbed imperiously through the dark. "Let's unass this joint, gate!"

Stoneland motioned to the figures standing hesitantly behind the truck, expecting directions, their eyes clouded with suspicion and resentment at their helplessness. Their shadowy appearance reminded Schade of all the refugees he'd seen since the end of the war: gray ghosts bumping about the landscape, dependent and frail, shuffled from one place to another, driven on by the hope of an anonymous existence in some town or countryside where legality meant protection from savagery, not deliverance to it. For the older ones, the resentment at their dependence would come later; the younger among them had already rebelled against these conditions: they became leaders in the camps or criminals in the larger societies to which they attached themselves like limpet mines with unregulated timing devices. (Later, Makepeace wondered aloud about the percentage of Soviet agents nestled in the wandering groups of the DPs from the east. "They can't be that well organized," Schade replied, but wondered about that answer.) The Jews among the displaced population faced a somewhat different set of circumstances: they could not expect to disappear into anonymity, and for the most part they wanted to leave Europe for Palestine or America. And the necessity for the illegal brichah activities forced many of them to become criminals as they maneuvered their way through the twilight clandestine world of the wasteland's underground.

Shifting their few possessions, they climbed into the truck bed wondering if they would safely arrive at yet another transit point so they could move on to the next, and the next.... Barry Green turned on the motor and lightly prodded the gas pedal. The refugees had not seemed startled at the presence of the black men: they had seen too much already and guardian angels came in all colors and shapes: their ability to be surprised would have to be replenished.

Sitting by the passenger side window, Schade asked: "What do you fellows get out of this?"

Barry Green snorted and Stoneland turned to him, examining his features in the pale light of the dashboard. "We get free circumcision for all our male children." The black men laughed softly. "Just a break in the monotony, man."

"Hardly relaxing, though. My stomach is as tight as a drumhead."

"Not relaxing, just different."

Barry Green's high-pitched voice grated with the barely controlled anger that ruled his memory. "It's a chance to *do* something, man!"

"You are Zionists?" Schade tried not to permit his smile to sound in his question.

"Why not?" Barry Green said, laughing sharply. "Didn't even know what it was until a couple of weeks ago. I mean it's a chance to *do* something, understand? To move, to break out sometimes, to do what the Man says can't be done, you dig?"

Stoneland shifted his thin frame between the other two. "Reminds me of Marcus Garvey's con about going back to Africa."

"Same thing, man, except these people are doing it. That's the difference."

"It's also like paying back for help received. Jews have helped us for a long time, lawyers and such, raising money for the NAACP -"

"Yeah, they feel bad about paying us peanuts for working ten hours a day in their factories all these years,"

Barry Green said flatly, his thick arm jamming the stick into second gear.

"Listen, man, we've been through this before. Nothing's that simple. They had a bad time of it at home too. But I don't want to argue about it now. What are you in it for, Lieutenant?"

To this question he had no ready answer. "I don't know. Sympathy for them, some form of restitution, support for the underdog...."

"As long as the dog is white," Barry Green said as if to himself, but clearly audible above the sound of the truck's motor. "Like that Mister Morgan Tahni said once, 'Never trust the bilagáana, my boy, ever.' As if a honky, even a weird one like him, needs to tell mose about trusting bilagáana! Shit."

Schade stiffened and swallowed an angry response. Stoneland quickly said, "Cool it, man. Don't be such a schmuck. That's a word we learned from Chuck, Lieutenant. Very useful sometimes."

"Where are we going?" Schade asked, wishing he were not so cramped between Stoneland's bony figure and the hard metal of the door so he could find a cigarette.

"One more stop to make, then straight to the other side of town. We don't want to drive around in the city with this load any longer than we have to. We may be crazy, but we're not stupid."

A few blocks further on near the Hallesche Tor, Barry Green stopped the truck and let the motor idle. Manipulating his bulk into a more comfortable position and opening the window, he said to no one in particular: "If he's not here in one minute we split without a blink."

"I'm here, friend, just as arranged." Wilson Tomkin's voice came from the driver's side of the cab. He wore his foreign correspondent trench coat with identification patches sewn to the shoulders indicating his status as an accredited representative of the US press corps. "Hello, Lieutenant. I really didn't expect you on these runs. Fear not. My lips are sealed, mum's the word, and all that. I'm going with them to the other side. I'll tell you about it when I get back." Tompkin nodded, wagging his beard, and walked to the back of the truck. They could hear him climb into the bed and ask if any of the refugees spoke English, then the rising sound of the motor blanketed the conversation in the rear.

Schade's annoyance distorted his voice when he said, "I wasn't informed that the press would be here."

"It's okay," Stoneland said. "Don't worry, Lieutenant, your name, rank and serial number won't be in the papers. They made a deal with him. All names changed in the papers."

"Why would they want anything printed about it? That doesn't make any sense."

"Hell, I don't know. No skin off my ass as long as my name's not in it."

"And he don't mention any moses being along," Barry Green added.

They drove on through the darkened city in silence, keeping to the less trafficked streets, carefully observing the speed limit. Several times MP jeeps passed them but did not pause. Each time Schade's heart stopped beating and his intestines froze. After the second jeep had gone by, he asked, "Have you been stopped often?"

"A couple of times," Stoneland answered with a grin, "but we've always got an officer with us and we always stop when they tell us to. Don't give them a chance to start blasting away. They shoot first, especially when they see Negroes. The officer gets us through with the papers and, besides, a lot of real DP transports go through the city all the time. Don't worry." Schade believed the words about the ease with which some MPs used their weapons in the city. At the end of the summer, a nervous MP had shot and killed Leo Borchard when the British civilian driving the car in which the conductor of the Berlin Philharmonic was riding for some reason did not stop when the young soldier signaled him to do so. Oscar Monday spent much of his time thereafter frantically attempting to find a replacement with both talent and an unbrown past so the Americans did not fall behind the Russians in the "cultural affairs front." The Philharmonic's rehearsals at the Titania Palast fell into lethargic chaos until the Americans finally appointed a colorless but experienced former party member as a transition conductor. The fact that Borchard earlier that summer defended the man before the denazification board allowed Monday to obtain a speedy clearance. The man served briefly and routinely as head of the orchestra and Monday breathed more deeply for a while, filling in guest conductors as often as possible, one of whom was decidedly an odd choice for the time and place. "Unfortunately, I can't take credit for the idea. Borchard had already invited the fellow to do the concerts." The American-trained, British Guiana-born Negro musician, Rudolf Dunbar, flew on a military airplane to Berlin from his home in London and set the city's cultural scene on its ear. Dunbar was the first black man to conduct the 65-year old Philharmonic, whose members responded positively and with enthusiasm to his direction, as he had been the first "coloured man" to conduct the London Philharmonic in 1942). The German audience applauded wildly, especially the final piece on the program, William Grant Still's *Afro-American Symphony*, hitherto unheard in the city.

(When they finally had put all the pieces in their proper places and had made the required arrangements, Monday and Makepeace had experienced a puff of euphoria. Descending the stairs to the Milinowskistrasse furiously chewing a wad of gum, Makepeace yelled, "Hi yo, Silver!"

"Awaayyy…" Monday shrieked waving his right arm about the air above his head and pressing his left arm to his side as he followed his stern-faced colleague into the battered blue Opel on their way to pick up Dunbar for the first rehearsal.

Harrigan shook his head and said to Schade, "I suppose Oscar should more appropriately have responded with 'Gettumup, Scout', but why complain."

With a straight face, Schade had replied, "I don't savvy that palaver, kemosabe.")

But afterward Monday said to Makepeace, "It's a goddamn shame that he won't be able to fulfill that talent because he won't be offered a decent orchestra. He'll end up teaching and writing on the race problem instead of conducting or playing the clarinet." Vasart's response bordered on condescension. "Not that I'm particularly chauvinistic at the boy's British background, you know, but it does put you Yanks on the spot, so to speak, doesn't it? Conducting the great orchestra in your sector. What would they say in Cleveland?" Now Schade wondered what his companions in the truck thought about the event, but with Barry Green on such a short fuse he thought it better not to ask.

By the time they reached the southwestern edge of the city Schade's stomach muscles had relaxed somewhat but his eyes still flitted up and down the streets scrutinizing anything that moved in the gloom. It was cold in the cab, the heater malfunctioned, but they kept the windows open to maintain a steady flow of fresh air. Schade had felt suffocated by the tension earlier and now spasms gripped his bowels each time another vehicle passed them.

    Barry Green stopped the truck at the American checkpoint on the border of the US sector and Soviet Zone south of the Schlachtensee. An American military sedan in front of them had just been cleared and started its journey toward Helmstedt in the American Zone two hundred kilometers down the potholed highway. A half a kilometer beyond their truck, around a bend in the road, the Soviets checked travel papers at their own guard house. The young American soldier with a carbine walked up to the passenger side of the truck, white puffs of breath visible in the cold air. Schade found it difficult to breathe and suddenly had to urinate.

    The soldier looked past Schade at the two Negroes. He grinned. The Negroes nodded. "Lieutenant. Haven't seen you on this run before, sir." The young guard's Duluth accent rolled around the constricted cabin and Schade wished he could tell Makepeace about it. He smiled weakly and said: "Not on this run, Corporal," trying to control his own accent, which always thickened in moments of tension and pressure.

    "Sir, there's been a change in plans. They don't want you to go through the Russian checkpoint. Cargo's too valuable to risk an incident." Barry Green muttered a foul oath and both Stoneland and Schade drew in sharp breaths. "It's not so bad, sir. Take the first right before the bend in the road and follow the left curve at the fork. Same route back. I get relieved in an hour. You can go back to the city with me. Is that clear, sir?" Despite his best efforts, the soldier was pleased with the change: it gave him an opportunity to participate, however briefly, in the adventure beyond just passing the truck through the checkpoint.

"That is clear, Corporal. Thank you. We'll appreciate the ride." He nodded to Barry Green who started the truck moving again. As they made the right turn, Schade asked: "Does this happen often?"

After a moment Stoneland answered: "No. We always meet them after the Russian Zone checkpoint. Sometimes we drive through to our zone when the papers say we can go there and back to the base in the city, and when we have the time off."

"A lot of sweet poon in the Zone, man," Barry Green said.

"But this is the first time we've made the turnover before the Russky checkpoint. Usually after we get through that we give the truck to two other guys who drive it through the Russians to our zone and bring the truck back with a real load of supplies and stuff. One of the Jews drives us back to the base."

"Don't like this at all," Barry Green announced.

They followed the curve to the left at the fork and their headlights picked up two figures in Army fatigues standing at the side of the road. Barry Green brought the truck to a stop, shoved the gearshift into neutral, pulled up the handbrake, and they climbed out of the cab. The two sergeants, both very young, nodded in greeting. Schade wondered idly at their youth and motivation. Tompkin would undoubtedly get that information, anonymously of course.

"We'll take it from here."

"Why the change?" Stoneland asked.

"Damned if I know, but it should be a piece of cake. There's a lotta roads around here and at the other end too. They're not so well organized yet."

"Okay, fay, the whole shebang is all yours. You got tonight's password?"

"Yeah. What's 'shalom' mean?"

"Peace, man, peace."

Walking back to the American checkpoint along the frosty road, Schade felt a hollowness in his chest and frustration in his mind. The tension and excitement had given way to a sour emptiness. There had been no satisfying resolution of the tension: expectation had not been fulfilled. Now the events of the night made no sense. The pain returned to his temples. The thrill of illegality and danger would recur on each of the several further occasions he participated in the nighttime crossings, but now he felt a deep disappointment as if he had somehow been cheated. As he passed by the sign, he automatically checked the ground in front of him.

Achtung! Vorsicht!
Bomben nicht anfassen!
Aufpassen oder sterben.

* * * *

Some time after Ogilvy Vasart's abrupt departure for the more hospitable climate of occupied Vienna, his replacement arrived at the Milinowskistrasse office to, as Harrigan explained it, "put his credentials to the real test – not to face the German clients, but to determine how well he'll work with his closest Allies on this vast and unpredictable enterprise." Captain Levon Bornholm, born Ludwig Bernheimer into a business man's family of observant but not intensely religious Jews in Vienna ("Ironic given my predecessor's current whereabouts."), cut his deep black hair short to balance his thick black eyebrows dotting a long sallow face under a forehead furrowed with creases ("Comes from concentrated thinking, or so I'm reliably informed.") His dark brown eyes contained the burden of his family's exile and hard times, though he often noted that his had been a better experience than many due to his father's business connections. "After March 1938, of course he had no business to connect, and I had none either. I'd been in the theater as a young man acting minor roles with the family's blessing. None of the usual 'follow in the father's footsteps'. Then there were no footsteps to follow. But the connections did remain, especially in London. How many of us wouldn't have gotten out without business connections all over the world? For such things the nazis defamed us as 'rootless cosmopolitans' and 'international communist atheists'. Some of us were very fortunate in our internationalism. At first my father worked as a milkman for a while and I delivered newspapers, learning English until they interned us as enemy aliens. I got out of that by volunteering for the army. Dad they let go because he had those connections, and was harmless in any case. He's now in the insurance business, as he was in Vienna, but not so successfully. His English isn't the best. My mother died in an air raid so the nazis finally got one of us after all.

"I learned English quickly and that helped a great deal. They interned me in a primitive camp near the border with Wales in October '39. Released me to the army which schooled me in signals and communications, whatever that means. Some clever personnel officer had me transferred to a theater group performing for the troops and that was fun, but also primitive in accommodations, the beginning of the war, y'know, not well organized at all. Finally I landed in an intelligence unit and set to translating and analyzing German intercepts very quickly. Still don't know where they came from or how they were deciphered but we had those two tasks and kept at them constantly. The first was relatively easy once one got the hang of military jargon. The second was well-nigh impossible without a context for the messages and our superiors were forbidden to provide this to us. Damned stupid, of course, but such things happened all the time. It's a wonder we won the war. Perhaps the other side made more stupid moves than we did.

"Ah, no, I didn't change my name. The army did me that favor. The sergeant who interviewed me took great pleasure in the power he had to say that no proper Englishman could have such an unenglish name, forgetting the very proper English families called Rothschild, Warburg, Disraeli, Montagu, Wolfson, Montefiore, Sassoon, but *Schwam drüber*, what? He looked in a little book and came up with Bornholm. Not very English either to my ear. I added Levon because it sounded neutral but contained Lev. My own miniscule protest against the small minds."

After the traditional first greetings, Captain Levon Bornholm asked a question of Captain Felix Harrigan, which under other circumstances would have appeared to be a relatively innocent social faux pas of a minor order. "Tell me, Mr. Harrigan, what is the origin of your rather unusual first name?"

Harrigan smiled and replied, "My mother loved bizarre cats and my father instinctively foresaw that I would be a pussy cat as an adult."

"Did his instinct fail him?" Bornholm said with a blank look.

"You know, I've not yet discovered the answer to that question."

"Don't let him fool you, Levon, old pal, he's tougher on the Germans than many of us and we don't let him go to the Kommandantura meetings anymore because he won't let the French and the Russians get away with obscure reasons for their recalcitrance." Makepeace paused, rattled his ID bracelet and turned to Schade. "Did I actually say that, John?"

Poker-faced, Schade nodded. "I believe you did, my dear colonel. Did you hear the same thing, Felix?"

"Only if Mr. Bornholm can confirm the statement will I agree." Harrigan wiped his lips with his monographed silk handkerchief. "Otherwise it all remains speculation, doesn't it?"

"Gentlemen," Bornholm pronounced in his best learned English accent, "I am now convinced we shall get along splendidly and offer each other the necessary support when confronting the problems of joint occupation of the former – and for some the still – enemy capital."

"What we need is a drink before we choke on the rhetorical treacle the British are so good at providing," Harrigan laughed.

"The émigré must be more English than the British," Bornholm said in an offended tone.

Schade said, "What part of Austria do you come from, Captain?"

"Is it so obvious?"

"American children have a cogent saying appropriate to situations such as this: takes one to know one, usually shouted in derision, which is not the case here."

"But you are not Austrian – or Jewish?"

"Neither. Breslau for the first thirteen or so years, long enough, then New York."

"Vienna until April '38. We were very lucky to have business associates in London and Liverpool who helped with the affidavits and other paperwork."

Makepeace touched the crown of his head, clearly impatient. "John here was also lucky in that sense. Felix and I have seen a bit of the old Fortuna in our lives as well, haven't we, Captain Harrigan?"

"Oh, yes indeed, Lieutenant Colonel Makepeace, we have, we have. Especially you in your endlessly flexible promotions and demotions. Rarely in the history of the west have we seen so many fluctuations in rank as we experience every week here in this city of flux and jetsom."

"A fine Irish tongue on you, lad, but sometimes I wish your silent Torah-study Yeshiva side was more prominent in your personality."

"The curse of coming from two worlds, the heritage of the wild city of Boston in the great state of Massachusetts."

Through the vise of repressed laughter Bornholm sought to break the flow of patter. Almost choking, he said, "I understand you gents had a solid working relationship with my predecessor – "

"Well, John here used to get drunk with him from time to time," Makepeace offered as confirmation.

"Ah, yes, indeed. Perhaps we can continue that tradition at some point, but about the level of cooperation between your office and mine…?"

"We are about to be reorganized yet again," Harrigan said with mild distaste. "Consequently and ergo, we are not quite sure what our offices will in fact be, in order to cooperate with anyone."

"And that," pronounced Schade popishly, "is the true gen and nothing but the true gen, so help me General Ike."

"You may with some degree of safety ignore the rantings of this benighted refugee from further east," confided Makepeace. "He occasionally knows not whereof he speaks."

"But you all do speak a great deal. Or so I've been told."

"Calumny!"

"So you've spoken with our erstwhile and former colleague currently dealing with our neighbors to the south east," Harrigan said.

"No, no, I've never had the pleasure of meeting Captain Vasart. Pity, I suppose. He might've been able to give me some tips on the job."

"You're better off learning on the job," Harrigan laughed.

"And stay away from the Countess," Makepeace added, lighting a Fatima. "Have a fag."

"They're surely better than the Woodbines we're issued. I've heard tell of the Countess, but I'm not sure I've got the details of the story."

Schade smiled. "I'm not sure any of us have. There are so many of them that contradict all the others. One isn't quite sure which ones to believe."

"Quite, quite. Just so, but our Manning-Lehman – you know him I think, yes – tells me they made a thorough investigation of the matter, but he is rather mean with the details."

"Manning-Lehman is not quite sure the right side won the war."

"Now, John," Makepeace swiftly interposed, "no excessive bitterness. We've got too much to do."

"That fascist railroaded Ogilvy out of town with no cause."

"John's still not forgiven the British army for transferring Captain Vasart," Harrigan explained. "Despite the uproar he caused."

"Loudmouthed drunken officers every day smash up far more furniture than Ogilvy ever did."

"But you see," Bornholm said quietly, "Ogilvy Vasart smashed some of the furniture in their minds. An unforgiveable offense in a British officers' mess."

Makepeace laughed. "But you don't have all the details, of course."

"Exactly, Lieutenant Makepeace. That puts it in the proverbial nutshell. You wouldn't happen to have something stronger than this military issue coffee around, would you? Not that this isn't better coffee than German coffee, mind, or would be if the Germans had any real coffee."

"We might if the *Putzfrauen* haven't been nipping at the supply again."

With an elaborate flourish Harrigan produced an unlabeled dark green bottle from the file cabinet against which he'd been conveniently leaning. "Prepare mugs for launch," he announced and pulled the cork from the bottle with a sweep of his arm. Into the white porcelain coffee mugs he poured the light yellow liquid intoning, "*E pluribus unum illegitimati non corrundum in paceat files mundo*. Bottoms up, as it were."

They drank. Bornholm smacked his lips and stared thoughtfully at the bottle. "Gentlemen, this is without an iota of a doubt the worst dreck I've ever had the unpleasant experience of allowing into my mouth. I will not ask a thing about its origins, *aber was für 'ne Scheissdreck*, if you'll excuse my Viennese."

"Actually," Harrigan held up the bottle to the fading sunlight, "we're not quite sure what this is, but for the moment it's all we seem to have."

"Put ice in it," Schade suggested.

"And ruin a good ice cube? Never!" Harrigan expostulated.

"Look here, I've got a concert to attend at one of the churches in our sector. Nights are chilly now and of course there's no heat. And tomorrow I have to interview twenty-three clients, cellists, all of whom want to perform in a recital next month, none of whom have been cleared except by the Russians so we've got to by Christ do it ourselves."

"So what you are saying is - ?" Schade began.

"Perhaps I could have one more small jot of this dreck to keep me warm tonight and give me a headache tomorrow so I'll keep the meetings short and sour."

"A man after my own heart," Makepeace said.

"Where is the concert?" Harrigan asked.

"In the Church of the Epiphany in Charlottenburg. A small orchestra, no conductor, hungry musicians, eyes ablaze with plans for the future, no sense of reality. Just as well, of course."

"Sounds like Woller," Makepeace said and poured another round of the dreck.

"Ah, the great sour breath machine." Bornholm sighed. "I've met him once or twice. He was very annoyed that at first I refused to speak German with him. Not very polite on my part, I know, but he damned well annoyed me from the start. No, not his breath, though I dare say that's a powerful enough reason to stay as far away as possible. No, his adamant conviction that all nazis should be considered on the same level of guilt and punishment greatly put me off because of its unreasonable and unrealistic foundation. Lord knows I've no sympathy with any of 'em here, but that fellow gets on my bloody nerves."

"We all have our crosses to bear, although that is the wrong metaphor for you and Harrigan here," Makepeace murmured.

"Doesn't bother me. Come from an observant family but not orthodox, and I rarely attend services. But that's not what you meant, I realize. I'll bear the metaphor, if not the wood."

Schade asked, "What are they playing, these starving artists?"

"Oh, the usual stuff they think we'll approve, post facto, of course, since we don't really tell them what to play ahead of time. There is a list of banned stuff, but we only 'suggest' they don't play the pieces on it. It's easier with the larger, established orchestras who need a dedicated hall in which to perform and other amenities like sheet music. We can always 'intimate' that there might be a problem with their tenure in the hall if they ignore our suggestions. We British like the subtle approach, y'know."

"What are they going to play?" Schade asked.

"Oh, yes, sorry. A bit of Elgar, a bit of Vaughn-Williams – "

"Old Rafe," Harrigan murmured.

"Ah, Ralph, actually. It's a ridiculous pretention to pronounce it 'Rafe' as if he were, hmm, raffish, which he isn't at all, if you know the music. Ralph it is and Ralph it shall ever be. Now Manning-Lehman one might at the extreme edge describe as raffish. He no doubt would love to be called Rafe. Try it and see."

"Don't know about that," Makepeace said. "He doesn't strike me as the type one can easily joke with."

"Perhaps not, but now that the bottle of this dreck is empty, perhaps we might find another source for my future well-being as a well-heated control officer in His Royal Highness's army at work during the cold winter nights in this desolate city, humm?"

"Vienna is no better, I fear," said Harrigan sadly.

"Nor Paris," added Schade snuffling briefly.

"Gents, I can tell you without hesitation that London is also a place not to be at present. Perhaps Edinburgh..."

"No, no," Schade said brightening. "Manhattan: food lights music laughter Leslie Archer, Jack Liddell, cocktails, Fats Waller – sniff – "

"Ahoy!" Makepeace interrupted Schade's increasingly larmoyant litany, pointing with a sudden gesture to the open doorway. "Deux ex machinery! In the very figure of U.S. Navy Lieutenant Kenneth Farisse, soon to be relegated to the rank of civilian, upholder of the American press policy against the nefarious activities of the defeated who resist guidance in the ways of democratic ideals – "

"What the hell, Makepeace, what the hell! Has the dreck bottle been emptied again? Are you hard up for liquid refreshment of a certain strength, a powerful reminder of my miraculous way with the scotch and the ice cube? Is that the meaning of the two in the machinery? Speak, Oh Baffled One!"

Thus spake an extremely slender man in a high pitched but pleasantly modulated voice, smiling brightly at the others with a look of complete innocence on his pale face. He pushed his thin blonde hair off his forehead. "Eh, whot?"

Bornholm joined in the general hilarity, but harbored a suspicion that all was not as it appeared to be. He wondered for a brief moment how well he would be able to work with these clowns and took comfort if not courage from the fact that each of the Allies seemed to be operating their sectors of the city in increasing isolation from the others.

"What, indeed, is the question to the fair mariner posing as a journalist of repute and reputation. Wherefore we know already, what ho, is what we want to know – "

"In short," Harrigan broke into Makepeace's harangue, "in brief: what have you got to drink?"

"And where, pray tell, is the mythical Vasart flask with its endless source of human comfort and happiness?" Farisse asked without losing the bright smile of innocence. "You guys should really open the windows when you fog up the place like this. Jesus!"

Schade walked with elaborate caution to the window behind his desk and, as Harrigan later described it, threw up the sash so hard a pane cracked, a fact that none of the assembled then noted, but one which caused some trouble the following day when the glass fell out and could not easily be replaced. "There," Schade intoned, "you have the open door, ah, window, a veritable *offene Fenster* through which all the toxic nasty can seep into the urban landscape to dissipate in the noxious fumes of a formerly great metropolis now posing as a cultural backwater currently under renovation and repair – "

"Shit, John, no wonder the dreck bottle is empty," Farisse grumbled.

"Where *is* Ogilvy's flask when we need it?"

"Major Makepeace, it is perhaps gone with the breezes over Capri – or are they over Tivoli? I always associate flasks with cold aquavit."

"Listen, Felix, I was a major an hour ago. Now I'm general one star soon to be field marshal, so watch yer tongue."

"I wonder if we might find something to *eat*. I mean something real; perhaps at the French officers' mess?" Bornholm smiled in sympathy.

"You guys are too far ahead of me," Farisse complained. "The French have garlic and red wine of quality even better than Rheingold."

"Wine from the Rheinland?" Bornholm asked.

"Beer from New Jersey," Farisse replied, hoping it did not originate in Seattle.

"I've had American beer. Rather like one of our weaker lagers – Whitbread or so. The name fooled me, you see. I thought it came at least indirectly from Czecho, but I was wrong. Only the name is the same. Fraud, if you ask me."

"Let's eat, I agree," Makepeace said.

Bornholm placed his hat haphazardly on his head and gave them a sweeping mock British salute. "Being in perfect shape to attend a concert in a chapel in my official capacity, I will remove my official self to said center of worship to indulge my ears in musical baksheesh, perchance to doze perchance, but unlikely to dream of steak and kidney pie drowning in HP sauce."

"You know," Makepeace told his colleagues after Bornholm departed with stiffened back and hazy mind, "I think we'll get along just fine with that tommy."

"Where *does* the word limey come from?" Harrigan wondered vaguely.

* * * *

Schade's meeting with Colonel Darkley on the occasion of his promotion to first lieutenant did nothing to relieve the grating irritation upsetting his equilibrium. After handing him the official letter and mouthing the usual phrases of congratulations, the older man's eye held Schade captive.

"I can *praise* the help certain *gentiles* are giving to the *aliyah* movement, but of course I don't know *anything* about that." Darkley's hard brown eye maintained its grip on Schade's mind.

"After what has happened that kind of help is understandable, isn't it?" Schade responded in as neutral a tone as he could muster. Darkley always evoked a slight feeling of discomfort in him, as if he had not accomplished a task with the necessary verve and expertise.

"Few people, including *most* American Jews, have really understood what happened. They *haven't* made all the connections yet. And maybe it's better they don't. What we've taken to calling 'the atrocities' are still *generalized*. Think of the film about the *camps* we've just made, doesn't mention the Jews as victims *at all*. Certainly in the States the Jews are not *singled* out in the popular mind. And perhaps it would be better for the Jews in America not to insist too loudly on their European brethren as the great victims. We've made *tremendous* progress, but our assimilation remains a *goal* rather than a *fact*."

"Assimilation?"

"Yes. I don't mean losing our *identity* as Jews, but the acceptance of our being Jews as *normal*. The war is over. The great common cause which held Americans together is gone."

"White Americans."

"Yes, yes. No society is *perfect*, but that's not the *point* at the moment, Lieutenant."

"No sir, it is not."

"You have *caught* my drift, Lieutenant."

"Yes sir, I think so." But he knew he had comprehended only a portion of the message being delivered, perhaps the most important part, but only a part of the whole.

"There is a *delicate* balance to the forward march of our circumstances at *home*. It would not be particularly helpful if we Jews stood too far out in the spotlight at the moment. The Jews here are part of the great *mass* of DPs who require assistance and attention."

"Do you really believe that, sir?"

"Whether I believe it or not is *irrelevant*, Lieutenant. More importantly, I believe the strategy is the correct one. There is so much going on at *home*, the times are turbulent and slippery. We have to deal with the *present*, the past will have to wait."

"I'm not sure that can work...."

"It must, Lieutenant, it *must*. And those of us who write for the public have to be particularly *sensitive* to the issue."

"Ur."

"I'm not speaking as a *ranking* officer now, Mr. Schade."

"I understand that, Colonel."

"*Thank* you, Lieutenant."

* * * *

A short while after the trip through the city with the Jewish refugees Tompkin called Schade to arrange a meeting in the journalist's shabby but comfortable room on Kalckreuthstrasse near Nollendorfplatz. The room's appointments took Schade back in time to his childhood in the over furnished living room of the family apartment in Breslau, where heavy dark curtains shrouded the window casings, thick dark rugs covered the hardwood floor, and heavy dark armoires towered over him as the deep dark upholstered chairs and couch threatened to swallow him down into their dark intestinal depths. The differences brought him back immediately to the present: the Russians had long since confiscated any rugs, the doors of the bookcase contained no glass, and two straight-backed chairs replaced the confiscated upholstered armchair. But the massive armoire remained as did the large bed with its pale yellow feather-filled cover. No fire burned in the iron stove in the south corner of the room and an icy drizzle smashed bits of frozen rain against the windows.

They sat on the wooden chairs and drank whisky to create the illusion of warmth in the room. Tompkin's large hand almost hid the glass, enveloping it with an army of fingers. "I'm saving the coal for when it really gets cold. Which it will. I'm lucky to have gotten glass in the windows. That required dropping the name of a quartermaster sergeant into an article about supplying the garrison here, and the promise that it would appear in his hometown newspaper. Oh yes, it did: always keep your word to the quartermaster people. They can be extremely useful. The previous tenant left suddenly after I had a word with the landlord. Mid-level city bureaucrat, but a very active long term party member. I believe he's living with a sister and her family in a small room in Friedrichshain. He may be out of work for a while, but his kind always land on their feet. Swine." They sipped the whisky and smoked Russian luxury cigarettes. "A gift from a Soviet colleague. I did him a small favor."

"It must have been very small. The question is," Schade said, pushing his spectacles closer to the bridge of his nose, "are you going to do me a favor?"

"How much longer are you going to be in the city, John? When does your time run out?"

"Next winter. Why?"

"Any plans to extend or convert to civilian status as Harrigan and Makepeace threaten to do?"

"I doubt it. What difference does it make?"

"If you're leaving the army, does it matter what I print?"

"I may want to come back to the city someday. Of course it matters."

"No need to get huffy. You needn't worry about it in any case." He arched his back against the chair and grimaced. "I hope I never get assigned to Moscow without my own cigarette supply."

Schade laughed. "They're not so bad. Try the local Rot-Händel. Tear your throat up."

Grinning, Tompkin said, "Yeah, they're all prewar now. No wonder." He scratched his full corn silk colored beard. "You're rather touchy about the Soviets, aren't you?"

"You can't believe everything Makepeace tells you. Let's just say I'm not automatically anti-Soviet."

"Have you heard about the boar hunt? There's something not quite believable about that. The Berliners are starving and the Russians organize a boar hunt for selected Allied personnel, not including your world famous foreign correspondent, I might add. Not that I feel in the least bit slighted, mind you."

"I can't see any difference between that and a cocktail party in the officers' club with enough food to feed two blocks of Germans for a week. The club is warmer most of the time. The spoils of victory. It's disgusting regardless of who does it, but you can't expect anything else, can you. I've not been invited either: too low on the totem pole."

"You certainly can throw those Americanisms around with flair, John." Tompkin laughed loudly and filled their glasses to show he meant no offense. Wrapping his huge paw around the glass, he asked: "Notice anything unusual about this glass? No? Take a better look at it.

See? This is actually a jar, a mason jar, used for preserving fruits and vegetables by your grandmother, or mine at least, perhaps German grandmothers did not have the advantage of mason jars. I've had this jar for ten years. Regular glasses never hold enough and it's embarrassing to pour another drink long before anyone else is ready. People might think I'm addicted to the stuff. I learned this trick in San Francisco back in the Twenties when I was a cub reporter there. High times."

The whisky burned Schade's throat and exploded softly an expanding ball of warmth in his stomach. He rarely drank hard liquor before lunch and his head already felt lighter than it should. The water had not yet been restored to the building. "How can you drink this stuff so early and still get anything done?"

"Practice, of course, as anyone will tell you. Long years of practice. It's part of the image of the foreign correspondent, which unfortunately has become part of me. Never missed an appointment or a deadline, though. The mason jar is part of me, never go anywhere without it. A prized possession, you might say." He sighed and crushed out the Russian cigarette in an ashtray with the letters "Hotel Bristol" on the bottom. "But let's get to the point of this. I've got a press conference to cover in an hour. You want to know about the other night, right?"

"I don't understand why they would want any publicity about their activities. It doesn't make sense."

"Right. First of all, they *don't* want any open coverage, not now. The point is that eventually they'll get what they want, a Jewish state of some sort in Palestine. They believe this and so do I. So what I'm doing is storing up stuff for the future. When the time comes it will make a hell of a series of articles and then a bestselling book. I'll have all the material I need. This story is my retirement, you see, my pension, so to speak. It's a good one. I'll make a lot of money and the Mossad Le Aliyah Bet people will be heroes to the world. David against Goliath redux. Everyone is served and ends up happy. A felicitous conjoining of interests, as I explained to them at great length and considerable passion when we set it up."

"Except Arab and British interests."

"That's not my problem, is it?" He slowly shook his head and the shock of gray and silver hair fell over his forehead. Even in his ill-fitting civilian uniform the journalist managed to look distinguished, somewhat shabby, but distinguished. "Objectively a problem, no doubt, but not mine. Our arrangement is a business deal as far as I'm concerned. In any case, you don't have to worry about it. I'll change most of the names. That's part of the deal, how I got the soldiers to agree to my going along. We got through without a hitch the other night, even with the change in route, but I hear the checkpoints are going to be strengthened in the future. They're going to try to close off the entire border to stop the movement. Arab pressures on the Brits and the Brits ask the Americans for a favor. Impossible. They'll never be able to close all the roads. Not enough MPs. Not enough desire to do it, either."

Schade remembered the stories he'd heard in New York from the exiles who had left Germany in the late Thirties about how well the European states had closed their borders. "Perhaps. You're not going to mention that those fellows are Negroes, are you? They seemed concerned about that."

"I assured them on that point, but who knows what the situation will be when the time comes. Maybe they'll want to have the fact noted. Another spot of this eau de vie?"

"Ah, no thanks. I've not had the necessary practice. How did you get to them?"

"The Jews? Ah, that goes back to before the war when I was first in Berlin. Very simple actually. A Mossad group worked underground here smuggling Jews out to Palestine. Not on the same scale, of course. I was able to be, how shall I put it, helpful to them from time to time. They did not forget it. That's all."

No, Schade thought, that was hardly "all," but he did not pursue the matter: Tompkin would tell him no more. "Did you know a Mossad agent named Lev in Berlin then?"

The reporter's face behind his beard fell into an expressionless mask. He studied Schade for a moment, veiling whatever emotions passed behind that fragilely constructed facade, but Schade saw the pain in his eyes before the burly figure got up and busied himself with his cap and trench coat. "Yes, I knew him a bit. Do you know anything about what happened to him?"

Schade, too, rose and buttoned up his overcoat. "Only that he died in the war fighting for the British."

The reporter turned to Schade, his face still a mask, but disbelief colored his voice which sounded tight and rasping. "*For* the British?"

"That's what I've been told."

Tompkin lifted and dropped his big shoulders as if dismissing the information. Clearing his throat he asked: "Where did you hear that?"

"I'd rather not say, really."

The reporter smiled absently and nodded his large head. "Well, you are a regular d'Artagnan then."

"Scarlet Pimpernel is more like it."

"Not quite, Lieutenant, but I know what you mean."

Tompkin shrugged his shoulders again and they went out into the half-frozen city.

PART SEVEN

> He's a thin-pisser. And his eyes are old potatoes. Can't trust a thin-pisser.
> --Mister Morgan Tahni to Eden the Perfect Bartender in The Edge Bar, August 27, 1946

As winter expanded and deepened its cold, damp domination of the city, movement became more difficult for the refugees, but almost impossible for the *Kriegsbeschädigte*, those maimed by the war and the concentration camp system who had lost arms or legs, the blind and the halt in their thousands throughout the city hobbling about in the ice and the snow, evading further damage from military vehicles speeding erratically through the streets more or less under the control of their drivers. Winter forced people off the streets into their cold, spare living quarters, making criminals of the citizens who stole every piece of combustible material they could scrounge from the increasingly inhospitable landscape, as both the victors and the defeated struggled to assemble the fragments of time and energy that made their lives into coherent wholes. The Brandenburg plains shot the snarling wind into the maimed canyons of the city, whipping victor and defeated alike, the former suffering less from the cold than the latter. Both the victors and the defeated busied themselves with their public functions but as winter slowed the velocity of life, private concerns occupied a proportionately larger part of their time and thoughts. The year's end would not elicit the usual summing up and inventorying of the debits and credits of the last twelve months. Few in the city thought of the approaching year's end as anything other than another day in the life they would prefer not to be living. Escape for most was impossible except through the traditional mechanisms of self-deceit: alcohol, drugs, sex, and madness: the first two of which were not readily available to many; the third had lost its savor in the cold and rubble; the last was reserved for those beyond fear and hunger. So most of the inhabitants of the charnel house called Europe devoted themselves to surviving the winter as best they could, as the suicide and death rates climbed. The European Christians who celebrated Christmas did so without enthusiasm. The surviving remnant of European Jewry devoted more of their prayers to Kaddish than those celebrating the fact they had survived. The Allies welcomed the end of the year in various ways commensurate with their traditions as optimists or pessimists, each to his own. No one in the city escaped the cold.

(As a shivering Harrigan complained to a red-nosed Manning-Lehman one frozen evening as they trudged through the snow to the theater, "That much vaunted razzamatazz in the Twenties surely all took place at night and the heating bills must have been astronomical. All those naked girls prancing around the stages of the music halls and cabarets. Must have been colder than that proverbial part of the witch's anatomy. This burg is always cold and damp!")

The Kronauers moved about the city collecting affidavits and talking to as many occupation officials as they could corner about the necessity for a newspaper of the center to balance the coverage of political affairs and present an un-political review of cultural developments.

The Russians showed no interest in supporting another bourgeois publication. Because the Kronauers and their advisors believed they had the best chance in the British sector, they maintained as much pressure as they could muster on the British press control authorities who appeared to be so satisfied with the success of their official newspaper, *Der Berliner*, that they felt no compelling urgency in licensing a German product in their sector. ("Dear Sir ... While we of course continue to support the policy of licensing appropriately cleared German newsmen to conduct ... we are at the moment for technical reasons unable to process the required paperwork within ... as we are sure you will understand....") Ironically, the success of the licensed papers in the American and French sectors, *Der Tagesspiegel* and *Der Kurier*, indicated the days of overt military government papers as the only source of hard news were coming to a close. In the first seven months of the Allied occupation the city had progressed from no newspapers (for the first time in more than 300 years Berlin had been without a paper for seventeen days in the final weeks of the war) to twelve with a circulation of two million, nine of these published in the Soviet Sector, including the flagship *Die Tägliche Rundschau* (the daily review), called in the vox populi *Die Klägliche Rundschau* (the pitiable review) because it contained so little real news but voluminous praise of the Soviet Union. But it had also become clear that the three western sector publications found more readers in the Soviet part of the city than the reverse. In an attempt to counter this trend and to compete with *Der Kurier* in the early evening, the Soviet Military Administration licensed *Die Nacht-Express*, a noisy, sensationalizing, big headline Boulevardblatt that polemicized with increasing sharpness against the western powers.

"That is no doubt a mistake," Kronauer noted. "That rag may be read in the western sectors but in the long run it can only reduce the level of quality in all the city's papers. We have the opportunity to begin again on a high level of quality; we shouldn't throw it away for whatever reason." Boltzmann, who when sober wrote occasional pieces for the *Kurier* and assisted Kronauer in preparing plans for the latter's publication, disagreed with a spongy vehemence: "When this city has its share of sensationalist newspapers written for illiterates, we'll know it has returned to normal. Forty years ago over 800 newspapers and magazines were being published in the city, 36 of them dailies! Besides, all the Allies care about is their own positions, not the quality of Berlin's newspapers."

"I don't believe that. Furthermore, my friend, I don't think Berlin will ever be normal again in the old sense."

"That may be just as well."

("I tell you, Villum, we are trapped in, what do you call it, a straight-jacket? We follow the line of complete and open cooperation with our Allies, of course. But these stupid Germans, what do they understand after so many years of nothing but propaganda? They have not had to think in twelve years. For the common Berliner we have to send messages in a form he'll comprehend." "Yuri Vladimirovich, my mind reels in awe at the multitude of responses that statement brings forth." "Ach, I grow tired of this buggered city and its canalized inhabitants!")

Buchdow, along with every other theater producer, struggled with a lack of material to construct sets, performers hungry in belly and ego, and the cold, which accompanied each day's progress as the city marched inexorably deeper into winter. "Actually, it is probably good we don't have as much as we need for the sets: this means I can keep everyone physically busy taking apart the old and building the new, which keeps them warm." He maintained a constant if prickly relationship with Gisela after she started rehearsals for *Hokuspokus* and they met to discuss the difficulties of their profession and their lives. She played to a certain extent upon his guilt for his behavior toward her during their months in hiding, and from time to time confided to him some of her more frightening nightmares, asking his opinion but not his advice about possible solutions to her situation. Thus their acquaintanceship continued, if in a different form, as long as he did not mention Schade as part of the problem that she tried so desperately to define and resolve. Schade himself felt an ambivalent relief at their relationship; it drew off some of his own guilt over his position vis à vis Gisela. He felt relieved because the time for him to decide on his future edged closer and he knew he would leave the city before the next winter. He did not again talk to Buchdow about Gisela, but the director somehow knew, perhaps from Gisela herself, that he would eventually leave. The feeling between the two men remained distant and formal, but both realized an uncomfortable bond connected them: having been lovers of the same woman they came to care about each other in a strange unspoken but understood fashion, in which intimacy played no part at all.

    Once Buchdow took Schade to what the owners claimed *soto voce* to be "the new improved Eldorado." "Just for a drink; you probably don't get to these places very often," said with a sly smile as they walked down the Budapester Strasse away from the ruin of the Gedächtniskirche. "We are both too young to have known the real Eldorado, but it must have been so extravagant, so overboard. Couldn't last with the nazis of course, though many of them would have loved to go there. Perverts. Would never admit their own tastes, repressed little twits banged us with 175 and took it out on the Jews and the rest of Europe and the Russians."

"The war machine in action because they suppressed their homosexuality? That's a new one."

"Why not? It's as good as any other theory, isn't it?"

Schade laughed. "Probably not. What's the name of this place?"

"I'm not sure it has one."

They noticed a change in the rhythm of the darkened street as the whores began to move faster than usual, congregating in suddenly formed groups to discuss things in quick, whispered hisses of Berlinerisch before fluttering apart to swiftly move on to reform further down the street. A young man in ragged clothes passed by them and whispered "Razzia!" This happened several times with different fast moving young men until Schade and Buchdow turned a corner and left the neighborhood. "It doesn't make any sense to keep arresting those women. They should be organized and checked by doctors regularly, that would prevent more VD than arresting them."

Buchdow laughed gently. "You've missed the point, Lieutenant. It's not the whores the police are after. It's the rough trade and their customers. Those thoughtful boys must have taken us for queers on the prowl! Imagine that."

"We should give the German police more to do. They're not busy enough if they take time to harass the queers."

"Your uniform offers you protection."

"Not against the MPs."

"I doubt you have to worry overly much on that score."

"You never know."

The bar resembled any other small anonymous *Kneipe* in any German big city during the months and years after the war: sparsely furnished with a motley collection of tables, chairs, and a zinc bar, bereft of wall decorations, dimly lit, especially during the hours of reduced electricity, smelling of stale beer, wax candles, and acrid cigarette smoke, such places offered a provisional haven for those whose living quarters were unbearable and a venue in which to relax for those who could only do so among their own kind, however that might be defined. In this case, the "kind" was the homosexual underworld in a country whose laws made such men criminals if they acted out their true natures, and in a city occupied by foreign armies whose leaders threw out great chunks of German law as being undemocratic but left in the infamous paragraph 175 of the civil code, which criminalized homosexual behavior. Thus the bar viewed from the outside and from the inside when empty in no way differed from hundreds of others in the city, but filled with clientele it presented a rather different aura and milieu.

Most of the regulars in the bar did not react with surprise to Schade's uniform when he and Buchdow entered the narrow doorway and sat at a table along the brownish yellow wall. The uniform alone told them nothing since the US Army had not drafted recruits on the basis of sexual orientation (although one could get out of the army by openly stating such, but that carried its own dangers with it) and Allied homosexuals frequented bars in which they too could relax, as much as they could under the nervous conditions of sudden razzias and potential malicious denunciations. The presence of Buchdow further lowered the anxiety level and, aside from a brief lull in the volume of conversation when they first entered, everyone returned to their previous pursuits, verbal and otherwise. Occasionally the skat players, thumping the table as they discarded their cards, glanced at the young American officer whose only sign of discomfort, if it could be described as such, was the regular brushing of his thumb across his brown mustache. Smoke stung and watered their eyes, and Schade removed his horn-rimmed glasses to wipe his face with a clean khaki GI handkerchief. Buchdow used a piece of red and white checkered cloth from an old table covering he saved from a bombed Italian restaurant. The ancient waitress snuffled in a constant state of mild but runny influenza.

"Order the beer, the whiskey is watered," Buchdow said in newly learned English.

"Makes no difference," the snuffling crone responded also in English, "it's all watered."

Schade said to her in German: "See if you can find the least watered whiskey for us. And dare one hope for an ice cube or two?"

"*Nein*," she mumbled and stumbled off to the bar.

Buchdow laughed. "Some things never change. Suzanna was once an attractive trapeze artist in the last century. Then she took up with one of the city's grande dames which created such a scandal that they had to leave and live in Paris where things are easier like that if you have enough money, and the fine lady's family made sure she has sufficient cash to keep her out of Berlin. When the war started in 1914 they had to return but agreed to live in Munich. Something happened during the war and they split up. Suzanna's life slipped ever down the path of poverty and somehow she survived the last war and ended up here. A sad story. Ah, thank you. Not bad, lieutenant, you have a way with old women. Such charm brings almost unwatered whiskey."

"It is a sad story. The whiskey is all right. What was this place like during the war?"

"I've no idea. The new government shut down most of the queer joints before the summer of 1933. Some reopened in different places and camouflaged themselves as best they could, but queers no longer had any public places to go to. Everything had to be done in private. It all reinforced our guilt about being perverse, of course, and many left the tribe, so to speak, in one way or another: marriage and children, the lonely life of the celibate, and after September '39 hiding out in the army, which usually meant death if you got sent to the eastern front. A nasty time. Some were protected somehow, if the Bonzen needed them: Gründgens, and others. They had to be very careful, but they got through all right.

"It was all quite different up to '33. The guidebooks even bragged about nightclubs for transvestites and the queer life-style in general, all of which apparently thrilled the boobs from the provinces. One of the most popular guides, I recently looked into it at Count Vlady's, went something like this." Buchdow's voice squeezed itself into a thin wavering squeak. "You could hear the piano music as you walked up the few stairs into the bar where young blonde boys drank beer and smoked cigarettes. The air is clogged with blue smoke. Wool jackets and pullovers at the tables leaning close to older types in well-brushed suits and stiff collars bordering on the middle class, businessmen, civil servants, soaking up the decadence, whispering to their young companions trying so hard to have a good time. And the young and old moving together back and forth between the tables in a parody of dancing, for which there is really no space. The young ones throw inviting looks at the tables out of kohl-rimmed eyes. No powder or make-up here, just their youth and freshness, only mildly paled from sitting too long at bars in bad smoky air waiting for the next offer. One of them tosses his blonde curls back from his forehead imitating the female movie stars, he wears lederhosen but they're not made from leather but gray silk, and everyone admires his lovely round knees."

He returned his voice to its normal timbre and grimaced. "*Bouf*! It's enough to make you gag. The old Eldorado on the corner of the Motzstrasse and the Kalckreuthstrasse, the Silhouette in the Geisbergstrasse, the Pyramide in the Westend, the Kabaret die Spinner, the Kurfürsten-Kasino, the huge Alexander-Palast, they all became tourist attractions where everybody performed for the trade and nothing was real. All those garlands of flowers ... The clubs were choked with those bourgeois types out for a bit of outré and the others who were out to perform it for them, paid or not. Herr und Frau Apotheke with their tight mouths denying the clandestine pleasures which broke briefly through their stiff moral watchman to satisfy their little aches for little debaucheries. God, what cretins! Small groups of secretaries and department store clerks with bobbed hair and no corsets yearning for an atom or two of titillation to relieve the monotony of their shallow existences spent at dull work and worshipping dull movie stars, and the elegant women from the moneyed aristocracy genteelly scratching the itch of their hesitant curiosity about the seamy side of the city's underworld. They all rushed about seeking the luminous effervescent beauty of Anita Berber's bare ass! One could almost have felt sorry for them. Did you ever hear the song about that?

Was interessiert das Publikum?

> *Hunger, Elend, Not von Millionen?*
> *Dass Tausende im Zuchthaus verrecken?*
> *Interessiert das das Publikum?*
> *I wo, der nackte Hintern der Anita Berber*
> *Der interessiert das Publikum!*[36]

Well, that all went underground after '33, or stopped altogether. It's fitting that the Eldorado became a nazi propaganda office, don't you think?" Smiling casually he said, "Things are almost back to normal, almost, but we've no tourists now, except of course the soldiers, some of them. Some of the older homos make pilgrimages to the old buildings and complain about the lost paradise. They long for the old times and old songs. 'Ich küsse Ihre Hand, Madame,' 'Das Lila-Lied,' and 'Schöner Gigolo, armer Gigolo.' Have you been to Count Vlady's apartment? Quite an experience."

> *Wir sind nun einmal anders als die andern,*
> *die nur im Gleichschritt der Moral geliebt,*
> *neugierig erst durch tausend Wunder wandern,*
> *und für die's doch nur das Banale gibt.*
> *Wir aber wissen nicht, wie das Gefühl ist,*
> *denn wir sind alle andrer Welten Kind.*
> *Wir lieben nur die lila Nacht, die schwül ist,*
> *weil wir ja anders als die andern sind.*[37]

---

[36] What interests the public?/Hunger, squalor, the misery of millions?/That thousands croak in prison?/Nah, Anita Berber's naked bottom,/That interests the public!

[37] After all, we are different from the others/who've only been loved by the moralists,/who blindly walk through a thousand wonders,/and who only know life's banality./But we of course

"But I did want to mention one bit of business, Lieutenant. Sorry, but things are still extraordinarily difficult running the theater and rehearsing the casts for the next two plays all at the same time. We desperately need an administrator to operate the theater."

"Do I detect a hint of the ubiquitous and egregious Hagen Reger in the back of your sentences?" Schade said.

"I would welcome Reger; he is very good at the job."

"He is a nazi swine and a swine in general."

"No worse than many others, but better than most at his work."

"We'll try to find you someone else."

"Whoever he is, he's unlikely to be as good."

"But cleaner, Herr Buchdow, cleaner."

Buchdow remained silent for a moment, then smiled with sudden and unexpected shyness. "You know, in a way I've been forced to become a 20th century Iffland. Do you know him? No? A great all-round man of the theater at the start of the 19th century. August Wilhelm Iffland, playwright, producer, director, manager, actor. The king put him in charge of the National Theater and then added the Royal Opera to his responsibilities. Incredible. There are all sorts of stories about him, but the one I like best is his honoring Schiller on a visit to Berlin just before the great poet died. Iffland staged a cycle of all Schiller's plays and the author attended every performance. They say

don't know what that feeling is,/because we come from another world./We only love the lavender, sultry night,/ for, after all, we're different from the others.
(See also endnote.)

he contemplated moving from Weimar to Berlin, but in the end thought it would be too expensive. Too bad for Berlin." Buchdow sighed with theatrical emphasis. "I am writing a play to go on next season. I regret you won't be able to see it. I'm trying to get both Gisela and Claudia Kaufmann to play the lead female roles. Should be interesting chemistry."

Schade laughed. "Very interesting."

* * * *

The detached intimacy Schade shared with Makepeace did not diminish as they saw less of each other during the second year of the occupation. Schade's involvement with the Brichah, his official duties which developed into increasingly standardized bureaucratic patterns but nonetheless often confusingly spilled over into his private life, his ambiguous affair with Gisela, and his increasingly hoarded spare hours devoted to making endless desultory notes and outlines for his book - all these things left little time or energy for devoted friendships, especially after he began to spend evenings in Schadow's room talking about things that troubled him and all manner of other subjects that interested the old man. Makepeace himself rarely visited his old office; officially he continued to be attached to Lt. Colonel McCrae's information control unit, but Schade knew less and less about his friend's activities, which concerned various intelligence matters considered to be secret. They achieved an unspoken agreement that Schade would not ask for details and Makepeace acknowledged he had become an intelligence operative doing whatever he did. ("Why they call it intelligence work I'll never know, much of it is not very intelligent.")

One Monday morning in the first autumn of the occupation, they walked across the Köpenicke-Strasse at the Schlesische Tor to attend yet another meeting with their Soviet counterparts intended to mediate a difference of policy regarding licensing American films in the Soviet Sector and Soviet films in the American Sector. As they stepped on to the sidewalk, they noticed two skinny men in carefully blocked and creased fedoras, striped ragged KZ-jackets, khaki-green Red Army trousers, and wooden shoes clacking in their direction. Makepeace muttered, "This country is a perfect example of what my father always said when some parking lot attendant in a military-looking hat insisted we park in a slot away from the one he drove into: 'Give a nobody a badge and a uniform and he becomes a goddamn dictator!' Everybody is a Hauptmann von Köpenick." They watched the DPs move down the sidewalk. A beggar dressed in a shiny tuxedo jacket, a shirt that had once been white, and greenish gray Wehrmacht trousers held by two rusty safety pins around the stump of his left thigh leaned against a lamp post, the stump resting in the cross bar of a wooden crutch, his open hand outstretched. As the DPs walked closer to the building to keep as much distance as possible between them and the beggar, the latter pulled back his hand and looked down at the cement. The DPs clacked up to Makepace, stood to rigid attention and executed a burlesque British salute. In the garble of several Eastern European languages their message gradually emerged, fuzzy around the edges but clear enough in intent: they had extremely valuable information for Colonel Meckpiz which they had to deliver that evening at the latest, should the Colonel not possess sufficient time at that very moment and place, information they did not want the *"tschinowniks,"* a pejorative for Russian civil servants and other officials, to know. Embarrassed by the salutes if not the radical promotion in rank, Makepeace arranged another time and place that evening for the meeting. The two skeletons with wary eyes and the stale breath of the camps still clinging to them saluted again, turned as sharply as possible in wooden clogs, and clacked away down the street. "Don't ask, John, don't even ask," Makepeace pleaded, rattling his ID bracelet. "Why, Colonel, I wouldn't think of it for a minute." "Poor sods, they remind me of a toothless dog." "Not so toothless, just shell-shocked."

The incident reminded Schade of the meeting between Makepeace and the Italian liaison officer, whose business in the city no one really knew anything about. Late one afternoon following a fruitless and boring conference at which the four-power cultural control representatives continued the frustrating process of negotiating a common denazification policy, the Italian cornered Makepeace in the hot corridor of the Allied Kommandantura building. "*Scusi, scusi, Tenente*. A favor, *perfavor*. I am Lieutenant Guilio Tristano. I am supposed to have a relative in New York. I think he teaches the piano. Do you know him?"

"I don't know anyone in New York. The people from New York I know are all in Berlin. Or Paris. Maybe Roma."

"If you do ever hear of him, perhaps you will be so good as to inform me."

"You will be the first to know, Capitano Tristano."

"So I might get into contact with him, you understand, so he can sponsor my application to go to the famous Little Italy to eat well fresh pasta and real tomatoes."

"I understand completely, *Senor Majorico*."

"That is a very fine thing, *Tenente*." Some form of charm Schade could not quite comprehend drew the oddest

549

assortment of people to Makepeace to ask favors. This magnetism amused his colleagues.

Nonetheless, Schade and Makepeace continued to find each other's company stimulating and amusing, and both were glad when they both had time for a drink and the games of one-upmanship they played. Schade trusted Makepeace not in his political judgments, but his personal insights into the characters of those Schade thought he needed to understand. Makepeace clearly enjoyed the other's ability to dissect and explain matters with which he was not emotionally concerned.

So they continued to agree to disagree about certain matters ("You must come to understand that the Soviet Union is a voracious predator that cannot live on its own resources so preys on its neighbors for its own survival and represses its own people." "What is more important is the fact that socialism is the only system to liberate all the people from the chains of human greed; that's the goal to which we all must aspire."), but their arguments contained sufficient humor and wit to limit the occasions when they developed into acrimonious confrontations.

"You blind leftists make me laugh," Makepeace said, shaking his head in mock sadness. "You never learn."

"That's a gross generalization, which means nothing at all, a lot of hot air – "

"All you would-be Stalinists – "

"Who's a Stalinist, for Christ sake? Trotsky? *The Partisan Review*? Schumacher? Kramer? My father, perhaps? All on the left but no Stalinists."

Makepeace squinted and leaned forward. "Were you ever a member of the Young Communist League? Eh?"

"Just because I went to City College? What a farce!"

"City College is a well-known hive of communist youth conspiracies and recruitment for the CPUSA. Everybody knows this."

"Everybody in St. Paul maybe. City College is the Harvard of the proletariat! And there is no everybody."

"There's just you and me, pal."

"And I wonder about you, brother."

"Don't ask me for a dime, friend, all I've got is occupation marks." Makepeace drank Eden the Perfect Bartender's new cocktail containing rum and coconut milk purloined from the French commissary. "Are you sure you never were a member of the YCL?"

"My politics are my private possession and I, personally, am accountable to no one or thing except my very own conscience for my political affiliations and my voting records."

"You've never voted in any election except for the dictators of the YCL!"

"How can you drink this stuff? It tastes like chemicals."

"This is an eminently liberal cocktail, perfect for those of us in the vital center of political life."

"Let me tell you a story. I did not join the group that boarded the *Bremen* and ripped up the swastika flag in protest against the nazis. The CP organized the whole thing and most of the group were YCL members. I did not participate."

"Ur?"

"The German ship *Bremen*, 1935, New York harbor. Big demonstration. Anti-fascist protest. Six protesters arrested. Trial. Five let off. One charged with battery against a policeman. Judge said for many that flag symbolized everything contrary to American ideals. Lots of publicity for the cause."

551

"Nineteen thirty five? You were too young."

"And my parents would never have tolerated such a deviance from their norms of public protest, especially since the CP organized the action."

"That really doesn't answer the question, y'know."

"But it is my onliest answer."

Makepeace remained one of the rare exceptions to Schade's discomfort when talking to dogmatists because that bedrock of humor mediated the vehement expression of firmly held belief sufficiently to allow the conversation to continue or swerve into less controversial subjects. They most resembled two academics in the university club who refused to allow deeply held antagonistic opinions to darken the bright atmosphere of civilized discourse, though neither would have then agreed with this analogy. However, they liked each other. They agreed that boot camp represented the only true melting pot in the United States despite the opinions of certain blinkered academics and thoughtless patriotic boosters. This period was for most of the men the only time in their lives they would hear the voices and tones of all the corners of America, where they would meet every conceivable type of American in every possible craft and profession from short order cooks to librarians, from truck drivers to plumbers, from university professors to shoe salesmen, from pimply adolescents with high-pitched Brooklyn accents just out of high school to forty year old cowboys whose mother tongue was Spanish ... Only here where the great varieties of citizens were forced by external circumstances to live and work together for the common good, could one find a true commingling of all the various strains that constituted the great American republic. "Yes, well, with one big exception of course: the army is still segregated." "Yes, there is that, isn't there?"

Their continued discussions of things American flowed logically from their two manifestly different positions on the subject of cultural nationalism. Makepeace viewed the world and its unpredictable behavior from the point of view of a considered and deeply implanted patriotism. He unhesitatingly believed in his personal responsibility for defending and protecting the source of his patriotism, which a competing ideology threatened with obliteration. No intellectual argument could dent the security of his loyalty to his definition of his country's interests and safety.

Schade did not possess such an emotional and mental fortress of patriotic faith and belief: his political beliefs denied capitalism the properties of righteousness and superiority, and his divided cultural heritage precluded a rock hard submission to the icons of either German or American cultural systems. Unsurprisingly, then, despite his earlier New York writing in English, he had not yet decided in which language to write his serious works in the future.

These differences informed their persistent talk about the possibilities of that mythic leviathan, the Great American Novel. Less a rational discussion than a series of fragmented statements and questions posing examples for the title Great American Novel, which they then examined briefly before moving on to the next. It gradually became clear to them that they would never agree on one book deserving of the title and that it did not matter because the conversation itself became its own justification. They simply enjoyed themselves too much to want to achieve a resolution of the question.

Schade sipped from the surprisingly unwatered whiskey at The Edge Bar and fired another cigarette. "All the good writers are trying to write the Great American

Novel. But what exile whose native language isn't even English could hope to achieve it. How many Conrads can there be? I doubt I could be a contender, even though I might write in English. My roots are too ambiguous not to preclude my entering the race with any chance of winning, placing, or showing up at all. But who knows? Despite the handicaps it might be possible. I do practice a lot."

"Try simplifying your language," Monday suggested helpfully.

"It's the notion of the novel as containing responsibility and morality, not the style. The requirement is quite difficult to comply with, but the necessity of doing so is incontrovertible. The writer has to be serious about a serious enterprise, even though huge elements of it may be comedy. The work has to approach the totality of the society, even if symbolically. But it can't preach. It has to describe reality. In a non-realistic manner, perhaps, but reality must be at its core."

Eden the Perfect Bartender stopped in front of them and leaned through the smoke across the bar as if he had private information of a sensitive nature to impart to them. "Have you heard the writer Mithman is lecturing on Rilke and Goethe at the Centre des Beaux-Arts? Why they don't call it the Zentrum der schönen Künste is beyond my capability to grasp the essence of things so arcane."

"Is he lecturing in French?" asked Makepeace.

"No, English, I think."

"Well, then, there's your answer. Wonder what he did during the war?"

"Some meat and potatoes would be more appropriate these days than lectures on poetry," Schade said.

"Philistine!" Makepeace yelled. "*Kulturbanause*. What d'you think, EP?"

Eden looked thoughtful as he pushed the gray rag around the bar in ever tightening circles. "I am not privileged sufficiently with knowledge to answer the question with satisfaction, I fear."

"A perfect bartender is a perfect diplomat, eh?" Makepeace smiled.

"Something like that, I think, yes. Another drink perhaps?"

Makepeace turned to Schade and said, "It's food for the soul, pal, can't do without that."

"Hard to appreciate with your stomach growling and your mind full of dry sex and Bratwurst."

They smoked and drank in thought. Schade worried about his ability to move the English language about the page to make it say what he wanted it to say. He wondered if an American novel could be written in a language other than English. Makepeace repressed the guilt that from time to time gnawed at his conscience, berating him for paying insufficient attention to his original calling. He said firmly, "What American lit needs is a good Künstlerroman like the German has Novalis's great fragment *Heinrich von Ofterdingen* and the Irish have *Portrait of the Artist as a Young Man*."

"Novalis wrote that when Jefferson was president; the Republic is young."

"That's what I mean, we're still incompletely formed. American lit hasn't come of age as yet."

*

At some point in the meandering conversation Eden brought them plates of boiled potatoes and turnips seasoned with a batch of piquant green leaves of indeterminate origin, and chunks of fresh white bread purchased that morning from the black market supplier at the French officers' mess. Schade cut into the meal with the knife in his right hand, laid the knife down, picked up the fork and ate the cut portion, where after he repeated the procedure, the choppy ballet of hands and arms at which Europeans smiled with condescension: amusing but hardly efficient and uncomfortable to practice. Being left-handed, Makepeace ate by maintaining his cutting knife in the left hand and the fork in the right, thus satisfying at least half the traditional demand. "John, you choose the dumbest Americanisms to imitate."

"When amidst Amis, eat like Amis. Helps to feel part of the group and less a furriner."

"There's got to be better ways than that."

"But I don't really like fried chopped meat in a clump misnamed because there's not a bit of ham in them. Now Nathan's kosher hot dogs, that's something else again. Doesn't matter what hand you hold them in."

Later, as Eden began to clean up the detritus of the evening, Makepeace said in a clear demonstrative voice, "The Great American Novel must be written by an Indian, one of the first Americans."

Schade looked askance. "Is there such a book?"

"Not yet. They've all been written by white eyes and palefaces. But someday it will be."

"Maybe, but I won't hold my breath. All this talk about redskins and palefaces is exhausting. Literature is supposed to be exalting, or is it exulting. Perhaps both. And why just the Great American Novel? What about the Great European Novel, or the Great Oriental, or African Novel?"

"Never read a Jap novel, or Chink one for that matter. Do they write novels in Indochina in Indo Chinese? There's something about dreaming in a red chamber, dallying in the boudoir of the province governor or something. Has to do with pillows, as I recall. Chinese or maybe Japanese, but that hardly qualifies. Who knows anything about inscrutable oriental culture?"

"The Orientals maybe?"

"It's all opaque and barbarous. As for African literature, it doesn't exist. Savages don't create literature; oral traditions maybe, but the only stuff written about Africa's been done by white men or Arabs, and I'm not too sure about the Arabs. Some Frenchman wrote a book about Algeria, I think. Haven't read it. Now Europe, that's another story, especially if we exclude British novels."

"Maybe we just don't know enough about the other non-European literatures to say anything meaningful about them."

"They are either too decadent or too primitive to be able to create anything we'd understand as great literature. But think of *Tom Jones*."

"I'd rather think of *Tristram Shandy*. Shakespeare has to be considered here."

"Not at all. He wrote plays, if he wrote anything at all." Makepeace decided not to contain the deep-seated, well-founded, highly literary fart which steamed down his large intestine, gathering not at all fictional pressure as it rose to the height of its tightest peak and exploded through the tan cloth of his regulation G.I. uniform trousers into the fetid air of the Edge Bar in its latest Shanghai incarnation, adding olfactory weight to the heady atmosphere already diverting the minds of the wavering clientele. "And so we come by diverse and diverting routes to the nut of it all, eh? What makes literature literature?"

Schade pondered pontifically for a brief smoke-filled moment and finally pronounced, "Let us ask Schadow about this. He reads a lot of literature for a historian." When informed of this free-floating discussion,

Schadow smiled and said something to the effect that "Volleying names about like an unguided tennis ball is not a serious consideration of anybody's literature tradition, but it does make for harmless if inebriated fun for the participants." "Typical German academic, can't imagine fun is also a way to wisdom," Makepeace snarled in return.

* * * *

One of the more immediately pressing political matters they argued about was Reinhard Woller and his increasingly shrill public pronouncements of ideas and plans for the new Germany. Ironically, Woller agreed with Makepeace's hard line on the denazification issue, but the latter rejected Woller's adherence to the doctrines of Marx and Lenin as warped through the diseased mind of the great Marshal Stalin and his paranoid henchmen. ("How do you know they're paranoid? You have a direct connection to the Kremlin, do you." "Have you never heard about the show-trials, ever heard of the NKVD?") While Woller occasionally criticized individual aspects of Moscow's German policy, his loyalty to the fundamentals of the ideological twists and turns of the Russian policy makers remained steadfast, at least in public. Makepeace did not trust the young firebrand. "Besides, John, how can you take anyone seriously who suffers from an incurable case of terminal halitosis. It's absolutely foul. We ought to get him a ton of Sen-Sen, and even that would barely dent the poison." Schade, however, thought Woller interesting enough to meet him from time to time in the Möwe and elsewhere in spite of his wretched breath and dogmatic opinions. Woller possessed not one iota of humor and this fascinated Schade. The younger man's harsh coughing laugh adumbrated only sarcasm and a profound cynicism which his experience in the resistance and the camps partially explained, but was rare in a man only twenty-three who rigidly professed a belief in an essentially optimistic ideology. "Have you ever met a Red with a sense of humor?" Makepeace wildly pontificated after a meeting with Woller and several of his colleagues. "Especially a German Red?"

During one of their discussions Woller made a request of Schade which the latter for a brief instant thought might prove them wrong about his sense of humor. "Would it be possible for you to accompany me to the Femina?" The utter seriousness of the question caused Schade himself to smile. "I mean this very earnestly, Herr Schade."

"I can see that, but why on earth do you want to go to that joint? And why should I go with you?"

"I think I should see one of the signs of the bourgeoisie's collapse first hand. Perhaps I could learn something of value there. And with a uniformed American officer I would be treated differently from other Germans."

"No problem with consorting with the class enemy? And what about using that despicable Vitamin B?"

"What is more efficient in gathering intelligence than using the enemy's own system and customs, don't you think?"

"Did you obtain the approval of the politburo for this excursion?"

"That is hardly necessary, Lieutenant."

"That was a joke, Herr Woller."

Boltzmann denied Woller the status of Berliner. "The real Berliner," he muttered one evening in the newly installed bright lights of the Florian, the press bar where Kirshhof had met "his" German months before, "the true Berliner really loves the city but doesn't take it seriously - or didn't in the past, and if we ever reach a point of being able to live relatively normal lives again this healthy attitude will come back in all its cynical warmth. Even their blasphemy had a large dollop of humor in it. Do you know the little verse by Otto Reutter about the old Berliner who went to heaven and didn't think too much of it compared to the city. When Peter at the gate asked him if he thought the place delightful, the old guy answered 'Ah, I want to go home again; you've no idea what Berlin is like!' Young Woller would not understand such verses."

> *Kommt ein Berliner mal nach oben*
> *Zum Petrus vor das Himmelstor,*
> *Denn fragt ihn der: "Kommt dir die Gegend*
> *Hier oben nicht entzückend vor?"*
> *Doch dann schaut der Berliner nieder,*
> *Und flehend ruft er auf den Knien:*
> *"Ach, nach der Heimat möcht' ich wieder.*
> *Habt Ihr 'ne Ahnung von Berlin!"*[38]

Since Schade never took Woller to the Femina, he never knew if the energetic philosophy student ever visited that symbol and locus of bourgeois decadence to discover if something valuable awaited him there. By the end of the year Woller gave up his position with the Chamber of Creative Artists and started to write articles for the *Tagesspiegel* as the resident leftist chronicler of the city's cultural scene. ("They asked him to leave the Chamber," Makepeace related with amusement. "Even the

---

[38] Reutter's verses can be translated into prose as "When a Berliner ascends to Peter at heaven's gate, Peter asks him, 'Don't you find the neighborhood here delightful?' But the Berliner looks back down and pleadingly he calls out on bended knee: 'Ach, I'd like to go home again. You've no idea about Berlin!'"

commissars couldn't take his breath. No, actually they became too uncomfortable with his ranting about the new Germany. He won't last long at the *Tagesspiegel* either, it's too middle class and our influence there is too powerful.") Ulrich Kramer, employed now by the *Kurier* as its theater critic, remarked after reading several of Woller's pieces: "His style is a pleasure to read until he interrupts things with his ideological pronouncements. That in itself wouldn't be so bad, but then he starts writing like Marx or Hegel and the editors sweat blood to make the stuff comprehensible. He's learning, though, and much of what he writes is interesting. He sees things differently than most of us in the press, communist or not, of course. We need such differences after twelve years of one-sided propaganda. Sometimes I envy his insights."

In the end, Woller too much liked the association with the Communist Party policy makers and the high-ranking political officials in the city, whose main base remained the Soviet Sector. He argued continually with these apparatchiks, but over time his own judgments, tempered by argument and reality, folded into the evolving system, which demanded a depth of loyalty from him beyond his intelligence and this became the main tension in his life.

*****

It was Kramer who introduced Makepeace to Claudia Kaufmann shortly before she began working in Buchdow's theater near the Hallische Tor in Kreuzberg. The friendship between the theater critic and the American officer developed slowly as they occasionally met at various functions, then at cafés where they went to continue their discussions of state of culture in the city and the state of literature in general. Despite Makepeace's initial suspicion that Kramer leaned too comfortably toward the policies of the Soviets and their German "brothers," he found the critic's mind to be vigorously independent and conscientiously rational. The American also warmed to Kramer's project to re-write many of his theater reviews in an attempt to present truths he could not print when he wrote them. "Someday I'll publish them under the title *What I Dared Not Write: The Truth. Theater Criticism 1933-1944. Revised for Honesty*. Instead of the dishonest reviews the newspapers printed this will be honest criticism. Well, it's nice to think this will be possible. I've already begun the revisions. And I could use some sheets of paper. I'll submit the revisions as a supplement to my denazification file." Kramer's short barking laugh shot into the air. "By then you won't need them," Makepeace said, opening a copy of the *Berliner Zeitung* to the international news.

Kramer served the American as a source of information about the city and its history in addition to being a highly intelligent discussion partner. From his point of view, Kramer could not reconcile the other's appreciation for the broad spectrum of modern literature with his narrowly dogmatic opinions in politics and music: Makepeace was increasingly anti-communist in his political views and thought listening to most music of any period as a waste of time, but would occasionally find pleasure in the work of the Comedian Harmonists, Artie Shaw and Igor Stravinsky. Kramer considered himself a liberal in politics and a conservative in music: musical works composed after the end of the 19th century he thought did not deserve the name since they resulted in nothing more than cacophony. "Dissonance does not soothe, nor does it lead to a productive use of the mind when listening to it. This primitive noise and its counterpart, abstract art, are indications of a debased civilization which cannot be supported by anyone concerned with the development of man's mind."

"Are you calling this degenerate art and music?"

"Not in the same sense as the nazis, but I do believe they are developing in the wrong direction. And no, I do *not* think they should be forbidden. That is a ridiculous notion that never works, as the nazis discovered to their dismay and our Schadenfreude. Banning things only calls attention to them."

So their friendship skated over the thin ice of opposing dogmas which added a certain edginess to their discussions. As Kramer became more comfortable and thus open with his American friend, as it became clear to them that friendship could indeed exist between them, their talks took on the characteristics of a debate in which neither side tried to absolutely convince the other but rather attempted to so completely explain their own opinions that the other would abandon his own position. That neither of them gave any indication of being swayed by the other's arguments only added to the willingness of each to continue the debate.

As leaden clouds choked the sky over the city and the air crisped into brisk points of late autumn wind gusts, Makepeace stopped briefly in Kramer's office one afternoon to make a further point in their floating roundtable. Claudia Kaufmann and the critic stood in the narrow room talking as Makepeace came to the door. Kramer had known Claudia before the war and had followed her career acclaiming her talent in print. A recent particularly lavish review of her performance at the Schiffbauerdamm theater had moved her to thank him personally for this attention. Their conversation ended as Makepeace joined them. Startled at the acute reality of his vision of the woman in the rain, he offered to drive her whatever her destination. During the short ride in the Opel sedan, Makepeace sped through the stages of acquaintance and burgeoning intimacy of friendship to the plateau of infatuation, telescoping periods of development usually requiring weeks or months into a brief forty-five minutes. When he left her at the theater she had totally beguiled him with her rare combination of self-possession, detachment, and ease, which overlay the aura of sexuality she unsuccessfully attempted to hide. She only nibbled at her fingernails once during the ride; Makepeace with great effort resisted the urge to rattle his bracelet. He began attending theater performances all over the city to be able to compare her abilities with others on the stage and arranged to be at social events he thought she might attend. When it became obvious that she rarely went to such public receptions or appeared at the parties her colleagues organized, he brashly asked her to dinner.

  The relaxation of the non-fraternization edicts altered the contours of German-Allied social relationships as official policy evolved into something more akin to the real and the possible. Thus Makepeace risked no such scene as caused by Ogilvy Vasart and the Countess many months earlier when he took Claudia for a drink at the Harnack House, the former home of the Kaiser Wilhelm scientific institute requisitioned by the Americans as an officers' club. A few eyebrows lifted slightly when they walked into the bar, but Makepeace's visible pleasure at being with her and her own equipoise diminished her squeamishness almost to the point where she could relax and enjoy his company in that place. "Next time we'll go to The Edge Bar. They've fixed it up quite a bit recently." Makepeace was no fool and she appreciated his being that perceptive.

Then they went to a small, dimly-lit restaurant in the Werbellinstrasse near the Neuköln Rathaus which the black market supplied with food and drink as well as coal pilfered from the stores of the occupying powers. No sign identified the restaurant known as the Weisser Schwann to those few who held memberships and dollars or Swiss francs. Inside, the decor might have been called "postwar wreck," but the cook prepared fine if simple dishes and the wine was drinkable if expensive, and candles cast a light and shadow play which offered privacy for the diners amidst the smells of melting wax, roasted meats, and American cigarettes. A shabby, but under the circumstances romantic rendezvous with the vague atmosphere of danger to stimulate the sensuous appetites. Claudia found it delightful and, of course, thoroughly enjoyed the meal of lightly salted marinated herring served with a glass of rum of only a slightly suspicious provenance and freshly baked brown bread, grilled steak and fried potatoes with which they drank a well-preserved 1934 Bad Durkheimer red. "No real vegetables or fruit, and the Germans refuse to learn how to do a steak without grilling it to death, but on the whole, not bad, especially after I threatened the chef with reopening his denazification process if the beef showed up at the table gray all the way through."

"Listen, please," she said with a smile as they sat after dinner drinking coffee from true brown beans and sipping from Ogilvy Vasart's ubiquitous silver flask that he had donated to his friends in his hasty departure for Vienna. "We must understand each other. I don't plan to sleep with you in return for decent food and a warm restaurant. There's more of that available as time goes on. If we are going to be friends, it must be on a different basis. It's not that I don't like you or think it wouldn't be fun, but I won't submit myself to that kind of affair, not under these circumstances. It is too demeaning."

"That is not necessary. Perhaps things will change, perhaps not. Let's see what happens."

So they met when the demands of their professions allowed them time and discovered they could slake each other's mental if not physical needs: he received from her knowledge of the city and life during the nazi years from a vantage point he could not have gotten elsewhere and she received from him knowledge of the nations which were shaping and changing the future of the city and its inhabitants. Given his propensity for seeing the caustic possibilities of comedy in life's twists and turns they also laughed a great deal: it gave him a thrilling satisfaction to watch her shake her head and break the neutral set of her features with a smile. For her part she found this increasingly easier to do as she came to know him better: she lost none of her self-control in laughing at his witticisms and she felt increasingly relaxed, less threatened in his presence. They spoke in German inserting occasional English words and phrases when Makepeace could not find the equivalent in her tongue, talking with a vague sense of unease about the future and with some wistfulness of the present, but with a growing comfortableness in each other's company. Neither escaped from the sexual attraction that grew in both of them, but they fended it off with strength of will and mental effort. The image of her in the rain, head arched back, hands crushing her breasts, became sharper and clearer, bedeviling his senses as often as he evoked it in his mind.

After a while, both of them realized that their physical coupling could not be avoided if they continued to develop the emotional and intellectual intimacy which shaped their affair, but neither wished to consciously accept this realization: she continued to refuse to add herself to the number of the city's women in the beds of the occupying victors and he continued to respect her refusal. Since he decided to remain in the city as a civilian employee of military government after his duty tour ended, he did not feel the cloying pressure to argue the point with her: he had time to wait upon events.

But when she said to him: "You are laying siege to me whether you want to or not," he recognized the truth of the statement. "Do you feel besieged?" "A little, but I think it only human to feel some satisfaction in that, don't you? Surely there would be something wrong if I didn't feel it." Probability thus gradually gave way to inevitability as their feelings for each other extended beyond the original impetus that brought them together. Still, as the days turned colder and grayer and the air began to snap in their noses and water their eyes, they maintained the refusals, even making whimsical jokes about their positions. The attribute that allowed them to be in each other's presence in a flow of enveloping intimacy, dependence and desire was their capacity for laughter. Their relationship lacked the heavy drag of neurosis and labyrinthine emotional wrangling that occluded the minds and hearts of Gisela and Schade. Thus they were able to dive ever more deeply into each other's beings without disturbing the superficial equilibrium of their natures. What they constructed together was free of doubt because they offered the depths of their personalities in small increments, testing the responses cautiously before proceeding further along the chain of binding involvement. Their concrescence had the characteristics of organic growth and while they convinced themselves they could control the speed of development by intellectual effort, it was beyond the power of their minds to determine the final shape of their affair. They accepted the fact that events might interfere with the progression of links they traveled in that chain, but assumed they held destiny in their own hands.

Schade professed to be surprised by the affair. "Consorting with the enemy! I would hardly have believed it of you, Bill. Are you sure she's been thoroughly vetted? Did you check her *Fragebogen*? Think of all the American women around here who will be terribly put out, disgruntled in fact, maybe even downright jealous. Hmmm...." But Marybeth Mullen, the American woman he knew best in Berlin, regarded him with sympathy. "Well, I'm not surprised. Love, even if it's foolish, doesn't have any restrictions on citizenship, does it? You may not call it love, but I see it. You're both very serious people, even you under that sarcastic front of yours. Some of my dormmates wouldn't agree, of course, but what do you care about them? Have on, Macduff! Or whatever that saying is."

* * * *

The information regarding Gisela's father came transmitted in a curiously incomplete form, but Schade found nothing errant in this because the confusions of the war's end still maintained a nebulous but effective grip on many aspects of life in Europe. A letter took fourteen days to reach Munich from Berlin, if it arrived at all. To obtain a permit to travel by inter-zonal train to the American or British zones from the city required four weeks of paperwork and visits to various Allied and German offices. Little wonder that much of the population suffered from island fever. The banker had survived the last months of the war physically intact barring a considerable loss of weight and a ruined digestive system, in part as a result of the food he ate during his sojourn in an American prison camp for lesser VIPs considered to be jailable nazis nonetheless. The tall, sandy-haired CIC Captain Feldman with whom Makepeace had argued over Boltzmann's clearance and who conducted many of the background investigations for Information Control appeared one morning in Schade's office. After ascertaining that Albrechtsburg was in fact the object of Schade's interest, the Texan leaned back and puffed his cigar with an erotic pleasure.

"One of my colleagues in Munich who talked to you on the phone asked me to pass on the gen about this fellow. He said to tell you that this is the true gen as far as he knows. We've got the guy at a camp near Bad Tölz for the nazi financial leaders. Something like the holding pens we've got here, but bigger I guess. Anyway, he's there, or was. They kept him in the pen until they squeezed him dry. He cooperated and they let him go. He gave Berlin as his address, so they think he's on his way. Could get here any time now. That's it. You know, these Germans certainly knew how to import the best cigars, Havana-Havanas straight from the guest room at Göring's apartment, nothing better. Puff, puff. So long for now." The gangly captain disappeared in a tall Texas-sized cloud of blue-gray smoke while the telephone on Schade's desk shrilly demanded attention and the list of appointments on his calendar crawled across his blotter to anchor him to the uncomfortable chair for the next several hours.

When he finally got away, cursing the general lack of telephone connections in the city, he had to search for her, racing in the Opel to her room, then to the Schlossparktheater in Lichterfelde where he found her skipping rope backstage to keep warm between scenes, her ever longer blonde hair swinging about her head. Quickly he told her what little he knew and they thought of places where the elder Albrechtsburg would possibly go upon arrival in the city. The family house in Weissensee lay in ruins, but he had left Berlin before Soviet artillery leveled it. Neighbors would offer him room if he asked, but he might head for the Kronauers or to other friends or former colleagues who possessed livable quarters. "The only thing to do is let them know he's on the way. They'll tell him where you are when he gets here." Schade's advice did nothing to lessen the excited frustration she felt, but there was little else they could do. If he saw one of the advertisements for the play in the newspapers or on the hoardings around the city, he would look for her at the theater in any case.

The visibly ill banker, reduced by eighty pounds to just over fifty kilograms, arrived on a wooden bench in a frigid passenger train car filled with travelers as cold, hungry, and exhausted as himself. Shocked at the destruction of the city, but not surprised that his house no longer existed except as an imploded pile of wet plaster and stone, he made his way by foot and streetcar to the Kronauers, where Mathilde Kronauer gave him a bowl of warm broth with pieces of frankfurter sausage and hot ersatz coffee in addition to the assurance that his daughter had survived the catastrophic early end of the Thousand Year Reich. "*Dankeschön*, Mathilde," he said in a tone flattened by fatigue and the resigned acceptance of loss. "That makes me feel much better. Not knowing is worse than anything else. I'll sleep if I may. Please wake me when Helmuth comes home. We have much to talk about. Can you get word to Gisela?" His eyes closed before he finished the last sentence; relief drained the little energy left in his body and his mind closed down. Mathilde Kronauer crossed the street to a villa in which an American colonel and his newly arrived family lived. They had a telephone that worked with some regularity with which she called Schade's office, trying unsuccessfully to banish the animosity from her voice because she loathed him for her own reasons he did not completely understand. "Herr Schade, Axel Albrechtsburg has arrived."

Axel Albrechtsburg had spent the greater part of his adult life dealing with people whose materialism he detested and whose philistinism he abhorred. That he achieved great success in a business choked with such people was due to his ability to project an image of detached charm and concern for others' financial gain, and a capacity for hard work and toughness in negotiating with his fellow financiers. This he clothed in a graceful articulateness of language, a wealth of functional expertise, and a sympathetic demeanor, which hid his contempt for most of those with whom his profession required he meet. This carefully nurtured detachment allowed him to exhibit a modicum of affability when he met Schade a week after his arrival in the city. His months of incarceration in the prison camp did not increase his meager supply of tolerance for the Americans, and to his hostility toward them caused by his country's defeat, he shared Mathilde Kronauer's opinion regarding those émigrés who returned to Germany in the uniform of the enemy. This and his instant distaste for the idea of his beloved if difficult daughter "fraternizing" with one of the occupiers, exacerbated by the fact that he was a "former" German, made it hard for him to accept Schade as anything other than another one of those from whom he must camouflage his true emotions and thoughts, whose presence he must endure for a longer or shorter periods of time, preferably of course the latter.

(One night, slightly tipsy from bourbon whiskey, Schadow smiled at Schade and said, "You would be surprised how many Germans devoutly hoped the non-fraternization edict would be rigorously enforced. Even anti-nazis tasted ashes in their mouths at the thought of dealing with those who had just beaten the shit out of them - I mean who had just decisively defeated them. Yes. Nationalism in the older generation is still a virulent bacillus, you see, and it does not *look* good to appear to be kowtowing to one's cultural inferiors.")

Although Albrechtsburg did not fundamentally alter his opinion of his daughter's relationship with Schade, he possessed sufficient insight to recognize that they were exhausting each other, that the affair could not last, and that her ferocious ambition would turn any emotional damage she might suffer into another form of her art. That Schade might be severely bruised or worse by the affair never entered his mind. No warmth of friendship developed between them, but a certain neutral acquiescence in each other's existence tentatively grew on the almost barren soil of their common attachment to Gisela and one day, on finding themselves in the Kronauer's chilly living room, the banker explained his internment in Bad Tölz, or at least as much of the story as he thought Schade should know.

Sitting stiffly erect, one leg draped over the other, dressed in an elegantly cut but frayed suit too large for his shrunken figure, Albrechtsburg absently smoked an English cigarette, occasionally touching the scar on his right cheek. "Gisela has told me of your efforts to discover my whereabouts and I wish to thank you for that. It eased her mind, I think, just to know something was being done about it."

"I had nothing to do with your release."

"That is immaterial. The effect on my daughter of your attempt to locate me was positive, that is the important thing. Did your colleagues explain my situation? No?

Then let me briefly tell you something about it. You deserve that at least.

"I left Berlin when it became clear to many of us that total defeat might be postponed for a month or two, but it was inevitable. Some held out the foolish hope of joining forces with the western Allies against the Russians, but those of us with any sense knew that was out of the question. My departure was prompted by two considerations, one official, one not. In fact, the latter might have been considered traitorous in those paranoid days. My official mission involved the transport of a large sum of counterfeit foreign currency that had been printed for various reasons years earlier. Someone's grandiose idea of how to destroy the stability of the enemy's economy. It might have worked, I suppose, but by then, of course, the time had passed. In fact, the idea of moving the stuff to Bavaria had little to recommend it at all. Rationality in government and the party was at a premium then and could rarely be found anywhere in the city. I certainly would not have involved myself with such stupidity had the mission not given me the opportunity to do other things, the other non-official reason for making such a hazardous trip. You see, I wished to be captured by the Americans, not the Russians or the others who suffered so much from our war. I had information for the Americans.

"While I was not a government official, my bank dealt regularly with the Finance Ministry and I had a number of friends who held high positions there. A small group of us met whenever our schedules allowed to discuss mutual problems, the war, and increasingly, what would happen to the country afterward, when we had been defeated. We had no way of knowing what plans the Allies had for us in any detail, of course, but rumors about such things as the Morgenthau plan for pastoralizing Germany, an absurd idea under any circumstances, and the dismantling of industry, and so on, did filter through to us from the neutral countries. Regardless of any such plans, and assuming more intelligent opinions would prevail, at least in the higher levels of the American government, some kind of stable currency system would have to be established. Our small group began to make plans toward this end, various options that could stabilize the economy and prevent a repetition of what happened after the last war. These we planned on presenting to the Allies. We were being naive, I suppose, but we did not realize that at the time. When we discovered that the counterfeit currency was being shipped, it was arranged that I and one of my colleagues would accompany the shipment and see to its proper disposition. This would also give us the chance to meet with like-minded men concerned with financial matters and continue our planning.

"As you may imagine, events overtook our deliberations and in the confusion of the capture of Munich I was arrested. First, they sent me to a jail in Augsburg, a city where I have only ever found happiness when leaving it. This experience did not alter my opinion. Some perverse quirk in my nature refused to let me destroy my identification papers, especially my party book. Stupid perhaps, since my membership meant nothing and I was never an official of the government. After a week they moved me to the Bad Tölz prison. Finally, after a great deal of tedious interrogation I was brought before an officer who had been a banker in Chicago in civilian life. He is now a high official in your military government finance department. This man had the foresight to see that men of my position could be of assistance to both the occupation forces and the new Germany at the same time. It necessitated some time before we reached an agreement of sorts, with the details of which I will not bore you. Suffice it to say that I had certain information which this man's department needed, information I was quite willing to give in return for my being denazified quickly and sent back to Berlin where I could be of help in creating the new financial structure. In this way we would all benefit from whatever talents I possess. I also requested that my daughter be protected as far as possible during the denazification process. That, at least, seems to have worked out without undue problems. I understand you had something to do with that as well, for which I thank you.

"The whole process took a great deal of time and the interrogators were quite Germanic in their industriousness and thoroughness. They extracted information from me I had long since forgotten. It was often not very pleasant, but on the whole I suppose it could have been much worse. Now I understand I must formally go through the entire business again here. Very tiresome, Lieutenant. The standards of judgment seem to change from location to location. I will not be able to return to the bank for a while, or what remains of it, but I will consult with city officials and the appropriate committees in the Kommandantura when the paperwork is completed. I thought you should at least be informed of that much." Albrechtsburg seemed to age in a very gradual but constant evolving process, which made him paler than before he began his narrative. He sank back into the upholstered chair and Schade thought he might disappear altogether. Clearly the banker suffered from various forms of physical debilitation, which exhausted him and fed tremors into his hands. His fingernails curved downward at their ends, which his old friend Hans-Manfred Rau had assured him in a letter from a Texas prisoner of war camp several years ago was a sure sign of someone suffering from tuberculosis.

Schade thanked the ailing Albrechtsburg for the information, but before the conversation could develop any elaboration the others returned to the house. Schade doubted that the man had given him a complete account of his experience, or that the story he had told was accurate, but this did not unduly disturb him. The banker obviously knew how to ingratiate himself with the new powers and possessed something of value to offer them. The younger man coldly appreciated the other's visible struggle to be formally correct with him. Albrechtsburg's condescending arrogance annoyed him, but he smiled in his mind's eye at the thought that the older man would quickly learn a lesson in humility from those with whom he would be working, both Allied and Berlin officials, who would not tolerate such attitudes from anyone as compromised as this man. Schade allowed himself a muted sense of satisfaction that compensated for the anger he felt toward the man who would no doubt at some point once again stride through the halls of power after making himself invaluable to the new establishment.

On his way out he spoke briefly with Kronauer to whom he passed on a letter from his father, the specific contents of which he did not know; what he did know was that the subject revolved around plans for the reconstruction of the country, about which the New York exiles and their counterparts in Berlin differed considerably. After a few private words with Gisela and a fleeting kiss (the touch of a cool transient breeze on a warm afternoon), he left to return to his office and the increasing number of forms requiring completion. He had seen the knowledge of their breakup in her eyes, although they had not spoken of it.

* * * *

Mathilde Kronauer's reproach against those Germans who left the country after Hitler's appointment as chancellor and the formation of the right-wing coalition government in January 1933 boiled in Schade's mind, nagging at his conscience, forcing him to contemplate his way through the labyrinth of the subject. The clash between the exiles and the so-called inner emigration was inevitable after the defeat of nazi Germany and fascist Italy; the only unknown factor was the form in which the conflict would be carried out. Although he had been too young to participate in his parent's decision to emigrate, he felt Mathilde Kronauer had personally attacked him as well as the more general phenomenon. If politeness restrained his response at her table, no such obstacle blocked his mental processes as he wrestled yet again with the problem.

On the level of public discussion the issue had become controversial in an oblique way, buried in the argument over the return of some of the well-known exiles to their former homeland. Now as the debate in Germany expanded, the issue had been reduced to two contradictory formulations. One openly requested the exiles' return to help reconstruct the nation and present the necessity of that reconstruction to the world; the opposing view questioned whether the exiles could contribute anything valid to reconstruction because they had perforce become foreigners with no experience in that Germany upon whose ruins the nation had to be rebuilt. The implication was that they had ceased to be true Germans and should have no say in the matter because they had not experienced the tragedy as Germans in their own country, much as Mathilde Kronauer expressed it.

The exiles themselves never doubted that the sneering brown-shirted creatures with torches and whips in their fists had expelled German culture from the nation; the soul of the true Germany fled reluctantly across its borders by night and fog taking the traditions of German humanism and poetry with it -- the other alternatives: deathly silence, moral complicity, the concentration camps, atrophy, and for many sure torture and death, as the terrible examples of the poet Erich Mühsam and the journalist Carl von Ossietsky clearly proved. The image of the bonfires in the streets of the university towns into which the "new Germany" happily tossed German and European culture never left the inner eye of the exiles scattered throughout the world. They also remembered the exiled poet Heinrich Heine's prophetic words, "Where they burn books, in the end they also burn people." For the most part, they agreed with Thomas Mann that the books allowed to be published in Germany during the nazi era were less than worthless and impossible to hold in one's hand: they stank of blood, ignominy, and desecration.

Had he not shied away from an open confrontation with Mathilde Kronauer, Schade could have responded to the egocentric ignorance of the exiles' lives held by most Germans who did not experience the tribulations of a forced removal from the homeland. He had stated his opinion on many occasions, on some of which he received a sympathetic hearing, on others not. "It wasn't easy for us either, you know," he always said, although he personally suffered little in comparison with the older exiles including his parents. "You think we lived in the land of roses and sunshine, streets in Harlem made of gold, dollar bills growing on the bushes of Central Park for everyone to pick. Look at the suicide rate. We went into exile because the alternative was jail or the KZ and probably being killed;

definitely being killed if we were Jewish. And to what did we flee? Men selling apples on the street corners, women selling themselves, misery on the streets, no work available, after we got there, wherever there was. And before we got there wherever that was? Poverty, gray days of not knowing where your next meal would come from, sleazy cheap hotels where the permanent guests were big cockroaches who resented our intruding, shoddy clothing and no soap to wash our stinking bodies, in whatever country we could find to take us in Europe while we desperately tried to gather the necessary papers and visas and affidavits, running from country to country, consulate to consulate, battered by dozens of bureaucratic systems that seemed designed to specifically keep us from being saved. The crushing hopelessness and daily despairing until some miracle blessed the fortunate, the lucky among us with the right number of papers and a ship's ticket to somewhere away from Europe which for us had become worse than a prison, more like an inescapable morgue. It got worse after September 1939 when the Germans marched in one safe haven after the other until it became impossible to get out and we went underground, a way of life none of us was prepared for and most of us did not survive.

"But those of us who did get out, yes, most of us survived one way or the other. We did not go to prison, no, and our lives were certainly not easy but we didn't have to fear the Gestapo with every breath, but most who stayed didn't either if they behaved, did they? They had to fear the war and dying or being maimed and the humiliation of a well-deserved defeat.

"But the most important thing about the exiles is that we kept the real cultural heritage alive and untainted, and we moved it along its true lines of development, we kept it vital, we saved it from degradation and for a post-nazi Germany. We thought the rebuilding would be done upon this fundament because it was that German culture not perverted by the nazis. We were rather naive I now think; we didn't calculate the resistance to us and our return by those who remained, anti-nazi or indifferent. The lack of knowledge about our exile lives and the distorted views of our experiences in exile are making the reconstruction more difficult in ways we did not consider seriously enough. So we have to allow the Germans to learn about these phenomena, perhaps even before we conduct any 're-education' programs the Allies, at least the Americans, are so anxious to begin."

In New York in 1942, shortly after he read of Stefan Zweig's suicide in Brazil, Schade began to compile a list of those members of the exiled German intelligentsia who died in exile, either by suicide or murder or natural causes (which of course under the circumstances were not natural at all). Circumstances forced him to expand the list to include those murdered in Germany, information about all of which he noted on individual cards, which he maintained in scrupulous alphabetical order. While he attempted to maintain a scholarly distance between himself and his material, his manner of presenting the facts as he discovered them betrayed the inadequate attempt at academic objectivity. He considered his quest as an effort to identify at least some of the victims to ensure that they would not be forgotten as the march of history chugged on, overriding the past with the necessities of the present and the perceived requirements of the future. The list constituted his homage to those whose culture had been violently ripped from their hearts and minds while their bodies suffered the pains of hunger and deprivation of sleep and language, and finally to the ultimate indignity of death in forced exile from all they considered valuable in their homelands.

He considered it incomplete and open ended because the list continued to expand as he learned about additional men and women who fell within one or another of his categories, and he filled in each entry with new information as he gathered it. The list, he realized, was sadly far from complete. He gradually realized that the compiling of the list became an obsession, and that after the conversation with Mathilde Kronauer he added the list to his arsenal of arguments on the question of the role of the exiles in the postwar reconstruction of the nation. (Inevitably the fate of the cultural figures who did not go into exile also engaged his curiosity, but not obsessively. Shortly after arriving in Berlin, he'd asked Yuri Tamirov if he knew anything about Roma Bahn. "Nothing, Lieutenant, but I can certainly find out and inform you of the results of the investigation. As a friendly gesture among Allies." "She played Polly in the first *Dreigroschenoper*." "I am aware of that, Lieutenant, thank you. She also appeared in Georg Kaiser's *Europa* with the unfortunate Heinrich George. Do you remember the year? The piece is not very well known," the Russian said with a grin. "Ah, no, before my time." "Mine also, but I believe it was 1920." Later, Tamirov provided Schade with some information about several Germans who disappeared in the purges of the late 1930s and early in the war. "Strictly on the quiet, Lieutenant, on the very quiet, *nicht wahr*?")

Some of Schade's facts may not have been entirely accurate, but his passion drove him to continually add to the collection of index cards, increasing the volume of his memorial to the dead. These meager facts, the bare skeletons of full, rich lives so barbarously ended before their times, gnawed at his mind, demanding enrichment, expansion, demanding that their memory at least be remembered in some form beyond the minds of their families and friends. He did not know everything, but he knew enough to speculate on the immensity of the tragedy his tattered index cards memorialized. He realized that the list would never be finished: too many exiles lived and died in obscurity. Was it his task to compile the complete list? He would have to devote the rest of his life to the project. The thought depressed him: someone else would have to do it. To be able to do anything coherent with the names, he limited the list in general to those related in one way or another to writing, literature, and the visual arts.

The sheer weight of the names of those exemplars of German culture dead in exile always astonished and depressed him. He remembered his personal hero, Ernst Toller, the dazzling Cassandra of exile, a deeply contradictory personality, lonely and overly sensitive (when someone asked him why he lived in an expensive hotel near Columbus Circle in New York City, he snapped, "*Ich muß doch eine gute Adresse haben, nicht wahr?*"), as if having a good address would benefit his fundraising activities. The individualist revolutionary who spent five years in prison for his participation in the doomed, almost farcical Munich Soviet Republic in 1919 (the writer as Minister of Culture!), the passionate artist whose expressionist plays not only mirrored the *Zeitgeist* of the 1920s darker side, but also brought him success if not satisfaction, and in exile, the brilliant speaker in German and English at countless congresses and fund-raising meetings for the Spanish Loyalists, for those fleeing from fascism's creeping spiritual death and the very real possibility of physical extinction.

No one doubted the power of Toller's eloquence when he spoke of his murdered friends and colleagues in

Germany and Austria. Schade heard him speak on many occasions in Manhattan and came to revere and trust him with a teenager's enthusiasm. From time to time he sat in on meetings with the older man and talked with him at the wearying receptions held to raise funds. The younger man felt himself drawn in to the other's spiritual aura and thought of him as a heroic figure.

Shortly before the end, in mid-May with the war less than four months away, he traveled to Washington with an international delegation of anti-fascist writers who had attended the meetings of the PEN Club in New York during the World's Fair. Mrs. Roosevelt had invited them to lunch at the White House. Klaus Mann told Schade later that Toller had made a visible effort to wrench himself out of a depression into which he periodically fell, and that he actually seemed rather happy or at least animated, particularly after a brief meeting with the president and a tour of the building led by the First Lady. During a visit to Arlington National Cemetery and a reception for the delegation at the house of the owners of the *Washington Post*, he continued to participate in the conversation in a witty and lively manner. But on the train back to New York that night the black depression returned to shroud his mind and he could not sleep.

Between his return to the city and ten days later when he hanged himself in his hotel room, young Schade brought him an envelope full of money his mother's organization had raised to help those trapped in the cities of Europe, desperate prisoners of every country's administrative procedures which required feedings of endless streams of paper and forms and expensive stamps to maintain a bare minimum of hope for a transit visa or residence permit. Those large expressive eyes that burned with some inner glow when he spoke at meetings now sat like lumps of coal in his skull, dulled and deep. In the oppressive humid heat of early summer, the man appeared exhausted, as if life had already left his body and only concentrated will power kept him going. His blank expression never altered during Schade's brief visit; his depression dragged him into an endless tunnel of blackness into which an increasingly dimming light barely penetrated. His bags, packed days ahead of time for a trip to England, stood scattered haphazardly around the room awaiting departure. His actress wife had left him and was then in Hollywood working and worrying about him, but Schade did not know this at the time.

    The older man sat on the bed and looked through Schade into a future he could not describe. In an absent-minded tone he thanked the young man for the contribution but did not ask him to sit down, and added that it was too late to help too many who would never make it out of hell. Schade felt himself tumbling into a void, but he struggled to hide his confusion: this was not the man he had admired for his passionate commitment, and lightning energy on the podium. Later Schade came to understand, but at the time his immaturity stood in the way of his comprehension. After a stumbling attempt to express his continued admiration for Toller's work and hope for its success, he left the writer's room in flushed embarrassment. He never learned exactly what had extinguished the fire, and he came to doubt that Toller could have expressed it in any way comprehensible to another. Several days before his trip to England, they found his body at midday hanging by his own belt in the hotel room in a city that had remained alien to him. Schade and his mother went to the funeral along with the great figures of German, American and Spanish literature and assorted hangers-on, each claiming to have been the last to see the writer alive, to have lent him money, or bought him dinner. Toller might have appreciated the irony in the situation: during his lifetime he had never experienced such a grand amount of sympathy and comradeship. Schade remembered the proceedings as a grotesque farce: the corpse lay in an open coffin hardly recognizable because they had died his hair and put rouge on his cheeks and lips. Schade believed Toller would not have appreciated this travesty.

Schade absorbed Toller's death as a personal insult, an affront to his amour propre, for he refused to understand how this man whom he considered so important to the cause and whom he so admired could leave him so completely. Long after the younger man had rejected this self-defensive response, he remained unable to totally comprehend that act of self-annihilation Toller performed in that desolate hotel room. Schade believed that on the day he could say, "Herr Toller, now I understand why you did this," on that day he would be able to consider himself a fully formed adult. Until then the formation of his life would remain incomplete.

Since the Gestapo could not readily dig their venomous claws into Toller while he was in New York, Schade and his friends simply assumed he had private reasons for killing himself. Why would a courageous militant who had spent years in jail for revolutionary activity, written some of the great avant-garde works of the 1920s and a flowing elegiac memoir of his youth, then thrown himself into the hurleyburley of the anti-fascist movement, constantly on the move from one speaking tour to the next, raising funds and morale, how could this dashing, glamorous figure, who appeared so confident about his place in the universe, why would this man hang himself leaving the struggle unfinished?

"He simply could not take the life any longer," Schade's mother told him. "Perhaps a variety of secondary things caused it. Perhaps this was his way of sticking his tongue out at the world, a final form of revenge against a world that refuses to understand what is happening to it, a world in which he had completely lost faith. Last year Queens College took back an invitation for him to speak about 'Social Drama' because he was suspected of being a communist. How do you think that made him feel? Perhaps he was just exhausted."

"I don't think he had the right to hang himself." Schade stubbornly persisted. His mother turned to other matters, but later in Europe, Makepeace asked him: "Was it the hanging or the suicide that bothered you?" - a question he did not then choose to answer.

But what of those who remained in Germany? If the best did not suffer the terrible variations of torture with death often as a welcome release, they fell silent, and those who did continue to write produced mediocre work at best. What did Germans in Germany produce comparable to Heinrich Mann's *Henri Quatre*, Anna Segher's *Siebten Kreuz*, the novels of Hermann Broch and Alfred Döblin, Arnold Zweig's *Erziehung vor Verdun* or Thomas Mann's *Lotte in Weimar*? Germany's "inner emigration" had nothing to equal the work of the exiles, German culture existed outside the borders of the Reich during the nazi years, of this Schade had no doubt.

Mathilde Kronauer was right, he thought, at least in one sense: the experiences of the two Germanys had been different, both suffered in different ways, but both had suffered, and the Germany in Central Europe, the geographical Germany, continued to suffer. But this Germany stood before the dock as the greatest national criminal in human history. Mathilde Kronauer had not yet completely realized this, or thought it relevant to her argument. In responding to her attack, Schade could justifiably note that this Germany also had no understanding of what exile meant, no comprehension of the pain and often fatally profound despair at being ejected from one's homeland to wander stateless about the earth, hounded from one country to the next, unable to work or breathe freely. To be uprooted from one's homeland was a deeply traumatic experience for almost all the exiles, no matter where they settled, particularly so because they believed that the national culture they had been forced to leave was being systematically and deliberately destroyed from within. If the Germans were ever to become whole again, shriven and healed, they would have to understand this shattering experience. The quality of suffering was not the issue, Schade believed, but the very fact that the exiles had been deeply wounded in their patriotism and violently rejected by their national culture would have to be comprehended by those who remained, as would the fact that the exiles had taken the best of German tradition and culture with them. This would be hard to digest in the aftermath of total defeat, but Schade remained convinced it must be accomplished for Germany to have any spiritual or intellectual future.

At some point during his meditations on the subject a painful knot in his mind loosened and a sudden illumination grew in brightness and clarity. He found the answer to the question of the theme of his book: the experience of exile, expressed in a work of art capable of containing the vast complexities of the subject. In the modern novel, resplendent with all its multitudinous techniques and styles, he would bear witness to the sufferings, sacrifices and quiet heroism of the exiles. But not just that side, no, he would show the darker side of the exile experience: an exile is not ipso facto an admirable human being. The mean, soulless even criminal behavior of many exiles would also have to be shown. The loving father and husband, exhausted and filthy, who lied to the consular official in Lisbon about his friend and former colleague's past association with the German Communist Party ... there were, after all, only a limited number of visas available. The setting would be New York City, of course, the metropolis about which he knew most, the center of a large German exile community. He would show the rough-and-tumble of city life, the struggles of those with little material base for their lives to pay the rent and feed their hungry families, the wrenching fight to learn to live and succeed in remaking their lives in a foreign, often frightening environment, in an alien language. And he would show that so many of these very tormented people also continued the other struggle to defeat the barbarian usurpers of their culture and national spirit. This would be something new, something original: Others had written novels about the exiled and shunned, but they either hadn't been translated into English (Klaus Mann's *Der Vulkan*, Leon Feuchtwanger's *Exil*) or dealt only the exiles experience in Europe (Anna Seghers's *Transit* published in English in 1944).

How could he not have seen this earlier? He even briefly thought of this as being his contribution to the rejoining of the Germans' split psyche. He stood up from his desk and shuffled a few steps while whistling fragments of *How High the Moon*. Then he sat again, hands trembling slightly, he lit a cigarette and reached for paper and his fountain pen. The growing pile of notes had found a direction and a form.

Somewhere there's music

How faint the tune
Somewhere there's heaven
How high the moon

* * * *

He had sat with Schadow in a small café near the old man's room suffering the morning chill in the unheated space as winter slowly came upon the city like a great bear stalking its supper. The oily coffee remained in the cups untasted and Schade smoked one cigarette after another. They talked desultorily as if spending an hour or so relaxing after a leg of a journey to a destination they did not care to reach too soon. Schade had shown him the collection of dog-eared and battered index cards that comprised the "Ominum Gatherum" and the old man had swiftly read through them, then handed the pile back and folded his hands. Looking directly into Schade's eyes, he said, "Some of these unfortunate souls seem not to have died in exile, but here."

"They either had no chance to go when they wanted to or the Gestapo kidnapped them or they were turned over to the Germans, but it comes to the same thing."

"I expected you to say that they suffered as well here, as so many did."

"I don't deny the suffering of those in the so-called 'inner emigration,' but one cannot equate the two groups in terms of art and value. The nazis forced the best of German culture into a brutal exile."

"Or closed it down temporarily."

"That amounts to the same thing. It no longer existed here; it went elsewhere, and that's the tragedy of the whole thing. It will take generations to recuperate." Schade sounded more positive in his judgment than he had when talking to Mathilde Kronauer or his other German acquaintances.

Schadow decided not to pursue the question then. "Let me think about this some more and then we'll talk about it again. You know the Pestalozzistrasse? Yes, well, you know that Toller lived in Ernst Niekisch's apartment there after his release from prison, 1924 I think. Niekisch had been in prison with him for taking part in the Bavarian soviet republic, that deadly romantic enterprise. I met Toller at Niekisch's one afternoon. He did not appeal to me. Too much full of himself, a great 'ladies' man,' to use an Americanism."

"After four years in jail, one can sympathize with that."

"'One' could, perhaps; I could not. What are you going to do when you leave?"

Before his revelation, Schade had constantly asked himself the same question. He tended to think of it as a coiled serpent lying in his brain, striking at unexpected moments. He had too many half-formulated answers, all of them involving writing. His inability to settle on one or another caused him to repress the whole subject until the snake uncoiled and struck: the pain stung him anew into the flux of his indecision forcing a confrontation. "I have been thinking of writing a book," he had replied then. "It grows inside like a tumor, but I don't know yet whether it is benign or malignant."

"And the traditional subject for a young author? Autobiography? Suitably clothed of course."

"Of course. What else is there to begin with except potboilers? Do you know that English word? Very appropriate." But many months later, now that he had discovered a subject in which he could passionately believe, to which he could energetically and enthusiastically devote himself, the notion of a potboiler dissipated into the air like steam from a teakettle. In the house of fiction there are many writing desks, he thought, and the last 50 years had shown how the house could bear so many varied weights and shapes without collapsing under the pressures of the heterogeneity of styles and the electric fragmentation of the century's consciousness. He had no doubt, however, that autobiography would play a role in the fiction.

Unfortunately for Schade they never did find another occasion to discuss the matter of the "Ominum Gatherum."

* * * *

At the end of that first postwar winter, as its icy forces continued to assault the northern European plains, Schade received an invitation to attend a boar hunt organized by the Soviet political commissariat to belatedly celebrate the end of the war. Cynics among the western Allies wondered about the ethical situation of celebrating the end of shooting humans with an event involving the shooting of helpless animals, but few who received an invitation refused it.

Yuri Vladimirovich Tamirov officiously bustled into Schade's office one cold morning rubbing his hands together complaining about the weather. His steel-rimmed spectacles reflected the muted light of the room and his massive body overflowed the chair in front of Schade's desk. "This climate is mad, like Germans. No wonder they went insane. Neither cold nor warm, no real winter like in Soviet Union. *There* it is cold. Here everything is in between, ambiguous, eh? One cannot be comfortable in this city when one is accustomed to clear changes in the weather. There is a lack of definition here, don't you think, Lieutenant?"

Schade's relations with Tamirov had evolved into an arrangement of personalities that worked on the surface levels of their jobs, but rarely entered into the private aspects of their lives. He understood the Russian's bluff and boisterous character to be a facade behind which functioned a cold, analytical mind limited only by the ideological constraints the man accepted and, Schade thought, even welcomed. Schade possessed a natural reserve and propensity toward cautious thought before expressing himself on political matters. This hesitation, as most viewed it, stemmed from his lack of determined and programmatic political commitment beyond his strong leftist sympathies. Thus he was not at his conversational best in the presence of hard line dogmatists. This trait did not allow him the same forms of banter and joking by-play in conversation with Tamirov that the Russian enjoyed with Makepeace. ("He is, after all, a German: very serious fellow," as Tamirov explained to Makepeace.) Schade could also never be sure whether Tamirov's phrases hid meanings behind the banalities on the surface, whereas Makepeace simply assumed those hidden meanings and spoke to them from a position behind his own façade of jocular sarcasm. Consequently, Schade often responded with such hesitation and precision of language that Tamirov thoroughly enjoyed talking to him. He found Schade's intellection, the necessity to think about an issue from all sides before reaching a conclusion, amusing and indicative of western liberals for whom en masse he essentially felt the contempt of the committed ideologue. Nonetheless, he liked Schade in an unconsidered way and enjoyed discussing things other than job-related matters with him.

One early autumn afternoon as they waited for a meeting to begin, they discussed in a desultory fashion the effects of photography on how people perceive things they think they see. Schade mentioned the well-known image of Red Army soldiers raising the Soviet flag over the Reichstag during the final bloody fighting for the city. "That is certainly a great photograph; the spontaneity is almost palpable. The best images are those that are snapshots taken on the edge of the moment."

"Lieutenant, you are a fooling idealist who could get himself killed thinking that way. Comrade Khaldei posed that photograph and kept pressing the shutter button until he ran out of film. He even brought that with him from Moscow. He is one of our great photographers. Have you seen the one of the people in the bathing costumes lying in the sun amongst the rubble? Sevastapol, in May 1944. Someday people will think it is Berlin now. How important is Sevastapol? You see?"

"In any case, it *looks* spontaneous and that's what attracts people to it."

"Art and propaganda are both manufactured, Lieutenant. It is a wonder you ever even landed in North Africa. Such naïveté. How wonderful. How sweet. How deadly." Tamirov shook his head and laughed.

With a small smile, Schade retreated into a diplomatic silence.

Now, behind his glasses he observed Schade's discomfort, brief but palpable, with his opening gambit about the weather. What does he think I mean?

"Most of us are able to adjust to the changes in climate, I think. If not, we move to a more accommodating area."

"Nicely done, Lieutenant. Unfortunately I have no time at the moment for our usual thoughtful exchanges.

I've only stopped by to tell you that you are invited to our celebration." He placed a square buff envelope on the desk.

"I thought only the brass was asked to such events."

"The brass, hummm, odd word. But no, not only generals, Lieutenant, mostly generals and diplomats, true, but some of us lower ranks are included. Democratic, eh? What do you think? You will come?"

"I thank you for the invitation, Captain, that is kind of you. Certainly I will come if I can get the day off."

Tamirov smiled sagely. "That should be no problem for you. By the way, I am now major. Another reason to celebrate perhaps. You will find it interesting, I am sure. Have you ever hunted before?"

"Not for anything like wild boar."

"Ah, that is only the most dangerous part, for generals. For us there will be rabbits and smaller prey. That way everyone of importance is able to shoot something. Everyone leaves with satisfaction. Tactful, eh?"

Having elicited a burst of unfeigned laughter with this sally, Tamirov departed in a whirl of glittering eyeglasses and huge gray coattails, leaving Schade gnawing at the question as to why they had invited him, seeking as usual the motivations behind the obvious. One by one all the possible reasons flitted through his mind and out again like blackbirds fleeing a fox in the meadow. Finally, he lit a cigarette and vigorously blew smoke at the inkwell on his desk: what difference did it make? Perhaps they had an extra invitation. But where in this ravaged city, in which every warm-blooded thing not human that moved was scavenged for food, would they find rabbits?

On the appointed day he rose before dawn and hurried through his morning ablutions ritual wondering if he would be required to shoot anything and if so how well he would be able to do it. He had never shot anything before except targets at Coney Island and during basic training in that horrible Louisiana swamp (quaintly called a "bayou" by the natives, who in turn called themselves "Cajuns," a word that Schade discovered to be a corruption of "Arcadian," those French Canadians who emigrated on the long trek to southern Louisiana), where the Army did teach him to drive a motor vehicle, which previously he had no need to learn. Officer training school at Fort Benning, Georgia had taught him nothing about shooting, but a great deal about how whites of all social levels treated the Negroes. Perhaps he would not have to shoot at all, just sit in the appropriate place to think and freeze, or talk and freeze if he had a partner with a common language. If he had to shoot he would try to do it as cleanly and as quickly as possible and not feel bad about it. His only knowledge of game hunting came from that book about Africa Hemingway had written as an experiment during a time when his art dried up. Schade knew that reading about hunting surely was not the best way to learn to do it. But this did not overly concern him because in the future he would not be doing any further hunting of animals: unless the experience of this day changed his opinion, he would continue to have no interest in shooting animals with heavy caliber rifles. His interest in this particular event lay not in the hunting itself but in the circumstances surrounding it.

    He limited himself to one cup of hot bitter coffee and urinated just before leaving the building: the discomforts of peeing outside in freezing temperatures held little appeal for him. Then he walked swiftly several blocks to the street corner where some other officers gathered before driving to the rendezvous point at the Brandenburg Gate where the Russians planned to pick up their Allies and move them in a convoy to the forest southeast of the city. The broad pulsing winds off the great Brandenburg plain to the north drove the cold snapping dark air through their winter greatcoats. If they were lucky the sun would appear and lightly reduce the penetrating ache of the frosted atmosphere.

They drove slowly through the broken brick and mortar, avoiding the potholes, hugging themselves for warmth: the jeep had no heater, but a major had brought a flask of whiskey and that helped a little. A group of British soldiers reeled noisily down the street and waved to them as they passed by, the dregs of an all-night party given to stave off boredom. A few Berliners moved quickly in the chill toward their matutinal destinations, work if they were lucky to have it, long lines at the employment office if not. A lone streetcar, a torn advertisement for Odol mouthwash flapping erratically on its side, slowly clanked its way over loose rails, its passengers huddled together behind glassless windows. The dull monochromatic gray dawn began to lighten the sky in the east, the direction in which they were driving. The pockmarked blasted carapace of the Gate assumed a ghostly dimension in the dim illumination as they drove into the Potsdamer Platz to take their places in the convoy. Thick-wasted Red Army women in bulky overcoats and thin clouds of iced breaths before their faces directed the vehicles into what appeared to be organized chaos: an incredible variety of civilian automobiles and trucks and military vehicles sped back and forth, scuttling in and out of the spiraling line as heavily clothed figures leapt nimbly out of their paths in the half-light. A blue or red or yellow car confiscated from some unlucky German, who would not have been able to purchase fuel for it even if he possessed the money, occasionally broke apart the dun column of military colors. The light from the headlamps swerved in erratic patterns becoming dimmer as the natural light filled the streets.

    Schade saw no one he recognized in the apparent disorder of people and vehicles in which bursts of sound, shouts in a dozen languages, to organize, line up, and go forward struggled to be understood against the roaring of the motors. None of the four commanding generals who constituted the Allied Control Authority for Germany would be there: no one expected that celestial level of command to submit to the winter's frigid embrace. Soviet officials had organized the hunt for the Berlin-level commands and the Kommandantura staffs, but they issued the invitations in what seemed to be a thoroughly haphazard manner. As a junior officer Schade had to clear his acceptance with his commanding officer: Lt. Col. McCrae had asked no questions, but had looked oddly at him for a moment. Apparently, EB himself had not received an invitation, nor had Makepeace, and somewhere in the mass of people and vehicles Schade's other colleagues struggled to repress their bewilderment and astonishment at the nature of the event. Leseur had mentioned to Schade that his commanding officer had refused to grant permission for anyone in his office to attend until a higher level not so gently suggested that the value of intelligence resulting from social contacts with France's allies was of sufficient import to change the officer's mind. Leseur later said he became so drunk that he almost shot himself in the leg and could remember none of the conversations he had during the hunt. The higher-ranking officers drove in closed automobiles with functioning heaters; at Schade's level they drove in jeeps and their toes and fingers became numb.

At one point he thought he saw Oscar Monday, and some others he vaguely knew from the Kommandantura, but the light was too diffuse to be certain. He did notice the tall, bulky figure of Wilson Tompkin, but the distance was too great to hail him before he stepped into one of the Russian command cars, a wide grin splitting his face. Then, at some unseen signal or command, the vehicles started to move out along Unter den Linden in the direction of Alexanderplatz. The major in Schade's jeep passed the nickle-plated flask around and everyone sipped at the warm, harsh liquid, praising him for his foresight. Schade thought of Vasart, transferred out of the city because of his Untoward Outburst at the officers' club. Ogilvy would have loved the hunt at which he could have thought himself one of the aristocratic figures he so intensely wanted to be. But the Englishman had been frightened to the point of incoherence that he would be cashiered and sent to London in disgrace, and his relief had been monumental when he discovered his punishment was to be a transfer and nothing more. ("It would have been a disaster, old man, an absolute disaster to have gone home under those circumstances. I'd never have lived it down. Probably have had to move to Liverpool or some other unholy place just to find a position. You can imagine my relief, John. We must have a drink on it.")

Led by a lend-lease jeep with a red star replacing the original white design and a 50 caliber machine gun jutting up from its center, followed by two open jeeps full of soldiers with automatic rifles and a confiscated luxury model Mercedes-Benz carrying the commandant of the Soviet sector of the city and his personal staff, the convoy moved as quickly as possible through the almost deserted thoroughfares. The sky began to lighten now, but with a leaden gray winter illumination that cloyed the eyes like a thick fog. Schade successfully controlled a sour belch, glad he had remembered to put on two pairs of heavy socks; if he had owned long angora underwear he could have kept reasonably warm with the whiskey in his empty stomach. The Russians would feed the members of the hunting party when they arrived at the forest and he hoped that by then he would not be feeling too good from the alcohol. He vowed not to shoot at all if he was feeling too good.

As the landscape began to shift from modern urban devastation to countryside farmlands unchanged for a millennium, the day finally suffused the convoy with a lighter hue of the omnipresent winter gray of northern Germany. Splashes of green now fused with brown and gray as they picked up speed along the less severely damaged country road. In Schade's jeep they commented on the fact that with the light it seemed warmer and complained about their inability to get out of the city except through the labyrinth of military bureaucracy and paper shuffling. The Russians had it easier, they said with voices of open envy: their zone was contiguous with their sector of the city, all they had to do was zip out of the city and into the countryside; they sure had it easier. Schade said nothing about that situation: he was not entirely sure that the Russian soldiers could so easily move in and out of the city to relax in the countryside. Army bureaucracies respected no nationality and the Soviet military appeared to be tougher than most from what he had seen in the past months. He settled back in the stiff seat and let the whiskey warm him as the countryside merged into an undefined panorama of colors and shapes. He tried not to think of Gisela, the novel, or his job and he concentrated on the diffuse and blurred rural scenes as they sped past his vision. He did not want to spoil the day, however it would turn out. He dozed on and off and let his body respond to the rolling movement of the jeep, until a sharp left turn almost threw him out of the vehicle, after which he stiffened and held on to the frame.

Some time later the convoy turned off the road into a narrow hardpacked dirt lane that led into the forest of evergreens and leafless trees: the traditional Deutsche Mischwald of beech, pine, and birch, drooping now in the early morning graylight. A few kilometers deeper in the forest they stopped and got out of the vehicles. The road narrowed and the group walked in irregular clusters talking and flapping their arms to retain the warmth of the cars, their boots cracking the frost and shallow ice that formed in the ruts of the packed dirt. In needled grandeur the tall pines loomed over the line of men: the Germans had not been allowed to cut any wood in this forest. Tamirov later told Schade that the Soviet high command had reserved the forest for the leisure hours of its generals: it reminded them of the countryside outside Moscow where some of them had dachas for their off hours and leave time. The wood would have been of little use that winter in any case, it was too green to burn well. ("For a German without any heat at all, even green wood is welcome," Kronauer expressed the popular local opinion.)

Without warning they came to a clearing in the woods filled with long refectory tables covered with startling white linen table cloths on top of which overflowed piles of food and an army of bottles: cold smoked meats and sausages, an assortment of fresh vegetables such as Schade had not seen in months, high mounds of round dark bread, fruits from the Crimea, buckets of unnamed but richly brown stew heated by electric plates plugged into a series of groaning generators, bottles of vodka, fruit juices and mineral water. Waiters in tails or red jackets and bow ties, and waitresses in black skirts and white blouses stood shivering behind the tables waiting to be of service. Schade never found out if they were Red Army soldiers pressed into this duty or German personnel shanghaied for the occasion: none of them spoke a word, but seemed to know enough Russian to respond to commands given them. At the sight of all this largesse in the midst of the devastation of central Europe, the western Allied personnel showed the appropriate astonishment. (One American general muttered to his British colleague: "This is going to be difficult to duplicate when we reciprocate." "Oh yes, Parliament will never approve the budget; we'll have to hide the expenses.") The Soviet officers moved among their allies urging them to sit and eat and drink, the hunt would begin when the food had been dispatched. A collective murmur of appreciation rose from the clearing as the men settled into the food and drink. The Russians had organized the affair with efficiency and industry: a Soviet officer presided over a small group in his charge, assuring a constant flow of delicacies to his guests, speaking to them collectively and individually in a polyglot of Russian and western languages, including German phrases and words. It became obvious that the Soviet command wished the affair to be a grand success and if the amount of food and drink being consumed with open enthusiasm represented a measurement of the achievement, the Russians were well on their way to meeting that goal. The cold air had been forgotten as the hunting party bent en masse to the task of satisfying their hosts' hearty request that they enjoy themselves. Roweled by vodka, the relaxed laughter and reckless goodwill increased in volume and intensity with shared jokes, backslapping and half-understood phrases of praise for the gustatory and combat experiences of each other's armies: the scene was reminiscent of that short moment of elation and comradeship when the American and Red Armies met at the Elbe River near the end of the war.

The only things Schade found to be missing were portable toilets. But if the Russian bear could shit in the woods, then so could the American eagle, the British lion, and the French ... what was the French national animal? Did they have one? A frog? Ouf! Their symbol was Marianne of the bared breast in the Delacroix painting: he could not imagine that lady defecating in the cold forests of the German north in winter, even as a gesture of contempt. He leaned across the table to ask the major who shared the flask in the jeep about the French national animal, but the man was deeply engaged with their group's Soviet officer explaining with exaggerated seriousness of the early stages of intoxication how the game of baseball worked. Schade laughed out loud and realized the vodka on top of the whiskey had warmed him beyond the point of comfort: he had come to the border of the condition he defined as feeling too good. He shook his head and reached for the fruit juice; he had consumed enough alcohol for the time being. He noticed the reporter Tompkin sitting at the table of the thin, sharp-eyed Latvian who served as the Soviet city commandant conversing at ease through an interpreter. Schade marveled again at the reporter's talent for getting everyone to talk to him. How had he gotten an invitation to the hunt? He had no official status in the city. The alcohol brought Schade to the edge of admiration.

"How do you like our social graces, Lieutenant? Not quite like in Chekov, but nonetheless...." Tamirov's bulk darkened the table in front of Schade and he looked up into the flat blue eyes barely restraining their expression of amusement behind the metal-rimmed spectacles.

"You certainly know how to throw a bash," Schade replied with a smile.

"'Throw a bash...' ah yes, I shall remember that one. You should learn some of our idioms, Lieutenant, to add to your collection."

"I have trouble enough with the American idioms. The Russian would defeat me."

"Perhaps, perhaps." Tamirov smiled his mysterious smile indicating that he read another meaning into Schade's words. Before the smile could become offensive, he leaned closer to Schade's ear and lowered his voice. "We will begin the hunt soon. If you come with me we can talk. Unless of course you wish to shoot some animals."

"Just me, Captain?" Schade did not conceal his surprise.

"I like you, Lieutenant. I enjoy our conversations. I've not been assigned to any particular group so I have flexibility. Do you really wish to shoot these harmless animals." The Russian made this a statement, not a question. "Originally humans sacrificed animals for ritual purposes to propitiate the gods. The operation could only be carried out by priests who knew the secrets of the gods' desires."

"So who are the priests now? And to what gods are these poor animals being sacrificed?"

"International, anti-fascist cooperation. If you wish, we can indulge in some more of our dangerous national drink. Potato juice I believe you once called it. Not altogether unfitting perhaps, but often equal to your bourbon whiskey, I think."

Schade did not like the sweet harshness of bourbon whiskey, another American habit he had been unable to acquire. "I think I've had enough of that for a while, but it will get cold again."

"I shall come for you when it is time. And please remember, I am now major." Tamirov moved away and one of Schade's table partners asked a question intended to begin a conversation about the man's profession of sanitation engineer. Schade absently followed the other's discussion of the most efficient, correct, and safest method for cleaning out the Landwehr Canal, nodding and grunting when necessary, thinking about what it would be like to shoot a boar, satisfied that he would not find out today, but wondering nonetheless.

Then simultaneously the Soviet officers signaled for silence and the laughter and the talk died away in the frosted air. The sun forced its way through the overcast sky and vaguely supplemented the chemically produced warmth in the party. Many had achieved various stages of intoxication, but not the Russians: they had drunk the toasts along with the others but they were not drunk. Some of them may have been slightly tipsy, but they would not dare to have been drunk, at least not visibly so. The Soviet commandant turned to his three colleagues seated at his table (the Frenchman puffing a pipe and holding his tumbler of vodka as if it contained hydrochloric acid, the American flushed and distant with wandering eyes, the Englishman attempting with aplomb to disguise his boredom and trying hard to pay attention) and barked out a further toast to Allied cooperation which two translators immediately put into French and English. Without allowing for counter-toasts, for which each of those men quietly breathed in relief, he proceeded to explain the method of the hunt to the hunters. ("Would have been more accurate to call it the shoot and them the shooters," the disgusted Tompkin said later.)

Just beyond the clearing in the forest lay a wide meadow of bush and undergrowth, a farmland that no one had planted for two seasons, nor had it been torn up very much in the fighting. The hunters would be spaced along the edge of the meadow in rickety blinds with guns supplied by the Red Army, while a company of soldiers who served as beaters drove the animals along the forest line through the meadow. One animal would be allowed for each member of the party and they would stop shooting as the beaters went past their positions. It would not be difficult, the translators reported the general as saying, even for those who had not previously hunted. With that the commandant wished everyone luck and indicated his Kommandantura colleagues should follow him to the ranking generals' shooting dugout. An increased gray chill invaded the clearing as clouds again obscured the sun, darkening the remnants of food and empty bottles lying on the soiled white linen tablecloths. Another set of soldiers distributed an eclectic assortment of guns, including some genuine hunting rifles with fine silver chasing from German villas and castles, and a small amount of ammunition for each. The scarcity of bullets for the more obscure types of weapons and a sensitivity for the democratic pretensions of the western allies served the Russians as an excuse to limit everyone's capability to do damage with the guns. The men all but stopped talking as they moved out of the clearing toward the meadow to take up their positions in the blinds. Occasional bursts of laughter punctuated the morning offering some relief from the tension of anticipation and expectations. The guns felt cold in their hands and the reality of the hunt reduced the effect of the vodka on their brains. The Soviet officers efficiently guided their charges to the appropriate places spaced far enough apart so that determining who shot which animal would not cause later argument.

  Tamirov reappeared at Schade's table and led him through the woods to a position not far from the clearing overlooking the flat bottom land. "If they had planted this, we could feed half the city this winter," he said with some bitterness. Schade looked out over the meadow seeing nothing but weeds and bush. The Russian produced a small bottle of vodka, but when Schade shook his head he returned it to his gray-green overcoat. "It will take some time before they have everyone in place. What do you think of the guns? A strange collection, eh?"

"What will happen to them when this is finished?"

"You mean the hunt?" Tamirov asked with a grin.

"For the moment."

"The better pieces will be stored away for the next time when the general and the commissars want to shoot again. You know, the icons of our age are weapons, and the atomic bomb is the greatest icon of them all: it will dominate us in the future. We, all of us, will come to worship it in a way. Perhaps we shall even come to see in it a way of salvation, a perverse way, of course, but still ... It is fitting, don't you think, that America invented the bomb? It is the most democratic of all weapons, it kills indiscriminately all classes, it is the great leveler of the 20th century. Nothing survives its devastation. It removes all uncertainty. It reappropriates everything into nothing. Everything is reduced to the same level."

"That level is zero. I find that extremely depressing. And frightening." Schade looked into the trees and saw nothing move.

"Infinity, my friend, infinity is cosmically angst-making."

"We couldn't imagine it, I suppose."

"We no longer have to imagine it: we have the photographs, the reports, films...." Tamirov shrugged.

"I think they are insufficient, they become pieces of paper, unreal. They are too difficult to believe, and who wants to believe such a thing. It is too much all the way around."

"We will have more, you know. It will not stop here."

"How so?"

The Russian breathed in sharply. "Do you think for a minute we will not have the bomb one day? Do you really think we can allow you to have it and not us? There would be no balance that way. Do not be naive, Lieutenant. We cannot afford to let you have that kind of power over us. Why are all you foreign leftists so innocent and blind to the power balance?"

"That's hardly a fair statement, Captain, ah - Major."

"Thank you. Lieutenant, because I like you I will tell you a secret. Only the Bolsheviks, starting with Lenin and Stalin, know the real world as it is. Not even Marx and Engels understood the international power balance. How could they? No Soviet Union existed then. Now it exists, a great power and for its own security it must behave like a great power. Why can you people not see this? Your reactionaries have no trouble in that regard."

"Some of us saw the Soviet Union as a great power and comprehended that it acted accordingly, but we also viewed it as the motherland of socialism in which we urgently believed. And these two things conflicted too often."

"The past tense, Lieutenant?" Tamirov smiled sadly. "Have you lost your faith in socialism, in the socialism of the Soviet Union, because it must protect itself like any other great power against its enemies? That is a shallow faith."

"I never believed the Soviet model was the only socialist alternative to capitalism. My family has been social democratic since 1848."

Before the Russian could respond a gun exploded in the distance and a red flare burst beneath the overcast sky signaling the beaters to begin driving the animals through the meadow. As they neared the first of the blinds the sound of other guns gradually filled the air with a spectrum of explosions ranging from sharp cracks to dull thuds as the hunters blasted away at objects they could barely see in the weeds and undergrowth. The din swelled and ebbed as the beaters forced the rabbits, pheasants, wild boar and others creatures down the line of the guns. Cries and shouts joined the noise of the beaters and the guns as the men ran into the meadow to collect the corpses matted with fresh blood and torn fur.

"You believe the slander written about the Soviet Union in the bourgeois press?" Tamirov assumed an expression of mock disbelief and raised his voice above the rolling din.

"Major, I believe the Soviet Union has slandered itself far more than the bourgeois press: the Moscow trials, the pact with the nazis, the commissars killing in Spain ... But I also believe that we must work together now. If we don't work together here in Europe, in Berlin, then all the fighting and dying was hardly worth it. We'll not have solved anything in middle Europe, the so-called German question will not have been answered." Schade spoke with an intense earnestness and Tamirov responded with an equal gravity.

"There is not very much you and I can do about the increasing lack of such cooperation between our countries, Lieutenant. That is unfortunate, but it is so. Not on our level. Oh, we can work many things out locally, you and I, exchange a film or an actress here and there, agree to certain aspects of policy in the Kommandantura, investigate war criminals, even find relatives for each other. But otherwise what is left for us to do, eh? We are prisoners of our government's policies, are we not? Whether we agree with them or not."

To avoid falling into the usual unprofitable and irresolvable argument, Schade deliberately lightened his rejoinder. "At least we can vote the government out from time to time. And we can elect not to stay here and carry out policies we disagree with when our tours are finished."

"You may have the latter alternative," the Russian replied dryly, ignoring the former. "We have few such opportunities. Perhaps it is easier for those of us who believe our governments are correct in their assessments of the situation and make policy accordingly."

"It is not going to be easy at all. I am well aware of that, but the will to make cooperation happen, at least to negotiate our differences, this must be there. And that we see less and less of on both sides."

Tamirov thought for a moment, then said over the final wave of gunshots and shouting: "You know, Lieutenant, the symbol of the city of Berlin is a bear. It is our national symbol as well."

Schade did not smile. "We had better find new icons, Major, for all our sakes."

Tamirov shrugged his wide shoulders and again produced the narrow vodka bottle: a decision had been made. "One for the road, Lieutenant? I learned that one recently. Dangerous habit, if you are driving." Schade drank from the bottle and handed it back. The Russian took a long swallow and replaced the now half-empty container in the folds of his overcoat. "*Okhota okonchena.* Let us see about the results, shall we. Oh, by the way, about the actress Roma Bahn -"

"Yes, we found her in the Deutsche Theater," Schade admitted. "We thought she might be fit to return to the stage."

"I meant to tell you some time ago, but it slipped from my mind."

"She wants to revive Toller's plays."

"Bad timing, Lieutenant."

"Exactly what my superiors said, Major."

"Well, there you are: agreement, cooperation among us Allies."

"Ah...." Schade brushed his mustache with his left thumb as they walked back to the staging area, now emptied of chairs, tables, and food.

"You asked about this Bahn. You might well have asked about the fate of Günther Schiffer and Martine Ragwitz, who made real contributions to the class struggle against the fascists. Your colleague, *tovarich* Makepeace, has an interest in them. Curious, no? Given his ideological position?"

"I must admit, I have not heard of either one of them."

"Writers, Lieutenant, proletarian writers, exiled in the Soviet Union. You comprehend exile, so I need say no more." Schade could not clearly read the message in the pale blue eyes behind the thick sheltering lenses of the Russian's glasses.

"But," Schade said softly, "there is no doubt much to be said."

"At another time, perhaps. *Les jeux sont faits.*"

Most of the shooters had shot nothing. Some, like the British city commandant, had bagged a rabbit with a gun much too big for that small animal. A lesser number had come back with pheasants, most of which had been blown apart by the high caliber bullets and unfit even for stuffing and presentation on the mantlepiece. Only the Soviet and French commandants had shot boars. The Soviet general from Latvia ordered his trophy's tail cut off and wrapped in cloth, which his orderly placed in the glove compartment of his automobile. The carcasses of the two boars, the generals agreed to give to the beaters, like feudal lords in a gesture of generosity and praise for a job well done, imitation noblesse oblige. Then it was over. Those with trophies stuffed the ragged bodies of the animals in the game bags and, after a last swallow of vodka, climbed into the vehicles with their fellow hunters who had not had any luck that day. As the vehicles began the trip back to the city in a winding irregular formation, snow began to fall in swirls of small elegant flakes, blurring vision in the lowering darkness of late afternoon. Some of them lost their way and did not arrive until well after dark that night. Schade's jeep took only an hour longer to return than it had required for the trip out, but the extra hour was filled with verbose joking and laughter: the major had not only shot a rabbit, but had also refilled his silvery flask with vodka. As the jeep slipped and slid from one side of the street to the other, Schade pretended to sleep and drank no more vodka. That night he ate no dinner and walked in the cold snow-laden Berlin air for a long time before he crawled into bed and attempted to sleep. He dreamed of spring and bright colored flowers and a slender young blonde woman with long flowing hair lying naked in a meadow smiling a golden smile in the bright warm sunlight: try as he might, he could not see her face.

Und wer kein Mädel hat,
Dem hilft nur eine Stadt:

Das ist Berlin, das ist Berlin.[39]

* * * *

They began to prowl around the impossibility of their relationship each time they were alone together. The subject that caused the argument had lain like a snake at the center of their feelings for each other from the beginning: their relationship rested on the external pillars of need and sexual gratification, not on any fundamental emotional commitment which could be defined as love. Therefore no basic foundation for a lasting relationship they could believe in existed, therefore they had the choice of accepting their being together as a superficial if satisfying passionate friendship that included both filling their stomachs and gratifying the genital itch without creating the traditional structure called love. Or, if they could not accept such a reasonable arrangement, viewing it as a betrayal of the deeper emotive give and take of what they could actually define as love, they could end the intimacy and either continue as social friends or end the affair completely.

But neither was able to simply end the affair and each selfishly desired to maintain the relationship as long as possible, even if this meant arguments and guilt piling up like sand in the bottom of an hourglass. At certain moments her consuming devotion to the theater convinced him that she was using the pain of their increasingly tortured affair to support and nurture her art. At times his mind pulled up short, aghast at the thought: was he falling in love with her? That, he knew, could lead to nothing but

---

[39] For whoever had no girl/ only the city can help/This is Berlin, this is Berlin."

emotional disaster for them both. That situation would only add to her guilt and neurosis, and drive her to break with him immediately: she could not stand the responsibility and it would desiccate his emotional resources. They had to maintain the proper perspective: they still saw each other, their behavior imitating that of lovers, because they fed on each other's depths of strength and weakness. This, he convinced himself, was not per se harmful to either of them as long as they both continued to view the affair within its real limits, namely that there was and could be no love between them: love would break both of them emotionally and mentally. Neither of them, if for differing reasons, could give that final part of themselves beyond sexual passion that solidified the vapors of feeling and thought into the crystalline structure we call love. They could accept but not give the gift of love; they had as yet been unable to reconcile their individual persona with the demands of another. Too intelligent to fool themselves, they attempted to fool each other, but the ruse became so transparent it disappeared into the dust of the city leaving them only their passion and diminishing need for each other and the lacerating togetherness they willfully refused to give up.

One night in the first winter after the war, as they walked from the theater after a performance, she turned to him and said, "This cannot go on. It makes me feel cheap, soiled."

"What is that supposed to make me feel?"

"You are the victor, you get the spoils."

"And what have you gotten? This isn't a one-way street, you know."

"Oh I know all right, I know what I've got and I'm grateful for it all, but that doesn't change the matter. The exchange hasn't been exactly equal and that is not acceptable."

"It's not up to you to decide whether what I've gotten is sufficient or not. I decide that."

"I am tired of feeling guilty about it. I'm sick of feeling like a common Amimädchen."

"Then don't feel that way."

"That's easy for you to say."

"Don't you think I feel uneasy about us, about the way you feel, but that doesn't mean the answer is breaking off, dammit, it means changing the way we react."

"I'm not going to argue with you in the middle of the street. It's too demeaning."

Schade took her to her room but did not stay that cold winter night. Now with his tour of duty edging toward its conclusion the banality of their previous conversation shocked him and he found it all but impossible to accept that this incandescent wildly passionate affair had come to such a narrow quotidian standpoint. The realization left him breathless and disoriented. After not seeing her for a fortnight and with his tour of duty edging toward its conclusion, he could no longer postpone the decision whether to transfer to civilian duty in the city or return to New York. She did not immediately question him about the decision because he did not speak to her about it for some time, but she comprehended a subtle sequence of changes in him. After a day of terrifying panic, she began to accustom herself to the realization that he had listened more carefully than she thought to her painful attempts at resolving the conundrum of their lives together. This did not make it any easier to accept, despite her relief, nor did his continued inability or unwillingness to speak to her about it, but she felt lighter in her spirit, felt a sense of liberation and a confidence in her ability to deal with the other wounds in her personality, and the prospect of healing compensated to some as yet unknown extent for her future loss of his passion and attention. Surprising herself she began to feel a freer affection for Schade now that she knew they would release each other. But she could not explain this to him until he spoke to her about his decision.

> *Nimm dich in acht vor blonde Frauen, Johnny*
> *Sie haben so etwas Gewisses.*
> *'s ist ihnen nicht gleich anzuschau'n,*
> *Aber irgendetwas isses.*[40]

* * * *

Snow fell in small persistent flakes the night Schade visited Schadow to talk about his ideas for the novel he now knew he could write. He had already written a mass of unconnected fragments of notes and thoughts for characters and plot lines, but except for the idea behind it nothing had fallen into place. As he drove slowly along the slippery street running alongside the Spree River toward the Treptow section of the city where Schadow lived, uncomfortable thoughts of Gisela nudged the book out of his mind and he called up his shamanic moving images sequence to replace her in his inner vision: a crouched cowboy holding a Winchester repeating rifle in his right hand, loping quickly along a dry desert arroyo moves up to the lip of the arroyo and peers over the edge. Sometimes it took him a while to reach the lip of the arroyo, sometimes it happened very fast, depending upon Schade's need for respite or escape; he never knew what the cowboy saw on

---

[40] Watch out for blonde women, Johnny/They've all got a certain something/You can't see it at first sight/but it certainly is something

the other side of the arroyo's edge. There was no necessity for him to see it: the cowboy was a gunman and would raise the Winchester to his shoulder, aim and shoot whatever it was on the other side. Schade must have watched the scene at a Saturday matinee when he was about twelve years old. He usually brought this image to mind to dispel other pictures and thoughts that threatened to make him uncomfortable or question his view of himself.

"*Sie Vollidiot!*"

The old woman's scream lashed him back to the present and the awareness that he had allowed the car to drift so close to the river that he had almost run down the woman trudging along the embankment with her wheelbarrow full of broken pieces of coal and mortar. He yanked the wheel to the left and continued down the street followed by the sharp invective of the old Berliner's tongue, the heat of embarrassment and shame flushing his neck and face. The enforced slowness of the car, not his swift reaction had saved both of them from worse than frightened anger and hot humiliating embarrassment. Complete idiot. Yes, he had to agree he had been that. The remainder of the way around Treptowpark he drove with complete attention to the road.

The old man's room faced the small garden in the back of the house on a residential street which had been spared total destruction and in which the ground fighting had been minimal. The textile manufacturer who owned the house, a friend of Axel Albrechtsburg's, had offered the room after nazi housing officials had ejected Schadow from his apartment following his wife's death. The manufacturer removed himself and his family to the south before the Red Army encircled the city and when the soldiers encountered the building, by then without roof and side wall, they found only the bent elderly man with thin-rimmed spectacles dressed in an old black suit, soiled white soft-collar shirt and faded silver necktie, who walked with difficulty and spoke a few words of out-of-date Russian. This expertise was of no immediate service to Schadow since the soldiers spoke as little Russian as he, but they did not harm him as they stripped the house of everything they thought of value. Having in his small room off the garden little except a bed, chair and writing table, piles of foolscap covered with his crabbed handwriting, some books and an old fountain pen, he lost nothing to this plundering because he hid the pen. They left him what little food remained in the kitchen and departed. Succeeding groups of soldiers found nothing to plunder and after urinating on the walls to show their dissatisfaction also moved on to greener pastures. Finally, the military command stabilized the city and the soldiers came no more. Schadow was left alone except for sporadic visits from Gisela after she left the cave, the Kronauers, some former colleagues asking for affidavits attesting to their anti-nazi attitudes, and now Schade. All of his visitors brought some provisions, especially Schade who had access to more of them than the others. The manufacturer of textiles did not return and a neighbor, the poet Mechtild Piekheim, informed Schadow that he and his family had been killed when airplanes strafed the train outside the city on its way south. The city Magistrat confiscated the house and placed a young couple and a communist party official in the two other rooms still inhabitable. The couple worked long hours while remaining healthy and well-fed, from which Schadow deduced without any concrete evidence that they had some connection with the party official. Party membership played a crucial but not always hegemonic role in determining who obtained which position in the city's public civilian hierarchy. The surviving KPD leaders reappeared in Berlin from their exile in Moscow in the baggage of the Soviet armed forces and worked hard in the early days of the occupation to organize a broadly based center-left coalition to arrange postwar life in the Soviet occupied zone and Berlin. In any case, Schadow saw little of his house-mates and when their paths crossed their reciprocal greetings were pleasant if cool and brief. He tended to forget their existence as he got out and about more often until the winter forced him to remain inside near the small metal and porcelain stove, his only source of heat in the house with no central heating system.

"Welcome to my modest scriptorium. It is always a pleasure to greet Americans bearing gifts. And at my age there is little left to beware of, except perhaps ill-tempered soldiers with guns. *Treten Sie ein, bitte*." His chuckle sounded like sandpaper scraped across rusty metal.

Schade handed over the sack of canned food and tin of Prince Albert pipe tobacco, and gazed out the window to the barren waste of the garden now white with the soft snowflakes while Schadow busied himself opening a bottle of wine. The old man jested on occasion: "With all this help I eat almost as well as before the war. My appetite has always been that of a bird, a very small bird. But what would I not do for an orange!" Even the Americans, the best fed of the victors, rarely had fresh fruit. He was particularly grateful for the tobacco. From a collection of a dozen good pipes he had been able to save one, but had not smoked it during the war because he could not obtain tobacco. Now he rationed himself to one pipe a day, smoked after his iron-ration dinner, one of the few physical pleasures that remained to him on the wintry heights of his age. "When I see the young girls dressed in their summer clothes, I like to think that wild, wild horses could not drag me away, but of course at this point in my life that is all in my head, the red doors have long since been painted black."

Neighbors had reduced the trees in the garden to stumps and the remnants of the summer vegetables Schadow and Gisela had grown had long since been cooked and eaten. Preparing for winter they cut down everything that could be burned. They left a fair portion of the wood for his use in the old stove sitting in the corner of his room and cleaned the flue for him. Pages of various sizes and colors covered with his tiny but legible script, those precise essays he wrote to maintain his sanity but did not expect ever to publish, lay in two squared piles on the small table he used as a writing desk before the window. "It will take years before academic work by a German can be published unless it directly concerns the recent past, and that from the correct point of view, of course. Although I understand my former fellow professor, Herr Meinecke, has just published an analysis of the deeply rooted socio-historical reasons for the nazi phenomenon's advent. Given his ego and various points of view, the answers should be interesting, if not useful. But by the time other work can be printed, I will be dead and it will be of no matter to me. I have published a great many words as it is. I have accustomed myself to writing for the desk drawer." Later he said, "That Meinecke, you understand, had no choice in dismissing Hedwig Hintze from the journal *Historische Zeitschrift*. She was a full Jew and he could not keep her on. Her husband was more than twenty years older than she and long since emeritus because of his health. He resigned from his position as co-editor. A brave man, very old. She was able to escape to the Netherlands just before the war started. Otto died the following year. I don't know what happened to her."

Schade voiced concern over the professor's wellbeing during the remaining winter days. "I shall survive this winter, Herr Schade. I have decided to feed my still large ego by writing some reminiscences and that will ensure my continued breathing for a while, another year, perhaps. How could I leave the world without giving it the benefit of my life, an exemplar for the man of tomorrow?" His frail laughter came in short gasps sounding like old paper being crumpled.

They clicked the small glass Mason jars Tomkin had given Schade for that purpose ("What an idea! If we had had these things before 1914, do you think, Lieutenant, that the panther would have jumped differently? Or would it have remained the same dangerous piss and vinegar?") and sipped the mildly sweet cold Rheingau. "Not the best of years," Schade said with a grin. "And I think I'm going to leave Berlin; return to New York after my tour is finished."

Schadow adjusted his spectacles and rubbed his left earlobe between thumb and forefinger. "Yes, the odd years seem to be the best. The return is inevitable, I suppose, though I must honestly admit that I will be sad to see you go. Not just the goods, of course, but I've grown to like and depend upon our talks. When will you go?"

"The end of the summer next year, early September. The details haven't been settled yet and I've officially informed no one."

"Then we have several months to talk. You could also change your mind, I suppose. No doubt the military government could use you here."

"Yes, that's a possibility of course, but I don't think I will. I've come to think of America as my home, New York City. I've not even tried to visit Breslau since I've been here. My intellectual roots may be German, Central

European, perhaps, but emotionally my connections are all with America. I can't help making comparisons. My bouts of nostalgia concern New York, not Germany."

"You have no desire to return to Breslau?"

"Why don't I go back there? It doesn't exist any longer. Now it's some foreign place called an unpronounceable Polish name. I wouldn't remember it anyway, would I? Not having been there in much more than a decade. I was too young, I'm sure of it. Yes, that's why, you see? And getting there now is practically impossible in any case: too much suspicion and paperwork."

Schadow chuckled lightly. "You remember what Tucholsky said?"

"Of course," Schade smiled crookedly. "But I've just forgotten it."

"*Die meisten Berliner stammen aus Breslau.*"

"Most Berliners come from Breslau. How clever."

Schadow settled as comfortably as his age and the wooden chair allowed, reached for his pipe and in a soft murmur said, "Tell me, if you wish."

Without trying to organize his thoughts, Schade plunged into his explanation and justification for leaving the city. His sentences took on a logic of their own, following an inner rationality which made sense to him and appeared to be comprehensible to Schadow as well. He spoke of his desire to write the novel not only as a work of literature ("Yes, literature. I want to write a Work of Art; I'm not ashamed of it but of course I'd like to earn a living from it as well; I'm not a fool either."), but as a piece of history that had to be understood if the exiled and inner emigration Germanys were to combine again into a healthy, progressive culture. He spoke of his increasing disenchantment with American policy on the denazification question and the increasing acrimony among the Allies over various occupation policy directives, especially French and Soviet obstructionist maneuvers; of his desire to be a writer, not a cultural bureaucrat; of his wish to see his family again ... all the motivations clanking against each other in his psyche, seeking some form of release or realization. When he began to speak of Gisela, he hesitated.

"You know she visits me quite often; she has mentioned you of course. I mean, I know something about your relationship, the problems...," Schadow said kindly.

"It isn't easy for me to speak about it. I am still confused to some extent about the balance of good and bad, healthy and sick, the rights and wrongs of it. I think I welcome the prospect of the book taking up more of my time, and the end of my tour, ways out of the affair ... otherwise I might not have the strength ... there's still so much pleasure and good."

"It is entirely possible that *she* would, or will, end it from her side. She is a very intelligent young woman and is as aware as you are of the 'balance,' as you put it. She is perhaps less confused about it than you are, but given the circumstances she is weaker at the moment. When her confusion is cleared up, when she regains her own balance, she will be strong enough to make such decisions herself."

"And you think she would decide to end it?"

"What I think hardly matters, but I believe she would. If I ever felt I could give her a piece of undiluted advice that would be my recommendation. I hope this is not too painful for you. I presumed you wished me to be honest."

"Yes, of course." Schade hesitated. "It is disconcerting to think of oneself being the cause of pain and disturbance in a person one is very fond of."

"You are not the complete cause of Gisela's troubles, do not credit yourself with too much. The origins of her troubles lie in the deeper past. But you contribute to the prolongation of arriving at a solution, or a series of solutions, to the problems. Surely you can see that."

"That I can understand it intellectually does not make it easier to act on that understanding."

"You are a young man, not even thirty. And what choice have you as a man of honor?"

"I don't know that I am such a man."

Schadow's voice tightened in annoyance. "I think you are, Herr Schade. I take her side in this matter without apology. Your presence in her life at this time is rendering her incapable of making decisions she must make and disrupting the healing process. That you contributed to the start of that process is not in question, but now you are not advancing the solution, you are blocking it. You know this and so does she. If she cannot act, then you must." The old man sighed and slumped against the back of his chair. "But this is academic, as it were, isn't it? You obviously have made the decision, and I fully support it."

"Yes, I think I have."

"Then you must act on it, regardless of how much longer you remain in Berlin."

"I must tell her soon, yes. That will not be an easy conversation."

"No, of course not, but to fall into the sickly sweet comfort of self-pity will be of no help either."

Schade drew in a sharp breath but banished the flash of annoyance and smiled. "No, one mustn't allow oneself that."

"Perhaps you will find it less difficult than you think. After all, she will be relieved." Schadow swirled the wine in his Mason jar and watched the pale screen of residue slowly descend into the well of the container. Then he drank the remainder in one satisfying swallow. "You see, increasing age may not bring with it any great wisdom, but it does have an emptying effect. It does bring about a massive indifference to one's own fate. This makes dealing with others much easier. One's own emotions no longer become obstacles in relationships with others. Concern for one's own heart no longer blocks the ability to sacrifice for loved ones. It is something we all learn and my admonishing you with this knowledge may not add to yours, but it may encourage you to think about some things differently. I see I have not lost my tendency to lecture. Some characteristics we never rid ourselves of. If you will pour me just a small tot of wine I will give you my reaction to your ideas for the novel.

"Ah, thank you." He drank the wine now in brief sips and edged his chair closer to the stove, into which Schade shoved a trowel full of coal. "I do not know whether or not a reconciliation between the two Germanys you spoke of can take place at present. Too much bitterness and guilt have stifled any objective analysis of the situation, on both sides. The émigrés feel bitterly betrayed at being cast out, deprived of their citizenship, forced to live in exile ... the experience cannot have been very pleasant for most of them and I know many of them died from it. It is a rare human who can make an adjustment like that when it is not of his own choosing. You could give us that experience to some extent, better in a work of fiction than with reportage or biography. We know so little about it here. That would surely be of value. I suppose you must also consider whether or not such fiction has already been written. I vaguely recall Feuchtwanger writing something about France, but you will work that out.

"But what of the other side? Those who remained for whatever reason, I mean those who consider themselves to have gone into the inner emigration, these people cannot easily accept that German culture was violently forced out of the country with the émigrés. They have to feel and believe that they, not the unfortunate exiles, protected and saved that part of our heritage. They feel profoundly insulted in their deepest sense of being German by the speeches and writings of those outside who did not suffer through the brown years at home. They believe they are the true carriers of German culture, the true Germans per se, not those who lived in relative safety abroad for so long. They believe it is they themselves who must revive our music, our literature, our morality. And are they so wrong? Should they move aside and let the exiles return, set up shop and continue as if they had never been gone? This is asking too much surely. They also carry a different weight of guilt about the atrocities committed in their names, don't they? That is something the émigrés can only feel in the abstract, at a distance, precisely because they were not here then. Will those who stayed work together with the returnees? As long as the Allies force the situation, but how long can that last?

"You are correct, I think, in the assumption that there is a vast abyss between the two and that anything that can be done to bridge it should be done. Too many ties have been slashed, you see, so much psychic devastation ... I don't know. Perhaps I am too old to be optimistic any longer; I have seen too much. We so rarely learn from our experiences. I truly envy you your age. Even though I think your generation is far more cynical and pessimistic than mine at your age, you at least have the chance to do something. I hope you are successful as we were not. I am beginning to wander. One tires too quickly; the old gray matter loses its spring after a while. But I urge you to write your novel. And the one after that and after that. We need all the help we can get, don't we?

"Just guard against nostalgia. Make it strong and real, not an elegy. We have a sufficient number of those." The old man's voice began to lose its edges. "One more thing, a citation from Goethe about books, which might be of help to you. '*Gewisse Bücher scheinen geschrieben zu sein, nicht damit man daraus lerne, sondern damit man wisse, dass der Verfasser etwas gewusst hat.*' Perhaps …"[41]

His pipe had long since gone out and dangled from his blue-veined fingers. His eyes closed and he mumbled something about taking a short nap. Schade sat for a while longer then gently helped the old man to his bed and covered him with a blanket. He decided he would not be offended at the implication he might write a book just to show what he had learned. After seeing to the coal stove, he quietly left the house and later thought he had heard the sleeping ancient in a barely audible voice say, "Come again." The sour feeling returned to his stomach, physically expressing the disgust he felt at his weaknesses. Schadow was right, of course: now he had to act on what he already knew. He drove cautiously back to the American sector suppressing a desire to weep.

* * * *

The last time he visited Schadow, at the end of their conversation, the old man walked him to the door and with a small smile recited some lines from a Heine poem.

---

[41]"Certain books appear to have been written not so that one can learn from them, but rather that one realize the author knows something."

Verlass Berlin, mit seinem dicken Sand
Und dünnen Tee und überwitz'gen Leuten,
Die Gott und Welt, und was sie selbst bedeuten,
Begriffen längst mit Hegelschem Verstande.[42]

"He could just as well have mentioned thin Berlin beer, and today Hegel is out of style, but it still works, don't you think? Goodbye, Lieutenant, thank you for your consideration and your company. I have enjoyed it."

* * * *

Winter continued to clasp the city in an embrace of ice. The young linden trees planted only a few months ago struggled to survive the wind-driven snow and the strangle hold of the bitterly frigid air blowing across northern Germany from the Baltic Sea and Finland. Encouraged by the British Military Government, the citizens of the city had cut all the wood remaining in the Tiergarten to heat their rooms, yet everyone suffered from chilled blue extremities and running red noses: the colors of winter framed the sounds of phlegm-rending coughing. Even the occupiers rarely spent a completely comfortable warm night and awoke in the mornings to see their breaths white in the air and a thin layer of ice formed in any vessel left with water overnight. No one walked in the streets unless it was unavoidable. The Berliners who worked for the Allies arrived early and departed late absorbing the damp warmth of the heated offices as long as possible. "*Amiherd ist*

---

[42]"Depart Berlin, with its thick sand/and thin tea and super-clever people/who have long since comprehended with Hegel's logic/the meaning of god, the world, and themselves."

Goldes wert" - so went the winter cliché in the American Sector: an American stove is worth gold.

Ulrich Kramer had made a correct prognosis: audiences sat wrapped in whatever winter clothing remained, shivering in unheated theaters and movie houses, but they continued to fill up the performances. Actors and actresses came to prefer roles that required them to move about the stage as much as possible. The wind whipped through the streets and the holes in the city made by the war, driving snow and freezing rain into the narrowest of crevices, through windows boarded with inadequate pieces of cardboard, into the marrow of the city's bones, while the unending gurgle of empty bellies continued its ulcerating accompaniment to the daily life of the city. Unexploded bombs suddenly burst fatally into life at odd moments during the day and night, unwelcome memories of half-forgotten terror, tearing the flesh of the innocent and the guilty with massive indiscrimination. The death rate climbed as the Allied and city authorities labored under increasing hardship to feed and minister to the health of the inhabitants.

"To some extent the stage in the theater has become the world of normality, where all the values and desires for a life without the war can be realized. The war destroyed everything of material value; now only the illusions remain, and they appear each night on the stage of the city's theaters. The stage has replaced life with all its horrors. How could it be otherwise?" Kramer shook his head sadly. "We are all such cowards."

Everything was at a premium, there was never enough of anything except whiskey, cigarettes and sex, provided one was lucky in friends and finances.

Mit einer Schachtel Chesterfield,

da macht er meine Schwester wild.[43]

    Although the Allied authorities cracked down on black market activities and withdrew the original occupation currency, the wheel of human avarice and ingenuity continued to turn, ignoring the sheets of ice on the streets. The real currency of the city remained the American cigarette, redeemable for anything. ("Did you ever try to imagine," Oscar Monday asked Makepeace shortly after the composer arrived in the city, "what a package of cigarettes must look like after a couple of weeks in the trade? Doesn't anyone ever smoke the damn things?") The black market in drugs expanded as people lashed themselves to extremes to reduce the dull ache of hunger, cold and despair. When the Allies lifted the curfew the day before Christmas the services offered by the criminal element grew in scope and volume allowing those Berliners with something to trade to survive. Packages of clothing and canned goods from America began to appear at distribution points organized by charitable groups (followed quickly by their appearance in smaller numbers on the black market), small amounts at first sent by individuals through members of the occupying forces, then in larger numbers through more organized channels for the children and the aged of the city. The towns and cities of America had not been bombed and no armies had battled on the American earth and city streets. The citizens of the other Allied nations did not have enough for themselves that winter.

    And the city continued to dig itself out of the frozen rubble. Driving through the streets, Schade noted the small

---

[43]"With a pack of Chesterfield he drives my sister wild." It rhymes, more or less, in German.

changes: more newspapers available as the Allies licensed "denazified" Germans to publish them; increased traffic (although this consisted mainly of the expanding numbers of refugees and DPs, motorized traffic remained military since the rare German with a wood or coal burning motor car now used that fuel to heat his home); more men in public as the POW camps emptied and their inmates returned home to complain they ate better in the camps; schools for the children began to reopen, the texts purged of nazi ideas, and each family that could afford the loss packed a coal brick in the children's knapsack to help heat the classroom; and, while the architecture of the city did not change (no construction took place in an economy based on cigarettes and the decisions of the victors who could not reach agreement on the industrial level to be allowed the defeated) and the debris of war still infested the city, the streets appeared cleaner even as the *Trümmerfrauen* worked shorter hours as they moved stones block by block for such work meant the highest calorie level ration card ... These changes could be seen, and occasionally one could detect a reflection of hope in the eyes of the people, both German and Allied. Tompkin reported he even noticed a return of the city's famous gallows humor that he had missed on arriving months before. (On the relation of the Berliners to the Allies, one citizen noted: "*Früher habe ich den einen oder anderen vorgezogen, jetzt sind sie mir alle gleich lieb.*"[44] And Monday remarked on a similar alteration of the city's peoplescape: "There's an old Cuban saying I learned from my friend Martino Cruz in Havana: you want to advertise, you move your ass. Of course, he was talking about girls.

---

[44]"Earlier I took one or another of them, now they are all my favorites."

The girls in Berlin were all starved so thin when we got here that if they tried to move their asses you'd have heard their pelvic bones click against each other like a marimba band playing a dirge. Things have gotten better. Now the band is playing rumbas and they've added saxophones!")

But not everyone defined these small changes as progress. As the winter continued its dagger-edge sharpness confusion also multiplied: many people in the city thought that while the Allies had won the war they were losing the peace. The occupation had done less to change German minds through its policies of reorientation and denazification than it had the minds of the occupiers, at least among the American soldiers. A number of surveys conducted by intelligence units appeared to show German resentment of the US occupation forces increasing in bitterness while at the same time the GIs were becoming more sympathetic to the Germans.

To illustrate this, Harrigan told the story of a young blonde German woman, apparently *au currant* with the customs of the army who, a few hours after the lifting of the ban on fraternization, sat perched on a barstool in the Harnach House officers club enjoying rye whiskey in a glass of iced cola and the attention of half a dozen junior officers. "You know," she pontificated in clear if haphazard English, "our countries must remain together, *nicht wahr*. Germany and America *sind grosse* countries and have many samenesses. We are *sehr* alike. The Germans are busy folk, good peoples but maybe a little stupid some times. But when you meet an intelligent German *er ist* really very intelligent, *ja*. World class type, *ja*?" At the peak of her twenty-one years she gently tossed her hair, smiled professorly, and graciously accepted a light from one of her attentive students before continuing her lecture. "*Sehen Sie*, now that this silly policy is finished, you will be able to meet real Germans, you will learn our *Kultur und* our methods. Then you will see how we are more like Americans than the others. We will get along wonderfully, I am sure, *nicht wahr*." She smiled again and they rushed to buy her another drink and placed the plate piled with salted peanuts before her.

Harrigan dredged his voice in the flour of sarcasm and commented: "I can see these creatures all over the place, 'explaining Germany' to the GIs. And they're all very serious and well-meaning; they believe what they're saying. Frightening, isn't it? Not only the substance, but the effectiveness. Soon we'll start believing that poor Germany is a victim of slander and misunderstanding. It was all somebody else's fault and, my goodness, no one was a nazi. Well, the story may be apocryphal, but it's still frightening. When you stop to think about all the Fräuleins looking for what they themselves now call 'a meal ticket'. My god, what are we doing here?"

Schade discovered that it was not only the uneducated and thus vulnerable common soldiers who were changing their views and attitudes toward postwar conditions. Men like Kronauer, whose anti-nazi credentials could not be faulted, questioned the wisdom of the Allies in arranging for Germany to be a weak nation yet expecting it to regain its former levels of great cultural creativity in a peaceful and essentially passive development. "Can we become a world nation of culture without becoming a world power at the same time? Has any nation from the ancient Egyptians to the present given us an admirable civilization without being a powerful state economically and politically? I think not. A nation can be powerful without being civilized, look at nazi Germany or Soviet Russia or, some would say, the United States, but no nation can give the world high culture without being a world power as well, not for very long." ("They damned well better learn," was Makepeace's comment.)

Schadow disagreed. "No, you are wrong, I think. That notion, as Nietzsche pointed out, is the result of the political defeat of Athens (the true Greece) by Sparta. That one can nurture and spread culture only when one puts on boxing gloves and is fully armed is a destructive theory which too many people unfortunately believe."

"It is unfortunate that the theory has been shown to be true since the Egyptians."

"What we need is a new form, less dependent upon the past, perhaps, but not neglecting the past. Such neglect leads to the debasing of our heritage and we end by studying and imitating dead cultures, as we do with Latin, though that is harmless enough and one learns certain styles of *value*. But what has this to do with the state, a form that has lost its raison d'être in our language? The more firmly the state is entrenched, the less secure is humanity."

"My old and good friend," Kronauer said with a warm smile, "you have been at your books for too many years. Nietzsche no longer speaks for our century."

"He not only still speaks to us, he is a symbol of our poor century. That, too, is unfortunate, but one cannot ignore the fact."

* * * *

Schade gradually realized that he belonged to a part of the human race that finds it difficult to think clearly in complex situations without putting pen to paper. He began to understand men who, like the old historian, never stopped jotting things down on scraps of paper, fragments of obiter dicta reflecting their experiences, who in some way worked out their personal conundrums even in their scholarly activities. He sat smoking and sipping whiskey in that ambiguous transition climate as the winter's last acerbic attempt to resist the intrusion of summer's phalanx of warm cottony comfort faltered. Bent over a stack of blank paper, pen and ink to hand, he tried to make sense of his recent history. After many false starts at composing a structured explication, he began to jot down notes on what he thought germane to his circumstances. He hoped this action would break through the monochromatic landscape of his mind and fill it with the bright colors of comprehension. In this he failed. The fragments added up to nothing coherent, they remained broken pieces of his mind unable to come to terms with itself or the emotional life it could not completely control.

Over the last several years his father had become an increasingly shadowy figure in his son's mind, loved but rarely present. The image of his father had not so much faded as broken into bits and pieces so that, when he thought of his father at all, the pictures came in time capsules of specific instances of remembered events, usually banal in themselves, all of which never cohered into a composite. Perhaps this ultimate vagueness made writing the letter to his father less troublesome.

He began to write in English, "Dear Dad..." but he could not continue, so he wrote "*Lieber Papa...*" and the block dissolved and his hand moved the fountain pen across the page forming the German words with an ease that astonished him. Later he wondered if the fact that his parents had given him the pen on the occasion of his graduation from college played any role in the release of his language.

"The problem on the whole seems to be one of commitment, or the lack of it, which might allow me to get off the periphery into the center of something, something worthwhile and satisfying, a cause worth fighting for beyond the end of the war. Statements about contributing to the betterment of mankind always sound pretentious and superficial, but without some kind of faith in what one does, one does nothing.

"I have been on the periphery of things all my life, never truly committed and in the center of events. I was too young to really know what was happening before we emigrated. In New York I was always on the edges of the anti-fascist activities mama was so deeply concerned with, too busy with school and jobs and trying to figure out what I wanted to do with my life. Too immature perhaps to really know what was happening then, not comprehending the fullness of the situation. Then I turned into myself and tried to be a writer, then partially out of myself again with Leslie, but that didn't last. With the writing I thought I had found something to which I could commit myself with the knowledge of what I was doing, but too many things were happening, too much flux, too little stability, I suppose.

"After I graduated and the army drafted me I committed myself to winning the war, to finally defeating the fascists and perhaps bringing about some kind of real socialism in Germany, but we were all just cogs in the machine over which we had no control. I never saw any combat, as you know, because they put me in the psychological warfare section where I made propaganda, not death. Important enough, at least we thought so then. How we'll ever know is a mystery.

"Here in Berlin for a time I thought I was in the center of things, doing work of value, being useful. Perhaps this was true in the beginning, but now everything has become routine in detail and the wartime cooperation among the Allies is falling apart. The pages of my life are turning brown, the ink is fading. (I hope you understand, papa, that this is my way of thinking; I don't usually talk this way, but I think and write like this in both languages, god help me.)

"Even the movement of Jews through the city developed into a routine. Perhaps others received more satisfaction from doing that, but for me, except for the thrill and tension of action, it ended in disappointment even though I realized I placed myself in a dangerous situation. Of course I believe mentally in what they are doing and I want to continue to help, but emotionally I do not seem to be able to connect with the cause. If I stayed in Berlin I would continue to work with the Brichah, but my commitment is intellectual, not emotional. Perhaps if my participation were more directly related to the mission and its dangers the situation would be different. But I remain on the periphery. If the MPs had caught us and tossed us into the stockade (this is what the army calls its jail, papa) I might feel differently. Martyred for the cause. But is it my cause?

"My regular work? Again, I made a commitment, but we've been so often frustrated by inept and misguided regulations and policies with which I cannot agree ... we seem to be running things, but I think we're running in place, not making much progress, and we do things that curtail our ability to implement our programs. Now it's all become so much routine, the spontaneity is gone. No doubt this is inevitable, but we're increasingly imprisoned deeper in a maze of regulations and paperwork. If I could stir up the requisite cynicism, like deliberately provoking acid in the stomach, perhaps I could get along better here. But why should I? I don't want to approach everything behind the protection of the cynic. That is not living one's life. Where is the commitment there? We allowed too many nazis into too many jobs, the black market is a disgrace, the attempt to Americanize the Germans in our sector under the rubric of 're-educating the Germans into the democratic way of life' is absurd when all they have to do is take the streetcar (the system is running fairly well now) to the French or Soviet sectors for culture. This program is doomed to fail.

"In fact, as an example, my theater control ('control' is of course a joke by now, though in the first summer here we did exert more than just a little influence) colleague recently told me that a nazi theater manager, who we've consistently refused to license because of his early party membership and faithful support for the regime, is going to be cleared because we allegedly need experienced personnel in those jobs. This one is a real swine who feels no remorse. I'm told we need 'an experienced hand not tainted with the red brush'! What about the brown brush? But we keep changing the rules in the name of expediency and now we've given the entire process over to the Germans themselves (the so-called Spruchkammer) to handle. This is not what we came here to accomplish; at least it is not what I came here to do.

"And we don't seem to be able to agree as a four-power authority either. This also was doomed from the start. I can see now that the interests are too divergent.

"Some even considered this to be an opportunity for a true social revolution to radically remake Germany: up from the ashes with a new classless, peaceful society. How naive, foolish, given the strategic interests of the powers. How could anyone believe that the western governments would allow the creation of such a potentially competitive example? And Moscow does not seem to be very interested in such a revolution either. Makepeace remarks that I came to the work in Berlin with the attitude of a romantic idealist and got bashed about by reality, which has to be negotiated on the basis of many things but evidently not the clear ideals for which we fought the bloody war. Perhaps.

"And what about my 'sentimental life', as one of my Italian colleagues calls it? The volatile Gisela, who sometimes loses the ability to differentiate between acting and reality, the enraged consciousness atoning for the sins of her fatherland by giving herself to remaking the future ... how we all are obsessed with remaking the German mind, the German soul, the German spirit, German this and German that. At some point it becomes boring.

"How comforting it would be to write 'It was nice while it lasted, but now it's over, adieu, auf wiedersehen, and inkadinkadoo.' (Am I actually gaining a sense of humor?) But of course this is impossible. Like acid splashed on the skin she has eaten her way through my emotions into my consciousness. As long as we were together the ambiguity was bearable, even perversely enjoyable, but what now? No doubt we could both live here and never see each other again, but that is unreal. It would be too difficult to watch her move about the city with her growing sense of assuredness and of her own worth, and not be part of it. The attachment is too great, like an addiction one knows one shouldn't have, but there it is. We ran from love into each other's bodies and found a strange sort of comfort and excitement there, but we could not cross the line of giving required to complete the circle to reach the fullness of love. Our tenderness was of a different variety: it protected us from the wreckage around us and allowed us to believe for a while that we complemented each other's desperation. Our kisses brushed each other like leaves falling from the linden trees while our minds ransacked our emotions under the guise of needing to understand. We slaked our needs with our embarrassing concentration on the surface of sexuality and ended with a more profound thirst left unsatisfied. The mistake we made was to think we could continue that greatly off-center passion without the balancing weight of giving. Two parasites feeding on the other's inadequacies must fall away from the coupling in frustration with the taste of copper on the tongue. We used each other for our own ends and exhausted the circumstances in which we acted. There was really no alternative.

"Did I think, after a while, of Gisela as my own private project to create an example of the 'new German culture'? Was I so arrogant without being consciously aware of it? The towering Olympian molding the lesser creatures into my own image for their own benefit? So full with hubris that a fall was inevitable? And what was the fall? The end of the affair? How trite. How misguided. We had nowhere to go but down, too intelligent not to eventually realize what we were doing and become disgusted with the falseness of it.

"So, the eternal question of youth: 'What shall I make of my life?' should have been answered long ago, but I never made the opportunity happen. Shaving in the mirror I hardly looked myself in the face. But now I think I have asked the question properly and found an answer. I must do something in which I can perceive myself as being in the interstices of the process, at least feel myself moving centripetally toward the core of experience, toward an illuminating task to which I can commit myself without reservation or the backbite of conscience. The risk is not only material (I have no desire to starve), but psychological, spiritual as well: will I live up to my own conception of my worth? Will I betray my faith in myself? If I do not resolve these questions I will never be able to love, will I?

"Thus I move from such considerations to the action which I believe and hope will resolve them: I am going to write the novel about the exiles and make a contribution to ... what? The betterment of mankind? Not likely. To the enrichment of the universe of literature? That is my ambition. (You remember the lines from Milton above the main reading room entrance at the 42nd Street library:

A Good Booke Is The Precious Life-Blood Of a Master Spirit,
Imbalm'd and Treasur'd Up on Purpose To a Life Beyond Life.

I've never forgotten them. And I've also formed a motto from the old Royal Library here. Schadow, the old historian I've written you about before, added this to the collection. It comes from Adolf von Harnack, the keeper from 1904 to 1921: '*Biblioteca docet*'. And the newspaper reporter Tompkin tells me that the line on the façade of the National Archives in Washington reads: 'The past is prologue'. Now there's a frightening thought. Finally, I have from Kronauer, whom I think you know, an aphorism from Erasmus: 'When I get some money I buy books, and if any is left over, I buy food and clothes.' Is there a lesson in there somewhere?)

"To the rapprochement between the exiles and those who remained in Germany? I believe I can do this. Certainly anything that contributes to this end is of value. Perhaps it is that simple. I have put aside the idea of writing a novel about the early 1920s in Germany to be called 'Paranoia Rising', which is the name of a middleweight boxer character who personifies the era. Putting this idea away in the drawer will give me a project for later in my life when I've achieved a higher state of humor. In the meantime, I will put into the book that bitter exile joke, you probably remember it: Two dachshunds meet in Central Park while out walking. One says to the other 'Here, it is true, I am only a dachshund, but in the old country I was a Saint Bernard!'"

Few brilliant colors filled his mind when he laid the pen aside, but if he could not fully or adequately answer all the questions attendant to his decision, he at least had set his direction. That in itself, he thought, showed progress, that elusive human need so easily mistaken for substance. Where he would finally arrive he would discover in due time. What response could his father give to such an outpouring of confusion and confession? He never knew the answer, of course, because he never mailed the letter.

I'm gonna sit right down and write myself a letter
And make believe it came from you
I'm gonna write words, oh, so sweet,
They're gonna knock me off my feet.

* * * *

The city seemed to slide from winter directly into summer without the transition of spring. For most of the civilians who had not been able to heat their ramshackle rooms during the frozen months straddling the years 1945-46, spring felt so much warmer it might have well have been summer. All of the city's inhabitants welcomed the thawing warmth as it eased the stress of muscles and nerves contracted against nature and their destinies. Those among the defeated who survived the winter realized they would not die from the punishments of the weather and they felt liberated at the thought of having one less problem in their miserable lives. The more foresightful of them also realized that the next winter would return them to the icy hell from which they had just emerged, and this thought tempered their joy in wallowing in the heat of the summer days and nights.

Having decided finally what he must do, Schade experienced the sharp tines of impatience as the days creaked on deeper into the summer. He quickly wore out the sense of emotional liberation he had felt at making the decision to leave the city, and he began to strain against the daily routine that fed on itself and no longer served any useful purpose. He also rebelled against the constant physical reminders of his time in the city: he longed for the freedom from the past months and the release from memory, but this would not come until the end of the year when he had accumulated sufficient points for discharge. The summer raised his level of sensual awareness and desire as the women, both civilians and military, shed their heavy confining winter clothes for the lighter freedoms of thin dresses and less inhibited laughter. The lack of sexual intimacy with Gisela frustrated him each time they met, but he hesitated to form an attachment with any other woman. To escape the pressure of failure he was impatient to begin the next chapter of his life.

("You know," Leseur told him one warm silvery night as they sped in an open jeep down the empty Havelchaussee toward the Schlachtensee, "I know for a fact that Marybeth has friends who would be happy to be petted by you. Only necessity is to make the effort, n'est-ce pas." "It is not fear of being turned down that bothers me, Claude-Jean, quite the opposite." They drove on in silence, Leseur shaking his head at lost possibilities and the smashed summer insects spreading like diamonds across the windshield in the moonlight.)

His colleagues had swept into the city riding on the proud vehicles of history and victory, feeling full of power and the ability to remake the conscience of the defeated nation. He had not fully shared this sense of dominance, and now he cringed at the ignorant arrogance of that embarrassing attitude. Somewhere in the long months that followed these grandiloquent sentiments withered as they suffered the varied climate of the city's reality, which prevented most of them from being transformed from theory into practical policy and solutions. Now the only satisfaction he found lay in his conviction that he could personally rise above that reality and commit himself to a course of action that might in the future make a contribution toward meliorating its harshness. He rationalized that the failure had been of a grander nature than the level of the individual; the failure had come about through the misuse of power and an arrogance shared by the victors and the defeated, which resulted in a lack of cooperation and understanding. This allowed the truculence and the will to survive of the defeated to partially reverse the decision of the war. Perhaps Makepeace had been right: each victor had its own Germans and would attempt to remake them in its own image. If Kirshhof had his German...? And the Berliners, like most Germans, played their own survival games, many of which aimed at keeping those forced into exile when the nazis came to rule out of the new Germany they were in the process of creating.

To balance what he perceived as a sense of general failure he could only hold up his idea for the novel, his immediate justification for leaving the city at the end of the summer: the book would contribute through character and drama to a clearer understanding of the German problem. His deeper notion was, of course, that of creating a work of art that spoke to a slowly developing sense of aesthetics that could make a difference to individuals who read it; he even allowed himself, in his innermost private self, to think that such a creative act would ensure his own immortality. Of this he could speak to no one, as trite as the thought may have been and as universal as it was: every serious artist coddled the same thought. None of this helped with the resolution of his emotional turmoil in radically altering his relationship with Gisela.

Shortly before he left the city, they walked late one afternoon in the pale winter sunlight down the Kurfürstendamm. Ill at ease, they ambled past the sparsely decorated shop windows, stopping to stare at the shoddy merchandise behind the glass but seeing only their own reflections. They stopped to look through the window of the Galerie Gerd Rosen, one of the first modern art show rooms to open in the city during the summer of 1945. A large collage by Hannah Höch glared back at them under the sign

Fotomontage von Dada bis heute

The sun did not afford them much warmth and they pulled their overcoats tighter.

"You should wear a hat. Forty percent of your body heat – "

She laughed briefly. "Yes, so my mother told me every winter."

He pulled off his overseas cap and offered it to her with an exaggerated bow. She could not but smile and shake her head as she made as graceful a curtsy as she could in her winter clothes.

Against the building to their left a street vendor sat on a worn cushion behind a shallow wooden box, the top of which held his wares: three rolls of thick green thread, innumerable ancient rubber bands, three packets of

Woodbines, and eleven pencil stubs with no erasers on the ends. The box covered the stumps that remained of his legs and he shivered in a regular rhythm. She looked away and walked faster. "I thought they kept them off streets like the Ku-damm. Too many negative reminders, like the signs in the trams 'Reserved for the war mutilated.' But we are all that, aren't we?" They walked on in silence and turned into the Fasanenstrasse where they found a café whose antiquated tile stoves provided a hint of warmth.

"You don't have to leave the city altogether, you know," she said, ignoring the ersatz coffee, but deeply smoking a Chesterfield. They kept their overcoats on, but unbuttoned them as a gesture toward the pretension of heat. Her just-washed hair swirled around her head in waves of golden brilliance and he could not help but admire her ability to transcend her shabby skirt and blouse. No longer painfully thin, her body would never contain more than a nominally sufficient amount of flesh. "It's in my genes. Mother was the same way, always thin." He wanted very much to touch her.

They had chosen this café where they had never been before because it represented a form of neutral territory with no physical expression of memories to upset their precariously balanced emotions. The tension between them rose and fell with the tides of their abilities to maintain the equipoise, but say what they thought they had to say nonetheless. In his mind's eye he smiled wryly at the situation so drenched in the cliché of the cinema: each lover makes what each thinks is the bigger sacrifice for the other. He thought: if I can think of that at a time like this I must be well on the way out of the city already. But then why is my heart choking me with unshed tears? Where does this anger come from? Clichés, dammit, they fit too well when you can't think clearly.

"You could stay, whether we are together or not. You don't absolutely have to leave."

"Yes. It will be better this way. We won't be stumbling over each other."

"Like blind people in a room full of furniture," she said with just a hint of sarcasm at the touch of literature in her analogy.

"Yes," he replied softly, "like blind people."

"But we are not blind," she cried. "That is just the problem. We see all too well."

"When I am gone you can concentrate – "

"I can do that now. Let's not lie to each other."

"We aren't lying, Gisela, we're evading and that's not always such a bad thing. We save ourselves much pain by evasion."

"That doesn't change the situation, does it? You are going to leave me. That's the situation."

"The situation is that we have fed on each other for whatever comfort and pleasure we could find, but we move in circles. We're not going anywhere."

"Why is it absolutely necessary to go anywhere? As long as we are aware of the circumstances, we cannot really be hurt by them. We don't have to go *anywhere*, all we have to do is *exist*."

"Please don't make it anymore difficult than it is."

"Why not? It doesn't seem to be so hard for you."

"We both understand what we are doing. Why act out this charade as if we didn't?"

"Understanding is not everything, you know. It is a disease of you bastard intellectuals who can't love anyone other than yourselves, who have time only for their own messy little thoughts. You create art, you hope, but you've no idea how to live. No, don't tell me. I know. I know." She caught her breath and said softly with great bitterness:

"I know. I'm describing myself as much as you. Sad, isn't it. Could we get a whiskey here? I must go to work soon."

He walked with her to the streetcar stop. A light brush of chilled kisses like fine dry snowflakes skipping across the pavement, an awkward embrace, a few mumbled words, the clang and screech of the streetcar. "Come see the play before you leave. But don't tell me when."

"I will and I won't."

Then with a quick intake of warm air as she boarded the wooden cabin: "You *are* right, Jonathan. We have nothing of substance to give each other any longer. We've exhausted our little supplies of love. Otherwise it makes no sense." A brief smile containing the weight of the past and the promise of the future and the streetcar clattered away. He remembered the smell of her hair for a long time: it would come to him unbidden, in bursts of memory when he least expected it.

>*Goodbye, Johnny,*
>*Goodbye, Johnny,*
>*Schön war's mit uns zwei,*
>*aber leider, aber leider,*
>*kann's nicht immer so sein.*
>*Goodbye, Johnny,*
>*Goodbye, Johnny,*
>*Macht's mir nicht so schwer.*
>*Ich muß weiter, immer weiter,*
>*meinen Glück hinterher.*
>*Bricht mir heut' das Herz in zwei,*
>*In hundert Jahren, Johnny,*
>*Ist doch alles vorbei –*

Johnny![45]

* * * *

Most of the arrangements for his departure had been made as a matter of routine: with so many military personnel being transferred out for demobilization, 1st Lieutenant John Schade was just another statistic to the khaki bureaucracy that administered the gigantic machine called the U. S. Army. His replacement came from duty in Munich and did not have to be rigorously trained in the job. Oscar Monday shook his head with skepticism and said, "There's no way to train anyone to deal with Berliners. That's all balls. You either learn on the job or you don't. Don't forget to introduce him to Mister Morgan Tahni! That'll start him off right." Schade took the officer around to the people he had to know and tried to explain some of the local quirks of the assignment. He concluded that Monday had superbly summarized the situation. Just before Schade left, his replacement said, "These people are sure different. They suffer the general privations with more balls and wit. Smartasses, that's what the Berliners are. Jesus Christ Almighty." Makepeace looked at Schade and said, "How come we never thought of that?"

* * * *

---

[45] "We had a great time/ but it's too bad/ it's too bad/it can't always be so/I must go on/ever onward/chasing my fortune/today you break my heart in two/in a hundred years, Johnny/it'll all be over/Johnny!" There is no way of conveying the explosive effect of this song without hearing Hans Albers sing it on the soundtrack of the film *Wasser für Canitoga* (1938), which barely camouflages its homoerotic content.

Tamirov held the thin cardboard tube of the Russian cigarette between his thumb and forefinger and drew the acrid smoke into his lungs. Makepeace, attempting yet again to quit the noxious weed, watched with envy and sipped at his glass of sour mash. "I do miss the Dunhills from time to time, but you are right to do this thing, Villum. Much better for one's health, but this panther piss is no match for our vodka, even with cubed ice bergs."

"Can't agree with you there, Yuri Vladimirovich, but I will admit the last bottle of vodka you brought attained a higher level than the others."

"Rare Kremlin vintage, something we peasants rarely get. But tell me about Lieutenant Schade, why is he leaving? Had enough of the Germans?"

"He's one himself, but I don't think that's the reason. Perhaps he's confused and wants time and place to think about life."

"I must admit that I sometimes tire of them myself. They can be extremely irritating, can't they? Frankly, the only position for the Germans is prone so we can walk or piss on them whenever necessary. And the praise for our great Soviet culture must be never ending and full of hyperbole. This is the only acceptable behavior for our Germans. Lieutenant Schade could never accept that idea."

"Yuri Vladimirovich, I tremble with anxiety at the thought that you might be my Doppelgänger. Brr!" He softly rattled the links of his ID bracelet.

"More your mirror opposite, I should think." Tamirov grinned with only partially feigned pleasure.

"Yes, our methods differ considerably."

"But our goals here are the same, Villum, da?"

"Doubtful, Yuri Vladimirovich, doubtful, not in the long run."

"And that is the only run of value, isn't it?"

"Now there John would agree with you."

"Speaking of moving quickly, we've seen more of that odd Mister Morgan Tahni than usual recently. You wouldn't know …"

"Why don't we arrest him?"

Tamirov sat back in horror. "What? And lose a perfectly good local color? Besides he doesn't seem to do anything illegal. I think he is a spy."

"His being here is probably illegal. He moves from sector to sector with some ease."

"Doing what, we'd like to know."

"We could ask him, I suppose, but that would be too straight forward. And he's much too visible to be a spy."

"Visibility is the best cover of all."

"Well, he always has enough money to pay for drinks at The Edge Bar."

"But where does he get the money?"

"No one knows, apparently," Makepeace said with mock sadness.

"One hears he has a Belgian passport."

"We hear he's Eskimo, but that's not our problem, is it?"

"A man who without a nation is a sad thing," Tamirov said softly and Makepeace knew he meant it. "No loyalty, no protection."

"Spoken like a true believer."

"It could make him a *dangerous* man."

"Yuri Vladimirovich, are you going to arrest him?"

"Of course not."

"This isn't like you. Those Moscow Germans of yours will arrest him for sure one of these days."

"Not as long as we tell them what to do."

"I think I'll have a chat with him."

"If you discover anything of importance, let me know."

But Makepeace apparently never discovered anything of importance because he never passed on any additional information about the lanky former sea captain out of water.

Achtung! Vorsicht!
Bomben nicht anfassen!
Aufpassen oder sterben.

* * * *

He made the matter of farewell events clear to everyone: none would be held, and he felt only mild disappointment that no one disobeyed his wishes. He did, however, see several people alone or in small gatherings. At their last meeting, he listened as Kronauer, who had finally been given a license to publish his newspaper in the British sector, and Tompkin, suffering from a head cold, discussed the idiosyncrasies that characterized the city. The reporter's malaise had been brought on by a dip in the temperature during a sudden snowstorm as he returned on foot to his room from a romantic interlude in the Grunewald. "It's the air, for chrissake. When I first got here last year the air was choked with sex and the smell of defeat. Now the air is charged with the smell of sex and the invigorating swirl of revitalized artistic life and politics. The golden hunger years is what they'll call it in the next generation, wait and see."

Mathilde smiled her secret smile edged in the bitter lines of age she could not control and softly pronounced the words to the popular song.

Das ist die Berliner Luft, Luft, Luft

So mit ihrem holden Duft, Duft, Duft,
Wo selten was verpufft pufft, pufft,
In diesem Duft, Duft Duft,
Dieser Luft, Luft, Luft.[46]

After much argument, leavened by their old friendship, they agreed that speed best described the uniqueness of Berlin, at least in the past. No one could say what the future historian of the city would be able to say about it during its present crisis.

"Tempo! Tempo!" Tompkin shouted into his special whiskey jar.

Kronauer nodded. "Yes, that was the by-word of the Twenties. Tempo gave Berlin its big city character. Everything seemed to move faster here, even in comparison to New York, certainly to London or Paris. The Berliner possessed a *Drang nach Bewegung*, activity above all, always on the move at incredible speed. One theory has it that the Berlin air was such that Berliners could sleep long and deeply and awaken refreshed and ready to take off again."

Boltzmann, still eyeing Tompkin with some suspicion, shouted out the Walter Mehring verse that summed up the frenetic existence in the city before the war.

Die Linden lang,
Galopp, Galopp,

---

[46] The excerpts from the song might be very loosely translated as This is the Berlin air, air, air (atmosphere)/With its sweet smell, smell, smell (fragrance)/Where rarely anything fizzles out, out, out/In this smell, smell, smell,/This air, this air, this air.

See also end note.

> *mit der Uhr in den Hand,*
> *mit dem Hut auf'n Kopp;*
> *keine Zeit, keine Zeit, keine Zeit!*[47]

  This mass movement bordering on hysteria affected everyone including the street youth, those philosophers of the asphalt playground, whose behavior both threatened and amused the bourgeoisie. Makepeace, who picked up the anecdote on one of his excursions around the city, was fond of reciting the phrase of the Berlin youth: "*Hau dir selber 'n paar in die Fresse, ick hab' keene Zeit!*"[48] And Kronauer noted in a different context, "In those days everything moved so fast one barely knew whether one was coming or going; I mean during the twenties we were notorious for our speed, exemplified in that famous anecdote about the two youths who bumped into each other rushing in opposite directions."

  Not to be outdone, Schadow said, "Ah, but my dear Helmuth, you don't remember the nineties, you are too young. The city changed much more radically and faster then. Berlin developed from a rather austere garrison appendage of Potsdam into a modern European city. Too bad, of course, but inevitable."

  Boltzmann in his cups, dropped his gray head upon his increasingly expansive middle and whispered quite clearly, "All our clocks are destroyed. The Ivans have taken our wristwatches and pocket onions, and the others the war blasted away. How can we know we're ahead of

---

[47] The lines could be translated as "Along the Linden/Gallop, gallop,/with your watch in hand,/ with your hat on your head,/No time, no time, no time!"

[48] "Punch yerself a couple in da kisser, I got no time!"

time now? We must move even faster just to be sure, but we've no streetcars left, our feet suffer much more now. *Sic transit gloria mundi, oder umgekehrt!"*

Drinking Kronauer's good wine and not entirely sober, Schade intoned: "Berlin is doomed to always be in the process of becoming, never reaching, the state of complete being." They stopped and looked at him with something approaching astonishment, only Mathilde Kronauer retaining her usual look of slight distaste when in Schade's presence. He rarely entered into these conversations and disputations with strong opinions on one side or the other. With single individuals he might propound theories and venture ideas, but in groups he normally remained comparatively silent, adding bits and pieces in a quiet almost neutral tone, unless drunk or provoked. For him to interject this apparently profound statement with authority and finality surprised them. A new Schade? Now that he was about to leave? A more knowledgeable Schade? "Just a slightly drunk, feeling liberated Schade," Makepeace later informed Tompkin. "He's finally resolved the double schizophrenia that's blocked his progress; at least he believes he has. Perhaps there's no real difference."

At the time only Kronauer knew that Schade had cribbed the idea from a book on Berlin published in 1910 by a writer who did not particularly love the city.[49] But the notion fit so well into the conversation that he said nothing about its origins. Later they walked in the late summer rain for a short distance; Kronauer's stiff leg did not permit him

---

[49]The idea that Berlin would be forever in a state of becoming, never reaching a level of stasis, was expressed in 1910 by Karl Scheffler in the book *Berlin – Ein Stadtschicksal*.

lengthy perambulations, just long enough to exchange a few words about the future and for the newspaper publisher to give Schade a small package for his father in New York. Then they returned for a final glass of wine after which Schade made his farewells and he drove to his room in the Schlachtensee villa to finish packing. The city's smells had changed: now that its citizens no longer killed horses for stew meat, the streets reeked increasingly of the animals' excrement. Horsepower for transporting things and people had its price.

  The last time he met Tompkin, the journalist asked him, "Have you ever met Walburga Todtleben? She was a dancer and singer in the cabarets and music halls before '33, had quite a reputation as a nude dancer, or maybe naked would be more apt. Anyway, afterwards she made a hard living when she could get jobs in the shows the nazis allowed, but her reputation worked against her: all that puritanical dooblahdoo in public. So she scraped together some dough dancing at private parties. No, I don't think you *can* imagine. At least not from my experience, which I admit is limited, only saw her once. Very strange it was, and not very pleasant. For some reason I accepted an invitation in '35 or '36 to a party at which plenty of the press officials from the Propaganda Ministry celebrated something or other. Don't know why because I usually refused such things; then of course they stopped arriving like little packets of bacteria in my postbox.

  "It was out on the Wannsee, huge house with a big living room, plenty of space for the guests, a trio of musicians, and the dancers had room to move if they weren't too athletic. It was quite something with all the party uniforms and black suits and the women in their would-be Paris fashions, dresses cut on the oblique with deep cleavage, not at all attractive on most of the

Hausfrauen there, but some of the thinner ones fit the clothes like a silk glove. So about midnight, when else, the trio starts a slow drag number, which I guess they thought of as something like what might have been played in ancient Greece, because the three young dancers floated out in flowing smocks of velvet with garlands in their hair and they jumped and swayed around each other mimicking women courting and seducing one another. The smocks soon floated down and ended on the floor and the whole thing lasted about fifteen minutes. Embarrassing to me, but not to most of the others who drooled and got red in the neck watching, the women too. There was something perverse about it, something reaching into the depths of decadence, the aura of decay seemed to permeate the entire house. Strange. Even the nudity of the three girls seemed sterile, without any erotic attraction, no arousal there. But I didn't feel good. One of the dancers was Walburga Todtleben and I wondered if she applied for a license to work. No? Ah, well, perhaps in one of the other sectors. I'll ask there. And I'm glad you made no snide comment about her name. But, then, you wouldn't, would you."

Caught up in his own life, Schade mentioned the woman to Harrigan and Monday, then he promptly forgot about her.

* * * *

Makepeace watched him fiddle with his duffle bag, books, and socks, sipping slowly from Ogilvy Vasart's flask. The Englishman's brief missives from Vienna complained bitterly about the Countess for cutting off their relationship after he had Spoken Out to protect her person in a Dangerous Situation, and for having made him a farewell gift of a dose of the clap in addition. He had left the flask to his friends saying, "Someday, lads, you'll return it to me and we'll drink together from its endless depths. Perhaps even in The Edge Bar somewhere. One of us will always have it with him, and that's enough for me to know." Ogilvy Vasart, the true romantic. What disgrace could void his chipper stereotype?

Makepeace said with some asperity, "Politics aside, John, you're leaving at a very interesting time and I wish you would reconsider. These are interesting times and they'll only get more interesting. The lines are drawn and we're in a great competition for the German soul. What's it going to be? Capitalist or communist? Things are going to get hotter before they cool off. The struggle will be on the cultural front as well and you could be a big part of it."

"Politics aside, of course!" Schade mumbled into the suitcase searching for the unfindable. "What ever happened to literature, Bill? Your first love?"

"I've had to make a schedule adjustment. You don't sit around writing lectures when the house is burning down."

"So you're saving the house?"

"You bet. *We* are saving the house. The other comes later."

"But I'm not saving the house?"

"You're not pouring kerosene on the fire either. Maybe you're running to get the fire trucks. All things considered."

Schade stopped pawing about in his bag and sipped from the memorial flask. "All things considered. Drive me to the station, I'm taking the late night duty train to Frankfurt. But I want to make a stop first."

As they dragged Schade's luggage down the stairs, Makepeace sang in a neutral tone,

Get out of town before it's too late, my dear...

* * * *

He stood in the back of the theater watching her movements, her perfectly timed gestures, her ability to react with the ensemble, especially with blonde Bicycle Fred playing opposite her, while simultaneously emphasizing her own role and talent. Her concentration left no emotional or mental space for anything extraneous to the performance itself: no hesitation prompted a false movement or inadequate tone of voice. She carried the audience out of the cold shabby theater into a timeless climate of fiction where the weather never intruded upon the nature of pleasure: they roared with laughter and wept with abandon as she led them through the scale of responses with a grace and ease that drew the viewers to her with a naturalness that made the interaction seem serendipitous rather than contrived in the uncomfortable artificial setting of the theater itself.

In the scene he now watched, Gisela and another actress playing old friends meet after a long absence. Their dialogue encapsulated the wry submerged humor of the city.

"Hallo, darling! What have you been doing?"

"My dearest friend! I married a banker in Hamburg named Johann John-Jahn."

"No wonder you look so fresh and rested. I married an Argentine race car driver named Gonzales."

"Poor dear! No wonder you look so exhausted!"

The Berliners burst with laughter as they always had at such jokes, and thus lived for a few moments out of time, emptied of history.

"She is brilliant and strong," Buchdow had said, "and she is only really happy when she's acting." Schade believed this assessment to be correct and it reinforced his decision to leave the city: he concentrated on the pain and frustration they had caused each other, and tried to repress the memories of the moments of joy and elation.

He shivered as the cold crept through the gaps in the theater's roof and walls. With a toss of her foaming honey blonde hair, she swept off the stage in a grand yet funny exit accompanied by what in a warmer room would have been thunderous applause, but which now sounded like pieces of sandpaper being rubbed together. She and Fred had one further scene in this last act and he would be gone before the piece finished. They had made their farewells and had nothing further to say that would not repeat the same phrases they had given each other over the past weeks. He was somewhat surprised to discover he did not have a headache.

Now she strode on to the stage again for her last scene, integrating the essentially unnecessary movement all the city's actors had learned last winter to keep warm with the flow of the play's action, securely dominating the audience and fellow actors alike. Strong and brilliant. The weight she had gained over the last year reinforced the confidence with which she moved on the stage and off: the round bottom and firm thighs allowed that edge of self-assuredness to contrast her with others who lacked her profound belief in her own talent and appearance. Strong and brilliant, yes, but also somehow isolated in the aura of her success.

> *Ich weiss nicht zu wem ich gehöre*
> *Ich bin doch zu schade für einen allein*
> ....
> *Die Sonne, die Sterne gehören doch auch allen...*
> *Ich weiss nicht zu wem ich gehöre.*

Ich glaub, ich gehöre nur mir ganz allein.[50]

Nothing fades in Berlin: sunrise, sunset, winter into spring, love into indifference or its antonym: no, changes are accomplished with the slam of a door, the new arrives with a bang, it bursts into being and there, in less than a second of time the change is done – in the blink of an eye, in a heartbeat – and all is no more what it had been. Schade's departure would later seem to him to have followed this tradition; suddenly he was no longer there. He turned and walked out of the theater to the street where Makepeace waited to drive him for the last time through the fractured urban landscape that had so tightly possessed him and would do so even more intensely in his memory. Now he could leave it: a city full of ghosts. The blue Opel smelled of gasoline and burned oil and Makepeace drove at a moderate but consistent speed through the fissures in the cityscape.

Schade did not question his friend's curiously complex route, thinking: He's giving me the last tour, the bastard. At a busy street juncture in the Soviet Sector an unusually slender young Russian woman stood on a thin piece of wood in the middle of the crossroad enthusiastically working a yellow flag on a short stick in her right hand in conjunction with, appropriately if not intentionally, a red flag in her left: the shuffling civilians and the roaring military traffic both obeyed her signals.

---

[50]"Ich weiss nicht zu wem ich gehöre." This is one of saddest of all songs. The lines could be translated as "I don't know to whom I belong/ I'm too wonderful for just one person alone/The sun, the stars also belong to everyone…/I don't know to whom I belong/I guess I belong only to myself alone."

Dressed in a brown tunic, a black skirt to her knees and a pair of felt boots to mid-calf, she exercised her authority with a flamboyance that hinted at frustration in other aspects of her life: beneath the black cloth beret sitting atop her piled auburn hair her eyes sparkled with the pleasure of power and her flashing smile indicated to those who could read the signs that, while she took the job very seriously, she also saw the humor in the situation. Her elaborate movements also served to ward off the biting cold.

Makepeace pulled the jeep to a lurching stop as she brandished the red flag with an overhand swoop to allow three Russian soldiers and a one-legged civilian on crutches to cross in front of them. "They're usually so solemn," Makepeace said in admiration.

"Maybe she's got her discharge orders," Schade offered.

"More likely approval to extend her tour here." Makepeace slowly accelerated past the woman and smiled; she nodded in return but promised nothing. Makepeace guided them through small side streets back to the American Sector and as the jeep turned left from Lutherstrasse into Wittenbergplatz, a tall lanky figure in a faded blue blazer topped with a battered yachting hat striding south waved at them and made writing motions with his right hand over the left palm, eyebrows raised in an unspoken question. Makepeace did not see the strange message and did not slacken the jeep's pace as they moved past the now neatly painted sign in four languages:

> YOU ARE LEAVING
> THE AMERICAN SECTOR
> ВЫ ВЫЕЗЖАЕТЕ ИЗ
> АМЕРИКАНСКОГО СЕКТОРА
> VOUS SORTEZ
> DU SECTEUR AMÉRICAIN
> SIE VERLASSEN DEN AMERIKANISCHEN SEKTOR
> U.S ARMY

In front of the newly printed announcement three scraggly adolescents, cracking chewing gum between their brown-stained teeth and operating renegade yoyos from the American army stores, walked the dog and rocked the cradle with the ease and panache of professionals.

ENVOI

Berlin, September 1947

Dear John,
It has been some time since I last wrote. My apologies for not responding sooner about the manuscript of your book, which I understand is due to be published this winter. Wonderful news! As you know, life has been extremely hectic here since the early summer. I've simply not had the time to read the thing in one marathon sitting as I'd like to have done, but rather in a broken series of grabs at it as I get an hour or so. So it is only now that I have the chance to tell you how good I think it is. One really gets to know what the exile experience meant for your characters, and by extension the hundreds of thousands who suffered it (and you and your family?). I imagine there is a lot of autobiography in it, but, as we all know, a young man's first novel is always the story of himself. The book will, I think, serve the purpose you intended for it. (What are the plans for publishing it in German here?) But it is also a fine piece of writing. Did you write it in German first and translate it? If you have a German version send it to me and I'll see what I can do to find a publisher. Your ability with language is marvelous, given your crazy-quilt background. You might even become another Conrad!

Unfortunately, I don't have time to give you my professorial lecture-critique right now: too busy trying to hold things together. The situation here is reaching a critical point. There is a distinct chill in our relations with the Soviets (and of course some Germans leap to take advantage of this). When we announced the economic fusing of the British and the American zones last June (we seem to be calling it by the stupid name 'Bizonia'), and when General Marshall announced that month at Harvard the plan to help European states revive their economies, things here took a nose dive. I suppose the vicious attacks on the US by Molotov and his walkout at the Foreign Ministers Conference in Paris in the summer indicates the line of response in Moscow. The economic situation in the Soviet Zone is appalling, to the point where people there are not even interested in their ruling party's much ballyhooed second congress last week here in Berlin which was badly organized and sparsely attended. We are now waiting for the second Sov shoe to drop, if the first was the walkout in Paris.

I know you are aware of the general situation. I've been following your occasional articles in *Openings*. (Can't you find a more objective rag to write for?) It's a wonder the editors print your stuff, which I find surprisingly balanced and quite fair in the commentary on what's going on in central Europe. (But you're certainly not making any friends among the Brits and the Arabs with your pieces on Palestine and the Middle East.) I always thought you to be too soft on the communists. I've even entertained the idea from time to time that you might be one of those woolly-headed fellow travelers. I see now you are merely a romantic utopian - your mind is essentially in the right place but your emotions refuse to allow you to see the world realistically. Reading your recent stuff, and the sections of the novel on the Soviet attempts to control the exiles' anti-fascist groups, I am convinced you have learned to stop thinking that everything on the left is good and valuable, though I still think you're too soft on the reds. Yes, I know there are differences on the left, there is an anti-Stalinist left, and all that. But I still think you're straddling the political fence. Clearly you are too intelligent to fall completely for any particular line. And of course I like you in spite of your fuzzy politics.

You know, old pal, that notorious list of the dead in exile and the camps you're compiling has an echo on the other side. Think about the Russian writers and artists who got chewed up in the Ezhov Terror. We all know about the show trials, but what about Mayakovsky? Or Mandelstam? Meyerhold? Or Marina Tsvetaeva? Isaak Babel? I just had a chat with a British diplomat back from Moscow – oddly enough named Berlin, fascinating talker – who learned all about it. Maybe you should get up a second list: anti-communist artists killed in the line of duty. I know you mention a couple of people who died in the Sov camps, but you've hardly scratched the surface of this travesty. (And have you ever thought about their fact that the Japanese had no great mass of exiles as a result of the government's actions in the 30s? An interesting point, *nicht wahr*?)

In the year or so since you left the city, many things have happened with our former "clients," as we so jocularly put it then. Gisela is about to start making movies and I think there's no doubt she will become one of "the stars of stage and screen" before too long, so concentrated and so intense, especially if the Germans revitalize the film industry here. We're doing what we can, but it still takes time to approve all the details and get the equipment and supplies. And we thought putting the theater back together was tough! Claudia has become something of a cult figure in the theater, not the blazing success that Gisela is achieving, but she is one of the best stage actresses in Germany and just came back from doing a stint at the Burgtheater in Vienna, where by the way our old chum Ogilvy is still doing business, though one is never sure just what kind. Alas, no time to write now about all the others. You should come back and see for yourself.

The enclosed manuscript was written by the old historian, Schadow, before he died from last winter's horrors and old age. Actually he made it to the end of June, but he did not survive the effects of the severest winter in three generations. We did not get a chance to have an autopsy performed to see if something else other than heart failure may have been involved; our red colleagues refused the request. But there is a lingering doubt for some of us: the notion of suicide comes to mind, as much as one might want to reject it, but perhaps only in the sense that he simply no longer wanted to live.

In any case, the manuscript deals in fragments with his life and loves (yes, he actually had a couple!), but perhaps more to the point, the period of time you spent in Berlin, with many asides and digressions into German history attempting to explain Germany's paradoxical role as predator and victim. It also contains sections about all of us, sometimes painful passages which show the old man to have been extremely perceptive or incredibly dense, or both. The handwriting is rather bad at times, but you will understand it better than I did. He suffered greatly during the last couple of months of his life, but he kept a clear head. Some of us come off pretty badly in this summa vita (mainly he himself!), but since it presents us from an angle much different from our own I thought you would like to read it. No one else has seen it. As you will notice, I could not resist commenting on certain sections of the manuscript and I've inserted scraps of paper with my scribblings throughout. Let me know what you think.

I should say that the second section of papers in another hand was found at the same time the old man's manuscript was recovered. With some effort I discovered the writer was Helga Opladen, the painter's first wife. They bear directly on a certain part of Schadow's life and help to explain something about the complexity of human existence. Beneath the banal exteriors most of us show to the world around us there swirls a cauldron of passions and private perversions better left behind closed doors; or so we think. Clearly the old guy had several qualities we knew nothing about: some of this stuff is embarrassing to read and I skipped a lot. Helga was something of a firecracker, but a bit cracked as a political analyst. Apparently she was a fine sculptor, though it is impossible to see any of her work these days, and she certainly turned the Herr Professor around for a while. She died in the winter of 1918-19, but you will find this out for yourself when you read the old man's notes.

As for me, I've been making some notes for a novel about all this, and the city of course: how could it be otherwise? Everybody's writing these days. No title yet, but several characters have vaguely formed in my mind and I'm trying to figure out the connections among them. Too bad I don't have more time for the project. Someday....

You really ought to think about coming back to work here, see what is really going on, first-hand, on the front line. Since you seem to be drifting along with the tumbling wild west weed, why not drift over this way? Return to the thrilling days of yesteryear where the snow still falls but the summers are not too lazy. It would be fun to work with you again, and the work is still worthwhile. Who was it who said, "The war didn't stop, it just changed its form"? Perhaps you don't agree with the notions behind that statement, but things here are looking more war-like with the passing of each day.

You remember Ken Farisse, Kirshhof's successor? Turned out to be an interesting character after all. Quite the card with, as you know, two major preoccupations, namely his job and women. He wrote a poem the other day about an Arab potentate communing with Allah that contains a line going something like "I would love thee without limit loved I not nooky more." Now he's threatening to force the newspapers in the US sector to publish the thing in English with his own translation into German. The guy's demented of course, but who isn't these days?

I've been writing this letter on and off for three days and will send it off now, but there's one Berlin story you, of all people, will appreciate. It concerns the bad-breath man, your old pal, Woller - how could you forget him? It seems that the new theater critic for the *Klägliche Rundschau*, for that is what he currently indeed is, lives at 56 Im Dol, two houses away from General Clay himself. Well. Can we tolerate this "leading exponent of pro-Soviet government policy" occupying a "Soviet Military Government command post" from which the comings and goings of the American Military Governor and CINCEUR can be readily observed? (You recall the military obsession with acronyms: "Commander-IN-Chief-EURope".) Not only that, but this Sov spy has a telephone! Imagine that. At least you can't smell him on the phone. It has been recommended that he be removed from that house, natürlich. Stay tuned for the next thrilling chapter, or more seriously and better yet, pay a visit and see what happens.
Meeting with Tamirov is becoming ever more difficult.

Keeping up the façade of bantering repartee is harder to do when he stands for all that is warped in the Soviet system. After months of denying they use the old nazi camps to hold their own political prisoners, he finally admitted to "a few malcontents and criminals" being under arrest. How many people have disappeared from the city into the silence of the GPU camps? But I soldier on; it's my job.

    I hope your book sells a million copies. (It won't, of course, too good for the mass public, but it should sell well enough to make you some royalties.) By the way, I should tell you that Mister Morgan Tahni threatened to write you a letter to give you encouragement. Send me a copy of the book for him, will you? What language are you writing in now? And don't you still have a valise in Berlin? Can't you see the Berolina waving to you?

               All the best,
               Bill

END MATTERS

The Dreams They Had

Gisela dreamed she stood naked at the edge of a field of golden wheat, each stalk of which suddenly transformed into a soldier holding a rifle across his chest. The machine gun in her hands spit out its deadly flowers and the soldier fell down in a sea of blood. The dream always ended with her on the stage bowing to the frenzied clacking applause of the formally dressed audience of skeletons and she awoke with a shriek.

Oscar Monday dreamed he appeared as Apollo in a great mural on the wall of the Metropolitan Museum of Art in Manhattan. He was naked in glorious color and around his erect penis was wrapped a deep green ribbon the ends of which putti held in their chubby little hands and grinned with lascivious intent.

Felix Harrigan dreamed of a granite-edged pool of chilled water in the depths of a dark green forest whose pine trees smelled penetratingly of old scents and decayed flora. He swam in his dream from one point in the circle to another counter-clockwise in a long slow crawl; the water puckered his flesh with its cold embrace and he smiled just before the alarm clock rudely awakened him.

Tamirov never dreamed, much to his dismay.

Woller dreamed of standing at the podium in a gigantic closed arena passionately orating but no sound left his throat, the arena held not one other soul, and he could not determine the subject of his emotional lecture, nor could he stop the waterfall of silent words.

Schadow dreamed of his dead son at the age of five standing at the top of the staircase in the old Steglitz apartment building, unwilling to take the first step to descend to the front door. Schadow waited impatiently at the bottom of the stairwell to help his son. The older man awakened with watery eyes and a ferocious headache.

Tompkin dreamed of a furry cat lying on the hill of his belly moving slowly up and down with his breathing, a secretive grin on its tabby face.

Mathilde Kronauer dreamed a lizard-like animal was crawling up the inside of her left thigh. She shivered and when she awakened she found the sheet between her legs damp and strangely odorous.

Makepeace dreamed of a narrow but swiftly moving stream of icy cold blue water tumbling down a thickly forested mountainside. He stood in the middle of the stream catching one large trout after the other with a net and his bare hands, stuffing them into an endlessly deep shoulder bag of tan Spanish leather.

Claudia dreamed she stood on the edge of a blazing hot yellow desert in the shimmering middle of which she could barely make out a small figure that seemed to be running away from her. She awoke with a cry strangling her dry throat.

Their Favorite Artworks

Helga Pechhold Opladen: Erich Heckel's "Nude (Dresden)" 1910. "Heckel learned from Matisse, what better mentor? Look at this painting and think of the green stripe nose. Cubism? A dead end. Picasso will commit suicide before too long, but Braque will live to be an old man."

Helmuth Kronauer: Adolphe von Menzel's "Das Balconzimmer". "Look at the gorgeous light flowing into the room. We have so few of these days in the city."

Mathilde Kronauer: Caspar David Friedrich's "Artic Shipwreck". Her husband notes, "She won't say anything beyond the fact that this is her favorite, but I think she identifies with the scene. It fits her at times."

Marybeth Mullen: "That painting of the emaciated family in the ruins looking for their next meal; it's the perfect expression of the times. She painted it, not him, though he signed it. Poor guy."

William Makepeace: Whistler's self-portrait with monocle painting. "All artists are mad and this exemplifies that truth."

Heinrich Opladen: "One of my own, especially the bright colors and brilliant, ever so slightly distorted draftsmanship of that painting of the Jardin du Luxembourg in the snow. I wish I had it still. As good as any Matisse or Dufy."

Ulrich Kramer: Gauguin's "Jacob Wrestling with the Angel". "I go through this almost every day and sympathize with the angel, poor thing."

Ursula Opladen: Renée Sintenis Small Daphne. "The figure strains to reach the heights of life's experiences, ever upward, to the heaven of true fulfillment."

Emil Schadow: "I prefer Dürer's self-portraits, they are so burdened with the weight of the man and the times, and they follow him from youth to deep age. They overflow with his connection to his time and place. I also admire ancient Greek statuary, so clean and straightforward."

Claudia Kaufmann: Max Liebermann's 1901 "Samson and Delilah". "Because, well, that should be obvious. Not the typical woman-man relationship, is it? And Liebermann was a very brave man."

John Schade: I don't know much about art but I like things to be straightforward so I guess Mondrian's "Broadway Boogie-Woogie" would come at the top of my list.

Buchdow: Holbein the Elder's drawing "Young Man with a Hat", "because he has such a soulful look, one would like to comfort him. On the other hand, Kranach the Elder's nude wild man holding a club has a wonderfully tight bottom."

Gisela Albrecht: None. "Visual art is too static, to have real beauty things must be dynamic, like the film Berlin, *Symphonie einer Großstadt*." "But, my dear," Schadow murmured, "we are talking about your favorite work of art, not what is most beautiful." "Then it must be me. After all, I created myself, didn't I?" "Yes, you and many others one way or another."

Yuri Vladimirovich Tamirov: "No, not what you think, my friend; no image of a healthy peasant fucking a tractor in a field of swaying wheat with a great factory belching gobs of black industrial shit into the air. I personally and privately prefer the gorgeous pink flesh of Titian's women. For that alone I would like to visit Venice. Does that surprise you?"

Oscar Monday: "I have seen a painting of Salome by a totally unknown American who lived in France, Henry Tanner, and it bowled me over. Such a sexual threat. It fits Strauss's damp opera perfectly. Has anyone ever compared her song to the severed head to Isolde's Liebestod? The man's a genius. I'd give a lot to see more of this work."

Claude-Jean Leseur: "Despite my bohemian manner, I am a traditionalist and I think the work of Claude Lorrain is the height of artistic creation, although Poussin is also great …"

Ogilvy Vasart: Julia Margaret Cameron's photograph portrait of Mrs. Herbert Duckworth (1867). "It so plangently expresses the Victorian desire for adult innocence and a return to an edenic time what of course never existed. It is an exemplar of the escape from the realities of the era – and she is so beautiful."

Wilson Tompkin: Francisco Masriera Manoven's "Harem Beauty". "There's something provocative about her but at the same time distancing. Either she can't make up her mind, or we can't. Intriguing."

Reinhard Woller: "Les Demoiselles d'Avignon because they foresee the destruction of European culture by the barbarians. Now we must rebuild."

Walter Boltzmann: "Anita Berber's naked ass, of course! A lovely piece of pulchritude I once very briefly held in my hands, when I had two of them."

Washington DC – Avignon/Tavel – Berlin – Key West, 1981-2017

END NOTES

P. 271: Orson Welles used this idea in *Mr. Arkadin* (*Confidential Report*) (1955) where the dying character played by Akim Tamiroff has one last wish, but the warm sausage gets to him too late.

P. 309: The complete lyrics for The Sanjak of Novi Bazar are:
        All
When you're feeling blue and low
And have no sweeter place to go
Move your mind around, my friend
And your ear to my song do lend
And prepare to go right round the bend.

    Carlo
If you're looking for a place not too far
Where all the types meet to greet
    The Edge Bar
Is just right to be your meat
So bizarre.

    Chorus
    (It is)
In the Sanjak!
In the Sanjak!

In the Sanjak of Novi-Bazar.

   Mitzi
If you're looking for someone with clout
Or a fine round popo to mount
They're easy to find, if you're of a mind
To visit this one of a kind

   Chorus
In the Sanjak!
In the Sanjak!
In the Sanjak of Novi-Bazar.

   Jacko
If all this perversity makes you so thirsty
Don't look for water here in the sand
Booze there's a plenty the long a day
And always, always look out for the bey

   Chorus
  In the Sanjak, etc.

   Feeno
Here you'll find your heart's desire
If that muscle survives the fire
Of those pulsing Albania loins so dire
Hidden in this deep Byzantine mire.

   Chorus
  In the Sanjak, etc.

   Maria
This is that dusty mysterious place
Where bright eyes see behind the lace

Where worry-beads are made of jade
And tiresome Parisians come to get laid
Where the sharpest outlines tend to fade

    Chorus
    In the Sanjak, etc.

    Alioop
    Here we shall meet
After we've done out big feat
I know where I want to meet you
I know you want me to tell you
Where the smoke makes you high
Where the whiskey makes you lie
So, my darling, there is no choice
You must meet me

    Chorus
    In the Sanjak, etc.

    Benami
I know a place
Where all the swells go to the well
I know a place
Where those on the lam fit into the jam
And the jury stays out till it finds all about
Where the corpse died away in the face of the day.

    Chorus
It's the Sanjak!
In the Sanjak!
The Sanjak of Novi-Barzar.

P. 448: The lyrics Makepeace sings from "Hoppla, jetzt komm' ich" (Werner Richard Heymann, Gilbert, Kolpe) are:

    Hoppla, jetzt komm' ich
    Alle Türen auf, alle Fenster auf
    Hoppla, jetzt komm' ich
    Und wer mit mir geht, der kommt bald auf
    Hoppla, jetzt komm' ich
    Und die Straßen frei, für mich!

(Hey, it's me on my way
Throw the doors open! Throw all the windows up!
Hey, it's me on my way
And whoever follows me, makes it to the top
Hey, it's me on my way
Clear all the streets, for me!)

P. 545: *Das Lila-Lied*, the anthem to the homosexual life in the city played with the phrase "anders als die Andern" ("different from the others") which was the title of an eponymous 1904 novel by Bill Forster and a 1919 silent film sympathetic to homosexuals with Anita Berber and Conrad Veidt. Weimar authorities suppressed the film. The song was originally published in 1920 with text by Kurt Schwabach and music by Arno Billing (pseudonym for Mischa Spolansky), dedicated to Dr. Magnus Hirschfeld, a well-known and widely published sexologist and a public supporter of legalizing homosexuality. It is possible that Marcellus Schiffer added some lyrics in 1928.

P. 652: The irony is the fact that Berlin air never smelled sweet even before the introduction of the internal combustion, gas-powered engine: garbage, unwashed bodies, horse manure, beer, etc.

CREDITS

I Surrender Dear: Music, Harry Barris, lyrics Gordon Clifford (1930)
Blue Skies: Music & lyrics Irving Berlin (1926)
Brother, Can You Spare a Dime: Music Jay Gorney, lyrics E. Yip Harburg (1931)
What is This Thing Called Love: Music & lyrics Cole Porter (1929)
Die Dreigroschenoper: Music Kurt Weill, lyrics Bertolt Brecht (1928)
Wenn sich zwei lieben: Music Kurt Levaal, lyrics Hedwig Knorr (1932)
Berlin kommt wieder: Music and lyrics Heino Gaze (1945)
Melodie der Strasse: Music Heino Gaze, lyrics Bruno Balz & Curth Flatow (1948)
Wenn die beste Freundin: Music Mischa Spolansky, lyrics Marcellus Schiffer (1928)
Veronika der Lenz ist da: Music Walter Jurmann, lyrics Fritz Rotter (1930)
Lieber Leierkastenmann: Music & lyrics Willi Kollo (1928)
Singt eener uffin Hof: Music Olaf Bienert, lyrics Kurt Tuckolsky (1929)
Ich bin die fresche Lola: Music Friedrich Hollaender, lyrics Robert Liebmann & Hollaender (1930)
Es gibt nur ein Berlin: Music Willi Kollo & lyrics Kollo & Hans Pflanzer (1933)
Jonny: Music & lyrics Friedrich Hollaender (1920)
Das war sein Milljöh: Music & lyrics Willi Kollo (1930)
How High the Moon: Music Morgan Lewis, lyrics Nancy Hamilton (1940)

Hoppla, jetzt komme ich: Music Werner Richard Heymann, lyrics Robert Gilbert & Max Kolpe (1932)

Das Lila Lied: Music Arno Billing (pseudonym for Mischa Spolansky), lyrics Kurt Schwalbach (1920); later attributed to Marcellus Schiffer.

Nimm dich in acht vor blonde Frauen, Johnny: Music Friedrich Hollaender, lyrics Richard Rillo & Hollaender (1930)

I'm Gonna Sit Right Down and Write Myself a Letter: music Fred E. Ahlert, lyrics Joe Young (1935)

Ich weiss nicht zu wem ich gehöre: Music Friedrich Hollaender, lyrics Robert Liebmann (1932)

Goodbye, Johnny: Music Peter Kreuder, lyrics Hans Fritz Beckmann (1938)

Berliner Luft: Music Paul Lincke, lyrics Heinrich Bolton-Baeckers (1904)

Heimat Berlin (Mit der Hand übern Alexanderplatz): Music Friedrich Hollaender, lyrics Walter Mehring (1930)

Get Out of Town: Music & lyrics Cole Porter (1938)

Made in the USA
Middletown, DE
12 September 2017